Collected Essays on Human-Centered Computing, 2001–2011

IEEE computer society

IEEE Computer Society Products and Services

The world-renowned IEEE Computer Society publishes, promotes, and distributes a wide variety of authoritative computer science and engineering books, e-books, journals, magazines, conference proceedings, and professional education products. Visit the Computer Society online at www.computer.org for more information.

To submit questions about the books and e-books program, or to propose a new title, please e-mail books@computer.org or write to Books, IEEE Computer Society, 10662 Los Vaqueros Circle, Los Alamitos, CA 90720-1314. Telephone +1-714-821-8380.

Additional information regarding the IEEE Computer Society Press program can also be accessed from our web site at http://computer.org/cspress.

Collected Essays on Human-Centered Computing, 2001–2011

Edited and Coauthored by Robert R. Hoffman

With Coeditors Pat Hayes, Kenneth M. Ford, and Jeffrey M. Bradshaw

IEEE computer society

Page design by Monette Velasco.

ISBN-10: 0-7695-4715-X
ISBN-13: 978-0-7695-4715-2
IEEE Computer Society Order Number: P4715

Contents

Acknowledgements

When I joined the Institute for Human and Machine Cognition in 1999, its Director Ken Ford challenged me with specifying the principles of human-centered computing (HCC). At that time I was primarily concerned with specifying the methodology of cognitive task analysis for the study of domain experts. I had not thought much beyond that, in terms of possible implications at a systems level. I had begun a collaboration with David Woods that emerged from my studies of the history of task analysis, and as a part of that I was asking him about what he called "process tracing." But he cared less about the specifics of methodology than about how cognitive task analysis fits into a broader picture, which we now refer to (comfortably) as the design of macrocognitive work systems.

Fortunately for me, these influences led to waves of metamorphosis that shredded and re-knit my tattered soul. First, proposing some "principles," then backing off and wondering what it means to call them principles in the first place. First, focusing on cognitive task analysis, then broadening to a concern with systems analysis and design. First, focusing on the individual thinker who is ranting at his workstation, then broadening to questions of how the procurement process guarantees that computational tools will be user-hostile.

I feel deeply indebted to Ken Ford and the Institute for Human and Machine Cognition for their support, allowing me to metamorphose.

I am deeply grateful for my collaborations with David, with Gary Klein, Peter Hancock, Jeff Bradshaw, Brian Moon, Stephen Fiore, and Paul Feltovich, all of whom contributed to multiple essays. I thrive on collaboration, and I try always to reach for it in otherwise competitive situations. Collaborations are always more fun. I am deeply grateful to all my newly found colleagues whose ideas and accomplishments are presented in these essays.

I am deeply grateful to Nigel Shadbolt. Back in the heyday of expert systems he was sponsor on my Fulbright. Something must have come of that, since some 15 years later it was he who, for worse or for better, nominated me to take point in an HCC Department for *IEEE Intelligent Systems.* Nigel lived. I have heard rumors about what happened when my name was placed in nomination. I have repressed my memory of what I heard about the rumors. I prefer to feel good about myself. I trust that in the course of time I have manifested myself as a proper gentleman.

I am grateful for the support of the Editors who followed Nigel: Jim Hendler and Fei Yue Wang. I am deeply grateful for the efforts of *IEEE IS* editorial and production staff, including Dennis Taylor, Dale Strok, Margaret Weatherford, and Cheryl Baltes. They suffered through my eccentricities and rants. Cheryl in particular had to adapt to my penchant to treat words as potatoes and the rules of syntax as carving knives.

I would like to thank Jeff Yerkes of IHMC for his help in editing the galleys, and Robin Hoffman for helping prepare the author index.

I am deeply grateful to Pat Hayes and Jeff Bradshaw, who were always critical and supportive as they donned their Department Editor's cap to review draft essays. All the essays ended up far better than the drafts because of their input. Which is to say, the first drafts were pretty good to begin with, and their input was minimal. (Forgive my humor.) Rest assured, some essays were completely panned and never went beyond a first draft.

Quite a few essays were determined, after all, to be appropriate for some other outlet since they did not really fit the HCC theme. I say this because my experience with this Department makes me believe strongly that fields such as cognitive systems engineering and intelligent systems engineering need more "short essay" outlet opportunities such as that afforded by the Department on HCC.

As work on these essays progressed, with Yours Truly suffering but only occasionally from the stress of producing under a regular deadline, we Department Editors started to refer to our intellectual goal in terms of "epiphanies per fortnight." If that number was 1.0 or greater, things were OK. Well, in the ebb and flow of efforts and distractions, we had to hedge, to include a category of "minor epiphanies." (Obviously, we were not afraid of oxymorons.) Minor epiphanies would be 2.0 or even 3.0 per fortnight. That made us feel better about ourselves. These essays contain some ideas that were scary at that moment when a penumbra of epiphany wafted out from the cerebral cobwebs. These essays contain some ideas that are still scary. My mantra has been a statement that, with regret, I can no longer attribute, but that I absolutely love:

> "That idea seems ridiculous at first, but after you think about it you realize it makes no sense whatsoever."

It has been empowering to be able to have an interesting idea, formulate it as clearly but succinctly as possible, and then "get it out there." We're not done yet.

Robert R. Hoffman
Pensacola, Florida
November 2011

About the Department Editors

Robert R. Hoffman is a Fellow of the American Psychological Society, a Fulbright Scholar, and an Honorary Fellow of The British Library, Eccles Center for American Studies. He received his BA, MA, and PhD in experimental psychology at the University of Cincinnati, where he received McMicken Scholar, Psi Chi, and Delta Tau Kappa Honors. After a Postdoctoral Associateship at the Center for Research on Human Learning at the University of Minnesota, Hoffman joined the faculty of Adelphi University. There, he received awards for outstanding research and service, and also served as Chair of the Institutional Review board and the University Grants Officer. He joined the IHMC as a Research Associate in 1999.

Hoffman's early research was in the area of psycholinguistics, where he helped pioneer the experimental study of the comprehension of figurative language (metaphor, proverbs). His first book, *Cognition and Figurative Language,* coedited by his mentor Richard Honeck of the University of Cincinnati, is now regarded as a classic. Hoffman went on to help found the journal, *Metaphor and Symbol,* for which he remains Associate Editor. Another focus of Hoffman's early work, an interest that continues to this day, is the psychology and history of science. Hoffman has published analyses of the use of metaphor in science, the philosophy of contextualism, and reviews of the histories of task analysis, cognitive psychology, and applied psychology.

After his Postdoctoral Associateship, Hoffman's research took an applied direction. Hoffman helped launch an Annual Conference on Applied Experimental Psychology—one of which was the

Ebbinghaus Centennial Conference (Gorfein & Hoffman, 1987), and another of which was an initial meeting of what would become the International Society for Ecological Psychology.

Hoffman has been recognized internationally for his research on expertise, on the methodology of knowledge elicitation, and on human factors issues in the design of workstation systems and knowledge-based systems. He is series editor for the book series "Expertise: Research and Applications." To realize his goals for research in applied cognitive psychology, Hoffman received grants from the US Army and US Air Force to receive training in remote sensing, including aerial photo interpretation, terrain analysis, radar interpretation, and meteorological satellite image interpretation. Ultimately, Hoffman qualified to teach remote sensing in environmental science, as well as human factors psychology.

Current projects include an effort to define the methodologies for human-centered computing and cognitive technologies, an effort to forge a general theory of macrocognitive work systems, and an effort to develop measures and metrics for evaluating cognitive work.

Hoffman is a member of Human Factors and Ergonomics Society, the American Association for Artificial Intelligence, the IEEE, and the American Meteorological Society. He is a member of the Board of Editors for the journal *Human Factors* and member of the Advisory Board for the *Journal of Cognitive Engineering and Decision Making.*

Hoffman has published widely, in journals including *Human Factors, Memory & Cognition, Organizational Behavior & Human Decision Processes, The Bulletin of the Psychonomic Society, The Journal of Psycholinguistic Research, Ecological Psychology, Applied Cognitive Psychology, Metaphor and Symbol, The AI Magazine, Weather and Forecasting,* and *The Journal of Experimental and Theoretical Artificial Intelligence.*

Also an award-winning teacher, Hoffman has offered courses in General Psychology, Experimental Psychology Laboratory, Cognitive Psychology, Developmental Psychology, Problem Solving, Psycho-linguistics, Philosophy of Science, Philosophy of Psychology, History of Science, Human Factors, and Remote Sensing. Hoffman has also worked as a Ranger/Naturalist in the Green Mountains of Vermont and is an accomplished blues drummer. In his spare time he likes to restore Art Deco period furniture.

Jeffrey M. Bradshaw is a Senior Research Scientist at the Florida Institute for Human and Machine Cognition (IHMC). His PhD is in Cognitive Science, from the University of Washington. At IHMC he leads the research group developing software agents systems. His first book on the topic, *Software Agents,* became a classic in the field and a best-seller for The MIT Press. Formerly, Jeff led research groups at The Boeing Company and the Fred Hutchinson Cancer Research Center. With Ken Ford, he edited the seminal volume *Knowledge Acquisition as a Modeling Activity,* and became well known for his role in helping develop a suite of successful methodologies and tools for automated knowledge acquisition. While at Boeing, he founded the emerging technologies group of the Aviation Industry.

Jeff has been a Fulbright Senior Scholar at the European Institute for Cognitive Sciences and Engineering (EURISCO) in Toulouse, France; a visiting professor at the Institut Cognitique at the University of Bordeaux; is former chair of ACM SIGART; a member of the National Research Council (NRC)

Committee on Emerging Cognitive Neuroscience Research; and was an advisor to technology initiatives in Germany and Japan. He currently serves as a member of the Board on Global Science and Technology for the National Academies and as an external advisory board member of the Cognitive Science and Technology Program at Sandia National Laboratories. He is an Honorary Visiting Researcher at the Center for Intelligent Systems and their Applications and AIAI at the University of Edinburgh, Scotland. In 2011, he received the Web Intelligence Consortium Outstanding Contributions Award.

Kenneth M. Ford received a PhD in Computer Science from Tulane University and is Founder and CEO of the Institute for Human & Machine Cognition (IHMC)—a not-for-profit research institute located in Pensacola, Florida. IHMC has grown into one of the nation's premier research organizations with world-class scientists and engineers investigating a broad range of topics related to building technological systems aimed at amplifying and extending human cognitive and perceptual capacities. Richard Florida has described IHMC as "a new model for interdisciplinary research institutes that strive to be both entrepreneurial and academic, firmly grounded and inspiringly ambitious." IHMC headquarters are in Pensacola, and a branch research facility has recently opened in Ocala, Florida.

Dr. Ford is the editor or coauthor of hundreds of scientific papers and six books. Ford's research interests include: artificial intelligence, cognitive science, human-centered computing, and entrepreneurship in government and academia. He is Emeritus Editor-in-Chief of AAAI/MIT Press and has been involved in the editing of several journals. Dr. Ford is a Fellow of the Association for the Advancement of Artificial Intelligence (AAAI), a member of the American Association for the Advancement of Science, a member of the Association for Computing Machinery (ACM), a member of the IEEE Computer Society, and a member of the National Association of Scholars. Dr. Ford has received many awards and honors including the Doctor Honoris Causas from the University of Bordeaux in 2005 and the 2008 Robert S. Englemore Memorial Award for his work in artificial intelligence (AI).

In January 1997, Dr. Ford was asked by NASA to develop and direct its new Center of Excellence in Information Technology at the Ames Research Center in Silicon Valley. He served as Associate Center Director and Director of NASA's Center of Excellence in Information Technology. In July 1999, Dr. Ford was awarded the NASA Outstanding Leadership Medal. That same year, Dr. Ford returned to private life and to the IHMC.

In October of 2002, President George W. Bush nominated Dr. Ford to serve on the National Science Board and the United States Senate confirmed his nomination in March of 2003. The National Science Board (NSB) is the governing board of the National Science Foundation (NSF) and plays an important role in advising the President and Congress on science policy issues. In 2004 *Florida Trend Magazine* named Dr. Ford one of Florida's four most influential citizens working in academia. In 2005, Dr. Ford was appointed and sworn in as a member of the Air Force Science Advisory Board (SAB).

In 2007, Dr. Ford became a member of the NASA Advisory Council (NAC) and on October 16, 2008, he was named as Chairman—a capacity in which he served until October, 2011. In August 2010, Dr. Ford was awarded NASA's Distinguished Public Service Medal—the highest honor the agency confers. In February of 2012, Dr. Ford was named to the Defense Science Board (DSB).

Pat Hayes has a BA in mathematics from Cambridge University and a PhD in Artificial Intelligence from Edinburgh. He has been a professor of computer science at the University of Essex and of philosophy at the University of Illinois, and the Luce Professor of cognitive science at the University of Rochester. He has been a visiting scholar at Universite de Geneve and the Center for Advanced Study in the Behavioral Studies at Stanford, and has directed applied AI research at Xerox-PARC, SRI, and Schlumberger, Inc. At various times, Pat has been secretary of AISB, chairman and trustee of IJCAI, associate editor of *Artificial Intelligence*, a governor of the Cognitive Science Society, and president of AAAI.

Pat's research interests include knowledge representation and automatic reasoning, especially the representation of space and time; the semantic web; ontology design; image description; and the philosophical foundations of AI and computer science. During the past decade Pat has been active in the Semantic Web initiative, largely as an invited member of the W3C Working Groups responsible for the RDF, OWL, and SPARQL standards. Pat is a member of the Web Science Trust and of OASIS, where he works on the development of ontology standards.

In his spare time, Pat restores antique mechanical clocks and remodels old houses. He is also a practicing artist, with works exhibited in local competitions and international collections. Pat is a charter Fellow of AAAI and of the Cognitive Science Society, and has professional competence in domestic plumbing, carpentry, and electrical work.

About the Authors

Irma Becerra-Fernandez, PhD, is Vice-Provost for Academic Affairs, Florida International University, and Founder/Co-Chair of the 2010 and 2011 Americas Venture Capital Conference, Fellow and former Director of the Pino Global Entrepreneurship Center and Professor of MIS, 2009 MIT Sloan/CISR Visiting Scholar, and 2007 FIU/Kauffman Entrepreneurship Professor. She has advised organizations, in particular NASA, about knowledge management (KM), KM systems, business intelligence, disaster management, and IT entrepreneurship. She is an author of numerous journal publications and four books. She received the 2004 Outstanding Faculty Torch Award, 2006 Faculty Teaching Award, and 2001 Faculty Research Award. Contact her at becferi@fiu.edu.

Steve Deal is a systems engineer with a background in space systems. Since 2005, he has been working on human systems in the areas of acquisition, distributed collaboration, test and evaluation, and information transfer. He is currently supporting BCI Dahlgren while conceiving and coding web-based health care and massively distributed decision applications. Contact him at steven.v.deal@gmail.com.

Sidney Dekker is professor in the School of Humanities at Griffith University in Brisbane, Australia. Author of several best-selling books on human factors and safety, he has recently been flying the Boeing 737 part-time as airline pilot. Contact him at s.dekker@griffith.edu.au.

Susan Eitelman was a researcher at CHI Systems, Inc. at the time she collaborated on an essay. It was only from her encouragement that it was decided to write up the concept of the "Janus Machine." She died unexpectedly and at a young age in 2012. The Editors of the HCC Department extend their condolences to her husband Matt Dean and all of her family.

William C. Elm is President and Cognitive Systems Engineering Fellow of Resilient Cognitive Solutions, LLC. RCS focuses exclusively on delivering revolutionary decision support systems for severe data overload/mission critical applications using the methods and tools of Cognitive Systems Engineering. He specializes in the pragmatic application of CSE as part of a complete Systems Engineering practice. Bill is one of the longest practicing cognitive systems engineers, combining over 30 years of experience in domains ranging from commercial nuclear power to national intelligence and over 20 years' active and reserve officer experience in the intelligence domain from Division level to Joint Command. He has BS and MS degrees in Electrical Engineering and PhD coursework in Artificial Intelligence from Carnegie Mellon University. He has several patents and numerous professional publications. He can be contacted at welm@resilientcognitivesolutions.com.

Mica R. Endsley is President of SA Technologies, a cognitive engineering firm specializing in the development of operator interfaces for advanced systems, including the next generation of systems for aviation, air traffic control, power, medical, and military operations. Dr. Endsley received a PhD in Industrial and Systems Engineering from the University of Southern California. She has published extensively in the areas of situation awareness, decision-making, and automation and is coauthor of *Designing for Situation Awareness* (2nd ed., 2012; CRC Press). She can be contacted at mica@satechnologies.com.

Anne Feltovich holds a PhD in Classics from the University of Cincinnati and is currently an assistant professor at Grinnell College in Iowa. She enjoys teaching Greek, Latin, and Classical archaeology and is always looking forward to her next trip back to Greece. She can be reached at feltovic@grinnell.edu.

Paul J. Feltovich is a Research Scientist at the Florida Institute for Human and Machine Cognition. Feltovich received his PhD from the University of Minnesota (Minneapolis) and a BS in mathematics from Allegheny College, PA. He was also a post-doctoral fellow at the Learning Research and Development Center of the University of Pittsburgh. He has conducted research on human expertise, learning and instruction for difficult subject matter, and Human-Agent-Robot Teamwork (HART). He is a coauthor of a designated Science Citation Classic article on problem solving in physics. He is also coeditor of the first *Cambridge Handbook of Expertise and Expert Performance*. Contact him at pfeltovich@ihmc.us.

Stephen M. Fiore, PhD, is a faculty member in the University of Central Florida's Cognitive Sciences Program in the Department of Philosophy and Director of the Cognitive Sciences Laboratory at UCF's Institute for Simulation and Training. He earned his PhD degree in Cognitive Psychology from the University of Pittsburgh, Learning Research and Development Center. He maintains a multidisciplinary research interest that incorporates aspects of the cognitive, social, and computational sciences in the investigation of learning and performance in individuals and teams. He is coeditor of recent volumes on *Macrocognition in Teams* (2008), *Distributed Learning* (2007), *Team Cognition* (2004), and he has coauthored over 100 scholarly publications in the area of learning, memory, and problem solving at the individual and the group level. He can be contacted at sfiore@ist.ucf.edu.

John M. Flach is Professor and Chair of Psychology at Wright State University. His curiosity about human performance stems from his failures at sports, ineptitude with music, and uneasiness with technology. He began graduate school in psychology at Ohio State seeking reasons why things that seemed to come so easily to others were difficult for him. He finally completed the PhD in Human Experimental Psychology in 1984 and joined the faculty at the University of Illinois, where he had joint appointments in Mechanical and Industrial Engineering, Psychology, and the Institute of Aviation. He found a home at WSU where supportive colleagues and talented students helped him to muddle his way over the tenure hurdle and up the academic ladder to the rank of Professor. Serendipitously, he became chair of the Psychology Department in 2004. He teaches graduate and undergraduate courses in the areas of cognitive psychology and cognitive systems engineering. He also helps to direct an interdisciplinary research specialization in Learning with Disabilities and continues to explore a wide range of issues associated with human performance in complex systems. Despite over 30 years of research, however, he remains a clumsy athlete, an inept musician, and always the last to learn how to use new technologies. He can be contacted at john.flach@wright.edu.

Jennifer Fowlkes is a training analyst at the Naval Air Warfare Center Training Systems Division. She has over twenty years of experience in areas of human factors and training, which includes team training and performance strategies, training effectiveness evaluations, and performance test battery development. Her recent work centers on training system requirements for training complex skills. Dr. Fowlkes holds a PhD in Experimental Psychology from the University of Georgia. Contact her at jennifer.fowlkes@navy.mil.

Peter Hancock is Provost Distinguished Research Professor and Pegasus Professor at the Department of Psychology and the Institute for Simulation and Training at the University of Central Florida, where he directs the "Minds in Technology, Machines in Thought" Laboratory. He is a Past-President of the Human Factors and Ergonomics Society and the Society for Engineering Psychology. He is the former Chair of the Board of the Society for Human Performance in Extreme Environments. His primary areas of study are the effects of stress on performance and the mystery of time. Contact him at peter.hancock@ucf.edu.

Lewis F. Hanes is a consultant working primarily in the electric utility industry. His most recent research has involved helping develop Decision-Centered Guidelines for the Design of Human System Interfaces. Contact him at lhanes@columbus.rr.com.

Erik Hollnagel, PhD, is Professor and Chair in Industrial Safety at the École des Mines de Paris—Pôle Cindyniques. He can be contacted at erik.hollnagel@cindy.ensmp.fr.

Matt Johnson, PhD, has been a researcher at IHMC since 2002. He has worked on numerous projects including the Oz flight display for reducing the cognitive workload in the cockpit, the NASA Human-Robot Teamwork project, the DARPA Augmented Cognition project for improving human performance, the DARPA Little Dog project developing walking algorithms for a quadruped robot on rough terrain, and several human-robot coordination projects for both NASA and the Department of Defense. Most recently he has worked on development of the NASA humanoid based on Robonaut. He is responsible for acquiring IHMC's first robots and has been the lead on integration of robots into several IHMC projects including both NASA and Office of Naval Research unmanned systems projects. His research interests focus on improving performance in human-machine systems and include the areas of teamwork, coordination, and human-robot interaction. Matt has a BS in Aerospace Engineering and an MS and PhD in Computer Science. Matt comes to IHMC after 10 years as a Naval Aviator flying both fixed wing aircraft and helicopters. When not working on robots for IHMC he is a Naval Reserve Flight Instructor. Contact him at m.johnson@ihmc.us.

Gary Klein, PhD, is a senior scientist at MacroCognition LLC. He is one of the founders of the field of Naturalistic Decision Making and has developed Cognitive Task Analysis methods for studying cognition in field settings. His research with firefighters resulted in a Recognition-Primed Decision model of how people actually make decisions. He has also studied sensemaking and replanning. He can be reached at gary@macrocognition.com.

Philip Koopman, PhD, is an Associate Professor at the Carnegie Mellon University Electrical and Computer Engineering Department. He has served as a US Navy submarine officer, has architected embedded control CPUs for Harris Semiconductor, and has created embedded system architectures for a variety of United Technologies applications such as elevators and automobiles. His current research interests include lightweight processes for embedded system design, security of deeply embedded systems, and architectural support for embedded system survivability and safety. He is the author of the book *Better Embedded System Software*. Contact him at koopman@cmu.edu.

Phil Laplante, PhD, is Professor of Software Engineering at Penn State's Great Valley Graduate Professional Center. He conducts research and teaches in the areas of software and systems engineering, project management, and software testing and security. Contact him at plaplante@psu.edu.

Ron Laughery, PhD, is the founder and former President of Micro Analysis and Design, Inc., now a Division of Alion Science and Technology. He received his PhD in Industrial and Systems Engineering from the State University of New York at Buffalo. His research focused on the development of computational models and supporting technology for representing human performance in complex systems. He applied and tested these models in a variety of environments including aviation, military systems, nuclear power, and finance. He is currently retired and living in Boulder, Colorado, and can be contacted at ron@laugherys.com.

John D. Lee, PhD, is the Emerson Electric Professor and Director of the Cognitive Systems Laboratory in the Department of Industrial and Systems Engineering at the University of Wisconsin-Madison. He conducts research on how technology mediates attention in complex human-machine systems. He is a coauthor of the textbook *An Introduction to Human Factors Engineering* (2nd ed., 2003; Prentice Hall), and he recently coedited the *Oxford Handbook of Cognitive Engineering* (2008). Contact him at jdlee@engr.wisc.edu.

Charlotte Linde, PhD, is a senior research scientist in the Intelligent Systems Division of the NASA Ames Research Center. She is a socio-linguist who has studied the relation of narrative and memory for both individuals and organizations. Her publications in this area include *Life Stories: The Creation of Coherence* and *Working the Past: Narrative and Institutional Memory*, both Oxford University Press. Her current research focuses on the social functioning of formal procedures, particularly systems engineering, as a form of group remembering. Contact her at charlotte.linde@nasa.gov.

Gavan Lintern has a PhD in Engineering Psychology (University of Illinois, 1978). His recent research employed Cognitive Work Analysis to identify cognitive requirements for complex military platforms. Gavan retired in 2009. He now works occasionally as an industry consultant and runs workshops in Cognitive Systems Engineering, otherwise filling in as minder of the home pets and general home roustabout. He published a book, *The Foundations and Pragmatics of Cognitive Work Analysis* in 2009. Contact Gavan at glintern@CognitiveSystemsDesign.net or visit his website, www.cognitivesystemsdesign.net.

Morris Marx, PhD, received his doctoral degree in mathematics from Tulane University. He has served as faculty member and administrator at Vanderbilt University, the University of Oklahoma, and the University of Mississippi. He was the third president of The University of West Florida, for fourteen years. He is a recipient of the Order of the Rising Sun, the highest award given by the Japanese Government to non-Japanese. On July 15, 2002, he became Trustees Professor and President Emeritus and continues to serve in that position. He is also a Senior Scientist at the Institute for Human and Machine Cognition. Contact him at mmarx@ihmc.us.

Janet E. Miller, PhD, is a Senior Electronics Engineering in the Sensors Directorate of the Air Force Research Laboratory. Her current emphasis is addressing human factors issues in sensors systems. She can be contacted at janet.miller3@wpafb.af.mil.

Brian M. Moon is the Co-Founder and Chief Technology Officer of Perigean Technologies LLC. He was formerly a Principal Scientist at Klein Associates/Applied Research Associates. Contact him at brian@perigeantechnologies.com.

Alex Morison, PhD, is a Research Scientist in the Integrated System Engineering Department at The Ohio State University. Prior to completing his doctorate in Cognitive Systems Engineering, he completed a BS in Electrical Engineering and Applied Physics from Case Western Research University and an MS in Computer Science and Engineering from The Ohio State University. He studies the growing challenge of coupling human observers to remote sensor systems. Specifically, he is using fundamentals from human visual perception to define a new paradigm in human-robot interaction called extending perception. Inspired by models of human perception and attention, he has invented solutions to the image overload, keyhole effect, and multiple feeds problems associated with layered sensing systems and mobile sensor platforms. He is currently developing new devices and algorithms that implement the basic principles of perspective control for surveillance systems, human-robot interaction, and layered sensing systems to help human decision makers use of the large volume and flux of data these systems generate. He can be contacted at morison.6@osu.edu.

Kelly Neville, PhD, is an Associate Professor of Human Factors and Systems at Embry-Riddle Aeronautical University in Daytona Beach, FL, where she teaches cognitive psychology, ergonomics, systems concepts, and cognitive systems engineering. Her research interests lie in team coordination, expertise in dynamic and complex domains, training requirements for complex work, and stress effects on cognitive performance. She can be contacted at nevillek@erau.edu.

James M. Nyce, PhD, received his doctorate from Brown University in 1987. Nyce, a cultural anthropologist, is associate professor at Ball State University (Muncie, IN, USA). He is a docent (in information science) at Linköping University, Sweden. Nyce is also a Senior Partner/Principal at CRiSM, a research group focusing on information systems for crisis response (see https://www.imh.liu.se/samhallsmedicin/socialmedicin/crisim?l=sv). He is also adjunct associate professor at the Department of Radiology, Indiana University School of Medicine, Indianapolis, and has been visiting professor in military technology at the Swedish National Defence College 1998 to 2000 and 2005 to 2011. Contact him at jnyce@rocketmail.com.

M. Birna van Riemsdijk, PhD, is Assistant Professor in the Interactive Intelligence group at Delft University of Technology, The Netherlands. She received her PhD in 2006 from Utrecht University (under supervision of John-Jules Meyer, Mehdi Dastani, and Frank de Boer). After her PhD she spent two years at LMU Munich as a postdoc in the Programming and Software Engineering group of Prof. Wirsing before moving to Delft in 2008. Her research interests include human-agent/robot teamwork, organizational reasoning, and agent programming languages. She can be contacted at m.b.vanriemsdijk@tudelft.nl.

Axel Roesler, PhD, is an Assistant Professor at the Division of Design at the University of Washington. He is the Chair of the Interaction Design program and holds an adjunct appointment at the Department of Human Centered Design and Engineering. He received his PhD in Cognitive Systems Engineering with a specialization in Human-Centered Design and MFA in Industrial Design from The Ohio State University. His research explores the role of design in the development of human/machine interaction systems for high-stakes settings—technology-driven, collaborative work environments in aviation, medicine, and process control. He can be contacted at roesler@u.washington.edu.

Emilie M. Roth, PhD, is Owner and Principal Scientist of Roth Cognitive Engineering. Her work focuses on analysis and design of joint cognitive systems, and particularly collaborative automation. She is currently an associate editor of the *Journal of Cognitive Engineering and Decision Making*. Contact her at emroth@mindspring.com.

Nigel Shadbolt, PhD, is a Professor of artificial intelligence and head of the Web and Internet Science Group in Electronics and Computer Science at the University of Southampton, and will be co-director of the Open Data Institute, London. His research interests are the Semantic Web, Web science, and knowledge technologies. He received his PhD in artificial intelligence from the University of Edinburgh. He is a fellow and former president of the British Computer Society, a fellow of the Royal Academy of Engineering, a director of the Web Science Trust and a director of the World Wide Web Foundation. He is an Adviser to the UK Government on Open Data and a Member of the UK Public Sector Transparency Board. Contact him at nrs@ecs.soton.ac.uk.

David D. Woods, PhD, is Professor in the Institute for Ergonomics, Department of Integrated Systems Engineering, Institute for Sensing Systems, and leads the university-wide initiative on Complexity in Natural, Social and Engineered Systems at The Ohio State University. Contact him at woods.2@osu.edu.

Wayne Zachary, PhD, is managing partner at CMZ Health Technologies, where he consults and conducts research in cognitive engineering and macroergonomics. His expertise lies in developing effective and efficient methods for cognitive task analysis and cognitive modeling, and in using macroergonomic analyses to minimize human total cost of ownership and maximizing return on engineering investment on large systems. He was previously founder and CEO of CHI Systems, which he sold in 2005. He can be contacted at wzachary@comcast.net.

David Ziebell is manager of human performance technology at the Electric Power Research Institute. His work is currently in support of EPRI's Nuclear Maintenance Application Center. Contact him at dziebell@epri.com.

Foreword

I began my first term as Editor in Chief of *IEEE Intelligent Systems* in 2001. The Board began looking to refresh the title, and we were on the lookout for new Departments that would tackle particular themes in a sustained fashion. One such theme was to be Human-Centered Computing—and I knew just the person to lead it.

I had known Robert Hoffman since the late 1980s, when we were both researching the area of knowledge elicitation—how to find ways to efficiently and effectively elicit human expert knowledge sufficient to build models of that expertise, which in turn would support the creation of decision support systems. Robert spent his Fulbright year in my lab at the University of Nottingham, and I saw first-hand how he deployed insight, intuition, and deep scholarship to the problems of how to understand and characterize human cognition. In particular, we were both seized by the challenge of understanding the opportunities of the relationship between humans and computing technology.

Robert was always committed to the view that we humans were the central marvel to be understood, a phenomenon to appreciate and a resource to harness. Long before the Web facilitated collective cognition or augmented intelligence, he understood that we were the measure of all things and must remain so if we are to use our technology effectively and humanely.

When I commissioned the Department I knew Robert would be a tenacious and committed leader of it. He immediately recruited his colleagues Pat Hayes and Ken Ford to coedit—Pat and Ken brought their own expertise and experience to bear—both deeply immersed in AI yet ever conscious of the complexity of context that made the human brain such an exquisite intelligent system.

Ten years later we can look back on the essays and see Robert's fingerprint on every one of them. He authored most of them and coauthored and commissioned all the others. They were prescient when they were written, and they are still relevant now.

The range of the essays' topics captures the full scope of Human-Centered Computing, from the Boiled Frog Problem—determining when a company has lost so much corporate knowledge that it is indeed in hot water—to the Borg Hypothesis that long-term space exploration requires machines that are biologically inspired and humans that are computationally augmented. The Department has featured essays on the woes of procurement when we ignore the cognitive element. Essays have touched on the cybersecurity threats that arise despite our best technology because of our social nature.

The nexus of computer science and cognitive science will remain a fruitful area for research and reflection. Humans, computers, and their context form a trinity that will require the sort of insight that these essays embody. If we are to realize the promise of intelligent systems in all their forms, we will need the concepts, methods, and reflections contained in this book.

Nigel Shadbolt
December 2011
University of Southampton

Introduction

The notion of Human-Centered Computing (HCC) was introduced as a named program at the NASA-Ames Research Center. As shaped by Kenneth M. Ford, then the Associate Center Director at Ames, the NASA HCC program had a new vision for Artificial Intelligence (AI).[1] The Turing Test criterion for AI seeks to develop machine capabilities to imitate (or substitute for) the human. This is in contrast to HCC, which, in our perspective, has the goal of creating technologies that amplify and extend human perceptual, cognitive, and collaborative capabilities.[2,3,4]

What Is Human-Centered Computing?

The term HCC is sometimes used as an umbrella, encompassing a range of research themes such as interaction design and intelligent systems, human-computer interaction, and so forth. Some identify HCC with social networking. Some uses of HCC terms and concepts come without any apparent commitment to HCC as an overarching conceptual framework for intelligent systems, other than a

1 K.M. Ford, *Personal Communication*, Florida Institute for Human and Machine Cognition, 2009.

2 K.M. Ford and P.J. Hayes, "On Computational Wings: Rethinking the Goals of Artificial Intelligence," *Scientific American*, Special Issue on Intelligence, Winter 1998, pp. 78–83.

3 P.J. Hayes and K.M. Ford, "Turing Test Considered Harmful," *Proc. Int'l Joint Conf. on Artificial Intelligence* (IJCAI 95), Morgan Kaufman, 1995, pp. 972–997.

4 R.R. Hoffman, P.J. Hayes, and K.M. Ford, "Human-Centered Computing: Thinking In and Out of the Box," *IEEE Intelligent Systems*, vol. 16, no. 5, Sep./Oct. 2001, pp. 76–78.

general interest in the development of complex human-machine systems that pay close attention to human and social factors. In this use of the HCC term, the field of HCC is simply the sum of its parts, so HCC can be described by an enumeration of the topics and sub-fields that make it up. For us, however, the phrase "human-centered" in such terms as "human-centered design," "human-centered systems," and "human-centered computing" implies a specific theoretical—and ethical—commitment for the design and development of technologies that augment human capabilities and expertise.[5,6]

In a memorable encapsulation of a few of these themes, Ford, Glymour, and Hayes argued that the accumulated tools of human history could all profitably be regarded as orthoses—not in the sense that they compensate for the specific disabilities of any given individual, but rather because they enable us to overcome the biological limitations shared by all of us.[7] With reading and writing, anyone can transcend the finite capacity of human memory; with a power screwdriver, anyone can drive the hardest screw; with a calculator, anyone can get the numbers right; with an aircraft, anyone can fly to Paris; and with IBM's *Watson*, anyone can beat the world Jeopardy champion. Eyeglasses, a familiar instance of an "ocular orthosis," provide a particularly useful example of three basic HCC principles:

- ***Transparency.*** Eyeglasses leverage and extend our ability to see, but in no way model our eyes: They don't look or act like them and wouldn't pass a Turing test for being an eye. Moreover, eyeglasses are designed in ways that help us forget we have them on—we don't want to "use" them, we want to see *through* them.
- ***Unity.*** Since our goal is not making smart eyeglasses but rather augmenting vision, the minimum unit of design includes the device, the person, and the environment. This mode of analysis necessarily blurs the line between humans and technology.
- ***Fit.*** Your eyeglasses won't fit me; neither will mine do you much good. Prostheses must fit the human and technological components together in ways that synergistically exploit their mutual strengths and mitigate their respective limitations. This implies a requirement for rich knowledge not only of technology, but also of how humans function.

Orthoses or prostheses are useful *only* to the extent that they "fit"—in fact, the "goodness of fit" will determine system performance more than any other specific characteristic. This is true whether one considers eyeglasses, wooden legs, or cognitive orthoses. One can identify two broad categories of fit—*species fit* and *individual fit*. In some cases, a particular aspect of human function can afford a consistent fit across most of a population of interest. In many other instances, however, an *individual fit* is desirable, and in these cases relevant differences amongst individuals must be accommodated.[8]

One important difference between eyeglasses and the kinds of sophisticated machine-based assistance usually envisioned in HCC is the active, adaptive nature of the assistance. This quality is often characterized in the AI literature by the word "autonomy." Autonomy, however, sounds like just the *wrong* word for characterizing systems that are designed to assist, rather than replace, people. Though

5 M. Cooley, *Architect or Bee? The Human Price of Technology*, Chatto and Windus, 1987.

6 T. Winograd, "Shifting Viewpoints: Artificial Intelligence and Human-Computer Interaction," *Artificial Intelligence*, vol. 170, 2006, pp. 1256–1258.

7 K.M. Ford, C. Glymour, and P.J. Hayes, "Cognitive Prostheses," *AI Magazine*, vol. 18, no. 3, Fall 1997, p. 104.

8 K.M. Ford, "Toward Cognitive Prostheses," Robert S. Englemore Memorial Award Lecture, *23rd AAAI Conf. Artificial Intelligence* (AAAI 08), Association for the Advancement of Artificial Intelligence, 2008.

we are certainly interested in making machines more active, adaptive, and functional, the point of increasing these proficiencies is not merely to make the machines more independent when independence is required, but also to make them more capable of sophisticated *interdependent* joint activity with people. In addition to being able to hand off their tasks to machines, people need to be able to work coactively with them, participating in joint activity in a fluid and coordinated manner.[9,10,11,12]

How Did This All Get Started?

The Federal High Performance Computing program was established in the mid-1990s, based on a report by the National Science and Technology Council that identified human-centered systems as an important program component.[13] Stemming from that was an NSF workshop on "Human-Centered Systems" held in Arlington Virginia in February 1997.[14] This workshop was motivated by the same general issues that had also motivated human factors and cognitive engineering:

> Human-centered systems have vast potential to... increase the effectiveness of computer technology... by making computers easier to use... In an era of unprecedented technological change and growth, basic scientific research is crucial to design appropriate interventions into complex human social systems and to analyze and evaluate the effects of such interventions. To be human-centered, a [computer] system should be based on an analysis of the human tasks that the system is aiding, monitored for performance in terms of human benefits, built to take account of human skills, and adaptable easily to changing human needs.[15]

"Human-centered systems" was not seen as a community of practice, but rather as a rallying point for an inter-discipline. This was reflected in the merging of three programs of the US National Science Foundation (Human-Computer Interaction, Universal Access, and Digital Society and Technology) into a cluster called Human-Centered Computing.[16] The interdisciplinary nature of HCC

9 J.M. Bradshaw et al., "Sol: An Agent-Based Framework for Cyber Situation Awareness," *Kuenstliche Intelligenz*, in press, due 2012.

10 J.M. Bradshaw, P.J. Feltovich, and M. Johnson, "Human-Agent Interaction," *Handbook of Human-Machine Interaction*, G. Boy, ed., Ashgate, 2011, pp. 283–302.

11 M. Johnson et al., "Beyond Cooperative Robotics: The Central Role of Interdependence in Coactive Design," *IEEE Intelligent Systems*, vol. 26, no. 3, May/June 2011, pp. 81–88.

12 G. Klein et al., "Ten Challenges for Making Automation a 'Team Player' in Joint Human-Agent Activity," *IEEE Intelligent Systems*, vol. 19, no. 6, Nov./Dec. 2004, pp. 91–95.

13 Computer Science and Telecommunications Board, *Realizing the Information Future: The Internet and Beyond*, National Research Council, 1994.

14 J. Flanagan et al., eds., "Human-Centered Systems: Information, Interactivity and Intelligence," Report, National Science Foundation, 1997.

15 Flanagan et al., "Human-Centered Systems," p. 12.

16 A. Sears et al., "Human-Centered Computing: Defining a Research Agenda," *International Journal of Human-Computer Interaction*, vol. 24, no. 1, 2008, pp. 2–16.

is also reflected in the Statement of Goals of the IEEE Computer Society's Task Force on Human-Centered Computing:

> The field... has emerged from the convergence of multiple disciplines and research areas that are concerned both with understanding human beings and with the design of computational devices and interfaces. Researchers and designers of human-centered computing include individuals from computer science, sociology, psychology, cognitive science, engineering, graphic design, and industrial design.[17]

In retrospect, HCC has a number of historical antecedents. Detailed reviews of this history appear in Hoffman, Bannon, and Sebe[18] and Hoffman and Militello.[19] Roots can be traced to the notion of "sociotechnical systems" developed at the Tavistock Institute in the 1950s, to DARPA-funded work in the 1960s,[20,21] and to European work analysis.[22,23] In the 1980s and 1990s, sentiments about the consequences of deficient design of information technology were expressed by many scientists in fields of computer science, psychology, and human factors.[24,25,26,27] Beginning in the 1980s and continuing for a decade or so, a flurry of catchphrases were introduced, such as "Human-Centered Design," "User-Centered Design," "Contextual Design," and literally dozens more.[28] The impetus came from both academic groups and private industry.

What Are These Essays About?

In 1999 when Hoffman joined the Institute for Human and Machine Cognition, he was charged by its Director, Kenneth M. Ford, to "lay out the principles of HCC." At the time, Hoffman was one of the applied cognitive psychologists who had turned their attention to the study of domain experts

17 IEEE Computer Society, "Task Force on Human-Centered Computing," 2009; www.human-centered-computing.org/.

18 R.R. Hoffman, L.J. Bannon, and N. Sebe, "Human-Centered Computing," *Encyclopedia of Software Engineering*, P.A. Laplante, ed., Taylor & Francis, 2010, pp. 395–403.

19 R.R. Hoffman and L. Militello, *Perspectives on Cognitive Task Analysis: Historical Origins and Modern Communities of Practice*, CRC Press/Taylor and Francis, 2008.

20 J.C.R. Licklider, "Man-Computer Symbiosis," *IRE Transactions on Human Factors in Electronics*, vol. HFE-1, Mar. 1960, pp. 4–11.

21 D.C. Engelbart, "Augmenting Human Intellect: A Conceptual Framework," Stanford Research Institute, 1962.

22 V. De Keyser, "'Shallow' versus 'In-Depth' Work Analysis in Human-Centered Design," *Human-Centered Systems: Information, Interactivity and Intelligence*, J. Flanagan et al., eds., Report, National Science Foundation, 1997, pp. 261–266.

23 C. Floyd et al., "Out of Scandinavia: Alternative Approaches to Software Design and System Development," *Human-Computer Interaction*, vol. 4, no. 4, 1989, pp. 253–350.

24 C.E. Billings, *Aviation Automation: The Search for a Human-Centered Approach*, CRC Press, 1996.

25 J. Goguen, "Towards a Social, Ethical Theory of Information," *Social Science Research: Technical Systems and Cooperative Work: Beyond the Great Divide*, G. Bowker et al., eds., Erlbaum, 1997, pp. 27–56.

26 T.K. Landauer, *The Trouble with Computers*, MIT Press, 1995.

27 T. Winograd and F. Flores, *Understanding Computers and Cognition*, Ablex, 1986.

28 R.R. Hoffman et al., "A Rose by Any Other Name... Would Probably Be Given an Acronym," *IEEE Intelligent Systems*, vol. 17, no. 4, July/Aug. 2002, pp. 72–80.

(versus the academic study of the college freshman) and a confident practitioner of knowledge elicitation for expert systems. But he was broadening his focus to general cognitive task analysis methodology and its applications. He was not sure what these principles might be, or what it would mean for there to be such a thing as a "principle."

Bradshaw, on the other hand, with his background in both cognitive and computer science, had turned his attention early on from building knowledge acquisition tools for domain experts to the task of developing policy-governed multi-agent systems capable of participating in mixed human-automation teams.[29] Though he was a latecomer as a Department Coeditor on these HCC essays, the hallway leading between his office and that of Pat Hayes at IHMC had, for years, been a conduit for frequent sharing of ideas and outlooks.

Some 45 essays later, we have begun to achieve some clarity about the "principles of HCC." Both the evolution of HCC and its current theoretical and research foundations are laid out in the essays that are compiled into this volume. We hope that this may be the first of other such compilations. Already, we are told, this column has a longevity record in IEEE journals.

The first section of the book includes some of the earliest essays, which focused on the question of what HCC is, and especially what its principles might be. As the diverse meanings and interpretations of HCC emerged, as we mentioned just above, we began to question what was meant by "principle" and began to look at broader systems-level issues.

The second section includes essays that focused on issues of teams and collaboration. The taxonomy of types of kludges and workarounds and the topic of design anti-patterns still present opportunities for empirical research that could lead to measures for evaluating usability and human-centeredness. We still see considerable potential here.

We are seeing indications that the distinction between requirements and "desirements" is coming to be recognized as having value for our understanding of procurement processes. A comment often made is that "users" have difficulty specifying their requirements, and that, as designs are prototyped, the requirements described by the user keep morphing or "creeping." This is the bane of project management. The word "requirements" here refers to descriptions that enable the software engineer to proceed with the programming. It is important to recognize that requirements creep is inevitable, not a thing to be avoided or managed away. Rather than bemoaning this fact, users and software engineers need to work collaboratively, with users specifying their desirements and with designers bearing some responsibility for creative design, rather than simply "building to the requirements." The issue of responsibility in design is crucial with respect to the ultimate goal of building human-centered technologies.

IEEE Intelligent Systems originated in the heyday of expert systems, and the field of Expertise Studies is where we all cut our teeth in the 1980s. HCC remains directly related to expertise, since the goal of amplifying and extending human abilities is to achieve and exercise expertise. The macrocgnition-microcognition distinction discussed in a 2003 essay has proven valuable as a means for people to frame their inquiries and goals. The theory of sensemaking is gaining traction as a way of understanding human reasoning, often characterized in contrast with the "heuristics and biases" approach that focuses on human fallibilities. Finally, the notion of *perceptual re-learning of meaningful patterns that exist across multiple dynamic data types*—while a mouthful—is a significant extension of traditional notions of perceptual learning. It is crucial in most domains of expertise and certainly the critical activity in such domains as cybersecurity.

29 J.M. Bradshaw, ed., *Software Agents*, The AAAI Press/The MIT Press, 1997.

HCC seeks to escape the traditions of measurement and performance evaluation that place the worker as John Henry racing the steam hammer. Measurements of such things as hit rate, errors, efficiency, and so on are certainly useful and necessary for some purposes, but do not do well at capturing more meaningful levels of human-automation interaction. The distinction between measures and metrics is crucial, but generally overlooked. Metrics do not emerge from measures, or from the conceptual measureables that are the subject of measurement. Rather, metrics come from policy. The HCC Department's essays that pertain to measurement are an invitation to push measurement to more meaningful, system levels of analysis.

This topic of measurement relates directly to issues of procurement, and the final set of essays in this collection address this topic. These discuss barriers to human-centeredness as well as schemes such as the "Practitioner's Cycles" for injecting human-centered considerations into procurement. This is more than "human-system integration," which seems to simply be a new phrase to express some basic considerations that have a long standing in human factors (e.g., safety, manpower, training). Human-centeredness is about making the work meaningful, about being *in* the problem rather than fighting the technology, and about human desires to achieve and grow.

In some of the essays we were deliberately tilting at windmills. With some sense of accomplishment—and astonishment—we see that some sails were actually moved.

The ten challenges for team players outlined in 2004 are still crucial considerations in work design and management for any sort of collective, whether humans and more humans, or humans and software agents and robots.[30] Related to the increasing development and application of robotic technologies, the notion of task allocation has given way to a notion of human-machine interdependence.[31] This crucial concept merits further exploration and application.

Stay tuned—we're not done yet.

30 Klein et al., "Ten Challenges for Making Automation a 'Team Player.'"

31 Johnson et al., "Beyond Cooperative Robotics."

Part I:

Human-Centered Computing Foundations and Principles

Chapter 1: Human-Centered Computing: Thinking In and Out of the Box

R.R. Hoffman, P.J. Hayes, and K.M. Ford, "Human-Centered Computing: Thinking In and Out of the Box," *IEEE Intelligent Systems*, vol. 16, no. 5, Sep./Oct. 2001, pp. 76–78. doi: 10.1109/5254.956085

The motion picture* AI *lets the AI profession squirm in the glory of misrepresentation. It's not fun, especially when one's field suffers from waves of innovation/hype/backlash. The problem is that the film *AI* reinforces the dream of the android just when many who work toward "truly" intelligent technologies are cutting loose from the dream's more surrealistic aspects. People are asking new questions: Is the Turing test really the right kind of standard? If not, what is better? Must we define intelligence in reference to humans? Must intelligent technology be boxes chock-full of this thing we call intelligence, or should it operate as a "cognitive orthosis" to amplify or extend human perceptual, cognitive, and collaborative capabilities? Must intelligence always be in some individual thing—either a headbone or a box—or is intelligence a system property that is definable only in terms of the triple of humans-machines-contexts?

Human-Centered Computing: Thinking In and Out of the Box

Robert R. Hoffman, Patrick J. Hayes, and Kenneth M. Ford,
Institute for Human and Machine Cognition, University of West Florida

This department will present brief essays on timely or important topics, innovations, and developments that fall at the nexus of computer science and cognitive science. From time to time we will invite others having particular experiences or views to discuss issues involving human-centered computing. This department's title is intended to anchor the discussions in multiple perspectives—not only examinations of what's inside heads and computers (and other black boxes) but also what heads and computers are themselves inside of. Furthermore, by double entendre, the title expresses our intent to promote out-of-the-box thinking.

So, what's first? Something completely different—a review of the motion picture *AI*. Before its release, you could quite easily guess what the film would generally be about, what with Steven Spielberg producing off of an idea from Stanley Kubrick. You could imagine cool special effects, perhaps with a hefty dash of antiscience, and then the pace to the climax, which would probably involve something like turning the boy off ... and Lo! and Behold!—robots do have souls. Or something equally syrupy.

It's scary to have a major film premised on your profession, your love. Although we have yet to see a major motion picture titled *Psychology*, psychologists get nailed with this sort of thing, overhearing the odd hallway comment on the latest film about someone having multiple personalities: "Yeah, but the therapy is *really* realistic," or some such. *AI* lets a new crowd squirm in the glory of misrepresentation. It's not fun, especially when one's field suffers from waves of innovation–hype–backlash. (Example: expert systems, then the hype about them, then the hubbub about brittleness and explanation, then the promissory notes about *n*th-generation expert systems.)

Of Galatea and golems

But another factor is also at work in this case. One of humankind's oldest and most persistent dreams is to build reasoning devices. In Greek mythology, Pygmalion fell in love with a statue he created (which he named Galatea), subsequently bringing it to life, defying the gods and resulting in his punishment (in one version of the myth). In Jewish legend, mystical incantations instilled life in a human-like form made of earth or clay (the Hebrew word *golm*).[1,2] The golem possessed neither a soul nor the power of speech—only God can give these. The golem developed powers, became a threat (for example, to innocent little flower-carrying girls), and had to be controlled (or returned to dust) by its creator.

Sound familiar? Mary Shelley acknowledged having been inspired by German "ghost stories" she and her associates amused themselves with during the summer of 1816 in Geneva, where only eight years earlier Jacob Grimm had written extensively about the golem legend along with all the other folktales.[3] (It is instructive to compare the 1920 Czech film *Der Golem* with the 1931 Hollywood version of *Frankenstein*.) In addition, the golem legend contributed to the notion of the "robot" or human-created servant, as originated in Prague and elsewhere in Europe.[1,4,5] In all these stories, a presumptuous human discovers the scientific (or alchemical) secret to life, plays God, and winds up in hot water.

Cogs and cogitation

Exploring another path to the dream of the human-created reasoning device, Blaise Pascal (1623–1662), Gottfried Leibniz (1646–1716), Joseph-Marie Jacquard (1752–1834), Charles Babbage (1791–1871), and others tried to create actual machines—calculating engines.[6] For example, Pascal invented the Pascaline (see Figure 1), a device for addition. The Pascaline couldn't beat hand calculation but stirred some furor by demonstrating that a machine could perform operations that many traditionally regarded as the sole purview of the rational soul. Subsequent machines included elaborate mechanical clocks replete with moving figurines, which still adorn cathedrals throughout Europe. These machines showed the value of this method of natural philosophy or "science" and served to concretize the root metaphor—the entire universe (including the biological one) as a clockwork machine, having parts that interact according to mathematically specifiable rules. This metaphor was important throughout the late Renaissance and the Enlightenment.

René Descartes (1596–1650) and Julien Offroy de la Mettrie (1709–1751), among others, applied this metaphor to the question of the nature of the human body and soul. In "Passions of the Soul" and elsewhere, Descartes made it clear that he regarded the body and brain as a kind of machine:

> Any movement we make without any contribution from our will—as often happens when we breathe, walk, eat, and indeed, when we perform any action which is common to us and the beasts—depends solely on the arrangement of our limbs and the route which the spirits, produced by the heat of the heart, follow naturally in the brain, nerves, and muscles. This occurs in the same way as the movement of a watch is produced merely by the strength of its spring and the configuration of its wheels.[7]

But he did not go so far as to apply this to the mind/soul (hence his basic "dualistic" view):

> [The notion of the body as a machine would not] appear at all strange to those who are acquainted with the different automata, or moving machines, fabricated by human industry.… [S]uch persons will look upon this body as a machine made by the hands of God, which is incomparably better arranged and adequate to movements more admirable than any machine of human invention.[8]

Descartes held to a distinction between humans and automata (self-moving machines):

> It is indeed conceivable that a machine could be so made that it would utter words, and even words appropriate to the presence of physical acts or objects which cause some change in its organs; as, for example, if it is touched in some spot that it would ask what you wanted to say to it, if in another that it would cry that it was hurt, and so on for similar things. But it could never modify its phrases to reply to the sense of whatever was said in its presence, and even the most stupid men can do.… [A]lthough such machines could do many things as well as, or perhaps better than, men, they would infallibly fail in certain others, by which we would discover that they did not act by understanding or reason, but only by the disposition of their organs. For while reason is a universal instrument which can be used in all sorts of situations, the organs have to be arranged in a particular way for each particular action. From this it follows that is it morally impossible and clearly incredible that there should be enough different devices in a machine to make it behave in all the occurrences of life as our reason makes us behave.[8]

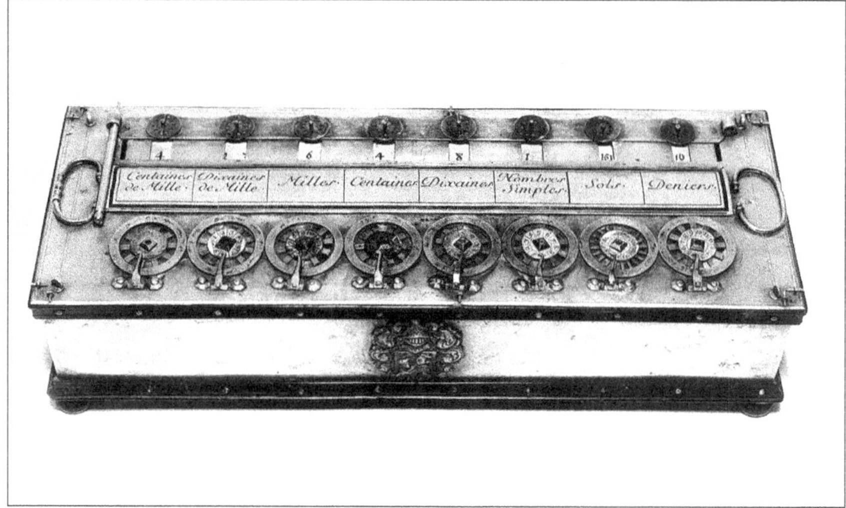

Figure 1. Blaise Pascal invented the Pascaline, an early device for addition.

Descartes set the stage for this discussion by supposing a man-made machine with all the outward appearance of a primate—based on and motivated by his view that animals did not possess rational souls. This shows why he is sometimes regarded as anticipating behaviorism:

> "So I may by chance look out of a window and notice some men passing in the street.… [W]hat do I see from this window except hats and cloaks which might cover automata?[9]
>
> And as a clock, composed of wheels and counter weights, observes not the less accurately all the laws of nature when it is ill made, and points out the hours incorrectly, than when it satisfies the desire of the maker in every respect; so likewise if the body of man be considered as a kind of machine, so made up and composed of bones, nerves, muscles, veins, blood, and skin, that even if there were in it no mind, it would not cease to move in all ways than it does at present when it is not moved under the direction of the will."[9]

Reflecting the impact of Descartes on the French Enlightenment, Julien La Mettrie (see Figure 2) pushed the mechanistic view of the universe to a monistic position regarding the mind–body relationship. In his essay "Man—a Machine." He went further than Descartes by rejecting all three dualisms: mind/body, human/animal, and mind/soul. Most of his evidence reflected his background as a physician—for example, the changes in mental state brought about by coffee or indigestion, or the mental incapacities caused by disease and fever. Putting a fine point on it:

> The diverse states of the soul are always correlative with those of the body.… [A] mere nothing, a tiny fibre, something that could not be found by the most delicate anatomy, would have made of Erasmus and Fontanelle two idiots.…[10]

Figure 2. Julien Offroy de la Mettrie.

> But since all the faculties of the soul depend to such a degree on the proper organization of the brain and of the whole body, that apparently they are but this organization itself, the soul is clearly an enlightened machine.[10]

Reading works such as those of Descartes and La Mettrie reminds us that we stand on the shoulders of the great thinkers who came before us. Descartes' arguments about the behaving simulacrum are suggestive of the Lovelace objection (machines can do only what we tell them

Robert R. Hoffman is a research scientist at the University of West Florida's Institute for Human and Machine Cognition and is a faculty associate in the university's Department of Psychology. He specializes in expertise studies, including knowledge elicitation and the design of human-centered systems. He is a Fulbright Scholar and a fellow of the American Psychological Society. He is on the editorial boards of *Human Factors* and *Cognitive Technology* and is a series editor for the book series *Expertise: Research and Applications*. He received his BA, MA, and PhD in experimental psychology from the University of Cincinnati. Contact him at the Inst. for Human & Machine Cognition, 40 Alcaniz St., Pensacola, FL 32501; rhoffman@ai.uwf.edu.

Patrick J. Hayes is a senior research scientist and the John Pace, Jr., Eminent Scholar at the University of West Florida. His research interests include knowledge representation and automatic reasoning, especially the representation of space and time and diagrammatic representations, and the philosophical foundations of AI and computer science. He received his BA in mathematics from Cambridge University and his PhD in Artificial Intelligence from the University of Edinburgh. Contact him at the Inst. for Human & Machine Cognition, 40 Alcaniz St., Pensacola, FL 32501; phayes@ai.uwf.edu.

Kenneth M. Ford is the founder and director of the University of West Florida's Institute for Human and Machine Cognition. He has an interdisciplinary interest in understanding cognition in both humans and other machines. He is the editor in chief of the AAAI/MIT Press, executive editor of the *International Journal of Expert Systems*, and associate editor of the *Journal of Experimental and Theoretical Artificial Intelligence*, and is a *Behavioral and Brain Sciences* associate. In 1999 he received the NASA Outstanding Leadership Medal. He received his PhD in computer science from Tulane University. Contact him at the Inst. for Human & Machine Cognition, 40 Alcaniz St., Pensacola, FL 32501; kford@ai.uwf.edu.

to). La Mettrie's discussion of the enlightened machine is suggestive of the distinction between strong and weak AI (weak AI: machines can be programmed to simulate intelligence; strong AI: machines can be programmed to have intelligence).

I, android

However, the prototype of the dream of the man-made rational device is not the calculating engines of Pascal or Leibnitz. It is the enlightened machine that looks just like us: the android (Greek for "man-like"). Not long before La Mettrie got himself into trouble for his views, one of his heroes, Denis Diderot (1713–1784), had written of the notion of the automaton in his *Encyclopedia*, during his discussion of the mechanical arts, including clockworking and machine fabrication.[11] Clockwork dolls of many varieties had been crafted to have an outward human appearance and were popular entertainments throughout Europe. A number of machines (boxes like the Pascaline—jammed with gear assemblies, rotors, and so on) had miniature humanoids on top, which did such things as copy handwriting or move the pieces in a chess game.[6] One craftsman, lacking neither bravado nor a sense of humor, made a robotic doll with a head that bobbed as the robot moved about on wheels. Covered with a monk's robe and holding prayer beads, it was a mockery, a dangerous device to build in dangerous times. (Upon hearing the news of Galileo's trial, Descartes decided to not publish his first book; La Mettrie's first book, *A Natural History of the Soul*, had been publicly burned, and La Mettrie had fled from France to Berlin.)

Today we suffer other ignominies, including the parodies produced in Hollywood. The problem is that the film *AI* reinforces the dream of the android just when many who work toward "truly" intelligent technologies are cutting loose from the dream's more surrealistic aspects. People are asking new questions: Is the Turing test really the right kind of standard? If not, what is better? Must we define intelligence in reference to humans? Must intelligent technology be boxes chock-full of this thing we call intelligence, or should it operate as a "cognitive prosthesis" to amplify or extend human perceptual, cognitive, and collaborative capabilities? Must intelligence always be in some individual thing—either a headbone or a box—or is intelligence a system property that is definable only in terms of the triple of humans–machines–contexts?

Implications and explorations of these sorts of questions will provide grist for the mill in this department. ■

References

1. C. Roth, ed., *Encyclopedia Judaica*, Macmillan, New York, 1971.

2. J. Trachtenberg, *Jewish Magic and Superstition: A Study in Folk Religion*, Behrman's Jewish Book House, New York, 1939.

3. G.L. Levine and U.C. Knoepflmacher, eds., *The Endurance of Frankenstein: Essays on Mary Shelley's Novel*, Univ. of California Press, Berkeley, Calif., 1982.

4. M. Idel, *Golem: Jewish Magical and Mystical Traditions on the Artificial Anthropoid*, State Univ. of New York Press, Albany, 1990.

5. R. Plank, "The Golem and the Robot," *Literature and Psychology*, vol. 15, Winter 1965, pp. 12–28.

6. W. Aspray, ed., *Computing before Computers*, Iowa Univ. Press, Ames, Iowa, 1990.

7. R. Descartes, "Passions of the Soul," *The Philosophical Writings of Descartes*, vol. 1, trans. J. Cottingham, R. Stoothoff, and D. Murdoch, Cambridge Univ. Press, Cambridge, UK, 1985, pp. 325–404.

8. R. Descartes, "Discourse on Method," *Descartes: Philosophical Essays*, trans. L.J. Lafleur, Prentice Hall, Upper Saddle River, N.J., 1964, pp. 2–57.

9. R. Descartes, "Meditations Concerning First Philosophy," *Descartes: Philosophical Essays*, trans. L.J. Lafleur, Prentice Hall, Upper Saddle River, N.J., 1964, pp. 61–143.

10. J.O. de la Mettrie, *Man—a Machine*, trans. G.C. Bussey, Open Court Press, Lasalle, Ill., 1912, pp. 89, 138.

11. D. Diderot and J. d'Alembert, eds., *Encyclopédie ou dictionnaire raisonné des sciences, des arts et des métiers* [*Encyclopedia or Systematic Dictionary of the Sciences, Arts, and Crafts*], Chez Briasson, David, Le Breton, Durand, Paris, 1751–1772.

Chapter 2: The State of Cognitive Systems Engineering

RR. Hoffman, G. Klein, and K.R. Laughery, "The State of Cognitive Systems Engineering," *IEEE Intelligent Systems*, vol. 17, no. 1, Jan./Feb. 2002, pp. 73–75. doi: 10.1109/5254.988462

The widespread introduction of the personal computer, beginning about 1970, helped spawn the field of inquiry called cognitive engineering, which concerns itself with such things as interface design and user friendliness. Since then, this field has taught us many important things, including two major lessons. First, the road to user-hostile systems is paved with designers' user-centered intentions. Even smart, clever, well-intentioned people can build fragile, hostile devices that force the human to adapt and build local kludges and workarounds. Worse still, even if you are aware of this trap, you will still fall into it. Second, technology developers must strive to build truly human-centered systems. Machines should adapt to people, not the other way around. Machines should empower people. The process of designing machines should leverage what we know about human cognitive, perceptual, and collaborative skills.

The State of Cognitive Systems Engineering

Robert R. Hoffman, *University of West Florida*
Gary Klein, *Klein Associates*
K. Ronald Laughery, *Micro Analysis & Design*

The widespread introduction of the personal computer, beginning about 1970, helped spawn the field of inquiry called *cognitive engineering*, which concerns itself with such things as interface design and user friendliness.

Since then, this field has taught us many important things, including two major lessons.

First, the road to user-hostile systems is paved with designers' user-centered intentions. Even smart, clever, well-intentioned people can build fragile, hostile devices that force the human to adapt and build local kludges and workarounds. Worse still, even if you are aware of this trap, you will still fall into it.

Second, technology developers must strive to build truly human-centered systems. Machines should adapt to people, not the other way around. Machines should empower people. The process of designing machines should leverage what we know about human cognitive, perceptual, and collaborative skills.

Time to rethink

We're in a new ballgame, in which the modern "socio-technical" workplace is characterized by changing collaborative mixes of humans and machines. Advances in technology have opened new horizons that are changing the nature of work and education, including distance learning, distance collaboration, training support, and performance support.[1–3]

Consider, for example, the notion from human factors engineering of *task analysis*: you can decompose jobs into invariant linear or tree-like sequences of actions (and some cognitions). This notion has a long history, dating to the applied psychological research in Europe dubbed *psychotechnics* in the late 1800s. (This notion of task differs from the AI notion of "generic tasks."[4])

Studies of the modern workplace suggest that significant problems can arise when you design systems based on a decomposition of tasks into invariant sequences of prescribed steps. Sometimes, people might appear to be conducting linear sequences of actions, when they are actually engaging in context-sensitive, knowledge-driven choices among alternative actions.[5,6] Would loss of the uplink to the weather radar keep a forecaster from crafting a forecast? No, the forecaster can work around it because knowledge permits the creation of alternative paths to the goal. When you are forced to adapt, kicking and screaming, to a new software upgrade and are frustrated by changes in functionality, are you totally paralyzed? No, you can craft a workaround.

The point is not that something is inherently wrong about the notion of a task as an expression of a particular goal, but that task analysis as it has been applied can sometimes be limiting. When regularly occurring sequences are regarded as invariant and therefore predefined, systems designed on this basis can run a substantial risk of being flawed. Specifically, you can expect them to lead to fragilities, hostilities, and automation surprises.[3,7] In short, they might not be human-centered.

Over the past decade, research activities have converged on new notions of "cognitive field research" and new frameworks that point toward methodologies for crafting human-centered systems.[8–13]

Understanding

Research over the past decade has led to

Editors: Robert R. Hoffman, Patrick J. Hayes, and Kenneth M. Ford
Institute for Human and Machine Cognition, University of West Florida
rhoffman@ai.uwf.edu

- Knowledge about the development of proficiency and the acquisition of skill leading to the achievement of expertise[13–17]
- Effective methodologies for eliciting and preserving the knowledge of domain practitioners[18,19]
- Clear ideas of how to describe the reasoning and decision-making skills of experts[20–22]

We also know the strengths and weakness of alternative methods and how to fit the methods to particular practice domains and research goals.[23–24]

Converging research and ideas from the cognitive, social, and computational sciences will lead to a concrete road map guiding the creation of human-centered technologies.

Application

- We are learning how to train people to become "expert apprentices"—that is, empowering them to enter into a domain or organization, arrive at a rich empirical understanding of work practice, and perceive the "true work" that must be accomplished.[13] This supports the process of revolutionary design.
- We know how to go from models of expert knowledge and reasoning to revolutionary designs for systems to display information and support both the learner and the practitioner.[25]

Where the rubber meets the road

Analyses of technology and its impacts have lead to an understanding of what it means for technology to be truly human-centered.[26–29] Converging research and ideas from the cognitive, social, and computational sciences will lead to a concrete road map guiding the creation of human-centered technologies. However, to reach this destination, system designers must refuse to cave in to penny-wise, short-term thinking in system development. They also must have zero tolerance for user-hostile systems. Who will step up to bat? ■

References

1. A.J. Cañas, D.B. Leake, and D.C. Wilson, "Managing, Mapping and Manipulating Conceptual Knowledge," *Exploring Synergies of Knowledge Management and Case-Based Reasoning*, tech. report WS-99-10, AAAI Press, Menlo Park, Calif., 1999, pp. 10–14.
2. A. Schaafstal, J.M. Schraagen, and M. van Berlo, "Cognitive Task Analysis and Innovation of Training: A Case of Structured Troubleshooting," *Human Factors*, vol. 42, 2000, pp. 75–86.
3. D.D. Woods and E. Hollnagel, "Mapping Cognitive Demands in Complex Problem-Solving Worlds," *Int'l J. Man-Machine Studies*, vol. 26, 1987, pp. 257–275.
4. T. Bylander and B. Chandrasekaran, "Generic Tasks for Knowledge-Based Reasoning: The 'Right' Level of Abstraction for Knowledge Acquisition," *Int'l J. Man-Machine Studies*, vol. 26, 1987, pp. 231–243.
5. P.A. Hancock and S.F. Scallen, "Allocating Functions in Human-Machine Systems," to be published in *Viewing Psychology as a Whole*, R.R. Hoffman, M.F. Sherrick, and J.S. Warm, eds., Amer. Psychological Assoc., Washington, D.C., pp. 509–540.
6. J. Rasmussen, "Skills, Rules and Knowledge: Signals, Signs and Symbols and Other Distinctions in Human Performance Models," *IEEE Trans. Systems, Man, and Cybernetics*, vol. SMC-13, 1983, pp. 257–266.
7. N. Sarter, D.D. Woods, and C. Billings, "Automation Surprises," to be published in *Handbook of Human Factors/Ergonomics*, 2nd ed., G. Salvendy, ed., John Wiley & Sons, New York.
8. W.J. Clancey, "The Knowledge Level Reinterpreted: Modeling Socio-Technical Systems," *Knowledge Acquisition as Modeling*, K.M. Ford and J.M. Bradshaw, eds., John Wiley & Sons, New York, 1993, pp. 33–49.
9. V. De Keyser, "'Shallow' versus 'In-Depth' Work Analysis in Human-Centered Design," *Human-Centered Systems: Information, Interactivity and Intelligence*, J. Flanagan et al., eds., Nat'l Science Foundation, Washington, D.C., 1997, pp. 261–266.
10. R.R. Hoffman and D.D. Woods, guest eds., special issue on cognitive task analysis, *Human Factors*, vol. 42, no. 1, 2000, pp. 1–95.
11. J.M.C. Schraagen, S.F. Chipman, and V.L. Shalin, eds., *Cognitive Task Analysis*, Lawrence Erlbaum, Hillsdale, N.J., to be published.
12. L. Suchman, *Plans and Situated Actions: The Problem of Human-Machine Communication*, Cambridge Univ. Press, Cambridge, UK, 1987.
13. K. Vicente, *Cognitive Work Analysis: Toward Safe, Productive, and Healthy Computer-Based Work*, Lawrence Erlbaum, Mahwah, N.J., 1999.
14. M.T.H. Chi, R. Glaser, and M.J. Farr, eds., *The Nature of Expertise*, Lawrence Erlbaum, Mahwah, N.J., 1988.
15. K.A. Ericsson and J. Smith, eds., *Toward a General Theory of Expertise*, Cambridge Univ. Press, Cambridge, UK, 1991.
16. R.R. Hoffman, ed., *The Psychology of Expertise: Cognitive Research and Empirical AI*, Lawrence Erlbaum, Mahwah, N.J., 1992.
17. J. Shanteau, "Competence in Experts: The Role of Task Characteristics," *Organizational Behavior and Human Decision Processes*, vol. 53, 1992, pp. 252–266.
18. K.M. Ford and J.M. Bradshaw, eds., *Knowledge Acquisition as Modeling*, John Wiley & Sons, New York, 1993.
19. R.R. Hoffman, B. Crandall, and N. Shadbolt, "A Case Study in Cognitive Task Analysis Methodology: The Critical Decision Method for the Elicitation of Expert Knowledge," *Human Factors*, vol. 40, 1998, pp. 254–276.
20. E. Hutchins, *Cognition in the Wild*, MIT Press, Cambridge, Mass., 1995.
21. J. Lave, *Cognition in Practice: Mind, Mathematics, and Culture in Everyday Life*, Cambridge Univ. Press, Cambridge, UK, 1988.
22. C. E. Zsambok and G. Klein, eds., *Naturalistic Decision Making*, Lawrence Erlbaum, Mahwah, N.J., 1997
23. R.R. Hoffman et al., "Eliciting Knowledge from Experts: A Methodological Analysis," *Organizational Behavior and Human Decision Processes*, vol. 62, no. 2, 1 May 1995, pp. 129–158.
24. S.S. Potter et al., "Bootstrapping Multiple Converging Cognitive Task Analysis Techniques for System Design," *Cognitive Task Analysis*, J.M. Schraagen and S.F. Chipman,

eds., Lawrence Erlbaum, Mahwah, N.J., 2000, pp. 317–340.

25. J.D. Novak, *Learning, Creating, and Using Knowledge*, Lawrence Erlbaum, Mahwah, N.J., 1998.

26. J. Flanagan et al., eds., *Human-Centered Systems: Information, Interactivity and Intelligence*, Nat'l Science Foundation, Washington, D.C., 1997.

27. K.M. Ford, P. Hayes, and W.J. Clancey, "Cognitive Prostheses," paper presented at the meeting of the Florida AI Research Soc., Melbourne Fla., 1998.

28. R.R. Hoffman, "How to Doom Yourself to Repeat the Past: Some Reflections on the History of Cognitive Technology," *Cognitive Technology*, vol. 2, 1997, pp. 4–15.

29. E. Hollnagel and D.D. Woods, "Cognitive Systems Engineering: New Wine in New Bottles," *Int'l J. Man-Machine Studies*, vol. 18, 1983, pp. 583–600.

Robert R. Hoffman is a research scientist at the University of West Florida's Institute for Human and Machine Cognition and is a faculty associate at the university's Department of Psychology. He specializes in expertise studies, including knowledge elicitation and the design of human-centered systems. He is a Fulbright Scholar and a fellow of the American Psychological Society. He is on the editorial boards of *Human Factors* and *Cognitive Technology* and is a series editor for the book series *Expertise: Research and Applications*. He received his BA, MA, and PhD in experimental psychology from the University of Cincinnati. Contact him at the Inst. for Human & Machine Cognition, 40 Alcaniz St., Pensacola, FL 32501; rhoffman@ai.uwf.edu.

Gary Klein is the chief scientist at Klein Associates Inc., a company he founded in 1978 to better understand how to improve decision making in individuals and teams. His work on recognitional decision making has been influential for the design of new systems and interfaces and for the development of decision training programs. He received his PhD in experimental psychology from the University of Pittsburgh. Contact him at Klein Associates, Inc., 1750 Commerce Center Blvd., North, Fairborn, OH 45324-3987; gary@klein-inc.com.

K. Ronald Laughery is the president and founder of Micro Analysis and Design, Inc., a consulting company specializing in the development and use of tools for analyzing human-centered systems. He has a BS, an MS, and a PhD in industrial engineering from the State University of New York at Buffalo. He is a member of the IEEE, ACM, Inst. of Industrial Engineers, and Human Factors and Ergonomics Society. Contact him at Micro Analysis and Design, Inc., 4949 Pearl East Circle, Boulder, CO 80302.

Chapter 3: The Sacagawea Principle

M. Endsley and R.R. Hoffman, "The Sacagawea Principle," *IEEE Intelligent Systems*, vol. 17, no. 6, Nov./Dec. 2002, pp. 80–85. doi: 10.1109/MIS.2002.1134367

Many software tools and systems restrict the availability of information and make information integration and exploration difficult. Poorly designed tools are often brittle, because they prescribe task sequences. But in complex sociotechnical contexts, workers do not perform tasks; they engage in knowledge-driven, context-sensitive choices from among alternative activities in order to achieve goals. So, good tools must be flexible—they must provide the information that workers need to generate appropriate action sequences by which they can achieve the same goal in different situations. Adapted from the writings of Donald Norman is a principle we call the Sacagawea Principle: human-centered computational tools need to support active organization of information, active search for information, active exploration of information, reflection on the meaning of information, and evaluation and choice among alternative activities. Context-conditional variation includes variation due to the worker—each worker has his or her own needs, entailing different requirements and constraints. This implies that individuals should be able to choose different trajectories to achieve the desired outcome in different ways. A good tool gives users discretion to generate various action sequences and express their preferences. As with many HCC principles, we have named this one after a person to give it a concrete and meaningful label. Sacagawea served as a guide, without whose help the Lewis and Clark expedition might not have achieved the successes it did. The name is also somewhat ironic, because Sacagawea was, for part of her life, a captured slave. The theme of machines and robots as slaves is arguably the oldest in the robotics literature, and it is still often used as a metaphor to describe the tools people use to accomplish their work. In this essay, we explore an approach for fulfilling the Sacagawea Principle in system design—an approach based on empirical study of the way in which people process their environments in complex worlds.

The Sacagawea Principle

Mica Endsley, *SA Technologies*
Robert R. Hoffman, *Institute for Human and Machine Cognition*

Many software tools and systems restrict the availability of information and make information integration and exploration difficult.[1] Poorly designed tools are often brittle, because they prescribe task sequences. But in complex sociotechnical contexts, workers do not perform tasks; they engage in knowledge-driven, context-sensitive choices from among action sequence alternatives in order to achieve goals.[2] So, good tools must be flexible—they must provide the information that workers need to generate appropriate action sequences by which they can achieve the same goal in different situations. Adapted from the writings of Donald Norman is a principle we call the Sacagawea Principle:

> Human-centered computational tools need to support active organization of information, active search for information, active exploration of information, reflection on the meaning of information, and evaluation and choice among action sequence alternatives.

Context-conditional variation includes variation due to the worker—each worker has his or her own needs, entailing different requirements and constraints. This implies that individuals should be able to choose different trajectories to achieve the desired outcome in different ways. A good tool gives users discretion to generate various action sequences and express their preferences.

Editors: Robert R. Hoffman, Patrick J. Hayes, and Kenneth M. Ford
Institute for Human and Machine Cognition, University of West Florida
rhoffman@ai.uwf.edu

As with many HCC principles, we have named this one after a person to give it a concrete and meaningful label. Sacagawea served as a guide, without whose help the Lewis and Clark expedition might not have achieved the successes it did. The name is also somewhat ironic, because Sacagawea was, for part of her life, a captured slave. The theme of machines and robots as slaves is arguably the oldest in the robotics literature, and it is still often used as a metaphor to describe the tools people use to accomplish their work. In this essay, we explore an approach for fulfilling the Sacagawea Principle in system design—an approach based on empirical study of the way in which people process their environments in complex worlds.

Situation awareness: Key to designing human-centered systems

One of the most important functions that people must perform, when they are using machines for exploring and understanding the world, is to maintain a state of *situation awareness* (SA). This is especially true in domains such as aviation, firefighting, and weather forecasting. The user must form what is often referred to as a *mental model* of the ongoing situation—a situational model or SA. Domain practitioners often report an imagistic experience, manifested as a 4D simulation of events that is driven or constrained by the practitioner's understanding of domain principles. Then, as things change, the person must continuously update that mental model, which is adjusted by anticipating how events will unfold. Attention must be directed to important events and situation features, with "importance" being a function of the situation itself. SA forms the critical input to decision making in these domains.[3–6] Maintaining SA depends on achieving and then maintaining a global understanding of some unfolding situation, while at the same time using that understanding to juggle goal-driven and data-driven activities, both of which can redirect attention to new goals or subgoals. Achieving high levels of SA requires a system that effectively supports this process.

SA operates at a number of levels,[3] as shown in Figure 1. Level 1 SA concerns the perception of needed information from the mass of data that is available. What constitutes

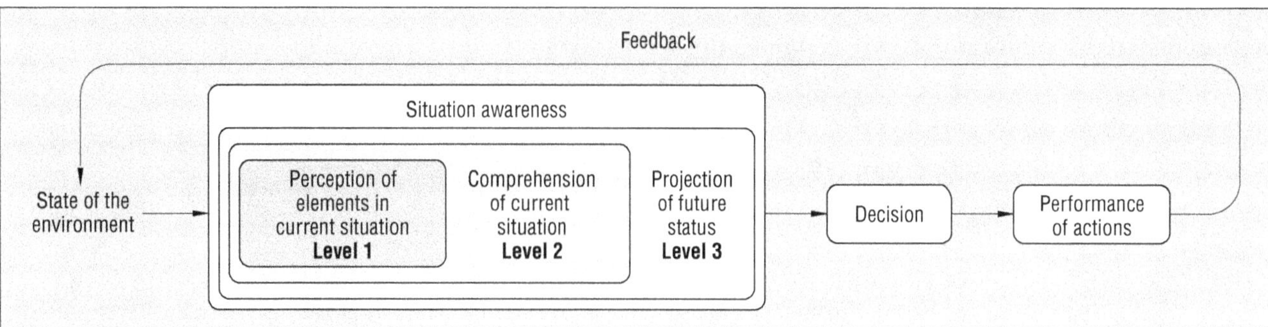

Figure 1. Three levels of situation awareness.

"needed data" is a function of the operator's goals and decision requirements. Level 2 SA concerns the degree to which the individual comprehends the meaning of that data, typically via the formation of a mental model of the system and environment. In complex domains, understanding the significance of various disparate pieces of data is nontrivial. It involves integrating many pieces of interacting data, forming a higher order of understanding—that is, information prioritized according to how it relates to achieving the goals.

Once the person is aware of relevant data in the environment and what they mean in relation to the current goal, it is the ability to predict what those elements will do in the future (at least in the near term) that constitutes Level 3 SA. Using current situation understanding to form projections requires a good understanding of the domain—which is often made possible by the formation of a highly developed mental model—and can be quite demanding mentally. In complex domains, the ability to project is a key to the ability to behave proactively and not just reactively. SA is critical to successful operation in these dynamic domains where accurately perceiving, understanding, and projecting actions and events in the environment is necessary for good decision making and performance.[4]

SA is a process conducted largely in the person's mind. Few domains have the kind of graphics "fusion box" that provides users with a 4D representation of their world; domains in which tools do provide at least some support (for example, weather forecasting and battlefield command and control) tend to be electronic chart-wall systems that let users merely combine and overlay various multiple data types. That is fusion in only a limited sense.

Given this primary reliance on human cognitive thinking, presenting a ton of data does no good unless users can successfully assimilate it in a timely manner. So, SA provides a mechanism—arguably the single most important mechanism—for fulfilling the HCC goals of the Sacagawea Principle. Because the requirements for SA in any given domain are operationally derived on the basis of operator goals and decisions, they provide a basis for determining what has meaning—that is, Level 2 SA. It involves going from data to information, and to the meanings that the operator really needs to know.

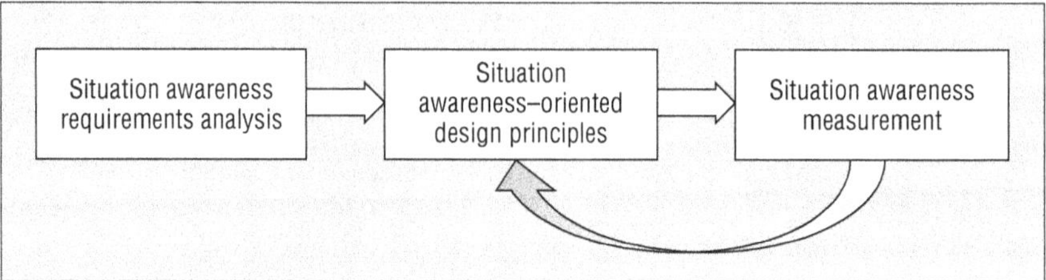

Figure 2. The situation awareness–oriented design process.

One of us (Mica Endsley), with colleagues, developed the *situation awareness–oriented design process* as a means for designing systems that support SA.[4,7,8] SAOD addresses the needs of pilots, air traffic controllers, power plant operators, military commanders, and others who must make decisions in the face of rapidly changing situations, large volumes of data, and system complexity. In these domains, not only must the operators be able to rapidly explore and integrate data but also do so on an ongoing basis as events (data) and their goals change.

SAOD embodies three main steps or phases (see Figure 2). SA requirements analysis provides the driver, or leverage points, for designing SA support systems. Evidence about the factors that lead to good and poor SA led to the creation of SA design principles, providing a means to translate SA requirements into systems designs. Finally, SA measurement forms the backbone of the process by providing data on the effects (usefulness, usability) of the design concepts that were developed on the basis of the design principles and requirements analysis.

Phase 1: SA requirements analysis

We have approached the problem of determining what aspects of the situation are important for a particular operator's SA using a form of cognitive task analysis that focuses on identifying the user's goals. *Goal-directed task analysis* is based on structured interviews, observations of operators performing their tasks, and detailed analysis of documentation on users' tasks.[9,10] GDTA first identifies the major goals of a particular job class. When we ask domain practitioners what their primary goal is and how they go about achieving it, they often couch their replies in terms of the technologies with which they must work, the "environmental constraints" on performance.[11] So, for instance, the practitioner might say, "Well, I have to determine the input to the DLN receiver, but first I have to access the MNBT files using the DPD system here, and then reinitialize the login files since the data types for the DLN do not conform to the

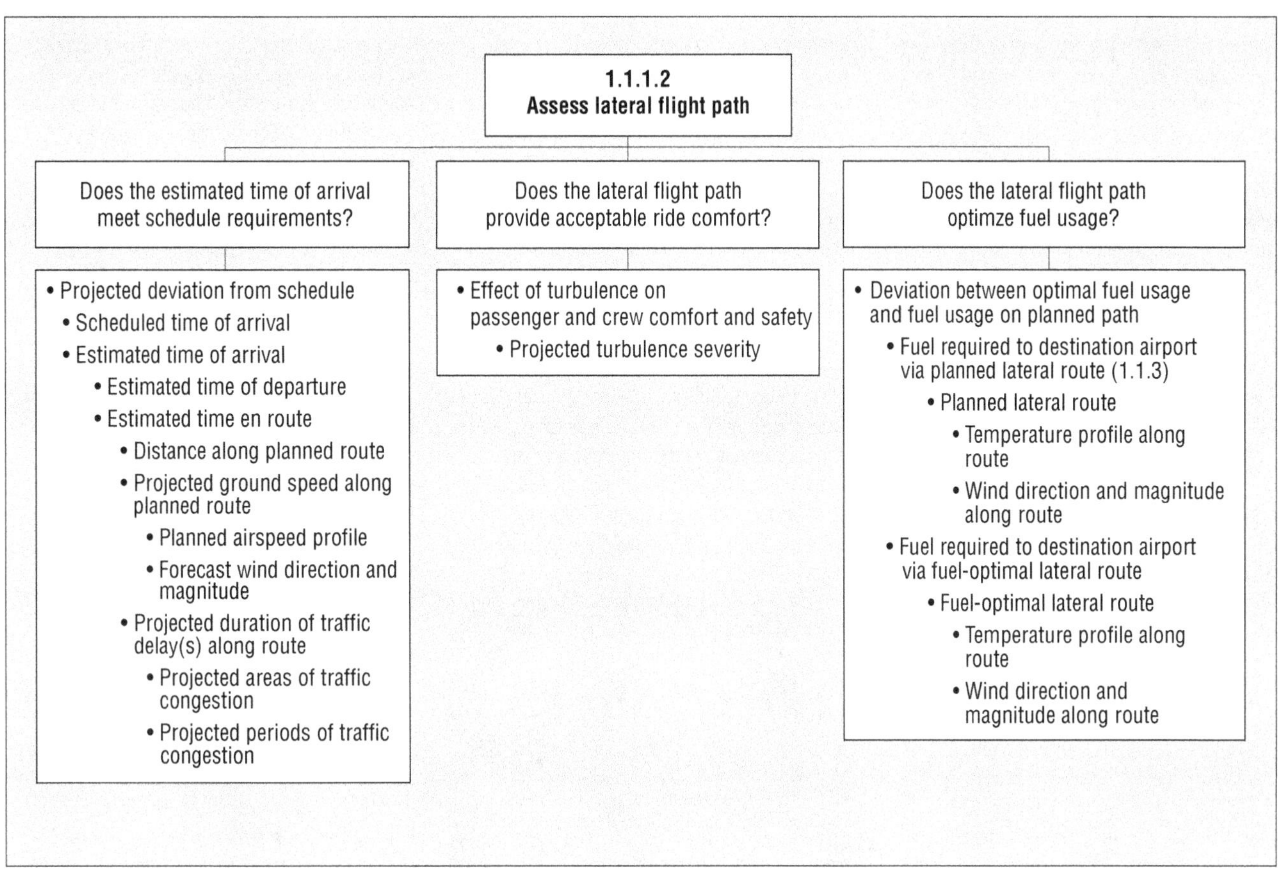

Figure 3. Goal-directed task analysis: A commercial pilot subgoal.[12]

input specifications for the data files ..."

At that point, the analyst interjects, "No, what is it that you really are trying to accomplish?" It invariably turns out that the true work they must accomplish falls at a more meaningful level, the knowledge level if you will—perhaps something like "What I am really trying to do here is find out what data types must be involved in this particular situation. But to do that, I have to format them according to the right categories before anyone else can use the information." It is this clear focus on the meanings of goals and task activities that perhaps distinguishes GDTA analysis from other forms of cognitive task analysis.

The analysis then moves on to specify the main subgoals necessary for meeting each major goal. We identify the key decisions that the user must make for each subgoal, as well as the SA needed for making these decisions and working toward each subgoal. Subgoal SA requirements often focus not only on what data the operator needs but also on how that information is integrated or combined to address each decision. This provides a basis for determining what meanings the user must derive from the data. Figure 3 presents an example of a partial goal hierarchy that came from a GDTA process for a commercial airline pilot.[12]

Phase 2: SAOD principles

Historically, most interface design guidelines focus on the individual component level—the size of the text, the type of dial or gauge, the size of a button, and so on.[13,14] Historically, guidelines for human–computer interaction focus on the design of physical components (for example, the shape of the mouse, or best uses for alternate input devices) or of specific software components (for instance, how a menu should function or be placed or the best way to fill in information on a screen).[15] Furthermore, most guidelines assume the "one person, one machine" scenario for HCI.

These features tend to make many interface guidelines insufficient for application in complex sociotechnical workplaces. Their grain of analysis, useful for the microscale design of specific interface features, is inappropriate for understanding the broader interactions and dependencies of cognitive processes such as attention and sense-making. Most guidance remains silent on the subject of how to determine or convey the meaning of information that is to be displayed.[16]

A number of design guidelines have been developed for creating systems that will support SA, based on a general model of how people process information in complex environments to form and maintain SA.[4] SA-oriented design principles do not supplant existing microscale design guidelines but rather augment and complement them. They do so by addressing such issues as the integration of information into knowledge and SA to support the operator in managing information on the basis of dynamically changing information needs associated with a dynamically changing situation. In some work contexts, a fixed task sequence can help constrain the layout of information. Yet, for most complex cognitive systems, the human must have the flexibility to bounce between different goals as events change. So, a goal-oriented approach tries to take into account how people actually work.

We illustrate SA guidance with an example—another HCC principle. To correspond with the Sacagawea Principle, we dub this one the Lewis and Clark Principle. It states that

> The human user of the guidance needs to be shown the guidance in a way that is organized in terms of their major goals. Information needed for each particular goal should be shown in a meaningful form, and should allow the human to directly comprehend the major decisions associated with each goal.

The Lewis and Clark Principle is somewhat different from Norman's notion of "naturalness of representation":

> Perceptual and spatial representations are more natural and therefore to be preferred but only if the mapping between the representation and what is stands for is natural—analogous to the real perceptual and spatial environment.[1] (p. 72)

The spirit of "naturalness" is similar to that of the Lewis and Clark Principle; that is, its displays must present meanings in a directly perceptible and comprehensible way. But ease and directness are differing meanings of "natural." What we might call immediately interpretable displays need not necessarily present information in the same way it is presented in the real world. We might computationally integrate displays of data from measurements made by individual sensors (for example, airspeed indicators and altimeters) into goal-relevant higher-order dynamic invariants (for instance, how a plane is flying in terms of its drag), and these might be presented as pictographic metaphors that look fairly unlike anything in reality.[17]

SA requirements analysis (Phase 1) provides the input needed to determine which information is required for addressing each goal. In turn, this guides the determination of how to follow the Lewis and Clark Principle to support the operator in goal attainment. That is, information should be grouped in displays (or across multiple displays), based on what is required for each goal—operators should not need to search through multiple displays or across disjointed areas of a display to find what they need.

In SAOD, the displays integrate data to directly present the operator with the Level 2 information that is needed. This might involve grouping information or creating higher-order representations, or the information might be directly evident from the confluence of the display of Level 1 data. For example, in today's cockpits, pilots can view their current airspeed and altitude but must remember their assigned altitude, terrain altitude, and planned airspeed (among other values) to derive meaning from that information. Is 10,000 feet good or bad at this point? By explicitly representing terrain altitude, assigned altitude, and current altitude graphically on the same display, deviations are immediately apparent without mental calculations or reliance on memory.[9] In dynamically evolving situations or situations involving potential data overload, the degree to which displays provide information for Level 2 SA can positively affect SA. For instance, directly portraying the deviation between a current value and its expected (or required) value is preferable to requiring the operator to calculate this information on the basis of data.

> **The spirit of "naturalness" is similar to that of the Lewis and Clark Principle; that is, its displays must present meanings in a directly perceptible and comprehensible way.**

Level 2 SA requirements vary in different systems but typically include considerations of prioritization, congruence between data and requirements, and the effect of various factors on other systems or on operator goals. In some cases, the machine has to do calculations to provide this information. In other cases, the presentation of the information in juxtaposition with other information (relevant comparators) can support comprehension.

Finally, displays must support global SA, a high-level overview of the situation across all operator goals. A frequent SA problem occurs when the operator directs attention to a subset of information and does not attend to other important elements, either intentionally or unintentionally. Designs that restrict access to information only contribute to this attentional narrowing. The use of many separate windows, for example, often obscures information that should signal operators to attend to other, more important information. The human–machine system can discourage attentional narrowing and loss of SA from windowing by using displays that provide the operator with the "big picture" or global SA. The human–machine system should provide global SA at all times as well as detailed information related to the subgoals of current interest, as required. Many machines might need a global SA display that is visible at all times. Global SA is critical for determining which goals should have the highest priority and for enabling projection of future events.

Phase 3: SA measurement

SA measurement is the capstone of SAOD. Many concepts and technologies are being developed and touted as enhancing SA; actually evaluating them for their effect on SA is critical. Prototyping and simulating new technologies are necessary for assessing the actual effects of proposed concepts. Evaluation must occur in the context of the task domain, and it needs the domain practitioner's participation. In concert with HCC's principles and goals, if SA is to be a design objective, then we must evaluate a design's impact on SA as part of the system development process. We emphasize this because

> [In the] tradition we might dub Technology-Centered Design (TCD), system developers specify the requirements for machines, they then implement or prototype the requirements, and finally they produce devices and software. And then they go away, leaving users to cope with what they have built. Indeed, experience has shown that devices that are designed according to the 'design-then-train' philosophy ... force users to adapt to the system. The user is entangled with the system terminology and jargons that are the designer's view of the world.[18]

We must determine whether a proposed concept actually helps SA, does not affect it, or inadvertently compromises it in some way.

Studies of avionics concepts and other display design and interface technologies have successfully used the *situation awareness global assessment technique* (SAGAT) to provide this information by objectively measuring operator SA.[19] Participants perform a simulated task; at random times the simulation is frozen, the displays go blank, and the researcher asks a few preplanned questions based on the SA requirements. For example, in an aviation scenario, the researcher might ask, "Where is the other traffic?" and "How far are you from your assigned altitude?" Freezing can occur about three or four times in a scenario trial of 20 or so minutes without disrupting the flow. Through SAGAT, we can assess the impact of design decisions on SA via their accuracy in responding to these questions, giving us a window on the quality of the integrated system design when used within the actual challenges of the operational environment. We can then use the information derived from the evaluation of design concepts to iteratively refine the system design.

SAGAT gives designers diagnostic information not only on how aware operators are of key information but also on how well they understand the significance or meaning of that information and how well they can think ahead to project what will happen. Simply providing displays that have all the needed data on them is not sufficient. Operators must be able to rapidly use and assimilate this information to support dynamically changing goals and decisions. The measure of merit is not just getting information to the screen or audio alarm, but helping the user understand.

SAOD and the Sacagawea Principle

The HCC principles we have presented in this essay offer basic guidance about what constitutes the ideal tool. So, how can SAOD lead to satisfying the Sacagawea Principle?

Active organization of information

SAOD provides a basis for organization that fits with the operator's dynamic needs (that is, his or her goals). A goal-oriented display allows rapid switches between information sets as goals change, rather than assuming a predetermined task sequence or organization that fits the technologies rather than the user.

Active search for information

We can simplify information search through the goal orientation of the displays—for example, information that is needed together should be presented together. By ensuring that global SA is maintained at all times, key information that is needed to trigger a switch in goals ("*this* information is now more important than *that* information") can be made readily apparent and thus much less likely to be overlooked without an active search.

Reflection on the meaning of information

The direct presentation of Level 2 SA information ensures that meaning and not just data are presented. Support for Level 3 SA goes a step further in extending meaning to the dynamics of the operation, providing the key projections upon which much of proactive decision making rests.

Simply providing displays that have all the needed data on them is not sufficient. Operators must be able to rapidly use and assimilate this information to support dynamically changing goals and decisions.

Active exploration of information

Because SAOD leaves the operator in control, he or she is free to explore information at will in the pursuit of different goals, or merely to update his or her situational model with what is happening with the system. There can be a fine line between doing things for the user and doing things to the user. Systems that automatically switch displays or take users through preset sequences severely restrict their need for information acquisition and often frustrate people by running contrary to the way they want to work.

Evaluation and choice among action sequence alternatives

Because the choice of what information to examine is in the user's hands, choice regarding action sequences in interface operation is supported. Because SAOD organizes information to support needed decisions together, it also directly supports choice among actions in system operations.

Although SAOD ideas and methods evolved independently, we used this essay to slip in something of a homage to Donald Norman.

We invite readers to correspond with the Human-Centered Computing Department (isystems@computer.org) concerning more candidate HCC principles. ■

Acknowledgments

We prepared this article through participation in the Advanced Decision Architectures Collaborative Technology Alliance, sponsored by the US Army Research Laboratory under cooperative agreement DAAD19-01-2-0009.

References

1. D.A. Norman, *Things That Make Us Smart*, Perseus Books, Cambridge, Mass., 1993.
2. J. Rasmussen, A.M. Pejtersen, and K. Schmidt, *Taxonomy for Cognitive Work Analysis*, tech. report M-2871, Risø Nat'l Laboratory, Roskilde, Denmark.
3. M.R. Endsley, "Design and Evaluation for Situation Awareness Enhancement," *Proc. Human Factors Soc. 32nd Ann. Meeting*, Santa Monica, Calif., 1988, pp. 97–101.
4. M.R. Endsley, "Toward a Theory of Situation Awareness in Dynamic Systems," *Human Factors*, vol. 37, no. 1, 1995, pp. 32–64.
5. G.A. Klein, "Recognition-Primed Decisions," *Advances in Man-Machine Systems Research*, vol. 5, W.B. Rouse, ed., JAI Press, Greenwich, Conn., 1989, pp. 47–92.
6. G.A. Klein, "A Recognition Primed Decision (RPD) Model of Rapid Decision Making," *Decision Making in Action: Models and Methods*, G.A. Klein et al., eds., Ablex, Norwood, N.J., 1993, pp. 138–147.
7. M.R. Endsley, "Designing for Situation Awareness in Complex Systems," *Proc. 2nd Int'l Workshop Symbiosis of Humans, Artifacts and Environment*, Japan Soc. for the Promotion of Science, Tokyo, 2001, pp. 176–190.
8. M.R. Endsley, B. Bolte, and D.G. Jones, *Designing for Situation Awareness*, to be published, Taylor and Francis, London.
9. M.R. Endsley, "A Survey of Situation Awareness Requirements in Air-to-Air Combat Fighters," *Int'l J. Aviation Psychology*, vol. 3, no. 2, 1993, pp. 157–168.
10. M.R. Endsley and D.J. Garland, eds., *Situation Awareness Analysis and Measurement*,

Lawrence Erlbaum, Mahwah, N.J., 2000.

11. K. Vicente, *Cognitive Work Analysis*, Lawrence Erlbaum, Mahwah, N.J., 2000.

12. M.R. Endsley et al., *Situation Awareness Information Requirements for Commercial Airline Pilots*, tech. report ICAT-98-1, Mass. Inst. Technology Int'l Center for Air Transportation, Cambridge, Mass., 1998.

13. M. Sanders and E. McCormick, *Human Factors in Engineering and Design*, McGraw-Hill, New York, 1987.

14. W.E. Woodson, B. Tilman, and P. Tilman, *Human Factors Design Handbook*, 2nd ed., McGraw-Hill, New York, 1992.

15. M.G. Helander and P.V. Prabhu, *The Handbook of Human-Computer Interaction*, 2nd ed., Elsevier, Amsterdam, 1997.

16. P.A. Kommers, S. Grabinger, and J.C. Dunlap, eds., *Hypermedia Learning Environments*, Lawrence Erlbaum, Mahwah, N.J., 1996, p. 127.

17. O.D. Still and L.A. Temme, *OZ: A Human-Centered Computing Cockpit Display*, tech. report, Inst. Human and Machine Cognition, Univ. West Florida, Pensacola, Fla., 2002.

18. C. Ntuen, "A Model of System Science for Human-Centered Design," *Human-Centered Systems: Information, Interactivity and Intelligence*, J. Flanagan et al., eds., tech. report, US Nat'l Science Foundation, Washington, D.C., 1997, p. 312.

19. M.R. Endsley, "Measurement of Situation Awareness in Dynamic Systems," *Human Factors*, vol. 37, no. 1, 1995, pp. 65–84.

Mica Endsley is president and founder of SA Technologies, a cognitive-engineering firm specializing in the development of operator interfaces for advanced systems, including next-generation systems for aviation, air traffic control, and medical and military operations. She is a fellow in the Human Factors and Ergonomics Society and serves on its Executive Council. She is also is a Certified Professional Ergonomist and a Registered Professional Engineer. She received a BS in industrial engineering from Texas Tech University, an MS in industrial engineering from Purdue University, and a PhD in industrial and systems engineering from the University of Southern California. Contact her at SA Technologies, 4731 E. Forest Peak, Marietta, GA 30066; mica@satechnologies.com, www.satechnologies.com.

Robert R. Hoffman is a research scientist at the University of West Florida's Institute for Human and Machine Cognition and a faculty associate in the Department of Psychology. He is a fellow of the American Psychological Society and a Fulbright Scholar. He is a member of the Human Factors and Ergonomics Society, the American Association for Artificial Intelligence, the Psychonomic Society, the International Society for Ecological Psychology, the American Meteorological Society, and the American Society for Photogrammetric Engineering and Remote Sensing. He received his BA, MA, and PhD in experimental psychology from the University of Cincinnati. Contact him at rhoffman@al.uwf.edu.

Chapter 4: The Triples Rule

R.R. Hoffman, P. Hayes, K.M. Ford, and P. Hancock, "The Triples Rule," *IEEE Intelligent Systems*, vol. 17, no. 3, May/June 2002, pp. 62–65. doi: 10.1109/MIS.2002.1005633

A fundamental stance taken in human-centered computing is that information processing devices must be thought of in systems terms. At first blush, this seems self-evident. However, the notion has a long history, and not just in systems engineering. In this new age of symbiosis, machines are made for specific humans for use in specific contexts. The unit of analysis for cognitive engineering and computer science is a triple: person, machine, and context. The triples rule asserts that system development must take this triple as the unit of analysis, which has strong implications, including a mandate that the engineering of complex systems should include detailed cognitive work analysis. It also has implications for the meaning of intelligence, including artificial intelligence.

The Triples Rule

Robert R. Hoffman, Patrick Hayes, and Kenneth M. Ford, *University of West Florida*
Peter Hancock, *University of Central Florida*

A fundamental stance taken in human-centered computing is that information-processing devices must be thought of in systems terms. At first blush, this seems self-evident. However, the notion has a long history, and not just in systems engineering.

The Industrial Fatigue Research Board

During World War I, the British Health and Munitions Workers' Committee presented the results of wartime studies of fatigue and efficiency, which motivated the establishment of the Industrial Fatigue Research Board. The IFRB's mandate—marking the beginnings of ergonomics in England—was to identify the causes of worker fatigue and boredom (due to mechanization, task automation, and the need for concentrated attention) and determine ways to alleviate it.[1]

Under the IFRB's aegis and the leadership of pioneer industrial psychologists, studies were conducted of diverse jobs, covering worker selection, product design, production procedures, delivery methods, environmental effects on productivity and safety, and so on.[2] In the pages of the Board's research reports—there were 90 in all, published up through 1947—we find the first use of the phrase "the human factor."[3] We also find the first explicit notion of a man–machine system. In his 1923 "personal contribution" to the IFRB's annual report, H.G. Weston foresaw a need for a program of psychological research:

> The introduction and development of power-driven machines has effected an enormous savings of time and energy, not only by increasing the rapidity of production through substitution of mechanical power for human effort, but also by changing the character of the manipulations which remain to be performed by the operative. So great has this economy been, that is has brought with it a tendency to overlook the possibility that, while industrial machinery may be admirably adapted to the performance of its mechanical functions, it may be incompletely adapted to the needs of the human organism, upon whose efficient co-operation it depends for its productive use.[4]

Weston goes on to mention research detailing the discovery of serious design flaws in various machines that led to inefficiency and physical debilitation. For example, even commonly used lever shapes could result in serious physical debilitation if they were in an improper position. Sometimes, attempts to correct one obvious problem led to another one that the design engineers did not recognize. For example, the lightening of a roller in a laundry machine was not accompanied by a lightening of the load needed to depress the foot pedal controlling the roller, making the roller mechanism more, rather than less, difficult to use.

> It is, therefore, most important that correct design should be secured in the first place. It is difficult to see how this can be obtained to the fullest extent except as the result of definite research, undertaken with the object of determining such physiological and psychological facts as should be borne in mind when designing machines, the forms of mechanism and mechanical combinations which will conform to the needs of the operative.[4]

We could therefore say that the basic concept of the man–machine system was already entrenched in industrial psychology as early as the 1930s. To say now that we must think of humans and machines in systems terms seems perhaps more than passé. However, technology has wrought many changes since the 1930s, entailing entirely new implications for the meaning of human–machine system.

Cognitive fit: The dawn of a new age

Computers do things with symbols that reflect the meanings of those symbols, forcing us to rethink the relationship between machines and humans—the cognitive fit as well

Editors: Robert R. Hoffman, Patrick J. Hayes, and Kenneth M. Ford
Institute for Human and Machine Cognition, University of West Florida
rhoffman@ai.uwf.edu

as the physical fit and how the two relate. For example, eyeglasses are an ocular prosthesis that improves vision. They must be fitted to the individual's head shape and vision; my eyeglasses won't work well for most other people. However, the use of the ocular prosthesis depends on context: If I am wearing my reading glasses and suddenly look up to examine something far away, the eyeglasses become a hindrance rather than a help. Extending this analogy to computers, we must be aware of contexts in which the human and machine collaborate and operate. This broadens the notion of context and makes it subtler; it now includes such things as goals and expectations, which are just as relevant as physical context. Also, the context can include other people in a way it hadn't before because the machine can facilitate new kinds of communication, and other peoples' concepts and ideas can be part of the context of use.

SRI International scientists in a mobile-agents research project are developing eyeglasses that do not magnify in the usual sense (see www.erg.sri.com/projects/sae/cars-poster.jpg). Rather, they can calculate where you're looking and project a virtual image onto the real scene—for example, to show you where to turn to get to the nearest convenience store. When such devices become commonplace, we will regard them as an extension of our vision and will wonder how we ever got along without them. To not have them—a failure to be able to see in new ways—will be regarded as a form of shortsightedness. However, to make such devices commonplace, we must totally reconceive what it means for a machine to have an interface.

Modern cognitive engineering has progressed through four "ages" over its 30-plus-year lifetime. During the Age of the Average Man, design was based on "one size fits all." During the Age of Adaptation, there arose a recognition of the need for flexibility. During the Age of Personalization, we realized that machine siblings could be adapted to single users. We are now entering a fourth age.

The Triples rule

In this new Age of Symbiosis, machines are made for specific humans for use in specific contexts. The unit of analysis for cognitive engineering and computer science is a triple: person, machine, and context (see Figure 1).

The Triples rule asserts that system development must take this triple as the unit of analysis, which has strong implications, including a mandate that the engineering of complex systems include detailed *cognitive work analysis*.[5–7] It also has implications for the meaning of intelligence, including artificial intelligence.

Intelligent ... in a sense

It is easy, perhaps too easy, to regard humans as intelligent, but we must keep in mind that the attribution of intelligence to a human is heavily context dependent. Sitting nearly naked on the ground and poking at ants with a stick would be regarded as odd in many contexts, but not when you're in the Kalahari Desert, looking for ant trails that might lead to a source of water. The world-class expert in any particular domain will not necessarily top the charts on a standard test of general intelligence.[8] Likewise, a computational device when taken out of its intended context of application can be useless—an extreme case being when it is dropped into a swimming pool. As a physical artifact, the device will still have affordances—it could plug a leak—but it would not interact with people on the basis of its computational capabilities. Or, try entering a chess machine in a natural language processing competition. Reductio ad absurdum examples such as these perhaps make the point less well than realistic examples. A geographic information system accepts data types x, y, and z, but the user needs (context of application) to integrate data types q, r, and s, which can't be done. Or, Box A cannot communicate with Box B. These sorts of problems are daily fare in complex sociotechnical workplaces plagued by mandated and legacy systems.

To continue with the triple analysis, replace the human who knows how to work with the computational device with a human who does not, and again the device becomes essentially useless. An extreme example would be a chess machine used by someone who knows nothing about games. The machine retains some of its affordances—the human could push buttons just to see what happens or could use the machine as a doorstop. To continue the triple, change the machine (its computational and interface capabilities), and you get entirely different patterns of interactions with the human and the context.

Changes to the human or the context can

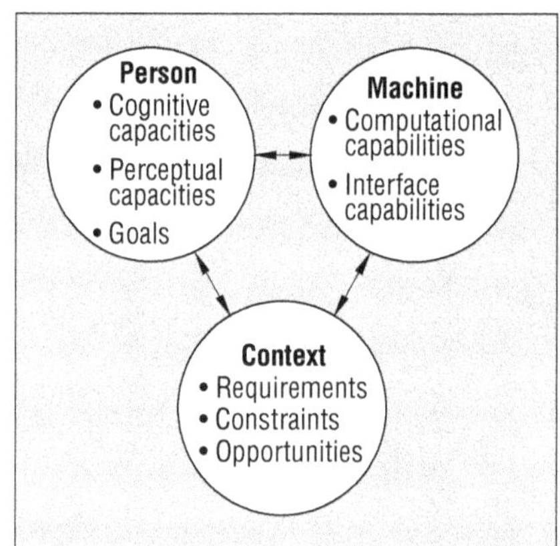

Figure 1. The triple.

render the machine useless or make the context inappropriate; the human is rendered less capable by changes to the context (for example, a PC user who finds himself surrounded by Macintosh users) or the machine. According to the Triples rule, intelligence emerges from the triple interaction. The rule thus runs head-on into the traditional definition of intelligence in AI: the Turing test.

Turing redux

Alan Turing's paper "Computing Machinery and Intelligence"[9] gave AI a vision and its first great challenge.[10] As Turing described it, the test is an imitation game that involves a man, a woman, and a judge, all communicating but unable to see one another. The judge's task is to decide which of the other two is the woman; the others try to persuade the judge that one of them is the woman and that the other is the man. Turing is usually understood to mean that the game should be played with the question of gender (being female) replaced by the question of species (being human). The judge is faced with the task of differentiating a human participant from a machine pretending to be human.

Borrowing from Patrick Hayes and Kenneth Ford,[11,12] we point out just three of the problems with the Turing test. First, from the standpoint of experimental design, it confounds the machine's intelligence with that of the judge. If a machine passes the test, is it demonstrated to be intelligent, or was the judge not intelligent enough to ask sufficiently telling questions? The game conditions say nothing about the judge, but the game's success depends crucially on how intelligent the judge is.

Second, the Turing test confounds intelligence with cleverness. To pass the test, a machine would have to not only give a human-like impression but also be an expert on making a good impression. It would have to avoid exhibiting any inhuman talents that it might have; it would always have to lie, cheat, and dissemble. The winner of the Loebner competition, for example, sometimes deliberately mistyped a word and then backspaced to correct it at human typing speed. This strategy is clever, but such tricks should not be central to AI.

A third difficulty with the Turing test is that the definition of intelligence keeps shifting. As AI progresses and machines increasingly perform tasks previously considered to involve human intelligence, those abilities are no longer taken to be definitive. When Eliza first appeared, some people found its conversational abilities quite human-like. No machine until then could have reacted even in a simple way to what had been said to it. But during the Loebner competition, many programs were instantly revealed as nonhuman precisely by the first hint of their behavior's resemblance to Eliza's. The ability to perform simultaneous translation could soon be reduced to the merely mechanical. Turing tests have become circular: They define the qualities for which they are claiming to be evidence.

We could argue that the Turing test should not be regarded as the defining goal for AI but as a spur to technological progress—constantly pushing us to reach for Rene Descartes' dream of the "enlightened machine."[13] But why should we take it as our only goal to build something that is just like us? A dog would never win any imitation game, but there seems to be no doubt that dogs exhibit cognition, and a machine with the cognitive and communicative abilities of a dog would be an interesting challenge for AI.[14] More importantly, our most useful computer applications (including AI programs) are often valuable by virtue of their lack of humanity. There are cameras, copiers, televisions, automobiles, battery rechargers, and laptop operating systems all incorporating algorithms that use AI ideas and techniques but are not usually advertised as "intelligent" or "expert."[12]

If we abandon the Turing test as the defining goal for AI, the goal can shift from making artificial superhumans that can replace us to making artifacts that we can use to amplify and extend our cognitive abilities. AI should play a central role in this exciting new technology of cognitive prosthetics,[15] but to do so it must turn its back on the Turing test. What, then, should be the test?

The Triples rule suggests that the problem here is with the question itself—there is no single test. In fact, there are boundless numbers of tests. In general, for any task x or y that a human or machine can do (each under the appropriate set of contextual constraints), the human–machine–context triple is "intelligent" if the task can be conducted better than if either the human or the machine were to conduct the task without engaging in a partnership with the other.[16] The word "better" is deliberately left open in this formulation. It might be instantiated by "more efficiently," "more rapidly," or "more economically," but it might just as well mean "more playfully." This is how it should be if the machine is human-centered. There is an appropriate fit between the human, the machine, and the context such that the human's cognitive, perceptual, and collaborative capacities are enhanced. AI thus becomes Amplified Intelligence.

This line of thinking helps put to rest the doomsaying about intelligent machines taking over the world, which is another story.[14] This is just the first of what we hope will become a series of essays that discuss candidate principles for this thing called human-centered computing. The Triples rule is one of the first such principles. We invite others to suggest additional ones.

References

1. S. Wyatt, J.A. Fraser, and F.G.L. Stock, *The Effects of Monotony in Work*, Report no. 56, Industrial Fatigue Research Board, His Majesty's Stationery Office, London, 1929.
2. M.S. Viteles, *Industrial Psychology*, Norton, New York, 1932.
3. E.M. Newbold, *A Contribution to the Study of the Human Factor in the Causation of Accidents*, Report no. 34, Industrial Fatigue Research Board, His Majesty's Stationery Office, London, 1926.
4. H.G. Weston, "A Note on Machine Design in Relation to the Operative," *3rd Ann. Report Industrial Fatigue Research Board, 31 December 1922*, Industrial Fatigue Research Board, His Majesty's Stationery Office, London, 1923, pp. 71–75.
5. D.D. Woods, "Coping with Complexity: The Psychology of Human Behavior in Complex Systems," *Mental Models, Tasks, and Errors*, L.P. Goodstein, H.B. Anderson, and S.E. Olsen, eds., Taylor and Francis, London, 1988, pp. 128–148.
6. D.D. Woods and D. Tinapple, "Presidential Address: Watching Human Factors People at Work," *Proc. 43rd Ann. Meeting Human Factors and Ergonomics Soc.*, Human Factors and Ergonomics Soc., 1998; http://csel.eng.ohio-state.edu/hf99.
7. K. Vicente, *Cognitive Work Analysis*, Lawrence Erlbaum, Mahwah, N.J., 2000.
8. R.R. Hoffman, "How Can Expertise Be Defined? Implications of Research from Cognitive Psychology," *Exploring Expertise*, R. Williams, W. Faulkner, and J. Fleck, eds., Macmillan, New York, 1998, pp. 81–100.
9. A.M. Turing, "Computing Machinery and Intelligence," *Mind*, vol. 59, no. 236,1950, pp. 433–460.
10. A. Hodges, *Alan Turing: The Enigma*, Simon and Schuster, New York, 1983.
11. P. Hayes and K.M. Ford, "Turing Test Considered Harmful," *Proc. 14th Int'l Joint Conf. Artificial Intelligence*, Morgan Kaufman, San Francisco, 1995, pp. 972–977.
12. K.M. Ford and P.J. Hayes, "On Computational Wings: Rethinking the Goals of Artificial Intelligence, *Scientific Am. Presents*, vol. 9, no. 4, Winter 1998, pp. 78–83.
13. R.R. Hoffman, P. Hayes, and K.M. Ford, "Human-Centered Computing: Thinking In and Out of the Box," *IEEE Intelligent Systems*, vol. 16, no. 5, Sept./Oct. 2001, pp. 76–79.
14. P.A. Hancock, *Essays on the Future of Human-Machine Systems*, Banta Information Services Group, Eden Prairie, Minn., 1997.
15. K.M. Ford, C. Glymour, and P.J. Hayes, "Cognitive Prostheses," *AI Magazine*, vol. 18, no. 3, Fall 1997, p. 104.
16. P.A. Hancock and S.F. Scallen, "Allocating Functions in Human-Machine Systems," *Viewing Psychology as a Whole*, R.R. Hoffman, M.F. Sherrick, and J.S. Warm, eds., Am. Psychological Association, Washington, D.C., 1998, pp. 509–540.

Robert R. Hoffman is a research scientist at the University of West Florida's Institute for Human and Machine Cognition and is a faculty associate at the university's Department of Psychology. He specializes in expertise studies, including knowledge elicitation and the design of human-centered systems. He received his BA, MA, and PhD in experimental psychology from the University of Cincinnati. He is a Fulbright Scholar and a fellow of the American Psychological Society. Contact him at the Inst. for Human & Machine Cognition, 40 Alcaniz St., Pensacola, FL 32501; rhoffman@ai.uwf.edu.

Patrick Hayes is a senior research scientist and the John Pace, Jr., Eminent Scholar at the University of West Florida. His research interests include knowledge representation and automatic reasoning, especially the representation of space and time and diagrammatic representations, and the philosophical foundations of AI and computer science. He received his BA in mathematics from Cambridge University and his PhD in artificial intelligence from the University of Edinburgh. Contact him at the Inst. for Human & Machine Cognition, 40 Alcaniz St., Pensacola, FL 32501; phayes@ai.uwf.edu.

Kenneth M. Ford is the founder and director of the University of West Florida's Institute for Human and Machine Cognition. He has an interdisciplinary interest in understanding cognition in both humans and other machines. He is the editor in chief of the AAAI/MIT Press, executive editor of the *International Journal of Expert Systems*, and associate editor of the *Journal of Experimental and Theoretical Artificial Intelligence*, and is a *Behavioral and Brain Sciences* associate. He received his PhD in computer science from Tulane University. Contact him at the Inst. for Human & Machine Cognition, 40 Alcaniz St., Pensacola, FL 32501; kford@ai.uwf.edu.

Peter Hancock is a professor at Central Florida University and president of the Human Factors and Ergonomics Society. His research interests include transportation safety, air traffic control, workstation design, mental workload, intelligent interfaces, simulator design, and other topics. He received a PhD in motor performance from the University of Illinois. Contact him at Dept. of Psychology, Univ. of Central Florida, Orlando, FL 32816; phancock@pegasus.cc.ucf.edu.

Chapter 5: The Janus Principle

R.R. Hoffman, G. Lintern, and S. Eitelman, "The Janus Principle," *IEEE Intelligent Systems*, vol. 19, no. 2, Mar./Apr. 2004, pp. 78–80. doi: 10.1109/MIS.2004.1274915

We find here an allegory to the apprentice-expert continuum in the acquisition of knowledge, and so we name a principle of human-centered computing after Janus. This principle deals with the distinction between performance and training, and its implications for intelligent technologies. The notion of a Janus Machine is the following: if a software tool works well as an intelligent training aid (for apprentices), it should also work as an actual operational support tool (for experts). We illustrate such machines.

The Janus Principle

Robert R. Hoffman, *Institute for Human and Machine Cognition*
Gavan Lintern, *General Dynamics*
Susan Eitelman, *CHI Systems*

The real Janus (Ianua) may have been an ancient king from Greece who encouraged his (adopted or conquered) people of Latium (now, a part of Italy) to acquire the skills of agriculture, industry, art, and religion. Over time, the Roman myth arose of a god who brought all things into the world, from the seasons to the ways of civilization. This god of gates and doorways opened and closed all things, including the gates of heaven. Janus was symbolized as a two-faced god, one face being that of a youth, the other of an elder. In his left hand, the youth held a key to open the gates. In his right, the elder held a scepter to master all comings and goings.

We find here an allegory to the apprentice-expert continuum in the acquisition of knowledge, and so we name a principle of human-centered computing after Janus. This principle deals with the distinction between performance and training, and its implications for intelligent technologies.

Training versus performance

We know from psychological research that performance and training are related in strong but complex ways.[1] For instance, accelerated training doesn't always transfer to the operational context.[2] Because of traditions including the separation of disciplines (for example, instructional design in education versus control systems design in cognitive engineering), there is a widespread distinction between training systems (TSs) and performance support systems (PSSs).

A moment's reflection reveals that this distinction runs counter to empirical fact. Consequently, it's misleading, even potentially dangerous. As we can deduce from the psychology of learning, TS versus PSS forces an unnatural separation:

- To train, you must have opportunities to perform. In fact, trainers and educators—indeed, all of us—take for granted the idea that learning must involve a performance component. In introductory biology, we dissect frogs. In learning command-and-control skills, warfighters practice in simulations. In general, current training systems always include performance and practice components. If a training system doesn't support practice, it's a good bet that the training won't transfer into the operational context.
- It's an empirical fact that for people to perform in complex sociotechnical contexts, they must continually learn new things. Such work contexts are always moving targets (new software, new task goals, and so on), so learning on the job is both inevitable and necessary. If a PSS system doesn't promote learning, or at least doesn't make learning any easier, then it won't lead to long-term performance enhancement. Furthermore, a defining aspect of expertise is the intrinsic motivation to learn and acquire new skills.

When training works and doesn't work

It is often assumed that aids and instructional materials that accelerate and maximize performance during training will result in optimized performance when the trainee is in the operational context. However, training in which performance is maximized (especially what's called "just in time" training) can actually fail to transfer when the trainee later confronts such things as multitasking, distractions, cascade failures, loss of data, and other factors of actual work contexts that often are sanitized out of the training context.

Conversely, training that allows for learner error and

Editors: Robert R. Hoffman, Patrick J. Hayes, and Kenneth M. Ford
Institute for Human and Machine Cognition, University of West Florida
rhoffman@ai.uwf.edu

then provides feedback based on domain knowledge—even if this extends the training time—can lead to better performance when the trainee is later confronted with tasks in the operational context. Neither a TS nor a traditional PSS on its own can accomplish this fit between human, machine, and context.

In his *Unified Theories of Cognition*,[3] Allen Newell argued that people learn continuously, so in his SOAR cognitive architecture, he modeled learning as a result of problem solving, implying performance. Thus, learning and problem solving (or performance) are necessarily intertwined.

One conclusion is possible.

The Janus Principle

We propose the following Janus Principle:

> Human-centered systems do not force a separation between learning and performance. They integrate them.

We know this is possible. Here are two examples.

Example 1: Oceanography

The US Navy's Naval Air Warfare Center sponsored the creation of a software and display tool to help train oceanographers and aerographers about sonar oceanography. The Interactive Multisensor Analysis Trainer (www.onr.navy.mil/sci_tech/personnel/cnb_sci/342/majapps/imat/imat5.htm) depicts a volume of ocean in horizontal view, with a ship at its surface. Sonar beams appear as ray tracings. Within the volume of water are colorized layers, representing different layers of temperature and salinity. These cause deflections in sonar-beam paths, which the learner can see after manipulating layer parameters.

The group that was trained using this system found it useful as a training aid and later as a performance aid. Indeed, they took it with them when they deployed to the fleet and were able to use it to visualize actual conditions. So, the system worked as a PSS. In this case, the training aid was well designed as a TS, so it also supported performance—and interestingly enough, it was the users, not the designers, who apparently discovered this.

Example 2: Satellite Systems Operations

The Air Force Research Lab, Human Effectiveness Directorate, is sponsoring the development of a PSS to help satellite operators maintain healthy satellites for the Space Tracking and Surveillance System.[4] The tool, called the Adaptive Decision Enabling Performance Tracking toolkit, is under development. The Adept design process has been iterative and involved the users, and it revealed opportunities to support training by having the tool used in an operational context.

Adept's overarching theme is to provide "one-stop shopping" for all the information that satellite operators might need while performing their work. The tool offers a usable alphanumeric data display (leveraging useful characteristics from the previous software system's data display), electronic availability and storage of forms, chat access to other team members, a visualization tool of the remote satellite environment, and electronic access to reference materials. To ensure a useful and usable tool, the developers identified and built these performance support functions in collaboration with subject matter experts.

> **The tool enhances performance, as intended, but it also supports performance by enabling operators to improve their abilities and acquire expertise.**

One of the performance support functions is a visualization tool that helps satellite operators understand the alphanumeric data they receive by comparing it with a real-time simulation of the remote environment, updated by live data. For instance, the tool facilitates recognition of an anomalous situation: if a satellite enters into eclipse before the appropriate preparation procedure is administered, alarms sound. In this case, an operator can access the visualization tool and recognize, for instance, that the satellite is safe and the alarms were simply not prevented before the expected eclipse occurred.

One of the participating experts asserted something that psychologists would underscore: The more proactive and curious learners perform better. The visualization tool lets operators explore prior and upcoming situations by using rewind and fast-forward buttons. Thus, the tool enhances performance, as intended, but it also supports performance by enabling operators to improve their abilities and acquire expertise.

Merging training and performance

What general guidance is there for crafting systems that merge TS and PSS?

Cognitive apprenticeship

The traditional apprenticeship model emphasizes a special form of situational experience. Apprentices start with small, peripheral tasks but can see, by observing the full scope of the work, where their individual efforts fit. As their experience grows, apprentices are given opportunities for involvement in more central, more significant, and more critical activities. Such active and responsible involvement in an authentic environment facilitates learning.

In reality, not all apprenticeships promote active involvement in meaningful tasks or allow steady progression to more central work activities. Jean Lave and Etienne Wenger noted the case of butchers' apprentices in a large supermarket who were separated from the experienced butchers.[5] These apprentices had few opportunities to assist with progressively more central tasks or get legitimate access to the experienced butchers or their work. In addition, much of the formal instruction was outdated and therefore irrelevant, because butchers who no longer worked actively in the trade directed that part of the learning process.

We can apply the apprenticeship model to intellectual skills.[6] Barbara Rogoff coined the term *cognitive apprentice* to make the point that development proceeds through appropriation of the intellectual tools and skills of the surrounding cultural community.[7] Skills and knowledge acquired through this process are more likely to be applicable to real situations. There should be fewer occurrences of inert or partitioned knowledge that cannot be applied successfully to situational problems. Cognitive apprenticeship involves activity that extends students slightly beyond their level of competence and engages a gradual transition from peripheral to central activities.

People acquire expertise by abstracting and relating lessons from individual experiences, but a training program should use an explicit organizing framework to connect

Robert R. Hoffman is a research scientist at the Institute for Human and Machine Cognition. Contact him at the IHMC, 40 Alcaniz St., Pensacola, FL 32501; rhoffman@ihmc.us.

Gavan Lintern is chief scientist of Advanced Information Systems at General Dynamics. Contact him at General Dynamics, 5200 Springfield Pike, Ste. 200, Dayton, OH 45431-1289; gavan.lintern@gd-ais.com; www.veridian.com.

Susan Eitelman is a cognitive engineer at CHI Systems. Contact her at CHI Systems, 12000 Research Pkwy., Ste. 120, Orlando, FL 32826; seitelman@chisystems.com.

and give meaning to specific experiences. Instead of students encountering a host of seemingly disparate facts, they'd discover and integrate facts as they explored the problem domain's structure. The learning challenge becomes one of discovery and integration versus one of memorization.

Some may feel that course material should be structured to discourage error, but the performance of errors in a safe context helps students learn to recognize the consequences of error as they unfold and to practice error recovery.[8]

Error feedback

The traditional perspective on error feedback is straightforward: We inform a student who errs as soon as possible about the error and possibly how to correct it. If the error persists, we might drill the student in the correct behavioral pattern. However, the treatment of error in the training context requires a more thoughtful approach.

Experimental psychologists and human factors professionals have known for some time that summarized, delayed, and adaptive feedback is more effective for learning in most circumstances. Feedback should be short and sweet (that is, don't beat up on the learner); it helps if there's a slight delay between the error and the feedback; and the feedback must empower the learner. Rather than just saying that the learner erred and how the learner erred, it must provide a concrete plan for how the learner can engage in corrective action.[9–11]

This is difficult for the trainer to implement because errors rarely provide direct evidence of the nature of the underlying knowledge gap or skill deficiency. Errors tell us that something is going wrong, but they don't inform us directly of the nature of the problem. For example, consider the problem of a weak and inaccurate tennis serve. The mechanistic approach would show each serve's strength and accuracy, implying that the server must strike the ball more accurately and with greater power. That, of course, is entirely consistent with the laws of physics, but it's not diagnostic. It doesn't tell the server how to correct the problem. Any direct attempt to generate more power will result in less accuracy, and vice versa. Worse, a direct attempt to generate more power will induce strain and eventually lend to injury. An experienced coach, in helping the server improve, will talk of body rotation, wrist snap, knee bend, and timing, which are properties of coordination. More generally, the nature of an error, taken by itself, rarely informs us directly about the required correction.

Human-centered intelligent systems merge training and performance. They must be demonstrably usable and useful in a training mode as well as a performance mode. This requirement is one more reason why the development of intelligent systems mandates full involvement of cognitive engineers. ■

References

1. NRC Committee on Developments in the Science of Learning, *How People Learn: Brain, Mind, Experience and School,* Nat'l Academy of Sciences Press, 2000.
2. R. Bjork, "How and Why Common Teaching Practices Fail to Foster Good Learning," presentation at the Conf. Applying the Science of Learning to the University and Beyond: Cognitive, Motivational, and Social Factors, Am. Psychological Assoc., 2001; www.apa.org.
3. A. Newell, *Unified Theories of Cognition*, Harvard Univ. Press, 1990.
4. S.M. Eitelman, K.J. Neville, and H.B. Sorensen, "A Performance Support System That Facilitates the Acquisition of Expertise," *Proc. Interservice/Industry Training, Simulation, & Education Conf.*, Nat'l Training Systems Assoc., 2003.
5. J. Lave and E. Wenger, *Situated Learning: Legitimate Peripheral Participation*, Cambridge Univ. Press, 1991.
6. R.R. Hoffman, "How Can Expertise Be Defined? Implications of Research from Cognitive Psychology," *Exploring Expertise*, R. Williams, W. Faulkner, and J. Fleck, eds., Macmillan, 1998, pp. 81–100.
7. B. Rogoff, *Apprenticeship in Thinking*, Oxford Univ. Press, 1990.
8. G. Lintern and N. Naikar, *Analysis of Crew Coordination in the F-111 Mission,* Defence Science and Technology Organisation Client Report DSTO-CR-0184, Aeronautical and Maritime Research Laboratory, Melbourne, Australia, 2001.
9. R.A. Schmidt and R.A. Bjork, "New Conceptualizations of Practice: Common Principles in Three Paradigms Suggest New Concepts for Training," *Psychological Science*, vol. 3, no. 4, 1992, pp. 207–217.
10. G. Lintern, "Transfer of Landing Skill after Training with Supplementary Visual Cues," *Human Factors*, vol. 22, 1980, pp. 81–88.
11. G. Lintern, "An Informational Perspective on Skill Transfer in Human-Machine Systems," *Human Factors*, vol. 33, 1991, pp. 251–266.

Chapter 6: The Pleasure Principle

R.R. Hoffman and P.J. Hayes, "The Pleasure Principle," *IEEE Intelligent Systems*, vol. 19, no. 1, Jan./Feb. 2004, pp. 86–89. doi: 10.1109/MIS.2004.1265891

The list of "concepts that psychology really can't do without" includes such notions as neuronal connectionism, degrees of consciousness, mental representation of information, and dissociation. Of the pantheon of contributors to the history of psychology, Aristotle outranks all others in terms of the number of critical concepts he introduced, including the notion of the association of ideas, the law of frequency and the affiliated concept of memory strength, the notion of stage theories of development, the idea of distinguishing types of mental processes or faculties, the idea of scales of nature and comparisons between humans and animals, and last but not least, the pleasure principle. Unfortunately, computers don't always provide an unmixed increase in pleasure. Recent evidence suggests, contrary to what we might hope or suppose, that the computerization of the modern workplace has actually led to productivity declines. The negative impacts are likely due, at least in part, to the user unfriendliness of computers.

The Pleasure Principle

Robert R. Hoffman and Patrick J. Hayes, *Institute for Human and Machine Cognition*

The list of "concepts that psychology really can't do without" includes such notions as neuronal connectionism, degrees of consciousness, mental representation of information, and dissociation. Of the pantheon of contributors to the history of psychology, Aristotle outranks all others in terms of the number of critical concepts he introduced, including the notion of the association of ideas, the law of frequency and the affiliated concept of memory strength, the notion of stage theories of development, the idea of distinguishing types of mental processes or faculties, the idea of scales of nature and comparisons between humans and animals, and last but not least, the Pleasure Principle.

History of the Pleasure Principle

In his *Physics*, Aristotle wrote, "All moral excellence is concerned with bodily pleasures and pains."[1–3] What he was getting at is that animals as well as humans experience pleasure and pain but that a human who lets such factors alone direct his or her behavior would be intemperate, impetuous, brutish, and self-indulgent to excess. He further said, "[In] the case of bodily enjoyments ... the man who pursues excessive pleasures and avoids excessive pains like hunger and thirst, heat and cold, and all the discomforts of touch and taste, not from choice but in opposition to it and to his reasoning, is described as incontinent [driven to excess by an uncontrollable appetite] without any added determinant [or cause of behavior]."[2] Humans are distinguished from mere brutes by having within them "a rational principle," but being the animals that we are, we still share the universal Pleasure Principle.

Based on his studies of trial-and-error learning in animals, Edwin Thorndike proposed a variant[4] of the principle: "Any act in a given situation producing satisfaction becomes associated with that situation, so that when the situation recurs, that act is more likely to recur," recapitulating Aristotle's notion of association and his law of frequency. This general idea for a causal explanation of behavior in terms of affect was so critical and useful that even the Behaviorists such as John Watson thought they could embrace it in a theory devoid of all the cooties of mentalism, referring to behaviors that get "stamped in" because they are "reinforced" and behaviors that get "stamped out" because they lead to punishment.[5] In Sigmund Freud's work,[6] which also echoed many Aristotelian notions, the principle was transformed to the more familiar "Humans behave so as to seek pleasure and avoid pain." This was the force of the id, in contrast to the "reality principle" that governed the ego. In the early 1900s, the often-misunderstood "efficiency experts" (such as Frank Gilbreth[7]) were likewise cognizant of the principle. They wanted to increase worker productivity—not just for its own sake but also to eliminate wasteful work practices and increase worker health and psychological satisfaction.

The Pleasure Principle remains a theme today. Kim Vicente subtitled his opus on cognitive work analysis *Toward Safe, Productive and Healthy Computer-Based Work,* implying that psychological satisfaction is an ingredient in "health."[8] Job satisfaction is a critical factor in determining worker morale, productivity, and health. When working either as individuals or as team members, people show higher levels of emotional investment in their projects, greater levels of commitment, greater staying power in the face of impediments, and higher levels of accomplishment if the group perceives itself to be functioning effectively.[9] So, as Aristotle pointed out, pleasure makes even rational work more effective.

Editors: Robert R. Hoffman, Patrick J. Hayes, and Kenneth M. Ford
Institute for Human and Machine Cognition, University of West Florida
rhoffman@ai.uwf.edu

How does this history lesson map to human-centered computing?

Unfortunately, computers don't always provide an unmixed increase in pleasure. Recent evidence suggests, contrary to what we might hope or suppose, that the computerization of the modern workplace has actually led to productivity declines.[8,10]

The negative impacts are likely due, at least in part, to the user unfriendliness of computers—for example, frequent changes in software, incompatibility of hardware and software systems, poor software and interface design, weak documentation and help support, and so on.[10] Many computer systems require effort to create work-arounds and local kludges.[11] All such features make both individual workers and teams feel less effective, and perceived self-efficacy is a critical factor in job satisfaction, motivation, and morale.[9]

Examples

Examples abound, but here's an example from Studs Terkel's classic book *Working*, in which he interviews a telephone operator:

> Half the phones have a new system where the quarter is three beeps, a dime is two beeps, and nickel is one beep. If the guy's in a hurry and he keeps throwing in money, all the beeps get mixed up together (laughs) and you don't know how much money is in the phone. So it's kinda hard. When you have a call, you fill out this IBM card. Those go with a special machine. You use a special pencil so it'll go through this computer and pick up the numbers. It's real soft lead, it just goes all over the desk and you're all dirty by the time you get off.[12]

Here's a second example to which we can all relate, this from newspaper columnist Dave Barry:

> The next day I booked another flight to Chicago ... I was flying with a ticket that said my name was "Barry White." Really. That is who the airline computer insisted I was. I pointed out to the ticket agent that Barry White is a famous soul crooner and does not resemble me in any way except that we are both bipeds. I asked if my ticket could reflect my real name; after tapping on his computer for a good ten minutes, the agent informed me—I swear—that this was not possible, and advised me to just get on the plane.[13]

A third clear example is one that arose during our research on HCC for weather forecasting.[14] NEXRAD (the Next-Generation Weather Radar system) is a marvel of technology, with capabilities yet to be fully explored. The NEXRAD Principal User Processor (PUP) workstation has the slick feel of *2001: A Space Odyssey*, but its appearance is misleading. Operation relies on a graphics pad that is anything but self-explanatory. Its colored sectors have functional significance, but that significance is totally hidden in the dozens of cryptic acronyms, abbreviations, and alphanumeric encodings that label the individual buttons. The user interface is a command line interface, requiring the operator to be familiar with dozens of commands, coding schemes, and so on. Operations manuals are always kept well within reach.

NEXRAD begs for both a graphical user interface (GUI) and a knowledge-based support system. It certainly need not suffer from an outdated assumption that the way to pack information into an interface is to abbreviate and encode. In the months after NEXRAD was installed (with initial enthusiasm) at the US National Weather Service's weather forecasting offices, the PUP went largely unused at some WFOs that one of us (Hoffman) visited. In some of those offices, the PUP still collects dust, and the forecasters work with NEXRAD products at their separate forecasting workstations. Only after the WFOs' science officers took NEXRAD training did the regional WFOs start really using the system (defining local thresholds, setting up special user functions, and so on). Even after that, WFO forecasters would refer to their one NEXRAD-trained colleague as their local "guru," meaning that only one forecaster was actually good at working with the interface, interpreting the NEXRAD products, and adapting the radar's operating characteristics to local weather regimes.

Others are often quite happy to work with a "guru" while they themselves almost proudly remain a "not-guru"—hence terms such as propeller-head, geek, hacker, turbine guy, and so on.

During one of the interview sessions in the Weather Case Study project, the following conversation took place:

> Interviewer: NEXRAD is so capable but there's no knowledge .... From a user point of view it's like having a Cadillac with all the bells and whistles but on the dashboard there are no labels, or the labels are like hexidecimal code, cryptic commands ....
>
> Forecaster: A lot of times you do not need to know how it works [which is primarily what is taught in the schoolhouse], you need to know how the radar reacts to things, different atmospheres ... actually how to use it. [But] it really doesn't invite you to have fun with it, no. Not at all. It's nice they have all the user functions ... the more you use it the more it invites you to use it. You can set up [your own] user functions.

This makes the point exactly. Once you start to use NEXRAD, it gets better and better because you can customize it. But it's too hard to get started. The forecaster must engage in experiential learning for a considerable time. This is unfortunate because NEXRAD has such fantastic capability. A workshop on NEXRAD human factors was held at the 1997 Meeting of the American Meteorological Society, and discussions at that workshop showed the promise of NEXRAD as an effort began to develop object-oriented GUIs. Until then, most NEXRAD users rely on one or two basic displays of the radar data, which they view at their workstations rather than at the NEXRAD PUP.

Being the guru

There is an additional subtlety here. Being the "guru" can be pleasurable. Others are often quite happy to work with a "guru" while they themselves almost proudly remain a "not-guru"—hence terms such as *propeller-head*, *geek*, *hacker*, *turbine guy*, and so on. So, these complex "usable-only-with-a-great-deal-of-training" systems actually can give pleasure but not in the way their designers had in mind. They encourage a kind of two-level workplace that is apparently stable socially but that can be inefficient in exactly the way the systems are not supposed to be—that is, they fail to provide user-friendly functionalities. No doubt, this is in part because of the designer-centered approach in which interfaces are designed by engineers who often have exactly the kind of personality that would have taken the training course and taken pleasure from playing the guru role. In extreme cases (we've all met these folks), they can be almost unaware of the existence of not-guru users, or maybe aware but contemptuous. This too illustrates the dangers of social instability that can make systems effectively useless in a socially healthier work situation.

Good tools self-explain to the greatest extent possible and don't assume that information must be crammed into data fields (at the expense of communicating meaning). Good tools make tasks neither so unnecessarily difficult as to instill hopelessness or frustration, nor so easy as to promote users' boredom or anger.[15] Good tools (and workspaces) motivate the worker. They don't involve distractions or disruptions (for example, having to look something up in a paper manual) that destroy the subjective experience of being "in the domain." They don't force the worker to create work-arounds and spend hours merely learning how to use the tool rather than getting the actual job done.

Are you having fun?

The role of emotion and aesthetics in HCC was raised a few times in the 1997 National Science Foundation workshop report on human-centered computing.[16] Pelle Ehn pointed out that quality in the workplace, like quality of life in general, necessarily involves aesthetic considerations.[17] Ross Jeffries defined HCC in terms of three characteristics:[18]

- The system does something that people want and need to do.
- The system is well integrated into real practice.
- The user is able to focus on the task rather than on the user interface.

But then Jeffries went a step further and added a fourth characteristic:

> I'll add to this a characteristic that may be somewhat controversial, but I have come to see as an important aspect of human-centered systems. The system should be fun to use. It's easy to see fun as an extra, an add-on (or even something frivolous, to avoid). By fun I don't mean "joke of the day" features or MTV-like presentations, although in the right context either of these could be a good idea. Rather, I mean that using the system leaves the user in a better state of mind than before. I don't know if fun is something we have to explicitly design into our systems, or if it is an emergent property of being sufficiently human-centered, but I have come to see it as an essential property of successful systems. (p. 277)

Here, Jeffries converges with Donald Norman on a cardinal principle of HCC, which we have formulated as a modern version of the Pleasure Principle:

> Good tools provide a feeling of direct engagement, flow, and challenge.

As we struggled to reach an integrative view of HCC,[19–21] we realized that something was missing from many discussions of such things as "user friendliness." When the Principle dawned on us, it felt dangerous at first. We took that as a clue that it was indeed important to information technology and intelligent systems. Since then, we've heard others allude to similar notions and now feel more comfortable discussing it.

This involves creating intelligent systems that let practitioners work problems rather than having to work their technologies in order to work problems.

HCC isn't about turning every complex sociotechnical workplace into a fun place to be, although it would be good if that happens where and when it's appropriate and possible. A retired senior naval officer commented to one of us (Robert Hoffman), "There ain't *no* place on board a ship where you *want* to go." This comment captures the fine line that must be walked in formulating the Pleasure Principle. "Fun" in the sense that we and Jeffries intend doesn't mean ho-ho-ho. It's more a feeling of engagement, an *integration* of Aristotle's animus with the rational process. You need them both—or perhaps better, the rational can't do nearly so well by itself if it has to do without the pleasure part.

The point of the Pleasure Principle is that human-centered systems must leverage domain practitioners' intrinsic motivation, especially the motivation that is definitive of expertise. This involves creating intelligent systems that let practitioners work problems rather than having to "work" their technologies in order to work problems. Indeed, the more important the job, the more important it is that the work environment let practitioners feel engaged in working toward a goal, experience no frustrations, and then feel satisfied that they have successfully, effectively, and effortlessly achieved their goal.

How the Pleasure Principle relates to other HCC principles

The Pleasure Principle relates to other HCC principles, including the following:[22]

- *The Sacagawea Principle*. Human-centered computational tools need to support active organization of information, active search for information, active exploration of information, reflection on the meaning of information, and evaluation and choice among action sequence alternatives.
- *The Lewis and Clark Principle*. The human user must be guided in a way that's organized in terms of his or her major goals. Information needed for each particular goal should be shown in a meaningful form and should allow the user to directly comprehend the major decisions associated with each goal.

Both are suggestive of a state in which practitioners are directly perceiving meanings and ongoing events, experiencing the problem they are working or the process they are controlling. The challenge is to live in and work on the problem, not to have to always fiddle with machines to achieve understanding.

Anyone practicing a skill has experienced this: musicians playing, dancers dancing, drivers driving, carpenters carpentering, even engineers engineering. But when it comes to the complex sociotechnical workplace, it's the rare piece of software that makes fiddling unnecessary for practitioners or that makes fiddling better for people who like to fiddle (unless of course fiddling happens to be programming or some bastardized version of it—for instance, when "work-around" really means "reprogramming").

The tool should let you see your problem or work better, not force itself on your attention. The tool "becomes part of you," as good tool users often say. This is the HCC point in a nutshell. The connection with the Pleasure Principle is that people in fact take pleasure from using a skill well and that a good tool should amplify and utilize this;

but a bad tool forces you to become skilled at using the tool. The tool becomes the subject matter. So nobody is better at doing the original job, but now we have a new kind of job (using the bloody tool!) that requires a new kind of skill. That can become kind of fun for some people, but it's not the actual job. Meanwhile, the original job is no more fun or any easier than it used to be.

The Pleasure Principle should be pushed for all it's worth, perhaps even to the point of being considered a criterion in requirements analysis and the procurement process. Aristotle, we assume, would see that as virtuous. ■

Acknowledgments

The authors' contribution to this article was made possible by participation in the Advanced Decision Architectures Collaborative Technology Alliance, sponsored by the US Army Research Laboratory under cooperative agreement DAAD-19-01-2-0009.

References

1. Aristotle, *Physics*, Book 7, Section 3, W.D. Ross, ed., Clarendon Press, 1908.
2. Aristotle, *Nicomachean Ethics*, W.D. Ross, trans. and ed., Clarendon Press, 1908.
3. G. Irbe, *Aristotle's Nicomachean Ethics*, 2000, www.interlog.com/~girbe/home.html.
4. E.L. Thorndike, "Animal Intelligence: As Experimental Study of the Associative Processes in Animals," *Psychological Rev. Monograph Supplements*, no. 2, 1898.
5. J.B. Watson, "Psychology as the Behaviorist Views It," *Psychological Rev.*, vol. 20, 1913, pp. 158–177.
6. S. Freud, *Civilization and Its Discontents*, standard ed., J. Strachey, ed., W.W. Norton, 1961.
7. F.B. Gilbreth, *Motion Study*, Van Nostrand, 1911.
8. K. Vicente, *Cognitive Work Analysis: Toward Safe, Productive, and Healthy Computer-Based Work*, Lawrence Erlbaum, 1999.
9. A. Bandura, "Exercise of Human Agency through Collective Efficacy," *Current Directions in Psychological Science*, vol. 9, 9 July 2000, pp. 75–78.
10. T.K. Laudauer, *The Trouble with Computers*, MIT Press, 1997.

Robert R. Hoffman is a research scientist at the Institute for Human and Machine Cognition. Contact him at the IHMC, 40 Alcaniz St., Pensacola, FL 32501; rhoffman@ihmc.us.

Patrick J. Hayes is a senior research scientist and John C. Pace Jr. Eminent Scholar at the Institute for Human and Machine Cognition. Contact him at the IHMC, 40 Alcaniz St., Pensacola, FL 32501.

11. P. Koopman and R.R. Hoffman, "Work-Arounds, Make-Work, and Kludges," *IEEE Intelligent Systems*, vol. 18, no. 6, Nov./Dec. 2003, pp. 70–75.
12. S. Terkel, *Working*, New Press, 1972, p. 37.
13. D. Barry, "There Is No Plane, but Your Flight Is Still on Schedule," *The Pensacola News J.*, 9 July, 2000, p. 4G.
15. D.A. Norman, *Things that Make Us Smart*, Perseus Books, 1993, p. 35.
16. J. Flanagan et al., eds., *Human-Centered Systems: Information, Interactivity and Intelligence*, US Nat'l Science Foundation, 1997.
17. P. Ehn, "Seven 'Classical' Questions about Human-Centered Design," *Human-Centered Systems: Information, Interactivity and Intelligence*, J. Flanagan et al., eds., US Nat'l Science Foundation, 1997, pp. 267–269.
18. R. Jeffries, "Position Paper," *Human-Centered Systems: Information, Interactivity and Intelligence*, J. Flanagan et al., eds., US Nat'l Science Foundation, 1997, pp. 277–279.
19. R.R. Hoffman, K.M. Ford, and J.W. Coffey, "The Handbook of Human-Centered Computing," a deliverable on the Human-Centered System Prototype contract, Nat'l Technology Alliance, 2000; available from Robert Hoffman, rhoffman@ai.uwf.edu.
20. R.R. Hoffman, P.J. Hayes, and K.M. Ford, "Human-Centered Computing: Thinking In and Out of the Box," *IEEE Intelligent Systems*, vol. 16, no. 5, Sept./Oct. 2001, pp. 76–78.
21. R.R. Hoffman et al., "A Rose by Any Other Name ... Would Probably Be Given an Acronym," *IEEE Intelligent Systems*, vol. 17, no. 4, July/Aug. 2002, pp. 72–80.
22. A. Endsley and R. Hoffman, "The Sacagawea Principle," *IEEE Intelligent Systems*, vol. 17, no. 6, Nov./Dec. 2002, pp. 80–85.

Chapter 7: Toward a Theory of Complex and Cognitive Systems

R.R. Hoffman and D.D. Woods, "Toward a Theory of Complex and Cognitive Systems," *IEEE Intelligent Systems*, vol. 20, no. 1, Jan./Feb. 2005, pp. 76–79. doi: 10.1109/MIS.2005.18

We present nine propositions that we've referred to as principles of human-centered computing. We discussed the reductive tendency, which is a necessary consequence of learning. We pointed out that this tendency also applies to those who are creating new information technologies, especially complex and cognitive systems. Indeed, the people who try to create new complex and cognitive systems are themselves prone to generate reductive understandings, in which complexities are simplified.

Toward a Theory of Complex and Cognitive Systems

Robert R. Hoffman, *Institute for Human and Machine Cognition*
David D. Woods, *Ohio State University*

Essays in this department have presented nine propositions that we've referred to as *principles* of human-centered computing:

- *The Aretha Franklin Principle*: Do not devalue the human in order to justify the machine. Do not criticize the machine in order to rationalize the human. Advocate the human-machine system in order to amplify both.[1]
- *The Sacagawea Principle*: Human-centered computational tools need to support active organization of information, active search for information, active exploration of information, reflection on the meaning of information, and evaluation and choice among action sequence alternatives.[2]
- *The Lewis and Clark Principle*: The human user of the guidance needs to be shown the guidance in a way that is organized in terms of his or her major goals. Information needed for each particular goal should be shown in a meaningful form, and should allow the human to directly comprehend the major decisions associated with each goal.[2]
- *The Envisioned World Principle*: The introduction of new technology, including appropriately human-centered technology, will bring about changes in environmental constraints (that is, features of the sociotechnical system, or the context of practice). Even though the domain constraints might remain unchanged, and even if cognitive constraints are leveraged and amplified, changes to the environmental constraints might be negative.[3]
- *The Fort Knox Principle*: The knowledge and skills of proficient workers is gold. It must be elicited and preserved, but the gold must not simply be stored and safeguarded. It must be disseminated and utilized within the organization when needed.[4]
- *The Pleasure Principle*: Good tools provide a feeling of direct engagement. They simultaneously provide a feeling of flow and challenge.[5]
- *The Janus Principle*: Human-centered systems do not force a separation between learning and performance. They integrate them.[6]
- *The Mirror-Mirror Principle*: Every participant in a complex cognitive system will form a model of the other participant agents as well as a model of the controlled process and its environment.[7]
- *The Moving Target Principle*: The sociotechnical workplace is constantly changing, and constant change in environmental constraints might entail constant change in cognitive constraints, even if domain constraints remain constant.[3]

The term "principle" doesn't actually do much work in science. Colloquially, it's used as a tacit reference to laws, as in "This device works according to the principle of gravity." What are these so-called principles? Our answer leads to additional considerations involving the use of the principles.

Cute mnemonics?

Are the principles we've proposed simply aids to help people remember some tips from people who've grappled with issues at the intersection of humans, technology, and work? Indeed, we've deliberately given the principles names that have both mnemonic and semantic value, even though we could have given them more technical designations. And yes, they are "tips."

But they're more than that.

Cautionary tales?

Are the principles merely signposts at the fork between

Editors: Robert R. Hoffman, Patrick J. Hayes, and Kenneth M. Ford
Institute for Human and Machine Cognition, University of West Florida
rhoffman@ihmc.us

paths to user-hostile and user-friendly systems? We and Paul Feltovich discussed the reductive tendency, which is a necessary consequence of learning: At any given time, any person's knowledge of a domain is bound to be incomplete and to some extent simplifying.[8] We pointed out that this tendency also applies to those who are creating new information technologies, especially Complex and Cognitive Systems (people working in teams, using information technology to conduct cognitive work to reach certain goals). Indeed, the people who try to create new Complex and Cognitive Systems are themselves prone to generate reductive understandings, in which complexities are simplified:

> The reductive tendency would be the assumption that a design principle has the same applicability and effects throughout the many different and changing contexts of work and practice. That is, the effects, embodied in the design principle, will hold fairly universally across differing practice environments.[8]

So, the principles are indeed important cautionary tales.

But they're more than that.

Guidelines?

Are the principles recipes that we can use to design human-centered or otherwise "good" information technologies? Take the Sacagawea Principle, for example. Can we go from that principle to a good design for a specific application? Hardly. The principles, as we've stated them, aren't entries in a cookbook that measure goodness in quarts or bytes or hours in the oven. They're not a substitute for empirical inquiry (for example, cognitive task analysis), design creativity, or proper software development. In discussing the application of human-centered computing notions to the design of intelligent systems, Axel Roesler, Brian Moon, and Robert Hoffman stated, "The principles of human-centered computing which have been discussed in essays in this Department are not entries for a cookbook; they are not axioms for design."[9]

Rather than being formulas, the principles imply design challenges. Looking back on the essays, we find one challenge expressed directly. An implication of the Fort Knox Principle is what we called the Tough Nut Problem[4]: How can we redesign jobs and processes, including workstations, computational aids, and interfaces, in such a way as to get knowledge elicitation as a "freebie" and at the same time make the usual tasks easier?

"Project managers or designers may choose to adopt [the principles] if their goal is to create good, complex cognitive systems."[9] The principles do serve as constraints on design.

But they're more than that.

Empirical generalizations?

The principles we've mentioned in this department's essays by no means exhaust the set we've generated. Consider another, for example, the Principle of Stretched Systems: Complex and Cognitive Systems are always stretched to their limits of performance and adaptability. Interventions (including innovations) will always increase the tempo and intensity of activity.

> It's certainly possible to create information technologies that don't support comprehension and navigation, don't integrate learning and performance, or fail to induce a feeling of joyful engagement.

Every system is stretched to operate at its capacity. As soon as some improvement, some new technology, exists, practitioners (and leaders, managers, and so on) will exploit it by achieving a new intensity and tempo of activity.

An example that should resonate with most readers goes as follows. "Gee, if I only had a robust voice recognition system, I could cope with all my email much better." We've heard this plea many times. But stop to consider what would really happen. Others would use the technology too, so the pace of correspondence would accelerate, and people would wind up right back where they were—in a state of mental overload. Systems always get stretched. This has happened whenever new information technologies have been introduced into, and changed, the workplace.[10]

The principles aren't just cautionary tales or design constraints; they're empirically grounded generalizations that have stood the test of time. If we tap into the literature on the philosophy of science,[11,12] we'd say that the principles are

- *Generalizations.* Referring to classes of things, not to individual things
- *Extensional generalizations.* Based on empirical or descriptive evidence

But they're more than that.

Scientific laws?

As we've stated them, the principles are what philosophers call *nomological generalizations*. That is, they're universal for the realm of discourse or for some specified boundary conditions. This criterion is important for physical law: It's literally impossible for matter to travel faster than the speed of light, for example. But it's certainly possible to create information technologies that don't support comprehension and navigation (Sacagawea, Lewis and Clark Principles), that don't integrate learning and performance (Janus Principle), or that fail to induce a feeling of joyful engagement (Pleasure Principle).

But it's impossible to create "good" human-centered systems that violate the principles. Thus, "goodness" sets a strong boundary condition and will prove, we think, to be a critical concept for cognitive engineering.

As we've stated them, the principles are what philosophers of science call *open generalizations*. That is, the evidence that's been used to induce the principles doesn't coincide with the range of application. If the evidence that is available were all the evidence there is, the science would stop. Kenneth Craik described this feature of scientific laws in the following way:

> Now all scientific prediction consists in discovering in the data of the distant past and of the immediate past (which we incorrectly call the present), laws or formulae which apply also to the future, so that if we act in accordance with those laws, our behavior will be appropriate to the future when it becomes the present.[13]

For all new applications and forms of Complex and Cognitive Systems, the principles should apply in the way Craik describes. So, what we've been calling principles are extensional, nomological generalizations whose fate is to be determined empirically. In other words, they're scientific laws.

But laws of what? This department is about making computational devices such as VCRs[14] human centered. But most of the essays have focused on technologies used in sociotechnical contexts. Complex and Cognitive Systems are systems in which multiple human and machine agents collaborate to conduct cognitive work. Cognitive work is goal-directed activity that depends on knowledge, reasoning, perceiving, and communicating. Cognitive work involves macrocognitive functions including knowledge sharing, sense making, and collaboration. Furthermore, Complex and Cognitive Systems are distributed, in that cognitive work always occurs in the context of multiple parties and interests as moments of private cognition punctuate flows of interaction and coordination. Thus, cognitive work is not private but fundamentally social and interactive.[10]

The principles—we should now say laws—are not just about HCC as a viewpoint or paradigm or community of practice; they're about Complex and Cognitive Systems in general. We do not refer to *complex cognitive systems* because that sort of adjective string would involve an ambiguity. Are they complex systems? Is it the cognition that's complex? Complex and Cognitive Systems, as we intend, uses the word "and" to express a necessary conjunction. The designation would embrace notions from "cognition in the wild"[15] and from distributed systems.[16]

So, we have a domain of discourse or subject matter. But a science needs more than that.

Steps toward a theory?

Salted throughout the essays have been statements implying that the principles hang together. An earlier essay on the Pleasure Principle stated that both the Sacagawea and the Lewis and Clark Principles

> are suggestive of a state in which the practitioner is directly perceiving meanings and ongoing events, experiencing the problem they are working or the process they are controlling. The challenge is to live in and work on the problem, not to have to always fiddle with machines to achieve understanding.[5]

This suggests that the principles resonate with one another. The interplay of the principles becomes meaningful.

The Envisioned World Principle and the Moving Target Principle have a strong entailment relation. New technologies are hypotheses about how work will change, yet the context of work is itself always changing. The Envisioned World Principle involves changes to cognitive constraints (for example, task requirements) brought about by changes in environmental constraints (that is, new technologies). The Moving Target Principle asserts that cognitive constraints are also dynamic (for example, new methods of weather forecasting and new knowledge of weather dynamics involve changes in forecaster understanding). Thus, all three sources of constraint can be in constant flux whenever new technologies are introduced into the workplace.

Another criterion philosophers of science hold out for postulates to be scientific laws is that laws must have entailment relations. They must hang together in necessary, interesting, and useful ways. Thus, what we seem to have been reaching for is a theory.

The principles—we should now say laws—are not just about HCC as a viewpoint or paradigm or community of practice; they're about Complex and Cognitive Systems in general.

But what is it for?

Why a theory?

We see two primary motivations for a theory of Complex and Cognitive Systems. The first lurks in previous essays in this department such as the discussion of kludges and work-arounds[17] and Kim Vicente's discussion of VCRs.[14] All sorts of smart, well-intentioned people are out there building new intelligent technologies, and have been doing so for years. The notion of user-friendliness has been around for over two decades. Yet, we're all confronted daily with technologies that are not only not user-friendly but also downright user-hostile. We're even tempted to assert this as another principle (law): *The road to user-hostile systems is paved with user-centered intentions.*[18]

Confronted with the problems that new technologies cause (apart from the problems they might solve) and new challenges entail, sponsors of systems development efforts have come to cognitive engineers crying for guidance in designing information technologies. Sponsors yearn for systems that will solve difficult problems in knowledge acquisition, collaboration, and so on, including such problems as how to enable a single person to control multiple robots or how to help weather forecasters build rich, principled visualizations of their mental models of atmospheric dynamics.

It would hardly do for cognitive engineers to reply with cute mnemonics, or cautionary tales, or cookbooks, or a disassociated collection of empirical generalizations. Cognitive engineers must present a coherent, empirically grounded, empirically testable scientific theory.

But aren't there already theories out there? Systems theory? A theory from cognitive psychology? The second motivation for a theory of Complex and Cognitive Systems is that the phenomena that occur in sociotechnical contexts are emergent and involve processes not adequately captured in either cognitive science or systems science. Explaining Complex and Cognitive Systems, and understanding their behaviors, will require more than the available perspectives and theories. Indeed, this is part of the motivation for the distinction between macrocognition and microcognition.[19]

Cognitive theory might tell us about the millisecond-to-millisecond process of attentional shift, but it doesn't say much about situational awareness. It might tell us about the processes of sentence comprehension, but it doesn't say much about sensemaking in real-world, dynamic situations.

Systems notions and notions of complexity are indeed critical for any understanding of Complex and Cognitive Systems. For instance, the Triples Rule (the unit of analysis of the human-machine-context triple)[1] and the Aretha Franklin Principle both involve systems concepts. But while systems theory can tell us about interactions and feedback, it doesn't say much about human collaboration or distributed cognition.

How do we extend the theory?

You might wonder whether the set of laws constituting a particular theory is complete. This is a high standard employed in logical or axiomatic theories, to which we might not be subject because the Theory of Complex and Cognitive Systems isn't a theory of logic or mathematics. But we might wonder, especially in light of the reductive tendency, to simply assert that the theory of Complex and Cognitive Systems is incomplete. The laws (formerly, principles) that we have mentioned in this department are certainly not all that there are—we know of some two dozen more that haven't yet been essay topics. But beyond this fuller list of laws, we assert that incompleteness is in fact a feature of the theory.

To the mathematically inclined, we might then be free to assert that the laws constituting the theory of Complex and Cognitive Systems are consistent. Rather than doing so, however, we assert that the theory's inconsistency is indeterminate. This affords one path to testability in the form of "forced inconsistency." If a Complex and Cognitive System is designed and initiated in accordance with any subset of the laws, doing so shouldn't force a violation of any other law. If that happens, the theory might need fixing.

Completeness, consistency, and testability are just three of the outstanding issues involved in creating a theory of Complex and Cognitive Systems. Obviously, more work is needed.[20] Numerous subtleties and nuances must be sorted out, involving operational definitions of key concepts and other paths to testability.

This essay aims to encourage people in the intelligent systems and cognitive engineering communities to reflect on the scientific foundations of HCC.

How do we forge a scientific foundation? Once forged, how do we use it? How do we extend, refine, and empirically test it? We invite you to correspond with this department's editors concerning more candidate laws and the challenges for a theory of Complex and Cognitive Systems.

References

1. R.R. Hoffman et al., "The Triples Rule," *IEEE Intelligent Systems*, May/June 2002, pp. 62–65.
2. M. Endsley and R.R. Hoffman, "The Sacagawea Principle," *IEEE Intelligent Systems*, Nov./Dec. 2002, pp. 80–85.
3. S.W.A. Dekker, J.M. Nyce, and R.R. Hoffman, "From Contextual Inquiry to Designable Futures: What Do We Need to Get There?" *IEEE Intelligent Systems*, Mar./Apr. 2003, pp. 74–77.
4. R.R. Hoffman and L.F. Hanes, "The Boiled Frog Problem," *IEEE Intelligent Systems*, July/Aug. 2003, pp. 68–71.
5. R.R. Hoffman and P.J. Hayes, "The Pleasure Principle," *IEEE Intelligent Systems*, Jan./Feb. 2004, pp. 86–89.
6. R.R. Hoffman, G. Lintern, and S. Eitelman, "The Janus Principle," *IEEE Intelligent Systems*, Mar./Apr. 2004, pp. 78–80.
7. G. Klein et al., "Ten Challenges for Making Automation a 'Team Player' in Joint Human-Agent Activity," *IEEE Intelligent Systems*, Nov./Dec. 2004, pp. 91–95.
8. P.J. Feltovich, R.R. Hoffman, and D. Woods, "Keeping It Too Simple: How the Reductive Tendency Affects Cognitive Engineering," *IEEE Intelligent Systems*, May/June 2004, pp. 90–95.
9. R.R. Hoffman, A. Roesler, and B.M. Moon, "What Is Design in the Context of Human-Centered Computing?" *IEEE Intelligent Systems*, July/Aug. 2004, pp. 89–95.
10. D.D. Woods and R.I. Cook, "Nine Steps to Move Forward from Error," *Cognition, Technology, and Work*, vol. 4, 2002, pp. 137–144.
11. A. Kaplan, *The Conduct of Inquiry*, Chandler, 1964.
12. W. Weimer, *Notes on Methodology of Scientific Research*, Lawrence Erlbaum, 1979.
13. K.J.W. Craik, "Theory of the Operator in Control Systems: I. The Operator as an Engineering System," *British J. Psychology*, vol. 38, 1947, pp. 56–61.
14. K.J. Vicente, "Crazy Clocks: Counterintuitive Consequences of 'Intelligent' Automation," *IEEE Intelligent Systems*, Nov./Dec. 2001, pp. 74–76.
15. E. Hutchins, *Cognition in the Wild*, MIT Press, 1995.
16. G. Coulouris, J. Dollimore, and T. Kindberg, *Distributed Systems: Concepts and Design*, 3rd ed., Addison-Wesley, 2001.
17. P. Koopman and R.R. Hoffman, "Work-Arounds, Make-Work, and Kludges," *IEEE Intelligent Systems*, Nov./Dec. 2003, pp. 70–75.
18. R.R. Hoffman, G. Klein, and K.R. Laughery, "The State of Cognitive Systems Engineering," *IEEE Intelligent Systems*, Jan./Feb. 2002, pp. 73–75.
19. G. Klein et al., "Macrocognition," *IEEE Intelligent Systems*, May/June 2003, pp. 81–85.
20. D.D. Woods and R. Hoffman, *A Theory of Complex Cognitive Systems*, tech. report, Inst. Human and Machine Cognition, 2005.

Robert R. Hoffman is a senior research scientist at the Institute for Human and Machine Cognition. Contact him at IHMC, 40 So. Alcaniz St., Pensacola, FL 32502-6008; rhoffman@ihmc.us.

David D. Woods is a professor of industrial and systems engineering and the coordinator of the Cognitive Systems Engineering Laboratory at Ohio State University. Contact him at the Cognitive Systems Eng. Lab, 210 Baker Systems, Ohio State Univ., 1971 Neil Ave., Columbus, OH 43210; woods@csel.eng.ohio-state.edu.

Chapter 8: Complex Sociotechnical Joint Cognitive Work Systems?

R.R. Hoffman, D.O. Norman, and J. Vagners, "Complex Sociotechnical Joint Cognitive Work Systems?," *IEEE Intelligent Systems*, vol. 24, no. 3, May/June 2009, pp. 82–89. doi: 10.1109/MIS.2009.39

This essay continues a tradition in this department: deconstructing the meanings of various buzz phrases. It calls out a cluster of phrases that use the word system. Notions of emergence and complexity are meaningfully related with regard to systems in general, and related in turn to notions of resilience, agility, and robustness. This is arguably true for engineered work systems and for biological systems. But a path to sorting all this out remains hidden by brambles. We are hostages to our language and especially to our fondness for Cartesian dualisms. We need to say that something is both a "structure" and a "dynamic." So far, the word "system" may be our best option even though the search for a definition continues. The editors of this department invite definitions of the word "system" and its modifiers.

"Complex Sociotechnical Joint Cognitive Work Systems"?

Robert R. Hoffman, *Institute for Human and Machine Cognition*
Douglas O. Norman, *Mitre*
Juris Vagners, *University of Washington*

This essay continues a tradition in this department: deconstructing the meanings of various buzz phrases."[1] It calls out a cluster of phrases that use the word *system*.

Kinds of Systems?

Consider the following six systems-related terms.

Sociotechnical systems emerged from research at the Tavistock Institute in the 1950s on the effects of the introduction of powered machines on the work, management-labor relations, and the lives, families, and societies of coal miners.[2]

Human-machine systems is the idea, originating in industrial psychology in the World War I era, that man and machine must be thought of as a single system. The tipping point was the design of a new machine tool's clutch, which required more force than a human lathe operator could muster. The engineers had to learn to design the human-machine as the unit of analysis. Researchers developed this idea further during World War II in work on control theory and cybernetics.[3] Use of the term *system* expanded after around 1950.[4]

Researchers have used the term *complex systems* to emphasize the importance of systems theory and issues of complexity in engineering and design.[5]

Human-system integration is the new kid on the block, initially a reflection of the US Navy's interest in reducing the crew complement on ships. More recently, the concept expanded in the systems engineering community to refer not only to the traditional goals of human factors such as safety, trainability, and reliability but also to such issues as usability, usefulness, and resilience (the key concerns of cognitive systems engineering).[6]

Joint cognitive systems describes this same general subject matter, with "joint" intended to focus on humans working collaboratively with information technology.[7]

Researchers at the Institute for Human and Machine Cognition proposed *complex cognitive systems* as the name of a theory based on the idea that we can reinterpret the "principles" of human-centered computing as empirical nomological generalizations—that is, scientific laws.[8]

All these terms relate directly and immediately to human-centered computing. Their point is to create technology and work methods that improve work processes and results, while also improving the human condition.

Since the notion of systems theory became coin of the realm, we've added many modifiers onto the word "systems." For example, some scholars refer to "dynamical systems," some to "large-scale systems." Both phrases are thought of as differing from run-of-the-mill systems.[9] "Self-organizing" systems are also considered more than plain old systems, in that they increase in complexity without an external guiding hand. Entire theories are built upon the notion of self-organization, largely (and perhaps not surprisingly) in biological systems.[10–12] Likewise, there are formidable theoretical scaffolds discussing "adaptive systems."[13]

Beyond their use as favored terms of particular disciplines and the carriers of historical baggage, what value or meaning do we add by prefixing "system" with any of these modifiers?

Editorial Changes

The editors and editorial board of *IEEE Intelligent Systems* extend our deepest appreciation to Patrick Hayes for his eight years of service as a coeditor of the Human-Centered Computing department. Through his perceptive contributions as both critic and colleague, he has helped to ensure that the essays presented here are substantive and thought provoking. Human-centered computing remains one of the most salient themes of modern technology, as evidenced perhaps by the department's longevity, now up to 36 essays. Dr. Hayes' guidance in crafting the essays has helped to shape what HCC is all about—its goals, its potentials, and its challenges.

We welcome Jeffrey M. Bradshaw, a new coeditor of this department. Jeff is a senior research scientist at the Institute for Human and Machine Cognition. His interests span both cognitive science and computer science, and he's considered a pioneer in the field of software agents. He leads the research group that developed the KAoS (knowledgeable agent-oriented system) policy and domain services framework now in use in several military, space, and scientific research programs. Among his many distinctions and contributions, he was a Fulbright senior scholar at the European Institute for Cognitive Sciences and Engineering, former chair of ACM SIGART, and former chair of the NASA Ames Research Institute for Advanced Computer Science council. He's a member of the National Research Council Committee on Emergent Physiological and Cognitive/Neural Science Research in the Next Two Decades. For more information, visit www.ihmc.us/users/user.php?UserID=jbradshaw.

Deconstruction

What follows isn't just an exercise in semantic deboning, although it is minimally that. The questions we ask are important because their answers can shape how we design cognitive work and the technologies that shape, and are shaped by, that work.[5]

So, let's start at the end of the phrase and work backward: "systems."

The classic approach to general systems theory says that we can define and fully understand systems in terms of sets and subsets.[14] Looking across the literature, we found that researchers have relied on two ideas in most attempts at defining a "system." According to Plato, a system is (1) a set of discriminable elements that are (2) meaningfully grouped (the group "carves nature at its joints").[15] These two basic assertions are the premises of a centuries-old worldview called *mechanism*.[16] This worldview includes three categories: particulars (parts), primary qualities (relevant to the machine's workings), and functional laws (that relate the parts).

Systems theory is not a single thing. It consists of many discussions of systems ideas and notions. One approach says that we can neatly describe systems using the mathematics of control theory.[17] Another approach, based on a biological metaphor, says we can understand systems as self-organizing dynamics.[10,12] Yet another says we can understand systems in terms of the mathematics of thermodynamics.[18] All these approaches highlight certain aspects of systems—sometimes philosophical, sometimes mathematical. Each approach provides interesting conceptual tools for analyzing systems. (Calculophobes beware!)

Complexities

Each approach must address the following three complexities head on.

Everything Is a System

The individual living cell is a system; so too is the organism, composed of many cells, and so on. When it comes right down to it, of course, we can think of anything and everything as a system, and systems are always nested. Systems thinking comes to be, more or less, just a "way of viewing the world."[13,19]

To get things off the ground, we have to assert some set of boundary conditions, or at least specify a spatiotemporal scale that's adequate for containing the main events of interest. But because there will always be cross-scale interactions (in which states and events at scales above and below will impact the system as defined), such bounding is slippery and sometimes next to impossible.

So, everything is a subsystem. For instance, we might think of NASA's launch-systems operations at the Kennedy Space Center as a system, perhaps with a focus on the technologies and decision making of flight controllers during launch. What about the status of the wildlife habitat and its implications for decisions to launch? Any analysis of a system must consider the influence of entities and events from outside its boundaries. Every shift in boundary conditions points to yet another possible shift. Once you start slicing and dicing systems into subsystems, you risk losing the very information that makes a system a system.[20]

Systems Are Relative to the Observer's Goals

The purposes and objectives of the observer or analyst shape the boundary conditions.[20,21] It's no wonder, then, that structural and mathematical approaches have multiplied. An observer's understanding of the system as a group of elements depends upon analysis of functions, causal interactions, and governing principles. Descriptions of the "parts" and the "functions" within a system are always relative. A system's boundary is imposed by an observer or analyst, who settles upon some sort of "closure" in which all the elements can be understood as being tied together into a whole. This depends on the scale of the observations, which is typically derived from the apperception of some sort of "functionally wrapped package" that the world might conveniently present.

Phenomena Are Often Emergent

We cannot predict an aggregate's properties and activities on the basis of knowing the properties of the separate elements and their functions. For example, thermodynamic treatments seek to explain how energy flows that are outside of regions of equilibrium can be a spontaneous source of "interacting structures" without any external intervention. Neurobiological treatments regard high-level cognition (such as perceiving, attending, and remembering) as emergent phenomena of the nervous system.[22] The field of resilience engineering is based on the idea that resilience is a requirement for work systems and must be designed in.[5,23] But resilience is also an emergent phenomenon that occurs as humans and machines adapt to variability and surprise:

> Normative performance is prescribed by the rules and regulations. ... *Normal* performance as well as failures are emergent phenomena. ... Outcomes sometimes differ from what is expected or required. ... The adaptability and flexibility of human work is the reason. (p. 13, italics added)[23]

But using the analysis of parts and functions as the foundation of theories of emergence is bound to prove insufficient. There's an element of surprise as new structures pop out from old ones.

The Modifiers

A possible conclusion from these complexities is that any carving, any notion of groups, elements, and relations, will have fuzzy borders and will come wrapped as a philosophical hornet's nest. Let's temporarily set aside additional questions about what a system is and look at some of the modifiers.

"Work"

What we commonly call a work system differs substantively from other kinds of systems. Of course, in a thermodynamic theory, all systems are about work—that is, transformations of energy, entropy, and so on.[18] But when researchers talk about "work systems," they're usually thinking about a process of *human* work—that is, goal-directed, willful activity in human affairs, especially in professional domains. Human work certainly is energy transformation and can be analyzed in such terms. But no theory that analyzes human work solely in thermodynamic terms can possibly be complete. Where would meaning and knowledge go? Intention? Consciousness? Skill?

Any carving, any notion of groups, elements, and relations, will have fuzzy borders and will come wrapped as a philosophical hornet's nest.

Like all the words we dance around in this essay, "work" has a fuzzy border. For instance, the local astronomy club might qualify as a sociotechnical system, since its activities are group activities and rely on relevant technologies (the Internet for communications and a Web site, computational devices to control the telescopes, and so on). But much of what the club does isn't "work." It's fun and edifying, such as field trips to a photon-sparse region to observe some astronomical phenomenon. On the other hand, sometimes the club's "fun" isn't so fun—it seems like work in the sense of being difficult or tedious, as in having to slog in updates to a Web site.

"Cognitive"

Adding "cognitive" onto the front end injects the mind-body problem into the mix, and that tends to be a game-changer. Things that happen inside individual "headbones," or minds, are causally related to individuals' goals, knowledge, and so on. (For ourselves, we cast aside any naive behaviorist notion that mental events don't have any causal power or efficacy.) We assert that a "cognitive (work) system" is a distinguishable kind of system. Purposefulness, mental models of reality, expertise, and changes in these all have significant causal impact on work system activity.

We can scan the major tomes on systems theory and not learn much about how cognition plays into the mix. We might take this as an argument, albeit a weak one, for the claim that the phrase "cognitive work systems" says something more than the phrase "work systems." In a chapter titled "Models of Mind," Yaneer Bar-Yam mentions the clash of behaviorism and mentalism and then launches into analyses of neural networks.[24] He refers to the "higher information processing functions" but regards these exclusively in terms of brain functions.

In *Autopoiesis and Cognition*, Humberto Maturana and Francisco Varela consider language and thinking as "states of a deterministic nervous system with a relativistic self-regulating organization."[10] In reaching for a relativistic description logic (is that an oxymoron?), Maturana and Varela ask many fascinating questions, such as

"How can the nervous system interact with its own states?" Their investigation of the dynamics and organizing principles of living beings is an attempt to explain the emergence of self-consciousness and linguistic meaning, but that's as far as their foray into *terra cognitionis* goes. For example, it tells us nothing useful about how we might design or analyze cognitive work systems.

In "An Essay on Understanding the Mind," Scott Kelso argues that "minds, brains, and bodies ... share a common and underlying dynamics."[22] He goes on to explain that

> dynamics refers here to equations of motion for key coordination variables or order parameters that characterize patterns of behavior on multiple levels of description: patterns of brain activity, patterns of cognition and emotion, patterns of human insertion, patterns of mind. ... Thoughts are a constantly shifting dynamic system. (pp. 183, 195)[22]

If only such analysis would proceed to actually say something interesting about the mind—or anything at all about it, for that matter (notice Kelso's casual retreat to the word "behavior"). These examples suggest that phenomena of cognition have only been hand-waved in the literature on systems thinking.

Another perspective, from the literature on expertise studies, suggests that "cognitive work systems" says more than "work systems."[25,26] Across studies of expert knowledge, reasoning, and performance in diverse domains, a distinction has percolated up between two classes of domains, for convenience called Type 1 and Type 2. In Type 1 domains, it's relatively easy to identify experts on the basis of operational definitions that specify what it means for a person to be an expert, in terms of performance at principal task goals. Examples would be medicine, weather forecasting, surgery, piloting, chess playing, musical performance, and industrial process control.

In Type 2 domains, it's much harder to come up with good operational definitions to identify experts. Here, the primary task goals involve understanding and predicting the activities of individuals or groups—counselors, astrologists, stockbrokers, clinical psychologists, personnel selectors, parole officers, economists, and so forth. (Consequently, Type 2 domains are also characterized by tasks involving a lack of timely feedback and few robust decision aids.) Both types of domains are complex, so the degree of complexity isn't the distinguishing feature.

Awareness dawns that the compound phrase "sociotechnical joint cognitive work systems" is getting a bit awkward.

"Sociotechnical"

The phrase "sociotechnical systems" focuses on two notions:

- work is conducted by groups, teams, organizations, societies, and cultures; and
- social factors are causally related to the goals, knowledge, activities, and work of individuals and groups.

One can scan the major tomes on systems theory and not learn much of anything about social stuff. The volumes of scholarship on social, organizational, and cultural phenomena reside in some other library. We might take this as an argument, albeit a weak one, for claiming that "sociotechnical work systems" says something more than "work systems." Ludwig von Bertalanffy proposed that sociology might benefit from using systems theory as its "logical skeleton."[14] But he was silent on the possibility that sociology might have something interesting to contribute to understanding how systems function in the world.

"Joint"

The phrase "joint cognitive systems" is intended to distinguish human-machine interaction from human-machine collaboration, emphasizing the interdependencies necessary for achieving the goals of work.[27] The intent is to extend human factors engineering from the focus on the one-person, one-machine context to broader contexts of work, especially complex contexts and systems. Thus, this modifier resonates with the other modifiers.

Pas de Deux

Awareness dawns that the compound phrase "sociotechnical joint cognitive work systems" is getting a bit awkward. We confess a temptation to resort to the two-word phrase "cognitive systems," with the view that "cognitive" embraces or entails "social." However, those whose disciplinary background includes social science might argue just the opposite—that the addition of "social" is meaningful and significant. We could use "cognitive" to distinguish systems that are considered and deliberate from social systems that merely evolve from cultural imperatives. We think, however, there's a better solution.

But before we present that solution, we wish to deconstruct one more adjective: "complex." Do we really need this adjective? Doesn't the notion of a system bring along with it the idea that systems come in varying degrees of complexity? Well, yes, but nevertheless,

> a vision shared by most researchers in complex systems is that certain intrinsic, perhaps even universal, features capture fundamental aspects of complexity in a manner that transcends specific domains. (p. 2538)[28]

Most discussions of complexity start with the premise that "complex systems" are somehow meaningfully different from run-of-the-mill systems.[13,29] A "complexity theory" seems necessary, and not merely possible.[20,30]

Most treatments regard complexity as a property, a property that can be defined in terms of a single scale (that is, the number of parts and part interconnections).[31] This is called "descriptive complexity."[32] We might define complexity in terms of the number of characters in an algorithm, the number of parameters needed in a "structural description,"[33,34] or the amount of information needed to describe all possible states of the system.[24] It's possible to define complexity using the notion of equifinality in a problem space—that is, a complex system is one in which there are many possible paths from problem to goal. One might define complexity in terms of the number of "design degrees of freedom."[28] This comes in handy:

> A 777 is sufficiently automated that it can fly without pilots ... so we could quite fairly describe the mechanism ... as an adaptive, emergent, self-organizing, far-from-equilibrium, nonlinear phenomenon ... [but] the same could be applied to a tornado as well ... [for the 777] design alternatives might have worse or even better performance, robustness and reliability.[28]

Another measure is based on the notion of dissimilarity: complexity isn't just a count of the number of parts or elements but a count of the number of dissimilar elements within a system.[28]

All the attempts to reduce complexity to individual measures seem to miss the point: complexity is complex. "There is simply no right answer when dealing with complexity."[35] It would be better to find some compound of multiple measures, perhaps integrating a measure of the self-dissimilarity of elements,[28] a measure of intricacy,[5] and a measure of the extent or rate of change of elements or subsystems as a result of forces applied to the system.[24]

If complex systems are what people seem to think they are, a theory of complex systems might forever and always be incomplete.

If complex systems are what people seem to think they are, then a theory of complex systems might forever and always be incomplete. This view contrasts with the worldview of mechanism and a view in science that complexity can always be understood as a consequence of the operation of some manageable set of simple, general laws or rules. This view argues that the appearance of complexity is due to our limited understanding.[21,36] At least one approach acknowledges this: it defines complex work systems as ones in which humans have to deal with wicked problems.[37,38] (However, this view seems to focus on complex cognitive work systems rather than complex systems in general.)

Let's move now from the physical-dynamics branch of systems theory to one focused on human affairs. The collectives of humans and machines whose purpose is to create complex (sociotechnical joint cognitive) work systems themselves constitute a complex (sociotechnical joint cognitive) work system.[1] One way this manifests itself is in the reductive tendency, the tendency of people to form mental models that simplify. In fact, the "dimensions of difficulty" that make problems especially hard for humans also express the features of complex systems: dynamic versus static, continuous versus discrete, nonlinear versus linear, interactive versus separable, simultaneous versus sequential, and so forth.

But are those not just the features of "systems"? Are we not back where we started? (Hint: Yes.) Any attempt to define "complex system" by defining complexity in absolute terms is doomed to fail: it will merely consist of words piled upon the relativities that are required to have any meaningful notion of a "system" in the first place.

Macrocognitive Work Systems

A previous essay in this department introduced the distinction between microcognition and macrocognition.[39] This distinction refers to both an approach and a subject matter. As an approach, macrocognition looks at extended problem-solving and the achievement of expertise, in contrast with microcognition research on such processes as moment-to-moment memory access and shifts of attention. Microcognition is a paradigm of laboratory research. Macrocognition is a paradigm of cognitive field research and a reaction to the limitations of what can be done in the laboratory.

Macrocognition is also a subject matter. In (complex sociotechnical joint cognitive) work systems, humans engage in many activities, including the management of their technology and the frustrations that it instills.[40] With regard to the work itself,

- some macrocognitive activities seem to be more individual and cognitive (forming mental models, sensemaking, identifying leverage points, detecting problems);
- some seem to be more social (coordinating, collaborating, maintaining common ground); and
- some insist on being both (replanning, adapting).

As a subject matter, macrocognition is defined as the adaptation of cognition to complexity. In addition to other dimensions that might be used to define complexity, we might say that a human work system is complex to the extent that it requires humans to continually adapt.[31] Thus, the term "macrocognition" gives us "complexity" as a freebie—that is, the first term encompasses the second. Macrocognitive processes are those of teams, organizations, and cultures, and not just individual "headbones." Thus, "macrocognition" gives us "social" and "sociotechnical" as freebies. In other words, we can wrap all of the "X systems" modifiers (cognitive, sociotechnical, joint, complex) in a nice pas de trois: *macrocognitive work systems*.

So, what difference might this make? In the introduction, we asserted that the semantic deboning is important because terminology can shape how we design the work and the technologies that shape, and are shaped by, the work.

Procurement

Someone must understand the work system from a particular vantage point and forge an expression of it so that it fits with their ability to understand and explain it to others. The explanation must cover the breadth of users and account for all the anticipated system modes and activities. The result is often an inaccurate model, but it is nevertheless required to get and maintain funding.[41]

One of the reasons often given for the waste of significant time and resources in the procurement of information technologies is the difficulty of managing the many complexities, dynamics, and interactions involved in designing and engineering a work system that is itself rich with complexities, dynamics, and interactions.[5, 42–44]

Traditional development paradigms assume and depend upon the early, unrealistic completion of a requirements generation stage, despite the dynamic nature of requirements. Macrocognition—the adaptation of cognition to complexity—can be a rallying point to motivate a change in the process of procuring information technologies.

> **We can wrap all the modifiers (cognitive, sociotechnical, joint, complex) in a nice pas de trois: macrocognitive work systems.**

In testimony before the US Congress (reported in a CNN interview on 3 April 2007), economist Alan Greenspan asserted that "complexity cannot be reduced." His point was that simple solutions for economic woes cannot work. David D. Woods and Erik Hollnagel stated a similar idea more in the form of a scientific law: Complexity is conserved under transformation and translation.[7] A classic example is the unintended effect of introducing automation in industrial process control. Although it simplified and improved some aspects of the work, it distanced the controllers from the machines, removing information sources that made work proceed smoothly. To get information, the controllers had to go from the control room (where they were isolated from the sound of the machines) out to the physical plant.[45] The form of the complexity changes, and burdens shift across roles, but the complexity itself doesn't go away.

Sources of complexity include the world that's being observed, influenced, or controlled by the macrocognitive work system as well as events outside the work system's defined boundaries. This might be the weather (observed), an insurgent group (influenced), or an industrial plant (controlled), or some combination of these. Especially salient in recent years has been the complexity added by the need for the military to engage in multiple types of missions in addition to combat (that is, humanitarian, economic, and so forth) and engage in different and new kinds of work in order to perform those missions (for example, networking, control of unmanned aerial vehicles, and so forth).

As the world shapes the work, so too do we struggle to create better work systems that are

- *robust*—able to maintain effectiveness across a range of tasks, situations, and conditions;
- *resilient*—able to recover from a destabilizing perturbation in the work as it attempts to reach its primary goals; and
- *adaptive*—able to employ multiple ways to succeed (as in Russell Ackoff's notion of purposefulness[46]), even as the nature of "success" is changing.

In reaching for human-centering as a goal and for revolutionary change in the procurement process, it's necessary to forge a general theory with macrocognitive work systems as its subject matter.

Notions of emergence and complexity are meaningfully related with regard to systems in general,[47] and related in turn to notions of resilience, agility, and robustness.[5] This is arguably true for engineered work systems[48] and for biological systems.[28] But a path to sorting all this out remains hidden by brambles. We are hostages to our language and especially to our fondness for Cartesian dualisms. We need to say that something is both a "structure" and a "dynamic." So far, the word "system" may be our best option even though the search for a definition continues.

The editors of this department invite definitions of the word "system" and its modifiers.

Acknowledgments

Robert Hoffman's contribution was through participation in the Advanced Decision Architectures Collaborative Technology Alliance, sponsored by the US Army Research Laboratory under Cooperative Agreement DAAD19-01-2-0009.

References

1. R.R. Hoffman et al., "A Rose by Any Other Name ... Would Probably Be Given an Acronym," *IEEE Intelligent Systems*, July/Aug. 2002, pp. 72–80.
2. R.R. Hoffman and L.G. Militello, "Sociological and Ethnographic Perspectives," *Perspectives on Cognitive Task Analysis: Historical Origins and Modern Communities of Practice*, Taylor & Francis, 2008, pp. 251–302.
3. K.J.W. Craik, "Theory of the Human Operator in Control Systems," *British J. Psychology*, vol. 38, 1948, pp. 142–148.
4. D.A. Mindell, *Digital Apollo: Human and Machine in Space Flight*, MIT Press, 2008.
5. D.O. Norman and M.L. Kuras, *Engineering Complex Systems*, tech. report 040043, Mitre, 2004; www.mitre.org/work/tech_papers.
6. Human-Systems Integration Working Group, "Appendix M: Human Systems Integration," *INCOSE Systems Engineering Handbook*, Int'l Council on Systems Eng., 2009; www.incose.org.
7. D.D. Woods and E. Hollnagel, *Joint Cognitive Systems: Patterns in Cognitive Systems Engineering*, Taylor & Francis, 2006.
8. R.R. Hoffman and D.D. Woods, "Steps toward a Theory of Complex and Cognitive Systems," *IEEE Intelligent Systems*, Jan./Feb. 2005, pp. 76–79.
9. M.A. Abramiuk, "Appreciating and Embodying the Dynamics of Large-Scale Systems: Some Examples from the Present and Past," *Ecological Psychology*, vol. 21, 2009, pp. 68–95.
10. H.R. Maturana and F.J. Varela, *Autopoesis and Cognition: The Realization of the Living*, D. Reidel Publishing Co., 1972, p. 42.
11. M.T. Turvey, "Introduction to a Special Issue: Philosophical Issues in Self-Organization as a Framework for Ecological Psychology," *Ecological Psychology*, vol. 20, 2008, pp. 240–282.
12. F.E. Yates, ed., *Self-Organizing Systems: The Emergence of Order*, Plenum, 1987.
13. J.H. Miller and S.E. Page, *Complex Adaptive Systems*, Princeton Univ. Press, 2007.
14. L. von Bertalanffy, *General System Theory: Foundations, Development, Applications*, George Braziller, 1968.
15. P. Plato, *The Dialogues of Plato Translated into English with Analyses and Introduction by B. Jowett in Five Volumes*, 3rd. ed., Oxford Univ. Press, 1892, pp. 265d–266a.
16. S.C. Pepper, *World Hypotheses: A Study in Evidence*, Univ. of California Press, 1942.
17. R.J. Jagacinski and J.M. Flach, *Control Theory for Humans: Quantitative Approaches to Modeling Performance*, Lawrence Erlbaum Assoc., 2003.
18. I. Prigogine, *Thermodynamics of Irreversible Processes*, Interscience, 1961.
19. G.M. Weinberg, *An Introduction to General Systems Thinking*, Wiley-Interscience, 1975.
20. L. Casti, *Complexification: Explaining a Paradoxical World through a Science of Surprise*, Harper Collins, 1995.
21. S.L. Schlindwein and R. Ison, "Human Knowing and Perceived Complexity: Implications for Systems Practice," *Emergence: Complexity and Organization*, vol. 6, 2004, pp. 27–32.
22. J.A.S. Kelso, "An Essay on Understanding the Mind," *Ecological Psychology*, vol. 20, 2008, pp. 180–208.
23. E. Hollnagel, "Resilience—the Challenge of the Unstable," *Resilience Engineering: Concepts and Precepts*, E. Hollnagel, D. Woods, and N. Leveson, eds., Ashgate, 2006, pp. 10–17.
24. Y. Bar-Yam, *Dynamics of Complex Systems*, Westview Press, 1997.
25. J. Shanteau, "Some Unasked Questions about the Psychology of Expert Decision Makers," *Proc. 1984 IEEE Conf. Systems, Man, & Cybernetics* (SMC 84), IEEE Press, 1984, pp. 23–45.
26. J. Shanteau, "Competence in Experts: The Role of Task Characteristics," *Organizational Behavior and Human Decision Processes*, vol. 53, 1992, pp. 252–266.
27. E. Hollnagel and D.D. Woods, *Joint Cognitive Systems: Foundations of Cognitive Systems Engineering*, Taylor and Francis, 2005.
28. J.M. Carlson and J. Doyle, "Complexity and Robustness," *Proc. Nat'l Academy of Sciences*, vol. 99, 2002, pp. 2538–2545.
29. D. Braha, A.A. Minai, and Y. Bar-Yam, *Complex Engineered Systems*, Springer, 2006.
30. A.S. Iberall and H. Sodak, "A Physics for Complex Systems," *Self-Organizing Systems: The Emergence of Order*, F.E. Yates, ed., Plenum, 1987, pp. 499–519.
31. D.P. Jenkins et al., *Cognitive Work Analysis: Coping with Complexity*, Ashgate, 2008.
32. N. Rescher, *Complexity: A Philosophical Overview*, Transaction Publishers, 1998.
33. G. Chaitin, *Algorithmic Information Theory*, Cambridge Univ. Press, 1977.
34. J.W.S. Pringle, "On the Parallel between Learning and Evolution," *Behaviour*, vol. 3, 1951, pp. 174–215.
35. P. Senge, *The Fifth Discipline: The Art and Practice of the Learning Organization*, Random House, 1990, p. 281.
36. I. Stengers, "The Challenge of Complexity: Unfolding the Ethics of Science," *Emergence: Complexity and Organization*, vol. 6, 2004, pp. 92–99.
37. H. Rittel and M. Weber, "Dilemmas in a General Theory of Planning," *Policy Sciences*, vol. 4, 1973, pp. 155–169.
38. D.D. Woods, "Coping with Complexity: The Psychology of Human Behavior in Complex Systems," *Mental Models, Tasks, and Errors*, L.P. Goodstein, H.B. Anderson, and S.E. Olsen, eds., Taylor & Francis, 1988, pp. 128–148.
39. G. Klein et al., "Macrocognition,"

IEEE Intelligent Systems, May/June 2003, pp. 81–85.

40. P. Koopman and R.R. Hoffman, "Work-arounds, Make-work, and Kludges," *IEEE Intelligent Systems*, Nov./Dec. 2003, pp. 70–75.
41. P.J. Feltovich, R.R. Hoffman, and D. Woods, "Keeping It Too Simple: How the Reductive Tendency Affects Cognitive Engineering," *IEEE Intelligent Systems*, May/June 2004, pp. 90–95.
42. J. Goguen, "Requirements Engineering as the Reconciliation of Social and Technical Issues," *Requirements Engineering: Social and Technical Issues*, M. Jirotka and J. Goguen eds., Elsevier, 1994, pp. 165–200.
43. R.R. Hoffman and W.C. Elm, "HCC Implications for the Procurement Process," *IEEE Intelligent Systems*, Jan./Feb. 2006, pp. 74–81.
44. K. Neville et al., "The Procurement Woes Revisited," *IEEE Intelligent Systems*, Jan./Feb. 2008, pp. 72–75.
45. D.A. Norman, *Things That Make Us Smart*, Perseus, 1993.
46. R.L. Ackoff and F.E. Emery, *On Purposeful Systems*, Aldine-Atherton, 1972.
47. J. Pariés, "Complexity, Emergence, Resilience ...," *Resilience Engineering: Concepts and Precepts*, E. Hollnagel, D. Woods, and N. Leveson, eds., Ashgate, 2006, pp. 43–53.
48. E. Hollnagel, D. Woods, and N. Leveson, eds., *Resilience Engineering: Concepts and Precepts*, Ashgate, 2006, pp. 43–53.

Robert R. Hoffman is a senior research scientist at the Institute for Human and Machine Cognition. Contact him at rhoffman@ihmc.us.

Douglas O. Norman is director of complex systems engineering at The Mitre Corp. Contact him at dnorman@mitre.org.

Juris Vagners is professor emeritus of aeronautics and astronomics at the University of Washington. Contact him at vagners@aa.washington.edu.

Part II:

Human-Machine Systems: From Interaction to Interdependence

Chapter 9: Work-Arounds, Make-Work, and Kludges

P. Koopman and R.R. Hoffman, "Work-Arounds, Make-Work, and Kludges," *IEEE Intelligent Systems*, vol. 18, no. 6, Nov./Dec. 2003, pp. 70–75. doi: 10.1109/MIS.2003.1249172

Paradigms are often defined partly in terms of what they are not, or in terms of what they are reacting against. The paradigm of human-centered computing is no exception. We discuss a user-hostile system. We decided that the terms kludge and work-around, and also the related concept of make-work, have yet to be clearly defined for the intelligent systems community. Human-centered systems are different from user-hostile systems as well as from systems based on a designer-centered approach. We try to clarify the senses of these three terms and suggest ways we might study work-around, make-work, and kludges as an integral part of human-computer systems—rather than as embarrassing necessities that are best swept under the computing research rug.

Work-arounds, Make-work, and Kludges

Philip Koopman, ***Carnegie Mellon University***
Robert R. Hoffman, ***Institute for Human and Machine Cognition***

Paradigms are often defined partly in terms of what they are not, or in terms of what they are reacting against. The paradigm of human-centered computing is no exception. In response to an essay in the Jan./Feb. 2002 Human-Centered Computing column "The State of Cognitive Systems Engineering,"[1] we had a lengthy discussion on the question, What is a *user-hostile* system? The following quote is from that essay:

> The road to user-hostile systems is paved with user-centered intentions on the part of the designers. Even smart, clever, well-intentioned people can build devices that are fragile and hostile, devices that force the human to adapt and build local kludges and work-arounds. Worse still, even if one is aware of this trap, one will still fall into it.

We decided that the terms *kludge* and *work-around*, and also the related concept of *make-work*, have yet to be clearly defined for the intelligent systems community. Human-centered systems are different from user-hostile systems as well as from systems based on a designer-centered approach.[2] In this essay, we try to clarify the senses of these three terms and suggest ways we might study work-arounds, make-work, and kludges as an integral part of human-computer systems—rather than as embarrassing necessities that are best swept under the computing research rug.

Editors: Robert R. Hoffman, Patrick J. Hayes, and Kenneth M. Ford
Institute for Human and Machine Cognition, University of West Florida
rhoffman@ai.uwf.edu

Work-around

We all have had to create and use a work-around at some point to get a user-hostile computer to do our bidding. Documented evidence attests to the pervasiveness of work-arounds.[3] Sometimes the work-around is inspired by a friend's hint; sometimes it's spelled out in a help page on the Web; sometimes it's discovered by flailing around until something just happens to work, more or less. Although work-arounds might seem inherently ad hoc, in many situations they make the difference between success and failure.

The *Concise Oxford Dictionary* definition of *work-around* is "a method for overcoming a problem or limitation in a program or system." (Neither the *Oxford Unabridged Dictionary* nor the *Oxford Dictionary of Computing* lists "work-around," but, ironically, the *Concise Oxford Dictionary* does. Go figure.) This definition doesn't go far enough to pin down the concept so that it might be more amenable for study. Does the "problem" being overcome mean a design defect or something as simple as a component failure due to wear-out? Does "limitation" mean an unimplemented (but clearly imaginable and clearly useful) feature, an intentionally precluded action, or an inability to use the tool to cope with an unanticipated operating environment? And is the work-around method written down, foreseen by designers, or made up on the fly?

Wikipedia, a Web-based encyclopedia (www.wikipedia.org), defines *work-around* as

> A bypass of a recognized problem in a system. A workaround is typically a temporary fix that implies that a genuine solution to the problem is needed. Frequently workarounds are as creative as true solutions, involving out-of-the-box thinking in their creation. A workaround is not a permanent solution. Typically they are considered brittle in that they will not respond well to further pressure from a system beyond the original design. In implementing a workaround it is important to flag the change so as to later implement a proper solution. Placing pressure on a workaround may result in later failures in the system. For example, in computer programming workarounds are often used to address a problem in a library, such as an incorrect return value. When the library is changed, the workaround may break the overall program functionality, since it may expect the older, wrong behavior from the library.

Whatis.com, a Web-based glossary (http://whatis.techtarget.com), defines *work-around* as

> A method, sometimes used temporarily, for achieving a task or goal when the usual or planned method isn't working. In information technology, a work-around is often used to overcome hardware, programming, or communication problems. Once a problem is fixed, a work-around is usually abandoned.

This last statement seems to point to an empirical base that, as far as we know, doesn't exist. Be that as it may, all three definitions seem to capture the usual intuitive notion and are all right as far as they go. However, they suggest trying to unpack the different senses of *work-around* might be useful.

Les Gasser defined three alternative senses of what he termed *adaptations*: *fitting*, *augmenting*, and *working around*.[4] Fitting jobs and work schedules to accommodate computing-resource limits is an adaptation you can make to avoid a computing-system failure due to overload. Augmenting involves removing anomalies from the computing environment to avoid triggering problems, such as scrubbing data and training users to avoid making certain types of mistakes. Working around involves users altering input data or procedures to compensate for system shortcomings, or using backup systems.

When a work-around is not readily available, people might even change their goal to something that they know the system can do. For example, if sending a file as an email attachment doesn't work, a potential work-around is putting it on an FTP or Web server and just sending a pointer to the intended recipient. However, we look at this solution simply as a work-around taking place at the next level up from a person's interaction with a computer. Gasser reported the common practice of using informal processes based on personal relationships to expedite organizational processes, with computer-based workflow activity backfilled after the actual task has been performed. Gasser gives the example of a purchasing manager handwriting a requisition to avoid delay and then having the requisition entered into a computer after the fact for tracking purposes.

We define the general sense of *work-around* as follows:

> When a path to a goal is blocked, people use their knowledge to create and execute an alternate path to that goal.

A block can occur when you don't know whether a path to your goal even exists (that is, you're working on a system with invisible and therefore unknown functionalities). A block can also occur when a known path is confusing, laborious, broken, or otherwise hostile. In this case, you might create a new path that you perceive as either more user friendly (for example, intuitive or transparent) or simpler and hence better able to expedite the work. In both cases, the method you create might or might not actually be simpler than that included in the existing functionality.

We propose grouping four alternative senses of *work-around*, hinging on the nature of the block:

A block can occur when you don't know whether a path to your goal even exists. A block can also occur when a known path is confusing, laborious, broken, or otherwise hostile.

- Completing tasks despite design flaws in a computational tool
- Completing tasks despite component failures
- Extending functionality to complete a new task
- Intentionally evading designed limits in an effort to overcome them

This set is based on the notion of a system problem or limitation as expressed in the dictionary definitions given earlier and on Gasser's emphasis on the intent of the person exercising the work-around. Of course, you can use the mechanisms for executing a work-around for more than one of these purposes, and we'll discuss them as we go.

(We've heard of a fifth meaning of "work-around," as a personality trait. Trainers might attribute this to their students, asserting that some individuals seem prone to ignore what they're told. We don't take seriously the idea that "working-around" is a personality trait, on par with, say, sociability.)

Sense 1: Completing tasks despite design flaws

Work-around (1): A procedural change in computer system use intended to compensate for a design flaw, typically a software behavior that is perceived to be a flaw.

Perhaps the most common experience of a work-around with computers is getting buggy programs to work well enough to accomplish a task or achieve a goal. Software companies often issue work-arounds to help users cope with bugs. While you can argue that almost any nontrivial software will have defects, desktop office automation software gets a lot of press for being plagued with bugs. An example that came up on a simple Web search was Microsoft Security Bulletin MS02-027, which states in part, "Customers using IE should implement the work-around detailed in the FAQ."[5] This particular work-around is a set of steps the user performs to reconfigure Internet Explorer.

Some definitions (for example, in Whatis.com) state that a work-around is a temporary compensation until a defect can be corrected. This is the meaning we also find in Eric Raymond's Jargon File.[6] MS02-027 is an example. It involves disabling Gopher service until a patch is released that eliminates a buffer overrun security vulnerability. Also, some work-arounds are only partial solutions. For example, MS02-027 actually disables a service and leaves users on their own if they must use Gopher for something, but it does improve the security of using IE for other tasks.

Sometimes work-arounds are put in place not because the software itself is defective or is perceived to be defective but because the software requirements or operating environment are inadequate. The designer's path through a system might be so confusing, laborious, or otherwise hostile that people create their own paths. These paths might or might not be "right," but are at least perceived to be friendlier (for example, intuitive or transparent), simpler, or less time-consuming.

Generally you can think of a work-around in Sense 1 as a situation in which a user tries to follow a set of well-defined steps to accomplish a particular goal, but something goes wrong that blocks the user from accomplishing those steps. For example, the user might encounter some mind-boggling complexity in the steps' description or a software design flaw that prevents completing those steps in a particular set of circumstances. For instance, Stephan Poelmans describes work-arounds as deviations from a defined workflow system, whether to overcome problems or to improve user experience.[7]

Sense 2: Completing tasks despite component failures

Work-around (2): A procedural change to using a computer system intended to compensate for a hardware or component failure.

We can expect most computer systems of reasonable complexity to suffer component failures, sometimes regularly. Work-arounds in such cases involve people diagnosing a failure or recognizing a pattern of system misbehaviors and then executing an alternate procedure to accomplish a goal. The simplest work-around strategy in the face of a component failure is to have a backup system (computerized or manual) you can use in a pinch, even though it might have limited functionality.[4]

Component failure work-arounds are similar to design defect work-arounds but differ in a few key ways. First, a completely redundant backup system is often helpful for component failures, but it might well have the same design defects as the primary system and thus might not help with design defects. Having heterogeneously designed systems is a way to provide at least some work-around capability for both design and component failures—for example, having both a Windows and a Unix desktop computer, or installing multiple Web browsers from competing vendors.

One good thing about component failures compared to design failures is that it might be possible to fix a component failure very quickly, whereas corrections of design problems can take a long time to create, and work-arounds for them might require trial and error. So, in some cases a simple adaptation strategy of rescheduling work hours to wait for a repair might be possible instead of using a bona fide work-around.

Sense 3: Extending functionality

Work-around (3): A new procedure that uses a computer system in a way not originally envisioned to accomplish a task.

Some work-arounds are necessary because the computer or software as originally designed simply doesn't address the problem or task at hand. This can be because the task you're trying to accomplish is "new" and there hasn't been time to make software changes. In some cases you can foresee this, and you can design work-arounds for existing software as part of a business process change. But at other times, this might not be practical. Working-around in Sense 3 is a common activity. An example would be to use spreadsheet software to compose an essay outline.

In the area of task analysis, Michael Albers argued that goal-driven approaches (that is, ad hoc activities) rather than a preplanned task analysis can be necessary when there are failures or exceptional operating conditions.[8] This reflects the fact that in many instances users are left on their own to determine a work-around because the great number of potential failure and use extension scenarios exceeds currently known techniques for analysis and documentation.

Users are left on their own to determine a work-around because the number of potential failure and use extension scenarios exceeds the currently known techniques for analysis and documentation.

Sense 4: Users intentionally misleading their computers

Work-around (4): A procedural deviation to circumvent an intentionally designed-in limit or constraint on computer system operation.

Sometimes we use work-arounds to evade a computer system's designed-in behavior. This can be because we're trying to use a computer to do something it wasn't intended to do, such as holding down the shift key to defeat a music CD copy protection scheme.[9] This differs from the other types of work-arounds in that the user is trying to do something that the system designers specifically intended the user to not do, or intended to prevent the user from doing, rather than accommodating to a design defect or gap in design requirements.

Some in the field of computer-aided design define *work-around* in this way, as a sort of subversion of a task:

> In subversion [as a constraint negotiation strategy], the user modifies the task approach to take advantage of known weaknesses in the tool, overriding the spirit but not the mechanism by which the constraint is imposed (also known as a "workaround").[10]

Indeed, in the context of CAD, a circuit design arrangement that exploits a loophole in automated design-rule checkers will likely result in a chip design that doesn't work. To increase productivity in safety-critical systems and other critical applications, people might use work-arounds to similarly evade safety features, but they do so at a cost of increased risk. Donald Day conducted a study of work-arounds in this sense of subversion, based on results from a questionnaire concerning the factors that affect flexibility when working under software-imposed constraints.[10] Approximately 200 professionals in computer-aided systems engineering completed the questionnaire. While most respondents reported that they didn't feel especially encumbered by their software tools, most also reported that they absolutely reserved the right to override or work around software-imposed constraints, assuming sufficient justification exists (for instance, to adhere to overriding professional standards or to deal with an obvious software design fault). Those who felt "controlled" by their software tended to report lower levels of satisfaction with it and a higher likelihood of being subversive. Conversely, those who felt that they were less controlled by their software tended to report greater levels of satisfaction with the software and a greater likelihood of conforming to the constraints that the software imposed.

By implication, Day is saying that evading design features is a constructive activity in some circumstances. Such instances abound in the area of graphics software. Alison Black studied how novice graphic designers get "sucked in" to the conventions and limitations of graphics software that was created without benefit of a user needs analysis.[11] She noted the work-arounds that users created to cope with awkward and inefficient commands in graphics software (for example, the problem of filling in enclosed objects that are created piecemeal).

Gasser interviewed approximately 60 professionals who worked at several manufacturing firms to study how they adapt to computing resources.[4] He reported several instances in which users "gamed" their computer systems by entering data known to be inaccurate, or otherwise not following expected normal system use. But the practitioners were able to get their systems to yield usable results, ones that sometimes were more "accurate" than those derived by "following the rules." An example of this in everyday life is booking a conference room for a critical meeting for a time block starting a half hour early on the expectation that any preceding meeting will run later than scheduled. Here's an example from Gasser's report:

> Engineering analysts working [at] a large firm which designed and constructed chemical plants, learned which analyses could go wrong in the package of complex analytical programs they used, and how to correct for untenable results. For example, they routinely input temperature coefficients for pipes carrying hot fluids as though the pipes were intended to operate cold, causing the analysis program to disregard certain heating stress calculations. Over years of experience with this program, the engineers had learned that entering the "correct" information would lead to erroneous results and the pipes would not work properly in the final design. They worked around the technical problems of the program by "running the hot pipes cold" when using it.[4]

The positive value of work-arounds is a recurrent theme in all the empirical work we found. One more example is a study by Gary Parish and William Sollfrey,[12] who examined work-arounds' effects on unmanned spacecraft, including performing reliability calculations that incorporated the expected benefits of work-arounds. They found that even the relatively primitive satellites of that era benefited from work-arounds, with 18 life-extending work-arounds recorded for 25 satellites studied. Their definition of the term emphasized procedural and software changes and specifically excluded built-in redundancy.

Kludge

Webster's Ninth Collegiate Dictionary defines *kludge* as a system (especially computers) made of components that are poorly matched or were originally intended for some other use. This source indicates that the word has unknown origins but cites 1962 as the earliest recorded use. This might refer to a paper in which Jackson Granholm,[13] his tongue firmly in his cheek, suggested several rules of applied "kludgemanship," exemplified by a number of ways in which hackers could create a variety of clever kludges. For example, when using magnetic tape as a storage medium, the "kludgeman" would use both odd and even parity and as many widths as he could find reels for.

Kludge and work-around are related in that both originated because an alternative solution that is either more elegant or more appropriate is for some reason unavailable.

We've seen the word spelled both "kluge" and "kludge" and have heard it pronounced both as "klooge"(as in "stooge") and "kludge" (as in "fudge"), with the former being the pronunciation most people prefer. Granholm traces the word to the German "kluge" (pronounced "kloo-ga"), meaning smart, witty, or clever. We wouldn't be surprised if the term was in fact an acronym for "*k*nowledge and *l*earning *u*sed to derive *g*ood *e*ffects." Nor would we be surprised if the term comes from the last name of an absent-minded German professor who was notorious for making electromagnets from hairpins, old tractor batteries, and fence wire. Raymond asserts that the term came into use in the 1940s in reference to a device called the Kluge Paper Feeder, a "fiendishly complex assortment of cams, belts, linkages ... devilishly difficult to repair ... but oh, so clever."[6]

The general difference between a kludge and a work-around is that a kludge is a set of design artifacts or elements, in one of these forms:

- A fix that is awkward or clumsy but is at least temporarily effective
- An overall design that is of questionable elegance or downright ugly

On the other hand, a work-around is generally considered to be a procedural variation that a person creates and uses. Raymond's Jargon File sees a kludge as an initial design approach and a work-around as a temporary bug fix.[6] On the other hand, most other sources, and our own experience, indicate that using "kludge" rather than "work-around" is more appropriate for temporary fixes. In any event, we feel that the distinction of procedure versus designed artifact is useful, one that accords with most documented definitions. This distinction seems largely consistent with various documented usages in which kludge applies only to hardware and work-around applies to both procedures and software.

Kludge and *work-around* are related in that both originated because an alternative solution that is either more elegant or more appropriate is for some reason unavailable.[13] These concepts are also related in that they are both, apparently, permanent residents of the technology landscape:

> Hardware and software products are sometimes the result of adding a new and basically incompatible design to an original design rather than redesigning the product completely. Users often have a different opinion than the designers do. To the extent that information technology products are combinations of elements originating from a variety of design philosophies and constraints, almost any product is bound to contain some element of kludginess.[14]

Make-work

Make-work activities are repetitive, boring, time-consuming activities that someone must engage in to accomplish something that could not be accomplished using a shortcut, or that one should be able to easily accomplish but cannot. An example is when a display of visualized scientific data relies on screen sectoring to permit the presentation of multiple data types or fields. Sectoring, an attempt to overcome screen real-estate limitations, places a great burden on the user, requiring repetitive point-click-and-drag minimization and maximization to view individual data fields. Another example is having to cut, paste, cut, then "paste as" to get a clean chart transfer from Excel to Corel Draw.

Opportunities

Now that our semantic deboning of the triad has played itself out, you must be asking just the sorts of questions that HCC advocates would raise. We began this essay with a reminder that human-centered systems differ from user-hostile systems in that user-hostile systems are often based on a designer-centered approach.[2] In this regard, Granholm was right on the money when he pointed to some of the reasons why kludges and work-arounds are necessary:

> It is sad, but true, that a kludge cannot be designed under just any old organizational structure. One of the most helpful atmospheres in which a kludge may arrive at full flower is that of complete, massive, and iron-bound compartmentalization. It is a good idea if the I/O men, say, are not only not allowed to talk to the mainframe designers, but also that they have, in fact, never met them. Interface cross-talk should, by all means, be done by edict and directive, and not by memo and design note. After all, someone has to hew the line on design philosophy, or people will go off in all directions.[13]

His sarcasm rings true. Day made a similar point in a literal tone:

> User dissatisfaction with some constraint management techniques may be attributable in part to a mismatch between builders' and users' views of appropriate and necessary design practices.[10]

Rather than simply bemoaning this state of affairs, we could see it as an opportunity. This involves adopting the goal of Day's[10] and Gasser's[4,15] empirical studies:

> Instead of studying how to eliminate problems ... we are attempting to describe and explain the dynamics of computer use over time. This leads us to focus on how circumstances persist and evolve, rather than why they exist in the first place.[4]

Might not research on work-around, kludging, and make-work (WKM) activities reveal ways we could achieve human-centering? Might it not suggest new methods for studying or evaluating human-centeredness?

Also wide open for research are the social and organizational aspects of work-arounds. When and why do organizations choose to ignore subversive, work-around activities? Individuals aren't the only ones who create work-arounds. As Day pointed out, teams and project managers also create them. Why? When? Inspired by Parish and Sollfrey,[12] can we quantify the effects of work-arounds on system dependability and usability?

There's no denying that WKMs will exist as an enduring part of the computing experience. But much software culture today is based on the notion of trying to achieve perfect software, which of course is an in-your-face manifestation of designer-centered design. Perhaps it's time to start treating WKMs as first-class citizens in terms of research topics, development efforts, and teaching. Gasser captured this point beautifully:

> Much software culture today is based on the notion of trying to achieve perfect software, which of course is an in-your-face manifestation of designer-centered design.

> A fundamental assumption of design-oriented literature is that managers, designers, and system proponents define what are "rational" actions in dealing with a computing system —rational procedures for using a system, getting problems fixed, etc. From this viewpoint, workers in our study who worked around formal systems were "escaping" from the constraints of the system, and acting "irrationally" with respect to system goals and managers' expectations. But we have discovered that, far from acting irrationally, the informal practical actions of participants actually make systems more usable locally. Informal fitting, augmenting, and working around are essential and locally rational parts of system use. Appropriate and rational action is defined by the demands of the work situation and the institutional arrangements surrounding computing, not by the ideologies of managers or the presumed necessities of system structure.[4]

This clearly places WKM behavior in the legitimate arena of "adaptive design," in which users help to finish the system design.[16] Researchable topics abound for studying the deliberate, systematic creation and deployment of WKMs. It might be useful to explore ways to build compensation mechanisms into software to make the user-plus-software system more resilient—that is, ways to make work-arounds easier for users to create, document, and share. For example, an online help system might notice that a user is repeatedly getting a particular error message and might offer advice on work-arounds relevant to that error. Help systems today assume that the user is making a mistake and offer canned tutorial advice, but typically do not consider that the real problem might be a software defect, limitation, or user hostility. Users must search the Web or other databases to find work-arounds, if they're published at all.

Although foreseeing all possible failure modes might be impossible, it's probably useful to catch and represent likely failure modes at design time. The only way to do that is to empirically study the "envisioned world"[17] and evaluate software for usefulness and usability. Indeed, safety-critical systems use Failure Mode Effects and Criticality Analysis[18] to represent the effects of hardware component failures and subsystem functional failures. We can extend this to look at the ways that users are blocked and frustrated as they try to complete sequences of steps.

In addition to possible practical applications, research along the lines we propose might lead to a scientific understanding of WKM behavior and a formal representation of work-arounds and kludges.[19]

WKMs are here to stay, perhaps even after computer scientists take notions of human-centering to heart. Intelligent and human-centered systems do not blame or punish users for making mistakes. Perhaps it's time for researchers and technologists to start including WKMs more explicitly in their agendas. *IEEE Intelligent Systems* should be the home for that agenda. ■

Acknowledgments

Phil Koopman's contribution to this article was supported in part by the General Motors Collaborative Laboratory at Carnegie Mellon University. Robert Hoffman's contribution was supported through his participation in the Advanced Decision Architectures Collaborative Technology Alliance, sponsored by the US Army Research Laboratory under cooperative agreement DAAD19-01-2-0009.

References

1. R.R. Hoffman, G. Klein, and K.R. Laughery, "The State of Cognitive Systems Engineering," *IEEE Intelligent Systems*, vol. 17, no. 1, Jan./Feb. 2002, pp. 73–75.
2. R.R. Hoffman et al., "A Rose by Any Other Name ... Would Probably Be Given an Acronym," *IEEE Intelligent Systems*, vol. 17, no. 4, July/Aug. 2002, pp. 72–80.
3. R. Kling and W. Scacchi, "Recurrent Dilemmas of Computer Use in Complex Organizations," *Proc. 1979 Nat'l Computer Conf.*, AFIPS Press, vol. 48, 1979, pp. 107–116.
4. L. Gasser, "The Integration of Computing and Routine Work," *ACM Trans. Office Information Systems*, vol. 4, no. 3, July 1986, pp. 205–225.
5. "Microsoft Security Bulletin MS02-027," 28 Feb. 2003, Microsoft, www.microsoft.com/technet/security/bulletin/MS02-027.asp.
6. E. Raymond, *The New Hacker's Dictionary*, MIT Press, 1991.
7. S. Poelmans, "Workarounds and Distributed Viscosity in a Workflow System: A Case Study," *ACM SIGGROUP Bull.*, vol. 20, no. 3, Dec. 1999, pp.11–12.
8. M. Albers, "Goal-Driven Task Analysis: Improving Situation Awareness for Complex Problem-Solving," *Proc. 16th Ann. Int'l Conf. Computer Documentation*, ACM Press, 1998, pp. 234–242.
9. J.A. Halderman, "Analysis of the MediaMax CD3 Copy-Prevention System," tech. report TR-679-03, Princeton Univ., Oct. 2003, http://ncstrl.cs.princeton.edu/expand.php?id=TR-679-03.
10. D. Day, "User Responses to Constraints in Computerized Design Tools: An Extended Abstract," *Software Eng. Notes*, vol. 21, no. 5, Sept. 1996, pp. 47–50.
11. A. Black, "Visible Planning on Paper and on Screen: The Impact of Working Medium on Decision-Making by Novice Graphic Designers," *Behavior and Information Technology*, vol. 9, no. 4, 1990, pp. 283–296.
12. G. Parish and W. Sollfrey, *Preliminary Analysis of the Effect of Work-Arounds on Space System Performance and Procurement Requirements: A Proposal*, Rand Corp. report N-1260-AF, 1980.
13. J. Granholm, "How to Design a Kludge," *Datamation*, vol. 8, Feb. 1962, pp. 30–31.
14. L. Swanson and M.J. Warden, "Kludge," Whatis.com, 2003; http://whatis.techtarget.com.
15. F. Darses, "The Constraint Satisfaction Approach to Design: A Psychological Investigation," *Acta Psychologica*, vol. 78, 1991, pp. 307–325.
16. D.D. Woods and S.W.A. Dekker, "Anticipating the Effects of Technological Change: A New Era of Dynamics for Human Factors," *Theoretical Issues in Ergonomic Science*, vol. 1, no. 3, 2000, pp. 272–282.
17. S.W.A. Dekker, J.M. Nyce, and R.R. Hoffman, "From Contextual Inquiry to Designable Futures: What Do We Need to Get There? *IEEE Intelligent Systems*, vol. 18, no. 2, Mar./Apr. 2003, pp. 74–77.
18. C. McCollin, "Working around Failure," *Manufacturing Engineer*, vol. 78, no. 1, Feb. 1999, pp. 37–40.
19. C. Martin, *Functional Fault Simulation for Distributed Embedded Systems*, master's thesis, Electrical and Computer Eng. Dept., Carnegie Mellon Univ., 2001.

Philip Koopman is an associate professor at Carnegie Mellon University. He is affiliated with the Department of Electrical and Computer Engineering, the Institute for Software Research International, and the Institute for Complex Engineered Systems. Contact him at the ECE Dept., Carnegie Mellon Univ., 5000 Forbes Ave., Pittsburgh, PA 15213; koopman@cmu.edu.

Robert R. Hoffman is a research scientist at the Institute for Human and Machine Cognition. Contact him at the IHMC, 40 Alcaniz St., Pensacola, FL 32501; rhoffman@ihmc.us.

Addendum

The September/October 2003 installment of this column was titled "The Borg Hypothesis." Jane Abbate, historian of technology at the Chemical Heritage Foundation, points out to us that the term *cyborg* was first introduced in 1960 by Manfred Clynes and Nathan Kline ("Cyborgs and Space," *Astronautics*, vol. 5, pp. 26–27, 74–76). They had a similar mission to that described in our essay: preparing humankind for space travel.

But this early vision of a cyborg future did not include the crucial concept of fitting the human body with intelligent technologies, as opposed to merely adding cybernetic mechanisms such as artificial limbs or even artificial eyeballs. The notion that control theory ala Norbert Wiener (that is, types of feedback loops) is sufficient for intelligence is at least arguable. The point of our essay was to consider the integration of intelligent technologies into humans and the implications this might have for human evolution.

—Robert R. Hoffman

To be continued ...

Chapter 10: Ten Challenges for Making Automation a "Team Player" in Joint Human-Agent Activity

G. Klein, D.D. Woods, J.M. Bradshaw, R.R. Hoffman, and P.J. Feltovich, "Ten Challenges for Making Automation a 'Team Player' in Joint Human-Agent Activity," *IEEE Intelligent Systems*, vol. 19, no. 6, Nov./Dec. 2004, pp. 91–95. doi: 10.1109/MIS.2004.74

We propose 10 challenges for making automation components into effective "team players" when they interact with people in significant ways. Our analysis is based on some of the principles of human-centered computing that we have developed individually and jointly over the years, and is adapted from a more comprehensive examination of common ground and coordination.

Ten Challenges for Making Automation a "Team Player" in Joint Human-Agent Activity

Gary Klein, *Klein Associates*
David D. Woods, *Cognitive Systems Engineering Laboratory*
Jeffrey M. Bradshaw, Robert R. Hoffman, and Paul J. Feltovich,
Institute for Human and Machine Cognition

We propose 10 challenges for making automation components into effective "team players" when they interact with people in significant ways. Our analysis is based on some of the principles of human-centered computing that we have developed individually and jointly over the years, and is adapted from a more comprehensive examination of common ground and coordination.[1]

Requirements for joint activity among people

We define *joint activity* as an extended set of actions that are carried out by an ensemble of people who are coordinating with each other.[1,2]

Joint activity involves at least four basic requirements. All the participants must

- Enter into an agreement, which we call a *Basic Compact*, that the participants intend to work together
- Be mutually predictable in their actions
- Be mutually directable
- Maintain common ground

The Basic Compact

To carry out joint activity, each party effectively enters into a Basic Compact—an agreement (often tacit) to facilitate coordination, work toward shared goals, and prevent breakdowns in team coordination. This Compact involves a commitment to some degree of goal alignment. Typically this entails one or more participants relaxing their own shorter-term goals in order to permit more global and long-term team goals to be addressed. These longer-term goals might be shared (for example, a relay team) or individual (such as highway drivers wanting to ensure their own safe journeys).

The Basic Compact is not a once-and-for-all prerequisite to be satisfied but rather has to be continuously reinforced or renewed. It includes an expectation that the parties will repair faulty mutual knowledge, beliefs, and assumptions when these are detected. Part of achieving coordination is investing in those actions that enhance the Compact's integrity as well as being sensitive to and counteracting those factors that could degrade it.

For example, remaining in a Compact during a conversation manifests in the process of accepting turns, relating understandings, detecting the need for and engaging in repair, displaying a posture of interest, and the like. When these sorts of things aren't happening, we might infer that one or more of the parties isn't wholeheartedly engaged. The Compact requires that if one party intends to drop out of the joint activity, he or she must signal this to the other parties. Breakdowns occur when a party abandons the team without clearly signaling his or her intentions to others.

While in traffic, drivers might have defensible motives for rejecting a Compact about following the rules of the road, as when they're responding to an emergency by rushing someone to the nearest hospital. At such times, drivers might turn on their emergency blinkers to signal to other drivers that their actions are no longer as predictable. But in most kinds of joint activity, the agreement itself is tacit, and the partners depend on more subtle signals to convey that they are or aren't continuing in the joint activity. In a given context, sophisticated protocols might develop to acknowledge receipt of a signal, transmit some construal of a signal's meaning back to the sender, indicate preparation for consequent acts, and so forth.

Editors: Robert R. Hoffman, Patrick J. Hayes, and Kenneth M. Ford
Institute for Human and Machine Cognition, University of West Florida
rhoffman@ai.uwf.edu

Mutual predictability

For effective coordination to take place during the course of the joint activity, team members rely on the existence of a reasonable level of mutual predictability. In highly interdependent activities, planning our own actions (including coordination actions) becomes possible only when we can accurately predict what others will do. Skilled teams become mutually predictable through shared knowledge and idiosyncratic coordination devices developed through extended experience in working together. Bureaucracies with high turnover compensate for lack of shared experience by substituting explicit, predesigned, structured procedures and expectations.

Directability

Team members must also be directable. This refers to the capacity for deliberately assessing and modifying other parties' actions in a joint activity as conditions and priorities change.[3] Effective coordination requires participants' adequate responsiveness to the others' influence as the activity unfolds.

Common ground

Finally, effective coordination requires establishing and maintaining common ground.[4] Common ground includes the pertinent knowledge, beliefs, and assumptions that the involved parties share. Common ground enables each party to comprehend the messages and signals that help coordinate joint actions. Team members must be alert for signs of possible erosion of common ground and take preemptive action to forestall a potentially disastrous breakdown of team functioning.

As an example, we had occasion to observe an Army exercise. During the exercise, a critical event occurred and was entered into the shared large-format display of the "common operating picture." The brigade commander wasn't sure that one of his staff members had seen the change, so he called that person because he felt it was important to manage his subordinate's attention and because the technology didn't let him see if the staff member had noticed the event. The commander had to act like an aide to ensure that the staff member had seen a key piece of information. Special language, often used in noisy, confusing environments (such as "acknowledge" and "roger that"), serves the same function.

Ten challenges

Many researchers and system developers have been looking for ways to make automated systems team players.[3] A great deal of the current work in the software and robotic-agent research communities involves determining how to build automated systems with sophisticated team player qualities.[5–7] In contrast to early research that focused almost exclusively on how to make agents more autonomous, much current agent research seeks to understand and satisfy requirements for the basic aspects of joint activity, either within multiagent systems or as part of human-agent teamwork.

Given the widespread demand for increasing the effectiveness of team play for complex systems that work closely and collaboratively with people, a better understanding of the major challenges is important.

> **Agents must also "understand" and accept the enterprise's joint goals, their roles in the collaboration, and the need for maintaining common ground.**

A Basic Compact

Challenge 1: To be a team player, an intelligent agent must fulfill the requirements of a Basic Compact to engage in common-grounding activities.

A common occurrence in joint action is when an agent fails and can no longer perform its role. General-purpose agent teamwork models typically entail that the struggling agent notify each team member of the actual or impending failure.[8]

Looking beyond current research and machine capabilities, not only do agents need to be able to enter into a Basic Compact, they must also "understand" and accept the enterprise's joint goals, understand and accept their roles in the collaboration and the need for maintaining common ground, and be capable of signaling if they're unable or unwilling to fully participate in the activity.

Adequate models

Challenge 2: To be an effective team player, intelligent agents must be able to adequately model the other participants' intentions and actions vis-à-vis the joint activity's state and evolution—for example, are they having trouble? Are they on a standard path proceeding smoothly? What impasses have arisen? How have others adapted to disruptions to the plan?

In the limited realm of what today's agents can communicate and reason about among themselves, there's been some limited success in the development of theories and implementations of multiagent cooperation not directly involving humans. The key concept here usually involves some notion of shared knowledge, goals, and intentions that function as the glue that binds agents' activities together.[8] By virtue of a largely reusable explicit formal model of shared "intentions," multiple agents try to manage general responsibilities and commitments to each other in a coherent fashion that facilitates recovery when unanticipated problems arise.

Addressing human-agent teamwork presents a new set of challenges and opportunities for agent researchers. No form of automation today or on the horizon can enter fully into the rich forms of Basic Compact that are used among people.

Predictability

Challenge 3: Human-agent team members must be mutually predictable.

To be a team player, an intelligent agent—like a human—must be reasonably predictable and reasonably able to predict others' actions. It should act neither capriciously nor unobservably, and it should be able to observe and correctly predict its teammates' future behavior. Currently, however, agents' "intelligence" and autonomy work directly against the confidence that people have in their predictability. Although people will rapidly confide tasks to simple deterministic mechanisms whose design is artfully made transparent, they are usually reluctant to trust complex agents to the same degree.[9] Ironically, by making agents more adaptable, we might also make them less predictable. The more a system takes the initiative to adapt to its operator's working style, the more reluctant operators might be to adapt their own behavior because of the confusions these adaptations might create.[10]

Directability

Challenge 4: Agents must be directable.

The nontransparent complexity and inadequate directability of agents can be a formula for disaster. In response to this concern, agent researchers have focused increasingly on developing means for controlling aspects of agent autonomy in a fashion that can be both dynamically specified and easily understood—that is directability.[3,11] Policies are a means to dynamically regulate a system's behavior without changing code or requiring the cooperation of the components being governed.[6,9] Through policy, people can precisely express bounds on autonomous behavior in a way that's consistent with their appraisal of an agent's competence in a given context. Their behavior becomes more predictable with respect to the actions controlled by policy. Moreover, the ability to change policies dynamically means that poorly performing agents can be immediately brought into compliance with corrective measures.

Revealing status and intentions

Challenge 5: Agents must be able to make pertinent aspects of their status and intentions obvious to their teammates.

Classic results have shown that the highest levels of automation on the flight deck of commercial jet aircraft (Flight Management Systems or FMSs) often leave commercial pilots baffled in some situations, wondering what the automation is currently doing, why it's doing that, and what it will do next.[12] To make their actions sufficiently predictable, agents must make their own targets, states, capacities, intentions, changes, and upcoming actions obvious to the people and other agents that supervise and coordinate with them.[13] This challenge runs counter to the advice sometimes given to automation developers to create systems that are barely noticed. We are asserting that people need a model of the machine as an agent participating in the joint activity.[14] People can often effectively use their own thought processes as a basis for inferring the way their teammates are thinking, but this self-referential heuristic is not usually effective in working with agents.

Interpreting signals

Challenge 6: Agents must be able to observe and interpret pertinent signals of status and intentions.

Sending signals isn't enough. The agents that receive signals must be able to interpret the signals and form models of their teammates. This is consistent with the Mirror-Mirror principle of HCC: *Every participant in a complex sociotechnical system will form a model of the other participant agents as well as a model of the controlled process and its environment.*[15] The ideal agent would grasp the significance of such things as pauses, rapid pacing, and public representations that help humans mark the coordination activity. Few existing agents are intended to read their operator teammates' signals with any degree of substantial understanding, let alone nuance. As a result, the devices can't recognize the operator's stance, much less appreciate the operator's knowledge, mental models, or goals, given the evolving state of the plan in progress and the world being controlled.

Charles Billings[16] and David Woods[17] argue that an inherent asymmetry in coordinative competencies between people and machines will always create difficulties for designing human-agent teams. Nevertheless, some researchers are exploring ways to stretch agents' performance to reduce this asymmetry as far as possible, such as exploiting and integrating available channels of communication from the agent to the human and, conversely, sensing and inferring the human's cognitive state through a range of physiological measures in real time. Similarly, a few research efforts are taking seriously the agent's need to interpret the physical environment. If they accomplish nothing more, efforts such as these can help us appreciate the difficulty of this problem.

To be a team player, an intelligent agent—like a human—must be reasonably predictable and reasonably able to predict others' actions.

Goal negotiation

Challenge 7: Agents must be able to engage in goal negotiation.

In many common situations, participants must be able to enter into goal negotiation, particularly when the situation changes and the team has to adapt. As required, intelligent agents must convey their current and potential goals so that appropriate team members can participate in the negotiations.

If agents are unable to readily represent, reason about, or modify their goals, they will interfere with coordination and the maintenance of common ground. Traditional planning technologies for agents typically take an autonomy-centered approach, with representations, mechanisms, and algorithms that have been designed to ingest a set of goals and produce output as if they can provide a complete plan that handles all situations. This approach isn't compatible with what we know about optimal coordination in human-agent interaction.

Collaboration

Challenge 8: Support technologies for planning and autonomy must enable a collaborative approach.

A collaborative autonomy approach assumes that the processes of understanding, problem solving, and task execution are necessarily incremental, subject to negotiation, and forever tentative.[18] Thus, every element of an "autonomous" system will have to be designed to facilitate the kind of give-and-take that quintessentially characterizes natural and effective teamwork among groups of people.

James Allen and George Ferguson's research on collaboration management agents is a good example.[5] CMAs are designed to support human-agent, human-human, and agent-agent interaction and collaboration within mixed human-robotic teams. They interact with individual agents to

- Maintain an overall picture of the current situation and status of the overall plan as completely as possible based on available reports
- Detect possible failures that become more likely as the plan execution evolves, and invoke replanning
- Evaluate the viability of proposed changes to plans by agents
- Manage replanning when situations exceed individual agents' capabilities, including recruiting more capable agents to perform the replanning
- Manage the retasking of agents when changes occur

- Adjust their communications to the agents' capabilities (for example, graphical interfaces work well for a human but wouldn't help most agents)

Because the team members will be in different states depending on how much of their original plan they've executed, CMAs must support further negotiation and replanning at runtime.

Attention management

Challenge 9: Agents must be able to participate in managing attention.

As part of maintaining common ground during coordinated activity, team members direct each other's attention to the most important signals, activities, and changes. They must do this in an intelligent and context-sensitive manner, so as not to overwhelm others with low-level messages containing minimal signals mixed with a great deal of distracting noise.

Relying on their mental models of each other, responsible team members expend effort to appreciate what each other needs to notice, within the context of the task and the current situation.[19] Automation can compensate for trouble (for example, asymmetric lift due to wing icing), but currently does so invisibly. Crews can remain unaware of the developing trouble until the automation nears the limits of its authority or capability to compensate. As a result, the crew might take over too late or be unprepared to handle the disturbance once they take over, resulting in a bumpy transfer of control and significant control excursions. This general problem has been a part of several aviation incident and accident scenarios.

It will push the limits of technology to get the machines to communicate as fluently as a well-coordinated human team working in an open, visible environment. The automation will have to signal when it's having trouble and when it's taking extreme action or moving toward the extreme end of its range of authority. Such capabilities will require interesting relational judgments about agent activities: How does an agent tell when another team member is having trouble performing a function but has not yet failed? How and when does an agent effectively reveal or communicate that it's moving toward its limit of capability?

Adding threshold-crossing alarms is the usual answer to these questions in automation design. However, in practice, rigid and context-insensitive thresholds will typically be crossed too early (resulting in an agent that speaks up too often, too soon) or too late (resulting in an agent that's too silent, speaking up too little). However, focusing on the basic functions of joint activity rather than machine autonomy has already produced some promising successes.[20]

Cost control

Challenge 10: All team members must help control the costs of coordinated activity.

The Basic Compact commits people to coordinating with each other and to incurring the costs of providing signals, improving predictability, monitoring the others' status, and so forth. All these take time and energy. These coordination costs can easily get out of hand, so the partners in a coordination transaction must do what they reasonably can to keep coordination costs down. This is a tacit expectation—to try to achieve economy of effort. Coordination requires continuing investment and hence the power of the Basic Compact—a willingness to invest energy and accommodate others, rather than just performing alone in one's narrow scope and subgoals. Coordination doesn't come for free, and coordination, once achieved, doesn't allow us to stop investing. Otherwise, the coordination breaks down.

> How does an agent tell when a team member is having trouble performing a function but hasn't yet failed? When does an agent communicate that it's moving toward its limit of capability?

Keeping coordination costs down is partly, but only partly, a matter of good human-computer interface design. More than that, the agents must conform to the operators' needs rather than require operators to adapt to them. Information hand-off, which is a basic exchange during coordination involving humans and agents, depends on common ground and mutual predictability. As the notions of HCC suggest, agents must become more understandable, more predictable, and more sensitive to people's needs and knowledge.

The 10 challenges we've presented can be viewed in different lights:

- As a blueprint for designing and evaluating intelligent systems—requirements for successful operation and the avoidance or mitigation of coordination breakdowns.
- As cautionary tales about the ways that technology can disrupt rather than support coordination: Simply relying on explicit procedures, such as common operating pictures, isn't likely to be sufficient.
- As the basis for practicable human-agent systems. All the challenges have us walking a fine line between the two views of AI: the traditional one that AI's goal is to create systems that emulate human capabilities, versus the nontraditional human-centered computing goal—to create systems that extend human capabilities, enabling people to reach into contexts that matter for human purposes.

We can imagine in the future that some agents will be able to enter into some form of a Basic Compact, with diminished capability.[6] Agents might eventually be fellow team members with humans in the way a young child or a novice can be—subject to the consequences of brittle and literal-minded interpretation of language and events, limited ability to appreciate or even attend effectively to key aspects of the interaction, poor anticipation, and insensitivity to nuance. In the meantime, we hope you might use the 10 challenges we've outlined to guide research in the design of team and organizational simulations that seek to capture coordination breakdowns and other features of joint activity. Through further research, restricted types of Basic Compacts might be created that could be suitable for use in human-agent systems.

Acknowledgments

Klein Associates, Ohio State University, and the Institute for Human and Machine Cognition prepared this work through the support of the Advanced Decision Architectures Collaborative Technology Alliance, sponsored by the US Army Research Laboratory under cooperative agreement DAAD19-01-2-0009. David Woods' participation was also made possible by an IBM Faculty Award.

References

1. G. Klein et al., "Common Ground and Coordination in Joint Activity," to be published in *Organizational Simulation*, W.R. Rouse and K.B. Boff, eds., John Wiley & Sons, 2005.

2. H. Clark, *Using Language,* Cambridge Univ. Press, 1996.

3. K. Christoffersen and D.D. Woods, "How to Make Automated Systems Team Players," *Advances in Human Performance and Cognitive Eng. Research*, vol. 2, 2002, pp. 1–12.

4. H.H. Clark and S.E. Brennan, "Grounding in Communication," *Perspectives on Socially Shared Cognition*, L.B. Resnick, J.M. Levine, and S.D. Teasley, eds., Am. Psychological Assoc., 1991.

5. J.F. Allen and G. Ferguson, "Human-Machine Collaborative Planning," *Proc. NASA Planning and Scheduling Workshop,* NASA, 2002.

6. J.M. Bradshaw et al., "Dimensions of Adjustable Autonomy and Mixed-Initiative Interaction," *Agents and Computational Autonomy: Potential, Risks, and Solutions*, M. Nickles, M. Rovatsos, and G. Weiss, eds., LNCS 2969, Springer-Verlag, 2004, pp. 17–39.

7. M. Tambe et al., "Teamwork in Cyberspace: Using TEAMCORE to Make Agents Team-Ready," *Proc. AAAI Spring Symp. Agents in Cyberspace*, AAAI Press, 1999, pp. 136–141.

8. P.R. Cohen and H.J. Levesque, "Teamwork," *Nous*, vol. 25, 1991, pp. 487–512.

9. J.M. Bradshaw et al., "Making Agents Acceptable to People," *Intelligent Technologies for Information Analysis: Advances in Agents, Data Mining, and Statistical Learning*, N. Zhong and J. Liu, eds., Springer-Verlag, 2004, pp. 361–400.

10. G. Klein, *The Power of Intuition*, Currency Book/Doubleday, 2004.

11. K. Myers and D. Morley, "Directing Agents," *Agent Autonomy*, H. Hexmoor, C. Castelfranchi, and R. Falcone, eds., Kluwer Academic Publishers, 2003, pp. 143–162.

12. D.D. Woods and N. Sarter, "Learning from Automation Surprises and Going Sour Accidents," *Cognitive Engineering in the Aviation Domain*, N. Sarter and R. Amalberti, eds., Lawrence Erlbaum, 2000, pp. 327–254.

13. P.J. Feltovich et al., "Social Order and Adaptability in Animal and Human Cultures as Analogues for Agent Communities: Toward a Policy-Based Approach," *Engineering Societies in the Agents World IV*, LNAI 3071, Springer-Verlag, 2004, pp. 21–48.

14. D.A. Norman, "The 'Problem' with Automation: Inappropriate Feedback and Interaction, Not Over-Automation," *Philosophical Trans. Royal Soc. London*, vol. 327, 1990, pp. 585–593.

15. R.R. Hoffman and D.D. Woods, *The Theory of Complex Cognitive Systems*, tech. report, Inst. for Human and Machine Cognition, Pensacola, Fla., 2004.

16. C.E. Billings, *Aviation Automation: The Search for a Human-Centered Approach*, Lawrence Erlbaum, 1996.

17. D.D. Woods, "Steering the Reverberations of Technology Change on Fields of Practice: Laws That Govern Cognitive Work," *Proc. 24th Ann. Meeting Cognitive Science Soc.*, Lawrence Erlbaum, 2002, pp. 14–17; http://csel.eng.ohio-state.edu/laws.

18. J.M. Bradshaw et al., "Teamwork-Centered Autonomy for Extended Human-Agent Interaction in Space Applications," *Proc. AAAI Spring Symp. Interaction between Humans and Autonomous Systems over Extended Operation*, AAAI Press, 2004, pp. 136–140.

19. N. Sarter and D.D. Woods, "Team Play with a Powerful and Independent Agent: A Full Mission Simulation," *Human Factors*, vol. 42, 2000, pp. 390–402.

20. C.-Y. Ho et al., "Not Now: Supporting Attention Management by Indicating the Modality and Urgency of Pending Tasks," to be published in *Human Factors*.

Gary Klein is chief scientist at Klein Associates. Contact him at Klein Associates, 1750 Commerce Center Blvd. North, Fairborn, OH 45324; gary@decisionmaking.com.

David D. Woods is a professor at the Institute for Ergonomics at Ohio State University. Contact him at the Cognitive Systems Eng. Laboratory, 210 Baker Systems, 1971 Neil Ave., Ohio State Univ., Columbus, OH 43210; woods.2@osu.edu.

Jeffrey M. Bradshaw is a senior research scientist at the Institute for Human and Machine Cognition. Contact him at IHMC, 40 S. Alcaniz St., Pensacola, FL 32502; jbradshaw@ihmc.us.

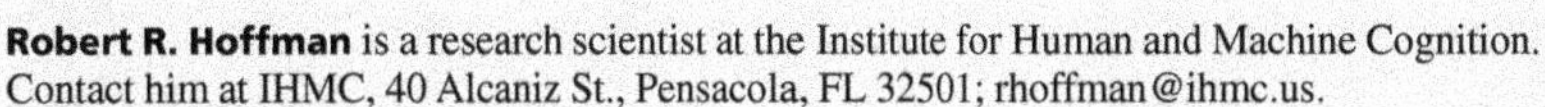

Robert R. Hoffman is a research scientist at the Institute for Human and Machine Cognition. Contact him at IHMC, 40 Alcaniz St., Pensacola, FL 32501; rhoffman@ihmc.us.

Paul J. Feltovich is a research scientist at the Institute for Human and Machine Cognition. Contact him at IHMC, 40 S. Alcaniz St., Pensacola, FL 32502; pfeltovich@ihmc.us.

Chapter 11: Antipatterns in the Creation of Intelligent Systems

P. Laplante, R.R. Hoffman, and G. Klein, "Antipatterns in the Creation of Intelligent Systems," *IEEE Intelligent Systems*, vol. 22, no. 1, Jan./Feb. 2007, pp. 91–95. doi: 10.1109/MIS.2007.3

A design pattern is a named problem-solution pair that enables large-scale reuse of software architectures or their components. Ideally, patterns explicitly capture expert knowledge, design trade-offs, and design rationale and make these lessons learned widely available for off-the-shelf use. They can also enhance developers' vocabulary—for example, by easing the transition to object-oriented programming. Conventionally, patterns consist of four elements: a name, the problem to be solved, the solution to the problem (often termed the refactored solution), and the consequences of the solution. Numerous sets of patterns (collectively known as pattern languages) exist for software design, analysis, management, and so on. Shortly after the notion of design patterns emerged, practitioners began discussing problem-solution pairs in which the solution did more harm than good. These have come to be known as antipatterns, and they are well known in the design and management communities.

Antipatterns in the Creation of Intelligent Systems

Phil Laplante, *Pennsylvania State University*
Robert R. Hoffman, *Institute for Human and Machine Cognition*
Gary Klein, *Klein Associates Division of ARA*

A design pattern is a named problem-solution pair that enables large-scale reuse of software architectures or their components (that is, interface designs[1]). Ideally, patterns explicitly capture expert knowledge, design trade-offs, and design rationale and make these lessons learned widely available for off-the-shelf use. They can also enhance developers' vocabulary—for example, by easing the transition to object-oriented programming.[2]

Conventionally, patterns consist of four elements: a name, the problem to be solved, the solution to the problem (often termed the *refactored* solution), and the consequences of the solution. Numerous sets of patterns (collectively known as pattern languages) exist for software design, analysis, management, and so on; a Web search on "pattern language" yields many hits.

Shortly after the notion of design patterns emerged, practitioners began discussing problem-solution pairs in which the solution did more harm than good.[3,4] These have come to be known as *antipatterns*, and they are well known in the design and management communities.

Antipattern examples

In 1998, researchers discussed three kinds of antipatterns: design, architectural, and management.[2] More recently, Phil Laplante and Colin Neill introduced 27 environmental antipatterns, which describe toxic work situations that can lead to organizational or project failure.[5] For example, the boiled frog syndrome discussed in this department a few years ago describes a situation in which an organization's members cannot perceive a slow loss of organizational expertise because of the subtlety of the changes.[6] Another example is the procurement problem, discussed in this department last year.[7]

Anyone can declare an antipattern—it's just a matter of whether others accept it. The pattern community relies on a "rule of three" before a new pattern or antipattern is generally accepted; that is, someone must have experienced and reported each pattern or antipattern (and a successful refactoring) in three separate instances (www.antipatterns.com/whatisapattern).

Many antipatterns take the form of cautionary tales about how day-to-day activities in human organizations can have serious repercussions. Examples include

- Email Is Dangerous—we've all wished we could retrieve one we've sent; and
- Fire Drill—months of monotony followed by a crisis, then more monotony.

Several management antipatterns remind us of *Dilbert* cartoons about bad business management practices:

- Intellectual Violence—using a buzzword or arcane technology to intimidate others. Because no one really understands the technology, methodology, or practice, dismissing it is difficult.
- Blowhard Jamboree—too many industry pundits influencing technology decisions.
- Viewgraph Engineering—too much time spent building flashy presentations for customers and managers rather than working on the software.
- Death by Planning—too much planning, not enough action.
- Throw It over the Wall—management forces the latest practices or tools on the software staff without buy-in.

Other antipattern classes refer more specifically to processes in the development of information technology, especially intelligent systems. There are two reasons why we can use human-centered computing to analyze antipatterns and examine the antipattern literature to see if any design challenges or regularities of complex cognitive systems might lie therein:

- antipatterns fall at the intersection of people, technol-

Editors: Robert R. Hoffman, Patrick J. Hayes, and Kenneth M. Ford
Institute for Human and Machine Cognition, University of West Florida
rhoffman@ihmc.us

Table 1. Some programming development and architecture antipatterns (adapted from W.H. Brown et al.[2])

Programming development		
Name	**Description**	**Negative consequence**
Lava Flow	Dead code and forgotten design information, frozen in an overall design that is itself constantly changing	Unfixable bugs
Poltergeists	Proliferation of classes	Slower code
Spaghetti Code	Use of GOTO statements and obfuscating code structures	Code that is difficult to understand and maintain
The Blob	Procedural design leading to one giant "God" class	Code that is difficult to understand and maintain; loss of object-oriented advantages
Functional Decomposition	Structural programming in an OO language	Loss of OO advantages
Golden Hammer	Using the same design over and over again ("If all you have is a hammer, everything is a thumb.")	Suboptimal designs
Metric Abuse	Naive or malicious use of metrics (for example, using the wrong metric or choosing a metric to get back at someone)	Unanticipated consequences; inability to control the project; fear, uncertainty, and doubt
Road to Nowhere	Regarding plans and requirements as rigid roadmaps; development teams failing to adapt	Creating superficial plans such as Gantt charts and PERT (Program Evaluation and Review Technique) charts to depict event sequences as if plans are actually followed; as artifacts, plans aren't a substitute for the evolving activity itself
Architecture		
Name	**Description**	**Negative consequence**
Architecture by Implication	Lack of architectural specifications for a system under development	Difficulties in maintaining and extending the system
Design by Committee	Everything but the kitchen sink	Political or policy factors dominating technical issues
Reinvent the Wheel	Failure to use acceptable existing solutions	Increasing cost and time to delivery
Stovepipe System	Legacy software with undesirable qualities	Difficulty in understanding and maintaining the system
Vendor Lock-In	Captive system(s) with mandated legacy components	Higher overall cost, loss of flexibility, and systems hostile to users
Penny Foolish	Focusing on short-term cost considerations	Burden is placed on the users, who have to kluge around hostile software.

ogy, and cognitive work (including the work of creating new intelligent technologies); and
- antipatterns' negative consequences tend to involve making systems toxic (that is, unusable) for humans.

Table 1 presents two classes, programming development antipatterns and architecture antipatterns.

Two new classes

Here, we add two new classes to the roster: procurement antipatterns and unintelligent-systems antipatterns (see tables 2 and 3). Many of these derive from recent experience in cognitive systems engineering.

Procurement antipatterns

One procurement antipattern we see far too often is Buzzword Mania. Sponsors of research and development programs ask for the world, and providers gladly promise it, using jargon-laden phrases that no one really understands, such as the following: "[insert acronym here] will provide near-real-time interoperability using a robust framework leveraging a multimatrix solution to inference that will use adaptive configuration management to ensure …."

Note the widespread use of the word "will" when in fact the proposer should use words such as "might" or "could," or even more honestly, "we hope will." Alas, we have no clear cases of successful refactoring to point to, but we are hopeful that some are out there.

Unintelligent-systems antipatterns

Unintelligent systems purport to provide "intelligent" functionality through some combination of hardware and software but are really created by relying on designer-centered design rather than on the empirical realities of cognitive work and sociotechnical organizations. Such systems require significant numbers of workarounds and kluges; at worst, they're useless.

Unintelligent-systems antipatterns differ from poor design—they are ways in which machines actually make people dumb. We've seen the consequences of unintelligent-systems antipatterns many times. Here are just two examples:

- The FBI spent a lot of money to develop the Trilogy system as a part of an information technology modernization program. The resulting software doesn't support the analysts' "operational needs"—that is, the actual cognitive work they do.[8]
- In the aftermath of the destruction of the World Trade Towers, massive amounts of funding have gone into creating new software systems to aid intelligence analysts' work. A new generation of technologists was led to believe that analysts need systems to help them overcome human limitations. This opinion was based on an older psychology theory[9] that describes cognition in terms of dozens of reasoning biases, such as the

Table 2. Five procurement antipatterns (adapted from W.H. Brown et al.[2]).

Name	Description	Negative Consequence
Fools Rush In	Rushing to use a new methodology, tool, or platform. The IT and software development world is ever-changing, and new ideas, technologies, methodologies, and practices arise all the time. Being one of the earliest adopters is often unwise.	Usually the "latest and greatest" is based more on hype than trusted evidence—more "sizzle" than "steak."
Emperor's New Clothes (also known as Smoke and Mirrors)	Those who perceive instances of Buzzword Mania are inhibited from speaking up. No one wants to point out the obvious, embarrassing truth about a situation or claim. It's often convenient to lay our hopes on a technology or methodology about which we know little, thereby providing plausible hope for a miracle.	Overly aggressive use of demonstration systems for sales purposes. The sponsor is sold a bill of goods. The truth emerges finally when users start using the new software.
Metric Madness (also known as John Henry and the Steam Hammer)	Evaluating software systems by measuring easily measured things (such as efficiency, accuracy, and raw productivity) and generally regarding the human user as an output device.	Failure to look at things that are hard to measure but critical (such as accelerating the achievement of expertise, facilitating problem recognition, coping with goal trade-offs, and reinforcing intrinsic motivation)
The Rolling Stone (also known as I Can't Get No Satisfaction)	Evaluation by satisficing (some people like it, more or less, some of the time) based on one-off and superficial interviews, with little awareness of issues of interviewing (such as biasing) or the effect of task demand characteristics. Is someone who has invested time and effort in building a system really going to fess up and say "It's lousy"?	Failure to objectively, empirically investigate usability and usefulness issues.
Potemkin Village (Around 1772, Potemkin built a façade village to fool Catherine the Great into thinking that all was well in the poverty-stricken Ukraine.)	A fancy but superficial facade hides substantial defects or shortcomings. People reach for a solution before the problem is even fully described. Many tool sets, frameworks, and off-the-shelf products allow for the quick manufacture of sophisticated-looking solutions but fail to promote robust designs and belie proper testing throughout the life cycle.	Highly staged demos and presentations; reluctance to let the customer "look under the hood;" systems that don't do anything useful and end up collecting dust.

> disconfirmation bias or the base rate fallacy.[10] The new software systems encourage (we might say *force*) analysts to juggle probabilities and evaluate likelihoods, all for the sake of shoehorning reasoning into a "rational" mode, such as Bayesian inference. Word on the street seems to be that analysts simply don't like the tools. The tools have little apparent value-added for the analyst and create what is perceived to be a considerable amount of make-work.[11]

We present three salient unintelligent-systems antipatterns, which we've adapted from Gary Klein's work.[12]

`The Man behind the Curtain` (from the Wizard of Oz). Information technology usually doesn't let people see how it reasons; it's not understandable.[13] If human users can't understand and their easiest path is to accept the machine's judgment, they are opted out of opportunities to practice their own mental model formation and evaluation skills. We aren't suggesting that all users must always be able to see how code is executing. But we've seen many cases where algorithms' mysteries nullified the potential benefits from human reasoning and collaboration:

> The [US] Air Force developed [AI] programs to generate Air Tasking Orders. Ordinarily, generating ATOs takes days ... the program could produce one in just hours .... The Air Force planners, however, did not like the new system .... [When we investigated how the planners made ATOs] we did not observe anyone evaluating an ATO once it was finished, but we did see planners evaluating the ATO while it was being prepared. One planner would suggest an approach, others would debate the suggestion, perhaps make some improvements. When the ATO was finished, the planning team would have a thorough appreciation for the nuances .... But when the [AI] software produced the ATO, the users lost their opportunity to conduct an evaluation, with no way to appreciate the rationale behind the order. (p. 263)[12]

`Hide-and-Seek.` On the belief that decision-aids must transform data into information and information into knowledge, data are actually hidden from the decision maker. The negative consequence of this antipattern is that decision makers can't use their expertise. The filtering and transforming of data, for the sake of protecting the decision maker from being overwhelmed, prevents the decision maker from drilling down and forces him or her to rely on other people's (or machines') decisions. On the belief that computers can miraculously present the decision maker with "the right information at the right time," data are (in one way or another) filtered into essential versus nonessential categories (on the basis of the judgments of the software designer—the person behind the curtain). The decision maker sees only the information that the computer (as a stand-in for the designer) thinks are important. Ideally this filtering is at least done in a smart, context-sensitive way, but however it is done, there is always a risk of turning humans into passive recipients. Experts like to be able to control their own searching and learning, and with good reason. We have seen many instances where experts did not believe the massaged data, went back to search the raw data, and made decisions—correct decisions—that differed from those coughed up by the computer, or by other decision makers who weren't skeptical and didn't do their own drill-down.

> One of the expert weather forecasters we followed complained bitterly about a new computer system that had replaced his old machine. The new system could show trends and plot curves and do all kinds of computer tricks. And that was the problem. If the temperatures in a region were very variable, some high and some low, the computer would smooth these out to provide a uniform temperature curve for the region. The program developers had wanted to provide operators with a sense of the trends, and to do that they had filtered out the "noise."

Table 3. An unintelligent-systems antipattern.

Name	What happens	Negative consequence
Shoeless Children (The shoemaker is too busy earning a living to make shoes for his own children.)	In some cases, systems engineers conduct what we might call cognitive task analysis, but they use weak methods (such as interviewing) that are not rich and continuous throughout project development. In other cases, where cognitive systems engineers are involved, they aren't given sufficient time or resources to use their expertise. In both cases, the result is that the development team is deprived of the use of and potential benefit from the tools needed to do the job right, usually in the guise of conservation.	Systems that aren't usable, useful, or understandable; systems that force users into a make-work mode far too much of the time and require significant numbers of kluges and workarounds.

> But the expert had always depended on seeing these areas of turbulence. To him, they signaled some sort of instability. Whenever he saw this cue, it triggered a reaction to watch these fronts much more carefully because it was a sign that something was brewing. As this forecaster said, "In reality, the fronts 'wiggle' as they move across the land. And it's in those whorls and wiggles that weather happens." The new system had erased this cue, making him less sensitive to the way the weather was developing and hurting his ability to do his job. (p. 252)12

As we suggested in the essay on sense-making in this department,[14] only human minds can drill down to find out what the right cues are in the first place, especially in non prototypical situations.

The Mind Is a Muscle. In the attempt to acknowledge human factors in the procurement process, some guidelines end up actually working against human-centering considerations: "Design efforts shall minimize or eliminate system characteristics that require excessive cognitive, physical, or sensory skills."[15] We find this astounding—that information systems should, in effect, prevent people from working hard and thereby progressing along the continuum of proficiency. Ample psychological evidence shows that we achieve expertise only after lots of "deliberative practice," in which we're intrinsically motivated to work hard and work on hard problems.[16]

> Information technology can diminish the active stance found in intuitive decision makers, and transform them into passive system operators. Information technology makes us afraid to use our intuition; it slows our rate of learning … passivity is bad enough but it can degenerate to the point where decision makers assume that the computer knows best … they follow the system's recommendations even in those cases where their own judgment is better than the system's solution. (p. 265)[12]

Recognizing unintelligent-systems antipatterns and giving them names might lead to system remediation more quickly, or at least the chance that a repository of lessons learned might be put to some use. And the advantages of avoiding unintelligent-systems antipatterns altogether is clear—successful system delivery, reduced costs in the long run, and reduced user frustration. In the spirit of what we might call the Penny Foolish antipattern (see table 1), reduced costs must include the human costs that are incurred after systems are "delivered": the costs to users in terms of frustration, the costs to human resources in terms of retraining personnel. Instead of computing the *total cost of ownership*, sponsors should calculate the *total human cost of ownership* by taking into account factors such as (re)training costs, costs of worker turn-around, costs of loss of expertise, and so on.

How can unintelligent-systems antipatterns be refactored? In some cases, unfortunately, refactoring involves throwing away or completely redesigning the system. In some cases, we can perhaps, just perhaps, repurpose the system's intent. Only by conducting cognitive task analysis in the first place can we have a path to creating human-centered systems that are useful, usable, and understandable and that help in growing expertise and maturing the cognitive work. This is true for many of the antipatterns we have mentioned in this essay: Only by doing it right the first time do we have a chance at a solution. Thus, we conclude with one unintelligent-systems antipattern, called Shoeless Children (see table 3).

In IT and software development, commentators and luminaries have long advocated the pursuit of excellence and the application of best practices. In recent years, however, what we have seen is a weakened, tacit view that "best is the enemy of good enough." Perhaps we misconstrue the true sentiment, but to suggest that computer scientists provide or offer anything but their best in any situation seems alien to most people. We would accept "best, time permitting" as a compromise, but never that the best is the enemy of good enough, or that the goal, especially for intelligent systems, is to be merely good enough. ■

References

1. T. Stanard et al., "HCI Design Patterns for C2: A Vision for a DoD Reference Library," *State-of-the-Art Report*, Air Force Research Laboratory, Wright-Patterson Air Force Base, 2006.

2. W.H. Brown et al., *Anti Patterns: Refactoring Software Architectures and Projects in Crisis*, John Wiley & Sons, 1998.

3. C.A. Dekkers and P.A. McQuaid, "The Dangers of Using Software Metrics To (Mis)Manage," *IT Professional*, Mar./Apr. 2002, pp. 24–30.

4. T. DeMarco, *Why Does Software Cost So Much?* Dorset House Publishing, 1995.

5. P.A. Laplante and C.J. Neill, *Antipatterns: Identification, Refactoring, and Management*, Auerbach Press, 2006.

6. R.R. Hoffman and L.F. Hanes, "The Boiled Frog Problem," *IEEE Intelligent Systems*, July/Aug. 2003, pp. 2–5.

7. R.R. Hoffman and W.C. Elm, "HCC Implications for the Procurement Process," *IEEE Intelligent Systems*, Jan./Feb. 2006, pp. 74–81.

8. J.C. McGraddy and H.S. Lin, eds., *A Review of the FBI's Trilogy Information Technology Modernization Program*, tech. report, Computer Science and Telecommunications Board Div. on Eng. and Physical Sciences, Nat'l Academies Press, 2004.

9. R. Heuer, *Psychology of Intelligence Analysis*, Central Intelligence Agency, 1999.

10. J. Flach and R.R. Hoffman, "The Limitations of Limitations," *IEEE Intelligent Systems*, Jan./Feb. 2003, pp. 94–97.

11. B. Moon, A.J. Pino, and C.A. Hedberg, "Studying Transformation: The Use of CmapTools in Surveying the Integration of Intelligence and Operations," *Proc. 2nd Int'l Conf. Concept Mapping*, 2006, pp. 527–533; available from proteaed@cariari.ucr.cr.

12. G. Klein, *Intuition at Work*, Doubleday, 2003.

13. D.D. Woods and E. Hollnagel, *Joint Cognitive Systems: Patterns in Cognitive Systems Engineering*, CRC Press, 2006.

14. G. Klein, B. Moon, and R.R. Hoffman, "Making Sense of Sensemaking 1: Alternative Perspectives," *IEEE Intelligent* Systems, July/Aug. 2006, pp. 22–26.

15. *Mandatory Procedures for Major Defense Acquisition Programs and Major Automated Information Systems Acquisition Programs*, instruction 5000.2-R, paragraph C5.2.3.5.9.1, US Dept. of Defense, 1996.

16. K.A. Ericsson, R.Th. Krampe, and C. Tesch-Römer, "The Role of Deliberate Practice in the Acquisition of Expert Performance," *Psychological Rev.*, vol. 100, 1993, pp. 363–406.

Phil Laplante is a professor of software engineering at Pennsylvania State University. Contact him at plaplante@psu.edu.

Robert R. Hoffman is a senior research scientist at the Institute for Human and Machine Cognition. Contact him at rhoffman@ihmc.us.

Gary Klein is chief scientist in the Klein Associates Division of Applied Research Associates. Contact him at gary@decisionmaking.com.

Chapter 12: The Dynamics of Trust in Cyberdomains

R.R. Hoffman, J.D. Lee, D.D. Woods, N. Shadbolt, J. Miller, and J.M. Bradshaw, "The Dynamics of Trust in Cyberdomains," *IEEE Intelligent Systems*, vol. 24, no. 6, Nov./Dec. 2009, pp. 5–11. doi: 10.1109/MIS.2009.124

This essay examines some human-centering issues for the Networld, placed primarily for convenience into five categories: antitrust in technology, a concensus on what "trust" is, interpersonal trust versus trust in automation, trusting as a dynamic process, and resilience engineering for the active management of trust. We describe our approach for designing the active management of trust in cyberdomains and generating multiple measures for different forms of trust relationships.

The Dynamics of Trust in Cyberdomains

Robert R. Hoffman, *Institute for Human and Machine Cognition*
John D. Lee, *University of Wisconsin–Madison*
David D. Woods, *The Ohio State University*
Nigel Shadbolt, *University of Southampton*
Janet Miller, *US Air Force Research Laboratory*
Jeffrey M. Bradshaw, *Institute for Human and Machine Cognition*

All economic, social, and legal interactions are based on assumptions that individuals can verify identities; that they can rely on rules, institutions, and normative practice; and that they can be assured that their private space will remain protected. Monitoring, managing, verifying, auditing, and enforcing these assumptions are difficult online.

How are "cydentities" (cyber-identities) affirmed when they are constantly changing and are sometimes human, sometimes machine, and sometimes virtual? How can individuals and organizations derive persistent and valuable digital identities? How does digital activity change when threats to privacy and trust assumptions arise? How can trust be repaired? Is trust actually stronger once repaired? Is it trust we actually want from our digital systems, or is it accountability and the opportunity for recourse or redress?

Many such empirical and technological questions are raised by cyberstories that have become well known.[1–4] Some of the more widespread cyberattacks are phishing and e-mail scams. Research from Get Safe Online (www.getsafeonline.org), published 9 February 2009, found that 23 percent of Internet users in the United Kingdom had either been a victim of a phishing scam in the preceding 12 months or knew someone who had been affected by the crime. Recent months have witnessed denial-of-service cyberattacks such as those on Facebook and Twitter.[5] A Google search reveals numerous Web sites that provide advice about avoiding scams at Web sites.[6] "Spoofs abound on the Internet. Web sites about hoaxes cover bogus science and technology ... and report hoax computer viruses."[7] Thus, we see the advent of "trust evaluation tools" and protocols for a common language for online trust.[8]

An account in the *Washington Post* of the recent cyberattacks on South Korea and the United States points to how difficult it is to protect from attacks and even to identify the perpetrators.[9]

> Cyberspace is a primary medium for the way the Air Force does business, whether it is used for command, control, communications ... Almost everything I do is either on the Internet, an Intranet, or some type of network—terrestrial, airborne or spaceborne ... Yet, everyone out there knows that hackers can potentially get into my network and slow down or corrupt it or cause me to lose faith in the networks or shut them down completely.[10]

The Lesson and Its Implication

For some decades now, cybersecurity has been a continuous game of catch-up. Clever hackers find some new scheme for malware, the malware is sent out and does its thing, the malware is sniffed out, and then the security people come up with a new software or hardware patch. This "clever game" is not likely to end. Indeed, attempts to improve software and hardware must continue.

But the real lesson is this: *the window of vulnerability never closes.* We must ask, therefore, what else might be done in addition to playing the clever game? With this question we find issues that are directly pertinent to human-centered computing, both in leveraging what we know about humans, and in leveraging technology to amplify humans.

The cultural, social, psychological, and computational are merging into a Networld. Trust in and through technology will likely mediate the effectiveness of software and hardware in maintaining security. In this essay, we examine some human-centering issues for the Networld, placed primarily for convenience into five categories: antitrust in technology, a consensus on what "trust" is, interpersonal trust versus trust in automation, trusting as a dynamic process, and resilience engineering for the active management of trust.

Antitrust

Previous essays in this department have discussed how so-called intelligent technology triggers frustration and other types of negative affect. Frustration leads users to create kludges and workarounds.[11,12] Antitrust—the skeptical assessment of a technology-reliant work system—is another form of negative affect that can trigger an effort to adapt. In a study of weather forecasters the experts were asked, "Do you trust your technology?" Frequently, they immediately responded, "Never!"[13] This is antitrust: confidence (to the point of certainty) that the technology *will* choke, *will* frustrate, and *will* trigger a need for workarounds. It is no surprise, therefore, that psychologists and human-factors engineers have devoted considerable effort to understanding the circumstances of automation underuse, misuse, and even abuse.[14,15]

This suggests a combinatoric of justified versus unjustified trust and justified versus unjustified distrust. The calibration of trust in automation involves finding the sweet shifts within this constantly morphing space.[16] For instance, novice users sometimes assume that computers are infallible. While they can adapt to the fallibilities of a human teacher, they are stymied when the computer gives what seems to be wrong feedback. People sometimes need help to understand how and when to shift from unjustified trust closer to justified distrust. On the other hand, experienced domain practitioners can become jaded, and are more likely to benefit from information that helps them calibrate their trust by shifting them from unjustified distrust to justified trust.

This is antitrust: confidence (to the point of certainty) that the technology *will* choke, *will* frustrate, and *will* trigger a need for workarounds.

Trust calibration is captured in one of the laws of macrocognitive work systems,[17,18] which we dub Mr. Weasley's Law, after that fictional character's admonition of his wizarding daughter, "Never trust anything that can think for itself, if you can't see where it keeps its brain."[19] Formally stated, the law is this:

Mr. Weasley's Law: *Workers in macrocognitive work systems develop unjustified trust and unjustified mistrust in their technology and the work system as a whole when the factors governing the technology's activity are not visible.*

What the cyberresearch community needs is a set of powerful principles to guide people in reaching for desired states on such polarities as antitrust (unjustified mistrust) versus skeptical trust (justified trust); and contingent trust (conditional trust) versus unconditional trust (faith).

We also need to try to define some terms, as impossible as that often is.

A Consensus on What "Trust" Is

The concept of trust has been a topic of analysis in many disciplines, including philosophy (especially ethics), sociology, management science, and psychology. As Kieron O'Hara has noted, any comprehensive account of trust would have to "plunder many sources; the philosophy of Socrates and Aristotle, Hobbes and Kant; the sociology of Durkheim, Weber and Putnam; literature; economics; scientific methodology; the most ancient of history and the most current of current affairs."[20]

Nevertheless, we find it interesting that, of all the fuzzy and abstract concepts inhabiting terra cognita (and ripe for debate in human-centered computing), there actually seems to be a consensus on how to define the multifaceted concept of trust.[16,21,22] Trust has aspects of

- an attitude (of the trustor about the trustee),
- an attribution (that the trustee is trustworthy),
- an expectation (about the trustee's future behavior),
- a feeling or belief (faith in the trustee, or a feeling that the trustee is benevolent, or a feeling that the trustee is directable),
- an intention (of the trustee to act in the trustor's interests), and
- a trait (some people are trusting and more able to trust appropriately).

Table 1. Some of the possible trust relationships.

Type of trust	Beliefs for interpersonal trust	Beliefs for trust in automation	Trustor certainty that the trustee (or automation) will carry out the directives
Unconditional trust (faith)	The trustor takes the trustee's assertions as true.	The trustor is confident that the automation is directable. The trustor takes the automation's actions as correct.	Certain.
Skeptical trust	The trustor takes some of the trustee's assertions as possibly true.	The trustor takes some of the automation's actions as possibly correct.	Somewhat certain.
Circumscribed trust	The trustor takes the trustee's assertions as true, for the time being, or with respect to a certain class of activities.	The trustor takes the automation's actions as correct for the time being, or correct with respect to a class of functions.	Certain for the time being, or certain with respect to certain activities.
Contingent trust	The trustor takes the trustee's assertions as true, depending on the circumstances.	The trustor takes the automation's actions as correct, depending on the circumstances.	Certain depending on the circumstances.
Antitrust	The trustor takes all of the trustee's assertions as false and potentially misleading.	The trustor might take some of the automation's actions as possibly correct, but also anticipates some to be wrong.	The trustor is certain that the technology will choke, will frustrate, and will trigger a need for workarounds.
Swift trust	The trustor has to take the trustee's assertions as true, because of urgent circumstances, often on the basis of trustee authority or position.	The trustor has to take the automation's actions as correct, because of urgent circumstances.	Somewhat certain.
Swift antitrust	The trustor takes the trustee's assertions as false and potentially misleading, because of emerging events or circumstances that reveal the trustee's genuine intentions.	The trustor takes any of the automation's actions as possibly wrong.	The trustor is certain that the technology will provide misleading information.

There are many perspectives on how trust plays a role in human relations,[21,22] in human-machine interaction,[16] and in decentralized sensing and networked systems.[23,24] Analyses generally converge on the concept that *trust reflects an assessment of the trustee's capabilities and competencies to respond to uncertain situations to meet common goals.* The outcome of the assessment is not always a single trust/do-not-trust judgment, but rather an assessment of what particular roles and tasks the trustee can be counted upon to accomplish successfully. The assessment is contingent; it is dynamic and evolves (or degrades) as events occur in the world and information and outcomes feed back to influence the trustor-trustee relation.

Trust can be thought of as a family of relations, certainly not a single relation. For instance, trust can be *about* different things: beliefs (information, data, knowledge), resources (such as valuables), or actions. Trust can be directional (the trustor trusts the trustee) or reciprocal (each party is both trustor and trustee). Trust can be general or contingent. Table 1 expresses some of the many relations.

There is also a consensus on the danger of anthropomorphism in generalizing ideas or research findings about interpersonal trust to the domain of trust in automation.[14,16]

Interpersonal Trust versus Trust in Automation

Interpersonal trust is both fundamentally and subtly different from trust in automation. Trust between people typically involves expectations of intent and reciprocity. But while such basic aspects of social relationships might seem irrelevant to human-automation relationships, people often behave as if technology is a social actor.[25] A direct comparison of trust in humans to trust in automation showed the dynamics of trust to be qualitatively similar.[26] For instance, an aspect of interpersonal trust is directability—that is, that the trustor can direct the trustee. Directability also contributes to human-computer relations.[27]

The feeling that the automation is a partner or a personality is sometimes enhanced by graphic personas. These can promote unjustified trust, and can be an undercurrent in automation abuse (that is, wanting an uncooperative machine to feel pain). The starkest differences between interpersonal trust and trust in automation have to do with the many and powerful effects of menus, graphic objects, and the like on automation misuse and underuse—effects that have no direct analog in interpersonal trust.[28]

How trust (in either a human or a technological agent) develops depends on context and experience. Early evidence that a trustee might be untrustworthy (or that automation might have a high false-alarm rate) can subsequently make it hard for the trustor to develop trust in the trustee (or in the automation). On the other hand, if the trustee (or the automation) provides explanations of the untrustworthy behavior (or why the automation makes false alarms), the effect of fallible performance can be mitigated.

These empirical findings link trust concepts to two additional laws of macrocognitive work systems. First, people are explanation generators. If they are not given sufficient information to make satisfying explanations, they will make explanations anyway.

> The Cognitive Vacuum Law: *Workers develop mental models of the macrocognitive work system, including the technology.*

Thus, in most cases, a worker's mental model of the automation is likely incomplete and not entirely veridical with respect to the designer's intent. The potential for error is increased when the designer's intent actually mismatches the worker's goals and needs. This latter situation is often brought about by the reliance on a designer-centered design approach instead of human-centered design approach. Operators will develop a level of trust in the automation, but it can be over- or under-trust if the designers do not fill the vacuum to make the automation trustable. This leads us to another law:

> Law of Surrogate Systems: *Macrocognitive work systems embody the stances, agendas, and goals of the designers.*

Across all the research on trust in automation, a finding that percolates up consistently is that information allowing the user to understand what the automation does, why it does what it does, and what the designer's intent is significantly promotes trust in the automation. Such information promotes a better understanding of the automation and leads to an appropriate level of trust, which in turn mediates between the feeling that the automation is trustworthy and the actual intention to go ahead and rely on the automation.[14,16,29,30] Without this information, trust or distrust will still develop, but it will likely be disconnected from the automation's actual capability.

Repaired trust relationships might be stronger than relationships in which a breakdown of trust has not occurred.

A third perspective on trust is to think of trust using a verb rather than a noun form. What Table 1 points to is not just that trust is a family of relations, but that any given trustor–trustee relation is a dynamic thing.

Trusting

Both interpersonal trust and trust in automation take time to develop. Early experiences contribute to understanding, which eventually can become a more stable relation of faith.[16] On the other hand, sometimes there can be swift trust, where a trustor automatically trusts a trustee on the basis of authority, confession, profession, or even exigency (see Table 1). Novice belief in the infallibility of computers is an instance of swift (and unjustified) trust. Swift trust can be prominent early in a relationship, with contingent trust developing over time, as people experience the automation in different circumstances.

Trust, whether human–human or human–machine, is dynamic, though it can be temporarily stable. Trust is always context-dependent, though it can be temporarily invariant. Trust can appear to be insulated, though it is actually contingent. Trust, like common ground, must be maintained and even managed. Likewise, mistrust is dynamic, and it too can be maintained (which is unfortunate) or managed.

The dynamics of trust are complex. Factors that contribute to this complexity include, first, threshold effects relating the level of trust to changes in reliance, and, second, contingencies between reliance and the information that guides the evolution of trust.[31]

Threshold effects are reflected in the tendency to maintain a fixed level of reliance even as the level of trust changes, resulting in a dichotomous pattern of reliance. This pattern of reliance can in turn affect the information an operator has regarding the automation's performance. In some cases, the automation's performance is only perceivable when the person is relying on the automation. Threshold effects and contingent information availability complicate the dynamics of trust, and both can undermine the calibration of trust.

There are also interesting findings on the repair of trust.[32] The role of apology and forgiveness as a means to repair trust have been extended to online transaction systems. This line of inquiry entails the possibility that repaired trust relationships might be stronger than relationships in which a breakdown of trust has not occurred.

Opportunities and Dangers

Cybersecurity and defense issues, including social deception, misdirection, influence, and manipulation, span all the venues of macrocognitive work in the Networld. How can we analyze networks to detect poorly calibrated trust, or increases and declines in trust? All networks are vulnerable to malicious attack, motivating our earlier comment, that the window of vulnerability never closes.

A direct implication of this is that the vulnerability of macrocognitive work systems to malware must be continuously evaluated and experimented on *within the operational context* where networks are being used, generated, grown, and adapted. How can net work continue when one believes that the network has been corrupted? Indeed, clever adversaries seek to maintain networks' overall integrity so that they can manipulate data or applications and go undetected. For the individual net worker, how do we calibrate trust and distrust in technology when the technology is potentially compromised? For macrocognitive work systems, how do we create work methods and work processes for active management of trustworthy communities and work groups?

We might change our perspective from that of victim to that of influencer, from defense to offense. If you remove the highly connected individual nodes in a network you can do much damage, but you can also do damage by removing nodes that are "weakly" connected to other nodes. To concretize this, consider law enforcement combating organized crime, which by tradition has tight and secure networks. If the law can inject swift mistrust or antitrust somewhere into an organized crime network, tweaking a weak link, the mistrust might spread or cascade, to the benefit of law enforcement.

All the challenges and questions we have raised point to the human element and the cognitive terrain of decision making, as much as they point to challenges for computer science and intelligent systems.

Trust in Macrocognitive Work Systems

Trust emerges from knowledge about the resilience (or brittleness) of the macrocognitive work system—how work systems composed of humans and machines adapt when events challenge their boundary conditions.[33] To achieve resilience, the technology and work methods must be created to support directability, responsiveness, reciprocity, and responsibility.[27]

To achieve resilience, the technology and work methods must be created to support directability, responsiveness, reciprocity, and responsibility.

Workers must appropriately trust those parts of the work system that will respond adaptively to disrupting events, events that alter plans and activities in progress. Coordinating the adaptive responses makes decentralized systems resilient.[34] Thus, trust in work systems can be thought of as confidence in this ability of different units at different echelons to act resiliently. Low levels of trust among units of a work system could play a critical role in maintaining a resilient system by signaling the need for additional resources or reconfiguration.

In macrocognitive work systems, trust can also be thought of as the expectation of reciprocity from others.[35] The parties involved in joint activity enter into a "basic compact," an agreement (often tacit) to facilitate coordination, work toward shared goals, and prevent coordination breakdowns.[27] In a reciprocal cooperative relationship, one human or machine agent relies on another to reciprocate in the future by taking an action that might give up some benefit in order to make both agents better off than they were at the starting point. Coordination and synchronization in distributed systems require reciprocity; otherwise, distributed systems are brittle and exhibit one or more maladaptive behavior patterns.

Both responsiveness and reciprocity emphasize anticipation, which introduces a forward temporal dimension of trust interactions. Both concepts point out that strategies change with changes in trust. For example, when one risks counting on others but anticipates little reciprocity or responsiveness, the result will be unstable, and the responsible party will shift to more conservative, independent strategies.

All the workers in macrocognitive work systems benefit if they can coordinate their activities, but coordination has costs. The challenge is to sustain the commitment to coordination and counteract any tendency to take advantage of others so as to benefit only one role. Decision making always occurs in the context of an expectation that one might be called to account for decisions. Expectations about what are considered adequate accounts, and the consequences for people whose accounts are judged inadequate, are critical parts of a cycle of accountability. Breakdowns in responsiveness or reciprocity encourage role retreat and break the basic compact.

Models of resilient work systems emphasize how interdependent activities are co-adapted to each other and to changing short-term and long-term conditions.[17] We need new control architectures to manage these resilient, distributed, multi-echelon, human–automation systems.

Finally, the issue of information accountability is arousing new interest in computer science. As we noted at the start of this essay, it is difficult to guarantee privacy when the technologies for information storage, aggregation, and analysis develop so rapidly. We live in an increasingly open information environment, in an increasingly linked Networld. Perhaps we need our technologies to be accountable such that the use of information is apparent, thus making it possible to determine whether a use is appropriate or legitimate in a particular context.[36]

The laws of macrocognitive work systems, which we have presented in this and previous essays in this department, can be thought of as signposts along the path to resilience. The approach of designing for resilience offers some guidance and foundation for the active management of trust in cyberdomains.■

References

1. K. Raina and A. Harsh, *eCommerce Security: A Beginner's Guide*, McGraw Hill, 2001.
2. B. Ortutay, "Don't Post That: Web Etiquette Evolves," Associated Press, 4 Sept. 2009, www.dailynews.com/news/ci_13273951.
3. C. Rhoads and L. Chao, "Iran's Web Spying Aided by Western Technology," *Wall Street Journal*, 22 June 2009, p. 2, http://online.wsj.com/article/SB124562668777335653.html.
4. B. Stelter and B. Stone, "Web Pries Lid of Iranian Censorship," *New York Times*, 22 June 2009, www.nytimes.com/2009/06/23/world/middleeast/23censor.html.
5. N. Gammeltoft and R. Garner, "Twitter, Facebook Resume Online Services after Cyber Attacks," Bloomberg.com, 7 Aug. 2009, www.bloomberg.com/apps/news?pid=20601102&sid=aEVBXs9eH8Gg.
6. "Finding Information on the Internet: A Guide," Teaching Library Internet Workshops, Univ. of California, Berkeley, 2009, www.lib.berkeley.edu/TeachingLib/Guides/Internet.
7. N. Shadbolt, "A Matter of Trust," *IEEE Intelligent Systems*, vol. 17, no. 1, 2002, pp. 2–3.
8. E. Naone, "Adding Trust to Wikipedia, and Beyond," *Tech. Rev.*, 4 Sept. 2009, www.technologyreview.com/web/23355/?a=f.
9. L.C. Baldor, "US Officials Eye North Korea in Cyber Attack," Associated Press, 8 July 2009, www.usatoday.com/news/washington/2009-07-08-hacking-washington-nkorea_N.htm.
10. J. Weckerlein, "Cyberspace Warfare Remains Serious Business," *Air Force Print News Today*, 2 Mar. 2007, www.af.mil/news/story_print.asp?id=123043232.
11. P. Koopman and R.R. Hoffman, "Work-Arounds, Make-Work, and Kludges," *IEEE Intelligent Systems*, vol. 18, no. 6, pp. 70–75.
12. R.R. Hoffman, M. Marx, and P.A. Hancock, "Metrics, Metrics, Metrics: Negative Hedonicity," *IEEE Intelligent Systems*, vol. 23, no. 2, pp. 69–73.
13. R.R. Hoffman et al., "A Method for Eliciting, Preserving, and Sharing the Knowledge of Forecasters," *Weather and Forecasting*, vol. 21, no. 3, 2006, pp. 416–428.
14. M.T. Dzindolet et al., "The Role of Trust in Automation Reliance," *Int'l J. Human-Computer Studies*, vol. 58, no. 6, 2003, pp. 697–718.
15. R. Parasuraman and V. Riley, "Humans and Automation: Use, Misuse, Disuse, Abuse," *Human Factors*, vol. 39, no. 2, 1997, pp. 230–253.
16. J.D. Lee and K.A. See, "Trust in Automation: Designing for Appropriate Reliance," *Human Factors*, vol. 46, no. 1, 2004, pp. 50–80.
17. D.D. Woods and E. Hollnagel, *Joint Cognitive Systems: Patterns in Cognitive Systems Engineering*, CRC Press, 2006.
18. R.R. Hoffman and D.D. Woods, "Steps Toward a Theory of Complex and Cognitive Systems," *IEEE Intelligent Systems*, vol. 20, no. 1, 2005, pp. 76–79.
19. J.K. Rowling, *Harry Potter and the Chamber of Secrets*, Scholastic Press, 1999, p. 329.
20. K. O'Hara, *Trust: From Socrates to Spin*, Icon Books, 2004, p. 5.
21. R.C. Mayer, J.H. Davis, and F.D. Schoorman, "An Integrative Model of Organizational Trust," *Academy of Management Rev.*, vol. 20, no. 3, 1995, pp. 709–734.
22. J.A. Simpson, "Psychological Foundations of Trust," *Current Directions in Psychological Science*, vol. 16, no. 5, 2007, pp. 264–268.
23. T.D. Huynh, N.R. Jennings, and N.R. Shadbolt, "An Integrated Trust and Reputation Model for Open Multi-Agent Systems," *Autonomous Agents and Multi-Agent Systems*, vol. 13, no. 2, 2006, pp. 119–154.
24. R. Stephens, A. Morison, and D.D. Woods, "Trust, ATR, and Layered Sensing: Models, Metrics, and Directions for Design," report to the US Air Force Research Laboratory, Sensors Directorate, from the Cognitive Systems Engineering Laboratory, Inst. for Ergonomics, Ohio State Univ., 2009.

25. C. Nass and Y. Moon, "Machines and Mindlessness: Social Responses to Computers," *J. Social Issues*, vol. 56, no. 1, 2000, pp. 81–103.
26. S. Lewandowsky, M. Mundy, and G. Tan, "The Dynamics of Trust: Comparing Humans to Automation," *J. Experimental Psychology: Applied*, vol. 6, no. 2, 2000, pp. 104–123.
27. G. Klein et al., "Ten Challenges for Making Automation a 'Team Player' in Joint Human-Agent Activity," *IEEE Intelligent Systems*, vol. 19, no. 6, 2004, pp. 91–95.
28. C.L. Corritore, B. Kracher, and S. Wiedenbeck, "On-Line Trust: Concepts, Evolving Themes, a Model," *Int'l. J. Human-Computer Studies*, vol. 58, no. 6, 2003, pp. 737–758.
29. A.M. Bisantz and Y. Seong, "Assessment of Operator Trust in and Utilization of Automated Decision-Aids under Different Framing Conditions," *Int'l J. Industrial Ergonomics*, vol. 28, no. 2, 2001, pp. 85–97.
30. V. Riley, "Operator Reliance on Automation: Theory and Data," *Automation Theory and Applications*, R. Parasuraman and M. Mouloua, eds., Erlbaum, 1996, pp. 19–35.
31. J. Gao and J.D. Lee, "Extending the Decision Field Theory to Model Operators' Reliance on Automation in Supervisory Control Situations," *IEEE Trans. Systems, Man, and Cybernetics*, vol. 36, no. 5, 2006, pp. 943–959.
32. A. Vasalou, A. Hopfensitz, and J. Pitt, "In Praise of Forgiveness: Ways for Repairing Trust Breakdowns in One-Off Online Interactions," *Int'l J. Human-Computer Studies*, vol. 66, no. 6, 2008, pp. 466–480.
33. E. Hollnagel, D.D. Woods, and N. Leveson, eds., *Resilience Engineering: Concepts and Precepts*, Ashgate, 2006.
34. J. Watts-Perotti and D.D. Woods, "Cooperative Advocacy: A Strategy for Integrating Diverse Perspectives in Anomaly Response," *J. Collaborative Computing*, vol. 18, nos. 2–3, 2009, pp. 175–198.
35. E. Ostrom, "Toward a Behavioral Theory Linking Trust, Reciprocity, and Reputation," *Trust and Reciprocity: Interdisciplinary Lessons from Experimental Research*, E. Ostrom and J. Walker, eds., Russell Sage Foundation, 2003.
36. D. Weitzner et al., "Information Accountability," *Comm. ACM*, vol. 51, no. 6, 2008, pp. 82–87.

Robert R. Hoffman is a senior research scientist at the Institute for Human and Machine Cognition. Contact him at rhoffman@ihmc.us.

John D. Lee is a professor in the Department of Industrial and Systems Engineering at the University of Wisconsin–Madison. Contact him at jdlee@engr.wisc.edu.

David D. Woods is a professor in the Cognitive Systems Engineering Laboratory at the Ohio State University. Contact him at woods.2@osu.edu.

Nigel Shadbolt is a professor of artificial intelligence in the School for Electronics and Computer Science at the University of Southampton, UK. Contact him at nrs@ecs.soton.ac.uk.

Janet Miller is senior cognitive systems engineer at the US Air Force Research Laboratory. Contact her at janet.miller3@wpafb.af.mil.

Jeffrey M. Bradshaw is a senior research scientist at the Institute for Human and Machine Cognition. Contact him at jbradshaw@ihmc.us.

Chapter 13: Beyond Cooperative Robotics: The Central Role of Interdependence in Coactive Design

M. Johnson, J.M Bradshaw, P.J. Feltovich, R.R. Hoffman, C. Jonker, B. van Riemsdijk, and M. Sierhuis, "Beyond Cooperative Robotics: The Central Role of Interdependence in Coactive Design," *IEEE Intelligent Systems*, vol. 26, no. 3, May/June 2011, pp. 81–88. doi: 10.1109/MIS.2011.47

This article argues that the concept of levels of autonomy is incomplete and insufficient as a model for designing complex human-machine teams, largely because it does not sufficiently account for the interdependence among their members. Building on a theory of joint activity, we introduce the notion of coactive design, an approach to human-machine interaction that takes interdependence as the central organizing principle among people and agents working together as a team.

Beyond Cooperative Robotics: The Central Role of Interdependence in Coactive Design

Matthew Johnson, Jeffrey M. Bradshaw, Paul J. Feltovich, and Robert R. Hoffman, *Institute for Human and Machine Cognition*
Catholijn Jonker and Birna van Riemsdijk, *Delft University of Technology*
Maarten Sierhuis, *Xerox PARC*

As automation becomes more sophisticated, the nature of its interaction with people will need to change in profound ways. Inevitably, software and robotic agents will become so capable that they will function less like tools and more like teammates.[1–3]

Many approaches to designing more team-like cooperation between humans and machines have been proposed, including function allocation, supervisory control, adaptive automation, dynamic task allocation, adjustable autonomy, mixed-initiative interaction—most recently regrouped under the rubric of *cooperative robotics*. All these approaches rely on the levels of autonomy concept as the benchmark for machine performance and the criterion for decisions about human-machine task allocation.

In this article, we argue that the concept of levels of autonomy is incomplete and insufficient as a model for designing complex human-machine teams, largely because it does not sufficiently account for the interdependence among their members. Building on a theory of joint activity,[4,5] we introduce the notion of coactive design,[6] an approach to human-machine interaction that takes interdependence as the central organizing principle among people and agents working together as a team.

What Is Autonomy?

The word *autonomy*, derived from a combination of Greek terms signifying self-government (*auto* means self, and *nomos* means law), today has two basic senses in everyday use.[7] The first sense, self-sufficiency, is about the degree to which an entity operates without outside help. For example, a Roomba robot can vacuum a room without assistance. The second sense refers to an entity's self-directedness, or the degree of freedom from outside control. The Mars Rover, which was tightly controlled by NASA engineers, is such as example.

In our discussion, we will use the terms self-sufficiency and self-directedness to distinguish between these two senses of autonomy.

Pervasiveness of the Levels of Autonomy Concept

The concept of levels of autonomy is usually attributed to the pioneering work of Thomas Sheridan and William Verplank.[8] Their ideas were derived from a teleoperation study with underwater robots. Although the original 1978 work is often cited, the original three page table is usually condensed and simplified as shown in Table 1. The "levels" were used to describe the space of design options, as they saw them. They range from tedious and error-prone manual operation, where humans are required to do everything (level 1), to fully autonomous operations, where the machine can perform the entire task without assistance or direction (level 10). Sheridan and Verplank realized the unlikelihood of achieving a completely autonomous solution because they "simply [did] not

Table 1. Levels of automation.*

Level	Description
High	10. The computer decides everything, acts autonomously, ignoring the human.
	9. The computer informs the human only if it, the computer, decides to.
	8. The computer informs the human only if asked, or
	7. The computer executes automatically, then necessarily informs the human, and
	6. The computer allows the human a restricted time to veto before automatic execution, or
	5. The computer executes that suggestion if the human approves, or
	4. The computer suggests one alternative
	3. The computer narrows the selection down to a few, or
	2. The computer offers a complete set of decision/action alternatives, or
Low	1. The computer offers no assistance; the human must take all decisions and actions.

*Adapted from an earlier work.[11]

have available at [that] time such devices or the understanding to build such devices" (p. 1–10) for their demanding environment. Given this realization, they suggested two things:

- levels of automation as a means to gain some of the benefits of autonomy while not requiring a fully autonomous solution and
- supervisory control, in which humans allocate tasks to one or more machines and then monitor them.

For the second suggestion, once control is given to the machine, it is ideally expected to complete the tasks without human intervention. The job of the machine's designer is to determine what needs to be done and then provide the capability (self-sufficiency) for the machine to do it. This is often described as finding the appropriate level of autonomy.

Although the supervisory-control approach fulfilled its initial purpose, its static nature did not address requirements for variable task allocation in different situations, which spurred interest in research on dynamic and adaptive function allocation. Dynamic interaction of this sort has been suggested as a unifying theme in human-robot interaction[9] and has led to numerous proposals for dynamic adjustment of autonomy level[10]—in this case, the self-directedness aspect. Such approaches have been variously called adjustable autonomy, dynamic task allocation, sliding autonomy, flexible autonomy, and adaptive automation. In each case, the system must decide at runtime which functions to automate and to what level of autonomy.[11]

Mixed-initiative interaction is defined as "a flexible interaction strategy, where each agent can contribute to the task what it does best" (p. 14).[12] Its contribution is in the perspective that people can work in parallel alongside autonomous systems, so it adopts the stance that the perception, problem-solving, and task-execution processes are subject to an ongoing give and take that can be initiated by either the human or the machine, rather than explicitly determined by the original system designer. Although it is more sophisticated in some ways than function allocation, in practice this approach still tends to be autonomy-centric, focusing on fluid management of task assignment and the authority to act—the self-directedness aspect of autonomy. The influence of the levels of autonomy concept is apparent in James Allen's proposal for mixed-initiative interaction levels.[12]

The classic Sheridan-Verplank levels are widely cited and have had a significant impact on the outlook of robot designers. A recent survey of human-robot interaction concluded that "perhaps the most strongly human-centered application of the concept of autonomy is in the notion of level of autonomy" (p. 217).[9] This seems counterintuitive. Why should the independence of a given robotic partner play a more dominant role in human-centered design of joint activity than the interdependence among the set of human-robotic team members?

Problems with the Levels of Autonomy Concept

Significant nuances in the original Sheridan-Verplank work have been forgotten through frequent use of the simplified list shown in Table 1. As a basis for our discussion, Figure 1 illustrates the richer detail in the original work. In this excerpt from the complete model, we have altered Sheridan's level 6 by adding the tell functions and associated text from level 8. We did this to incorporate all the basic elements in a single level for discussion purposes, but it does not significantly alter the original intention because the original table had a footnote indicating other possible variations.

The first column is the description that corresponds to an item on the simplified version of the list from Raja Parasuraman, Thomas Sheridan, and Christopher Wickens.[11] The second column represents the human functions in the activity and the third represents the functions the computer performs. Interestingly, arrows were used between the second and third columns in the original work, creating a small causal diagram. This representation more clearly shows that two parties are involved in the activity, as opposed to the list in Table 1, which focuses solely on the computer. Additionally, these arrows represent a

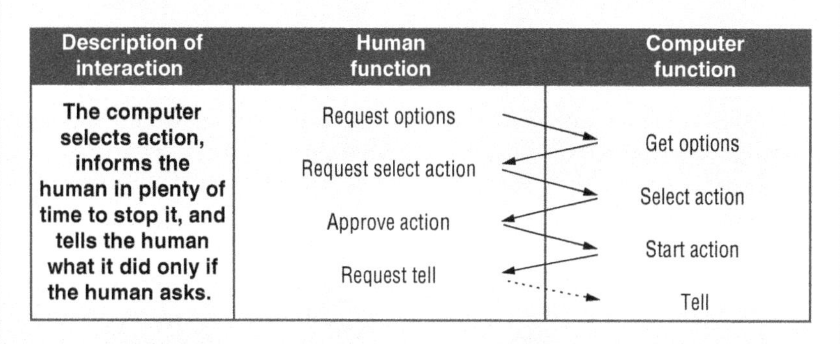

Figure 1. Altered excerpt of Sheridan-Verplank's level 6 automation. Our goal was to incorporate all the basic elements in a single level for discussion purposes and more clearly show that two parties (computer and human) are involved in the activity. The solid arrows depict hard constraints that enable or prevent the possibility of an activity. The dashed arrow indicates soft interdependence, which includes optional commands. (Adapted from an earlier work.[8])

workflow with dependencies connecting the functions. Insightfully, Sheridan and Verplank understood that even their original richer description had limitations and stated that "as computer control and artificial intelligence become more sophisticated, certain human functions in teleoperation may be replaced, but greater need and demand will be placed upon other human functions, and in these respects the need for improved man-computer interaction will increase, not diminish" (p. 1–10).[8]

With this in mind, we have outlined several problems with the simplified concept of levels of autonomy as it is usually formulated.

Problem 1: Functional Differences Matter

There are significant differences between performing an action and making a decision as well as between different kinds of actions. Sheridan and Verplank's original work provided a table of behavior elements that can be used to characterize a system. Their list included request options, get options, select action, approve action, start action, and tell functions. In this regard, the original levels model mixes apples and oranges—task work and teamwork. For example, in their level 1, the human handles the entire task without automation by performing the get options, select action, and start action functions. These are task-work components. On the other hand, the request options, approve action, and tell elements engage both parties in a simple form of teamwork.

The model also mixes reasoning (get options), decisions (select action), and actions (start action). Moreover, the entire approach reinforces the erroneous notion that "automation activities simply can be substituted for human activities without otherwise affecting the operation of the system."[13]

Parasuraman, Sheridan, and Wickens' work attempted to address some of these problems by associating activity types with the 10 levels.[11] They proposed four types (acquisition, analysis, decision, and action), but this merely highlights the importance of functional differences between the elements and ignores the issues of interdependence relating to such activities.

Problem 2: Levels Are Neither Ordinal nor Representative of Value

Another problem is that the term *level* implies an ordinal relationship. Authors who reproduce the condensed version often add the low and high labels to levels 1 and 10, respectively, as in our Table 1. These labels imply that the levels are of increasing autonomy, but are they really? The get options function seems like a lower level of autonomy than the select option. However, if the "getter" of the options can filter the options and the receiver has no other means to know what the options are, is it really a lower level? Who holds the power in this relationship? Which has a higher value: a start action or tell? It probably depends on the criticality of what is being started and the importance of what is being told. For these and other reasons, it is more productive to think about autonomy in terms of multiple task-specific dimensions rather than in terms of a single, unidimensional scale.[7]

The perspective in which we view a system can also affect our assessment of autonomy. For example, ambiguity about the term autonomy comes into play in Figure 1. Because the level shown is six out of 10, we could consider the machine semiautonomous—that is, at a mid-level of autonomy. However, with respect to the self-sufficiency perspective on autonomy, the machine could be viewed instead as fully autonomous because it can perform all aspects of the task work. On the other hand, from a self-directedness perspective, a machine functioning at this level would have no autonomy since the performance of its task work is completely subject to the direction and initiative of the human.

Our assessment of a system's autonomy also depends on the way we define the boundaries of its sphere of action. Consider the vehicles that competed in the DARPA Urban Challenge, which were designed to find their way over a given course in "fully autonomous" fashion. Although fully autonomous with respect to this one particular task, they might be far from autonomous with respect to related tasks, such as going to the store and getting groceries.

This also applies in the other direction. Several entries in the Urban Challenge were unsuccessful at completing the task but were successful at aspects of the task. For example, some could follow the road but not deal with traffic. These might be called semiautonomous, but all this term tells us is that the machine could not do everything on its own. If we redefine the task as something simpler, such as following a road without traffic, then we could once again describe the car as fully autonomous. In fact, virtually any machine could be considered fully autonomous if we define the grain size of its task to be sufficiently small. These examples make it obvious that the property of autonomy is not a mere function of the machine, but rather a relationship between the machine and a task in a given situation.

Problem 3: Autonomy Is Relative to the Context of the Activity

Autonomous capabilities are relative to the context of the task for which they were designed. When a designers consider what level of autonomy is appropriate, they are assuming some level of granularity and using that to define activity boundaries. Sheridan and Verplank's original table title was "Levels of automation in man-computer decision making for a single elemental decisive step." In other words, level 10 represents full autonomy relative to the single elemental decisive step or activity. Unfortunately, over time researchers have generalized this to all activity in complex systems involving teams of humans and machines. This goes far beyond the original scope and might explain Sheridan's comment that "surprisingly, the level descriptions as published have been taken more seriously than were expected" (p. 206).[14]

Functions are not automated in isolation from task context. Therefore, when system designers automate a subtask, they are really performing a type of task distribution and, as such, have introduced novel elements of interdependence within the system. This is the lesson to be learned from studies of the *substitution myth*,[13] which states that reducing or expanding the role of automation in joint human-automation systems can change the nature of interdependent and mutually adapted activities in complex ways. To effectively exploit automation's capabilities (versus merely increasing automation), we must coordinate the task work—and the interdependence it induces among players in a given situation—as a whole.

As an example, consider the major assumption underlying the Sheridan-Verplank levels that the human, in a supervisory role, is the initiator of the activity and has an implied obligation to monitor the activity. Although this is not explicit in the model, it can be derived from the fact that the request options action is only available to the human and that the tell option is only available to the computer. Roles are not simple titles; rather they are mechanisms by which we describe capabilities and their interdependence.

Problem 4: Levels of Autonomy Encourage Reductive Thinking

Previous essays in this department have raised the issue of "keeping things too simple" in the design of cognitive systems.[15] The levels of autonomy concept demonstrates several of these oversimplifications. Some have already been mentioned, such as ignoring functional differences, which could include treating heterogeneous elements as homogeneous and ignoring task context. Another problem is the tendency to view activity as sequential when it is actually simultaneous. Although task work often entails sequential dependencies and can be reasonably decomposed by looking at individual capabilities, we cannot uniquely describe or design teamwork in this way. Teamwork is necessarily based on the interaction among the participants, whereas a simplifying notion of levels treats elements as cleanly separable.

Using Figure 1 as an example again, there seems to be a sequential ordering of the task elements. This might be appropriate for some tasks but not in general. Most teamwork occurs concurrently. Looking at the description of level 6 in the first column of Figure 1, it includes the phrase "informs the human in plenty of time to stop it." This implies the human is concurrently monitoring and assessing the computer's activity on some level. It would also suggest the need for a stop function, although none is included. The simplification here might explain the apparent oversight of including a stop behavioral element, and it is indicative of the problems faced when using a model with a solitary focus on levels of autonomy.

Problem 5: The Levels of Autonomy Concept Is Insufficient to Meet Future Challenges

Many of the challenges facing designers are related to teamwork. An earlier article in this department proposed 10 challenges for making automation a "team player."[5] These challenges include directability, transparency, and predictability. These challenges deny the intrinsic validity of any levels of autonomy concept. Each of these challenges must be addressed not by making the machines more independent, but by making them more capable of supporting system interdependence.

Many supportive behaviors are what might be called soft system constraints and are not essential to task completion—that is, although the performer is, strictly speaking, self-sufficient, it can benefit from support. Joint activity is not exclusively about the hard constraints that enable or prevent the possibility of an activity, as the solid arrows in Figure 1 depict. Joint activity also includes soft interdependence, which includes optional commands, such as the ability to request the final status of the action (see the dashed arrow in Figure 1). Soft interdependence also includes helpful things that a participant might do to facilitate team performance. For example, team members can signal progress appraisals[16] ("I'm running late"), warnings ("Watch your step"), helpful adjuncts ("Do you want me to pick up your prescription when I go by the drug store?"), and observations about relevant unexpected events ("It has started to rain").

Our observations suggest that good teams can be distinguished from great ones by how well they support requirements arising from soft interdependence. Although social science research on teamwork indicates it as an important factor in team performance,[17] interdependence (particularly soft interdependence) has not received adequate attention in the research literature.[6]

Teamwork is largely about enhancing each member's performance, not merely effective task distribution. In response to the MABA-MABA (men-are-better-at/machines-are-better-at) Fitts' List model,[18] an alternative human-centered view was expressed in this department as the Un-Fitts List.[19,20] The intent was to emphasize the ways in which people and machines cannot simply divide up the

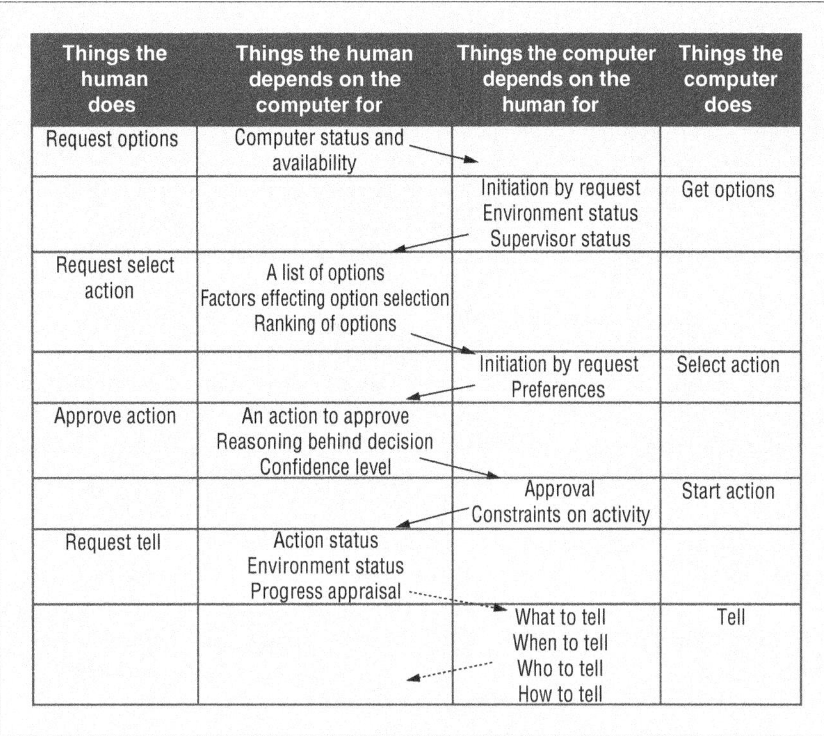

Things the human does	Things the human depends on the computer for	Things the computer depends on the human for	Things the computer does
Request options	Computer status and availability		
		Initiation by request Environment status Supervisor status	Get options
Request select action	A list of options Factors effecting option selection Ranking of options		
		Initiation by request Preferences	Select action
Approve action	An action to approve Reasoning behind decision Confidence level		
		Approval Constraints on activity	Start action
Request tell	Action status Environment status Progress appraisal		
		What to tell When to tell Who to tell How to tell	Tell

Figure 2. Example of an interdependence analysis based on the Figure 1 example. We added some potential interdependence and allow the sequential-work-flow assumption to persist only to maintain consistency in the discussion. The solid arrows depict hard constraints, and the dashed arrow indicates soft interdependence. (Adapted from an earlier work.[8])

work, but rather mutually enhance their competencies and mitigate their limitations. Such a view is consistent with our view of interdependence and its role in design.

Consider the hypothetical level 6 in Figure 1. If we consider the interdependence in the activity, we can concoct a table patterned after the Sheridan-Verplank levels of automation but based on the Un-Fitts List (see Figure 2). We have added some potential interdependence that might be appropriate for such an activity. We allow the sequential-work-flow assumption to persist only to maintain consistency in the discussion. The focus of Figure 2 is the diversity of interdependence among the activities.

Although we apply this process to a single level within the original Sheridan-Verplank list here, it can be applied to any of the levels with different results, based on the varying interdependence within the activity. If we move beyond the single decisive element portrayed by the Sheridan-Verplank list toward activity to support the future envisioned roles, the interdependence become much more complex and generating such a table becomes even more interesting. Such a construction calls out the ways in which changes to the level of autonomy affect interdependence and how the interdependence affects the total work system. Levels by themselves do not provide this information, which leads to the next problem.

Problem 6: Levels Provide Insufficient Guidance to the Designer

Levels of autonomy do not provide principles or guidelines for designers as they build human-machine systems. Previous articles have discussed the challenge of bridging the gap from cognitive engineering products to software engineering.[21] The levels of autonomy concept provides no assistance here. Parasuraman, Sheridan, and Wickens suggested using levels of autonomy in combination with human performance as an evaluative criterion for automation design.[11] Although we agree that human-performance measures are important and useful, it is unclear what value the descriptive levels of autonomy provide other than as a labeling mechanism. They provide no assistance to the designer, whose only option is to build it and try it, then build something else and compare the results.

Interdependence, however, affords a great deal of predictive power. It can inform the designer of what is and is not needed, what is critical, and what is optional. Most importantly, it can indicate how changes in capabilities affect relationships.

This extends the human-centered approaches where designers typically ask, "How can we keep the human in the loop?" or "How do we reduce the burden on the human?" These types of questions lead designers to focus on usability issues. Understanding the interdependence in the human-machine system in the context of the anticipated activity can provide a wealth of guidance to a designer. In fact, we posit that it is through understanding the dynamic interdependence within the macrocognitive work that the system developer can answer such questions as "What should be automated?" and "How do we reduce the burden on the human?" More importantly, it has the potential to answer richer questions, such as "How will this change affect the work system?"

As an example, consider our level 6 in Figure 1. What is the impact of allowing the computer to move from the get options to select action functions without requiring the human request function? Here, some amount of risk analysis might be required to assess the consequences of leaving it completely to the system. Making this change might enable a higher level of autonomy, but is it better? How does it affect the system?

Now look at Figure 2. Identifying the interdependence suggests several impacts. Not only does allowing the computer to select the action reduce the directability of the automation by eliminating the computer's dependence on the human to initiate action selection, it also reduces transparency because the human no longer has access to the options. Both of these limit the work system's ability to leverage the human's ability to improve the overall work system's effectiveness.

Coactive design takes interdependence as the central organizing principle among people and agents working together as a team.

Toward Coactive Design

Building on the theory of joint activity,[4,5] we are working on a *coactive design approach*[6] that is intended to provide prescriptive guidance to designers of sophisticated human-machine systems. Coactive design takes interdependence as the central organizing principle among people and agents working together as a team. The approach also embraces the idea that effective coordination in human-machine activity has much to learn from the various forms of social regulation that enable people to work well together.[22]

Besides implying that two or more parties are participating in an activity, the term coactive is meant to convey the reciprocal and mutually constraining nature of actions and effects that are conditioned by coordination. In joint activity, individual participants share an obligation to coordinate, to a degree sacrificing their individual autonomy in the service of progress toward group goals.

By its nature, joint activity implies the greater parity of mutual assistance, enabled by intricate webs of complementary, reciprocal affordances, and obligations. Thus, coactive design considers the mutual interdependence of the all parties instead of merely focusing on the dependence of one of the parties on the other. It recognizes the benefits of designing agents with the capabilities they need to be interdependent.

As we try to design more sophisticated human-machine work systems, we move along a maturity continuum from dependence to independence to interdependence. The process is a continuum because a small level of agent independence through autonomy is a prerequisite for interdependence. However, independence is not the supreme achievement in human-human interaction,[23] nor should it be in human-machine systems. Imagine a completely capable, autonomous human possessing no skills for coactivity—how well would such a person fit in most everyday situations?

This maturation process cannot only be seen in individual systems but also in the human-machine systems field as a whole. Consider the history of unmanned aerial vehicle (UAV) R&D. The first goal in development was a standard engineering challenge to make the UAV self-sufficient for some tasks (such as stable flight and waypoint following). As the capabilities and robustness increased, the focus shifted to the problem of self-directedness by the machine ("What am I willing to let the UAV do autonomously?"). The future developments of UAVs suggest yet another shift, as discussed in the "Unmanned Systems Roadmap,"[24] which states that unmanned systems "will quickly evolve to the point where various classes of unmanned systems operate together in a cooperative and collaborative manner" (p. 2). This requires a focus on interdependence ("How can I get multiple UAVs to work effectively as a team with their operators?").

This progression of development is a natural maturation process that applies to any form of sophisticated automation. Awareness of interdependence was not critical to the initial stages of UAV development, but it becomes an essential factor in realizing a system's full potential.

We believe that increased effectiveness in human-agent teamwork hinges not merely on trying to make machines more independent through their autonomy, but also in striving to make them better team players[5] by making them more capable of sophisticated interdependent joint activity with people.■

References

1. J.M. Bradshaw, P.J. Feltovich, and M. Johnson, "Human-Agent Interaction," *Handbook of Human-Machine Interaction*, G. Boy et al., eds., Ashgate, 2011, pp. 283–302.
2. C. Breazeal et al., "Social Robots: Beyond Tools to Partners," *Proc. 13th IEEE Workshop Robot and Human Interactive Communication*, IEEE Press, 2004, pp. 551–556.
3. T.W. Fong, *Collaborative Control: A Robot-Centric Model for Vehicle Teleoperation*, tech. report, Robotics Inst., Carnegie Mellon Univ., 2001.
4. G. Klein et al., "Common Ground and Coordination in Joint Activity," *Organizational Simulation*, W.B. Rouse and K.R. Boff, eds., John Wiley, 2004, pp, 139–184.
5. G. Klein et al., "Ten Challenges for Making Automation a 'Team Player' in Joint Human-Agent Activity," *IEEE Intelligent Systems*, 2004, vol. 19, no. 6, pp. 91–95.
6. M. Johnson et al., "Coactive Design," to be publishing in *Coordination, Organisation, Institutions and Norms 2010*, M.D. Vos et al., eds., Springer, 2012.
7. J.M. Bradshaw et al., "Dimensions of Adjustable Autonomy and Mixed-Initiative Interaction," *Agents and Computational Autonomy*, M. Klusch, G. Weiss, and M. Rovatsos, eds., Springer, 2004, pp. 17–39.
8. T.B. Sheridan and W. Verplank, *Human and Computer Control of Undersea Teleoperators*, tech. report, Man-Machine Systems Lab., Dept. of Mechanical Eng., Massachusetts Inst. of Technology, 1978.
9. M.A. Goodrich and A.C. Schultz, "Human-Robot Interaction: A Survey," *Foundations and Trends in Human-Computer Interaction*, vol. 1, no. 3, 2007, pp. 203–275.
10. P.A. Hancock and S.F. Scallen, "Allocating Functions in Human-Machine Systems," *Viewing Psychology as a Whole*, R.R. Hoffman, M.F. Sherrick, and J.S. Warm, eds., Am. Psychological Assoc., 1998, pp. 509–539.
11. R. Parasuraman, Y. Sheridan, and C. Wickens, "A Model for Types and Levels of Human Interaction with Automation," *IEEE Trans. Systems, Man and Cybernetics, Part* A, vol. 30, no. 3, 2000, pp. 286–297.
12. J.F. Allen, "Mixed-Initiative Interaction," *IEEE Intelligent Systems*, vol. 14, no. 5, 1999, pp. 14–16.
13. K. Christoffersen and D.D. Woods, "How to Make Automated Systems Team Players," *Advances in Human Performance and Cognitive Engineering Research*, vol. 2, E. Salas, ed., Elsevier Science, 2002, pp. 1–12.
14. T.B. Sheridan, "Function Allocation: Algorithm, Alchemy or Apostasy?" *Int'l J. Human-Computer Studies*, vol. 52, no. 2, 2000, pp. 203–216.
15. P.J. Feltovich, R.R. Hoffman, and D.D. Woods, "Keeping it Too Simple: How the Reductive Tendency Affects Cognitive Engineering," *IEEE Intelligent Systems*, vol. 19, no. 3, 2004, pp. 90–95.
16. P.J. Feltovich et al., "Progress Appraisal as a Challenging Element of Coordination in Human and Machine Joint Activity," *Engineering Societies for the Agents World VIII*, A. Artikis et al., eds., Springer, 2007, pp. 124–141.
17. E. Salas, N.J. Cooke, and M.A. Rosen, "On Teams, Teamwork, and Team Performance: Discoveries and Developments," *Human Factors*, vol. 50, no. 3, 2008, pp. 540–547.
18. P.M. Fitts et al., *Human Engineering for an Effective Air-Navigation and Traffic-Control System*, Committee on Aviation Psychology, Nat'l Research Council, 1951.
19. R.R. Hoffman et al., "A Rose by Any Other Name ... Would Probably Be Given an Acronym," *IEEE Intelligent Systems*, vol. 17, no. 4, 2002, pp. 72–80.
20. D.D. Woods, "Steering the Reverberations of Technology Change on Fields of Practice: Laws that Govern Cognitive Work," *Proc. 24th Ann. Meeting of the Cognitive Science Soc.*, Erlbaum, 2002, pp. 14–16.
21. R.R. Hoffman, "Influencing versus Informing Design, Part 2: Macrcognitive Modeling," *IEEE Intelligent Systems*, vol. 23, no. 6, 2008, pp. 86–89.
22. P. Feltovich et al., "Social Order and Adaptability in Animal and

Human Cultures as an Analogue for Agent Communities: Toward a Policy-Based Approach," *Engineering Societies in the Agents World IV*, LNAI 3071, Springer-Verlag, 2004, pp. 21–48.
23. S.R. Covey, *The Seven Habits of Highly Effective People*, Free Press, 1989.
24. "Unmanned Systems Roadmap: 2007–2032," memo, US Office of the Secretary of Defense, 10 Dec. 2007.

Matthew Johnson is a researcher at the Institute for Human and Machine Cognition and a PhD student at the Delft University of Technology, The Netherlands. Contact him at mjohnson@ihmc.us.

Jeffrey M. Bradshaw is a senior research scientist at the Institute for Human and Machine Cognition. Contact him at jbradshaw@ihmc.us.

Paul J. Feltovich is a research scientist at the Institute for Human and Machine Cognition. Contact him at pfeltovich@ihmc.us.

Robert R. Hoffman is a senior research scientist at the Institute for Human and Machine Cognition. Contact him at rhoffman@ihmc.us.

Catholijn Jonker is the head of the Man Machine Interaction Group of the Department of Mediametics at the Delft University of Technology, The Netherlands. Contact her at C.M.Jonker@tudelft.nl.

Birna van Riemsdijk is an assistant professor in the Man Machine Interaction Group of the Department of Mediametics at the Delft University of Technology, The Netherlands. Contact her at m.bvanriemsdijk@tudelft.nl.

Maarten Sierhuis is area manager in the Intelligent Systems Laboratory at the Palo Alto Research Center. Contact him at Maarten.Sierhuis@parc.com.

Part III:

Design of Human-Machine Systems: From Requirements to Desirements

Chapter 14: A Rose by Any Other Name… Would Probably Be Given an Acronym

R.R. Hoffman, P.J. Feltovich, K.M. Ford, D.D. Woods, G. Klein, and A. Feltovich, "A Rose by Any Other Name… Would Probably Be Given an Acronym," *IEEE Intelligent Systems*, vol. 17, no. 4, July/Aug. 2002, pp. 72–80. doi: 10.1109/MIS.2002.1024755

In this article, we concern ourselves with characterizations of the "new" approaches to the design of complex sociotechnical systems, and we use a biological classification scheme to organize the discussion. Until fairly recently, the design of complex sociotechnical systems was primarily known as "cognitive engineering" or "cognitive systems engineering" (CSE), a term introduced to denote an emerging branch of applied cognitive psychology. A number of new terms have since emerged, all of which might be considered members of the genus "human-centered computing" (HCC). A number of varieties have entered the fray, resulting in an "acronym soup" of terms that have been offered to designate "the" new approach to cognitive engineering. Using the rose metaphor, and taking some liberties with Latin, this article is organized around a set of "genuses" into which the individual "varieties" seem to fall.

A Rose by Any Other Name...Would Probably Be Given an Acronym

Robert R. Hoffman, Paul J. Feltovich, and Kenneth M. Ford, *University of West Florida*
David D. Woods, *Ohio State University*
Gary Klein, *Klein Associates*
Anne Feltovich, *Grinnell College*

Rosaceae Cogitationis Multiflorae

Rosaceae: The rose family
Cogitationis: Thoughts or ideas
Multiflorae: Trans-species root stock

In this essay, we concern ourselves with characterizations of the "new" approaches to the design of complex sociotechnical systems, and we use a biological classification scheme to organize the discussion. Until fairly recently, the design of complex sociotechnical systems was primarily known as *cognitive engineering* or *cognitive systems* engineering (CSE), a term introduced in the 1980s to denote an emerging branch of applied cognitive psychology.[1,2]

Research focused on such topics as human–computer interaction, the psychology of programming, display design, and user friendliness. Although some have sought to make the term *cognitive engineering* seem less of an oxymoron by doing work that somehow looks like actual engineering, a number of new terms have emerged, all of which might be considered members of the "genus" *Human-Centered Computing*. Researchers, research organizations, funding sources, national study groups and working groups, and even entire national funding programs espouse these approaches. A number of varieties have entered the judging competition, as the "acronym soup" in Figure 1 shows.

Editors: Robert R. Hoffman, Patrick J. Hayes, and Kenneth M. Ford
Institute for Human and Machine Cognition, University of West Florida
rhoffman@ai.uwf.edu

The rose is a rose,
And was always a rose.
But the theory now goes
That the apple's a rose,
And the pear is, and so's
The plum, I suppose.
The dear only knows
What will next prove a rose.
You, of course, are a rose—
But were always a rose.
"The Rose Family," Robert Frost, 1928

This variety has come about for many reasons. Some individuals have proposed terms to express views that they believe are new. Others have proposed terms as a consequence of the social and competitive nature of science and science funding, leading to turf wars and the need for individuals to win awards and claim niches that set themselves and their ideas apart from the crowd. The obvious, and obviously incorrect, question is, "Which term is the right one?" As we hope to suggest in this essay, this question is rather like the quest for the blue rose. Using the rose metaphor, and taking some liberties with Latin, we organize the essay around a set of "genuses" into which the individual "varieties" seem to fall.

Rosaceae Traditionum Contrarium

Rosaceae: The rose family
Traditionum: The act of handing over
Contrarium: Opposite or contrast

This genus includes those varieties that express a reaction against some less desirable alternative, often left unnamed (we will make up names to fill the voids). A proposed umbrella term is *Human-Centered Systems*, which people have used to denote

- Programs of college study—for example, at Cornell University[3]

- System development funding programs—for example, the 2001 program at the US National Coordination Office for Information Technology Research and Development[4] and the 1999 program at the US Department of Transportation[5]
- A journal's subtitle—*AI & Society: Journal of Human-Centered Systems and Machine Intelligence*

A report to the US National Science Foundation presented proceedings from an HCS workshop, which included position papers from 51 researchers spanning disciplines including electronics, psychology, medicine, and the military.[6,7] Although all said their work and ideas were human-centered, they had diverse opinions about precisely what *human-centering* is all about. To some, human-centering is

- A philosophical and humanistic position regarding workplace ethics and aesthetics
- A software design process that results in *really* user-friendly interfaces
- A description of what makes for a good tool, that is, the computer does all the adapting
- An emerging interdiscipline, requiring institutionalization and special training programs

To some, a *human-centered system* is

- Any system that enhances human performance
- Any system that plays any kind of role in mediating human interactions

Two main themes underlie this discussion: First, HCS is really technology driven, with human issues and concerns being an add-on rather than the primary engine of change. Second, HCS is driven by a reaction against what is perceived to be a naughty tradition in the design of information-processing technology—a tradition we might dub *Technology-Centered Design*. In TCD, system developers specify the requirements for machines, then implement or prototype the requirements, and finally produce devices and software. Then they go away, leaving users to cope with what they have built. Indeed, experience has shown that devices that are designed according to the design-then-train philosophy "force users to adapt to the system. The user is entangled with the system terminology and jargons that are the designer's view of the world."[8]

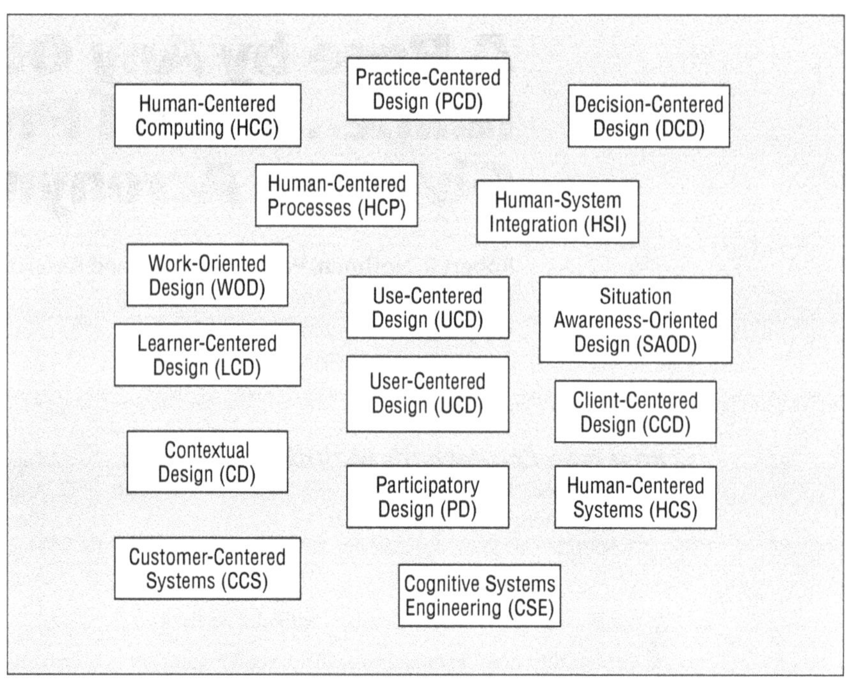

Figure 1. The acronym soup of terms that have been offered to designate "the" new approach to cognitive engineering.

Many lessons learned over recent decades have pointed toward a need for an alternative to TCD, sometimes tagged as *Participatory Design*. These lessons span a range, including insights from significant accidents caused by differences between designers' intentions and users' understanding and cognitive capabilities (for instance, the Three-Mile Island incident). But the lessons also come much closer to home.[9] We have all experienced, for example, the frustrations of learning to use upgraded software, advertised and lauded for its new capabilities by those who designed it and are therefore familiar with it. The new capabilities, however, usually require significant relearning, backpedaling, kludging, and work-arounds. Bells and whistles often go unused and even unnoticed. The vision for HCS is to create systems on the basis of an analysis of human tasks and an awareness of human capabilities, and then determine that the systems result in a performance gain and are adaptable to changing human needs.[7]

At about the time that the NSF began its HCS work, NASA Ames launched an effort on what it called *Human-Centered Computing*.[10,11] This designation is more forthright than HCS in that the "systems" being designed and built clearly are computational systems (and not other things, such as teapots). HCC also more directly reflects a reaction against a tradition that we might dub *Machine-Centered Computing* (MCC). HCC's core idea is to build systems that amplify and extend human cognitive, perceptual, and collaborative capabilities.[12] In this approach, system design must be leveraged by known facts and principles of human psychology and not just by the decontextualized principles that computer scientists or electronics engineers are accustomed to using as guidance (that is, MCC). Human-Centered Systems must complement humans and are not intended to imitate or replace them, as the Turing model for AI would have us believe.[13,14]

Even more speciated than HCC is the designation *Human-Centered Processes* (HCP), the term used by a Working Group of the European Association for Operational Research. At first blush, the HCP designation seems odd in the present context: Humans engage in cognitive processes, so how could a process *not* be centered on (or in) them? The answer is that this group focuses on the design of systems for manufacturing and industrial-process control. The Euro Group shares the sentiments of the HCS and HCC communities regarding goals such as support for distributed teams and dissatisfaction with user-hostile systems.[15]

HUMANS SURPASS MACHINES IN THE:

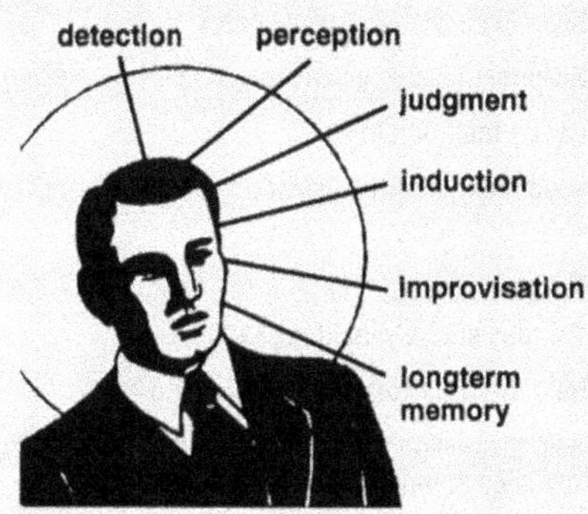

- Ability to detect small amounts of visual or acoustic energy
- Ability to perceive patterns of light or sound
- Ability to improvise and use flexible procedures
- Ability to store very large amounts of information for long periods and to recall relevant facts at the appropriate time
- Ability to reason inductively
- Ability to exercise judgment

MACHINES SURPASS HUMANS IN THE:

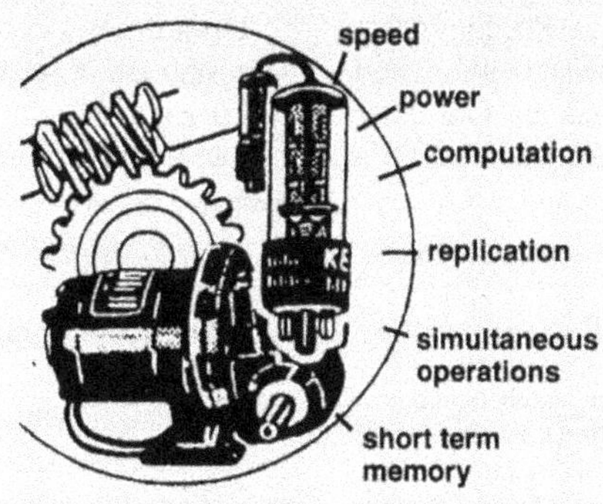

- Ability to respond quickly to control signals, and to apply great force smoothly and precisely
- Ability to perform repetitive, routine tasks
- Ability to store information briefly and then to erase it completely
- Ability to reason deductively, including computational ability
- Ability to handle highly complex operations, i.e., to do many different things at once.

Figure 2. The original Fitts' List. Reprinted with permission from *Human Engineering for an Effective Air Navigation and Traffic Control System*, National Academy of Sciences, Washington, D.C., 1951. Reproduced courtesy of the National Academy Press.

Contextual Design (CD) also expresses a reaction in computer science, but focused against what might be called *Laboratory-Based Design* (LBD), for want of a better term. The basic idea in CD is that the design process cannot be conducted by cloistered designers and programmers feeding designs to the user.

Rather, designers must become field researchers and immerse themselves in the application domain to fully understand domain practice and the context of the prospective designs' use.[16] CD advocates represent the impact on computer science of ethnography (also known as cognitive anthropology, situated cognition, and "cognition in the wild"),[17] especially the works of such people as Edwin Hutchins[18] and Jean Lave.[19]

Related to the spirit of CD are two additional varieties in the genus *Rosaceae Traditionum Contrarium*, called *User-Centered Design* and *Participatory Design*, which express a reaction in human factors psychology, ecological psychology, and applied cognitive psychology against the traditional approach, TCD. The UCD concept traces its origins to cognitive engineering around 1980[20] and is alive and well in the software engineering community.[21] The core idea is that that the machine must satisfy the needs of the people who will use the system, and therefore those people need to be involved in the system's design.[9,22,23] (Ironically, UCD as it is manifested in the software engineering community is actually somewhat designer-centered: It relies heavily on decontextualized principles of usability, interface design, and so on, rather than trying to deeply understand actual work contexts. Furthermore, users' involvement often only takes the form of user commentary on design ideas and clever prototypes—the "satisficing" criterion—rather than something more powerful such as a full empirical study of performance to assess usefulness and usability.)

Similarly, in the field calling itself *Human-Computer Interaction*, some use the terms *Client-Centered Design* (CCD) and *Customer-Centered Systems* (CCS) to express the idea that designers must interact with and satisfy clients and customers (who are not necessarily the end users but can be the ones paying for the work).[16]

In a moment of reflection on the ecological approach to human–machine integration,[24] John Flach and Cynthia Dominguez realized that the goal for systems designers is not really to build tools that support particular users, as the UCD designation suggests, because more than one individual might use any given system.[25] The goal is to provide information (possibilities for perception) and "affordances" (possibilities for action)—to support *uses* rather than users. Hence, we find the term *Use*-Centered Design. Some have suggested the term *Work-Oriented Design* (WOD),[2,26,27] and more recently *Practice-Centered*

Table 1. An "Un-Fitts" list.

Machines	
Are constrained in that	**Need people to**
Sensitivity to context is low and is ontology-limited	Keep them aligned to the context
Sensitivity to change is low and recognition of anomaly is ontology-limited	Keep them stable given the variability and change inherent in the world
Adaptability to change is low and is ontology-limited	Repair their ontologies
They are not "aware" of the fact that the model of the world is itself in the world	Keep the model aligned with the world
People	
Are not limited in that	**Yet they create machines to**
Sensitivity to context is high and is knowledge- and attention-driven	Help them stay informed of ongoing events
Sensitivity to change is high and is driven by the recognition of anomaly	Help them align and repair their perceptions because they rely on mediated stimuli
Adaptability to change is high and is goal-driven	Affect positive change following situation change
They are aware of the fact that the model of the world is itself in the world	Computationally instantiate their models of the world

Design (PCD), to clarify this subtle but important point.[28–30]

The Theme to the Contraria

The contrast of Technology-Centered and Machine-Centered Design with all the others—HCS, HCC, HCP, UCD, UCD, CCD, CCS, WOD, and PCD—shows perhaps most clearly in David Woods' analysis of Fitts' List, reproduced in Figure 2.[31,32] This list was developed during and just after World War II by human factors psychologist Paul Fitts and others who were designing cockpits, radar devices, and the like for the US Army Air Force. Fitts' List emphasizes the things that machines and people do well, but it clearly slants toward the view that we humans need machines to make up for our human frailties, limitations, and penchant for error. The focus of design according to this tradition is to have machines mitigate human error, emotionality, memory limitations, and so on.

Advocates of the new approaches have reacted against the Fitts' List tradition:

> It has sometimes appeared as if the central role of human factors has been to catalogue the limitations of the human information processor so that these limits could be taken into account in the design.... However, we would argue that ... the human is currently the most valuable resource for linking information and action ... it is not a question of protecting the system against human variability ... but how to fully utilize the intelligence, skill, and imagination of the human against the complexities inherent in these domains.[25]

Woods formalized this view by offering a different kind of list that is much in accord with HCC advocates.[33] Woods' "Un-Fitts List" presents a rich view, one that does not concentrate on human shortcomings. Table 1 contains one version of this list that emphasizes what people do well and how they create machines to enhance those competencies. They do so, for example, by creating algorithms that are well suited to bounded conditions and thus balance people's tendency to get stuck in "local" views and action patterns.

The idea that motivates an Un-Fitts list is this, paraphrased:

> Approaches to design will not succeed if they maintain one conceptual space for the environment (machine, world) and another conceptual space for the human (information processing). Cognitive Engineering rests on a foundation of treating people and machines that do cognitive work as a single unit of analysis. Success depends on creating a conceptual space in which humans and the environment are jointly represented.[25]

We express the spirit of the Un-Fitts' List in a nutshell by what we call the Aretha Franklin Principle, named after the singer because of her well-known recording of the song "Respect":

> Do not devalue the human in order to justify the machine. Do not criticize the machine in order to rationalize the human. Advocate the human–machine system in order to amplify both.

Rosaceae Urgentis Paniculae

Rosaceae: The rose family
Urgentis: Urgent
Paniculae: A type of flower shape, used also to denote a type of swelling; etymologically related to the word used to denote the fear induced by the Greek God, Pan—hence, "panic"

Terms that belong to this next genus represent panic attacks in reaction to the perception that the engine of change (technology) is overwhelming. A clear case is the term *Human-System Integration* (HSI). Professional meetings that have used this term (for example, the November 2001 Human Systems Integration Symposium, sponsored by the American Society of Naval Engineers) have resounded with excited and ardent cries for the computer science community to cope with the design challenges for the next generation of systems, in which fewer people will have to do more work using more computers. A great deal of concern has been expressed over an imminent potential disaster when people (more or less poorly trained) are confronted with new and highly complex technologies (more or less human-centered) that themselves run new and highly complex systems (for example, ships to be manned by only 90 people).

Rosaceae Foci Explicationis

Rosaceae: The rose family
Foci: Fireplace or hearth
Explicationis: Analysis or explanation

A number of terms express a particular focus point for empirical analysis. These terms fall into two subspecies. One is *Rosaceae Foci Explicationis Psychologicus*.

Varieties in this subspecies focus on the empirical investigation of certain psychological faculties and the design of systems that support the exercise of those faculties. *Decision-Centered Design* (DCD), for instance, focuses the empirical analysis on revealing the decisions that domain practitioners have to make, and the information requirements for those decisions.[34,35] The *Psychologicus* species also includes varieties designated as *Situation Awareness-Oriented Design* (SAOD)[36] and *Learner-Centered Design* (LCD).[37]

Additional varieties fall in the other subspecies, *Rosaceae Foci Explicationis Individualis*, which focuses on individual differences. This includes a local variant of User-Centered Design, which emphasizes such things as autoadaptive systems and expert systems. Both are systems that interact with users on the basis of models of the individual users (that is, their learning history).

Having laid out the acronyms using the rose metaphor of varieties (for terms) and genuses (for the themes and origins behind these terms), we can now attempt to clarify the "acronym soup."

Rosaceae Foci Explicationis Pluralis

Rosaceae: The rose family
Foci: Fireplace or hearth
Explicationis: To analyze and explain
Pluralis: Plural

Our analysis leads to the question of why there are not more varieties, rather than fewer. We can easily imagine quite a few new hybrids. For instance, much research that uses methods of cognitive field research aims to reveal the mental models of domain practitioners, models of their knowledge, and models of their reasoning and strategies. So, we might have *Mental Model-Oriented Design* (MMOD). For the *Individualis* species, we might invoke *Individual Differences-Centered Design* (IDCD) and *Trainee-Centered Design* (TCD). Indeed, we might create as many new varieties as there are psychological faculties to analyze.

This conclusion leads us to recognize a problem with the acronym soup having to do with the difference between the words

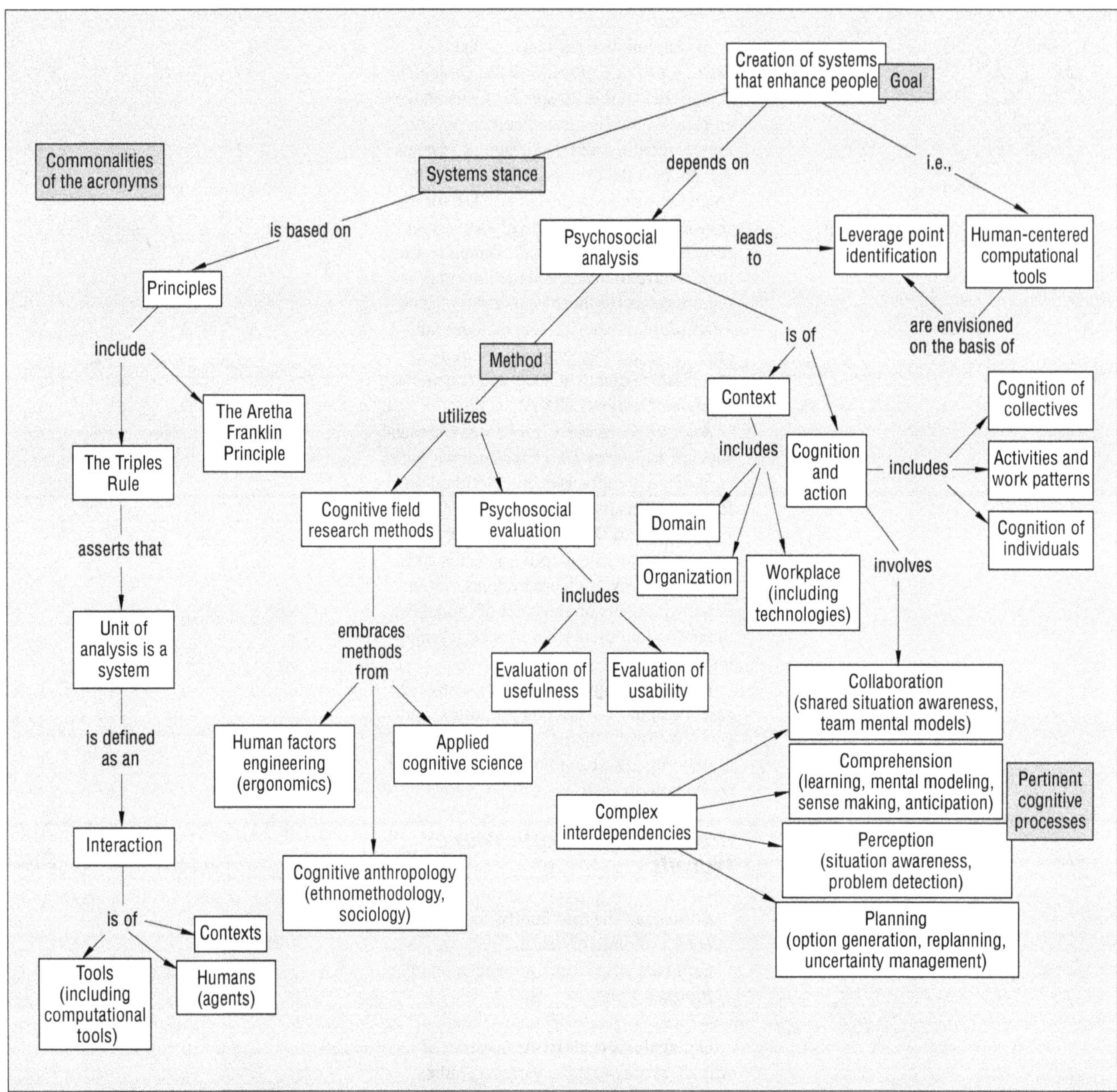

Figure 3. A Concept Map illustrating commonalities among the soup's acronyms.

"analysis" and "design." Empirically oriented researchers commonly generate data and identify leverage points that might lead to ideas for new tool designs, but they do not actually build tools. Indeed, so-called design activities are often analytical research activities that are intended to yield critical information for generating design ideas. This information can include things such as domain practitioners' reasoning, where new technology might be brought to bear. Thus, some activities whose name includes "design" should really be called something using the word "analysis." For instance, some activities that have been referred to as *Decision-Centered Design* should be called *Decision-Centered Analysis*. Some activities that are referred to as *Situation Awareness-Oriented Design* should be called *Situation Awareness-Oriented Analysis*—and so on. Furthermore, we could invoke notions such as *Mental Model-Oriented Design* versus *Mental Model-Oriented Analysis*. Each type of analysis is conducted in the service of design.

However, this begs a larger, more important question. What *is* the design process? Has anyone laid out a process, perhaps to complement the many detailed published descriptions of the empirical methodology that is used in analysis (for example, methods of cognitive task analysis and knowledge elicitation)?[38,39] Often, individuals who have conducted analyses seem to identify a leverage point and then recognize how they might adapt a known idea or innovation to the case at hand. In short, there is no specific design "process." What makes this issue

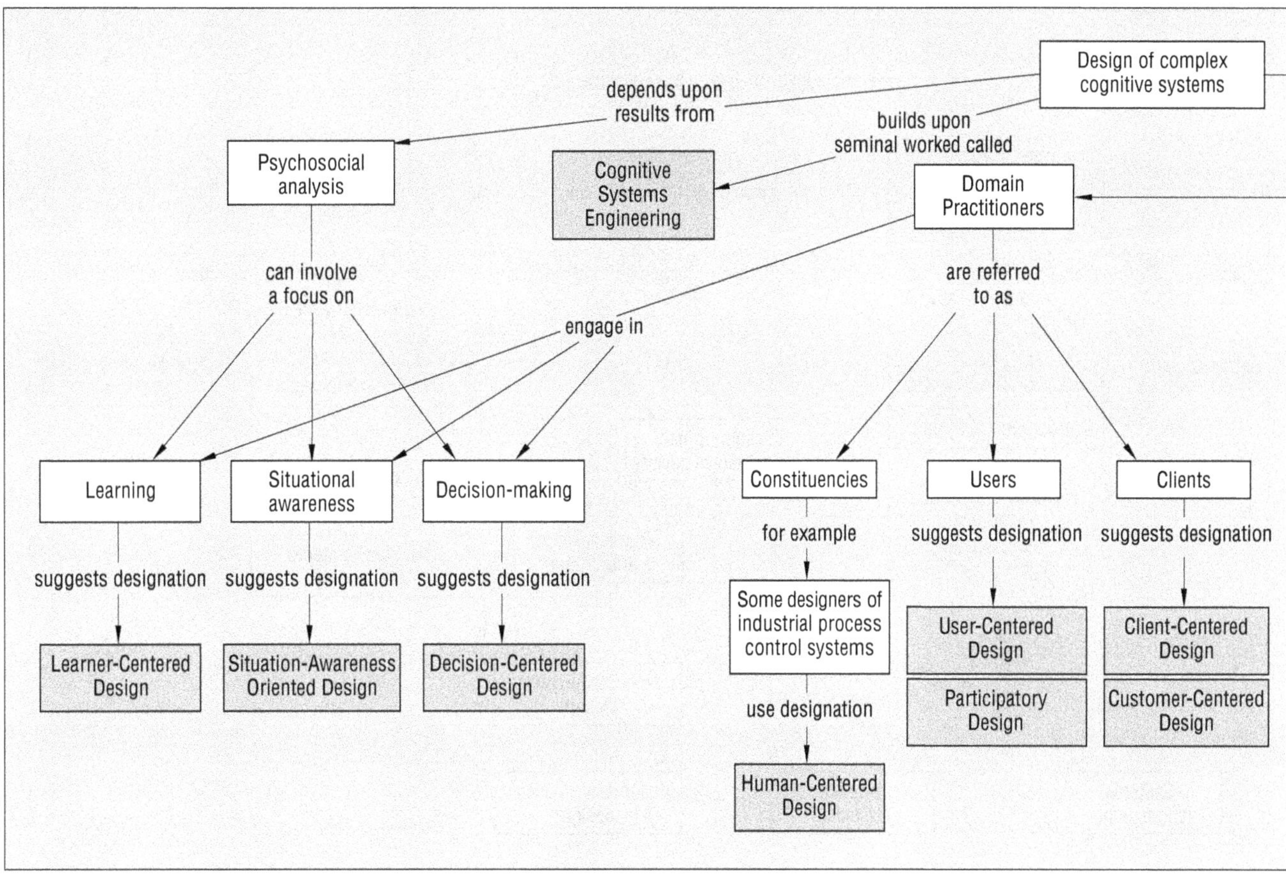

Figure 4. The acronym soup formatted in a Concept Map that lays out the underlying relationships.

important is that customers in government say that what they most desperately need is a specification of the design process. This is a topic to be pursued in a future column.

Rosaceae Cogitationis Multiflorae

Rosaceae: The rose family
Cogitationis: Thoughts or ideas
Multiflorae: Trans-species root stock

We return to the initial genus and the idea of a root stock—that is, that all the designations in the acronym soup have some commonalities. The Concept Map in Figure 3 depicts these commonalities: the goal, the systems stance, the cognitive processes that must be the focus for analysis, and the method. Method includes both the analytical method (cognitive field research in the service of design) and the evaluative method (that is, that new designs must be empirically evaluated for usefulness and usability).

At least one more difficulty remains. If we begin with the overall premise that design is the design of tools (including information systems) and that tools by definition involve humans-at-work, then what is actually gained by referring to either Human-Centered Design or Practice-Centered Design? After all, if the design is not for humans and does not support human practice, what good is it? Referring even to the hybrid Human Practice-Centered Design would be redundant and could be reduced to the single word "Design." Thus we find ourselves unable to completely escape our genealogical history. The designation of Practice-Centered Design speaks to tradition in human–factors engineering, mandating that we avoid all the pitfalls of Technology-Centered Design and Machine-Centered Design. The designation of Practice-Centered Design also serves as a reminder that not all the tools that we build are necessarily computational tools. The designation of Human-Centered Computing speaks to tradition in computer science, also mandating that we avoid all the pitfalls of Technology-Centered Design and Machine-Centered Design.

The Concept Map in Figure 4 places all the acronyms in the soup into a meaningful framework based on these considerations.

We thus have differently hued variants of the same variety of rose. They are all rooted in the same soil. All drink the same water. All reach toward the same light. To turn a phrase, ex uno plura. From one comes many.

Acknowledgments

We prepared this article through participation in the Advanced Decision Architectures Collaborative Technology Alliance, sponsored by the US Army Research Laboratory under cooperative

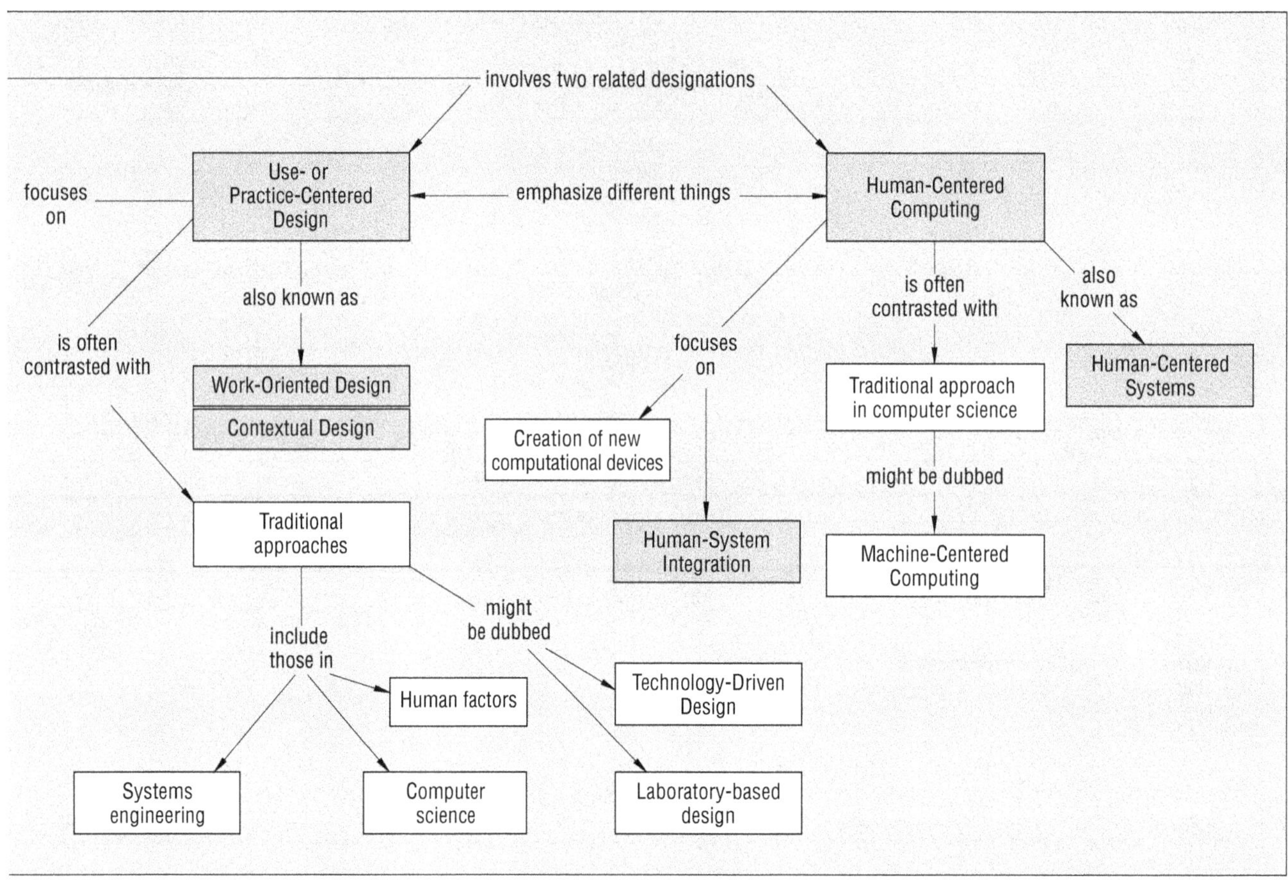

agreement DAAD19-01-2-0009.

"The Rose Family" by Robert Frost was reprinted by permission of Henry Holt & Co., which published it in *The Poetry of Robert Frost*, edited by Edward Connery Lathem. © 1928, 1969 by Henry Holt and Co., © 1956 by Robert Frost.

References

1. D.A. Norman, "Cognitive Engineering," *User-Centered System Design: New Perspectives on Human-Computer Interaction*, D.A. Norman and S.W. Draper, eds., Lawrence Erlbaum, Hillsdale, N.J., 1986, pp. 31–61.
2. J. Rasmussen, A.M. Pejtersen, and L.P. Goodstein, *Cognitive Systems Engineering*, John Wiley & Sons, New York, 1994.
3. Cornell Univ., "Undergraduate Program Courses in Human-Centered Systems," 2001; www.fci.cornell.edu/infoscience/human-systems.html.
4. "Networked Computing for the 21st Century: Human Centered Systems," Nat'l Coordination Office for Information Technology Research and Development, 2001; www.hpcc.gov/pubs/blue99/hucs.html#technologies.
5. "Human-Centered Systems: The Next Challenge in Transportation," US Dept. of Transportation, Washington, D.C., 1999.
6. J. Flanagan et al., eds., *Human-Centered Systems: Information, Interactivity and Intelligence*, tech. report, Nat'l Science Foundation, Washington, D.C., 1997, pp. 266–268.
7. R. Kling and L. Star, "Human Centered Systems in the Perspective of Organizational and Social Informatics," *Computers and Soc.*, vol. 28, no. 1, 1998, pp. 22–29.
8. C. Ntuen, "A Model of System Science for Human-Centered Design," *Human-Centered Systems: Information, Interactivity and Intelligence*, J. Flanagan et al., eds., Nat'l Science Foundation, Washington, D.C., 1997, p. 312.
9. D.A. Norman, *The Psychology of Everyday Things*, Basic Books, New York, 1988.
10. W.J. Clancey, *Situated Cognition: On Human Knowledge and Computer Representations*, Cambridge Univ. Press, Cambridge, U.K., 1997.
11. C.M. Seifert and M.G. Shafto, "Computational Models of Cognition," J. Hendler, ed., *Handbook of Cognitive Neuropsychology*, vol. 9, Elsevier, Amsterdam, 1994.
12. R.R. Hoffman, P.J. Hayes, and K.M. Ford, "Human-Centered Computing, Thinking In and Outside the Box," *Intelligent Systems*, vol. 16, no. 5, Sept./Oct. 2001, pp. 76–78.
13. K.M. Ford and P. Hayes, "On Computational Wings: Rethinking the Goals of Artificial Intelligence," *Scientific Am.*, Winter 1998, pp. 78–83.
14. R.R. Hoffman et al., "The Triples Rule," *IEEE Intelligent Systems*, vol. 17, no. 3, May/June 2002, pp. 62–65.
15. *European Working Group on Human-Centered Processes*, 2001; www-hcp.enst-bretagne.fr.
16. H. Beyer and K. Holtzblatt, *Contextual Design: Defining Customer-Centered Systems*, Academic Press, San Diego, 1998.
17. M. Cole, Y. Engeström, and O. Vazquez, eds., *Mind, Culture, and Activity: Seminal Papers from the Laboratory of Comparative Human Cognition*, Cambridge Univ. Press, Cambridge, U.K., 1997.
18. E. Hutchins, *Cognition in the Wild*, MIT Press, Cambridge, Mass., 1995.
19. J. Lave, *Cognition in Practice: Mind, Mathematics, and Culture in Everyday Life*, Cambridge Univ. Press, Cambridge, U.K., 1988.
20. D.A. Norman and S.W. Draper, *User-Centered System Design: New Perspectives on Human-Computer Interaction*, Lawrence Erlbaum, Mahwah, N.J., 1986.

Robert R. Hoffman is a research scientist at the University of West Florida's Institute for Human and Machine Cognition and a faculty associate at the university's Department of Psychology. Contact him at the Inst. for Human and Machine Cognition, 40 Alcaniz St., Pensacola, FL 32501; rhoffman@ai.uwf.edu.

Paul J. Feltovich is a research scientist at the Institute for Human and Machine Cognition, University of West Florida, Pensacola. His research interests include expert–novice differences in complex cognitive skills, conceptual understanding for complex knowledge, and novel means of instruction in complex and ill-structured knowledge domains. He received a BS in mathematics from Allegheny College and a PhD in educational psychology from the University of Minnesota. Contact him at the Inst. for Human and Machine Cognition, 40 Alcaniz St., Pensacola, FL 32501; pfeltovich@ai.uwf.edu.

Kenneth M. Ford is the founder and director of the University of West Florida's Institute for Human and Machine Cognition. Contact him at the Inst. for Human and Machine Cognition, 40 Alcaniz St., Pensacola, FL 32501; kford@ai.uwf.edu.

David D. Woods is a professor of industrial and systems engineering and codirector of the Cognitive Systems Engineering Laboratory at The Ohio State University. He received the 1995 Laurels award and the 1984 Westinghouse Engineering Achievement Award and is a fellow of the Human Factors and Ergonomic Society, the American Psychological Society, and the American Psychological Association. He received his degrees in experimental psychology from Purdue University. Contact him at Cognitive Systems Eng. Lab, Industrial and Systems Eng., 210 Baker Systems, Ohio State Univ., 1971 Neil Ave., Columbus, OH 43210; woods@csel.eng.ohio-state.edu.

Gary Klein is chief scientist of Klein Associates. His work involves recognitional decision-making. He received his PhD in experimental psychology from the University of Pittsburgh. Contact him at Klein Associates, 1750 Commerce Center Blvd. North, Fairborn, OH 45324-3987; gary@decisionmaking.com.

Anne Feltovich is a graduate of the Illinois Mathematics and Science Academy and is now majoring in classics at Grinnell College, anticipating graduate studies in classical archaeology. Contact her at Human and Machine Cognition, attn. Paul Feltovich, 40 Alcaniz St., Pensacola, FL 32501; pfeltovich@ai.uwf.edu.

21. A. Cooper, *The Inmates Are Running the Asylum: Why High Tech Products Drive Us Crazy and How to Restore the Sanity*, Sams Publishing, Indianapolis, Ind., 1999.
22. T.K. Landauer, *The Trouble with Computers: Usefulness, Usability and Productivity*, MIT Press, Cambridge, Mass., 1997.
23. K.L. McGraw and K. Harbison, *User-Centered Requirements*, Lawrence Erlbaum, Mahwah, N.J., 1997.
24. J.M. Flach et al., eds. *Global Perspectives on the Ecology of Human-Machine Systems*, Lawrence Erlbaum, Mahwah, N.J., 1994.
25. J.M. Flach and C.O. Dominguez, "Use-Centered Design," *Ergonomics in Design*, July 1995, pp. 19–24.
26. P. Ehn, *Work-Oriented Design of Computer Artifacts*, Arbetslivscentrum, Stockholm, Sweden, 1988.
27. K. Vicente, *Cognitive Work Analysis*, Lawrence Erlbaum, Mahwah, N.J., 1999.
28. D.D. Woods, "Designs Are Hypotheses about How Artifacts Shape Cognition and Collaboration," *Ergonomics*, vol. 41, 1998, pp. 168–173.
29. D.D. Woods et al., *Studying Cognitive Work in Context: Facilitating Insight at the Intersection of People, Technology and Work*, tech. report, Cognitive Systems Eng. Laboratory, Inst. for Ergonomics, Ohio State Univ., Columbus, Ohio, 2002; http://csel.eng.ohio-state.edu/woodscta.
30. D.D. Woods and N. Sarter, "Learning from Automation Surprises and Going Sour Accidents," *Cognitive Engineering in the Aviation Domain*, N. Sarter and R. Amalberti, eds., Lawrence Erlbaum, Mahwah, N.J., 2000, pp. 327–353.
31. S.S. Potter et al., "Bootstrapping Multiple Converging Cognitive Task Analysis Techniques for System Design," *Cognitive Task Analysis*, J.M. Schraagen and S.F. Chipman, eds., Lawrence Erlbaum, Mahwah, N.J., 2000, pp. 317–340.
32. D.D. Woods and D. Tinapple, "W3: Watching Human Factors Watch People at Work," *43rd Ann. Meeting Human Factors and Ergonomics Soc.*, Sept. 1999; http://csel.eng.ohio-state.edu/hf99.
33. D.D. Woods, "Steering the Reverberations of Technology Change on Fields of Practice: Laws That Govern Cognitive Work," *Proc. 24th Ann. Meeting Cognitive Science Soc.*, Lawrence Erlbaum, Mahwah, N.J., 2002.
34. G. Klein et al., "Applying Decision Requirements to User-Centered Design," *Int'l J. Human-Computer Studies*, vol. 46, 1997, pp. 1–15.
35. D.W. Klinger, "A Decision-Centered Design Approach to Case-Based Reasoning: Helping Engineers Prepare Bids and Solve Problems," *Advances in Agile Manufacturing*, P.T. Kidd and W. Karwowski, eds., IOS Press, Manchester, U.K., 1994, pp. 393–396.
36. M.R. Endsley, "Designing for Situation Awareness in Complex Systems," *Proc. Second Int'l Workshop Symbiosis of Humans, Artifacts and the Environment*, Japan Soc. for the Promotion of Science, Kyoto, Japan, 2001, pp.175–190.
37. E. Soloway, M. Guzdial, and K.E. Hay, "Learner-Centered Design: The Challenge for HCI in the 21st Century," *Interactions*, vol. 1, 1994, pp. 36–48.
38. R.R. Hoffman et al., "Eliciting Knowledge from Experts: A Methodological Analysis," *Organizational Behavior and Human Decision Processes*, vol. 62, 1995, pp. 129–158.
39. J.M. Schraagen, S. Chipman, and V. Shalin, eds., *Cognitive Task Analysis*, Lawrence Erlbaum, Mahwah, N.J., 2001.

Chapter 15: From Contextual Inquiry to Designable Futures: What Do We Need to Get There?

S.W.A. Dekker, J.M. Nyce, and R.R. Hoffman, "From Contextual Inquiry to Designable Futures: What Do We Need to Get There?," *IEEE Intelligent Systems*, vol. 18, no. 2, Mar./Apr. 2003, pp. 74–77. doi: 10.1109/MIS.2003.1193660

Human-centered systems result when software engineers or developers give attention to the orientations, expectations, and understandings of the people who will be part of the sociotechnical system. Human factors researchers often take certain agendas, terms, and theories for granted or rely on them out of habit. This paper takes a special look at contextual enquiry as a putatively (and indeed potentially) superior way of giving end users a serious say in the procurement process of complex cognitive systems.

From Contextual Inquiry to Designable Futures: What Do We Need to Get There?

Sidney W.A. Dekker, *Linköping Institute of Technology*
James M. Nyce, *Emporia State University*
Robert R. Hoffman, *Institute for Human and Machine Cognition*

So, what is an *end user*, really? And what do we really mean by the *procurement process*? Human factors researchers often take certain agendas, terms, and theories for granted or rely on them out of habit. This essay takes a special look at contextual enquiry as a putatively (and indeed potentially) superior way of giving end users a serious say in the procurement process of complex cognitive systems.

"End user"

Human-centered systems result when software engineers or developers give attention to the orientations, expectations, and understandings of the people who will be part of the sociotechnical system.[1] But this is far easier said than done. What are the orientations, expectations, and understandings of the "end user"? The term presupposes that humans and machines can and should be treated separately—assessed by different criteria. "End user" is a hangover label from computer science of the 1980s; it contradicts the systems stance of human-centered computing and the Triples rule, which specifies that stance.[2] Also, the term suggests that users involved in the design team are those, and only those, who will actually operate the machines. This is not necessarily true.

Editors: Robert R. Hoffman, Patrick J. Hayes, and Kenneth M. Ford
Institute for Human and Machine Cognition, University of West Florida
rhoffman@ai.uwf.edu

Take weather forecasting, for instance. To design a new workstation system to aid forecasters, the designers might rely on forecasters' participation in

- Identifying leverage points and decision requirements (the cognitive work analysis phase)
- Identifying and refining potential design innovations
- Evaluating and reprototyping

But if the new system does not help forecasters in their own work (for instance, evaluating forecast accuracy) and in the work of creating products that help *their* customers (pilots or the general public, for example), its usefulness will be restricted. Where is the "end" in "end user"?

"Procurement process"

Merely involving end users in the design process is not a panacea. Neither is overreliance on verification and validation, or on "getting human factors included early." Designs are hypotheses about an "envisioned world."[3] The Envisioned World Principle that David Woods and Sidney Dekker proposed can be stated as

> The introduction of new technology, including appropriately human-centered technology, will bring about changes in environmental constraints (that is, features of the sociotechnical system, or the context of practice). Even though the domain constraints may remain unchanged, and even if cognitive constraints are leveraged and amplified, changes to the environmental constraints may be negative.

Testing a "design as hypothesis" ultimately requires fielding the system, but this means prototyping the system at various levels (specific interfaces, software, user training, and so on). By this time, so much commitment and cost (psychological, organizational, political, financial) are involved that the potential for changing the design on the basis of end user feedback becomes almost impossible. Making things even more complex is what we call the Moving Target Rule:

> The sociotechnical workplace is constantly changing, and constant change in environmental constraints may require constant adaptation in cognitive work, even if domain constraints remain constant.

In other words, by the time you are ready to test an envisioned-world hypothesis, the sociotechnical workplace in which the work will be carried out will already have changed. Frustrations with the procurement process have led human factors researchers to *front-load* by trying to achieve a rich understanding of the nature of practice before beginning to develop new technology.

Front-loading, however, might not be able to address the dilemma that the Moving Target Rule poses for designers and developers. With the promise of privileged access to an understanding of what activities mean to the people who do them, designers have sought enlightenment by one or another form of *contextual inquiry*.[4] This includes bringing to bear methods from ethnography[1,5] and cognitive work analysis. These approaches involve finding out about people's work, about where they are doing that work while they are doing it, and about what doing that work means to them. Design, by extension, is not so much about building artifacts or systems as about creating new ways to work.

Is contextual inquiry really enough?

Ethnographers have often have failed to provide meaningful input into designers' choices.[6] They typically have difficulty jumping from the description and analysis of current practice to requirements capture, in part because of how ethnography has been defined as a method, but also because of analytic choices ethnographers have made with respect to design problems and design issues.

Those involved in design and development (including ethnographers) are often tempted to equate what informants do or tell them with what ethnography is and can tell them. Confounding informant understanding with ethnographic analysis has profound implications for ethnography's credibility and the contribution it can make to the creation of human-centered systems.

Of course, informants can claim privileged access to their operating world: What end users know and can tell us always *has* to be right in a sense; otherwise, they could not carry out their work. However, no set of practitioners, however expert, can be expected to be able to easily articulate analytic frameworks or categories strong enough to specify a complete design agenda. This is not to deny practitioners insight or analytic ability; it just acknowledges that experts in modern organizations are laypeople most of the time, no matter how reflective they are. According to Helena Karasti, "practitioners take the most fundamental aspects of their ordinary work practices for granted. It is not their task but the fieldworker's to reveal and make visible aspects of work practice that practitioners cannot make explicit."[7] In short, the analysis of complex work requires considerable second-order analysis to yield data and insight relevant to a given problem and design agenda.

Those involved in design and development, including ethnographers, are often tempted to equate what informants do or tell them with what ethnography is and can tell them.

Tying ethnography to pragmatic design hinges on two things:

- Understanding work's features and objects, not just cast in the informant's language but also recast by extracting, revising, and verifying the categories by which informants make sense of their world
- Finding ways to "build out" this revised, nuanced understanding into designable technology

Strong ethnography is more than "record and replay." The ethnographer must move back and forth between informant understandings ("native categories" is the term used in ethnography) on the one hand and analyses of the native understandings and categories on the other hand. This kind of ethnography must be informed by what designers require when they talk and think about human-centered requirements regarding work and systems. "To build out to the future"—in other words, to address the Moving Target Rule—requires that we have a principled understanding of the work that informants do and the resources they use to achieve it. It is only from knowledge such as this that we can extrapolate into the future.

Let's look at two contextual inquiries of a paper-based artifact that many system developers have wanted to replace with computerized variants: the air traffic control *flight progress strip*, which air traffic controllers use to display important flight data for a particular flight (planned altitude, destination, route, and so on). We examine these inquiries especially for their ability to go from contextual finding in the present to a designable future.

Study I: Strips help controllers build their mental picture of air traffic

Hailed as the exemplar of contextual flight progress strip studies,[5] a Lancaster University project[6] spent many person-months on the ethnographic observation and analysis of air traffic controller practice, with a focus on flight strip use. The grand conclusion of this often-cited project was that strips

> are the means by which controllers see and note what is happening, what they have already done, what needs to be done. They are an essential feature of "getting the picture," "organizing the traffic," which is the means of achieving the orderliness of traffic. The strips and their organization are a proxy orderliness of the configuration of the traffic flow.[6]

Strips help controllers "get the picture." Fine. But such an insight should not have taken longer to arrive at than half an afternoon spent observing air traffic controllers. This raises the question about what kind of ethnography the researchers were practicing. When we reduce ethnography to (or take it as) mere observation and description, we ignore the need to move to second-order work. In other words, neither the categories nor the "positions" of the natives (the people being studied) or the investigators themselves become objects of any sustained inquiry. The result is that this kind of ethnography never moves much further than the reproduction of what, for the investigators and informants, is common sense. Furthermore, if strips are adequate for letting a controller know what is going on, then there is no point in automating or developing anything new.

Such ethnography then, intentionally or not, privileges the status quo, even valorizing standard practice. It should be no wonder that designers often think they can do just as well or better themselves. As if to confirm the point, when the air traffic control system developers lost patience with the ethnographers, they gave them a set of guiding questions to answer, so that they (the developers) could get on with building their electronic substitute:[6]

- What characteristics of the existing manual system are unimportant and need not be supported in a computerized system?
- What are important manual activities that need not be supported in a computerized system because the activities are a consequence of the fact that no computer support is available?
- What characteristics of the manual system must be replicated without change in a computerized system?
- What activities from the manual system may be supported in a way which is different from that used in the manual system?

The developers missed the point. All the old biases of optimistic engineered positivism are here to see. The developers believed that they could simply substitute computers for paper—they just needed the ethnographers to tell them which parts to swap. The failure of ethnographers and developers to get along, or even understand each other, is not unique to the Lancaster project.[1] Confronted with challenges about such machine-oriented silliness, the ethnographers never quite recovered. Nor could they, given the way ethnography was defined in this project—as not requiring any second-order, analytic work.

The Lancaster project presents a particularly naïve form of ethnography: The researchers did not interrogate what was common sense to the air traffic controllers (or to themselves). They took practitioner categories as canonical and inherently correct, not requiring any second-order analysis. Informant competence, as expressed in domain terms and categories, can be strong and valid. It can also represent misconceptions or apocrypha.

Mistaking the domain practitioner's statements and categories for contextual understanding or analysis does not lead to strong ethnography. Nor does it generate meaningful design guidance. Tellingly, the title of the Lancaster project paper is "From Ethnographic *Record* to System Design ... ," not "From Ethnographic *Analysis* ... ." Clearly, ethnographic recording is not enough. Unless ethnography takes on the analytic question "What is really going on here?" the jump from ethnographic record to system design is too great for designers to deal with. Designers cannot and do not want to deal with it—indeed, it should not be their job.

On the other extreme, in their book on contextual design,[4] Hugh Beyer and Karen Holtzblatt prohibit the use of domain categories in design discussions, lest such characterizations trap developers into assumptions or lure them into believing that practitioner statements (such as "flight strips help me get the mental picture") can actually serve as design principles or analytic statements. Talking to designers meaningfully requires the person conducting the contextual inquiry to engage in a kind of strong ethnography, strong particularly in its analysis.[1] Only such higher-order analytical work can lead to designable futures. The question is, how?

Mistaking the domain practitioner's statements and categories for contextual understanding or analysis does not lead to strong ethnography. Nor does it generate meaningful design guidance.

Study II: Strips help compress complexity, manage dynamics, and support coordination

Informant remarks such as "flight strips help me get the mental picture" should serve as the starting point of a contextual inquiry, not as its conclusion. The revision of categories is a hallmark of strong ethnography, and Geoff Ross's study of flight progress strips in Australia can serve as an example.[8] Ross conducted a survey that many ethnographers derided for imposing the researcher's meaning on data rather than bringing out the domain practitioner's. But Ross conducted a stronger analysis and synthesis. He slowly treaded through the masses of survey data, abstracting and categorizing as he went along, relying at each step on previous categorizations for help.[9]

Ross's study shows the strength of second-order analytic work. It involved multiple intermediate steps of analysis and synthesis, each with an explicit trace that others could follow and critique. The typical way proposed is to move up from context-specific details to concept-dependent generalizations in successive steps—each more abstract than the previous one, each stated less in domain terms and more in design terms.[4,10] Furthermore, both the domain and design terms that emerge are grounded in the literature (that is, in prior analytic and design experience) as much as they are in informant meaning and understandings. This stepwise movement from context to concept is crucial for moving to designable futures, for linking ethnographic analysis and robust design guidance.

To use an example from Ross's study, context-specific controller activities such as "entering a pilot report; composing a flight plan amendment" reveal an intentional strategy (a slightly higher level of analysis), which is the "transformation or translation of information for entry into the system."[8] At an even higher level of analysis, this could be referred to as "coding" activity. Part of this coding is symbolic, in that it uses highly condensed markings on flight strips (red underlinings, black circles) to denote and represent "what is going on." Only from there can we make the (then no longer so large) jump to the highest level of abstraction—helping us identify the flight strip's role in making sense of workplace and task complexity. Unable to keep straight all the details of what a flight might do, the controller compresses complexity by letting one symbol stand for complex concepts and interrelationships, some even temporal.

Other high-level, concept-dependent roles of the flight strip would be to anticipate dynamics (what comes next) and support coordination (for example, in handing over flights to other controllers). Note how the language is no longer cast in that of context-specific details or artifact-related practices. Instead, second-order analysis provides developers with more general or abstract concepts that are informed by what these workers find to be significant in their work and world. It is with these concepts and categories that developers can open a window to a designable future.

Complexity and dynamics, as well as coordination, are critical features that make air traffic control what it is, including difficult. Developers must take into account the fact that controllers use their artifacts to help them deal with complexity, anticipate dynamic futures, and coordinate with other controllers. Ross shows us the paradox in contextual inquiry for HCC: Creating designable futures requires sensitivity to context. Yet it asks us to extract the description of people's work away from the current context that shapes it. Otherwise, designers will not understand what the ethnographic analyst is trying to say, so they will not know what to do next. This contrasts with the Lancaster project, which mistook the domain practitioners' language, categories, and understanding for analytic substance, and thereby assumed that the practitioners were self-reflective enough to do their ethnographic work for them. Strong ethnography is both analysis and synthesis, a working back and forth between informant statements and categories and concepts that capture reality and meaning.

Designable futures, and by extension HCC systems, can result if we succeed in describing people's work in terms that let designers proactively understand, even anticipate, the challenges of that work. Designers do not build artifacts or systems so much as they create new ways in which practitioners must handle the challenges associated with work. Involving users in the design and procurement process does not guarantee meaningful design input. Contextual inquiry, as a popular way of involving users, must not mistake informant understanding for analytic senses of work. Like any human performance data gathering, it must be backed up by strong, second-order analysis, lest designers and developers get misguided. ■

References

1. R.J. Anderson, "Representations and Requirements: The Value of Ethnography in System Design," *Human-Computer Interaction*, vol. 9, no. 2, 1994, pp. 151–182.
2. R.R. Hoffman et al., "The Triples Rule," *IEEE Intelligent Systems*, vol. 17, no. 3, May/June 2002, pp. 62–65.
3. D.D. Woods and S.W.A. Dekker, "Anticipating the Effects of Technology Change: A New Era of Dynamics for Human Factors," *Theoretical Issues in Ergonomics Science*, vol. 1, no. 3, 2001, pp. 272–282.
4. H. Beyer and K. Holtzblatt, *Contextual Design: Defining Customer-Centered Systems*, Academic Press, 1998.
5. R.H.R. Harper, "The Organisation in Ethnography: A Discussion of Ethnographic Fieldwork Programs in CSCW," *Computer Supported Cooperative Work*, vol. 9, no. 2, May 2000, pp. 239–264.
6. J.A. Hughes, D. Randall, and D. Shapiro, "From Ethnographic Record to System Design: Some Experiences from the Field," *Computer Supported Cooperative Work*, vol. 1, no. 3, 1993, pp. 123–141.
7. H. Karasti, *Increasing Sensitivity towards Everyday Work Practice in System Design*, doctoral dissertation no. A 362, Dept. Information Processing, Univ. Oulu, 2001, p. 66.
8. G. Ross, *Flight Strip Survey Report*, The Australian Advanced Air Traffic System Operations Instructor, Air Traffic Services Australia, 1995.
9. P.S. Della Rocco, C.A. Manning, and H. Wing, *Selection of Air Traffic Controllers for Automated Systems: Applications from Current Research*, tech. report DOT/FAA/AM-90/13, Nat'l Technical Information Service, Springfield, Va., 1990.
10. Y. Xiao and K.J. Vincente, "A Framework for Epistemological Analysis in Empirical (Laboratory and Field) Studies," *Human Factors*, vol. 42, no. 1, 2000, pp. 87–101.

Sidney W.A. Dekker is an associate professor at the Linköping Institute of Technology and director of studies at the Center for Human Factors in Aviation. Contact him at Linköping Inst. of Technology, SE-581 83, Linköping, Sweden; sidde@ikp.liu.se.

James M. Nyce is an associate professor in the School of Library and Information Management at Emporia State University, an adjunct associate professor in the Department of Radiology at the Indiana University School of Medicine, and a docent at Linköping University. Contact him at 9219 W 1250 N, Albany, IN 47320; jnyce@rocketmail.com.

Robert R. Hoffman is a research scientist at the University of West Florida's Institute for Human and Machine Cognition and a faculty associate in the Department of Psychology. Contact him at the IHMC, 40 Alcaniz St., Pensacola, FL 32501; rhoffman@ai.uwf.edu.

Chapter 16: The Borg Hypothesis

R.R. Hoffman, J.M. Bradshaw, P.J. Hayes, and K.M. Ford, "The Borg Hypothesis," *IEEE Intelligent Systems*, vol. 18, no. 5, Sep./Oct. 2003, pp. 73–75. doi: 10.1109/MIS.2003.1234774

What if intelligent computing were centered inside humans? Portending an even braver and newer world, it's now possible to insert wires into a person's nerves to control appliances. We can even send such signals over the Internet, where they are decoded by computer and then fed into another person's nervous system. Human bodies are getting more and more plugged in. It's not easy to set aside questions of ethics and choice. It is not even possible. However, in this essay we simply overlook them in order to work toward our hypothesis. To do that, we must take you on a trip into space. Our argument is that if humanity decides to continue human exploration of space, we will sooner or later—probably sooner—be forced to center some intelligent computing inside humans.

The Borg Hypothesis

Robert R. Hoffman, Jeffrey M. Bradshaw, Patrick J. Hayes, and Kenneth M. Ford,
Institute for Human and Machine Cognition

What if intelligent computing were centered inside humans? This essay's title is inspired by the nemesis of Jean-Luc Picard, captain of the starship Enterprise in the television series *Star Trek: The Next Generation*. The Borg are—or should we say "is"—a species consisting of organic beings symbiotically merged with technology. Each individual Borg is laden with all manner of appliances, ranging from laser eyeballs to appendages resembling drill presses to computational and communication devices implanted in their nervous systems. The Borg is a collective, meaning that they—or it—possess a single mind. That Borg mind has the single intent of "assimilating" all organic species into the collective. Assimilation involves first injecting nanoprobes that thoroughly transform the organic being down to the molecular level, then grafting on the various appliances (or else growing them de novo like so many cloned carrots in a hydroponic garden). Wending their way through the galaxy in huge Rubik Cube-like vehicles, the Borg assimilate entire planets at a time and carve up starships as if they were roast beef, making them (it) an especially nasty adversary.

In our real world, we already routinely replace hip joints with titanium and inner-ear structures with microcircuits; we can carry telephones comfortably on our heads, and Web-enabled eyeglasses can augment our view of reality. To counter the effects of drowsiness or inattention, DaimlerChrysler is developing prototypes that continuously monitor drivers' physical and mental states, while DARPA's Augmented Cognition Program is planning an even more ambitious reach to "plug in" the warfighter of the future (www.darpa.mil/ipto/programs/augcog/index.htm).

Portending an even braver and newer world, it's now possible to insert wires into a person's nerves to control appliances. We can even send such signals over the Internet, where they are decoded by computer and then fed into another person's nervous system.[1] Human bodies are getting more and more plugged in.

It's not easy to set aside questions of ethics and choice. It is not even possible. However, in this essay we simply overlook them in order to work toward our hypothesis. To do that, we must take you on a trip into space. Our argument is that if humanity decides to continue human exploration of space, we will sooner or later—probably sooner—be forced to center some intelligent computing inside humans.

Men into space

In 1959 and 1960, Ziv Television Productions and producer Lewis J. Rachmil produced a television series titled Men into Space. This series featured the space concepts of artist Chelsey Bonestell, whose works had a major impact on many writers, including Arthur Clarke, and motion pictures, such as Destination Moon and The Conquest of Space. For his TV series, Rachmil also relied heavily on advice from the US Air Force and the Surgeon General. Men into Space was intended to present the most realistic depiction of what it would be like to establish a space station or moon base and then begin the process of exploring the planets. Episodes included one in which a fold on an astronaut's space suit accidentally became crimped between two large pieces of a space station as he was assembling them in space. The problem: Is there a hole in the suit? If so, freeing the suit could kill the astronaut. In another episode, the crew was stranded at the bottom of a crater on the moon after a crash landing. The problem: Radio waves only move in straight lines, and there is no ionosphere to reflect them to receivers that are out of line-of-sight.

Editors: Robert R. Hoffman, Patrick J. Hayes, and Kenneth M. Ford
Institute for Human and Machine Cognition, University of West Florida
rhoffman@ai.uwf.edu

In one especially pertinent episode, an astronaut on a space walk at the space station becomes stressed out during a repair and botches a wiring job. As a result, a stabilizer rocket on the space station misfires, speeding up the rotation of the space wheel to the point where the crush of gravity makes movement, let alone repair, seemingly impossible. What makes this episode interesting is the explicit focus coming from ideas in human factors engineering circa 1960. The technology on the space station includes a polygraph-like device that constantly monitors the astronauts' stress levels. As the wheel spins faster, readings indicate that the station commander is stressed to the max. But our hero rises to the challenge and manually controls the wheel's stabilizing rockets. This study in human endurance begins with the following voice-over:

> The age of the conquest of space will be an age of men and machines probing far beyond our Earth. And just as some machines will probe deeply into space, others will probe the men who will travel in space. Yet, put to the ultimate test, no amount of machinery will be ever able to determine the measure of a man's inner strength.

As prescient as it was, the concepts presented in Men into Space now seem rather naïve because we have seen what real space flight, space walks, a space station, and a moon landing are like. However, all the accomplishments—and setbacks—of the last several decades represent just our first few tentative steps into space. We already know that traveling to the planets will be a very different affair in many ways than traveling to Earth's moon. Because our experience with long-duration space travel is so limited, our current ideas are almost certain to end up being as naïve as those of Rachmil's courageous space pioneers.

What will it really take?

Long-duration space travel is rather hostile to both our bodies and our machines. NASA still struggles to make systems that provide a lung-friendly atmosphere and stomach-friendly water (not to mention a human-centered interface for control and maintenance) and that will work for years with minimal maintenance. So far, we're working hard to do that right here on the good old Earth.[2] Because keeping an astronaut alive in space is so expensive and risky, we struggle to leverage the capacity of each member of the small crew through devices such as the Personal Satellite Assistant, an intelligent flying appliance.[3] And some of you may recall occasional glimpses of Shuttle astronauts using laptops to assist them in various ways. As a perspective on the challenge of getting the most advanced technology hardened for space, consider that an initial design for the International Space Station specified that the computer monitors would all be black-and-white.

On the biology side, we have a fairly clear idea about the effects of ambient radiation, and it isn't good. Radiation shielding means mass. Lots of it. That means the ship must be much heavier than we'd prefer. We also have some clear ideas about the effects of zero gravity, and they aren't good either. Irretrievable bone loss and muscle deterioration are two of the most obvious effects. A long-duration space mission will almost certainly have a gravity wheel habitat in which astronauts can get some respite from zero-g. But then, we have absolutely no clue about the effects on humans of frequent, repeated forays into and out of zero-g as astronauts go from the habitat wheel into the rest of the ship to perform various duties.

Long-duration space missions will not be possible unless and until human biological evolution has been forced.

We know all about gluing metal contacts onto bodies and measuring physiological indicators such as heart rate. We know a little about putting appliances, machines, and electronics inside bodies. Is it really that much of a step to imagine putting intelligent machines inside humans? But our "Borg Hypothesis" goes boldly beyond even this: Long-duration space missions will not be possible unless and until human biological evolution has been forced. What we are reaching for here is a new meaning of evolution. Geobiological evolution on Earth has yielded creatures (humans) that can reengineer their own physiognomy (for example, artificial limbs), their own anatomy (for example, cochlear implants), and even their molecular biology (for example, gene therapy). Through human-machine symbiosis, we are on an evolutionary threshold where our species is capable not only of deliberately affecting its own evolution but also of changing the rules by which evolution occurs.

Fundamental mechanisms of the evolution of new species include variation and "selection," meaning lots of death. Perhaps our technological advances have set the stage for a new form of evolution, one that does not require lots of death or even genetic change but might nonetheless entail speciation, if only because someone who has been "Borged" might not be able to procreate with someone who has not been "Borged." Once in space, might the transformed humans be stuck there? This brings to mind another idea from science fiction, that the best people to live and work in zero-g are those who have lost their legs (less work for the heart.)

By the traditional criterion in biology, such Borged humans would not be a different species. Biologists may have to change their criterion because survival and procreation will not necessarily be restricted to success in the reproduction of the biology alone. Borged humans might think that their offspring need more than this to be fully "human"—perhaps they would require being "born of woman and then properly engineered."

For long-duration space missions, we must approach Borgification from two directions:

- Machines, as we know them today, must become more biological in certain respects. They must possess functionalities such as self-repair and self-defense, for example. (Scientists at NASA's Jet Propulsion Laboratory are already working on systems that can train themselves to become new circuits.) Not just when the machines are in use, but also as they are created and decommissioned, processes must be more biological—that is, more like growing and recycling than manufacturing and discarding.
- Bodies, as we know them today, must become more machine-like in certain respects. We are already on that path, but taking it further, wouldn't it be nice, for example, to fix our bodies so that radiation and low gravity do less harm? Com-

putational technology also holds great and perhaps more immediate promise, for instance, using artificial intelligence technologies inside us.

For long-duration space missions, we may have to put intelligent technologies inside of us. Brave new worlds are usually described in a context implying choice, choice of paths that might lead either to utopias or to hells. Perhaps humanity made its choice already, eons ago when creatures first began wondering at the stars. ■

Robert R. Hoffman is a research scientist at the Institute for Human and Machine Cognition. Contact him at the IHMC, 40 Alcaniz St., Pensacola, FL 32501; rhoffman@ihmc.us.

Jeffrey M. Bradshaw is a research scientist at the Institute for Human and Machine Cognition. He currently is co-principal investigator for a DARPA-funded international experiment on agents for coalition operations and leads a DARPA Ultra*Log team studying agent survivability and policy-based security. Under grants from the NASA Cross-Enterprise and Intelligent Systems Programs, he leads research teams investigating principles of human-robotic teamwork. Contact him at the IHMC, 40 Alcaniz St., Pensacola, FL 32501.

Patrick J. Hayes is a senior research scientist and John C. Pace Jr. Eminent Scholar at the Institute for Human and Machine Cognition. Contact him at the IHMC, 40 Alcaniz St., Pensacola, FL 32501.

Kenneth M. Ford is director of and a computer science professor at the Institute for Human and Machine Cognition. Contact him at the IHMC, 40 Alcaniz St., Pensacola, FL 32501.

Acknowledgments

The authors dedicate this essay to the astronauts of the Space Shuttle Columbia: Rick Husband, Kalpana Chawla, William McCool, David Brown, Laurel Clark, Michael Anderson, and Ilan Ramon.

References

1. J. Selim, "The Bionic Connection," *Discover*, vol. 23, no. 11, Nov. 2002, pp. 49–51.
2. D. Schreckenghost et al., "Intelligent Control of Life Support for Space Missions," *IEEE Intelligent Systems*, vol. 17, no. 5, Sept./Oct. 2002, pp. 24–31.
3. J.M. Bradshaw et al., "Adjustable Autonomy and Human-Agent Teamwork in Practice: An Interim Report on Space Applications," *Agent Autonomy*, H. Hexmoor, C. Castelfranchi, and R. Falcone, eds., Kluwer, 2003, pp. 243–280.

Chapter 17: What Is Design in the Context of Human-Centered Computing?

R.R. Hoffman, A. Roesler, and B.M. Moon, "What Is Design in the Context of Human-Centered Computing?," *IEEE Intelligent Systems*, vol. 19, no. 4, July/Aug. 2004, pp. 89–95. doi: 10.1109/MIS.2004.36

We deal with design in human-centered computing. Problem solving often involves recognizing and fiddling with tacit assumptions. Such realization can often come from seeing things from new perspectives. Appreciating the human-centered perspective may offer some hope for enriching design's scientific foundations and for crafting new and better approaches to it. Certainly this suggests a constraint on or a goal for design, but how do we go from such statements to actual designs that accomplish the stated goals? We approach this class of question by considering the origins of and historical influences on the notion of design, then by considering the assumptions underlying our modern conception of design in light of the principles of human-centered computing.

What Is Design in the Context of Human-Centered Computing?

Robert R. Hoffman, *Institute for Human and Machine Cognition*
Axel Roesler, *Ohio State University*
Brian M. Moon, *Klein Associates*

There appears to be no reason to suppose that concepts as yet uninvented and unknown stand between us and the fuller exploration of those problem domains that are most obviously and visibly ill-structured. —Herbert Simon[1]

Problem solving often involves recognizing and fiddling with tacit assumptions. Such realization can often come from seeing things from new perspectives. Appreciating the human-centered perspective may offer some hope for enriching design's scientific foundations and for crafting new and better approaches to it. Essays in this department have introduced such notions as the Sacagawea Principle:[2]

> Human-centered computational tools need to support active organization of information, active search for information, active exploration of information, reflection on the meaning of information, and evaluation and choice among action sequence alternatives.

Certainly this suggests a constraint on or a goal for design, but how do we go from such statements to actual designs that accomplish the stated goals?

We approach this class of question by considering the origins of and historical influences on the notion of design, then by considering the assumptions underlying our modern conception of design in light of the principles of human-centered computing.

Editors: Robert R. Hoffman, Patrick J. Hayes, and Kenneth M. Ford
Institute for Human and Machine Cognition, University of West Florida
rhoffman@ai.uwf.edu

Evolution of the design concept

An investigation of word origins and current usage reveals a number of meanings of "design."

Making meaningful marks on things

The word "design" comes into English from the Latin *de signum* meaning "to mark out," with the root *signum* meaning "mark," "token," or "seal," and also having relations to Latin words meaning "to cut" or "to saw." *Signum* evolved, mostly through French, into words such as signify, assign, designate, signal, and many others. The original meaning of "design" was to physically make marks on something, marks that bear some signification. Current meanings of "design" preserve the notion of drawing representational marks (that is, sketches for artifacts such as machines or buildings).

Working with people

In the eras of the craft guilds, craftsmen gathered the design knowledge behind artifacts such as woodworking tools, farming equipment, and horse-drawn coaches by direct collaboration with the individuals who used their devices. The design knowledge was passed through generations of craft masters and apprentices. The knowledge and skill weren't freely available, at least until Denis Diderot produced *Le Encyclopedie*, which contained essays describing the guildsmen's knowledge and skills.[3] With the emergence of larger-scale designs, especially in the Industrial Revolution, the necessary skills had to be distributed among many specialists. This new task—designing for a class of people with whom the designer did not interact—helped mark the origin of industrial design.

Making machines for machines

Another factor added by the Industrial Age was a new responsibility of designers: To reshape formerly hand-crafted processes into ones that machines could do. Mass and assembly-line-based production stimulated, or necessitated, the creation of many designs for artifacts aimed at a broad mass of consumers and for machines designed to help in manufacturing other machines. In this context, design came to have a significant relation to the notion of *plan*.

Design as a plan

A design-as-plan lets the designer develop an entire artifact without having to change the actual things or parts referred to by the design. While making it possible to explore design alternatives, the design-as-plan serves as a design notation, because it defines the artifacts' overall structure as well as the detail required by the many craft disciplines involved in the manufacturing. This idea of design-as-plan was taken to new levels of complexity, or knowledge organization, by the large-scale technology development projects of World War II and the subsequent space program. These demonstrated the power of innovation and initiated directions that necessitated the systematization of design activity, ultimately justifying a scientific discipline of design in the 1960s. The availability of computers for tasks such as design optimization in constraint spaces stimulated an optimistic environment for rationalizing and formalizing design methods.

Design as radicalism

Design has also been used to refer to a *plan of attack* on a problem. This meaning originates from the French *desseigner*, an 18th-century term referring to political plotting or conspiracy. Design in this sense isn't just the mere act of defining and documenting a conceived plan to create artifacts. Rather, it involves imposing (not just suggesting or offering) radical alternatives, innovations that open up new classes of opportunities. This interpretation of design is illustrated in approaches that study the organizational aspects of designed environments in order to explore possibilities for change. Examples include participatory design and certainly any form of use-centered design, with implications that are intended to affect users, communities, or even societies.

Design as intent

Designs often become stand-ins for wishes and desires that are shared by the people involved in the design process or that are interpretations of the designed objects by those who use them. Designed objects can become representations of the mindset behind the design (that is, designer-centered design).[4] Design intent ranges from the attempt to simplify and economize (that is, functional design) to the attempt to provide first aid in order to hide and disguise—an ornamentation activity resulting in decoration.

Beyond the motif of design as a way of showing (or hiding) intent lies the ability of design to highlight or distinguish—that is, design as a deliberate expression of individualism. This ranges from referring to designs as archetypes (for instance, the "styles" of architecture) to expressions of fashion.

Debate continues today on the question of whether design is an art or can become a science.

Design as Gestalt

"Design" is often used to mean disembodied form (or, in German, *Gestalt*). The notion here is that artifacts possess properties that can be abstracted away from them. Hence, we can say, "This has a design," or "I'd like that kind of design for my house," or "I like the feeling of that design for sweaters."

Design as art

The notion of design as art takes the Gestalt notion a step further. Debates about this have raged for centuries. They include, for example, a debate in the 19th century between functionalists ("form follows function") and ornamentalists, who believed that there is no design without ornamentation and flourishes (things whose function is purely aesthetic). Debate continues today on the question of whether design is an art or can become a science. On one hand, some journals on the topic have published empirical studies of design[5]; on the other hand, academic and even industrial design programs are still typically housed in art colleges.

Donald Schön repeatedly encountered this notion of design in his study of architecture:[6]

> Like other practitioners, architects tend to value action over reflection. They tend to take for granted what is most exceptional about their own familiar practice. Perhaps more than other practitioners, they tend to mystify their artistry, treating it defensively as an indescribable something that "either one has or has not." … [T]hey may find it extraordinarily difficult to give explicit, accurate, and useful accounts of the understanding implicit in gradually learned competences that have become "intuitive." (p. 7)
>
> In 1972 [at] a colloquium on professional education … [the participants] disagreed about many things, but they held one sentiment in common: a profound uneasiness about their own professions.… Some were troubled by the existence of an irreducible residue of art in professional practice. The art deemed indispensable even to scientific research and engineering design seemed resistant to codification. As one participant observed, "If it's invariant and known, it can be taught; but it isn't invariant." (pp. 10–11)

Design as a profession

A theme in the history of the notion of design, and most of the notions we have discussed so far, is that design is concerned with change.[7] Designing involves envisioning a future that does not yet exist, but a future that designers predict by suggesting new artifacts for that future, a future that begins in the present. Today this theme has been taken to new levels, in part because the pace of change and the compartmentalization of knowledge have accelerated significantly. Seeds were sown for a fundamental change about the time of World War I. The challenge for the industrial designers in the first formalized academic design programs pioneered by the Bauhaus (1919–1933) was that they had to live in two worlds: the world of the engineer who is concerned with implementation, and the pragmatic world of the user. They had to be able to translate their sponsors' problem statements into innovative design solutions. At the same time, they had to present the implementing manufacturers with just the right degree of skill challenge without being too open to engineering compromise. To bring together the highest potential of innovation with the right justification in terms of technical and economic feasibility became the expertise of these professional designers of the first generation.

Good design is difficult and relies on training and experience. And people can get paid for doing it, so we can say, "She is a designer." Designers are supposed to know how to create novelty even five or more years into the future and are trained in orchestrating the means to bring the envisioned change about. Indeed, some people are very good at it and become famous, or come to be regarded as experts and so come under the psychologist's microscope to reveal their strategies and problem-solving methods. From this perspective, design is both an activity occurring in the medium of thought as well as a set of behaviors (such as keystrokes for a CAD system, making marks on a piece of paper, or scratching lines in the dirt).

Today we have a fragmentation of professions, a range of meanings of design in a number of disciplines. The understanding of design among the engineering disciplines differs from the understanding of industrial and visual communication designers. Consider, for example, the differences in meaning that the word "modeling" might have for an architect versus a software engineer. To the former, it's actually making something (for example, a scale model); to the latter, it's simulating something. As another example, the English use of "design" from an engineering point of view translates to at least three German semiequivalents: *entwerfen* (to envision and define after selection), *entwickeln* (to develop in order to add detail) and *konstruieren* (to commit to a detailed construction in order to implement). Such language-related subtleties surrounding the notion of design led European researchers to distinguish their design methods research from that conducted by the Anglo-American community.[8]

Design as a pervasive activity

Contrasting with the idea of design as a skill residing in select individuals is the notion that design is an element of all professions:[6]

> Among observers of the professions, it has become commonplace that all competent practice involves a kind of design. Indeed, the language of design has entered into the ordinary language of many professions other than those usually called "design professions." In medicine, practitioners speak of the design of a process of diagnosis and intervention; in law, cases and arguments are "designed." One eminent scholar [Simon[9]] of the professions has argued for a science of design as the fundamental knowledge base underlying all professional education.

The computer's impact

The older design credo "form follows function" has become obsolete. Artifacts now might not look like what they do, in part because their inner makings have shifted from a mechanical base to an electronic one. Much of the semantic coding in artifacts gets lost to the human who looks at the artifact, and designing meaningful artifacts for human–machine interaction becomes necessary to channel the vast growth in the belief that intelligent systems would provide means for collaborative technology. At the same time, the computer has entered the design office as a tool that has challenged traditional design expertise and extended the quest in defining what the activity of design entails. (Lore is that most design work is now done using computers.) Designers face challenges in designing new technologies, and they have to design with these new technologies. And they have to do so at an accelerated pace, using designer-centered technologies that require kludges, work-arounds, and make-work.

> **One of the themes in the history of design remains a driving force in current conceptions: the notion that there is a process of design.**

This state of affairs leads to consideration of the notions of human-centered computing. We approach this by focusing on one of the themes in the history of design, one that remains a driving force in current conceptions: the notion that there is a process of design. According to this view, we can look at people and say, "They are designing." This is an important assumption and a focus of our critical analysis.

What designers do and say they do

Psychological studies of how designers conduct design work have used a variety of research methods, including case studies. The most often used methods are interviews and think-aloud problem solving, combined with protocol analysis,[10–12] although observational methods have also been used (for example, teacher critiques of student designs).[6] Studies have looked at a range of design domains such as electronics, software, product design, mechanics, and architecture. Researchers have compared the strategies of domain practitioners with those of students (or apprentices), showing that the primary influence on design strategy is indeed the designer's level of expertise.[13] Such studies have revealed a variety of activities in which designers engage.

Problem finding

The role of problem finding in design work is highlighted in Schön's discussion of architecture education:[6]

> Given an architectural program and the description of a site, the student must first set a design problem and then go on to solve it. Setting the problem means framing the problematic situation presented by site and program in such a way as to create a springboard for design inquiry. The student must impose his preferences onto the situation in the form of choices whose consequences and implications he must subsequently work out—all within an emerging field of constraints.... Professional education emphasized problem-solving, but the most urgent and intractable issues of professional practice were those of problem finding. "Our interest," as one participant put it, "is not only how to pour the concrete for the highway, but what highway to build? When it comes to designing a ship, the question we have to ask is, which ship makes sense in terms of the problems of transportation?" (pp. 6, 11)

Top-down or hierarchical problem work

A widely held view is that designers approach design problems "systematically," by beginning at a functional level (goals, requirements, constraints, and so on) and then progressively working toward specific solutions, worrying about impasses along the way.[14,15] This design strategy fits well with the approach taken in most modern theoretical treatments of design, especially within engineering design, which have approached design problem solving as a matter of search in a problem space.[1] The codicil here is that design isn't always rigidly structured, even when it appears in this form of hierarchy. Linden J. Ball and colleagues have shown that highly experienced software designers deliberately deviate from a breadth-first approach to engage in deepening when they feel uncertain about the feasibility of a high-level solution or when they have encountered an impasse.[13]

Recognition and relaxation of assumptions

Herbert Simon argued that design problem solving involves the recognition of assumptions, that is, redefinition of the design problem.[1] Studies make it clear that this is a critical activity in creative design: As John Chris Jones said, "Changing the problem in order to find the solution is the most challenging and difficult part of designing."[7] Christopher Alexander described this process as involving a "satisficing" solution.[16] The designer decides what constraints to relax in order to respond to the most important ones. The design concept that emerges from this process of sacrificing secondary properties is a satisfying design solution, not necessarily an optimal one, as is generally approached by engineering optimization. The satisficing solution is a necessity when trying to address a complex design problem with so many parameters that optimization approaches would not be feasible.

Cognitive psychologists generally agree with this view or model of design. Linda Wills and Janet Kolodner refer to this as *design problem evolution*, a process in which the designer grapples with contradictions, ambiguities, and specification roadblocks and repeatedly reformulates the problem at hand.[17] Wayne Gray and John Anderson referred to this as *design cycles*:[18]

1. *Planning*—knowledge retrieval and the creation of an abstract solution
2. *Translating*—implementing or concretizing the abstract solution
3. *Revising*—modifying the implementation, the solution, or one's understanding

Recognition and relaxation of assumptions also figured prominently in Jones' discussion of design cycles:[7]

> A designer knows only too well the frustrating cycles of modification and remodification which have to be worked through before the delicate balance of his final design is achieved. The need to recycle continuously obliges a designer to progress towards novelty by modifying one design at a time instead of by comparing several alternative designs simultaneously. (p. 22)

Design by survival

Many designs reflect the survival of previous designs.[19,20] This can be design by reuse (which includes theft), design by adaptation, design by circumstance, or design by fitness. Design by reuse might be especially common in software design. During planning, the software designer's awareness of design goals and constraints brings to mind a known previous design. Along with it comes knowledge about the original context, including the design rationale and source situation. Such contextual knowledge, a "source situation model," is important, although it's rarely included in design documentation because reusable components are often believed to be generic.[11] François Détienne has provided a taxonomy of reuse situations based on the processes that seem to be involved, such as prospection (thinking ahead about how a design solution might be used in the future) and retrospection (realizing that a previous design might be adopted or adapted to a new problem).[11]

> "Changing the problem in order to find the solution is the most challenging and difficult part of designing."

Design by adaptation is when good and sometimes bad designs are adapted, diversified, and improved; an example would be the pencil.[21] Survival can also be a matter of circumstance. The history of the typewriter is a good example: The qwerty keyboard survived not because of its ergonomic soundness but because of mass production, the creation of a cadre of salesman, and the creation of a cohort of secretaries who taught other secretaries.[22]

Finally, design by survival can involve survival of the fit. An example would be the menu interface.

Design by deliberative recognition-priming

Research also shows that designers can recognize patterns, short-circuit any hierarchical or top-down strategy, and go right to a solution path.[13] In other words, they capitalize on their extensive conceptual knowledge of previous designs and design problems. Designers will opportunistically "take immediate advantage of solution opportunities."[13,23] Indeed, one technique that designers apply is that they constantly surround themselves with sketches. Often an entire wall is covered. The designer wants to be prepared for accidental discovery of a design solution that might already be present. In Alexander's pattern-based design technique,[16] complex designs are approached by recombining and orchestrating smaller and manageable modules that have proven appropriate for earlier, similar situations. This strategy is reminiscent of recognition-primed decision making,[24] which characterizes the decision making of experts in diverse fields other than design. It can also be regarded as a form of reasoning by analogy (though the distinction between analogy and case-based reasoning gets a bit fuzzy in the design context).[25]

Design by serendipitous recognition-priming

Recognition can go beyond comparison and refinement of existing designs. New designs can arise by serendipitous recognition stemming from the perception of just about anything—the ability to design "while walking down the street."[26] As Wills and Kolodner observed, "Creative designers often see solutions to pending design problems in the everyday objects surrounding them."[17] As in many arenas of human existence, people keep working on problems even when they aren't working on the problems. The human mind can be ravenously, if not just inherently, opportunistic. Comparisons, analogies, ideas pop up. Something is perceived, and an object gets thought of as serving some function other than the one ordinarily served. If the individual is prepared to recognize possible solutions, the serendipitous discovery may lead somewhere.

Design by collaboration and confrontation

A great many recent empirical studies have looked at design processes conducted by teams.[10] This research showed that patterns and cycles of individual and collective design activity do exist. These include not only collaborative interactions but also confrontations. Collaborative/confrontational design hinges on negotiation of acceptability and negotiation of trade-offs in light of constraints. Furthermore, collaboration can be opportunistic rather than patterned.[27,28]

Design via good, old-fashioned creativity

Each of these strategies hand-waves to creativity, in one way or another. Discussions of these strategies and stages typically acknowledge that they do not necessarily apply to creative design.[1] Creativity (as well as other design heuristics we've mentioned) has been and always will be needed, because design is a matter of coping with conflicting constraints that require trade-offs. Experienced designers concur; for example, Kenneth Grange says,[26]

> The creative mind that turns design toward production and away from the design for one off will have what I regard as true inventiveness. And that instinct—together with inquisitiveness—lies at the core of what produces useful and pleasing product designs.

The importance of the creative process for designing has fostered criticism of systematic design methods.[7,29] We now offer what we hope might be a first step toward a resolution.

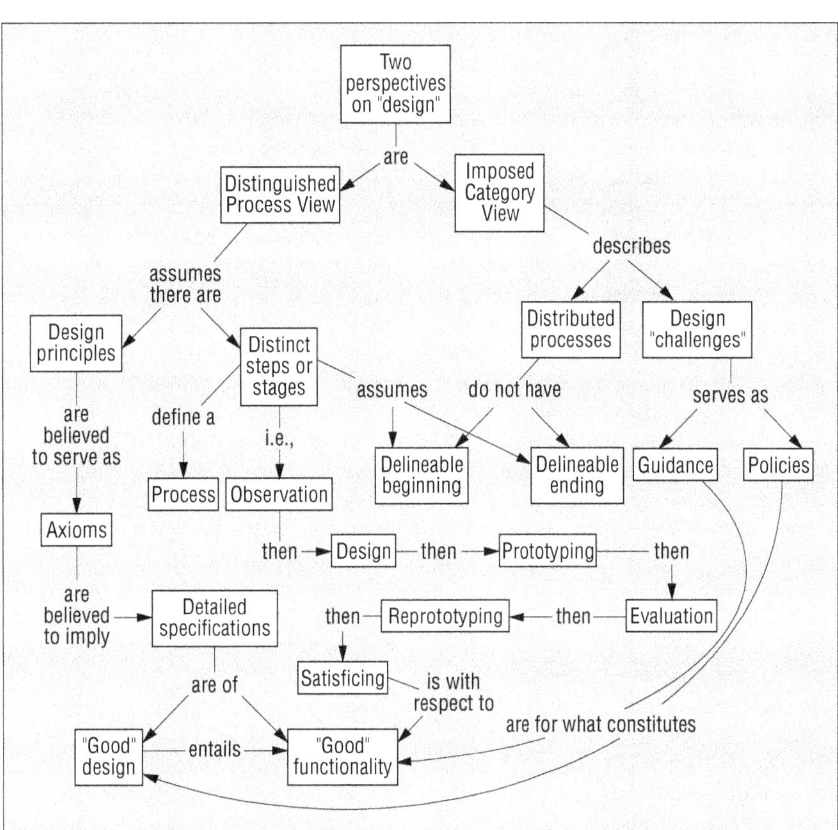

Figure 1. A Concept Map describing two views of design.

A macrocognitive view of design

Design qualifies as a phenomenon of macrocognition.[30] Designing isn't a basic building block of cognition that can be placed in a cause-effect sequence with such mental operations as associative priming, attention shifts, or retrieval of items from memory. But it does piggyback on microcognition. A clear example might be ravenous opportunism, which piggybacks on attentional phenomena and mechanisms.

Design (like essay writing) has been cited as an example of problems that can't be represented entirely in terms of problem spaces and stages of operations.[31] In fact, design work can be highly structured, have clear goals, and involve clear criteria for evaluating proposed solutions. It can involve many constraints (not too few), and these change over the problem-solving process. Design certainly involves great amounts of knowledge, even though we can't specify a priori what knowledge might be pertinent: New resources get induced during the course of problem solving, and "some information only shows up late in the design process after large amounts of search" (p. 188).[1] Hence, the problem spaces, if design were to be conceived in such terms, are indeterminate. Design is multiply structured. Try as we might, we can't shoehorn it into a single set of stages, or a single cycle. We can give key concepts in any given structural view alternative operational definitions from other structural views. Design is dynamically structured and depends on context. English lacks the non-Cartesian term we need here. Consider, for example, Détienne's struggle: "The overall process is cyclical rather than strictly linear.... [Design involves] phases of planning, translation, revision, implementing" (p. 19).[11] To cope with this conceptual/terminological problem, Détienne relies on Jens Rasmussen and Morten Lind's notion of levels of control.[32] Levels of control undergo multiple shifts, between activities that involve high-level knowledge to activities based on rules (for example, the execution of procedures such as trial-and-error).

These considerations suggest two fundamentally different views of design, depicted in the Concept Map in Figure 1. According to the Distinguishable Process View, design is a process we can distinguish by clear-cut beginning and ending points and that we can unpack into a sequence or series of stages or cycles. This view seeks design axioms or formulas. Ideally, the need for creativity, or at least the need to understand the role of creativity, would be minimized. According to this view, designers rely on heuristics such as recognition priming and ravenous opportunism, and design by survival is still the norm, because our notions of structured design haven't advanced far enough toward mechanization as part of the drive to emulate the human.

The Imposed Category View is that design is a category humans have imposed, not a category of the things-in-themselves. This view regards design as a macrocognitive phenomenon that is distributed, parallel with other macrocognitive phenomena, and highly dependent upon and highly interactive with them. It seeks design guidance, not design formulas. There is not, nor can there be, a yellow brick road to design. In some cases we can see design activity as having relatively clear-cut beginnings or endings, but phenomena such as ravenous opportunism caution us to avoid taking the exception to the rule and elevating it to the prototype. The Imposed Category View highlights Jones' caution about systematic approaches to design: There never was a promise of success guaranteed by systematic processing.[7] Indeed, design lore is that failures are often, if not usually, more useful and insightful than successes. Designers get lost while they explore. After a while, they might get lost in the wrong areas of exploration, areas that might not seem relevant for the design situation at hand. This is when they realize they must focus, and in order to do this, they might refer to design methods.

The human-centered design approach isn't to create microcognitive models that can be implemented as emulations of the human. Rather, it embraces the richness of human cognition so that it might be leveraged and extended by technologies that amplify. Human-centered design involves integrating technological novelty into the world of practice in a way that lets practitioners adapt to innovation. It must provide artifacts that embody innovation and the freedom to modify. In this way, human-centered design can be adjusted to the changing field of work.

With this spirit in mind, must we regard the relaxation of assumptions as an alternative to hierarchical problem work? Must we regard design by survival as an alternative to design by creativity? Are serendipity and confrontation mutually exclusive? Though none of these questions is entirely rhetorical, our answer in all cases is "no."

Design isn't a process. We aren't claiming that there are no interesting empirical phenomena involved in designing, but only rarely does designing have clear-cut beginnings and endings. While stages or cycles might be imposed, designing is never divorced from other ongoing mental activities. Designing involves all the strategies we've listed, and more. And these are typically parallel, highly interactive, and context-sensitive. The principles of human-centered computing discussed in earlier essays in this department aren't cookbook entries; they aren't design axioms. Rather, they are challenges for designers. Project managers or designers may choose to adopt them as policies if their goal is to create good, complex cognitive systems.[33] ■

Robert R. Hoffman is a research scientist at the Institute for Human and Machine Cognition. Contact him at the IHMC, 40 Alcaniz St., Pensacola, FL 32501; rhoffman@ihmc.us.

Axel Roesler is a PhD student at the Cognitive Systems Engineering Laboratory at Ohio State University's Institute of Ergonomics. Contact him at the Cognitive Systems Eng. Lab., 210 Baker Systems, 1971 Neil Ave., Columbus, OH 43210; roesler.1@osu.edu.

Brian M. Moon is a research associate at Klein Associates. Contact him at Klein Associates, 1750 Commerce Center Blvd. N., Fairborn, OH 45324; brian@decisionmaking.com.

Acknowledgments

We prepared this article through participation in the Advanced Decision Architectures Collaborative Technology Alliance, sponsored by the US Army Research Laboratory under cooperative agreement DAAD19-01-2-0009.

References

1. H.A. Simon, "The Structure of Ill-Structured Problems," *Artificial Intelligence*, vol. 4, 1973, pp. 181–210.
2. M. Endsley and R. Hoffman, "The Sacagawea Principle," *IEEE Intelligent Systems*, vol. 17, no. 6, 2002, pp. 80–85.
3. D. Diderot and J. d'Alembert, eds., *Encyclopédie ou Dictionnaire raisonné des sciences, des arts et des métiers*, Le Breton, 1751–1772; compact edition published by Readex Microprint Corp., 1969; selected articles appear at www.hti.umich.edu/d/did.
4. R.R. Hoffman et al., "A Rose by Any Other Name … Would Probably Be Given an Acronym," *IEEE Intelligent Systems*, vol. 17, no. 4, 2002, pp. 72–80.
5. N. Bayazit, "Investigating Design: A Review of Forty Years of Design Research," *Design Issues*, vol. 20, no. 1, 2004, pp. 16–29.
6. D.A. Schön, *The Reflective Practitioner*, Basic Books, 1983, pp. 7, 10–11.
7. J.C. Jones, *Design Methods: Seeds of Human Futures*, Van Nostrand Reinhold, 1970.
8. V. Hubka and E. Eder, "A Scientific Approach to Engineering Design," *Design Studies*, vol. 8, no. 3, 1987, pp. 123–137.
9. H.A. Simon, *The Sciences of the Artificial*, MIT Press, 1969.
10. N.H. Cross, H. Cristiaans, and K. Dorst, eds., *Analyzing Design Activity*, John Wiley & Sons, 1994.
11. F. Détienne, "Memory of Past Designs: Distinctive Roles in Individual and Collective Design," *Cognitive Technology*, vol. 8, 2003, pp. 16–24.
12. M. Suwa and B. Tversky, "What Do Architects and Students Perceive in Their Design Sketches? A Protocol Analysis," *Design Studies*, vol. 18, 1997, pp. 385–403.
13. L.J. Ball et al., "Problem Solving Strategies and Expertise in Engineering Design," *Thinking and Reasoning*, vol. 3, 1997, pp. 427–270.
14. L.B. Archer, "Systematic Method of Designers," *Developments in Design Methodology*, N. Cross, ed., John Wiley & Sons, 1965, pp. 57–82.
15. S.P. Davies, "Characterizing the Program Design Activity: Neither Strictly Top-Down nor Globally Opportunistic," *Behaviour and Information Technology*, vol. 10, 1991, pp. 173–190.
16. C. Alexander, *Notes on the Synthesis of Form*, Harvard Univ. Press, 1964.
17. L.M. Wills and J.L. Kolodner, "Explaining Serendipitous Recognition in Design," *Proc. 16th Ann. Conf. Cognitive Science Soc.*, Lawrence Erlbaum, 1994, pp. 940–945.
18. W.D. Gray and J.R. Anderson, "Change-Episodes in Coding: When and How Do Programmers Change Their Code?" *Empirical Studies of Programmers: 2nd Workshop*, G.M. Olson, S. Sheppard, and E. Soloway, eds., Ablex, 1987, pp. 185–197.
19. J.-M. Burkhardt and F. Détienne, "An Empirical Study of Software Reuse by Experts in Object-Oriented Design," *Proc. IFIP Int'l Conf. Human-Computer Interaction* (Interact 95), Chapman & Hall, 1995, pp. 38–138.
20. M.B. Rosson and J.M. Carroll, "Active Pro-

gramming Strategies in Reuse," *Proc. 7th European Conf. Object-Oriented Programming* (ECOOP 93), Springer-Verlag, 1993, pp. 4–18.

21. H. Petroski, *The Pencil: A History of Design and Circumstance*, Alfred A. Knopf, 1992.

22. R.R. Hoffman, "How to Doom Yourself to Repeat the Past: Some Reflections on the History of Cognitive Technology," *Cognitive Technology*, vol. 2, 1997, pp. 4–15.

23. R. Guindon, "Designing the Design Process: Exploiting Opportunistic Thoughts," *Human-Computer Interaction*, vol. 5, 1990, pp. 305–344.

24. G.A. Klein, "Recognition-Primed Decisions," *Advances in Man-Machine Research*, vol. 5, W. Rouse, ed., JAI Press, 1989, pp. 42–92.

25. M. Visser, "Use of Episodic Knowledge and Information in Design Problem Solving," *Design Studies*, vol. 16, 1995, pp. 171–187.

26. D. Gibbs, ed., *Pentagram: The Compendium*, Phaidon Press, 1993.

27. F. Détienne, *Software Design: Cognitive Aspects*, Springer-Verlag, 2002.

28. P. Falzon, "Dialogues Fonctionelles et Activité Collective [Functional Dialogs and Collective Activities]," *Le Travail Humaine*, vol. 57, 1994, pp. 299–312.

29. H.W.J. Rittel, "Second Generation Design Methods," *Developments in Design Methodology*, N. Cross, ed., Wiley Interscience, 1972, pp. 317–327.

30. G. Klein et al., "Macrocognition," *IEEE Intelligent Systems*, vol. 18, no. 3, 2003, pp. 81–85.

31. C.M. Eastman, "Cognitive Processes and Ill-Defined Problems: A Case Study from Design," *Proc. 1st Int'l Joint Conf. Artificial Intelligence* (IJCAI), AAAI Press, 1969, pp. 669–690.

32. J. Rasmussen and M. Lind, *A Model of Human Decision Making in Complex Systems and Its Use for Design of System Control Strategies*, tech. report M-2349, Risø Nat'l Laboratory, Roskilde, Denmark, 1982.

33. R.R. Hoffman and W.C. Elm, *The Procurement Woes: Handcuffs on the Development of Intelligent Systems*, tech. report, Inst. for Human and Machine Cognition, Pensacola, Fla., 2004.

Chapter 18: Keeping It Too Simple: How the Reductive Tendency Affects Cognitive Engineering

P.J. Feltovich, R.R. Hoffman, D. Woods, and A. Roesler, "Keeping It Too Simple: How the Reductive Tendency Affects Cognitive Engineering," *IEEE Intelligent Systems*, vol. 19, no. 3, May/June 2004, pp. 90–94. doi: 10.1109/MIS.2004.14

Certain features of tasks make them especially difficult for humans. These constitute leverage points for applying intelligent technologies, but there's a flip side. Designing complex cognitive systems is itself a tough task. Cognitive engineers face the same challenges in designing systems that users confront in working the tasks that the systems are intended to aid. We discuss these issues. We assume that the cognitive engineers will invoke one or more knowledge shields when they are confronted with evidence that their understanding and planning involves a reductive understanding. The knowledge shield phenomenon suggests that it will take effort to change the reductive mindset that people might bring to the design of a CCS.

Keeping It Too Simple: How the Reductive Tendency Affects Cognitive Engineering

Paul J. Feltovich and Robert R. Hoffman, *Institute for Human and Machine Cognition*
David Woods and Axel Roesler, *Ohio State University*

Certain features of tasks make them especially difficult for humans. These constitute leverage points for applying intelligent technologies, but there's a flip side. Designing complex cognitive systems is itself a tough task. Cognitive engineers face the same challenges in designing systems that users confront in working the tasks that the systems are intended to aid.

Research background

Research conducted under the rubric of Cognitive Flexibility Theory examined learning and performance in medical education and, in particular, how people learn and understand the cardiovascular system.[1,2] The research identified characteristics of learning material and performance situations that cause cognitive difficulty for learners and operators. It also determined how people respond to these elements of difficulty. That research found that learners and practitioners often deal with complexity through oversimplification, which can lead to misconception and faulty knowledge application.

The dimensions of difficulty

Eleven dimensions make tasks difficult and require mental effort.

Static vs. dynamic. Are important aspects of a situation captured by a fixed "snapshot," or are the critical characteristics captured only by the changes from frame to frame? Are phenomena static and scalar, or do they possess dynamic, vector-like characteristics?

Discrete vs. continuous. Do processes proceed in discernable steps, or are they unbreakable continua? Can we describe attributes by using a few categories (for example, dichotomous classifications such as large/small), or must we recognize and use continuous dimensions (such as size) or numerous categorical distinctions?

Separable vs. interactive. Do processes occur independently or with only weak interaction, or do strong interaction and interdependence exist?

Sequential vs. simultaneous. Do processes occur one at a time, or do multiple processes occur at the same time?

Homogeneous vs. heterogeneous. Are components or explanatory schemes uniform (or similar) across a system, or are they diverse?

Single vs. multiple representations. Do elements in a situation afford single or just a few interpretations, functional uses, categorizations, and so on, or do they afford many? Do we need multiple representations (such as multiple perspectives, schemas, analogies, models, or case precedents) to capture and convey the meaning of a process or situation?

Mechanism vs. organicism. Are effects traceable to simple and direct causal agents, or are they the product of more systemwide, organic functions? Can we gain important and accurate understandings by understanding just parts of the system, or must we understand the entire system to understand even the parts well?

Linear vs. nonlinear. Are functional relationships linear or nonlinear (that is, are relationships between input and output variables proportional or nonproportional)? Can a single line of explanation convey a concept or account for a phenome-

Editors: Robert R. Hoffman, Patrick J. Hayes, and Kenneth M. Ford
Institute for Human and Machine Cognition, University of West Florida
rhoffman@ai.uwf.edu

non, or does adequate coverage require multiple overlapping lines of explanation?

Universal vs. conditional. Do guidelines and principles hold in much the same way (without needing substantial modification) across different situations, or does their application require considerable context sensitivity?

Regular vs. irregular. Does a domain exhibit a high degree of regularity or typicality across cases, or do cases differ considerably even when they have the same name? Do concepts and phenomena exhibit strong elements of symmetry and repeatable patterns, or is there a prevalence of asymmetry and an absence of consistent pattern?

Surface vs. deep. Are important elements for understanding and for guiding action delineated and apparent on the surface of a situation, or are they more covert, relational, and abstract?

The consequences of complexity

The research also revealed serious consequences when the material to be learned or understood exhibits the latter alternative in each of the above 11 dimensions—that is, when

- Events are dynamic, simultaneous and parallel, and organic (evolving, emergent) rather than governed by simple cause and effect
- Event parameters are continuous and highly interactive
- Events involve heterogeneous components or explanatory principles, nonlinear dynamics, and multiple context-dependencies
- Events can be understood by multiple representations
- Cases show asymmetries and irregularities
- Key principles are abstract and nonobvious

In such cases,

- Learners and practitioners tend to interpret situations as though they were characterized by simpler alternatives
- Their understandings tend to be reductive—that is, they tend to simplify
- They tend to try to defend their simple understandings when confronted with facts that suggest that the situation is more complex than what they suppose
- Overcoming these defenses requires practice, experience, and mental effort

The reductive tendency

The term *reductive bias*[3] has been used to describe people's inclination to construct overly simplistic understandings and categories. However, we do not see this as a bias in the sense in which cognitive science frequently uses the term. Rather, this reductive tendency is an inevitable consequence of how people learn.[4] Of necessity, when people are forming a new understanding or developing a new category, their knowledge is incomplete. How else could it be? People perceive, understand, and learn distinctions only through additional experience and thought. So, at any point in time, a person's understanding of anything that's at all complex, even domain experts' understandings, is bound to be simplifying at least in some respects.

> When learners are confronted with evidence contrary to their views, they perform mental maneuvers to rationalize their faulty beliefs without fundamentally altering them.

In areas of complex cognition, the reductive tendency can lead to significant misconceptions and error-ridden performance.[5] In addition, the misconceptions might resist change. When learners are confronted with evidence contrary to their views, they perform mental maneuvers to rationalize their faulty beliefs without fundamentally altering them. These protective operations are called *knowledge shields*, and researchers have identified 23 of them.[5]

One such shield is the *demean effect.* When confronted with the evidence, learners acknowledge that the evidence might be true but dismiss it as trivial—"it's not a big deal." Here's an example:

> Instruction: As a vessel expands during the ascending phase of a pulse, this doesn't mean that all the blood in the expanded vessel simply flows downstream through a now larger vessel, since some of it, for instance, flows into the expansion of the vessel itself.
>
> Student response: (long pause) "Um, I'm going to agree. It makes sense that some of it would flow into the expansion of the vessel, but I'm sure it's not a big part of it."

Two other knowledge shields are *argument from faulty causal reasoning* and *extirpation*. In the first, the learner constructs a false causal explanation, consistent with his or her belief, for the anomalous evidence. In the second, the learner isolates the phenomenon to be explained from its real context. In the following example, the student uses both shields to avoid a real change in belief:

> Instruction: In the pulsing cardiovascular system, some of the energy produced by the heart is used up in making blood flow into and out of the expansion of vessel walls. Hence, factors associated with flow into and out of the vessel walls, such as stiffness and heart rate, contribute to opposition to blood flow.
>
> Student response: "And I agree with that, um, because when blood goes into the expanded area and then that expanded area contracts, the blood's gonna go both forward and backward, and this is going to create opposition to the other blood coming in."

Although Cognitive Flexibility Theory and the reductive tendency first had their impact in medical education, they have found wider application.[6,7] In particular, they have implications for our own understanding of the nature of *complex sociotechnical systems.* That is, what if our own (that is, cognitive engineers') understanding of CSSs is itself subject to a reductive tendency?

The nature of complex sociotechnical systems

CSSs are workplaces in which individuals act as collectives with the support of information technology, to conduct cognitive work.[8,9] Cognitive work involves obtaining, using, and sharing knowledge in the pursuit of goals under changing circumstances. Goals include empowering others to act according to that knowledge or a certain state of situation awareness. David Woods and his colleagues have identified consistent patterns ("Laws That Govern Cognitive Work") to activities and problems in CSSs, and to the principles governing human-machine interaction in cognitive work.[10,11] Previous installments of this department have presented some of these as principles of human-centered computing.

CSSs don't sit still, in at least two respects. First, new technologies provide new capabilities, but these spawn new expectations, roles, and ways of doing things. They can also introduce new complexities—for example, increased interconnectedness, interdependency, and need for coordination among players. Workers will employ various adaptations, including work-arounds, to function successfully in the new environment.[12] As Woods has written, "Whatever the artifacts and however autonomous they are under certain conditions, people create, operate and modify these artifacts in human systems for human purposes."[10]

Second, all the workplace participants operate from personally constructed models of the work to be done and of the other parties involved, including their roles, capabilities, and needs. This means that the CSS is inhabited by multiple viewpoints, multiple value systems, multiple ways of operating, multiple assessments of responsibility and authority, and the like. Different people will model the work environment's key elements differently, depending on such things as their backgrounds, experiences, responsibilities, personal agendas, and particular tasks.

This portrayal involves considerable complexity, including

- Constant readaptation, and hence constant dynamics and change
- Strong interaction and interdependence of processes and people
- Multiple interpretations, ambitions, and viewpoints
- Heterogeneous capabilities and methods
- The need to interpret and respond appropriately to high degrees of context sensitivity

This characterization of the complex workplace, at a general level, conforms precisely with the 11 dimensions of difficulty.

The implication for cognitive engineering: The "envisioned world" problem

If the reductive tendency affects the design, and redesign, of CSSs in the same ways it affects other complex domains of learning and knowing, what are the implications?

Static/dynamic

If the reductive tendency affects this dimension, cognitive engineers would be prone to construe dynamic situations as more static than they really are. The reductive assumption for CSSs would be that the way work is carried out might be improved but will be fundamentally the same after an intervention. This reduction probably also construes the day-to-day practice of work as being more routine than it actually is.

Discrete/continuous

The reductive tendency on this dimension would treat continuous processes as being more incremental than they really are. The cognitive engineer might be prone to think of continuous processes in terms of discernable steps. Perhaps most important, cognitive engineers might fail to anticipate that adaptive change will occur at all, and if it does, they might think that it consists of easily detected stages or steps.

> The CSS is inhabited by multiple viewpoints, multiple value systems, multiple ways of operating, multiple assessments of responsibility and authority, and the like.

Separable/interactive

Here, the reductive tendency would treat processes and people as functioning more in isolation and insulation than they actually do. The cognitive engineer might fail to appreciate the widespread interdependency of effects across workplace components. The reductive assumption would be that changing a component of the workplace would have only local, contained effects that wouldn't ripple throughout the operation following an intervention.

Sequential/simultaneous

The reductive tendency for this dimension resembles that for separability/interactiveness. However, here it emphasizes thinking of the work practice as a linear set of workplace steps, as in an assembly line, rather than a matter of interactiveness and simultaneity. This reductive assumption can, and often does, result in technologies that impose difficulties in coordination and communication, and in building common ground. This leads designers to be confident that demands for coordination have been reduced, whereas when the system is in use, the practitioners experience automation "surprises."

Homogeneous/heterogeneous

The reductive tendency would result in assumptions that the processes, values, ways of doing things, cultural norms, abilities, loyalties, and so forth are pretty much the same across the many diverse units of the CSS—a kind of uniformity tendency. This reduction's effect in design would be that the cognitive engineer fails to anticipate the diversity of reactions and adaptations to a workplace change.

Single/multiple representations (functions)

The reductive tendency would occur when the cognitive engineer doesn't realize that appraisals of the CSS, before and after an intervention, can vary greatly among different stakeholders. For example, a system's usability can vary across different perspectives, both with regard to the operation of the workplace itself (for example, its profitability, degree of stress, efficiency, and quality) and from the viewpoint of different stakeholders (for example, management, workers, unions, shareholders, the US Occupational Safety & Health Administration, and the US Internal Revenue Service). This tendency would also involve various kinds of fixations on the cognitive engineer's part—that is, envisioning the future (for example, how some device will be used or how some group will react to a change) in a rigid, fixed way.

Mechanism/organicism

The reductive tendency would treat CSS operation as a set of low-level, direct causes and effects. It would involve no consideration of complex, nonlinear, interactive, self-organizing characteristics that can emerge because the CSS has qualities and processes that are more than the sum of its component parts.

Linear/nonlinear

The reductive tendency would involve the assumption that changes, effects of interventions, and perturbations of various kinds to the CSS will have incremental, manageable consequences. This would entail failure to account for or anticipate the effects of tight coupling that produce cascading effects and other nonlinear responses. As a result, for example, developers can miss the complexity induced by the coupling (for example, how effects-at-a-distance complicate diagnostic reasoning), and their designed system would leave the practitioner unsupported.

Universal/conditional

The reductive tendency would be the assumption that a design principle has the same applicability and effects throughout the many different and changing contexts of work and practice. That is, the effects, embodied in the design principle, will hold fairly universally across differing practice environments. Indeed, one can sense this reductive tendency in operation in previous essays in this department.

The reductive tendency at work in design and envisionment

An example of how the reductive tendency affects the design of CSSs appears in the discussion of the "substitution myth."[13] As David Woods and his colleagues note frequently, the myth is that when some work system component is replaced by some device, the work's fundamental nature will remain essentially the same. That is, the replacement device will function in much the same way that the original component did (although it might be faster, more efficient, and so on). This is almost never the case; the work system changes dramatically, often in unintended, unanticipated, and undesirable ways.

Clearly, we can attribute the substitution myth's pervasiveness to the reductive tendency affecting designers on several of the dimensions of difficulty. For example, the myth involves treating dynamic work as static, treating interdependencies as being compartmentalized, and regarding the irregular nature of work as more regular and routine than it is.

So, what can we do about this? Is simple awareness of the reductive tendency and the dimensions of difficulty enough?

Mitigating the reductive tendency

Knowledge of the oversimplifications that designers will likely commit in CSS environments should influence the creation of intelligent instructional and performance support tools. This is already happening. There are systems that seem to acknowledge, and avoid, reductive tendencies. There are tools that help operators comprehend the implications of numerous, interdependent, and constantly changing variables that affect successful execution of a task—for example, flying an airplane.[14] Devices exist that warn doctors and patients about adverse interactions among drugs and activities. Instructional systems based on Cognitive Flexibility Theory are being built to help learners analyze and comprehend difficult material from multiple viewpoints.[15]

But the dimensions of difficulty themselves should provide explicit guidance for cognitive engineers who are confronted with challenges in CSS design. The dimensions, as well as people's known reactions to them, might help suggest leverage points, strategies, heuristics, and even technologies to help the cognitive engineer overcome reductive tendencies and effectively explore the envisioned world. A great opportunity exists here for creating tools that help those who design CSSs to anticipate and plan for the effects on work practice to be expected from new designs or redesigns.

Knowledge of the oversimplifications that designers will likely commit in CSS environments should influence the creation of intelligent instructional and performance support tools.

Finally, we must assume that cognitive engineers will invoke one or more knowledge shields when they're confronted with evidence that their understanding and planning involves a reductive understanding. The knowledge shield phenomenon suggests that it will take effort to change the reductive mindset that people might bring to designing a CSS and envisioning its nature after an intervention. ∎

Acknowledgments

We prepared this column through participation in the Advanced Decision Architectures Collaborative Technology Alliance, sponsored by the US Army Research Laboratory under cooperative agreement DAAD19-01-2-0009.

References

1. P.J. Feltovich, R.J. Spiro, and R.L. Coulson, "Issues of Expert Flexibility in Contexts Characterized by Complexity and Change," *Expertise in Context: Human and Machine*, P.J. Feltovich, K.M. Ford, and R.R. Hoffman, eds., AAAI Press, 1997, pp. 125–146.

2. R.J. Spiro et al., "Cognitive Flexibility Theory: Advanced Knowledge Acquisition in Ill-Structured Domains," *Proc. 10th Ann. Conf. Cognitive Science Soc.*, Lawrence Erlbaum Associates, 1988, pp. 375–383.

3. P.J. Feltovich, R.J. Spiro, and R.L. Coulson, "The Nature of Conceptual Understanding in Biomedicine: The Deep Structure of Complex Ideas and the Development of Misconceptions," *Cognitive Science in Medicine*, D. Evans and V.L. Patel, eds., MIT Press, 1989, pp. 113–172.

4. J. Feldman, "The Simplicity Principle in Human Category Learning," *Current Directions in Psychological Science*, vol. 12, no. 6, 2003, pp. 227–232.

5. P.J. Feltovich, R.L. Coulson, and R.J. Spiro, "Learners' (Mis)understanding of Important and Difficult Concepts: A Challenge for Smart Machines in Education," *Smart Machines in Education: The Coming Revolution in Educational Technology*, K.D. Forbus and P.J. Feltovich, eds., AAAI Press, 2001, pp. 349–376.

6. R.I. Cook and D.D. Woods, "Operating at the Sharp End: The Complexity of Human Error," *Human Error in Medicine*, M.S. Bogner, ed., Lawrence Erlbaum Associates, 1994, pp. 255–310.

7. C.E. Hmelo-Silver and M.G. Pfeffer, "Comparing Expert and Novice Understanding of a Complex System from the Perspective of Structures, Behaviors, and Functions," *Cognitive Science*, vol. 28, no. 1, 2004, pp. 127–138.

8. J.M. Carroll and M.B. Rosson, "Getting around the Task-Artifact Cycle: How to Make Claims and Design by Scenario," *ACM Trans. Information Systems*, vol. 10, no. 2, 1992, pp. 181–212.

9. T. Winograd and F. Flores, *Understanding Computers and Cognition*, Ablex, 1986.

10. D.D. Woods, "Steering the Reverberations of Technological Change on Fields of Practice: Laws That Govern Cognitive Work," *Proc. 24th Ann. Meeting Cognitive Science Soc.*, Lawrence Erlbaum Associates, 2002, pp. 14–17.

11. D.D. Woods and S.W.A. Dekker, "Anticipating the Effects of Technological Change: A New Era of Dynamics for Human Factors," *Theoretical Issues in Ergonomic Science*, vol. 1, no. 3, 2000, pp. 272–282.

12. P. Koopman and R.R. Hoffman, "Work-arounds, Make-Work, and Kludges," *IEEE Intelligent Systems*, vol. 18, no. 6, 2003, pp. 70–75.

13. K. Christoffersen and D.D. Woods, "How to Make Automated Systems Team Players," *Advances in Human Performance and Cognitive Engineering Research*, vol. 2, E. Salas, ed., JAI Press/Elsevier, 2002, pp. 2–12.

14. A. Gerold, "OZ: A Revolution in Cockpit Display," *Aviation Magazine*, Oct. 2003, pp. 27–32.

15. R.J. Spiro et al., "Cognitive Flexibility, Constructivism, and Hypertext: Random Access Instruction for Advanced Knowledge Acquisition in Ill-Structured Domains," *Educational Technology*, vol. 31, no. 5, 1991, pp. 24–33.

Paul J. Feltovich is a research scientist at the University of West Florida's Institute for Human and Machine Cognition. Contact him at the Inst. for Human and Machine Cognition, 40 Alcaniz St., Pensacola, FL 32501; pfeltovich@ai.uwf.edu.

Robert R. Hoffman is a research scientist at the Institute for Human and Machine Cognition. Contact him at the IHMC, 40 Alcaniz St., Pensacola, FL 32501; rhoffman@ihmc.us.

David Woods is a professor of industrial and systems engineering and the coordinator of the Cognitive Engineering Laboratory at Ohio State University. Contact him at the Cognitive Systems Eng. Lab, Industrial and Systems Eng., 210 Baker Systems, Ohio State Univ., 1971 Neil Ave., Columbus, OH 43210; woods@csel.eng.ohio-state.edu.

Axel Roesler is a PhD student at the Cognitive Systems Engineering Laboratory at Ohio State University's Institute of Ergonomics. Contact him at the Cognitive Systems Eng. Lab., 210 Baker Systems, 1971 Neil Ave., Columbus, OH 43210; roesler.1@osu.edu.

Chapter 19: Influencing versus Informing Design, Part 1: A Gap Analysis

R.R. Hoffman and S.V. Deal, "Influencing versus Informing Design, Part 1: A Gap Analysis," *IEEE Intelligent Systems*, vol. 23, no. 5, Sep./Oct. 2008, pp. 78–81. doi: 10.1109/MIS.2008.83

The collaboration of cognitive systems engineers with systems engineers is motivated by the goal of creating human-centered systems. However, there can be a gap in this collaboration. In presentations at professional meetings about cognitive systems engineering projects, we often hear that one or another method of cognitive task analysis was employed in order to inform design. But what software developers need is designs. This is the first of two essays about the gap between the products of cognitive task analysis and the needs of the software engineers. We discuss a success story of cognitive systems engineering for a large-scale system, a project that coped with the practical constraints of time pressure and the challenge of designing for an envisioned world when system elements could not be fully specified in advance. This project relied on a particular product from cognitive task analysis, the abstraction-decomposition matrix, that speaks in a language that corresponds with the needs and goals of the software designers.

Influencing versus Informing Design, Part 1: A Gap Analysis

Robert R. Hoffman, *Institute for Human and Machine Cognition*
Steven V. Deal, *Deal Corporation*

In this and the next essay in this department, we reflect on the mismatch that can occur between the promise of intelligent technology and the results of technological interventions. Cognitive task analysis (CTA) has been offered as a way of revealing actual work, especially macrocognition, but the system development process can fail to bridge the gap between the products of CTA and the needs of software engineers. This is the first of two essays about bridging this gap. In this essay we discuss a success story of cognitive systems engineering to illustrate a product from CTA that speaks in a language that's similar to that of software designers. The second essay is about bridging the gap going from the other direction, providing designers with a CTA method that they themselves can use to ramp up their understanding of end users' true work needs.

A gap analysis

Practitioners of cognitive systems engineering (many psychologists, but also anthropologists, sociologists, and others) conduct CTA and generate analytical outputs that are intended to inform the design of software systems (and other tools, of course).[1,2] Conclusions from the results of CTA take the form of general guidance, as the following examples show.

- Donald Norman, among others, has asserted that information technology cannot be designed without taking into consideration the full context in which the technology is used. Individual workers and the computational devices with which they work are nested in larger organizational contexts: "Social groups require flexibility, cooperation, and resilience, allowing diverse personalities, interests, and work styles to interact."[3]
- The Sacagawea Principle, discussed in a previous essay in this department, asserts, "Human-centered computational tools are ones that support active organization of information, active search for information, active exploration of information, reflection on the meaning of information, and evaluation and choice among action sequence alternatives."[4]

Such guidance is certainly valuable and useful. Guidance cautions us about the complexities of task allocation[5] and the ironies of automation.[6,7] Thus, guidance informs the design process. It could be taken as policy for design or a criterion for design success. But such principles can have only an indirect and limited influence on software design itself. In presentations about cognitive systems engineering projects at professional meetings, we often hear that one or another method of CTA was employed to inform design. But what software developers need is designs. That's the gap. The intent to inform frustrates both the practitioners who are on the giving end and the engineers who are on the receiving end of this transaction. Figure 1 shows the difference between the engineering path to design and the cognitive systems engineering path to design.

In the flow at the top, systems engineers decompose a system into subsystems that are handed off to design engineers. These engineers treat the design in progres-

Editors: Robert R. Hoffman, Patrick J. Hayes, and Kenneth M. Ford
Institute for Human and Machine Cognition
rhoffman@ihmc.us

sively more detail until they can provide diagrams, spreadsheets, and statements that enable manufacturers and software developers to cut metal or write code. So, at the time that requirements and specifications are crafted, the verification methodology is also specified. The engineering advantage of this is that the hardware and software producers have a means of determining when they've adequately completed the task. Their accomplishments are subsequently subjected to reviews that are progressively more integrated from configured items to operational system.

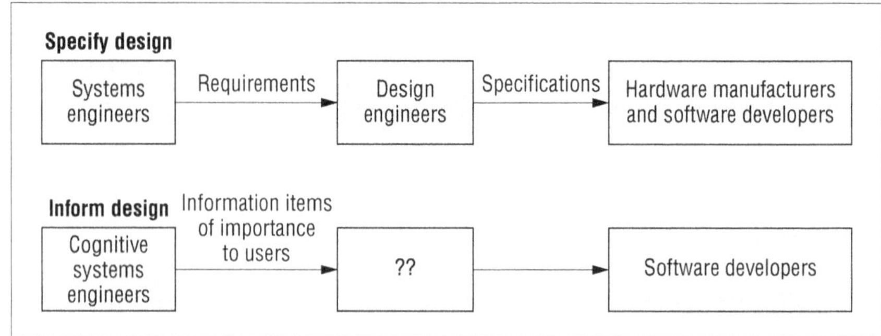

Figure 1. Specifying versus informing design. The engineering decomposition (top) involves specifications; the cognitive systems engineering decomposition (bottom) involves the requirements of the cognitive work.

In the flow at the bottom, cognitive systems engineers investigate the workers' decision requirements and information requirements. These engineers generate and deliver reports to the developers, but the latter can't proceed because the content isn't in the form they need. What's lacking in this progression is translation of the CTA content into a language that helps a product be built or coded.

We illustrate this situation with a hypothetical but realistic example.

Designing an interface

Cognitive systems engineers working on cockpit automation conducted a CTA and determined that the rate of change of aircraft altitude was a critical piece of information to include in a particular display. They presented this finding to engineers as a text report along with a drawing of the envisioned user interface. In theory, the software developer would replicate the drawing in the prototype user interface, and the design's success could be determined by inspection. But the developer couldn't proceed with interface development—a number of questions were unanswered. Here are two examples:

- The text mentioned an arrow indicating that the aircraft is ascending or descending. It's indicated statically on the drawing. What triggers the change? The aircraft is oscillating around a nominal altitude at all times; does the arrow change directions when the altitude moves up six inches, six feet, six yards, or a hundred feet?
- How does the representation play with other information items that must be integrated into the display? Is the graphic too large? Too small?

The information that informs design wasn't concise enough to enable the software expert to efficiently do his work with a high level of confidence that the job would be done correctly. The software engineer needs a specification statement describing an altitude object or altitude subroutine, including language that translates the cognitive requirements into build statements. Here are examples:

- The altitude subroutine shall output an altitude rate indicator of (horizontal and vertical) dimensions no less than 300 by 200 pixels.
- The altitude rate indicator shall provide an altitude-versus-time analog display (y, x) as well as a digital readout of current altitude.
- Analog altitude values shall be sampled and presented in one-minute increments.
- The altitude rate indicator shall include a red (RGB 255,0,0) directional arrow with dimensions no less than (horizontal, vertical) 5 by 200 pixels.
- When indicating a direction change, the directional arrow shall have a tolerance of ± 50 feet to prevent rapid changes in direction during level flight.

Even this set of bullets doesn't represent a fully fleshed-out design. It's meant to show that the specific language lets the software developer do a job with a high degree of confidence that the product is what the cognitive systems engineers intended. It's verifiable. Although the statements might not result in toto from the CTA, they're substantive expressions needed in the engineering world.

CTA guidance such as "enable the pilot to identify a track" refers primarily to the pilot's principal task goals. They are intended to be requirements, but at such a high level of abstraction they're desirements, subject to broad interpretation.[8] In fairness, a good deal of explanatory material customarily surrounds such guidance. To be effective, that material must be transformed into concise expressions that can be acted upon. Such specifications refer back to the text documents for traceability's sake, but designers shouldn't need to depend upon the text documents to do their jobs.

The user interface design that the cognitive systems engineers produced might have been preceded by a number of interviews and prototypes that examined the user's ability to perceive, interpret, and project the situation from the information presented. Storyboard prototypes used in this fashion can be very valuable, but a software developer still won't know which attributes of the prototype are the important ones. On the other hand, some developers prefer inputs in the form of storyboards or mock-ups because it lets them be creative. When developers interpret prototypes in a way that makes them aesthetically pleasing, they may have violated cognitive principles that went into the prototypes' creation. (This is one of the traps of designer-centered design.) When cognitive systems engineers collaborate with a software developer who has this approach, it must be made clear that what the software engineer first creates is a higher-fidelity prototype, not the operational code.

Although the software engineer might correctly apply user interface standards and conventions and even produce an exciting presentation, it might be uninformed by the work context that is the basis for cognitive engineering value. This means that the system will likely

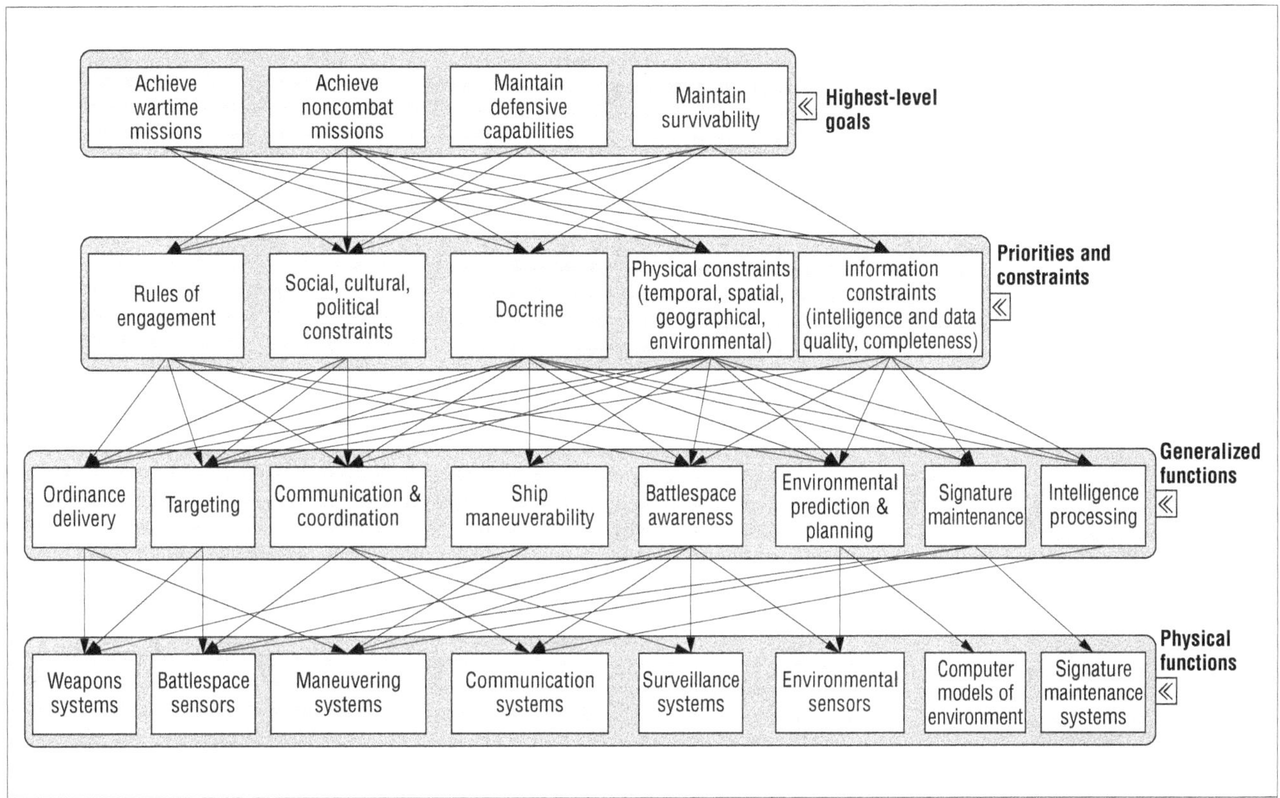

Figure 2. An example Abstraction-Decomposition Matrix for analyzing bridge operations. From top to bottom rows: Goals are constrained, constraints determine the general functions, and general functions are carried out by specific functions. (figure adapted from A. Bisantz and colleagues[10])

be less effective than it should be, that it might well be user-hostile, and that it will probably force the work to consume more resources than necessary. In a nutshell, it won't be human-centered.

Ultimately there must be a means for manufacturers and reviewers to assess that the job is done and that it has been done correctly and executed to greatest advantage. But not all requirements and specifications have to be in the form of "shall" statements. Model-based systems engineering generates executable replicas of a system that can also serve as specifications. Other people advocate the use of multimedia—drawings, interviews, videos—to communicate the design to manufacturers and developers. Whatever the form, the point of the specification is to communicate distinctively what must be produced and how to judge when it's completed correctly.

There are clear cases in which teams of researchers—cognitive systems engineers and systems engineers—successfully bridged the gap to research, design, and implement new technologies.[9]

A cognitive systems engineering success story

A study by Ann Bisantz and her colleagues used work analysis, CTA, and ethnographic methods to study distributed work: to design software, evaluate it for usefulness and usability, and then study the quality of the resulting new work methods.[10] Their project was motivated by the US Navy's Human–Systems Integration (HSI) program to develop next-generation surface ships with a highly reduced crew complement. The cognitive systems engineers had to define new roles and jobs, not just specify tasks and their interfaces. They had the opportunity to do all of this early in the development process. Although this presented the greatest opportunity to impact the design, it created new challenges. The overall "humans–machines" system was not yet pegged down and indeed was continually evolving. The HSI program used a rapid design cycle (sometimes on the order of a few weeks), limiting the opportunity for in-depth data collection and analysis. Thus, "a detailed mapping of ship goals to system functions, task responsibilities, and operator actions was impossible." Instead, what Bisantz and her colleagues did was focus on bridge operations, try to map higher-level information needs to potential functions, and then make recommendations regarding function allocation (human versus machine) based on human-centering considerations.

The researchers conducted interviews and documentation analysis resulting in a representation called the *Abstraction-Decomposition Matrix* (ADM). This analytical tool was developed by Jens Rasmussen and his colleagues in their research on process control,[11,12] research that contributed significantly to our current notions of work analysis methodology.[13] An ADM represents a work domain in terms of two dimensions. One is levels of abstraction, in which each level is a distinctive type of constraint—from highest-level system purposes, down to purpose-related functions, and finally down to the physical objects and tools of the workplace. The second dimension is levels of decomposition, from organizational context, down to social collectives (teams), down to the individual worker.[14,15] The matrix Bisantz and her colleagues developed described the work in terms of ship and mission goals to be accomplished, the many-to-many mapping between goals and available ship systems, choice points and complications in decision making, and collaborative activities. Completing the matrix are arrows that depict goal-means relationships. We created Figure 2 to give a high-level view of an ADM. (An actual ADM is far more detailed, and ADMs come in a variety of forms depending on the application.)

The representation explicitly showed how functions could relate to multiple ship goals and how multiple functions could rely on the same subsystem. For example, you could maneuver the ship to facilitate sensing of undersea contacts (supporting a defensive goal) while at the same time impeding the maintenance of the ship's signature (adversely affecting a defensive goal). Maneuvering could also restrict the use of some weapons systems, affecting both offensive and defensive goals. Thus, executing one mission could delay the execution of another.

Systems engineers often use functional analysis methods to generate something like the first ADM dimension, and use design decomposition methods to generate something like the second ADM dimension. Thus, one of the ADM's benefits is that it's essentially a kind of bookkeeping system that systems engineers recognize. Perhaps this isn't surprising, because the ADM originated in systems engineering research in industrial process control.[10,11] But the ADM adds the context and relationships that engineering representations often miss, thus making the ADM a good communication device between cognitive systems engineers and systems engineers.

Showing both constraints on design and opportunities for design, the matrix was used to guide further knowledge elicitation interviews with the experts about how goals could be decomposed (for example, how a radar system is managed and directed). It was also used to specify the design of display prototypes (as with multiple ship goals for a single weapon system) and communication channels (such as the need for bridge "watch standers" to communicate with sonar operators). An additional benefit was that each display entailed by the analysis (the information requirements and description of cognitive tasks) came wrapped along with the design rationale stated in terms of higher-order purposes and goals—valuable traceability for system verification and validation. For instance, we might assume that a watch stander wouldn't need a display showing activities in some other area of responsibility. However, the abstraction-decomposition analyses showed the potential for conflict among certain ship functions and goals, leading to specific recommendations about which area of responsibility's displays the various watch standers should be able to view.

This study could be considered a success story in CTA, one that coped with the practical constraints of time pressure and the challenge of designing for an envisioned world, a large-scale system when system elements could not be fully specified in the language that software engineers need.

Returning to Figure 1, the box of question marks shows the gap that must be filled. Thus far, we've argued that some gap filling is the cognitive systems engineer's responsibility, to generate products that get closer to designs rather than just documentation that "informs" design. In the next essay, we go in the other direction, that of helping the systems engineer understand the end user's cognitive work as the cognitive systems engineer would understand it. ■

Acknowledgments

Robert Hoffman's contribution was through participation in the Advanced Decision Architectures Collaborative Technology Alliance, sponsored by the US Army Research Laboratory under cooperative agreement DAAD19-01-2-0009. Portions of this material are based on work supported by the US Air Force under contract FA8650-06-C-6638.

Any opinions, findings, and conclusions or recommendations expressed in this material are those of the authors and do not necessarily reflect the views of the US Air Force.

References

1. B. Crandall, G. Klein, and R.R. Hoffman, *Working Minds: A Practitioner's Guide to Cognitive Task Analysis*, MIT Press, 2006.
2. R.R. Hoffman and L.G. Militello, *Perspectives on Cognitive Task Analysis: Historical Origins and Modern Communities of Practice*, CRC Taylor & Francis Press, 2008.
3. D.A. Norman, *Things That Make Us Smart*, Addison-Wesley, 1993.
4. M. Endsley and R. Hoffman, "The Sacagawea Principle," *IEEE Intelligent Systems*, Nov./Dec. 2002, pp. 80–85.
5. T.B. Sheridan, "Task Analysis, Task Allocation, and Supervisory Control," *Handbook of Human-Computer Interaction*, 2nd ed., M.G. Helander, T.K. Landauer, and P. Prabhu, eds., Elsevier Science, 1997, pp. 87–105.
6. L. Bainbridge, "Ironies of Automation," *Automatica*, vol. 19, no. 6, 1983, pp. 775–779.
7. D.D. Woods and N.B. Sarter, "Learning from Automation Surprises and 'Going Sour' Accidents," *Cognitive Engineering in the Aviation Domain*, N.B. Sarter and R. Amalberti, eds., Lawrence Erlbaum, 2000, pp. 327–353.
8. R.R. Hoffman and W.C. Elm, "HCC Implications for the Procurement Process," *IEEE Intelligent Systems*, vol. 21, no. 1, 2006, pp. 74–81.
9. N.J. Cooke and F. Durso, *Stories of Modern Technology Failures and Cognitive Engineering Successes*, CRC Press, 2007.
10. A.M. Bisantz et al., "Integrating Cognitive Analyses in a Large-Scale System Design Process," *Int'l J. Human-Computer Studies*, vol. 58, no. 2, 2002, pp. 117–206.
11. J. Rasmussen, A.M. Pejtersen, and L.P. Goodstein, eds., *Cognitive Systems Engineering*, John Wiley & Sons, 1994.
12. J. Rasmussen, A.M. Pejtersen, and K. Schmidt, *Taxonomy for Cognitive Work Analysis*, tech. report RISØ-M-2871, Risø Nat'l Laboratory, 1990.
13. K.J. Vicente, *Cognitive Work Analysis: Toward Safe, Productive, and Healthy Computer-Based Work*, Lawrence Erlbaum, 1999.
14. R.R. Hoffman and G. Lintern, "Eliciting and Representing the Knowledge of Experts," *Cambridge Handbook of Expertise and Expert Performance*, K.A. Ericsson et al., eds., Cambridge Univ. Press, 2006, pp. 203–222.
15. N. Naikar and P. Sanderson, "Evaluating System Design Proposals with Work Domain Analysis," *Human Factors*, vol. 43, 2001, pp. 529–542.

Robert R. Hoffman is a senior research scientist at the Institute for Human and Machine Cognition. Contact him at rhoffman@ihmc.us.

Steven V. Deal is vice president and systems engineer at Deal Corporation. Contact him at s.deal@sbcglobal.net.

Chapter 20: Influencing versus Informing Design, Part 2: Macrocognitive Modeling

R.R. Hoffman, "Influencing versus Informing Design, Part 2: Macrocognitive Modeling," *IEEE Intelligent Systems*, vol. 23, no. 6, Nov./Dec. 2008, pp.86–89. doi: 10.1109/MIS.2008.105

Cognitive-systems engineers study the cognitive work conducted in sociotechnical contexts and, from that understanding, provide guidance to software engineers. The previous essay in this department discussed how there can be a gap—the guidance from cognitive-systems engineers can inform design, but what software engineers actually need are designs. The gap has been successfully crossed in one direction, in projects in which cognitive-systems engineers expressed the requirements in a way that captured key functionalities and their rationale, thereby speaking to the software engineer's needs. This essay works in the other direction: providing systems engineers with an easy-to-use method—the macrocognitive modeling procedure—that might enable them to ramp up their understanding of the cognitive work. The procedure involves creating and then validating models of domain practitioners' reasoning. The method is easy to use and can enable software engineers to ramp up their understanding of end users' cognitive work.

Influencing versus Informing Design, Part 2: Macrocognitive Modeling

Robert R. Hoffman, *Institute for Human and Machine Cognition*

The human mind is like a black box—no one can directly observe or experience others' mental events. So, in any sort of flow diagram linking stimulus to response, at least one box remains unfillable. It has gone by many names—among them ego, apprehension, knowing, will, consciousness, the "executive," and reasoning. Psychologists and philosophers have labored for centuries to build a reliable foundation for a good (or "objective") view into the black box. Modern psychologists go to extreme lengths to design and execute supremely clever controlled laboratory experiments and procedures that provide us with glimpses into the box. What's needed in many venues, including human-centered computing for intelligent systems, is a fast track into that black box.

Software engineering is perhaps such a venue. A software engineer might start with the outputs of a documentation analysis, correctly apply user interface standards and conventions, and then produce an artifact that's exciting to look at. However, the artifact (and the work method it instills) might not be informed by the actual work context. The previous essay in this department discussed this gap in the systems-engineering process.[1] That essay illustrated how the gap has been successfully crossed in one direction, in a project in which cognitive systems engineers expressed the requirements in a way that captured key functionalities and the rationale for those functionalities, thereby "speaking to" the software engineer.

This essay works in the other direction: providing systems engineers with an easy-to-use method—the Macrocognitive Modeling Procedure (MMP)—that might enable them to ramp up their understanding of the cognitive work.

Editors: Robert R. Hoffman, Patrick J. Hayes, and Kenneth M. Ford
Institute for Human and Machine Cognition
rhoffman@ihmc.us

Macrocognition

Previous essays in this department have discussed the distinction between microcognition and macrocognition and its implications for intelligent systems.[2,3] Microcognitive and macrocognitive models take different forms and have different purposes. Microcognitive models present causal-chain understandings of mental events, built from mental operations such as short-term memory access and attentional shifts. Such laboratory-based models help us describe performance for known, fixed tasks. On the other hand, macrocognitive models describe the major goal-directed functions of cognitive work (deciding, replanning, sensemaking, problem detection, and so on) and the cognitive processes that support those functions (for example, developing mental models and maintaining common ground). Macrocognitive modeling is likely to be based on studies of the actual work and expert reasoning in complex and dynamic situations.

The creation of macrocognitive models of aspects of sociotechnical work systems could help systems and software engineers as well as cognitive systems engineers develop high-level understandings of the nature of the cognitive work. Through a deep, rich understanding of the actual cognitive work, we can increase the likelihood of creating human-centered technologies and work methods.

We can achieve an understanding of cognitive work through several broad cognitive task analysis methodologies:[4,5]

- Using largely ethnometric methods, we can study the workplace and work patterns and conduct documentation analysis. The general approach is called activity analysis or work analysis.
- Using largely psychometric methods, we can measure human performance and conduct cognitive task analysis. This is the general approach of human factors engineering and cognitive systems engineering.
- Using largely sociometric methods, we can interview domain practitioners, study communication patterns, and reveal social networks within knowledge-based organizations. This is the general approach of ethnomethodology, although it overlaps significantly with activity analysis and work analysis.

Applying these methods results in macrocognitive descriptions of practitioner knowledge and practitioner reasoning.

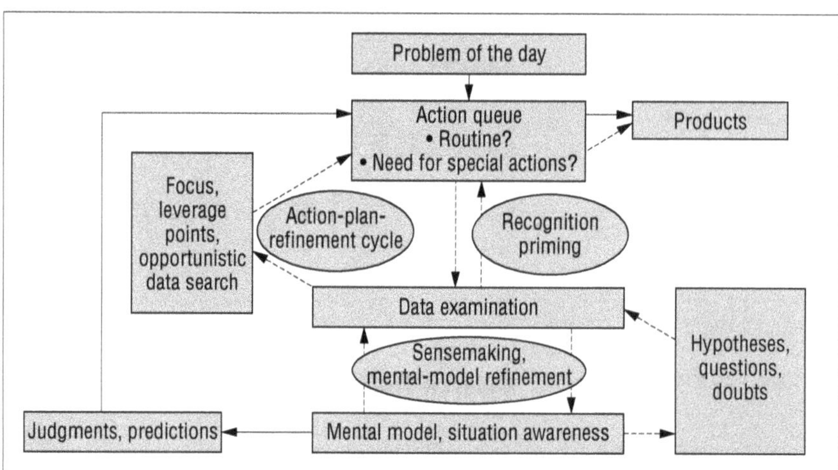

Figure 1. The base model of expert reasoning.[11] This model incorporates some basic macrocognitive functions. (reproduced with permission from Taylor and Francis)

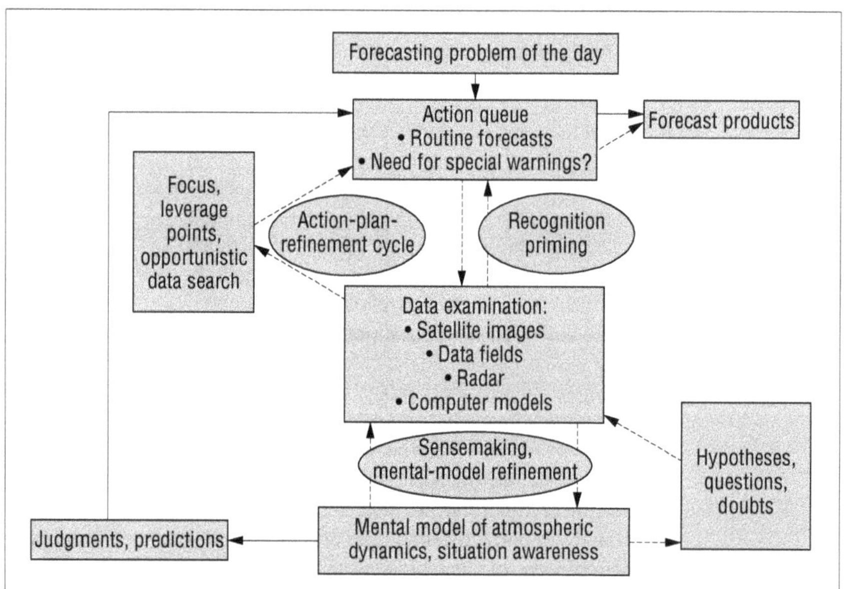

Figure 2. A macrocognitive model of expert reasoning. The base model is tailored to the domain of weather forecasting. (reproduced with permission[11] from Taylor and Francis)

The Macrocognitive Modeling Procedure

Software engineers don't need to carve time away from system development (whether at the high level of general architectures or the detailed levels of coding) to conduct all the research that cognitive systems engineers would like to conduct in order to come to a detailed and rich understanding of the work. What software engineers need is that fast track into the black box. Just as the creation of an Abstraction-Decomposition Matrix can bridge the gap from the language of the cognitive systems engineer to that of the systems engineer,[1] the MMP might efficiently help the systems engineer bridge the gap between his or her needs and those of the cognitive systems engineer.

My colleagues and I invented the MMP to support the efficient creation and subsequent validation of macrocognitive models of practitioner reasoning, thus avoiding labor-intensive protocol analysis. The MMP evolved after we had developed a general model of expert reasoning, which incorporated such processes as recognition-primed decision making, situational awareness, and mental model formation.[6,7] This general model of expert reasoning included Karl Duncker's notion of the hypothesis-testing refinement cycle.[8,9] The "base model," shown in Figure 1, captures (as variations on a theme) a considerable number of proposed hypothetical reasoning sequences taken from studies of diverse domains of expertise.[10] We also created a variation of this model to capture results from studies of expert weather forecasters' reasoning (see Figure 2).

My colleagues and I first conceived the MMP when we showed a weather forecaster the Figure 2 model and asked him whether it seemed appropriate to the domain. Ordinarily, an experimental psychologist's theoretical concoction would be foreign language to a domain practitioner. In this case we felt that discussing the model would be sensible because the weather forecasting community had for years relied on a distinction between conceptual (mental) models and computational models of the weather.[12] The forecaster we were working with spontaneously took the diagram as an opportunity to add domain-specific details to the process description and modify some of the relationships among the diagram elements. With this experience as a flash point, we created a more formal three-step procedure for the research method.

Step 1: Preparation

Adapt the base model (see Figure 1) to make it directly pertinent to the domain.

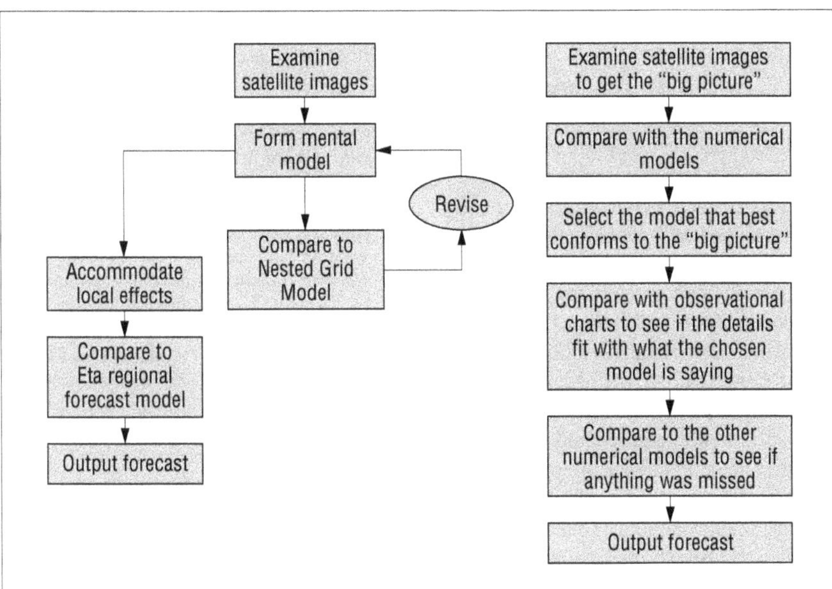

Figure 3. Example bogus models used in the study of weather forecasting. These models give the researcher a scaffold from which to probe the practitioner's goals.

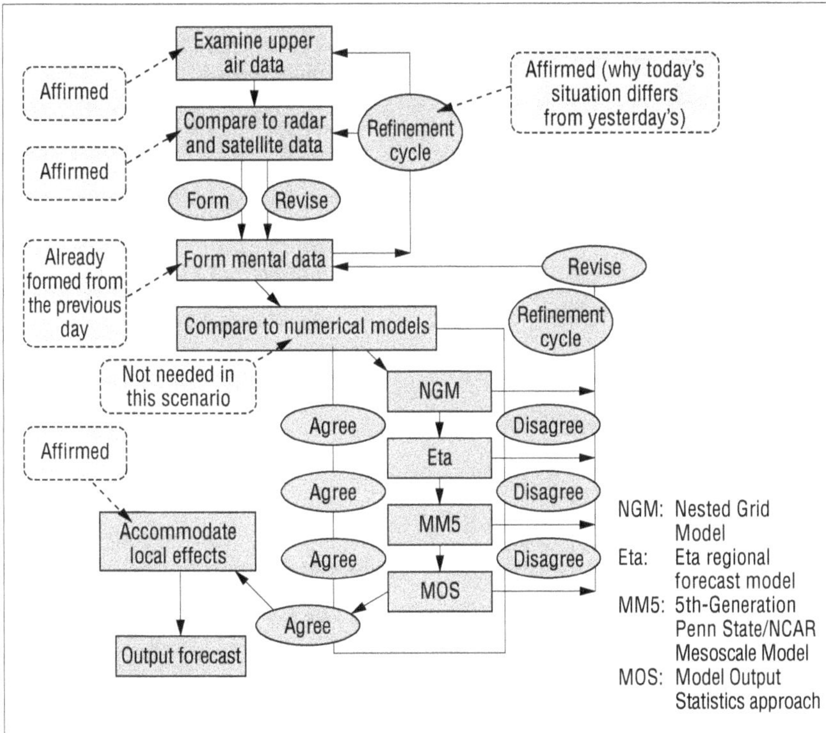

Figure 4. Results from an observational verification of a forecaster's model. Some elements can be verified by observation, others by probing questions.

Using weather forecasting—for example, comparing Figures 1 and 2—you'd specify the "problem of the day" as "the forecasting problem of the day," and "data examination" as "examination of images, data, radar." Next, create two alternative bogus models. At least one should include some sort of loop, and both should include some of the base model's elements. Taken together, the bogus models include core macrocognitive functions (for example, recognition priming, hypothesis testing, and so on). Ideally, these models aren't too unrealistic; nevertheless, expect the practitioner not to be entirely satisfied with either of them. Examples appear in Figure 3.

Step 2: Model Making

Show the domain practitioners (who span a range of proficiency) the bogus models, and invite them to pick the one best representing their strategy. Then, using the bogus models and their elements as a scaffold, invite each practitioner to concoct his or her own reasoning diagram.

Step 3: Verification

There is some likelihood that the model created in Step 2 might be a "just-so story," that is, a description of what the practitioner *says* their reasoning is. After a few days (or more), place yourself in the workplace and observe each practitioner as he or she arrives and begin their day's work. You can validate some elements of the model by observation (for example, "examine satellite images"). Other elements aren't so readily validated, but they might be subject to probing questions (such as "What are you thinking now?" and "What are you doing now?"). Figure 4 shows example results for one practitioner model, indicating the Step 3 results. The call-out balloons indicate results of the observation and probe procedure.

Our first use of this procedure, in the weather forecasting domain, resulted in models of the reasoning of seven proficient forecasters (experts and journeymen), validated by observations of actual forecasting activities. Developing and validating the models took 52 minutes on average. This is without doubt less than the time that other (widely used) methods need to reveal and verify reasoning models (for example, preparing and functionally coding a transcript of a think-aloud problem-solving protocol can take many hours[13]). We were also able to validate the general model of forecaster reasoning that we developed in our initial documentation analysis (see Figure 2). The results also clearly showed differences in proficiency, with less-experienced forecasters relying uncritically on computer forecasts and less likely to think hypothetically and counterfactually. Also, the less-experienced forecasters were more likely to rely on a fixed sequence for inspecting the outputs of various computer models of the weather.

Variations on the Theme

The three steps constitute a procedure that you can adapt for individual projects. For instance, you can insert a step between Steps 2 and 3 to create a form of sociogram, enabling you to discern patterns of knowledge sharing in the organization. After the individual practitioners have created their diagrams (Step 2), wait a couple of weeks or even longer, and then show each practitioner in the organization all the models that were devised and ask them to play a "guess who created this one" game. This step reveals the extent to which the practitioners have shared their knowledge and discussed their reasoning. This step also helps to identify individuals who possess special subdomain expertise or skills. This additional step is perhaps more useful to cognitive systems engineers than to systems engineers (who can skip it).

This forecasting study was a first attempt, and limited in some ways, but promising enough for further investigation and application. (You can download details on the MMP procedure at http://ihmc.us:16080/research/projects/CTAProtocols.) The MMP holds promise for developing reasoning models and for testing hypotheses concerning reasoning models, in less time than lab-based research methods take. But in addition to the benefits and applications for cognitive systems engineers, this method is easy and efficient enough to be useful in bridging the gap between systems engineering and cognitive systems engineering. In just a couple of days, systems engineers could come to a useful understanding of the cognitive work that would benefit from the new technologies (and work methods). Using the MMP, systems engineers could create macrocognitive models of the key cognitive activities involved in the work and, as an added benefit, gain rapport with the domain practitioners.

The MMP is likely inappropriate for studying some domains. But when it is appropriate, systems engineers and cognitive systems engineers could (and perhaps should) conduct MMPs collaboratively. There might be special value in such collaboration very early in a given system development project. This would serve to inform the systems engineers of the key or high-level aspects of the cognitive work while beginning to bootstrap the cognitive systems engineers into their further in-depth investigations using methods such as Abstraction-Decomposition Matrix analysis.[1]

A final caution. It makes little sense to think that any single macrocognitive model will effectively capture practitioner reasoning. One forecaster in the weather project looked at his own model some eight weeks after he had created it, and rejected it, explaining that the original model was no longer his preferred strategy because the weather trends had changed. The previously preferred computer models were no longer preferred. My colleagues and I speculated that a domain such as weather forecasting would require many dozens of macrocognitive models of reasoning strategies to present a rich and fair picture of practitioner reasoning.[6] Understanding this could be extremely valuable to the systems engineer. It could provide insight into the cognitive work's scope, diversity, and flexibility. It could also illustrate ways in which the work can't be captured just by using notions of tasks and fixed sequences of activities. ■

Acknowledgments

This work resulted from effort conducted under a contract from the National Technology Alliance and from participation in the Advanced Decision Architectures Collaborative Technology Alliance, sponsored by the US Army Research Laboratory under cooperative agreement DAAD19-01-2-0009.

References

1. R.R. Hoffman and S.V. Deal, "Influencing versus Informing Design, Part 1: A Gap Analysis," *IEEE Intelligent Systems*, vol. 23, no. 5, 2008, pp. 78–81.
2. G. Klein, B. Moon, and R.R. Hoffman, "Making Sense of Sensemaking 2: A Macrocognitive Model," *IEEE Intelligent Systems*, vol. 21, no. 5, 2006, pp. 88–92.
3. G. Klein et al., "Macrocognition," *IEEE Intelligent Systems*, vol. 18, no. 3, 2003, pp. 81–85.
4. B. Crandall, G. Klein, and R.R. Hoffman, *Working Minds: A Practitioner's Guide to Cognitive Task Analysis*, MIT Press, 2006.
5. K.J. Vicente, *Cognitive Work Analysis: Toward Safe, Productive, and Healthy Computer-Based Work*, Lawrence Erlbaum, 1999.
6. R.R. Hoffman et al., "Storm-LK: A Human-Centered Knowledge Model for Weather Forecasting," *Proc. 45th Ann. Meeting Human Factors and Ergonomics Soc.*, Human Factors and Ergonomics Soc., 2001, p. 752.
7. R.R. Hoffman et al., "A Method for Eliciting, Preserving, and Sharing the Knowledge of Forecasters," *Weather and Forecasting*, vol. 21, 2006, pp. 416–428.
8. K. Duncker, "On Problem Solving," *Psychological Monographs*, vol. 58, no. 270, 1945, pp. 1–113.
9. A. Newell, "Duncker on Thinking: An Inquiry into Progress on Cognition," *A Century of Psychology as a Science*, S. Koch and D.E. Leary, eds., Oxford Univ. Press, 1985, pp. 392–419.
10. R.R. Hoffman and L. Militello, *Perspectives on Cognitive Task Analysis: Historical Origins and Modern Communities of Practice*, CRC Press, 2008.
11. J.G. Trafton and R.R. Hoffman, "Computer-Aided Visualization in Meteorology," *Expertise out of Context*, R.R. Hoffman, ed., Lawrence Erlbaum, 2007, pp. 337–357.
12. R.R. Hoffman, G. Trafton, and P. Roebber, *Minding the Weather: How Expert Forecasters Think*, MIT Press, to be published in 2009.
13. R.R. Hoffman et al., "Eliciting Knowledge from Experts: A Methodological Analysis," *Organizational Behavior and Human Decision Processes*, vol. 62, no. 2, 1995, pp. 129–158.

Robert R. Hoffman is a senior research scientist at the Institute for Human and Machine Cognition. Contact him at rhoffman@ihmc.us.

Chapter 21: Once More, Into the Soup

P.J. Stappers, R.R. Hoffman, "Once More, Into the Soup," *IEEE Intelligent Systems*, vol. 24, no. 5, Sept./Oct. 2009, pp. 9–13. doi: 10.1109/MIS.2009.100

In one of the earlier essays in this department, we discussed a number of acronyms all having to do with system design, and all having the form "x-centered design." The purpose of that essay was to demonstrate a broad framework within which to understand human-centered computing (HCC), and also to show the various convergences and divergences of the communities of practice that have introduced their own x-centered-design designations. Among them are learner-centered design, client-centered design, designer-centered design, decision-centered design, and work-oriented design.

Once More, Into the Soup

Pieter Jan Stappers, *Delft University of Technology*
Robert R. Hoffman, *Institute for Human and Machine Cognition*

In one of the earlier essays in this department, we discussed a number of acronyms all having to do with system design, and all having the form "*x*-centered design."[1] The purpose of that essay was to demonstrate a broad framework within which to understand human-centered computing (HCC), and also to show the various convergences and divergences of the communities of practice that have introduced their own *x*-centered-design designations. Among them are learner-centered design, client-centered design, designer-centered design, decision-centered design, and work-oriented design.

Using a concept map, that essay converged on the things that the *x*-centered-design designations have in common:

- A shared goal: The creation of technologies to enhance humans. This is, of course, what HCC is all about.
- Shared methods (cognitive field research and psychosocial evaluation). This gives HCC a methodology to anchor the creation of intelligent systems in the empirics of cognitive work.[2]
- Shared focus on the high-level or "macrocognitive" processes that define cognitive work, processes such as situation assessment, replanning, problem detection, and decision making.[3]

It comes as little surprise that since the publication of that essay, even more acronyms have been put forth, as individuals and organizations struggle to make their ideas and contributions have an impact.[4]

Our purpose in this follow-up essay is to present an alternative view. To extend the soup metaphor from that earlier essay, what we seek to do here is clarify the broth and pick out the meaty bits. In this alternative view, we don't focus on historical origins of the *x*-centered-design designations in disciplines, or on the counterclaims and clashes of communities of practice. Rather, we take a functional approach,[5,6] in which we don't regard designing monolithically as a single activity. As in the first of the soup essays, we use a diagram.

Design

The research group at the Industrial Design-StudioLab (ID-StudioLab) of Delft University of Technology studies designers and design activities. It develops new methods, techniques, and tools to support design, including its own design processes. The researchers sometimes found it difficult to express what the ID-StudioLab was all about. In caricature, an unguarded moment could deliver, "We study how designers design in order to design methods to improve design." Responses included: "So, is what you do research, or is it design?" "Are you just designing for yourself?" and "Huh?"

These confusions arise often in discussions in this field. Short words such as "designer," "user," and "research" carry too many common connotations and denotations to be sufficient in themselves. Thus, ID-StudioLab created a diagram to depict the functional process of design and the lab's particular approach. The diagram iterated from a simple one into a larger one, as more and

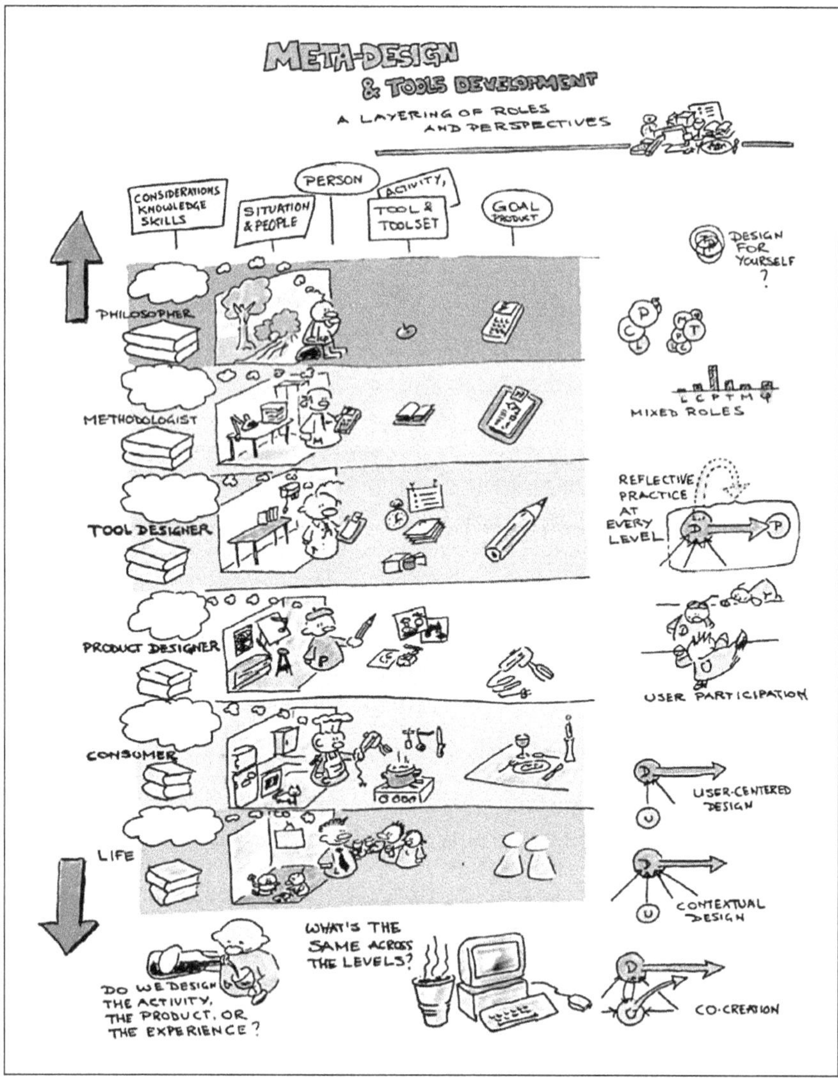

Figure 1. The metadesign diagram, which describes the design of technology as a distributed and collaborative process that involves multiple roles.

more issues and questions seemed to fit neatly into it. The end result is a sketch of the terrain that designers inhabit, a sketch that invites the viewer to look for parallels, similarities, and differences.

Figure 1 presents the final diagram, called the metadesign diagram. (Readers can contact the first author to download a poster-format high-resolution version.) The diagram is not a strict or precise graph; it is a sketch to aid thinking about the functional relations among many roles and goals. For example, it was not easy to concretize or symbolize the "product" of the "philosopher." The calculator in that position now is perhaps silly, but a better concept just didn't turn up. The calculator, like the other icons, has the value of being point-at-able, and it serves our purposes largely by its place in the diagram.

Working through the Diagram

Toward the center of the diagram is the product designer (cartoonishly identified by the beret) who uses tools (exemplified by the pencil, which stands for a variety of tools such as brainstorms, CAD, user studies, and so on) to create consumer products (the mixer).

The design techniques group at the ID-StudioLab deals with developing new "pencils" on the basis of understanding how designers do designing. The tools that the ID-StudioLab uses for this are design methods for conceiving and prototyping, and research methods for studying designing and evaluating the new concept tools. So the product designers are the tool designers' users, in the same way that the consumer who uses the mixer is the product designer's user. This parallel shows why the diagram refers to metadesign—that is, design applied to design.

The diagram is built on two principles: First, it makes sense to use the words "designer" and "user" to refer to roles relative to a specific product. These form a triad of *designer makes product for user:* <designer, product, user>. A common source of confusion in talking about design is that many discussions use the term "designer" to refer to a particular person with a particular professional education, in expressions such as, "designers are not users." Here we take "designer" and "user" to be people's roles with respect to a product or tool.[1,6] The diagram distinguishes several roles (such as product designer, tool designer, and consumer); none of these is called just "designer," but each of them plays a designing role with regard to the product to its right in the diagram. The diagram's second principle is that these designer and user roles can be extended and repeated on metalevels; and these "steps" (activities at many levels) can be repeated a few times, while still making sense.

With these basic ideas in mind, let's walk through the levels of the diagram. Starting first at the "product designer," the triad here is <product designer, mixer, consumer>. Moving downwards, the level below shows that the consumer is not just a passive receiver, but uses the mixer as a tool for preparing a meal (itself a designing activity), which may be used by a host <consumer, meal, host> to entertain his guests <host, party, guests>.

We can also work upward. We have already described how the ID-StudioLab provides new tools for designers, and this introduces the triad <tool designer, pencil, product designer>. In developing tools for design work, researchers use standard research and design methods, but they have to adapt them as well. This puts researchers in the role of adjusting (redesigning) their methods—for example, determining whether or how to use statistics or modeling and how to evaluate findings. This doesn't stop with using statistics handbooks as dictates and recipes; occasionally researchers make excursions into such fundamental questions as, "What is creativity?" "How exactly do we weigh proof?" and "How do we set the balance between relevance and validity?" Such questions touch upon the metaphysics of thinking. For this designing activity, we reserve a higher level, <philosopher, concepts, methodologist>.

The levels are an exercise in ordering thought, but they don't have the strict definition of a house built of bricks. We aren't claiming that there are exactly six levels, or that the separations can always be clearly made. Earlier, we used scare quotes around the word "steps" because all the activities in the diagram are parallel.[2] But the diagram does help to position some phenomena, call out the parallels, and clarify some misunderstandings that may be due to subtle shifts between levels. The diagram's visual form lets us see and point to elements about which we must be clear. Here are a few things that the levels can express.

Attention to Systems, Context, and Cultures

In the past decade, there has emerged a "contextualist" consensus that designers don't design objects to be used in a vacuum, or to be used for an isolated technical function.[7] In designing at the level of meanings for users, designers must take into account the situation in which the product is to be used, including the other tools and products in the domain (a mixer is used in a kitchen, together with a bowl and close to an electrical socket), the cultural values and needs that reign there, and the purposes (toward a lower metalevel, perhaps).

The relation between user and designer has changed over the past decades, in terms of who informs, who creates, and who decides. In user-centered design (UCD), consideration of the user's abilities, needs, and values are key to the definition of the new product. This was a step beyond classic "technology push," in which considerations of user and use were secondary. In the piece of the metadesign diagram reproduced in Figure 2, UCD is depicted as a thin arrow, indicating that the designer takes in information about the user, the task, and other tools involved before and during the time that product creation (thick arrow) takes place. The user's role may be that of either a passive object (observed, for example, with ethnographic techniques) or an active participant (taking part in a focus group, for example, or being interviewed).

With contextual design and context mapping, the designer takes into account a broader scope of factors about the user's environment, again with the user either passive or active.[6] With co-creation, or participatory design, the user not only informs the designer but closely interacts with the designer (double thin arrows), and participates not just in describing the current situation or future needs, but in the actual generation of the new product.

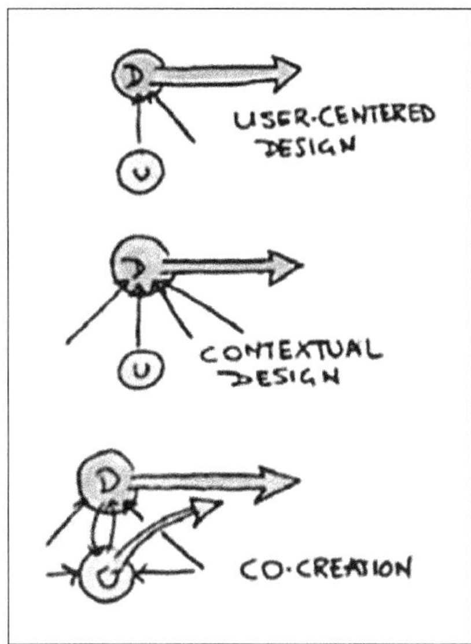

Figure 2. Relationships between design and user. In user-centered design, the designer takes in information about the user, the task, and other tools involved before and during product creation. With contextual design, the designer takes into account a broader scope of factors about the user's environment. In co-creation, the user closely interacts with the designer and participates in generating the new product.

Even close colleagues can differ in their opinions about which players should take which roles, but our jargon does not help us to be explicit about what we mean; being able to mark these roles helps to achieve clarity.

Specific Knowledge

At each different level there is specific knowledge (symbolized in the metadesign diagram by the books on the left). For instance, one expects the methodologist and academic researchers to come with relevant disciplinary theory, but the consumer's cooking activities also employ specific knowledge.

Values and Culture Differ across Levels

We've mentioned differences in consumer cultures; the divide between design and research is similar.[8]

Researchers and designers typically look for different things in a piece of research; they place different emphases on internal validity (truth) versus external validity (relevance). Distinguishing the levels of metadesign may help to clarify misunderstandings—for example, when two parties in a discussion are missing each other's point because they employ values from different contexts or levels.

Figure 3. Reflective practice means developing an awareness of the levels besides your own in the metadesign process so that you can work and communicate across levels.

Everyone Is a Designer in Some Things

In the last few years, the idea of "emancipating the user" has received attention, and design researchers, consumer activists, and corporate campaigns (such as Ikea's) have pointed out that everybody has creative abilities. In relation to the metadesign diagram, this would mean that at every level we see people create tools with the purpose of being used or enjoyed by others or themselves. The user-consumer is not just a passive digester of products. But when we focus on a single level, we tend to attribute less creativity and complexity to the levels above and below. Seeing users as passive digesters can be as wrong as seeing methods specialists as uncreative rulebook followers. The metadesign diagram helps us remain aware of that.

Importance of Ethnography to Design

Ethnography is closely tied to the attention to context mentioned earlier. All the confusion which led us to make the diagram arose when we started to apply ethnographic and contextual techniques in studying the way designers work in design studios. Then we were acting as designers, researchers, and users at the same time. Things became easier when we also inserted these ethnographic techniques in the educational program in industrial design, for then the research is aimed at consumers in general, and the results given to designers. In the last few years, the means to study or involve the users intensively in design are becoming popular, both in design education and in industrial practice.

Reflective Practice and Education

Donald Schön introduced the notion of the reflective practitioner to design theory, indicating that professionals acquire expertise by reflecting on the actions they take.[9] In design education, the implication is that a design student doesn't just learn the tools and techniques as strict procedures to execute as a computer would, but develops an awareness on a higher level (in the diagram, the tool developer level), so that he can later adapt and refine the methods according to shifting needs of the situation and growing personal skills. The reflective practitioner rises one level higher (Figure 3).

Participatory Design

Since the 1980s, the field or community of practice of participatory design has gained many advocates. This approach gives the user a more prominent role in the design process. Whereas earlier theories considered users unable to rise above their level of use, the participatory design movement proclaims that by giving users appropriate tools and training, they can become experts in their domain who can contribute on a par with other professionals in the design process.[6,10] These tools and training serve, as it were, to make them reflective practitioners.

Metadesign and Intelligent Systems

All of the levels in the metadesign diagram are about people acting, and this gives rise to many similarities across levels. We might mention the computer as a particular similarity: as computer technology has become more broadly intelligent, the computer is the "tool" used by people at all levels. But by reason of this very growth in intelligence capabilities, we don't include the computer in the metadesign diagram because the computer has become the thinking person's ubiquitous tool.

If we use Miller's law (that people can manage 7 ± 2 pieces of information in correct serial order in their short-term memory) to teach design students not to overload computer menus with too many items, shouldn't we apply the same principle to the way we design theories, including theories of design? The designers and researchers themselves also have limited mental capabilities, and the theories are their tools. Of course scientists do pay attention to this, calling upon Occam's razor or aesthetic principles to make theories manageable. But it would be worthwhile to train computer scientists involved in creating our design tools to devote more explicit attention to use-centered considerations.

Seeing that the "designer" at the different levels is a role—not an individual or a profession—may

Figure 4. The "designer" at each level of the metadesign process is a role, not an individual or a profession. Most participants in the design process shift among levels and play many roles to varying degrees.

help us realize how most of us shift among the levels (Figure 4). Still, some of us feel most comfortable at one level and spend most of our time there, while others specialize at another level. But each of us should understand the levels, and be able to bridge with others across the levels. We must teach our students to work across and between levels, and we must remember, ourselves, where we and others are.

References

1. R.R. Hoffman et al., "A Rose by Any Other Name ... Would Probably Be Given an Acronym," *IEEE Intelligent Systems,* vol. 17, no. 4, 2002, pp. 72–80.
2. G. Klein, "Macrocognition," *IEEE Intelligent Systems,* vol. 18, no. 3, 2003, pp. 81–85.
3. G. Klein, B. Moon, and R.R. Hoffman, "Making Sense of Sensemaking 1: Alternative Perspectives," *IEEE Intelligent Systems,* vol. 21, no. 4, 2006, pp. 22–26.
4. R.R. Hoffman, D.O. Norman, and J. Vagners, "Complex Sociotechnical Joint Cognitive Work Systems?" *IEEE Intelligent Systems,* vol. 24, no. 3, 2009, pp. 82–89.
5. R.R. Hoffman, A. Roesler, and B.M. Moon, "What Is Design in the Context of Human-Centered Computing?" *IEEE Intelligent Systems,* vol. 19, no. 4, 2004, pp. 89–95.
6. E.B.-N. Sanders and P.J. Stappers, "Co-Creation and the New Landscapes of Design," *Codesign,* vol. 4, no. 1, 2008, pp. 5–18.
7. H. Beyer and K. Holtzblatt, *Contextual Design: Defining Customer-Centered Systems,* Academic Press, 1998.
8. E.B.-N. Sanders, "Information, Inspiration and Co-creation," *Proc. 6th Int'l Conf. European Academy of Design,* 2005; http://www.ead.lancs.ac.uk/conf/EAD_06.html.
9. D.A. Schön, *The Reflective Practitioner: How Professionals Think in Action,* Basic Books, 1983.
10. P. Ehn, *Work-Oriented Design of Computer Artifacts,* Arbetslivscentrum, 1988.

Pieter Jan Stappers is a professor of industrial design engineering at Delft University of Technology, The Netherlands. Contact him at p.j.stappers@tudelft.nl.

Robert R. Hoffman is a senior research scientist at the Institute for Human and Machine Cognition. Contact him at rhoffman@ihmc.us.

Part IV:

Expertise and Cognitive Skill

Chapter 22: The Limitations of Limitations

J.M. Flach and R.R. Hoffman, "The Limitations of Limitations," *IEEE Intelligent Systems*, vol. 18, no. 1, Jan./Feb. 2003, pp. 94–97. doi: 10.1109/MIS.2003.1179200

The authors consider human-centered computing and argue that human factors and applied cognitive psychologists have not just been selective in regarding certain human characteristics as limitations, but have also selected the wrong things and for the wrong reasons. Throughout the literatures of cognitive science, computer science, and human factors, one finds all sorts of references to the idea that humans have limitations in memory, attention, and reasoning. Humans have many characteristics, any of which can be regarded as a limitation *if one chooses to*. The heart of the problem is a preference for easily quantifiable answers to the wrong questions and avoidance of the right questions because they are messy. There are many people within the human factors community who cling to the belief that their primary function is to catalog human limitations. We hypothesize that this resistance is partly due to a misconception about the needs of designers.

The Limitations of Limitations

John M. Flach, *Wright State University*
Robert R. Hoffman, *Institute for Human and Machine Cognition*

One of the principles of human-centered computing, the Aretha Franklin principle,[1] states,

> Do not devalue the human in order to justify the machine. Do not criticize the machine in order to rationalize the human. Advocate the human–machine system in order to amplify both.

The implication we pursue in this article has to do with the notion of human limitations.

In the introduction to his text on engineering psychology, Christopher Wickens wrote, "One major purpose of this book is to examine human capabilities and limitations in the specific area of information processing. The second purpose is to demonstrate how knowledge of these limitations can be applied in the design of complex systems with which humans interact."[2] The first sentence in this quotation clearly recognizes that humans have capabilities. However, the second sentence seems to imply that it is the limitations that are most relevant in the design of complex systems.

In a similar vein, Barry Kantowitz and Robert Sorkin wrote, "Indeed, many human factors analysts believe that *minimizing human error is the primary goal of any human factors design*. If people never made errors, there would be little need for a science of human factors" (italics added).[3] Such statements, and there are scads of them in the literature, portray the human as the weaker link in any complex system. And the design focus tends to be on protecting the system from the limitations and errors that are associated with that weak link.

In this essay, we argue that human factors and applied cognitive psychologists have not just been selective in regarding certain human characteristics as limitations, but also have selected the wrong things and for the wrong reasons.

Selecting the wrong things: The myths of human limitations

Throughout the literatures of cognitive science, computer science, and human factors, you can find all sorts of references to the idea that people have memory, attention, and reasoning limitations. The mind-set in human factors engineering has been cast along the dimensions that Paul Fitts and his colleagues established with their MABA-HABA (Machines Are Better At versus Humans Are Better At) List.[1] The capabilities and limitations of humans and machines are measured against each other, but there is also a tacit value judgment—that machines' capabilities compensate for human limitations. For example, Donald Norman attributes the focus on human limitations to a "machine-centered bias," in which the human is evaluated relative to machines' positive attributes and found to be wanting.[4]

In accordance with the entrenched tradition of Fitts' List, new PhDs in psychology are required be able to parrot the old saw, "Human working memory is limited." The notion of limited capacity in working memory goes back to the earliest studies of human memory, by Sir William Hamilton (memory for random scatterings of marbles) and Herrmann Ebbinghaus (memory for lists of syllables).[5] These pioneers in the study of memory discussed what they called the "span of immediate apprehension." With the rise of cognitive psychology, this came to be dubbed the "7 ± 2 chunks" limitation to short-term memory[6] or working memory.[7] The basic notion became entrenched with the advent of the modern computer and the affiliated metaphors for mind, in the classic works of such individuals as Herbert Simon.[8–10]

We know that with sufficient practice at immediate

Editors: Robert R. Hoffman, Patrick J. Hayes, and Kenneth M. Ford
Institute for Human and Machine Cognition, University of West Florida
rhoffman@ai.uwf.edu

recall for particular kinds of materials (for example, strings of numbers, restaurant orders, and so on), we can push this so-called "limitation" to accommodate surprisingly large amounts of material.[11] Studies of expertise have shown clearly that the amount of information people can integrate into chunks is rather flexible and domain-dependent. (We are tempted to say it is limitless, but this would be hyperbole.) So although there might be constraints on the number of chunks people can deal with effectively, and although 7 ± 2 might be a good ballpark estimate of that constraint, 7 ± 2 is hardly a limitation in the sense of a practical bound on the span of immediate apprehension. Rather, it might reflect a constraint on how that material must be organized.

As for the treatment of long-term memory in the literature, we find praise for human

- Memory in general,[12] with total memory capacity estimated to be approximately 10^8 to 10^9 "memories"[13]
- Memory for vocabulary[14]
- Ability to recognize thousands of pictures[15]
- Ability to become an expert possessing extensive, organized domain knowledge[12,16]

On the other hand, some claim that computers have much more extensive long-term memories than do people.[17] This might be true if by "memory" we mean the storage of bits of data. However, if we think about memory as the ability to coherently organize information into meaningful knowledge about the world, then human memory seems to far outstrip the capabilities, let alone the capacity, of current computers. The notions of "storage," "data," "information," "knowledge," and "meaningful" and the nature of the relations among these constructs are, to put it mildly, problematic in and of themselves. They are especially problematic when considered as limitations.

The bottom line is that we can regard any human characteristic as a limitation if we choose to. For any task that humans conduct, performance will have a ceiling at any given time, one that can with practice be pushed toward some asymptote that might represent a specieswide characteristic in the way information and meaning can be assimilated, or in the cognitive resources that are available at any given time.[18]

The selectivity in what is regarded as a limitation shows in the fact that humans have many characteristics that other entities have more of, but we do not choose to see these as limitations. For instance, people have only two eyes, whereas some creatures have more than two. Human vision is constrained to a portion of the electromagnetic spectrum; other creatures can perceive in the infrared and the ultraviolet. Most people have five digits on each major appendage, but some species have seven. Do these characteristics represent human limitations?

Two eyes, five fingers, or 7 ± 2 chunks might be "limitations" to the extent that they constrain how we look at the world, manipulate an object, or organize information. But they are not limitations in the sense of setting hard constraints on the span of seeing, doing, or remembering. Treating them as such results in a distorted view of how humans can fit into human–machine systems.

Human factors and applied cognitive psychologists have not just been selective in regarding certain human characteristics as limitations, but also have selected the wrong things and for the wrong reasons.

Selecting the wrong things for the wrong reasons

The heart of the problem is a preference for easily quantifiable answers to the wrong questions, and avoidance of the right questions because they are messy. Many in the human factors community cling to the belief that their primary function is to catalog human limitations. This resistance is due partly to their misconception that what designers and engineers need from psychologists is "numbers"—for example, the value of BHEPs (Basic Human Error Probabilities) to be entered into a THERP (Technique for Human Error Rate Prediction) analysis.[19] And the clearest numbers that human factors and applied cognitive psychologists have to offer typically reflect information-processing limitations (for example, the rate of information processing or the capacity of working memory). Approaches such as the GOMS (Goals, Operators, Methods, and Selection rules) model[19] are predicated on the belief that such numbers (for example, reaction time components) can be "integrated" in a way that will provide clear answers to design questions. Certainly the GOMS model and THERP analysis might be important tools for testing some qualitative intuitions about legacy systems, but to think that they can answer any question about the revolutionary redesign of human–machine systems is naïve. Rarely can an engineer or designer enter numbers into a formula and crank out a design solution.

Practical engineering and design are almost always heuristic processes driven by qualitative insights about a process. For example, control engineers rarely compute differential equations or use variational calculus to determine a design problem's solution. More typically, they begin with a heuristic judgment about the "style" of control logic (for example, lead–lag compensation) that will yield a stable solution based on a qualitative understanding reflecting their experiences with other control problems. They usually try this ballpark solution and iteratively tune it to see whether a satisfactory solution results. If not, they might reassess their heuristic judgment and reinitiate the iterative tuning process using a different style of control logic. So, what they need is help to gain a qualitative understanding of the important dimensions to consider when designing cognitive systems.

The challenge of the "chunk"

A second way in which a belief in "numbers" is naïve is that the numbers are considered to be concrete, practical answers. Let's return to the example of short-term memory. To what question is the number "7 ± 2 chunks" an answer? Is it an answer to questions such as

- How many chess pieces can an expert remember?
- How many aircraft can an air traffic control operator manage?
- How many state variables can a nuclear control room operator consider at one time?

After the human factors practitioner has confidently offered this "fact" (which she first encountered in her introductory psychology course), the engineers or designers ask, "What's a chunk?" The response is typically, "It depends on the domain and the person's experience."

The problem is not this answer, which is correct, but that the human factors practitioner abdicates responsibility for digging deeper to help the designer or engineer discover what might be the basis for "chunking" information in that particular domain. This is typically seen as a problem for the "domain experts," whoever they might be. The job of human factors typically ends with quantifying the limitation; the job of translating this "fact" into an effective representation is then left to others—until the human factors practitioner is again called when the system fails catastrophically. At this point, with the benefit of hindsight, the human factors practitioner can confidently count the "chunks" and blame the engineers for exceeding the limits of 7 ± 2 that the human factors researchers had "clearly" prescribed at the start!

So, the 7 ± 2 limit has little practical significance regarding how much information a person can handle in any particular work context. We don't see how any approach to human or machine expertise can progress without researching the different ways that information can be meaningfully integrated (chunked). Information or a database only becomes knowledge when we understand data as information and organize (chunk?) it in some way. Psychologists have focused on limitations and paid almost no attention to the human capability of integrating information into meaningful organizations. As an example of a more productive approach, Kim Vicente and Joanne Wang take an important first step to look at ways to chunk information as a function of structure within problem domains.[20]

Beyond limitations

The cataloging of limitations is such an important part of the conventional wisdom about human information processing that even approaches called "user-centered" design typically mean making sure that the automation doesn't create demands that exceed users' "limitations." Too often, "respect thy users" means adapt the system to this weak link. This is not respect.

Use-centered design[22] is an alternative to this limitations-based approach. In this view, we consider humans and machines as complementary resources for addressing problems of complex work domains. We measure the capabilities of each in terms of the work domain's demands and opportunities, not against each other's "limitations." Similar perspectives are reflected in the concepts of *situated and distributed cognition*[23,24] and cognitive systems engineering.[25–27] A key feature of all these approaches is that distinctions between human and machine components merge into higher-order invariants and conjoint variables, as the focus shifts to systems-level analysis. At this level, we measure "fitness" of the human–machine system against the demands of a situation or work context. And fitness implies more than the absence of error. As in holistic medicine, a systems perspective begins to move past questions of disease to consider questions of health. For design, this means beginning to think in terms of safety rather than exclusively in terms of the blame game of human error. It means shifting the emphasis—from protecting the system against human limitations to leveraging human capabilities most effectively relative to the functional work objectives.

Cognitive systems engineering and HCC should be about the exploration of work contexts and work domains. They should be part of a collaboration with engineers, operators, computer scientists, and designers.

Cognitive systems engineering and HCC should be about the exploration of work contexts and work domains. They should be part of a collaboration with engineers, operators, computer scientists, and designers in the search for qualitative insights into the dynamics of adaptive cognitive systems. How might we integrate information into meaningful chunks that reflect a work domain's demands? How can training or interface design help human operators achieve this integration? Consider not only experts' current thinking about a problem but also the possibility of even better approaches with the support of appropriate training or visualization and representation tools. As a side effect, discoveries resulting from this search might reflect back on theory in a way that offers insight into basic mechanisms of human performance. Clearly, Jens Rasmussen's constructs of skill-, rule-, and knowledge-based processing comprise one example of this.[25] Other examples include Gary Klein's construct of recognition-primed decision making[28] and Edwin Hutchins' ideas about distributed memory.[23]

In HCC, we rely on basic knowledge about human characteristics and then try to develop computational devices that leverage those characteristics. Negative evaluations, such as seeing human characteristics as limitations, are both misleading and unhelpful. Respect is what it is all about. Otherwise, we continue to fight the legendary battle of John Henry versus the steam hammer to see whether human or machine is the winner! Nobody wins when design problems are cast as a competition.

And most significantly, competition between human and machine typically overlooks an important design dimension. Somebody must take responsibility for describing domain constraints so that we can (at least qualitatively) understand the capabilities of both humans and machines relative to the opportunities and dangers that these constraints represent. Human factors engineers who confine their role to cataloging human limitations end up reducing both their opportunity to participate in the design process and their ability to more deeply understand the fundamental properties of complex cognitive systems. ■

Acknowledgments

The second author's contribution to this article was through his participation in the Advanced Decision Architectures Collaborative Technology Alliance, sponsored by the US Army Research Laboratory under cooperative agreement DAAD19-01-2-0009.

References

1. R.R. Hoffman et al., "A Rose by Any Other Name ... Would Probably Be Given an Acronym," *IEEE Intelligent Systems*, vol. 17, no. 4, July/Aug. 2002, pp. 72–80.

2. C.D. Wickens, *Engineering Psychology and Human Performance*, 2nd ed., Harper Collins, New York, 1992, p. 3.

3. B.H. Kantowitz and R.D. Sorkin, *Human Factors: Understanding People-System Relationships*, John Wiley & Sons, New York, 1983, p. 30.

4. D.A. Norman, *Things That Make Us Smart*, Addison-Wesley, Boston, 1993.

5. D. Gorfein and R.R. Hoffman, eds., *Memory and Learning: The Ebbinghaus Centennial Conf.*, Lawrence Erlbaum Associates, Mahwah, N.J., 1987.

6. G.A. Miller, "The Magical Number Seven plus or minus Two: Some Limits on Our Capacity to Process Information," *Psychological Rev.*, vol. 63, 1956, pp. 81–96.

7. A.D. Baddeley, *The Psychology of Memory*, Basic Books, New York, 1976.

8. H.A. Simon, "How Big Is a Chunk?" *Science*, vol. 183, 1974, pp. 482–488.

9. P.H. Lindsay and D.A. Norman, *Human Information Processing*, 2nd ed., Academic Press, New York, 1977.

10. E.A. Feigenbaum, "What Hath Simon Wrought?" *Complex Information Processing*, D. Klahr and K. Kotovsky, eds., Lawrence Erlbaum, Mahwah, N.J., 1989, pp. 165–182.

11. K.A. Ericsson and J. Smith, "Prospects and Limits on the Empirical Study of Expertise," *Toward a General Theory of Expertise*, J. Smith and K.A. Ericsson, eds., Cambridge Univ. Press, Cambridge, UK, 1991, pp. 1–38.

12. D.A. Norman, *Learning and Memory*, W.H. Freeman, San Francisco, 1982.

13. T.K. Landauer, *The Trouble with Computers*, MIT Press, Cambridge, Mass., 1997.

14. S. Pinker, *The Language Instinct*, Morrow, New York, 1994.

15. R.N. Shepard, "Recognition Memory for Words, Sentences, and Pictures," *J. Verbal Learning and Verbal Behavior*, vol. 6, 1967, pp. 156–163.

16. H.A. Simon and W.G. Chase, "Skill in Chess," *Am. Scientist*, vol. 61, 1973, pp. 394–403.

17. P. Fitts, *Human Engineering for an Effective Air Navigation and Traffic Control System*, Nat'l Academy of Sciences, Washington, D.C., 1951.

18. D.A. Norman and D.G. Bobrow, "On Data-Limited and Resource-Limited Processing," *Cognitive Psychology*, vol. 7, 1975, pp. 44–64.

19. D.P. Miller and A.D. Swain, "Human Error and Human Reliability," *Handbook of Human Factors*, G. Salvendy, ed., John Wiley & Sons, New York, 1987, pp. 219–250.

20. S.K. Card, T.P. Moran, and A. Newell, *The Psychology of Human-Computer Interaction*, Lawrence Erlbaum Associates, Mahwah, N.J., 1983.

21. K.J. Vicente and J.H. Wang, "An Ecological Theory of Expertise Effects in Memory Recall," *Psychological Rev.*, vol. 105, 1998, pp. 33–57.

22. J.M. Flach and C.O. Dominguez, "Use-Centered Design," *Ergonomics in Design*, July 1995, pp. 19–24.

23. E. Hutchins, *Cognition in the Wild*, MIT Press, Cambridge, Mass., 1995.

24. L. Suchman, *Plans and Situated Actions: The Problem of Human-Machine Communication*, Cambridge Univ. Press, Cambridge, UK, 1987.

25. J. Rasmussen, *Information Processing and Human-Machine Interaction: An Approach to Cognitive Engineering*, North Holland, New York, 1986.

26. J. Rasmussen, A.M. Pejtersen, and L.P. Goodstein, *Cognitive Systems Engineering*, John Wiley & Sons, New York, 1994.

27. E. Hollnagel and D.D. Woods, "Cognitive Systems Engineering: New Wine in New Bottles," *Int'l J. Man-Machine Studies*, vol. 18, 1983, pp. 583–600.

28. G. Klein, "Recognition-Primed Decision Making," *Advances in Man-Machine System Research*, vol. 5, W.B. Rouse, ed., JAI Press, Greenwich, Conn., 1989, pp. 47–92.

John M. Flach is a professor in the Department of Psychology at Wright State University, where he teaches cognitive psychology and its application. His research deals with understanding the basic nature of perceptual–motor coordination and implications for the design of human–machine systems. He received his PhD in experimental psychology from Ohio State University. Contact him at Wright State Univ., Dayton, OH 45435; john.flach@wright.edu.

Robert R. Hoffman is a research scientist at the University of West Florida's Institute for Human and Machine Cognition and a faculty associate in the Department of Psychology. He is a fellow of the American Psychological Society and an honorary fellow of the British Library, Eccles Center for American Studies. He is a member of the Human Factors and Ergonomics Society, the AAAI, the Psychonomic Society, the International Society for Ecological Psychology, the American Meteorological Society, and the American Society for Photogrammetric Engineering and Remote Sensing. He received his BA, MA, and PhD in experimental psychology from the University of Cincinnati. Contact him at the Inst. for Human & Machine Cognition, 40 Alcaniz St., Pensacola, FL 32501; rhoffman@ai.uwf.edu.

Erratum

In the Nov./Dec. 2002 essay by M. Endsley and R. Hoffman entitled "The Sacagawea Principle" (*IEEE Intelligent Systems*, pp. 80–85) is the following quotation:

> [In the] tradition we might dub Technology-Centered Design (TCD), system developers specify the requirements for machines, they then implement or prototype the requirements, and finally they produce devices and software. And then they go away, leaving users to cope with what they have built. Indeed, experience has shown that devices that are designed according to the 'design-then-train' philosophy ... force users to adapt to the system. The user is entangled with the system terminology and jargons that are the designer's view of the world.[18]

Reference 18 is listed as follows:

18. C. Ntuen, "A Model of System Science for Human-Centered Design," *Human-Centered Systems: Information, Interactivity and Intelligence*, J. Flanagan et al., eds., tech. report, US Nat'l Science Foundation, Washington, D.C., 1997, p. 312.

That is incorrect. The correct reference is as follows:

18. R.R. Hoffman et al., "A Rose by Any Other Name Would Probably Be Given an Acronym," *IEEE Intelligent Systems*, July/Aug. 2002, pp. 72–80.

Chapter 23: Macrocognition

G. Klein, K.G. Ross, B.M. Moon, D.E. Klein, R.R. Hoffman, and E. Hollnagel, "Macrocognition," *IEEE Intelligent Systems*, vol. 18, no. 3, May/June 2003, pp. 81–85. doi: 10.1109/MIS.2003.1200735

If we engineer complex cognitive systems on the basis of mistaken or inappropriate views of cognition, we can wind up designing systems that degrade performance rather than improve it. The results stemming from the application of any cognitive systems engineering methodology will be incomplete unless they include a description of the cognition that is needed to accomplish the work. Traditionally, cognitive researchers have conducted laboratory experiments on micro-level topics such as puzzle solving, serial versus parallel attention, and other standard laboratory paradigms for psychological research. In contrast, the methodology for macrocognition focuses on contexts such as the "field setting," the "natural laboratory." In such contexts the adaptation of cognition to complexity involves functions such as sensemaking and problem detection. Macrocognitive modeling also differs from modeling in the microcognitive distinction (e.g., stages, steps, flowcharts) in that the core processes are regarded as continuous, parallel, and highly interacting. This view has many implications for the goals of intelligent systems and for processes for creating human-centered work systems.

Macrocognition

Gary Klein, Karol G. Ross, and Brian M. Moon, *Klein Associates*
Devorah E. Klein, *Insight Product Development*
Robert R. Hoffman, *Institute for Human and Machine Cognition*
Erik Hollnagel, *Linköping University*

If we engineer complex cognitive systems on the basis of mistaken or inappropriate views of cognition, we can wind up designing systems that degrade performance rather than improve it. The results stemming from the application of any cognitive systems engineering methodology will be incomplete unless they include a description of the cognition that is needed to accomplish the work. The concept of *macrocognition* is a way of describing cognitive work as it naturally occurs.

Definition

Macrocognition is a term coined by Pietro Cacciabue and Erik Hollnagel to indicate a level of description of the cognitive functions that are performed in natural (versus artificial laboratory) decision-making settings.[1,2] Traditionally, cognitive researchers have conducted lab experiments on topics such as puzzle solving, serial versus parallel attentional mechanisms, and other standard laboratory paradigms for psychological research. We term these *microcognition* because they are aimed at investigating the building blocks of cognition, the processes that we believe are invariant and serve as the basis for all kinds of thinking and perceiving.

In contrast, the methodology for macrocognition focuses on the world outside the lab. This includes contexts designated by such terms as the "field setting," the "natural laboratory," and the "real world."[3] Key features of cognition in naturalistic contexts include the following:

Editors: Robert R. Hoffman, Patrick J. Hayes, and Kenneth M. Ford
Institute for Human and Machine Cognition, University of West Florida
rhoffman@ai.uwf.edu

- Decisions are typically complex, often involving data overload.
- Decisions are often made under time pressure and involve high stakes and high risk.
- Research participants are domain practitioners rather than college students.
- Goals are sometimes ill-defined, and multiple goals often conflict.
- Decisions must be made under conditions in which few things can be controlled or manipulated; indeed, many key variables and their interactions are not even fully understood.

In natural settings, domain practitioners rarely focus on microcognitive processes. Instead, they are concerned with macrocognitive phenomena, as Table 1 shows.

These types of functions—detecting problems, managing uncertainty, and so forth—are not usually studied in laboratory settings. To some extent, they are emergent phenomena. In addition to describing these types of phenomena (the left-hand column) on a macrocognitive level, we can also describe them on a microcognitive level. The two types of description are complementary. Each serves its own purpose, and together they might provide a broader and more comprehensive view than either by itself. We do not suggest that the investigation of macrocognitive phenomena will supercede or diminish the importance of microcognition work—just that we need research to better understand macrocognitive functions in order to improve cognitive engineering.

Another way in which the methodology for macrocognition differs from that of microcognition deals with assumptions about cognition's "building blocks." Microperspectives carry with them the notion of reductionism—that explanations come from reduction to a set of basic functions or components. Although we might want to reveal specific causal sequences of various memory or attentional mechanisms, this turns out to be difficult. When we try to describe naturalistic decision making, we quickly realize that it makes little sense to concoct hypothetical information processing flow diagrams believed to represent causal sequences of mental operations, because they end up looking like spaghetti graphs.

Table 1. Important macrocognitive phenomena and traditional microcognitive lab research.

Macrocognition phenomena of concern to domain practitioners	Parallel traditional microcognition topics of concern to cognitive scientists
Planning and problem detection	Puzzle solving
Using leverage points to construct options	Strategies for searching problem spaces
Attention management	Serial versus parallel processing models
Uncertainty management	Estimating probabilities or uncertainty values

Explaining cognitive phenomena by decomposing or reducing them to hypothetical building blocks might not always be necessary. If anything, supplementary explanatory concepts come from above rather than from below—for example, feedback/feedforward, self-organization, equilibrium, and so on. Macrocognitive functions can be considered as perspectives, but not in the sense that the constituent functions are necessarily elements, or elementary in any way. And they are rarely like the "basic" cognitive functions of microcognition. It is more like the phenomenon you often find in a functional analysis—that is, that function A is a precondition for function B, and function B is in turn a precondition for function A. In that sense, each one encompasses the other, but one is not more elementary than the other. Each description has a value in itself, and the fact that multiple descriptions exist only reflects that you can look at something from different viewpoints and different levels. The linkages we should look for are therefore dynamic ones that can explain how functions or behaviors can emerge and interact.

To some extent, macrocognitive phenomena take place over longer time periods than microcognitive phenomena, but the distinction is not time-linked. Some macrocognitive phenomena happen very quickly, and some aspects of microcognition, such as puzzle solving, can be drawn out. Macrocognition often involves ill-defined goals, whereas microcognitive tasks usually have well-defined goals.

As researchers learn more about macrocognition, they are likely to clarify its relationship to microcognition. However, the two levels might not line up neatly. Microcognitive research has posited a set of distinctions (for instance, the difference between memory and inference) that might not be useful as we study macrocognition. The study of macrocognitive functions will introduce new distinctions that will have to be evaluated on their own merits.

Why study macrocognition?

Some will object to postulating a distinction between micro- and macrocognition. If both levels address cognitive processes, why introduce new terms and a new distinction? One reason is that without it, most researchers would likely continue experimentation on microcognition and ignore macrocognition. Second, the study of macrocognition might require a different approach to research. Third, we believe that the field of microcognition will also benefit by being contextualized by macrocognitive functions.

Macrocognition comprises the mental activities that must be successfully accomplished to perform a task or achieve a goal. Other somewhat related terms have been used in this regard, such as *situated cognition* and *extended cognition*.[4] These terms describe the fact that macrocognitive functions are generally performed in collaboration—by a team working in a natural situation, and usually in conjunction with computational artifacts. The emphasis in macrocognition is on cognitive functions, and teams can perform these. Thus, we can study how the barriers to effective problem detection might be different for individuals than for teams. Macrocognitive functions can be performed using information technology, or without any technology at all, and we can study how technology helps us past some barriers but introduces others. We prefer the term *macrocognition* because in addition to broadening the focus to include the team and technology context, it also broadens the level of description of the cognitive functions themselves. General approaches such as situated cognition are important for explaining why cognitive functions must be studied in natural contexts, but they only point to the need to discover and understand the macrocognitive functions that operate in natural contexts.

Furthermore, one of a macrocognition framework's intended functions is to encourage the development of descriptive models of processes such as decision making, sensemaking, and problem detection. For example, a research program on decision making started by investigating the strategies used by experienced firefighters.[5] This research program used accounts of critical incidents to propose a new model of decision, called the *Recognition-Primed Decision* model. The RPD model tried to explain how experienced decision makers could generate effective courses of action without having to consider more than a single option. Normative models of decision making, such as utility theory, dictate that "good" decision making involves specifying all the action alternatives, all the possible outcomes, and their likelihoods, and evaluating all the alternatives for their costs and benefits. The RPD model postulates that we can use pattern matching to categorize a situation, so that the recognition of familiarity (case type) evokes a recognition of the typical way to respond. Furthermore, experienced decision makers can evaluate a single course of action by mentally simulating it rather than by deliberatively comparing it to other options.

After considerable research on recognition-primed decision making, we realized that the model was basically a combination of three decision heuristics that had already been well-studied from the microcognition perspective: availability and representativeness to identify the typical course of action, and the simulation heuristic to evaluate the course of action.[6] Therefore, in this case it was possible to trace the macrocognitive phenomenon back to hypothetical microcognitive components. However, several decades of research on the availability, representativeness, and simulation heuristics had not led to a discovery of recognitional decision making. That is why we see the macrocognitive functions as emergent. We discover them by investigating cognition in field settings rather than by continually pursuing explanations of lab findings.

A variety of macrocognitive functions

Our current list of the major macrocognitive functions appears in the center of Figure 1.[5,7–12] The circle around the primary functions shows a range of supporting macrocognitive processes.[13–19] We do not include them as primary functions because decision makers, at least those we have studied, do not carry out these processes as an end in itself but rather as a means for achieving the primary functions listed. This distinction is as much for pragmatic as for theoretical purposes: to highlight those functions that repeatedly emerge as ends in themselves across a variety of projects in various domains.

Additional macrocognitive functions and supporting processes will eventually be added to this set; some of the functions in the figure might be subsumed into others as researchers make new discoveries. For instance, we have not included situation awareness[7] in Figure 1 because it is a state rather than a process; it arises through sensemaking and situation assessment. Basically, we are less concerned with presenting an official list than with encouraging research at the macrocognitive level of description.

We considered trying to diagram the relationships between the different functions and supporting processes in the format of processing diagrams—the currency of cognitive science—but decided that such a representation is still premature. In most natural settings, the decision maker must accomplish most or all of these functions, often at the same time. A macrocognitive function such as problem detection can be an end in itself for a mission such as intensive-care nursing or intelligence analysis, or it can be a means toward an end of command and control replanning. Mental simulation and storybuilding are typical strategies for sensemaking but are also supporting strategies for naturalistic decision making. A mental model of a situation must be developed for decision making, sensemaking, effective planning and replanning, coordination, adaptation, and replanning. In other words, everything can be connected to everything. This makes any attempt at depicting a flow diagram either ad hoc or useless because cognition, as it occurs in the world, can't be "frozen."

Some of the functions that Figure 1 depicts have been studied to a level of specificity that enables the creation of specific models, whereas others are still in the early stages of modeling. An example of a specific model is the RPD model, mentioned earlier, which has generated several empirical generalizations about lawful relationships:

- People make most decisions using recognitional strategies, fewer decisions by comparing options analytically. This generalization is based on studies in domains such as firefighting, critical-care nursing, and military decision making and is tempered by the features of the domain.[5]
- Experienced people rely more heavily on recognitional strategies. When people are just learning about a domain, their approach tends to be more analytic and deliberative.
- If people have any experience in a domain, the first option they generate is usually plausible (and certainly not random).
- People typically evaluate options using mental simulation rather than analytical comparison.
- As people gain experience, they spend more time examining the situation and less on contrasting the options, whereas novices spend more time contrasting options and less on comprehending the situation.

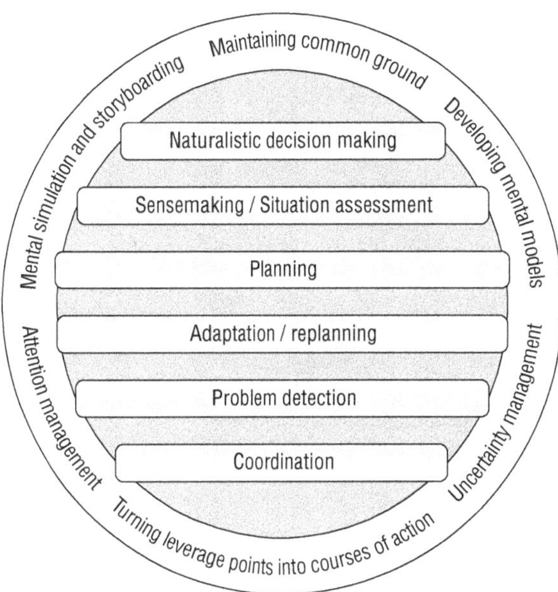

Figure 1. Macrocognitive functions and supporting processes for individuals, teams, and information technologies.

Many of the accounts researchers have provided of macrocognitive functions and processes are preliminary and tentative. Nevertheless, they are the best descriptions currently available—because macrocognitive processes have received so little attention. That is a major reason for calling out macrocognition as a distinct framework. We must study these types of functions and processes, even though they do not fit neatly into controlled experiments. We must find ways to conduct cognitive field research that can improve our understanding of the functions and processes encountered at the macrocognition level.

A natural science research approach

We propose that the naturalistic perspective is appropriate for studying macrocognition.[20,21] Naturalists develop theories, concepts, and methods by observing and interacting with the world. Research for the naturalist is a process—not a single, predefined procedure. The naturalist digs out the nature of the empirical world, continually revising conceptions of it and remaining flexible in methods of discovery and analysis. In the case of complex cognitive systems, the naturalist probes the world in which people actually live and work and the emerging situations in which they find themselves. The approach becomes most salient when contrasted with attempts to abstract or simulate a piece of the empirical world, as is typical in laboratory studies, or to substitute a preset image of it, as in many information processing accounts of cognition.

The naturalistic approach could yield an empirical basis for macrocognition. Yet, when someone proposes it to the research community as an investigative approach, standard methodological objections are often raised: Naturalism does not follow the experimental paradigm, it (therefore) lacks rigor, the procedures are (therefore) soft, and the results are (therefore) not generalizable. From our vantage point, these objections are wrong, a clear case of methodolatry. Many grand figures of science exemplify the naturalist at work—Charles Darwin, Jean Piaget, Galileo Galilei. It would be nonsense to say that Darwin contributed nothing to science because he did not formulate his theory of evolution as a consequence of a series of lab experiments. Nor would it make sense to criticize Galileo because he did not try to hold constant certain variables in the nighttime sky. Leading naturalists created rigorous observation methods, made valuable discoveries, and tested their hypotheses, leading to the conclusion that "more discoveries have arisen from intense observation of very limited material than from statistics applied to large groups."[22]

The naturalistic perspective qualifies as being scientific in the best meaning of that term. The long-held view that the study of cognition must adhere to tightly controlled studies using experimental methods would only serve to limit us in our attempt to study and describe macrocognitive functions. Our focus must turn now to formulating criteria for evaluating naturalistic studies, as other disciplines have done.[23] Our call for more macrocognition research is also a call for this research community to develop the science of understanding human cognition in natural settings.

The more we learn about macrocognition, the better should be the applications. We should be able to design better ways for using information technology, better interfaces, and better training programs. We should be able to discover strategies for enabling operators to control complex and highly dynamic systems, especially systems operated in distributed environments.

Researchers have empirically demonstrated that a range of cognitive functions and processes are central in complex cognitive systems, but these functions and processes have received little or no interest from the pertinent research communities. To a great extent, they are emergent phenomena—only obvious once researchers begin to investigate performance in natural contexts. The systems we would design to support decision making would be very different if we defined decision making as the process of multiattribute utility analysis or the collection of biases that must be continually corrected.

Researchers can probably be more effective working as naturalists to capture and study macrocognitive functions than by trying to impose an experimental structure. Furthermore, macrocognitive functions are linked; attempts to study individual processes in isolation from the others will probably result in distortions.

As we develop better tools and methods for cognitive systems engineering, we will have to gain a clearer sense of the cognitive functions we want to support. The macrocognition framework is intended to clarify what these functions are, so that we can do a better job of studying and supporting them. ■

Acknowledgments

We thank David Woods, Rob Hutton, Jeffrey Sanchez-Burks, and Amelia Armstrong for helpful discussions and criticisms of the ideas presented in this article.

The preparation of this article was supported by the Advanced Decision Architectures Collaborative Technology Alliance sponsored by the US Army Research Laboratory under Cooperative Agreement DAAD19-01-2-0009.

References

1. P.C. Cacciabue and E. Hollnagel, "Simulation of Cognition: Applications," *Expertise and Technology: Cognition and Human-Computer Cooperation*, J.M. Hoc, P.C. Cacciabue, and E. Hollnagel, eds., Lawrence Erlbaum Associates, 1995, pp. 55–73.

2. D.E. Klein, H.A. Klein, and G. Klein, "Macrocognition: Linking Cognitive Psychology and Cognitive Ergonomics," *Proc. 5th Int'l Conf. Human Interactions with Complex Systems*, Univ. of Illinois at Urbana-Champaign, 2000, pp. 173–177.

3. R.R. Hoffman and K.A. Deffenbacher, "An Analysis of the Relations of Basic and Applied Science," *Ecological Psychology*, vol. 2, no. 3, 1993, pp. 309–315.

4. E. Hollnagel, "Extended Cognition and the Future of Ergonomics," *Theoretical Issues in Ergonomics Science*, vol. 2, no. 3, 2001, pp. 309–315.

5. G. Klein, *Sources of Power: How People Make Decisions*, MIT Press, 1998.

6. D. Kahneman, P. Slovic, and A. Tversky, eds., *Judgment under Uncertainty: Heuristics and Biases*, Cambridge Univ. Press, 1982.

7. M.R. Endsley, B. Bolte, and D.G. Jones, *Designing for Situation Awareness: An Approach to Human-Centered Design*, Taylor and Francis, 2003.

8. G. Klein, "Features of Team Coordination," *New Trends in Cooperative Activities*, M. McNeese, M.R. Endsley, and E. Salas, eds., Human Factors and Ergonomics Soc., 2001, pp. 68–95.

9. G. Klein and T.E. Miller, "Distributed Planning Teams," *Int'l J. Cognitive Ergonomics*, vol. 3, no. 3, 1999, pp. 203–222.

10. G. Klein and L. Pierce, "Adaptive Teams," *Proc. 2001 Command and Control Research and Technology Symp.* (CD-ROM), Naval Postgraduate School, 2001.

11. G. Klein et al., "Features of Problem Detection," *Proc. Human Factors and Ergonomics Soc. 43rd Ann. Meeting*, vol. 1, Human Factors and Ergonomics Soc., 1999, pp. 133–137.

12. K. Weick, *Sensemaking in Organizations*, Sage Publications, 1995.

13. D. Gopher, "The Skill of Attention Control: Acquisition and Execution of Attention Strategies," *Attention and Performance XIV: Synergies in Experimental Psychology, Artificial Intelligence and Cognitive Neuroscience*, D.E. Meyer and S. Kornblum, eds., MIT Press, 1992.

14. G. Klein et al., *Cognitive Wavelength: The Role of Common Ground in Distributed Replanning*, tech. report AFRL-HE-WP-TR-2001-0029, Wright-Patterson Air Force Research Laboratory, 2000.

15. G. Klein and S. Wolf, "The Role of Leverage Points in Option Generation," *IEEE Trans. Systems, Man and Cybernetics: Applications and Reviews*, vol. 28, no. 1, 1998, pp. 157–160.

16. G.A. Klein and B.W. Crandall, "The Role of Mental Simulation in Naturalistic Decision Making," *Local Applications of the Ecological Approach to Human-Machine Systems*, vol. 2, P. Hancock et al., eds., Lawrence Erlbaum Associates, 1995, pp. 324–358.

17. R. Lipshitz and O. Strauss, "How Decision-Makers Cope with Uncertainty," *Proc. Human Factors and Ergonomics Soc. 40th Ann. Meeting*, vol. 1, Human Factors and Ergonomics Soc., 1996, pp. 189–192.

18. W.B. Rouse and N.M. Morris, "On Looking into the Black Box: Prospects and Limits on the Search for Mental Models," *Psychological Bull.*, vol. 100, no. 3, Nov. 1986, pp. 349–363.

19. J.F. Schmitt and G. Klein, "Fighting in the Fog: Dealing with Battlefield Uncertainty," *Marine Corps Gazette*, vol. 80, Aug. 1996, pp. 62–69.

20. H. Blumer, *Symbolic Interactionism*, Univ. of California at Berkeley, 1969.

21. B.M. Moon, "Naturalistic Decision Making: Establishing a Naturalistic Perspective in Judgment and Decision Making Research," Advanced Decision Architectures Collaborative Technology Alliance cooperative agreement DAAD19-01-2-0009, US Army Research Laboratory, 2002, http://arlada.info/uploads/62/286/KLEIN_Report_-_101402.doc.

22. W.I.B. Beveridge, *The Art of Scientific Investigation*, Vintage Books, 1957.

23. L. Athens, "Scientific Criteria for Evaluating Qualitative Studies," *Studies in Symbolic Interaction*, vol. 5, 1984, pp. 259–268.

Chapter 24: Decision(?)Making(?)

R.R. Hoffman and J.F. Yates, "Decision(?)Making(?)," *IEEE Intelligent Systems*, vol. 20, no. 4, July/Aug. 2005, pp. 76–83. doi: 10.1109/MIS.2005.67

Computers, including intelligent systems, assist human decision making in many ways. One aspect of decision making is the "final point" notion, that decision making leads up to a commitment to action. This aspect is what makes it too easy for us to think of decisions as things that are made. We argue otherwise, that all acts of deciding can be decomposed into a set of underlying issues and conditional dependencies. The decomposition we present has implications for the design of human-centered decision support systems.

Decision(?)Making(?)

Robert R. Hoffman, *Institute for Human and Machine Cognition*
J. Frank Yates, *University of Michigan*

Consider, for a moment, "What are we making intelligent decision aids *for*?" Computers, including intelligent systems, assist human decision making in many ways.[1–3] Decision aids can range from an online tool provided by *Consumer Reports* to help people choose a refrigerator, to a large system for monitoring an industrial process. Group decision aids focus on supporting communication.[4,5] Expert systems can be considered decision aids, as can systems that use statistical methods to assist in diagnostic procedures. Decision aids can provide information involved in deciding or information pertinent to evaluating states of the world. To support these situation assessment and monitoring activities, computers can integrate and display information and assist in replanning.[6] When we deconstruct such generic tasks, most of the component tasks reduce to option generation, option selection, and outcome evaluation.[7] For these, we can bring to bear various mathematical techniques such as utility analysis.[8]

But how well do such tools really help humans deal with the difficulties of deciding itself—for instance, adapting to changing circumstances or coping with situations that are both unfamiliar and infrequent?[7] While several good analyses of decision-making situations and situational factors exist that can help shape decision-aid architectures and functionalities,[9,10] has anyone done a corresponding analysis of what this thing called the *decision* is? After discussing this question, we'll sharpen the focus for new and potentially useful applications of intelligent systems technologies.

Editors: Robert R. Hoffman, Patrick J. Hayes, and Kenneth M. Ford
Institute for Human and Machine Cognition, University of West Florida
rhoffman@ai.uwf.edu

What's a "decision"?

The word *decide* gets a great deal of mileage in English, being critical in the definitions of dozens of other concepts, including *arbitrate*, *conclude*, *convict*, *declare*, *define*, *disagree*, *intervene*, and *judge*. Another use is adverbial: the idea of acting "decisively," achieving a final determination with clear and definitive intent. "Decide" also works as a transitive verb, meaning to influence or determine: for example, "This new development finally decided me," or "The vote in New Hampshire often decides the outcome of the presidential election."

The modern English word "decision" comes from the Sanskrit "/khidati/"—meaning to tear and then to Latin "caedare," meaning to kill or cut down (as in battle), and then to "de +caedere" meaning to cut off from or to cut thoroughly.[11–13] We see here a notion that the decision is a point, and a final point or action separating one thing from another (historically, a human head or limb from its body). All dictionary definitions preserve this sense of bringing a series of events, including a mental sequence, to a final, point-like conclusion.[11] For example, WordNet 1.7.1 (http://wordnet.princeton.edu/online) defines "decide" as "To make up one's mind, to reach, make, or come to a decision about something." While the circularity is obvious and troublesome, this essay starts with the idea that decisions are things that are "made."

You can't help but be struck by the irony that many scholarly books on judgment and decision making typically forego an attempt at defining this thing called "decision."[14–19] Only in one textbook[20] and one edited volume[21] do we find the word "decision" even as an entry in the subject index. Only in a few sources do we find an explicit discussion of the difference between "decision" and "judgment." (A "judgment" is an assessment or opinion as to what was, is, or will be the state of some decision-relevant aspect of the world—for example, whether a defendant committed a crime, whether a patient

Table 1. The received view of decision making, with examples.

Case	Step 1	Step 2	Step 3
General	Information that pertains to the decision is acquired.	Span of apprehension; the information is perceived and interpreted.	Commitment to action: the decision is made.
An everyday example	Dee arrives at the airport only to learn that her flight is delayed because of fog.	She apprehends or infers an impending threat—missing her meeting. She reasons that she should perhaps call ahead to Tom to ask for a delay in their meeting.	There is a mental act, not necessarily deliberative, and she begins to reach for her cell phone to make the call.
How can we get to the Moon? (known as the Apollo Mode Decision)[24]	US President John F. Kennedy decided, for political reasons, to begin a space program with the goal of getting to the Moon in a certain time frame—before the Soviets.	This implied the threat of not actually achieving that goal. So, the decision problem involved committing to a program intended to avert that threat. In months of debate, reports, and meetings, the participants discussed and debated many alternative plans, sometimes in the presence of President Kennedy.	Lunar-orbit rendezvous was chosen as the best chance of winning the race to the Moon because it involved relatively little technological innovation compared to the alternative schemes.
Where should the atomic bomb be dropped?[25]	The summer of 1945 was named as the most likely date when sufficient production would exist to make constructing an atomic bomb possible. A test in New Mexico was held six days after sufficient material was available for the first bomb.	Target selection began in the spring of 1945. Some important considerations were the aircraft's range, the desirability of visual bombing, probable weather, targets to produce the greatest military effect, target susceptibility, and, to determine an atomic bomb's effect, targets untouched by previous bombing.	It was decided that Hiroshima and Nagasaki met the criteria for the primary targets.

Table 2. Variations on the three-step scheme in various domains' literature.

Literature domain	Step 1	Step 2	Step 3
Decision aiding for process control	Situation assessment	Planning	Commitment[9]
Expert systems	Information acquisition	Modeling (via knowledge bases and decision trees)	Commitment[26]
Naturalistic decision making[27]	Situational awareness	Inference	Action
Problem solving	Staging activities, such as identifying problems and specifying goals	Apprehension, involving perceiving and comprehending activities such as the generation of possible solutions, implementation plans, and methods for evaluating outcomes	Selecting or choosing

Table 3. Unpacking the everyday example.

Case	Step 1. Information acquisition	Step 2. Perception and interpretation	Step 3. Commitment
The example	Dee arrives at the airport only to learn that her flight is delayed because of fog.	She reasons that she should perhaps call ahead to Tom to ask for a delay in their meeting.	She begins to reach for her cell phone to make the call.
The example unpacked	After hearing of the fog delay, Dee looks out of the panoramic window at the concourse to perceive the weather directly. How foggy is it? Did she pause to deliberatively decide, "Hey, I should look out the window"? Perhaps it was intuitive or automatic, perhaps not.	In thinking about the fog delay's implications, Dee mentally simulates possible futures. This takes into account the fact that she's hungry and she realizes that she has time to grab ... what? Perhaps a cup of coffee and a bagel.	While pushing the buttons on her cell phone, she's alert to signal strength ("What do I do if it's low?") and battery charge level ("What do I do if I forgot to recharge it last night?")

has a particular disease, or whether product sales will exceed the break-even point.[14,22,23]

The final-point notion

A decision can be defined as a commitment to a course of action having the intention of serving the interests and values of particular people.[23] A decision is generally understood as a mental event that occurs at a singular point in time—a psychological moment of choice—that leads immediately or directly to action (for example, push the button, or wait 30 seconds and then push the button). Most views of decision making in the literatures of psychology and of judgment and decision making locate the notion of decision in the final stage of a stage-theoretic framework. Table 1 provides three specific examples. Table 2 presents variations on the three-step scheme at the core of a number of both normative and descriptive models of decision making.[10,18]

The final-point notion allows us to say that decisions are "made," but even in apparently simple, clear-cut cases, the deciding process is much more than this.

Beyond three-step descriptions

The process of deciding (especially the big decisions as opposed to snap decisions) often entails making a number of component decisions. But more importantly, the decision process entails a host of significant cognitive, evaluative, and affective activities that are parallel and interactive. We illustrate this in table 3 by deconstructing one of table 1's examples.

While deciding involves acquiring information, that in and of itself might itself involve other decisions and deliberations over future possibilities, preferences, options, and goals. This shows in the Apollo Mode Decision (see table 1), which began with other decisions as the informational starting point. While most three-step views regard decisions as culminations, decisions are often expressions of contingencies and anticipations of unfolding events and ways in which future events might be surprising. Consider the atomic bomb decision. An initial decision problem was where to drop the bomb, but "the" decision that came out of the process wasn't just where to drop, but to try to develop a capability for generating accurate weather forecasts for Japan and then choose among targets and *then* decide *whether* to drop. Weather and weather-forecasting capabilities that would have to be created following the decision could not only affect the way the decision would be carried out but even forestall its implementation.

On this, three-step models are potentially misleading. You can always unpack any given three-step model into embedded three-steps, each having its own moment of choice. New decision problems constantly arise, either in the process of implementing a previous commitment or perhaps because that previous decision instigated new threats and opportunities. Often, there's no single "end" point. Notice in the Apollo Mode and atomic bomb examples that a network of contingencies and interdependencies existed. You might say there was a series of decisions, each of which could be unpacked as we did for the everyday example. It's perhaps possible to think of life as an endless chain of dominos—single commitments—each of which we can analyze, possibly to good effect. Despite the apparent popularity of three-step models, everyone would acknowledge that decisions are complex in this way. Thus, we could argue that in the table 3 reconstruction of the everyday example, we've merely decomposed each step into its own embedded three-step.

That might beg the issue because, as in the vast chunk of the modern scientific literature on decision making, "the decision" would still be regarded as a point-like thing, a singular commitment, that marks the end of a sequence of clear-cut mental operations.

In *Communication and Group Decision Making*,[28] editors Randy Hirokawa and Marshall S. Poole ask "What, exactly, is a decision?"

> Decisions are assumed to be discrete events, clearly distinguishable from other group activities .... Decision makers often can identify discrete decision points and feel a sense of completion at making a decision. These boundaries are not always as clear as they seem at first, however, and there is not always agreement on what events are involved in a given decision. Definitions of decision making episodes are ambiguous in several respects. (p. 9)

This volume comes from a different tradition than the psychology of judgment and decision making—specifically, the field of communications research. It also has a different emphasis: decisions' social context and "embeddedness" rather than the mental events that are believed to underlie decision making.

The scholarly volume, *Decision Making in Action*,[29] comes from yet another perspective—the field of "naturalistic decision making." This descriptive approach

> **Three-step models are potentially misleading. You can always unpack any given three-step into embedded three-steps, each having its own**

focuses on how experts perform and reason in real-world, complex domains where decisions are often high-stakes, high-risk, and made under considerable time pressure. The seminal studies in this area led to dissatisfaction with the literature's normative models. The authors latched onto a fact—that traditional decision research has been preoccupied with the issue of trade-offs:

> The basic cause of the mismatch is that traditional decision research has invested most of its energy in only one part of decision making, which we shall refer to as the decision event. In this view, the crucial part of decision making occurs when the decision maker (generally a single individual) surveys a known and fixed set of alternatives, weighs the likely consequences of choosing each, and makes a choice ... The decision making activities suggested by [the naturalistic studies] offer few clean examples of decision events. (p. 5)

Verbs, not nouns

We assert the following premises:

1. Whenever we carve out a three-step model, each step itself will be some other mental event involving judging or deciding.
2. The rule, rather than the exception, is that the commitment to action involves a contingency pointing to possible worlds and future contingencies, with the intention of scaffolding a capability to recognize when to be surprised.

These premises basically say that any individual three-step is necessarily incomplete as a description of a deciding event, even though one might be able to identify a moment of choice and call it "the decision."

We propose thinking of *decision making* in terms of *deciding*, regarding it as one of a number of macrocognitive processes that it supports and that support it.[27] This view hearkens to Franz Brentano's ideas,[30] who regarded all mental representations as interactions between constantly fluxing memory and perceptual activity, which always have a judgmental aspect. From Brentano's dynamic psychology comes the view that we should speak of mental phenomena using verbs rather than nouns—deciding, not the decision.

The richness of deciding

Deciding involves many factors beyond those notions that the main theories have captured.[8,31] In the real world,

- deciding involves instantiating intentions and purposes;
- deciding is usually about causing good things to happen;
- actions are intended to bring about states of affairs that serve the interests and tastes of particular individuals or groups;
- commitments to act must be distinguished from action because, for various reasons, not all decisions are actually implemented; and
- choice among alternatives is never equivalent to choice among consequences, because alternatives rarely lead to single consequences.

A decider's reasoning derives from a host of "deep" contributors that are important to understand in their own right—for example, unique personal experiences, constitutional factors such as inherited dispositions or abilities, training, and culturally transmitted local customs. Aspects of decision making that have received the most attention in decision research are the evaluation of options, the anticipation of possibilities, judgment and reasoning biases, and the motivating values that particularize and specify individual decision-making episodes.

However, before decisions are "made" and while they are being "made," the decider attends to one or more important preliminary issues. Empirical work in myriad fields (such as psychology, health care, management, finance, engineering, law, operations, anthropology, counseling, politics, and marketing) as well as analyses of many hundreds of incidents converge on a number of fundamental questions that arise in real-life decision problems. That's why we use the phrase *cardinal decision issues* to describe them.[31] We can characterize decision processes as the means by which these cardinal issues are addressed.

Need

Why are we (not) deciding anything at all? This issue is about whether and how decision problems are recognized in the first place, how people come to recognize that existing or developing circumstances constitute threats or opportunities. In the former case, unless something is done, those people will be harmed, and in the latter, they will miss out on the chance to improve their situation. Deciding, in this view, is about arriving at commitments to actions that are intended to meet impending threats or opportunities. This issue strongly links decision making to notions of vigilance, problem-finding, and recognition-primed decision making.[27,32]

Mode

Who will decide, and how will they approach that task? How will those individuals address the other cardinal issues that must be resolved? A major part of the "who" question concerns whether to defer authority and to whom authority is deferred. The "how" question of the mode issue is about the nuts and bolts of how deciders carry out their work. The decision-making literature discusses several broad categories of possibilities, including (but not limited to) analytic, rule-based, automatic, and so-called intuitive decision making. Another aspect of mode is deliberation over whether to seek opinions, and from whom. Deciding often benefits from opinion-seeking,[20,23] yet relatively little is known about how people evaluate and aggregate the verbal opinions and evaluations they receive.

Investment

What kinds and amounts of resources will we invest in the process of deciding? This issue is about how and how well we determine whether the investment of resources in the process of deciding—for example, time, expertise, or tools—is appropriate, neither too little nor too much. Two important considerations are as yet unstudied systematically:

- The evaluation of resources according to resource categories. Resources will rarely all be of the same type (for instance, human resources, time, and materiel), and evaluations of investment will differ for such categories.
- The strategy of minimizing the costs of deciding by deliberately engaging "direct," nonanalytic modes of deciding (such as intuitive decision making).[33]

> **We propose thinking of decision making in terms of "deciding," regarding it as one of a number of macrocognitive processes that it supports and that support**

Options

What are the different actions we could potentially take to deal with this problem? Evaluating options, especially in terms of their costs and benefits, has been a central focus in the field of judgment and decision making. But this isn't the activity we refer to here. The options issue is about how people come to apprehend some prospective solutions to their decision problems but somehow never even recognize the existence of others. The issue's significance is implicit in the truism that you can't choose an alternative you don't know about. It's essential to recognize that expert navigation of the options issue isn't about increasing the number of alternatives considered (a false assumption that many scholars make when asserting that people are limited in their ability to consider multiple options). The ideal "option consideration set" for a given problem consists of only a single alternative—the best one. Recognizing, let alone deliberating, over other options is often wasteful, requiring the decision maker to expend precious time and resources vetting alternatives that ultimately will (or should) be rejected. But recent work has demonstrated that deliberating over large consideration sets can do more than simply waste time. It can also exact significant psychological costs, such as turmoil over the possibility of failing to pick the best alternative.[34]

Possibilities

What are the various things that could happen if we took that action, and which ones do we care about? This issue also involves the macrocognitive functions of sensemaking and mental projection—recognizing outcomes of prospective actions that are capable of occurring, and which would matter greatly if they were to occur. The concern isn't with whether those outcomes will or would occur, only whether they could.

Judgment

Which of the things that we care about actually would happen if we took that action? Although this issue might logically follow the possibilities issue, in the real world the fuller process is macrocognitive. If a decider recognizes (accurately or otherwise) that some decision-relevant event can happen, there must then be a judgment as to whether it would happen. One of us (Frank Yates)[20] observed that there are two classes of judgment processes: formalistic and substantive. Formalistic procedures are exemplified by the application of rules such as those in probability theory or regression analysis. Significantly, such rules are largely indifferent to the content of judgment problems. Quite the opposite is true of substantive procedures, which entail the attempt to envision how the world would (or wouldn't) literally create the event in question. Recognition-primed decision making[29] is one such substantive procedure. There are many indications in the literature that people resort to formalistic procedures only when they can't use substantive ones, which seem to be more "natural."[20]

Value

How much would anyone really care—positively or negatively—if this particular outcome happened? The value issue is a special case of the judgment issue, albeit an exceptionally important case. That's because it centers on what makes decision problems so distinctive and difficult—individual differences in what people like and dislike. But what is a "good" decision depends on the parties involved. And this gets back to the core idea that deciding involves a commitment to actions that are intended to result in outcomes that are satisfying to particular people. In order for a decider to pursue actions that promise outcomes that the intended beneficiaries find satisfying—the goal of any decision-making effort—the decider must know those persons' tastes. That is, a decider must make judgments about how other people feel about things.

Trade-offs

All our prospective actions have both strengths and weaknesses. So how should we make the trade-offs that are required to settle on the action we'll actually pursue? This issue concerns the fact that in many (most?) real-world deciding situations, deciders eventually arrive at this reality: Every alternative has drawbacks. Expected utility theory, the point of reference for the field, is at heart about the trading-off of outcome value and uncertainty.[20,35] Decision research has been dominated by questions about deviations of people's actual decision behavior from what is predicted or prescribed by rules such as the expected utility, additive utility, and discounting models. This perspective reflects a narrow, idealistic, rationalistic conception of how people deal with trade-offs in real life. It's also a reflection of the reductive tendency.[36] The dominant models presume a "pick among these" stance by the decider. Evidence shows that a major tactic deciders use is to transform trade-off problems into options problems.[37] Specifically, people sometimes seek to avoid having to make an onerous trade-off altogether by finding or creating a new alternative that makes the trade-off unnecessary. In many cases, deciders have reached their decisions saying, for example, "So this is what we are going to do," once they've resolved the trade-offs issue. But that's never the end of things. In the "aftermath," often before anything else occurs, acceptability and implementation issues can take center stage—for example, how various other parties feel about how the decision was made.

Acceptability

How can we get the other stakeholders to agree to this decision procedure? In most high-stakes situations, the decider isn't a free agent but must contend with many stakeholders' sentiments concerning what's decided, how it's decided, and how it's implemented. Negotiations are the most familiar context where the acceptability issue figures significantly, but the acceptability issue assumes significance beyond the realm of formal negotiations. American automakers have lost several major lawsuits because they mishandled the acceptability issue in design decisions. In one prominent case, jurors were repelled by testimony that the decision to cut costs on certain features rested partly on a decision analysis in which a dollar figure (based on actuarial records) was attached to lives that might be lost in accidents linked to those features. The jurors responded by forcing the company to pay billions in punitive damages.[38]

> Disasters with respect to implementation generally result from the prior mishandling of one or more of the other cardinal issues when the original decision was being deliberated.

Implementation

That's what we decided to do. Now, how can we get it done? Or can we get it done, after all? While a decision aid might seek to get people to a point of commitment, events follow the commitment. As we suggested earlier in unpacking the "commitment to action," even acting has an element of deciding because it can and often does involve contingency. A commitment to act doesn't necessarily have action as its primary functionality. Rather, it's a resolution to accept a particular understanding in the hope that the understanding will serve to help the decider know when to be surprised after the action has commenced and the anticipated contingencies play themselves out, or not. The implementation issue is particularly important in decision situations where the selected alternative entails a nontrivial "project" that must be executed, as opposed to a single action that's virtually synonymous with the decision itself (for example, the final-point notion). Sometimes, a project proves to be difficult or even impossible to actually conduct and entails other decidings, even waves of decidings (as in the atomic bomb example). Disasters with respect to the implementation issue generally result from the prior mishandling of one or more of the other cardinal issues when the original decision was being deliberated—for instance, overlooking various implementation barriers and therefore failing to see them as possibilities. There's been little systematic research aimed at understanding how people address the implementation issue (as an exception, see Utpal Dholakia and Richard Bagozzi's work[39]).

Implications for intelligent systems

The modeling component of many decision aids basically involves taking input data; creating tabular representations of entities, attributes, and weightings; and performing mathematical operations predicated on notions of decision analysis.[3] Decision analysis has many benefits. It offers comfortable means to describe decision making in terms of choice among probability distributions. It offers techniques to mathematically specify preferences, derive and evaluate probabilities, and work on equations that balance gain and risk. It provides mathematical methods to achieve consistency by rules of logic. This approach prescribes a decision process that involves identifying promising prospective courses of action and their potential significant consequences (step 1), assessing the utility of those consequences and evaluating the likelihoods of all the recognized potential outcomes (step 2), and then selecting the alternative that's indicated to be best according to a "rational" decision rule (step 3).

Assuming this is what deciding is, then surely people must need help with these things.[8] Over the years, this view has had a substantial influence on the character of the literature on human biases and limitations. But the promise has not caught up to the reality:

> Behavior-focused decision aids have had little documented success ... decision quality entails myriad diverse facets ... yet the typical decision aid (and its theoretical underpinning) is predicated on a narrow conception. ... Deciders therefore often ignore such aids because they appear irrelevant to significant decider concerns. And when deciders do try the aids, the results disappoint them because the aids leave untouched the quality dimensions that matter to them.[3] (p. 13)

> The benefits of the system must be apparent ... The degree to which the judge will be held responsible for the judgment must be made evident, and the quality of the information the system is supplying must be indicated. In short, unless the judge sees a need to bother with the support system, the work put into its design will be of no avail.[40] (p. 124)

A case in point is the new decision aids that assist intelligence analysts. These take the analysts away from meaningful study of intelligence information and force them to engage in evaluations of probabilities and hypotheses. They do enough of that as is. The make-work and overhead necessitated by the new systems sometimes outweigh any value added.[41]

In the case of expert systems (regarded as decision aids), it was clear during so-called first-generation work that the structures of knowledge bases and brittle (or context-insensitive) procedural rules didn't capture the subtleties of expert deciding.[26] Likewise for aids based on decision analysis, there's been little if any concern about some of the tough and crucial aspects of deciding. These include determining whether there's a significant decision problem to solve in the first place, developing promising alternatives, envisioning nonobvious but critical potential side effects of alternatives, and discerning how key parties truly feel about possible outcomes of selected options as well as the decision process itself. When decision analyses acknowledge such matters at all, they assume that they've been addressed outside the analyses per se. But there is reason to believe that it's precisely these other tough and crucial aspects of deciding that often spell the difference between effective and ineffective deciding and thus are ones that people need help dealing with.

Table 4. Some possibilities for intelligent decision aids.

Cardinal issue	Intelligent systems might ...
Need	Help people monitor and recognize threats and opportunities that warrant efforts to make decisions that address them (for example, track trends in consumer needs and tastes for services).
Mode: Who?	Help people deliberate on whether and to whom authority should be delegated (for example, assess product proposal review skill requirements).
Mode: How?	Help people determine how well alternative procedures for addressing various other cardinal issues are suited to present circumstances (for example, monitor best practices databases for new product appraisal techniques).
Investment	Help people monitor and minimize decision process costs without jeopardizing other quality dimensions (for example, track trends in product appraisal expenses).
Options	Help people scan for and filter existing alternatives and organize their efforts to create new ones (for example, recommend participants in product creativity exercises according to their track records and personal characteristics, such as intellectual diversity).
Possibilities	Help people envision nonobvious but real and significant potential consequences of alternatives under consideration, such as "side effects" distinct from intended effects (for example, identify ways that potential new products might be misused, resulting in product liability claims).
Judgment	Help people anticipate the actual states of decision-relevant events and conditions (for example, structure the deliberations of supply chain buyers to best exploit their expertise in predicting future product component price changes).
Value	Help people assess how the various parties to a decision feel about potential consequences (for example, administer new product preference assessment and forecasting exercises under realistic product use simulation scenarios).
Trade-offs	Help people decide how to deal with trade-offs, including possibly obviating the need for trade-offs by identifying better alternatives or transforming trade-offs into opportunities (for example, manage interactive routines in which consumers can test their beliefs about new product feature trade-offs, such as style, convenience, and price, in vivid simulations).
Acceptability	Help people anticipate how various stakeholders will regard a prospective decision or the process used to make it and craft ways of achieving their acceptance (for example, guide a review of parties who have a stake in the introduction of a new product class and routines for negotiating with them).
Implementation	Help people anticipate common impediments to decision implementation before finalizing decisions, and respond quickly and effectively to impediments that occasionally arise despite those efforts (for example, guide impediment-anticipation exercises intended to surface new product manufacturing glitches after volume or scale ramp-up).

At one level, this is all terribly disappointing. But the perspective afforded by the cardinal decision issues may broaden the horizons for intelligent decision support systems. That perspective would point toward concrete ways that a new generation of systems might complement and extend human capabilities in ways that could result in decision processes that add significant, demonstrable value. Table 4 takes the cardinal issues one at a time and suggests the kinds of enhancements that intelligent technologies might make to how people ordinarily address those issues. For concreteness, we illustrate the ideas with a running product development illustration. Of course, not all of these suggestions are entirely new. For example, Lee Beach suggested a form of aid that would help decision makers construct explanatory narratives (that is, representations of their mental models).[40]

When the expert blacksmith hammers away at the anvil, he can make precise impacts time and time again, at just the right spot. Yet, measurement of the movements shows that the strokes are never exactly the same.[42] When we trace

Robert R. Hoffman is a senior research scientist at the Institute for Human and Machine Cognition. Contact him at IHMC, 40 So. Alcaniz St., Pensacola, FL 32502-6008; rhoffman@ihmc.us.

J. Frank Yates is a professor in the Department of Psychology at the University of Michigan, where he serves as acting director of the Afro-American Studies Program and director of the Coalition for the Use of Learning Skills. Contact him at 3038 East Hall, Univ. of Michigan, Ann Arbor, MI 48109; jfyates@umich.edu.

the history of a decision process, it's always possible to identify one or more moments of choice. We can then describe history in terms of causal steps leading up to that moment, creating a simple causal model that might then be amenable to specification in terms of rules. But when we look at deciding as it occurs, a different picture emerges. Like the blacksmith's process, people can reach moments of commitment that signal their occurrence clearly but are never achieved by following precisely the same path. People are not engaging a cause-effect chain or a rule-based process. They're navigating a space of constraints and issues, involving contingencies and contextual dependencies. Capturing such dynamics and interactions in ways that avoid making causal-chain theories is always a challenge.[43] Punctuated histories are what falls out as a result of our telling stories. Those who would create intelligent decision architectures might benefit from considering a macrocognitive view of deciding, one that's significantly richer than the domino three-step. To make intelligent decision aids that are maximally useful, designers might focus on trying to enhance consequential elements of the entire decision process, not just what occurs in the analysis of trade-offs to culminate in a single moment of commitment. ■

Acknowledgments

We thank John Flack for his comments on an early draft. Robert Hoffman's contribution was through participation in the Advanced Decision Architectures Collaborative Technology Alliance, sponsored by the US Army Research Laboratory under Cooperative Agreement DAAD19-01-2-0009.

References

1. G.E.G. Beroggi and W.A. Wallace, "Closing the Gap: Transit Control for Hazardous Material Flow," *J. Hazardous Materials*, vol. 27, 1991, pp. 61–75.
2. G. Wright and F. Bolger, eds., *Expertise and Decision Support*, Plenum, 1992.
3. J.F. Yates, E.S. Veinott, and A.L. Patalino, "Hard Decisions, Bad Decisions: On Decision Quality and Decision Aiding," *Emerging Perspectives on Judgment and Decision Research*, S.L. Schneider and J. Shanteau, eds., Cambridge Univ. Press, 2003, pp. 13–63.
4. P. Reagan-Cirincione and J. Rohmbaugh, "Decision Conferencing," *Expertise and Decision Support*, G. Wright and F. Bolger, eds., Plenum, 1992, pp. 181–202.
5. G. Rowe, "Perspectives on Expertise in the Aggregation of Judgment," *Expertise and Decision Support*, G. Wright and F. Bolger, eds., Plenum, 1992, pp. 155–180.
6. K. Hammond, "Explaining and Repairing Plans That Fail," *Artificial Intelligence*, vol. 45, 1990, pp. 173–228.
7. W.B. Rouse, "Design and Evaluation of Computer-Based Decision Aids," *Human-Computer Interaction*, G. Salvendy, ed., Elsevier, 1984, pp. 229–246.
8. B. Fischhoff, "Decision Making in Complex Systems," *Intelligent Decision Support in Process Environments*, E. Hollgagel, G. Mancini, and D. Woods, eds., Springer-Verlag, 1986, pp. 61–85.
9. G. Johanssen, "Architecture of Man-Machine Decision Making Systems," E. Hollgagel, G. Mancini, and D. Woods, eds., *Intelligent Decision Support in Process Environments*, Springer Verlag, 1986, pp. 327–339.
10. F.D. Rigby, "Heuristic Analysis of Decision Situations," *Human Judgments and Optimality*, M.W. Shelly and G.L. Bryan, eds., John Wiley & Sons, 1964, pp. 37–44.
11. *Webster's New Collegiate Dictionary*, G. & C. Merriam, 1979.
12. E. Partridge, *Origins: A Short Etymological Dictionary of Modern English*, Macmillan, 1958.
13. W. Smith, *Latin-English Dictionary*, John Murray, 1933.
14. H.R. Arkes and K.R. Hammond, eds., *Judgment and Decision Making: An Interdisciplinary Reader*, Cambridge Univ. Press, 1986.
15. P. Juslin and H. Montgomery, eds., *Judgment and Decision Making*, Lawrence Erlbaum, 1999.
16. D. Kahneman and A. Tversky, eds., *Choices, Values, and Frames*, Cambridge Univ. Press, 2000.
17. S. Plous, *The Psychology of Judgment and Decision Making*, McGraw-Hill, 1993.
18. K. Smith, J. Shanteau, and P. Johnson, eds., *Psychological Investigations of Competence in Decision Making*, Cambridge Univ. Press, 2004.
19. R.J. Sternberg and P.A. Frensch, eds., *Complex Problem Solving*, Lawrence Erlbaum, 1991.
20. J.F. Yates, *Judgment and Decision Making*, Prentice Hall, 1990.
21. O. Svenson and A.J. Maule, eds., *Time Pressure and Stress in Human Judgment and Decision Making*, Plenum Press, 1993.
22. K.R. Hammond, G.H. McClelland, and J. Mumpower, *Human Judgment and Decision Making: Theories, Methods, and Procedures*, Praeger, 1980.
23. J.F. Yates and M.D. Tschirhart, "Decision Making Expertise," *Cambridge Handbook on Expertise and Expert Performance*, A. Ericsson et al., eds., Cambridge Univ. Press, to be published in 2006.
24. P.E. Mack, "The Apollo Mode Decision," 1997; http://people.clemson.edu/~pammack/apmode.htm.
25. "Manhattan Project History: The Atomic Bombings of Hiroshima and Nagasaki by The Manhattan Engineer District, June 29, 1946," Manhattan Project Preservation Assoc., 17 Oct. 2003, www.childrenofthemanhattanproject.org/HISTORY/H-05.htm.
26. J. Gammack, "Knowledge Engineering Issues for Decision Support," *Expertise and Decision Support*, G. Wright and F. Bolger, eds., Plenum, 1992, pp. 203–226.
27. G. Klein et al., "Macrocognition," *IEEE Intelligent Systems*, May/June 2003, pp. 81–85.
28. R.Y. Hirokawa and M.S. Poole, eds., *Communication and Group Decision Making*, Sage Publishing, 1996.

29. G. Klein et al., eds., *Decision Making in Action: Models and Methods*, Ablex Publishing, 1993.

30. F.C. Brentano, *Psychology from an Empirical Standpoint*, A.C. Rancurello, trans., Humanities Press, 1874/1973.

31. J.F. Yates, *Decision Management*, Jossey-Bass, 2003.

32. S.M. Rostan, "Problem Finding, Problem Solving, and Cognitive Controls: An Empirical Investigation of Critically Acclaimed Productivity," *Creativity Research J.*, vol. 7, 1994, pp. 97–110.

33. G. Klein, *Intuition at Work: Why Developing Your Gut Instincts Will Make You Better at What You Do*, Doubleday, 2003.

34. B. Schwartz et al., "Maximizing versus Satisficing: Happiness Is a Matter of Choice," *J. Personality and Social Psychology*, vol. 83, no. 5, 2002, pp. 1178–1197.

35. R.L. Keeney and H. Raiffa, *Decisions with Multiple Objectives: Preferences and Value Tradeoffs*, John Wiley, 1976.

36. P.J. Feltovich, R.R. Hoffman, and D. Woods, "Keeping It Too Simple: How the Reductive Tendency Affects Cognitive Engineering," *IEEE Intelligent Systems*, vol.19, no. 3, 2004, pp. 90–95.

37. E. Shafir, I. Simonson, and A. Tversky, "Reason-Based Choice," *Cognition*, vol. 49, 1993, pp. 11–36.

38. J.L. Fix, "Memos Key in $4.9-Billion Verdict," *Detroit Free Press*, 13 July 1999, p. A1.

39. U.M. Dholakia and R.P. Bagozzi, "Mustering Motivation to Enact Decisions: How Decision Process Characteristics Influence Goal Realization," *J. Behavioral Decision Making*, vol. 15, no. 3, 2002, pp. 167–188.

40. L.R. Beach, "Epistemic Strategies: Causal Thinking in Expert and Nonexpert Judgment," *Expertise and Decision Support*, G. Wright and F. Bolger, eds., Plenum, 1992, pp. 107–127.

41. B.M. Moon and R.R. Hoffman, "How Might 'Transformational' Technologies and Concepts Be Barriers to Sensemaking in Intelligence Analysis?" presentation at the 7th Int'l Conf. Naturalistic Decision Making, 2005; available as a report from the Inst. for Human and Machine Cognition, www.ihmc.us.

42. N.A. Bernstein, "On Dexterity and Its Development," *Dexterity and Its Development*, M.L. Latash and M.T. Turvey, eds., Lawrence Erlbaum, 1996, pp. 1–246.

43. R.J. Jagacinski and J.M. Flach, *Control Theory for Humans: Quantitative Approaches to Modeling Performance*, Lawrence Erlbaum, 2003.

Chapter 25: Making Sense of Sensemaking 1: Alternative Perspectives

G. Klein, B. Moon, and R.R. Hoffman, "Making Sense of Sensemaking 1: Alternative Perspectives," *IEEE Intelligent Systems*, vol. 21, no. 4, July/Aug. 2006, pp. 70–73. doi: 10.1109/MIS.2006.75

Sensemaking has become an umbrella term for efforts at building intelligent systems. This essay examines sensemaking from various perspectives to see if we can separate the things that are doable from the things that seem more like pie-in-the-sky.

Making Sense of Sensemaking 1: Alternative Perspectives

Gary Klein and Brian Moon, *Klein Associates Division of ARA*
Robert R. Hoffman, *Florida Institute for Human & Machine Cognition*

A man was worried about his 72-year-old father, who had just had a pacemaker implanted. The man believed that his father's condition was serious, despite reassurances from the hospital staff. The man's father had shortness of breath, cardiac arrhythmia, mild congestive heart failure, an enlarged heart, water retention, mild high blood pressure, mild emphysema, and a heart valve replacement 10 years earlier. The combination of all these symptoms and problems seemed ominous. The man coaxed a physician to explain what was going on.

The physician said that the heart valve replacement was irrelevant. Basically, the father had a slightly enlarged heart. That wasn't a big problem except that the area of enlargement had stretched some of the nerves that controlled heart rate; this caused the cardiac arrhythmia. The arrhythmia, in turn, meant that the father's heart was less efficient at maintaining fluid levels, which is often a problem of aging. So, the fluid buildup resulted in mild congestive heart failure and shortness of breath. The mild emphysema didn't help. And that's why they installed the pacemaker. With that simple story, the various data elements fit together in a coherent causal scheme, satisfying the man that this was a treatable problem rather than a cascading breakdown of health.

This story is one of many that researchers use to illustrate the phenomenon of *sensemaking*. Although we can trace this notion to the early 1980s,[1] it has emerged since the 1990s as a subject for organizational research,[2–4] educational research,[5] and symposia on decision making.[6] Sensemaking has become an umbrella term for efforts at building intelligent systems—for example, the research on data fusion and adaptive interfaces.[7,8] Research requests are frequently issued for intelligent systems that will

- automatically fuse massive data into succinct meanings,
- process meaning in contextually relative ways,
- enable humans to achieve insights,
- automatically infer the hypotheses that the human is considering,
- enable people to access others' intuitions, and
- present information in relevant ways and defined in terms of some magically derived model of the human subconscious or its storehouse of tacit knowledge.

These envisioned capabilities appear to be good things to have, and the call for research on such capabilities might serve to throw down a gauntlet and thereby push the envelope of intelligent systems. But we see in various funding opportunities and program descriptions little actual relationship to the notion of sensemaking, especially to empirical-research findings from the field of naturalistic decision making. This essay examines sensemaking from various perspectives to see if we can separate the things that are doable from the things that seem more like pie-in-the-sky.

The psychology perspective

First, because sensemaking seems primarily to denote a psychological phenomenon, let's look at the psychology perspective.

Sensemaking has been defined as "how people make sense out of their experience in the world."[9] On the basis of this definition, you might easily conclude that sensemaking is merely a reinvented wheel, expressing concepts that have been common currency in psychology for decades, if not well over a century. Here are five of them.

Creativity

Sensemaking might essentially mean creativity. However, much research on creativity has focused on how peo-

Editors: Robert R. Hoffman, Patrick J. Hayes, and Kenneth M. Ford
Institute for Human and Machine Cognition, University of West Florida
rhoffman@ai.uwf.edu

ple generate novel solutions to individual problems and puzzles,[10] often expressed in terms of transformation within problem state spaces.[11,12] Others rely on the notion of creativity as a measurable individual difference in personality.[13] Even the research on how creativity relates to expertise[14,15] gives no indication that sensemaking might be reduced to a psychological notion of creativity. As most people seem to mean it these days, sensemaking sometimes might involve creativity but it's not the same thing.

Curiosity

Sensemaking might mean curiosity, long referred to as the trigger for "scientific imagination."[16] But in modern psychology, curiosity has typically been invoked to denote just the motivational aspect of exploratory behavior—that is, the physical-perceptual exploration of states of affairs or situations in the perceived environment.[17] As most people seem to mean it, sensemaking involves curiosity but is more than this.

Comprehension

Sensemaking might mean the same thing as the venerable psychological notion of comprehension, but the latter term has historically referred to the understanding of individual stimuli, especially words, sentences, or chunks of prose.[18] Sensemaking is generally understood as the understanding of more complex things—events, in particular.

Mental modeling

Sensemaking might mean the process of creating a mental model.[19,20] A mental model is generally considered a memory representation, with a salient mental-imagery component, depicting states of affairs but linked to or expressed in terms of concepts, principles, and knowledge (for example, a weather forecaster's mental model of the four-dimensional state of the atmosphere). Of all the psychological notions, this one seems closest to what people seem to mean today by sensemaking. Mental models are representations that explain events, not isolated stimuli. Indeed, researchers sometimes use the notion of a conceptual model to define sensemaking.[21]

Situation awareness

However, most discussions consider sensemaking to be even more than this—a process more than a stored memory representation. Psychology's focus has been on achieving a state, some sort of memory representation that constitutes an explanation. Here is the primary difference between sensemaking and situation awareness, although some have defined them as essentially the same.[6] Mica Endsley's work on situation awareness is about the knowledge state that's achieved—either knowledge of current data elements, or inferences drawn from these data, or predictions that can be made using these inferences.[22] In contrast, sensemaking is about the process of achieving these kinds of outcomes, the strategies, and the barriers encountered.

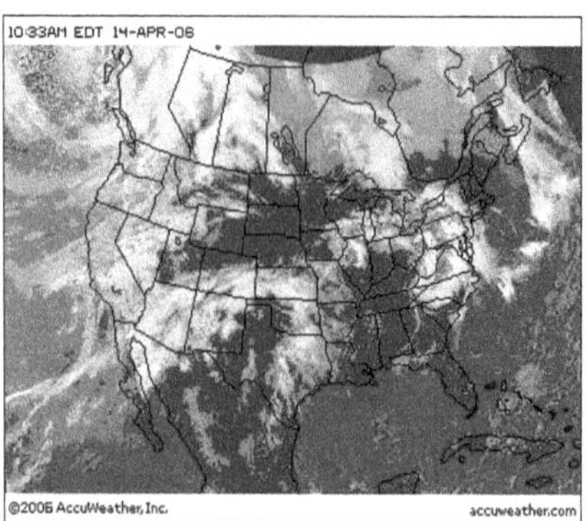

Figure 1. A representative SatRad image from Accuweather (downloaded 14 April 2006 from www.accuweather.com, reproduced with permission).

The verdict

By sensemaking, modern researchers seem to mean something different from creativity, comprehension, curiosity, mental modeling, explanation, or situational awareness, although all these factors or phenomena can be involved in or related to sensemaking. Sensemaking is a motivated, continuous effort to understand connections (which can be among people, places, and events) in order to anticipate their trajectories and act effectively.

The perspective of human-centered computing

From the HCC perspective, we don't assume that sensemaking capabilities of the kind we listed in the introduction (for example, data fusion) would actually be useful or usable. Indeed, they might even make people seem less able to act intelligently by limiting their ability to exercise expertise. For instance, fusing data effectively hides information from human analysis, and this cuts against what we know from studies of expert decision making: Experts must be able to explore data, and their analysis can suffer when data are hidden from them in layers of someone else's interpretations.

Let's look at a simple example of fused data. Televised weather forecasts often use a SatRad (satellite-radar) display, such as the one in figure 1. SatRad images are perhaps adequate to convey to the public where rain might occur, but if you ask a forecaster to generate a forecast based on such an image, the most likely response would be, "Show me the data." Why? For one thing, forecasting relies on many radar data types, and the "Rad" in SatRad is just one—base reflectivity.[23] Also, the satellite image—those graphical features that appear to represent clouds—isn't in fact a satellite picture of clouds; it's an infrared radiometric image, which carries particular nuances for correct interpretation. The fused data don't provide nearly enough information to support forecasting beyond mere guesswork. The task of building a rich mental model of atmospheric dynamics on the basis of fused data would trigger in the forecaster little more than frustration.

The sensemaking capabilities that people have envisioned have another potential problem. The technologies that spew out abductive inferences would almost certainly trigger some surprises, when the machine acts mysteriously without making its inner workings or intent apparent to the human. Certainly, data fusion algorithms can reduce information overload, but they also pose challenges to sensemaking if the human can't form an accurate mental model of the machine, to understand why and how the algorithms are doing what they're doing. The human will probably be multitasking. Managing and concentrating his or her attention will suffer when the machine is in the driver's seat. Unless the person has already developed trust in the technology and knows why the machine thinks something is important, the machine might be more of a nuisance than an aid.[24]

So, the verdict is this: For those who ask for the world, and those who promise it, caveat emptor.

The perspective of naturalistic decision making

The NDM perspective offers a way of finding some interesting questions about sensemaking. Perhaps even more important, it provides an empirical base that anchors the theoretical ruminations in concrete examples and findings. These, in turn, serve as a rationale for questioning some assumptions that underlie the drive to make intelligent sensemaking systems.

NDM research has used methods of cognitive task analysis in many studies of how domain practitioners make complex decisions in dynamic environments.[25–27] This research has yielded a large corpus of observations and cases in which phenomena might be ascribed to sensemaking. We began this essay with one such case, an explanation of the hospitalized father's symptoms. This and many other incidents[24,28,29] illustrate that sensemaking serves several functions:

- It satisfies a need or drive to comprehend.
- It helps us test and improve the plausibility of our explanations and explain apparent anomalies. Whether an explanation makes sense depends on the person who's doing the sensemaking. The property of "being an explanation" isn't a property of statements but an interaction of people, situations, and knowledge.
- It's often a retrospective analysis of events. It clarifies the past but doesn't make it transparent (that is, completely understood).
- It anticipates the future. This makes action possible, though uncertain. It helps us muster resources, anticipate difficulties, notice problems, and realize concerns.
- It isn't the choice of an explanation but a process of deliberating over alternative plausible explanations.
- It guides the exploration of information.
- It's often a social activity that promotes the achievement of common ground. It isn't just an individual activity.

The NDM research strongly suggests that several assumptions about sensemaking don't hold up under empirical scrutiny. Here we list and refute some of the myths.

Myth: Data fusion and automated hypothesis generation aid sensemaking

Research shows that when human decision makers are put in the position of passively receiving interpretations, they're less apt to notice emergent problems.[30]

Myth: Sensemaking is simply connecting the dots

We've often seen this metaphorical description of cognitive work, especially in reference to the intelligence analyst's job. It trivializes cognitive work. It misses the skill needed to identify what counts as a dot in the first place. Of course relating dots is critical, but the analyst must also determine which dots are transient signals and which are false signals that should be ignored.

Myth: More information leads to better sensemaking

Researchers have shown that more information improves performance up to a point, but after that point additional information isn't helpful and can sometimes even degrade performance.[31,32] Confidence continues to increase with additional information so that people become increasingly overconfident rather than increasingly correct.

> Sensemaking doesn't always have clear beginning and ending points. The simplified waterfall model of cognition runs counter to empirical evidence about expert decision making.

Myth: It's important to keep an open mind

Jennifer Rudolph presented anesthesiologists with a "garden path" problem—an initial setup that suggests one hypothesis, followed by a dribbling of contrary cues that indicate a different hypothesis.[30] The paradigm measures how long it takes for people to get off the garden path. Rudolph found that people who jumped to an early conclusion and fixated on it showed the worst performance, as she expected. But the participants who kept an open mind and refused to speculate were just mediocre, and not the best, which was contrary to Rudolph's hypothesis. The best participants were the ones who jumped to an early speculation but then deliberately tested it. Their initial hypothesis gave them a basis for seeking data that would be diagnostic. This approach was more useful than the "open mind" approach that's basically a passive mode of receiving data without thinking hard about them.

Myth: Biases are inescapable and prevent reliable sensemaking

This is the view posited by the "heuristics and biases" school of laboratory-based decision research.[33] However, W. Sieck and we three authors have recently completed research that shows this view's limitations in the analysis of real-world, expert decision making (*The Theory of the Handicapped Mind: Revisiting the Psychology of Intelligence Analysts*, to be published by the Institute for Human and Machine Cognition, 2006, is available from Robert Hoffman upon request). The so-called biases are mostly found in laboratory studies using artificial puzzle tasks and college freshmen as subjects, conditions that minimize expertise and context. In natural settings, biases can disappear or be greatly reduced.

Myth: Sensemaking follows the waterfall model of how data lead to understanding

This myth is that sensemaking follows the progression data → information → knowledge → understanding.[34]

Naive information-processing accounts assume that primitive data or isolated cues are successively massaged by inferential operations until they emerge from the other end as knowledge or wisdom. This is misleading in a number of ways. For instance, sensemaking doesn't always have clear beginning and ending points. The simplified waterfall model of cognition runs counter to empirical evidence about expert decision making, and it runs counter to evidence showing that data themselves must be constructed.

The verdict

All this suggests that the phenomena of sensemaking remain ripe for further empirical investigation and that the common view of sensemaking might suffer from the tendency toward reductive explanation.[35] What might be of help, therefore, would be a richer theory of sensemaking, one that gives shape to all the features of sensemaking listed earlier.

In the next essay in this department, we will present a theory of sensemaking that integrates our empirical understanding and points in new directions for the creation of intelligent systems.

Acknowledgments

Robert Hoffman's work on this essay was supported through his participation in the Advanced Decision Architectures Collaborative Technology Alliance, sponsored by the US Army Research Laboratory under cooperative agreement DAAD19-01-2-0009.

References

1. B. Dervin, "An Overview of Sensemaking Research: Concepts, Methods, and Results to Date," Int'l Communication Assoc., 1983; http://communication.sbs.ohio-state.edu/sense-making/art/artlist.html.

2. B. Dervin, "From the Mind's Eye of the 'User': The Sense-Making Qualitative-Quantitative Methodology," *Qualitative Research in Information Management*, J.D. Glazier and R.R. Powell, eds., Libraries Unlimited, 1992, pp. 61–84.

3. D.N. Greenberg, "Blue versus Gray: A Metaphor Constraining Sensemaking around a Restructuring," *Group and Organization Management*, vol. 20, 1995, pp. 183–209.

4. C.F. Kurtz and D.J. Snowden, "The New Dynamics of Strategy: Sense-Making in a Complex and Complicated World," *IBM Systems J.*, vol. 42, Sept. 2003, pp. 462–483.

5. C. Hulland and H. Mumby, "Science, Stories, and Sense-Making: A Comparison of Qualitative Data from a Wetlands Unit," *Science Education*, vol. 78, no. 2, 1994, pp. 117–136.

6. D.K. Leedom, "Sensemaking Symposium," final report to the Command and Control Research Program, Office of the Assistant Secretary of Defense for Command, Control, Communications and Intelligence, US Dept. of Defense, 2001; www.au.af.mil/au/awc/awcgate/ccrp/sensemaking_final_report.pdf.

7. T.L. Jacobson, "Sense Making in a Database Environment," *Information Processing & Management*, vol. 27, no. 6, 1991, pp. 647–657.

8. R. Savolainen, "The Sense-Making Theory: Reviewing the Interests of a User-Centered Approach to Information Seeking and Use," *Information Processing & Management*, vol. 29, no. 1, 1993, pp. 13–18.

9. M. Duffy, "Sensemaking in Classroom Conversations," *Openness in Research: The Tension between Self and Other*, I. Maso et al., eds., Van Gorcum, 1995, pp. 119-132.

10. M. Wertheimer, *Productive Thinking*, Harper and Brothers, 1959.

11. A. Newell and H.A. Simon, *Human Problem Solving*, Prentice Hall, 1972.

12. W.R. Reitman, *Cognition and Thought*, John Wiley & Sons, 1965.

13. T.B. Ward and K.N. Saunders, "Creativity," *Encyclopedia of Cognitive Science*, L. Nadel, ed., Nature Publishing Group, 2003, pp. 862–869.

14. M. Csikszentmihalyi, *Creativity: Flow and the Psychology of Discovery and Invention*, Harper Collins, 1996.

15. R.W. Weisberg, "Modes of Expertise in Creative Thinking: Evidence from Case Studies," *Cambridge Handbook of Expertise and Expert Performance*, K.A. Ericsson et al., eds., Cambridge Univ. Press, 2006.

16. J. Sully, *Outlines of Psychology*, Longmans, Green and Company, 1897.

17. L.S. Mark, "The Exploration of Complexity," *Viewing Psychology as a Whole*, R.R. Hoffman, M.F. Sherrick, and J.S. Warm, eds., Am. Psychological Assoc., 1998, pp. 191–204.

18. H.H. Clark and E.V. Clark, *Psychology and Language*, Harcourt Brace Jovanovich, 1977.

19. J.R. Anderson, *The Architecture of Cognition*, Harvard Univ. Press, 1983.

20. D. Gentner and A. Stevens, eds., *Mental Models*, Lawrence Erlbaum Associates, 1983.

21. "Sensemaking," *Curriculum on Interpersonal Relations and Communication*, Univ. of Twente, 2006, www.tcw.utwente.nl/theorieenoverzicht/Theory%20clusters.

22. M.R. Endsley, "Situation Awareness and the Cognitive Management of Complex Systems," *Human Factors*, vol. 37, no. 1, 1995, pp. 85–104.

23. R.R. Hoffman, G. Trafton, and P. Roebber, *Minding the Weather: How Expert Forecasters Think*, MIT Press, 2006.

24. G. Klein, *The Power of Intuition*, Currency, 2004.

25. G. Klein et al., "Macrocognition," *IEEE Intelligent Systems*, May/June 2003, pp. 81–85.

26. J.M. Orasanu, R. Calderwood, and C.E. Zsambok, eds., *Decision Making in Action: Models and Methods*, Ablex, 1993.

27. E. Salas and G. Klein, eds., *Linking Expertise and Naturalistic Decision Making*, Lawrence Erlbaum Associates, 2001.

28. K.E. Weick, *Sensemaking in Organizations*, Sage Publications, 1995.

29. D.J. Snowden, "Multi-Ontology Sense Making: A New Simplicity in Decision Making," *Management Today Yearbook*, vol. 20, 2005; www.kwork.org/Stars/Snowden/Snowden.pdf.

30. J.W. Rudolph, "Into the Big Muddy and Out Again," unpublished doctoral dissertation, Boston College, 2003; abstract downloaded 29 June 2006 from http://escholarship.bc.edu/dissertations/AAI3103269.

31. S. Oskamp, "Overconfidence in Case-Study Judgments," *J. Consulting Psychology*, vol. 29, no. 3, 1965, pp. 261–265.

32. M.M. Omodei et al., "More Is Better? Problems of Self-Regulation in Naturalistic Decision Making Settings," *How Professionals Make Decisions*, H. Montgomery, R. Lipshitz, and B. Brehmer, eds., Lawrence Erlbaum Associates, 2005, pp. 29–42.

33. D. Kahneman, P. Slovic, and A. Tversky, *Judgment under Uncertainty: Heuristics and Biases*, Cambridge Univ. Press, 1982.

34. R.L. Ackoff, "From Data to Wisdom," *J. Applied Systems Analysis*, vol. 16, 1989, pp. 3–9.

35. P.J. Feltovich, R.R. Hoffman, and D. Woods, "Keeping It Too Simple: How the Reductive Tendency Affects Cognitive Engineering," *IEEE Intelligent Systems*, May/June 2004, pp. 90–95.

Gary Klein is chief scientist in the Klein Associates Division of Applied Research Associates. Contact him at gary@decisionmaking.com.

Brian Moon is a research associate in the Klein Associates Division of Applied Research Associates. Contact him at brian@decisionmaking.com.

Robert R. Hoffman is a senior research scientist at the Institute for Human and Machine Cognition. Contact him at rhoffman@ihmc.us.

Chapter 26: Making Sense of Sensemaking 2: A Macrocognitive Model

G. Klein, B. Moon, and R.R. Hoffman, "Making Sense of Sensemaking 2: A Macrocognitive Model," *IEEE Intelligent Systems*, vol. 21, no. 5, Sep./Oct. 2006, pp. 88–92. doi: 10.1109/MIS.2006.100

In this paper, we have laid out a theory of sensemaking that might be useful for intelligent systems applications. It's a general, empirically grounded account of sensemaking that goes significantly beyond the myths and puts forward some nonobvious, testable hypotheses about the process. When people try to make sense of events, they begin with some perspective, viewpoint, or framework—however minimal. For now, let's use a metaphor and call this a frame. We can express frames in various meaningful forms, including stories, maps, organizational diagrams, or scripts, and can use them in subsequent and parallel processes. Even though frames define what count as data, they themselves actually shape the data. Furthermore, frames change as we acquire data. In other words, this is a two-way street: frames shape and define the relevant data, and data mandate that frames change in nontrivial ways. We examine five areas of empirical findings: causal reasoning, commitment to hypotheses, feedback and learning, sense-making as a skill, and confirmation bias. In each area the Data/Frame model, and the research it's based on, move us beyond commonsense views.

Making Sense of Sensemaking 2: A Macrocognitive Model

Gary Klein and Brian Moon, *Klein Associates Division of ARA*
Robert R. Hoffman, *Florida Institute for Human & Machine Cognition*

In our first essay on sensemaking,[1] we discussed various possible meanings of the concept and debunked some of the myths that seem current in discussions of cognitive work. The motivation for these two essays is to question whether it makes sense to envision certain kinds of intelligent sensemaking systems. None of the "verdicts" we announced in the first essay mean that intelligent technologies might not assist people in sensemaking. Indeed, intelligent technologies might help; they just won't be the sorts of technologies that people seem to seek.

Gary Klein and his colleagues have laid out a theory of sensemaking that might be useful for intelligent systems applications.[2] It's a general, empirically grounded account of sensemaking that goes significantly beyond the myths and puts forward some nonobvious, testable hypotheses about the process.

When people try to make sense of events, they begin with some perspective, viewpoint, or framework—however minimal. For now, let's use a metaphor and call this a *frame*. We can express frames in various meaningful forms, including stories, maps, organizational diagrams, or scripts, and can use them in subsequent and parallel processes. Even though frames define what count as data, they themselves actually shape the data (for example, a house fire will be perceived differently by the homeowner, the firefighters, and the arson investigators). Furthermore, frames change as we acquire data. In other words, this is a two-way street: Frames shape and define the relevant data, and data mandate that frames change in nontrivial ways.

Editors: Robert R. Hoffman, Patrick J. Hayes, and Kenneth M. Ford
Institute for Human and Machine Cognition, University of West Florida
rhoffman@ai.uwf.edu

Figure 1 shows that the basic sensemaking act is data-frame symbiosis. The figure captures a number of sensemaking activities. Sensemaking can involve elaborating the frame by adding details, and questioning the frame and doubting the explanations it provides.[3] A frame functions as a hypothesis about the connections among data. One reaction to doubt is to explain away troublesome data and preserve the frame.[4,5] These two aspects, elaborating the frame and preserving the frame, are part of the elaboration cycle of sensemaking (the left side of figure 1), akin to Jean Piaget's notion of assimilation.

Yet another sensemaking cycle is to reframe (see the figure's right side). Here, questioning the frame leads us to reconsider—to reject the initial frame and seek to replace it with a better one. We might compare alternative frames to determine which seems most accurate. Or we might simply be mystified by the events. The sensemaking activity here, akin to Piaget's notion of accommodation, is to find some sort of frame that plausibly links the events that are being explained.

Each of these aspects of sensemaking has its own dynamics, strategies, and requirements. Recognizing a frame and recognizing data are different from elaborating a frame that has already been adopted, and this is different from explaining away inconsistencies. Different still are the reactions to questioning a frame—choosing between alternative frames and constructing a frame where none exists.

The Data/Frame Theory posits a closed-loop transition sequence between

- mental model formation (which is backward looking and explanatory), and
- mental simulation (which is forward looking and anticipatory).

Think of the simplest transition sequence as a chain of closed loops. Each loop is triggered by a perceived subevent, leading to an effort to refine the existing mental model (backward looking) and an effort to run a new mental simulation (forward looking). You can construct a transition sequence retrospectively to generate an explanation of how events and subevents unfolded, or prospectively to imagine how a major causal factor or a situational mix of factors might play out. For illustration, envision a transition sequence using the metaphor of billiards, where a player would anticipate how hitting one ball would lead to motion in a second, and a third, to the shot's completion.

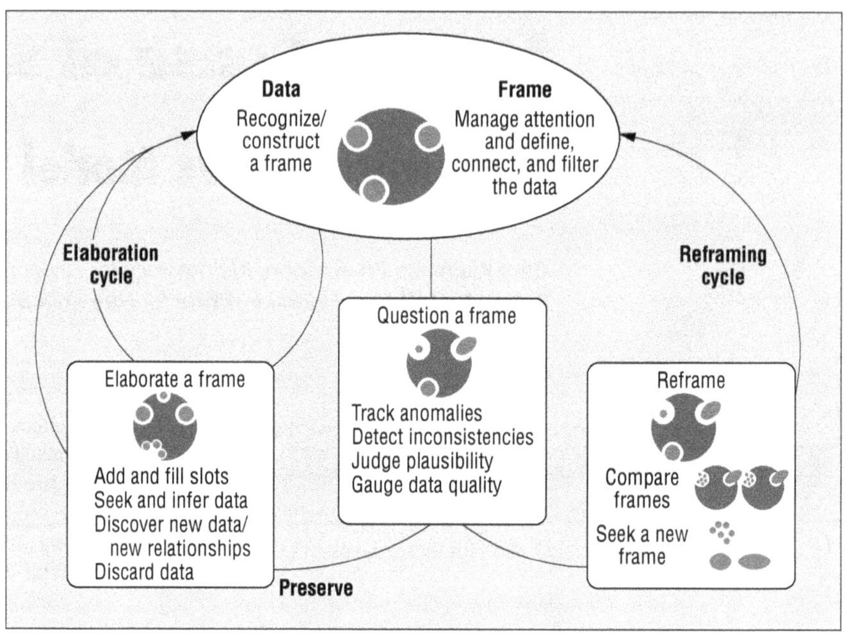

Figure 1. The Data/Frame Theory of sensemaking.

Empirical findings

We examine five areas of empirical findings: causal reasoning, commitment to hypotheses, feedback and learning, sensemaking as a skill, and confirmation bias. In each area the Data/Frame model, and the research it's based on, doesn't align with common beliefs. For that reason, the Data/Frame model cannot be considered a depiction of commonsense views.

Causal reasoning

Studies of domain practitioners' stories about how they understood real-life decision-making situations suggest that transition sequences—beliefs about what converts one situation into another—are typically based on about three to four causal factors. For example, in explaining why one sports team beat another, newspaper accounts typically focus on a single event such as a critical turnover ("and that cost them the game"), or perhaps that plus one or two other events, such as a star player doing poorly or well. Given the game's length, we can see these as oversimplifications, but most people would skim over any account that tried to capture a game's full complexity. That's why we introduced the billiards metaphor earlier, to illustrate a preference for chains of simple cause-effect relationships. A single causal factor at each junction might be the preferred form of explanation,[2,6] although such explanations open the decision maker up to the reductive tendency.[7]

Consideration of hypotheses

Decision makers are sometimes advised that they can reduce the likelihood of a fixation error by avoiding early consideration of a hypothesis.[8] But the Data/Frame Theory regards early consideration to a hypothesis as advantageous and inevitable. Early consideration—the rapid recognition of a frame—permits more efficient information gathering and more specific expectancies that can be violated by anomalies, permitting adjustment and reframing. Jenny Rudolph[9] found that decision makers must be sufficiently committed to a frame in order to be able to test it effectively and learn from its inadequacies—something that's missing from open-minded and open-ended diagnostic vagabonding. Winston Sieck and his colleagues have found that domain experts are more likely to question data than novices, perhaps because they're more familiar with instances of faulty data.[10] It might also mean that experts are more confident in their frames and therefore more skeptical about contrary evidence, in contrast to novices who are less confident in the frames they identify.

These observations would suggest that efforts to train decision makers to keep an open mind[11] can be counterproductive, and efforts to make machines that do the vagabonding for the human might be similarly unhelpful. We hypothesize that methods designed to prevent premature consideration to a frame will degrade performance under conditions where active attention management is needed (using frames) and where people have difficulty finding useful frames. Spoon-feeding interpretations to the human (via such methods as data fusion) can be counterproductive.

Feedback and learning

Another implication of the Data/Frame Theory concerns using feedback to promote learning. Frames are by nature reductive. And yet, frames can help overcome the reductive tendency. The commitment to a frame must be coupled with a motive to test the frame to discover when it's inaccurate. This process hinges on feedback of a certain kind. Outcome feedback ("you got it wrong") isn't nearly as useful as process feedback ("you did it wrong"),[12] because knowing *that* performance was inadequate isn't as valuable as understanding *what* to modify in the reasoning process. This includes the frame itself, because that will determine the way feedback is understood. In other words, people need sensemaking to understand the feedback that might improve sensemaking—the cycle as shown in figure 1. The implication is that people might benefit more from intelligent systems that guide the improvement of frames than from systems that generate alternative understandings and hypotheses and foist them on the human.

Sensemaking as a skill

We haven't seen evidence for a general sensemaking skill. Some incidents we've collected do suggest differences in motivation—an "adaptive mind-set" of actively looking to make sense of events, as illustrated in essay 1's example of the patient with a pacemaker. It might be possible to develop intelligent systems that acknowledge the Pleasure Principle of human-centered computing[13] and promote a positive motivation to question frames and to reframe, or at least not to frustrate the human and thereby detract from intrinsic motivation. Training might be better aimed at increasing the range and richness of frames, particularly causal mental models, and skill at noticing anomalies. Training scenarios and decision support might be developed for all the sensemaking activities in figure 1 (elaborating a frame, questioning a frame, evaluating a frame, comparing alternative frames, reframing a situation, and seeking anchors to generate a useful frame). Training would aim to provide a larger, richer repertoire of frames rather than to improve each aspect of sensemaking as if it were a separate skill.

Is there a confirmation bias?

The decision research literature suggests that people are inclined to look for and notice information that confirms a view rather than information that disconfirms it.[14,15] And yet more recent research looking at experts has shown just the opposite. For example, expert weather forecasters have sometimes been observed to deliberately look for information that might disconfirm hypotheses about future severe weather.[16]

The Data/Frame Theory provides a richer understanding of what's actually going on here. People don't engage in simple mental operations of confirming or disconfirming a hypothesis. Our cognitive task analyses of real-world decision making show that skilled decision makers shift into an active mode of elaborating a competing frame once they detect the possibility (or become worried) that the current frame is potentially inaccurate. What might look like a confirmation bias might be simply using a frame to guide information seeking. You need not think of it as a bias and assume that the purpose of an intelligent decision support system must be to help the human overcome some inherent reasoning bias.

Implications for AI: Reframing frames

Now, the other shoe must drop. Not only might the phenomenon of sensemaking illuminate the computational notion of frames—conversely, that computational notion might challenge our notion of sensemaking.

Reframing frames

As Marvin Minsky described frames, these organizing structures express the values of features that together define meaningful entities or categories—groups of slots into which the values of defined variables are entered.[17] The primary function of frames (in Minsky's original discussion) is recognition, to guide attention to fill in missing parts of the frame, to test a frame by searching for diagnostic information. To Minsky, frames are things you think with. In the Data/Frame Theory, frames are things that you think with but also things you think about. The Data/Frame Theory therefore blurs the border between phenomenological description and macrocognitive modeling.

We introduced the Data/Frame Theory by suggesting that when we try to make sense of events, we begin with some framework, however minimal. In the Cartesian view of things, sensory inputs (for example, a pattern of moving colored shapes) make contact with memory, lending them meaning in a process called perception ("it's a cat"). But there's a subsequent process, once called "apperception," which interprets the percept more broadly in terms of knowledge (for instance, "I like cats" or "cats can be a symbol for evil"). This is abductive inference, or something rather like it. So the challenge is, where do these frames come from in the first place? Here we see one of AI's outstanding problems, just as it has manifested in numerous views throughout psychology's history:[18] Any computational theory of how knowledge is formed as self-contained bundles should come with a full story about how these proposed "frame-ish" things are supposed to be created and what architectural assumptions underlie them. The AI systems Slate and Cyc both perform abductive reasoning to a plausible explanation using post-Minsky systems based on expressive logics. They both test their hypotheses by actively trying to refute them.

We introduced the Data/Frame Theory by suggesting that when we try to make sense of events, we begin with some framework, however minimal.

The phenomenon of sensemaking ties also to the notion that frames are chunks of knowledge abstracted away from computational details—symbolic descriptions that are taken off the shelf and used to perceive things, and thereby constitute understanding. However, what we see in studies of sensemaking doesn't fit with this view of frames in three ways. First, understandings shift; frames get changed. They aren't just "taken off a shelf." Frames change as data are acquired (so this isn't just a matter of frame reuse).

Second, even though frames define what count as data (which could be interpreted as a Minskyian notion), as we said earlier, frames themselves actually shape the data (so this isn't just a matter of data primitives). For example, skilled weather forecasters don't passively rely on the data presented by computational aids. Many computer models exist for forecasting weather. Some are based on climate statistics, others on computational models of the atmosphere. Each of these has known biases—for example, a model's tendency to overforecast the depth of low-pressure systems as fronts pass over the Appalachian mountains and the lows reform over the US East Coast. Experienced forecasters take these biases into account and adjust their interpretations of the computer forecasts accordingly.

Finally, frames sometimes have a just-in-time quality. Rarely do decision makers simply identify a relevant mental model. Instead, they construct the frame from smaller sets of causal relationships.

Here too is a challenge for both cognitive science and AI: Any computational theory of how knowledge is formed as self-contained bundles has to come with a full story about how these proposed "frame-ish" things are supposed to be manipulated. In the first essay on sensemaking, we referred to the similarity between sensemaking and mental modeling.[1] Most discussions of psychological research on mental models focus on comparing student and expert mental models, the student's use of mental models to make (erroneous) inferences, and the issue of how to train students to move beyond their naive analogies.[19] We need richer accounts of how the structures are constructed and manipulated.[20] In contrast, work in intelligent systems, such as the Structure Mapping Engine,[21] has specified some process mechanisms.

If frames shape data, how do data mandate any operation on the frame? What defines how frames get changed? Does this require using other frames to govern the frame-changing process? If not, how is it done? If so, what distinguishes the frames being changed from the frames mandating changes? What process can we use to question or doubt a frame? If frames are the vehicle that supports sensemaking, then any doubt would seem to require us to use a doubting-frame to represent the alternative hypothesis (that the frame might be incorrect or faulty). What kind of relationship between frames does this imply?

The phenomenon of sensemaking ties also to the notion that frames organize the large-scale structure of inference making—they're recipes for solving problems. What we see in studies of sensemaking is that frames aren't recipes, although they do play roles in inference making. In AI, the lesson was that knowledge packets are great when you can get them exactly right, so that all you have to do is use them, but you almost never can. For Minskyian frames to be useful, they had to have lots of details, but that would render them of little use across contexts unless they had some sort of internal machinery. Either that, or the frames would have to be chunks that you could pick apart by invoking some external inference machinery. When a frame actually gets used, you must be able to take it apart into the basic facts that constitute it and be able to use the flexibility that this gives you, because the chances of a frame being a perfect fit to particular circumstances are close to zero. Furthermore, if you want to use a frame to tell you what to actually do in a particular circumstance, you need some way to connect the general "type" to the particular exigencies. Computational versions of frames are notoriously poor at this, whereas decision makers are skilled at using frames in these ways.[22]

A pertinent idea from sensemaking studies is that thinking about frames in terms of an either-or (large chunks, with internal inference machinery, versus small chunks, with external inference machinery) might not be the best way to proceed. Indeed, we might think of the progression from novice to expert as a process of learning whereby individual cases, or small, contextually bound understandings with specific inference possibilities attached to them, might develop into larger, more organized understandings. In some cases, these understandings would have inference opportunities bound to them; in other cases, they'd be subject to inference machinery external to them. A process akin to logical inference or proof would assemble multiple small pieces into useful larger pieces. A process akin to pattern recognition might pick up big packets all at once, whereas a process more like mutual matching and fitting might assemble small pieces. In other words, there might be multiple assembly processes. The former might be a mechanism to explain "recognition-primed decision making," when the expert goes from an immediate understanding of a situation to a course of action. The latter would constitute the cycles described in figure 1. This is reminiscent of Cyc, in which bundles of related assumptions and concepts ("microtheories") are logic-like in their small structure but frame-like in that they're large and specific to a topic or concept and the knowledge inside them is specific to them.

We relied on the frame concept in the Data/Frame Theory as a metaphor to bootstrap a discussion of how people create, use, and manipulate organizing structures. We do not offer any clear path to a computational theory of how "frame-ish" things are created or manipulated. Our main goal in discussing the Data/Frame Theory is to point to empirical studies of how domain practitioners make decisions in complex, real-world contexts and then to mine these results for ideas that might invigorate and inform work on these fundamental issues. ■

Acknowledgments

Robert Hoffman's work on this essay was supported through his participation in the Advanced Decision Architectures Collaborative Technology Alliance, sponsored by the US Army Research Laboratory under cooperative agreement DAAD19-01-2-0009.

References

1. G. Klein, B. Moon, and R.R. Hoffman, "Making Sense of Sensemaking 1: Alternative Perspectives," *Intelligent Systems*, vol. 21, no. 4, 2006, pp. 70–73.
2. G. Klein et al., "A Data/Frame Theory of Sensemaking," to be published in *Expertise Out of Context: Proc. 6th Int'l Conf. Naturalistic Decision Making*, R.R. Hoffman, ed., Lawrence Erlbaum Associates, 2006.
3. K.E. Weick, *Sensemaking in Organizations*, Sage Publications, 1995.
4. C.A. Chinn and W.F. Brewer, "The Role of Anomalous Data in Knowledge Acquisition: A Theoretical Framework and Implications for Science Instruction," *Rev. Educational Research*, 1993, vol. 63, pp. 1–49.
5. P.J. Feltovich, R.J. Spiro, and R.L. Coulson, "Issues of Expert Flexibility in Contexts Characterized by Complexity and Change," *Expertise in Context: Human and Machine*, P.J. Feltovich, K.M. Ford, and R.R. Hoffman, eds., AAAI/MIT Press, 1997, pp. 125–146.
6. G.A. Klein and B.W. Crandall, "The Role of Mental Simulation in Naturalistic Decision Making," *Local Applications of the Ecological Approach to Human-Machine Systems*, vol. 2, P. Hancock eds., Lawrence Erlbaum Associates, 1995, pp. 324–358.
7. P.J. Feltovich, R.R. Hoffman, and D. Woods, "Keeping It Too Simple: How the Reductive Tendency Affects Cognitive Engineering," *IEEE Intelligent Systems*, May/June 2004, pp. 90–95.
8. R. Heuer, *The Psychology of Intelligence Analysis*, tech. report, CIA Center for the Study of Intelligence, 1999.

Gary Klein is chief scientist in the Klein Associates Division of Applied Research Associates. Contact him at Klein Associates, 1750 Commerce Center Blvd. N., Fairborn, OH 45324; gary@decisionmaking.com.

Brian Moon is a research associate in the Klein Associates Division of Applied Research Associates. Contact him at Klein Associates, 1750 Commerce Center Blvd. N., Fairborn, OH 45324; brian@decisionmaking.com.

Robert R. Hoffman is a senior research scientist at the Institute for Human and Machine Cognition. Contact him at IHMC, 40 So. Alcaniz St., Pensacola, FL 32502-6008; rhoffman@ihmc.us.

9. J.W. Rudolph, "Into the Big Muddy and Out Again," doctoral dissertation, Boston College, 2003; http://escholarship.bc.edu/dissertations/AAI3103269.

10. W.R. Sieck et al., "Basic Questioning Strategies for Making Sense of a Surprise: The Roles of Training, Experience, and Expertise," *Proc. 26th Ann. Conf. Cognitive Science Soc.* (CogSci 04), Lawrence Erlbaum Associates, 2004; www.cogsci.northwestern.edu/ cogsci2004/ma/ma305.pdf.

11. M.S. Cohen et al., "Dialogue as the Medium for Critical Thinking Training," *Proc. 6th Int'l Conf. Naturalistic Decision Making*, Lawrence Erlbaum Associates, 2003.

12. E. Salas et al., "Myths to Avoid about Crew Resource Management Training," *Ergonomics in Design*, Fall 2002, pp. 20–24.

13. R.R. Hoffman and P.J. Hayes, "The Pleasure Principle," *IEEE Intelligent Systems*, Jan./Feb. 2004, pp. 86–89.

14. C.R. Mynatt, M.E. Doherty, and R.D. Tweney, "Consequences of Confirmation and Disconfirmation in a Simulated Research Environment," *Quarterly J. Experimental Psychology*, vol. 30, 1978, pp. 395–406.

15. P.C. Wason, "On the Failure to Eliminate Hypotheses in a Conceptual Task," *Quarterly J. Experimental Psychology*, vol. 12, 1960, pp. 129–140.

16. R.R. Hoffman, G. Trafton, and P. Roebber, *Minding the Weather: How Expert Forecasters Think*, MIT Press, 2006.

17. M. Minsky, "A Framework for Representing Knowledge," *The Psychology of Computer Vision*, P.H. Winston, ed., McGraw-Hill, 1975, pp. 211–277.

18. H.L. Dreyfus, "A Framework for Misrepresenting Knowledge," *Philosophical Perspectives in Artificial Intelligence*, M. Ringle, ed., Humanities Press, 1979, pp. 110–123.

19. D. Gentner and A. Stevens, eds., *Mental Models*, Lawrence Erlbaum Associates, 1983.

20. J. Greeno, "Conceptual Entities," *Mental Models*, D. Gentner and A. Stevens, eds., Lawrence Erlbaum Associates, 1983, pp. 227–252.

21. B. Falkenhainer, K.D. Forbus, and D. Gentner, "The Structure-Mapping Engine: Algorithm and Examples," *Artificial Intelligence*, vol. 41, 1990, pp. 1–63.

22. G. Klein, *Sources of Power: How People Make Decisions*, MIT Press, 1998.

Chapter 27: Perceptual (Re)learning: A Leverage Point for Human-Centered Computing

R.R. Hoffman and S.M. Fiore, "Perceptual (Re)learning: A Leverage Point for Human-Centered Computing," *IEEE Intelligent Systems*, vol. 22, no. 3, May/June 2007, pp. 79–83. doi: 10.1109/MIS.2007.59

At least since Adrianus Dingeman de Groot conducted his pioneering work on the reasoning of chess masters, perceptual skill has been regarded as key to the advantage of experts. Here we explore the conjunction of two facts: 1. experts can perceive things that are invisible to the novice; 2. it takes a decade or more for someone to become an expert in most significant domains; 3. this conjunction represents a leverage point for intelligent systems—not from the Turing Test perspective of building machines that emulate humans but from the human-centered computing (HCC) perspective of amplifying and extending human capabilities.

Perceptual (Re)learning: A Leverage Point for Human-Centered Computing

Robert R. Hoffman, *Institute for Human and Machine Cognition*
Stephen M. Fiore, *University of Central Florida*

At least since Adrianus Dingeman de Groot conducted his pioneering work on the reasoning of chess masters,[1] perceptual skill has been regarded as key to the advantage of experts. Here we explore the conjunction of two facts:

1. Experts can perceive things that are invisible to the novice.[2]
2. It takes a decade or more for someone to become an expert in most significant domains.[3]

This conjunction represents a leverage point for intelligent systems—not from the Turing Test perspective of building machines that emulate humans but from the human-centered computing (HCC) perspective of amplifying and extending human capabilities.

Perceptual learning

James and Eleanor Gibson, champions of "ecological psychology," emphasized the importance of perceptual learning.[4] It's an interesting notion because it cuts across a Cartesian distinction between two processes that are believed to be distinct and fundamental to how the mind works. Today, there is a growing literature on psychophysiological changes, including demonstrations of the neural basis for cue imprinting.[5,6] With regard to cognition, however, the phenomenon of perceptual learning has been difficult to capture in the laboratory. It's not easily reproducible in a controlled experiment that can last only as long as a college class period and that uses undergraduates as "subjects." The only recourse has been to use simple, artificial materials (for example, geometric forms or schematic faces that fall into categories based on artificial rules)[7] and relatively simple discrimination tasks or similarity judgment tasks.

Researchers have conducted studies on somewhat more realistic tasks, such as learning to discriminate flavors of beer[8] or learning how to determine the sex of newborn chicks.[9] In one study, college students received six training sessions on recognizing species of birds (using photographs as stimuli).[10] Next, the students were tested in a same/different discrimination task. Those who had received training on discriminating species according to functional considerations (such as wading birds versus types of owls) rather than visual considerations showed better discrimination performance on a transfer task involving novel stimuli. A clear conclusion is that perceptual learning doesn't happen by mere exposure to exemplars but is acquired through deliberate acts of discrimination and differentiation combined with corrective feedback.[6]

Overall, the drive to capture phenomena in replicable, controlled circumstances has led psychological research to eliminate much of the richness of perceptual learning. Research hasn't looked much at the perception of real moving faces but has looked at the perception of pictures or static cartoons of faces. It hasn't looked much at the perception of real handheld chicks or flying birds but photographs of chicks and birds. Precious little research has attempted to capture perceptual learning across time spans longer than those of typical laboratory experiments, and only a fraction of studies have trained the participants for more than one day.

Perceptual knowledge, perceptual skill, and expertise

Although capturing perceptual learning in the lab is challenging, studies of expert-novice differences have illustrated perceptual learning in a variety of domains ranging from neonatal critical-care nursing to commercial fishing. Studies have looked at domains where perceptual skill is paramount, such as radiology[6,11] and baggage screening.[12] We know that experts' knowledge organization involves finer gradations of functional categories—their "basic object-level" categories fall at a finer level than for nonexperts. For example, for most people, limestone is simply a kind of rock, but to the expert, many variants (for example, tilted thinly interbedded limestone shale with limestone predominating) inform of geological dynamics.

Experts' categories fall also at a functional rather than literal surface feature level.[13] So, experts can rapidly evalu-

Editors: Robert R. Hoffman, Patrick J. Hayes, and Kenneth M. Ford
Institute for Human and Machine Cognition, University of West Florida
rhoffman@ai.uwf.edu

ate a situation and determine an appropriate plan of action, a phenomenon called *recognition-primed decision making*.[14] Within the first few seconds of exposure to a novel chess position, chess experts can perceive important information about the relations of the chess pieces' positions and begin identifying promising moves.[15]

This begins to get us closer to the heart of the matter: Perceptual learning isn't just about the perception of cues or reckoning of variables—it's about their meaningful integration. For example, a story is told in which an expert intelligence analyst inspected photos that had been used to show that Iraq was developing biological weapons. The expert disagreed with the original assessment that the photo showed a decontamination vehicle parked outside a chemical bunker: "I don't think it is—and I don't see any other decontamination vehicles down there that I would recognize."[16] He explained that the standard decontamination vehicle was a Soviet-made box-body van; this truck was too long. Another expert agreed, saying "If you are an expert, you can tell one hell of a lot from pictures like this."[16] The experts didn't just detect cues but understood the meaning and significance of cues that were present, and ones that were absent.

Here's another illustrative case. Terrain analysts interpret aerial photographs to assess soils, bedrock, vegetation patterns, drainage patterns, and so forth. In one experiment, an expert had two minutes to inspect a stereo photograph.[17] Ordinarily, the full systematic terrain-analysis process can take hours. After the viewing period, the expert had five minutes to report everything he could remember about the photo. In one particular trial, the expert began his retrospection by asserting that any personnel sent to the depicted area should be prepared for certain types of bacterial infection. The experimenter asked, "You can see bacteria in a photo of a pond taken from 40,000 feet?" The expert recounted the following reasoning sequence: The photo covered an area of tropical climate. The forest was mature and uniform, which meant that the contour of the tree canopy fairly mirrored the contours of the terrain surface (that is, the ground) and the underlying bedrock. Specifically, the expert could tell that the terrain was based on tilted interbedded limestone. The bedrock also determined the pattern of the streams and ponds, and it seemed one pond didn't have a tributary running away from it. Given the climate, vegetation (tropical legumes), and stagnant water, the presence of bacteria was a virtual certainty.

This appears to be a long chain of inferences, dependent on a great deal of declarative knowledge. Yet, in the actual interpretation exercise, the expert's judgment was the sort that you might be inclined to call direct or immediate, a perceptual phenomenon rather than a linear, deliberative process.

Psychological research on cue utilization illustrates the knowledge-based integration of cues. Expert decision makers don't always rely on all relevant cues; sometimes they seem to make decisions based on a limited number of available cues.[18,19] This finding feeds into the "biases and limitations" view of human cognition.[20] But what makes experts unique is "their ability to evaluate what is relevant in specific contexts. It's the study of that skill, not the number of cues used, that should guide future research on experts."[21] Furthermore, it's also likely that studies showing cue underutilization might be epiphenomenal to the subtle ways in which experts integrate information.[22] In other words, the informative cues might be separable in the sense that they can be operationally defined and measured independently of one another, but they link together for principled reasons and relate to one another in meaningful ways. In functional terms, they're integral.

Perceptual learning isn't just about the perception of cues or reckoning of variables—it's about their meaningful integration.

Consider a study involving livestock judges.[23] After viewing photos of young female pigs (gilts), the judges had to rate each gilt on its breeding quality. This is a typical task—agricultural extension experts can't possibly travel to all the regional farms to evaluate animals. By tradition and (extensive) training, judges rely on a set of 11 gilt features (including weight, length, ham thickness, heaviness of bone structure, and freeness of gait). However, the study's results suggested that the judges weren't relying on all 11 features. Sometimes, they seemed to ignore information. In a second condition, judges were given verbal descriptions of the gilts (reflecting a telephone conversation) that listed the values of the 11 attributes for each animal. This revealed the basis of the judges' reasoning: The cues interact. In the photo-based evaluations, the judges perceptually collapsed the 11 dimensions into three main judgments of size, meat quality, and breeding potential. Then they combined these to form an overall judgment. They could integrate the relevant stimulus attributes because they were, by nature, partly correlated for meaningful reasons (for example, tall gilts tend to be heavier and wider). Thus, even though a judge might have *seen* all the cues, he or she *perceived* meaningful cue integrations. The verbal descriptions, however, separated the cues, forcing a deliberative analysis and revealing the cue relations and the judges' sequential collapsing strategy. Robert Goldstone has referred to this as a process of *unitization*, in which a "single constructed unit represents a complex configuration."[6]

Now we begin to see the crux of the matter. Often, the patterns that bear meaning can't be defined in terms of the simple presence or absence (or values) of separable cues. Meaningful patterns are sometimes defined by the relations among functionally integral cues. Ludwig Wittgenstein was getting at this with his notion of featureless family resemblances. For instance, an expert weather forecaster can see a "gate-to-gate signature" in radar that is a clue to tornado formation. This signature is a function of a difference (which is a relation) in relative velocity (a second relation) of proximal (a third relation) winds, with strong (fourth relation) winds moving toward the radar (fifth relation) in very close proximity (sixth relation) to strong (seventh relation) winds that are moving away from (eighth relation) the radar.[24] Clearly, a considerable nexus of relations exists.

This is well known in other domains too. In medicine, it's captured by the phrase, "Diseases do not read the textbooks." Here, for example, is a passage from Malcolm Gladwell's interview with an expert radiologist about the process of interpreting mammograms:

> Some calcium deposits are oval and lucent. "They're called eggshell calcifications ... and they're basically benign." Another kind of calcium runs like a railway track on either side of the breast's many blood vessels—that's benign too. ... "There are certain kinds that are always associated with cancer. But those are the ends of the spectrum, and the vast amount of calcium is somewhere in the middle. And making that differentiation ... is not clear-cut."[16]

Mammogram interpretation is made complex and difficult for a number of reasons. This isn't just a matter of making better cameras or taking better pictures:

> You can build a high-tech camera ... [But] even then the pictures are not self-explanatory. They need to be interpreted, and the human task of interpretation is often a bigger obstacle than the technical task of picture-taking.[16]

As one expert said in discussing a tough case:

> That cancer shows up only because it is in the fatty part of the breast. If you take that cancer and put it in the dense part of the breast, you'd never see it. ... If the tumor was over there [by a few centimeters], it could be four times as big and we still wouldn't see it.[16]

You might expect such interpretive uncertainty and ambiguity to be frequently associated with things that are abnormal. However, "the overwhelming number of ambiguous things really are normal."[16]

Perceptual learning is what makes expertise possible: "There is good evidence that with more rigorous training and experience radiologists can become much better at reading X-rays."[16] For example, Alan Lesgold and his colleagues found that novice radiologists rather quickly acquired the ability to identify problem areas in an X-ray but were much slower in their ability to accurately interpret and diagnose the problem.[11]

From this brief review we can summarize that the patterns that are meaningful to experts sometimes involve

- individual cues,
- cues that are absent,
- sets of separable cues with some cues being necessary and some being sufficient,
- patterns that can be defined in terms of combinations of cues,
- patterns defined in terms of relations among cues,
- patterns defined in terms of the relations of cues that are present to cues that are absent,
- featureless family resemblances where cues are neither necessary nor sufficient when considered individually, and
- meaning that resides in the relations among cues that are integral, what Goldstone calls unitized cue configurations.

Now, let's up the stakes.

Dynamic cue configurations

When civil engineers who are experts in interpreting aerial photographs look at such photos to determine, for example, the best site for a dam, engineering requirements for building a new road, or a housing development's environmental impact, they see terrain features. However, they perceive geobiological dynamics: the complex, long-term processes that led the terrain to take its current form.[25] When expert radiologists look at mammograms, they see patterns of shades of white, gray, and black. But they perceive processes such as calcification.

> The expert bird watcher can identify a species even when all there is to see is a fleeting shadow of movement in flight. Meaningful patterns sometimes exist only over time.

The patterns that experts perceive, even in static images, are dynamic. Experts perceive processes. When expert weather forecasters look for tornadoes in a radar image, they see a pattern of colors and shapes, but that isn't what they perceive. The gate-to-gate signature we mentioned earlier looks like an owl's head (in its protoypical manifestation), but it rarely shows up in individual radar scans. More often, it appears only across a series of radar scans over time. The expert firefighter can determine a fire's location and cause by the movement of its flame and smoke; the expert bird watcher can identify a species even when all there is to see is a fleeting shadow of movement in flight. Meaningful patterns sometimes exist *only* over time.

Let's up the stakes again.

Dynamic cue configurations that exist across multiple data types

So far, we've talked about how experts perceive patterns in such things as x-ray films and radar images. But the patterns that experts perceive sometimes don't exist in individual data types. Indeed, the really critical information often is "transmodal"—that is, it exists only across data types. For instance, in weather forecasting, the radar images aren't the only thing that is guiding sensemaking activity and shaping the forecaster's formation of a mental model. A great many other data types are involved, such as satellite images, computer model outputs, wind fields, and pressure data. For example, indications of severe weather might lie in a combination of

- *Satellite image loops.* These show, on a space-time scale on the order of continent/week, the convergence of air masses of differing pressure, temperature, and moisture.
- *Wind fields as a function of height in the atmosphere.* These show, on a space-time scale on the order of states/days, the localized regions of potential instability.
- *Observational data.* These show, on a space-time scale on the order of regions/hours, where layers of the atmosphere are about to undergo inversion, releasing potential energy and triggering storm formation.

The "Aha!" moment might come when viewing radar, but the mind had been prepared in the sense that a mental model was based on an integration of meaningful patterns that only exist across data types. Likewise, the expert terrain analyst makes determinations when viewing aerial photos but also engages in the systematic analysis of other data, such as maps.

We should note that "multiple data types" can mean multiple perceptual modalities. In the case of a breast cancer diagnosis, "a skilled pair of fingertips can find out an extraordinary amount about the health of a breast, and we should not automatically value what we see in a picture over what we learn from our other senses."[16]

Now let's up the stakes even more.

Perceptual relearning

This final step involves bringing into the mix the Moving Target Rule:[26] The sociotechnical workplace is constantly changing, and constant change in environmental constraints (such as technologies in the workplace) might entail constant change in cognitive constraints (the work to be accomplished), even if the domain constraints remain constant. Change in cognitive work comes because of changes in goals (such as new tasks or challenges) but especially because of changes in technology, including changes in data types and display types. For instance, the Nexrad radar has revolutionized radar meteorology and forecasting, and new radar algorithms are being introduced all the time, resulting in new data products (hence, new displays) and new combinations of data types (such as those that combine satellite and radar images, called "Sat-Rad" displays). In the modern sociotechnical work context, the expert must engage in frequent, if not nearly continuous, perceptual relearning. Patterns previously learned and perceived in one way come to be perceived in a new way. New patterns pique the muse.

The crux of the matter

We can now return to the conjunction of the two facts with which we began this essay.

Fact one: *Experts can perceive things that are invisible to the novice.* We can be a bit more specific now: Experts engage in perceptual relearning of dynamic information defined over sets of integral cues that are transmodal (they exist over different data types). This is a holy grail for expertise studies because perceptual skill is critical for many, if not most, domains of expertise. A critical scientific gap is the paucity of research attempting to capture the perceptual relearning process as it occurs in the practice of domain experts. We need to know more about how it happens psychologically. Available research gives only the barest of clues.

Perceptual relearning of dynamic integral transmodal cue configurations (yes, we could give it an acronym, but we won't) is also important for intelligent systems. One way of thinking about it is that it takes the notion of pattern recognition to entirely new levels. Another way of thinking about it is that it's a cautionary tale about the rather nebulous yet popular notion of "information fusion."[27] We're reminded of the Sacagawea Law of HCC,[28] which asserts that effective complex cognitive systems support the integration, search, and active exploration of meaning. The law was invoked in the context of decision-aiding, but here we apply it to perception.

Fact two: *It takes years to achieve expertise*—thousands of hours of deliberate practice to reach world-class caliber in chess,[15] sports,[29] or weather forecasting.[24]

Now here is how these two facts come together: Any method for accelerating the achievement of expertise will hinge on the ability to support the processes of learning and perceptual relearning of dynamic cue configurations, including those that exist across multiple data types. Although the value of "on-the-job" training is clear,[30] it generally doesn't explicitly focus on perceptual learning and often lacks adequate organizational procedures and adequate management or organizational support.[31]

> In the modern sociotechnical work context, the expert must engage in frequent, if not nearly continuous, perceptual relearning.

Thus, we find a role for intelligent, human-centered systems. A key challenge is determining whether any shortcuts to mastery exist—that is, determining whether we can accelerate the perceptual learning process and facilitate the perceptual relearning process.

In domains of expertise where perceptual skill is paramount, such as radiology and baggage screening,[32] it seems reasonable to speculate that providing critical exemplars of targets makes the perceptual learning process possible. But it might not accelerate it. It might take upwards of 10 years to achieve expertise because experts (by definition) can deal with tough discriminations and challenging cases that are (by definition) rare.[2] If we could somehow compress the time needed to experience such cases, we might be able to accelerate perceptual learning. You might refer to this as "tough-case time compression." We predict that engaging in perceptual relearning will require effort and be disruptive even for experienced domain practitioners. But experienced practitioners should be able to reacquire expertise in less time than it takes less-experienced practitioners (students, journeymen) to acquire it.

Intelligent technologies will need to support the conduct of such research. Time-compressed case-based practice will depend on having at hand a large and navigable corpus of cases, in all their rich detail. Furthermore, the full corpus, and therefore both the training and testing sets of cases, will need to include cases that are routine and frequent, nonroutine and rare, easy and simple, and complex and tough. Generating sets of scenarios is a job for cognitive task analysis, which we know how to do.[33] What we need now are technologies through which the learner can experience the full range of meaningful event patterns.

The dynamics associated with this experience must be manipulable. Here is another role for computer science: Packaging case information and meta-information so that cases could be relived, explored as they are relived, and compared as they are explored ... but in "compressed" time. We might compress time through splicing or judicious speeding up to remove chunks of time or by shortening delays (for example, letting thunderstorms develop over a span of minutes rather than hours), but such an approach won't likely be the only—or even the consistently best—way to compress time. Cases find their meaning in how sequences or parallelisms of events hang together and unfold across time, thus making time one of the cues within a configuration. So "dynamic" isn't just a qualifier but also a variable that the learner might need to manipulate. In other words, we'll likely need multiple methods for compressing time, some of which might be domain or event dependent.

We hypothesize that a benefit from the research and development activity we're suggesting would be intelligent systems that have been referred to in this HCC department as *Janus Machines*[34]—human-centered machines that can facilitate learning (as training aids) and improve performance (as performance support systems). Acquiring the ability to make perceptual judgments will correlate with increasing knowledge about the underlying meanings, dynamics, and causal relations that are formative of the perceptible patterns. Conversely, increasing perceptual skill relates to a more sophisticated understanding and integration of the relevant perceptual dimensions. Strategies embodied in intelligent systems might help learners at all levels (initiates, apprentices, journeymen) ramp up their knowledge and skill more quickly when they move into an unfamiliar zone or when the nature of the work changes abruptly. Janus Machines for perceptual relearning would be of considerable benefit in many work domains, perhaps especially ones that are linked to significant workforce issues of our time, such as the loss of expertise. ■

References

1. A.D. de Groot, *Thought and Choice in Chess*, 2nd ed., Mouton, 1948 (reprinted 1978).
2. G.A. Klein and R.R. Hoffman, "Seeing the Invisible: Perceptual-Cognitive Aspects of Expertise," *Cognitive Science Foundations of Instruction*, M. Rabinowitz, ed., Lawrence Erlbaum Associates, 1992, pp. 203–226.
3. W.G. Chase and H.A. Simon, "Perception in Chess," *Cognitive Psychology*, vol. 4, 1973, pp. 55–81.
4. J.J. Gibson and E.J. Gibson, "Perceptual Learning: Differentiation or Enrichment?" *Psychological Rev.*, vol. 62, 1955, pp. 32–41.
5. M. Fahle and T. Poggio, eds., *Perceptual Learning*, MIT Press, 2002.
6. R.L. Goldstone, "Perceptual Learning," *Ann. Rev. Psychology*, vol. 49, 1998, pp. 585–612.
7. R.L. Goldstone, "Unitization during Category Learning," *J. Experimental Psychology: Human Perception and Performance*, vol. 26, 2000, pp. 86–112.
8. R.M. Peron and G.L. Allen, "Attempts to Train Novices for Beer Flavor Discrimination: A Matter of Taste," *J. General Psychology*, vol. 115, 1988, pp. 402–418.
9. I. Biederman and M.M. Shiffrar, "Sexing Day-Old Chicks: A Case Study and Expert Systems Analysis of a Difficult Perceptual-Learning Task," *J. Experimental Psychology: Learning, Memory, and Cognition*, vol. 13, 1987, pp. 640–645.
10. J.W. Tanaka, T. Curran, and D. Sheinberg, "The Training and Transfer of Real-World, Perceptual Expertise," *Psychological Science*, vol. 16, no. 2, 2005, pp. 145–151.
11. A. Lesgold et al., "Expertise in a Complex Skill: Diagnosing X-ray Pictures," *The Nature of Expertise*, M. Chi, R. Glaser, and M. Farr, eds., Lawrence Erlbaum Associates, 1988, pp. 311–342.
12. S.M. Fiore et al., "Perceptual and Conceptual Processing in Expert/Novice Cue Pattern Recognition," *Int'l J. Cognitive Technology*, vol. 5, 2000, pp. 17–26.
13. R. Glaser, "Thoughts on Expertise," *Cognitive Functioning and Social Structure over the Life Course*, C. Schooler and W. Schaie, eds., Ablex, 1987, pp. 81–94.
14. G. Klein, "A Recognition Primed Decision (RPD) Model of Rapid Decision Making," *Decision Making in Action: Models and Methods*, G. Klein et al., eds., Ablex, 1993, pp. 138–147.
15. N. Charness et al., "The Perceptual Aspect of Skilled Performance in Chess: Evidence from Eye Movements," *Memory and Cognition*, vol. 29, pp. 1146–1152.
16. M. Gladwell, "The Picture Problem," *The New Yorker*, 13 Dec. 2004, pp. 74–81.
17. R.R. Hoffman, "The Problem of Extracting the Knowledge of Experts from the Perspective of Experimental Psychology," *AI Magazine*, Summer 1987, pp. 53–67.
18. H.J. Einhorn, "Expert Judgment: Some Necessary Conditions and an Example," *J. Applied Psychology*, vol. 59, 1974, pp. 562–571.
19. P. Slovic, "Analyzing the Expert Judge: A Description of Stockbrokers' Decision Processes," *J. Applied Psychology*, vol. 53, 1969, pp. 255–263.
20. J. Flach and R.R. Hoffman, "The Limitations of Limitations," *IEEE Intelligent Systems*, vol. 18, no. 1, 2003, pp. 94–97.
21. J. Shanteau, "How Much Information Does an Expert Use? Is It Relevant?" *ActaPsychologica*, vol. 81, 1992, pp. 75–86.
22. M.M. Omodei et al., "More Is Better? A Bias Toward Overuse of Resources in Naturalistic Decision-Making Settings," *How Professionals Make Decisions*, Lawrence Erlbaum Associates, 2004.
23. R.H. Phelps and J. Shanteau, "Livestock Judges: How Much Information Can an Expert Use?" *Organizational Behavior and Human Performance*, vol. 21, 1978, pp. 209–219.
24. R.R. Hoffman, G. Trafton, and P. Roebber, *Minding the Weather: How Expert Forecasters Think*, MIT Press, 2007.
25. R.R. Hoffman and R.J. Pike, "On the Specification of the Information Available for the Perception and Description of the Natural Terrain," *Local Applications of the Ecological Approach to Human-Machine Systems*, P. Hancock et al., eds., Lawrence Erlbaum Associates, 1995, pp. 285–323.
26. R.R. Hoffman and D.D. Woods, "Steps toward a Theory of Complex and Cognitive Systems," *IEEE Intelligent Systems*, vol. 20, no. 1, 2005 pp. 76–79.
27. G. Klein, B. Moon, and R.R. Hoffman, "Making Sense of Sensemaking 1: Alternative Perspectives," *IEEE Intelligent Systems*, vol. 21, no. 4, 2006, pp. 70–73.
28. M. Endsley and R.R. Hoffman, "The Sacagawea Principle," *IEEE Intelligent Systems*, vol. 17, no. 6, 2002, pp. 80–85.
29. J.L Starkes et al., "Deliberate Practice in Sports: What Is It Anyway?" *The Road to Excellence: The Acquisition of Expert Performance in the Arts and Sciences, Sports and Games*, Lawrence Erlbaum Associates, 1996, pp. 81–106.
30. R.E. Derouin, T.J. Parrish, and E. Salas, "On-the-Job Training: Tips for Ensuring Success," *Ergonomics in Design*, Spring 2005, pp. 23–26.
31. T.W. Stanard et al., "Collaborative Development of Expertise: Evaluation of an On-the-Job (OJT) Training Program," *Proc. Human Factors and Ergonomics Society 46th Ann. Meeting*, Human Factors and Ergonomics Soc., 2002, pp. 2007–2011.
32. S.M. Fiore, S. Scielzo, and F. Jentsch, "Stimulus Competition During Perceptual Learning: Training and Aptitude Considerations in the X-ray Security Screening Process," *Int'l J. Cognitive Technology*, vol. 9, 2004, pp. 34–39.
33. B. Crandall, G. Klein, and R.R. Hoffman, *Working Minds: A Practitioner's Guide to Cognitive Task Analysis*, MIT Press, 2006.
34. R.R. Hoffman, G. Lintern, and S. Eitelman, "The Janus Principle," *IEEE Intelligent Systems*, vol. 19, no. 2, 2004, pp. 78–80.

Robert R. Hoffman is a senior research scientist at the Institute for Human and Machine Cognition. Contact him at rhoffman@ihmc.us.

Stephen M. Fiore is an assistant professor of cognitive science in the Department of Philosophy and a research scientist at the Institute for Simulation and Training, both at the University of Central Florida. Contact him at sfiore@ist.ucf.edu.

Chapter 28: Franchise Experts

R.R. Hoffman, D. Ziebell, P.J. Feltovich, B.M. Moon, and S.M. Fiore, "Franchise Experts," *IEEE Intelligent Systems*, vol. 26, no. 5, Sep./Oct. 2011, pp. 72–77. doi: 10.1109/MIS.2011.85

***This article harks back to the origins of this periodical as* IEEE Expert Systems.** Even while expert systems as a field or paradigm was morphing into intelligent systems, it was recognized that cognitive task analysis was critical in the design of new technologies. Furthermore, as a part of cognitive task analysis, it is crucial to conduct some form of proficiency scale to help identify the experts whose knowledge and skill might be revealed and specified in the creation of reasoning and knowledge-based systems. In this article, we will advance the claim that identifying and studying franchise experts can contribute to the design of intelligent systems. Of further interest is the possibility that the knowledge elicited from such experts might be invaluable for the practice of accelerated learning. We refer to "franchise" experts because they are not only expert in their chosen technical domain but also expert with regard to the organizations to which they belong. As a concept map organizer within a "knowledge model," some of the nodes are appended with icons that link to other concept maps that drill down into details, technical documentation, schematics, URLs, and so forth. This concept map shows that the franchise expert's knowledge refers to organizational structures and topics.

Franchise Experts

Robert R. Hoffman, *Institute for Human and Machine Cognition*
David Ziebell, *Electric Power Research Institute*
Paul J. Feltovich, *Institute for Human and Machine Cognition*
Brian M. Moon, *Perigean Technologies*
Stephen M. Fiore, *University of Central Florida*

This article harks back to the origins of this periodical as *IEEE Expert Systems*. Even while expert systems as a field or paradigm was morphing into intelligent systems, it was recognized that cognitive task analysis was critical in the design of new technologies. Furthermore, as a part of cognitive task analysis, it is crucial to conduct some form of proficiency scale to help identify the experts whose knowledge and skill might be revealed and specified in the creation of reasoning and knowledge-based systems.

In this article, we will advance the claim that identifying and studying *franchise experts* can contribute to the design of intelligent systems. Of further interest is the possibility that the knowledge elicited from such experts might be invaluable for the practice of accelerated learning.[1]

Defining Franchise Expertise

In professional sports, we sometimes hear of *franchise players*, individuals whose performance surpasses that of their best teammates and whose presence and contributions are identified with the spirit of the organization. The following example illustrates how we can apply this concept to experts:

> John Jones was a technical services manager at an electric utility. He supervised power quality engineers and district reliability engineers. Since childhood, he had an interest in electronics, mechanics, and engineering. While employed at the company, he sought out learning opportunities. "I learn on my own. I research and dig out the facts I need to know. Specialized training for engineering and construction is fun and neat to do." He worked for the company for about 30 years, in positions including distribution engineer, construction services supervisor, engineering division manager, power delivery manager, and reliability supervisor. He knew the company from top to bottom. Technology upgrades, staffing and training, production pressures, and the historical evolution of the system's complexity were all in play continuously, all needing to be orchestrated in the face of changing conditions to guard the corporate mission of reliable, safe electricity distribution. His knowledge of regulatory activities, including his knowledge of and strategies for liaising with the Public Services Commission, were tacit knowledge—undocumented and crucial to the company.

Thus, we refer to "franchise" experts because they are not only expert in their chosen technical domain but also expert with regard to the organizations to which they belong. The concept map in Figure 1 provides an overview of this individual's expertise. As a concept map organizer within a "knowledge model,"[2] some of the nodes are appended with icons that link to other concept maps that drill down into details, technical documentation, schematics, URLs, and so forth. This concept map shows that the franchise expert's knowledge refers to organizational structures and topics.

Proficiency Scaling

There is a classic claim that the development of high proficiency takes at least 10 years. No one spends all their time at work actually performing job-related tasks. A rule of thumb, based on classic studies of work,[3] is that only half of the time people are at work is actually spent doing job-related tasks. To achieve expertise, the metric generally cited is 10,000 hours of actual time on task.[4]

If we were to say "10,000 ± 2,000," this would be reasonable enough as a general estimate of the minimum time to achieve expertise.[5,6] There are

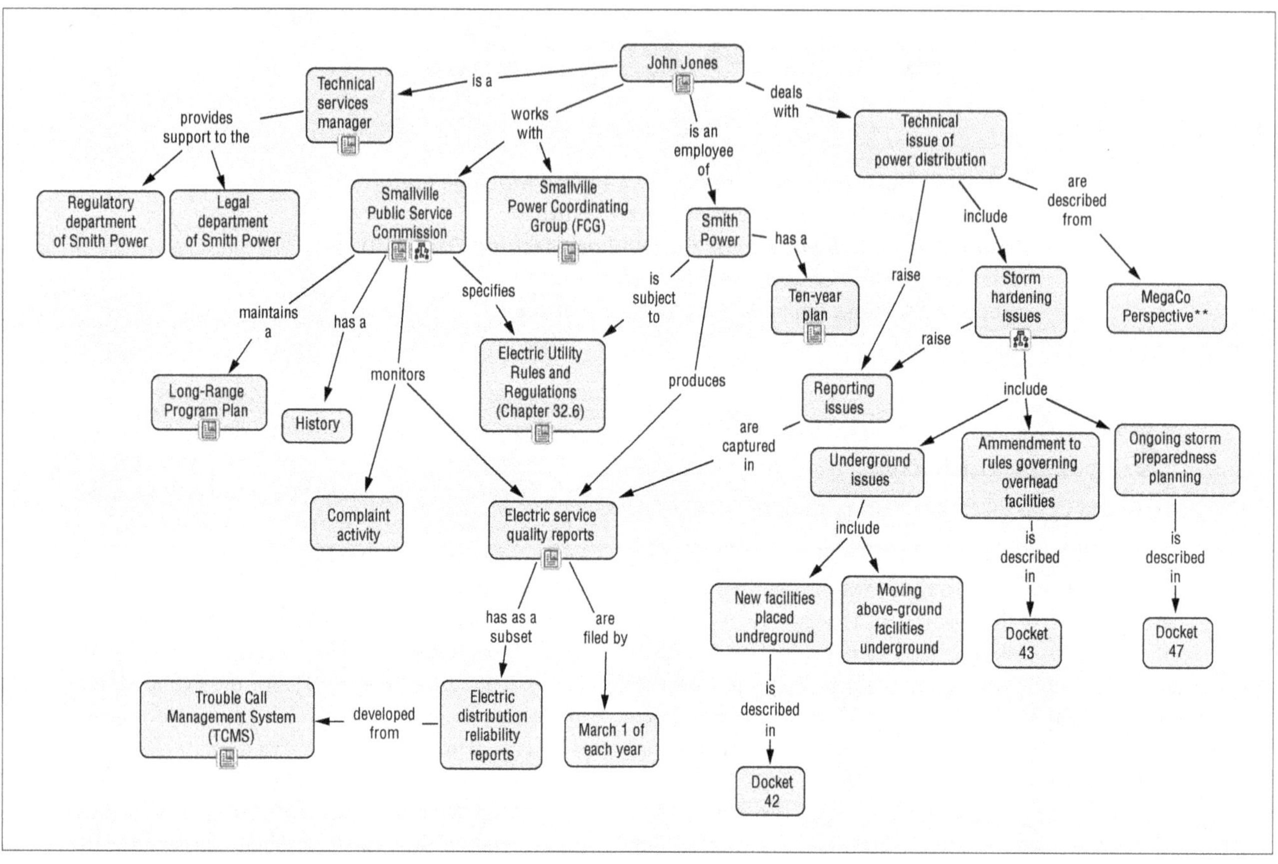

Figure 1. Concept map overview of a franchise expert's knowledge areas. The icons appended to some of the nodes link to resources, including other concept maps that drill down into details, technical documentation, schematics, URLs, and so forth.

additional considerations, however. For instance, an in-depth study of weather forecasters spanning the full proficiency range (from apprentice to journeyman to expert) estimated that the best forecasters—senior citizens—had spent as much as 50,000 hours on task.[7] In addition to looking at time on task, of course, we must consider actual performance (forecast skill scores for senior experts were greater than those for junior journeymen) and depth of experience as well (the senior experts had a greater variety of experiences, such as forecasting in multiple climates). Similarly, Jim Shanteau pointed out that someone might remain a novice in the judging of livestock even after 10 years of experience (typically at school and club training) and that experts are those with 20 to 30 years of experience.[8,9]

To achieve expertise, there needs to be

- a constant stretching of skills, defined by increasing challenges (such as tough or rare cases);
- high levels of intrinsic motivation to work hard, on hard problems, which pioneer educational psychologist Edwin Thorndike[10] called "practice with zeal;"
- practice that provides rich and meaningful feedback about both process and outcome; and
- opportunities to practice with the help of a mentor (for the apprentice-to-journeyman progression) or some form of more-expert instructional guidance (for the journeyman-to-expert progression).

These sorts of findings about expertise hold for domains ranging from musical performance to world-class sports performance to scientific and engineering domains.[6,11,12]

Robert Hoffman defined the expert as

> The distinguished or brilliant journeyman, highly regarded by peers, whose judgments are uncommonly accurate and reliable, whose performance shows consummate skill and economy of effort, and who can deal effectively with certain types of rare or "tough" cases. Also, an expert is one who has special skills or knowledge derived from extensive experience with subdomains.[13]

Some experts become extraordinary because of

- a personal choice to become a student of what interests them,

- a lack of barriers to their success, and
- some kind of positive feedback or mentoring that encourages their success.

This finding fits with results of previous studies of expert weather forecasters.[7,14] It is common for top performing weather forecasters to report an early fascination with the weather, leading in adulthood to an intrinsic motive to continue learning and developing higher levels of skill.

But not all experts have such an attitude and approach. Rebecca Pliske, Beth Crandall, and Gary Klein found that some weather forecasters were highly proficient, but were demotivated.[12] These had a *proceduralist attitude* of merely going through the motions in their job, whereas others had a *scientist attitude* marked by a desire to keep learning and improving.

Thus, it is possible to draw some distinctions within this single, grand category of "expert."

One-Percenters versus Five-Percenters

Across the literature, we sometimes see reference to experts who are *five-percenters*. A study of expert computer programmers affirmed a previous finding in expertise studies, namely that experts begin problem solving by thinking about general principles before moving to the analysis of details.[15] The researchers compared experts (determined to perform at the 70th to 80th percentile level) to super-experts, who were determined to perform in the top 95th percentile. The full proficiency scale created in a study of weather forecasters found it useful to distinguish junior and senior grades within each of the main categories of apprentice, journeyman, and expert.[7] On this expanded scale, we might informally refer to the senior expert as a *one-percenter*.

Although all experts have rich mental models, the one-percenters form mental models that go beyond those of their expert colleagues. When one-percenters generate an answer, they anticipate consequences throughout the work system or organization, in addition to the collateral consequences to other related systems or subsystems. Like all experts, one-percenters have knowledge and reasoning strategies that are not easy to write down. It might be difficult to formally model their knowledge and skills.

All experts learn from mistakes, but one-percenters retain a remarkably vivid recall of their errors. For example, proceduralists might be all too ready to forget their last faux pas, while one-percenters think about their past mistakes, which both gall and intrigue them. They revisit their performance, and revisit again, searching for the ways they were tripped up and considering what they could have done differently.

> One-percenters not only recognize the anomalous, they seek it out.

Like all experts, one-percenters can deal with tough cases. They recognize that to achieve the mission, work needs to be done at the edge of the familiar. They take satisfaction in opportunities to do work beyond their comfort zone, and examples of their best work are exhibited where the work is conducted beyond that edge of the familiar.

All experts are willing to improvise in challenging or unusual situations. However, one-percenters often demonstrate greater confidence and willingness in doing so. One-percenters not only recognize the anomalous, they seek it out. What they are not comfortable with is ignorance. They engage in problem solving to make sense of things and do not like to throw in the towel. When they say, "I've never seen this," their eyes light up, whereas others might say, "We do not have procedures for this."

One-Percenters versus Franchise Experts

Experts and senior experts in the utilities industry maintain that status for the last 15 to 25 years of their employment. This large proportion of utility personnel have simply become very, very good at what they do. This would not be inconsistent with the scientific conclusion about how long it takes people to achieve expertise as a five-percenter.[6]

We have elicited knowledge from dozens of utilities workers and have conducted workshops on workforce and training issues in the utilities. During the course of these interviews, we have encountered some individuals who triggered our thoughts about the concept of the franchise expert: a technical services manager, a training officer, a labor relations officer, a turbine repair technician, an environmental quality assurance officer, and a chief executive officer. The ways in which franchise experts stand apart from one-percenters have to do with the understanding they have about their organization and their relationships to it.

They have unique incentives. Franchise experts certainly expect to be compensated. But typical compensation packages are not the only, or even most important, rewards they seek. Technical achievements (such as problem solving and invention) are the things that motivate them.

They are an ad hoc solution provider. Franchise experts, by virtue of their continuously demonstrated success, become the go-to pro. People depend on them for mission critical, complex technical guidance or high-stakes decision making. Colleagues use the franchise expert's phone number as a hotline. Franchise experts routinely receive requests for help, to which they readily respond, even if the response requires additional effort.

A franchise expert's absence is traumatic. For colleagues that rely on the franchise expert, the absence of a franchise expert (due to a vacation or sick leave, for example) can be a traumatic event. The only circumstance that is more dreadful is to be placed in the role of the franchise expert during the franchise expert's leave.

They rarely say, "This is what I believe." Franchise experts do not support their actions or judgments by citing their own authority. They know that that is neither sufficient nor helpful to colleagues.

They appreciate the perspectives of others. While some experts become engrossed in the problem at hand, franchise experts consider the perspectives of others who are involved in the situation. They not only have the ability to do that, they pause to do it. Franchise experts understand (even to the point of sympathy) that other people simply cannot think the way they do and that others have to discover on their own things that the super-expert already knows or immediately discerns. Franchise experts display great patience with others, helping them to gain understanding from their own perspective, mentoring those who are developing their own expertise.

They create and own treasure maps. Franchise experts create and use memory artifacts that are unique organizing schemes that enhance their performance. These treasure maps reinforce the structure of the expert's knowledge, and they refer to the treasure maps as others would call for manuals. As an example, one of three gurus at a weather forecasting facility maintained a file drawer in which he kept data (images, charts, and so forth) on severe weather events that he had miss-forecast, with notes on what he got wrong and why. This was a goldmine for training material. As a second example, a technical services manager at a utility had a treasure map (which he referred to as an "informal documentation record") covering the history of the utility's relation with the Public Services Commission, policies concerning record retention, and notes about power outage metrics and outage reports that explained how the Public Services Commission interpreted the metrics and how the utility itself understood them. This material would be a crucial resource for anyone who might adopt this expert's role. The information existed in only two places, however: the expert's hard drive and the expert's memory.

Franchise experts create and use "treasure maps" that are unique organizing schemes that enhance their performance.

They lead, but usually by example. Franchise experts have the admiration of their peers and subordinates, and they develop a knack for employing their special position in furtherance of their organization's mission. Others follow them in order to learn and get their help. But franchise experts do not spend much of their time explicitly developing leadership qualities. Although they occasionally might find themselves in management roles, they are not always comfortable there.

They engage in continuous learning. Franchise experts thirst for knowledge. They self-select into learning opportunities, both formal and informal. They are students of their craft, and they practice with zeal. They go to great efforts to avoid getting stale in their domain of expertise. They are among the first to sign up for training events and the last to leave, staying behind to ask instructors for clarifications. They view all of life as an opportunity for development and often bring seemingly unrelated activities and knowledge to bear in the workplace.

They think in detail about training to high proficiency. Franchise experts think about what it would take for someone else to achieve their level of proficiency. The technical services manager we mentioned earlier had thought in great depth about the various "people skills" and interpersonal strategic considerations required for anyone who would represent the utility before the Public Services Commission. Another of the franchise experts we encountered was a nuclear chemist at a power plant. He was expert at radiation and effluent monitoring. He maintained computer programs and the radiation counting system, and he supervised procedures to meet industry requirements and reports to the Nuclear Regulatory Commission. He had thought in remarkable detail about entry-level requirements for his position (desired skills and abilities), training requirements to progress from the apprentice to journeyman level, and proficiency requirements for the journeyman and the expert.

All these factors defining franchise experts are certainly suggestive as things to consider in selection and in the promotion of aptitude, attitude, and motivation in order to make it easier to create new franchise experts and grow an institutional culture that rewards such attitudes.

Organizational Context

Some experts become extraordinary because of a personal choice to become a student of what interests them, but there are also organizational or situational factors. Franchise experts, by happenstance or by design,

- do not encounter organizational barriers (or they overcome or avoid them) and
- they receive some form of positive feedback or mentoring that encourages their success.

Achieving expertise is the purview of human resources departments. HR personnel have a keen interest in developing expertise through effective succession and workforce planning, training, information technology systems, and meaningful performance measurement approaches. We suspect that this is arguably true for organizations in all sectors of the economy.

However, the development of expertise often depends on chance and circumstance.[6] Many organizations have no institutionalized mentoring program. We know that the ability to effectively mentor is a skill set above and beyond that required for the domain expert.[16] Career development programs sometimes do not favor the development of technical expertise. And few incentives encourage the development of technical expertise. The labels *wizard* and *guru* are not necessarily signs of a rewarded status. The primary incentives that comprise many career development programs (including money) are not incentives that drive their self-development. Franchise experts, as we have pointed out, are motivated by the thrill of victory in solving problems or providing effective support to their teammates. Regrettably, improvisation might not only lack reward, it can actually be punished.

Although many organizations know that they rely on experts to achieve their mission, they often don't realize the degree of dependence until those experts leave.

Another challenge in career development stems from the fact that organizational and business cultures tend to track the development of specific skills into leadership. But experts, particularly technical experts (who might become franchise experts) might have little interest in leadership positions. This situation presents a catch-22 for the utilities because technical expertise can be useful in roles typically performed by corporate leaders, such as negotiation.

Another challenge organizations face lies in being attuned to the extent of the mission impact of experts, particularly their senior and franchise experts. Although many organizations know that they rely on experts to achieve their mission, they often don't realize the degree of dependence until those experts leave, often through retirement that is encouraged by workforce policies. Robert Hoffman and Lewis Hanes referred to this as the "panic attack mode."[17]

Utilities representatives we have interviewed (including leadership and technical experts) insist that utilities want to support continuous learning and want to have the achievement of expertise as a corporate goal. This too, we suspect, is an avowed goal of countless organizations across sectors of the economy. Attaining the goal, however, can be challenged by the need to accomplish the immediate mission, the lack of incentives for mentoring, and career and organizational stovepipes.

We have begun to develop notions of what is it about the nature of the cognition that makes it take upwards of 25 years to achieve the franchise expert level of proficiency. For intelligent systems, the "pull and push" on this is the requirement for information technologies to be adaptive and resilient.[18] This requirement mandates the study of how franchise experts (and the one- and five-percenters) are able to adapt. It also raises the human-centering issue of information technology. Technology based on designer-centered design fails to amplify the human abilities to know and reason.[19] It challenges the worker with frustrations and brittleness issues, and it limits the ability of workers to grow their expertise.

With regard to training and knowledge management, the pull and push is the payoff if we could reduce time-to-expertise from, say, 25 years to 20 years. Even junior experts are in a higher salary division, so any such time savings could have great practical significance. The window of risk, where loss of a particular expert could hurt the company's mission, could be reduced by accelerating the progression to extraordinary expertise.[1]

Specific achievements in the acceleration of expertise would be

- robust and efficient methods for identifying individuals who would be good candidates to receive training in how to be an effective mentor;
- application of knowledge capture and modeling tools to elicit and preserve the franchise experts' tacit knowledge, mental models, reasoning strategies, and treasure maps; and
- application of intelligent systems technologies to take that captured knowledge and generate training materials, exercises, and simulated decision problems.

To return to the origin of our term franchise experts, we note that sports clubs and professional organizations think of themselves in terms of building the future of their teams. Knowledge-based organizations might think about themselves in terms of nurturing the creation of franchise experts and building the organization around them.

References

1. R.R. Hoffman et al., "Accelerated Learning (?)," *IEEE Intelligent Systems*, vol. 24, no. 2, 2009, pp. 18–22.
2. A.J. Cañas and J.D. Novak, "Re-examining the Foundations for Effective Use of Concept Maps," *Proc. 2nd Int'l Conf. Concept Mapping*, A.J. Cañas and J.D. Novak, eds., 2006, pp. 494–502.
3. F.B. Gilbreth, *Motion Study*, Van Nostrand, 1911.
4. J.R. Hayes, "Three Problems in Teaching General Skills," *Thinking and Learning Skills, vol 2: Research and Open Questions*, S.F. Chipman, J.W. Segal, and R. Glaser, eds., Psychology Press, 1985, p. 391.
5. G. Colvin, *Talent Is Overrated: What Really Separates World-Class Performers from Everybody Else*, Portfolio, 2008.
6. M. Gladwell, *Outliers: The Story of Success*, Little Brown, 2008.
7. R.R. Hoffman et al., "A Method for Eliciting, Preserving, and Sharing the Knowledge of Forecasters," *Weather and Forecasting*, vol. 21, 2006, pp. 416–428.
8. J. Shanteau, "Some Unasked Questions about the Psychology of Expert Decision Makers," *Proc. 1984 IEEE Conf. Systems, Man, & Cybernetics*, M.E. El Hawary, ed., IEEE Press, 1984, pp. 23–45.
9. J. Shanteau, "Psychological Characteristics and Strategies of Expert Decision Makers," *Acta Psychologica*, vol. 68, nos. 1–3, 1988, pp. 203–215.
10. E.L. Thorndike, *Education: A First Book*, MacMillan, 1912.
11. K.A. Ericsson, ed., *Development of Professional Expertise*, Cambridge Univ. Press, 2009.
12. D.A. Schön, *Educating the Reflective Practitioner*, John Wiley and Sons, 1987.
13. R.R. Hoffman, "How Can Expertise Be Defined? Implications of Research from Cognitive Psychology," *Exploring Expertise*, R. Williams, W. Faulkner, and J. Fleck, eds., Macmillan, 1998, p. 85.
14. R. Pliske, B. Crandall, and G. Klein, "Competence in Weather Forecasting," *Psychological Investigations of Competent Decision Making*, K. Smith, J. Shanteau, and P. Johnson, eds., Cambridge Univ. Press, 2004, pp. 40–70.
15. R.J. Koubek and G. Salvendy, "Cognitive Performance of Super-Experts on Computer Program Modification Tasks," *Ergonomics*, vol. 34, 1991, pp. 1095–1112.
16. W.B. Johnson, *On Being a Mentor*, Erlbaum, 2007.
17. R.R. Hoffman and L.F. Hanes, "The Boiled Frog Problem," *IEEE Intelligent Systems*, vol. 18, no. 4, 2003, pp. 68–71.
18. E. Hollnagel, D.D. Woods, and N. Leveson, *Resilience Engineering*, Ashgate, 2006.
19. R.R. Hoffman et al., "A Rose by Any Other Name... Would Probably Be Given an Acronym," *IEEE Intelligent Systems*, vol. 17, no. 4, 2002, pp. 72–80.

Robert R. Hoffman is a senior research scientist at the Institute for Human and Machine Cognition. Contact him at rhoffman@ihmc.us.

David Ziebell is manager of human performance technology at the Electric Power Research Institute. Contact him at dziebell@epri.com.

Paul J. Feltovich is a research scientist at the Institute for Human and Machine Cognition. Contact him at pfeltovich@ihmc.us.

Brian Moon is chief technology officer at Perigean Technologies. Contact him at brian@perigeantechnologies.com.

Stephen M. Fiore is director of the Cognitive Science Laboratory at the University of Central Florida. Contact him at sfiore@ist.ucf.edu.

Part V:

Methodology and Metrics: Making What's Important Measurable

Chapter 29: Knowledge Management Revisited

R.R. Hoffman, D. Ziebell, S.M. Fiore, and I. Becerra-Fernandez, "Knowledge Management Revisited," *IEEE Intelligent Systems*, vol. 23, no. 3, May/June 2008, pp. 84–88. doi: 10.1109/MIS.2008.51

A number of social, economic, technological, and scientific trends have led to the emergence of communities of practice centered on the notion of the knowledge-based organization. However, the scientific foundation (knowledge elicitation methodology) and the commercial growth of knowledge management (KM) have largely developed in parallel. So, the creation of human-centered systems faces lingering challenges. In the KM process, company management establishes a program whereby experts who possess valuable knowledge collaborate with a knowledge engineer. Working together, they elicit the expert's wisdom for inclusion in the organization's knowledge base.

Knowledge Management Revisited

Robert R. Hoffman, *Institute for Human and Machine Cognition*
David Ziebell, *Electric Power Research Institute*
Stephen M. Fiore, *Institute for Simulation and Training and University of Central Florida*
Irma Becerra-Fernandez, *Florida International University*

A previous essay in this department[1] described how organizations are finding themselves in catch-up mode. They're losing their ability to conduct business as their workforce ages and critical knowledge walks out the door. A number of social, economic, technological, and scientific trends have led to the emergence of communities of practice centered on the notion of the knowledge-based organization. However, the scientific foundation (knowledge elicitation methodology) and the commercial growth of knowledge management (KM) have largely developed in parallel—that is, independently. So, the creation of human-centered systems faces lingering challenges. For each challenge, we ask, is this a matter of building intelligent technologies or of using technology intelligently?

Background

As the expert-systems field morphed into what's now broadly called *intelligent systems*, it became clear that we could preserve corporate knowledge by using the knowledge-elicitation methods that had been used to create knowledge bases and inference engines.[2] For all their limitations and brittleness, expert systems had pointed to the idea that organizations might create knowledge repositories.[3] We could then use the knowledge bases, including corporate "lessons learned," in training and corporate problem solving.[4]

Editors: Robert R. Hoffman, Patrick J. Hayes, and Kenneth M. Ford
Institute for Human and Machine Cognition
rhoffman@ihmc.us

Norman Kamilkow, editor in chief of *Learning Officer Magazine*, seems to agree. He said, "There is a growing role for a chief learning officer type within enterprise-level companies. ... There is a need to have somebody focused on how to keep the skills of the corporation's work force at a high level."[5]

In the KM process, company management establishes a program whereby experts who possess valuable knowledge collaborate with a knowledge engineer. Working together, they elicit the expert's wisdom for inclusion in the organization's knowledge base. In extreme cases, such as when a senior expert with specialized knowledge is soon to retire, the organization might retain or bring back the individual as a consultant.[3]

The KM literature on business management and the trade press on KM suggest that a wave of enthusiasm about KM hit in the 1990s but was followed by some disappointment.[1] The disappointment might have stemmed largely from limited KM software solutions, overzealous software sales personnel, or merely poor project implementations. For example, of over 220 KM implementations in 2000, at least half were "deeply suboptimized."[6] Certainly, issues of lack of trust and perceived effectiveness were and are in play.[7] However, at least some disappointment could certainly be due to failure to properly embed these KM software systems in the human activities and work processes they were intended to support—that is, lack of human-centering. Whatever the reasons were, various trends and forces have encouraged a renewed interest in KM.

Workforce issues

Workforce mobility and its implications for the transfer of expertise have made KM a hot topic ever since this HCC department last discussed it.[1] For example, in even the most highly technical military jobs, the tradition of regular change of duty assignment requires considerable relearning. Just when a weather forecaster achieves journeyman-level skill at one locale, the Navy transfers him or her to some other climate.[8,9]

Thus, there has been considerable discussion of the theory of organizational knowledge and KM,[10–12] and the topic is familiar to the pages of *IEEE Intelligent Systems*.[13] Researchers are interested in how social factors and organizational culture come into play in determining whether KM is successful and whether the organization shares knowledge effectively.[14]

Recent reports on the aging workforce have identified the upcoming retirement of baby boomers as the cause of an expected brain drain, in particular in specialized knowledge areas that have been unable to refresh their knowledge-worker base with recent graduates.[15,16] For instance, a NASA study revealed that the average number of years of service for all occupation groups at NASA has been increasing since 1995, partly because the most recent science and engineering graduates are taking jobs outside government and partly because of years of government downsizing and hiring freezes.[17] Most of NASA's employees today are 40 to 60 years old, and less than 5 percent of NASA's scientists and engineers are under 30. Currently, NASA has a number of programs of knowledge acquisition and KM, which includes the use of case-based-reasoning methods to form the architecture for a knowledge repository intended to help project managers find solutions to design, scheduling, and other problems.[7,18]

Another example comes from the US electric-utilities industry, which employs some 400,000 people in the US.[19] About half will be eligible to retire in the next five years.[20] A survey of managers representing 21 electric utilities found that 92 percent believed that loss of expertise would pose a problem within the next five years. But only 30 percent indicated that a planning effort was in place to retain knowledge.[14] Dale Klein, chairman of the US Nuclear Regulatory Commission, has said, "I have doubts about our ability to muster the workforce needed. … Where are we going to get the educated and skilled workers? … To a large extent, the knowledge reposes in the minds of older workers. … How do we transfer the knowledge to their replacements?"[21]

People have set up a number of commercial enterprises to provide services that address this question.

KM as a commercial enterprise

A Web search today shows considerable interest in KM activities and issues at international levels, reflecting the impact of global economic competition. KM is the topic of frequent meetings and Web forums (global brainstorming "Webjams"), hosted by institutes and government-industry partnerships. Numerous blogs and commercial Web sites offer a host of software products aimed at supporting KM in organizations. Web sites offer such things as "complete integrated design environments," "principles for KM success," "KM toolboxes," and "knowledge portals." Commercial e-magazines and monthly letters by authorities on "knowledge capital" give the impression that everyone sees value in retaining critical expert knowledge.

As a field, KM is undergoing refinement by subspecialization. The categories include knowledge capture, organizational learning, knowledge discovery, knowledge sharing, and knowledge application. Each of these is mated to a host of software systems, tools, and approaches ranging from more or less traditional management information systems to state-of-the-art Web-based virtual-community technologies and electronic knowledge networks.[3] Some providers focus on eliciting experts' knowledge; others focus on developing organizational staff to take on the knowledge-capture process.

If the knowledge-elicitation procedure provides proper scaffolding, experts can verbalize their tacit knowledge and express concepts they had never explicitly expressed before.

KM challenges

So, many are arguing that KM should be integral to an organization's operational infrastructure and culture. This presents challenges for the science underlying KM.

Challenge 1: Finding the knowledge

The differential-access hypothesis, from the early days of expert-systems knowledge acquisition, stated that different knowledge-elicitation methods might elicit different kinds of knowledge: declarative, procedural, and so on.[22] The philosophical notion of *tacit knowledge*[23] was associated with this topic,[24] along with the category "knowledge that cannot be verbalized."[25]

In time, tacit knowledge came to be regarded as a challenge for knowledge acquisition and KM, implying that human-to-human transfer (through collaboration and storytelling) would remain necessary because KM software can represent only codifiable knowledge.[26]

Research comparing knowledge-elicitation methods showed that most could yield information about domain-conceptual knowledge, including such things as causal principles and processes.[27] However, methods differ in terms of the elicitation of knowledge about the practitioner's procedures and strategies.[28]

Experts are sometimes well aware that they're having difficulty expressing their knowledge.[29] If the knowledge-elicitation procedure provides proper scaffolding, experts can verbalize their tacit knowledge and express concepts that they had never explicitly expressed before, including information about their procedures and strategies.[30] In other words, verbalizability doesn't seem to be an unavoidable problem in knowledge-elicitation practice. Overall, the findings might be more in line with the psychological notion of *inert knowledge*: knowledge that's accessed only in particular contexts and that might go unexpressed unless the right prompts or cues are provided.[31]

In contrast, tacit knowledge is regarded as a significant problem in the commercial KM world:[32]

> If an organization could capture the knowledge embedded in clever people's minds, all it would need is a better knowledge-management system. The failure of such systems to capture tacit knowledge is one of the greatest disappointments of knowledge-management initiatives to date. (p. 64)

The philosophical problem of tacit knowledge has given way to the practical problem of identifying individuals who possess knowledge that's unique to them, important to the organization, and tacit in the sense of being undocumented. This is key to KM's success.[14,33] In general, organizations lack agreed-upon robust methods for systematic, efficient identification of where critical knowledge might reside.

Knowledge-intensive organizations rely on decision makers to produce mission-critical decisions on the basis of inputs from multiple domains.[34] The decision maker needs an understanding of many specific subdomains that influence decision making, coupled with the experience that enables quick, decisive action based on such information.[11]

Is this an issue regarding intelligent technology or the intelligent use of technology? We think both. One of the many kinds of tools being used for KM is "expert locator" systems, which help people find experts who can consult on particular topics.[35] Another type of tool uses a thesaurus of concepts and relations, developed by experts, as a searchable ontology linked to a document repository. Searching is, in a sense, locating expertise. Another type of locator is based on a database search (keywords descriptive of jobs) to find frames that describe individuals. Knowledge locators and people locators strike us as a first step. Frames about people can yield a list of people's specializations, or a search on specializations can yield a list of people's names, but this is only a first approximation to locating critical expertise. Better are the various special services that help locate particular domain experts (such as vacation planners and political consultants) to enlist their services. Yet this too is only an initial step.

We might benefit from protocols and social software that support sociometry,[36] which could leverage recent advances in social-network analysis.[37] We've known for some time that sociometric methods can help determine where expertise resides in an organization.[38] A sociogram can be based on observations of people's interaction patterns, communication patterns, and workflows. Individuals in an organization can be interviewed and asked, for example, "If you have a problem of type x, whom would you go to for advice?" They might be asked to sort cards bearing domain practitioners' names into piles according to one or another skill dimension or knowledge category. We can think of a sociogram as a form of social-network analysis that identifies experts by revealing the organization's knowledge network (that is, who talks to whom, how often, and about what).

Once you know where the knowledge is, you have to get it.

Challenge 2: Eliciting the knowledge

Organizations view seriously a number of quick-fix solutions. Some organizations advocate just-in-time training, even though the literature on expertise (and especially demonstrations of the role of deliberate practice) suggests clearly that just-in-time training is a recipe for just-in-time failure. Many organizations seek software that claims to capture knowledge as it's created. The software might scan email, generate from it a repository of assertions to be posted on a Semantic Web server, and then generate computable ontologies and perform inferences.

In our experience, some organizations use weak methods for knowledge capture.

> Intelligent systems that merge the process of knowledge elicitation with the practitioners' ongoing work must make the work easier, not harder.

Typically, Human Resources personnel might grab the soon-to-retire expert, cloister him or her in a room, turn on a video camera, and ask, "Tell me everything you know." After 60 minutes, they label the videotape and put it on a shelf to collect dust. Knowledge might be on the tape, but it's neither usable nor useful. This seems like something of a caricature, but we've witnessed it more than once.

Less extreme are approaches that rely on various forms of structured interviewing, many of which are the essence of the practices of commercial companies that provide KM services.

So, is this a challenge for intelligent technology or for the intelligent use of existing technology? We think both. Reflecting the parallelism of scientific versus commercial KM, which we referred to earlier, knowledge providers can tap into the scientific foundations of knowledge elicitation and cognitive task analysis. We know that creating meaningful diagrams, in a process called Concept Mapping, is highly efficient at scaffolding experts in eliciting their domain knowledge.[39,40] We also know that methods such as the Critical Decision Method (CDM) effectively elicit knowledge about processes, procedures, and reasoning strategies.[41] Software for eliciting knowledge through Concept Mapping is growing in use, and the protocols for the CDM, including data collection forms, have been well specified.

Clearly, one limitation is that knowledge elicitation requires the active participation of a domain practitioner, who must forego his or her typical job obligations. These knowledge-capture initiatives "often fail because they make it harder, not easier, for people to do their jobs."[42] One idea is to forge intelligent systems that merge the process of knowledge elicitation with the practitioners' ongoing work in such a way as to make their jobs easier, not harder. This has been called the "tough nut" problem, for good reason: Envisioning how such technologies would work is difficult.[1] A software system for supporting physicians in the prescription-ordering process seems, on first look, like a good example.[42] It requires the physician to provide an explanation or rationale whenever an order deviates from the one generated by the computer (via a knowledge base and inference engine). However, such systems can be considered intrusive. Indeed, administrators removed a computerized system for physician order entry from the Cedars-Sinai Health System in Los Angeles after nearly unanimous protest from the physicians.[43]

The tough-nut problem remains tough. Nevertheless, once you've collected the knowledge, you must do something with it.

Challenge 3: Mentoring

A tradition in some organizations is mentoring, especially for new hires (apprentices). On the other hand, some believe that mentoring can be a waste of resources. In yet other cases, where knowledge organizations have entered the catch-up mode, there's a renewed recognition of the need to support mentoring processes. Increasing complexity, pace of change, pace of decision making, and worker mobility—all entail fewer opportunities for mentoring.[34] Because of these trends, national leaders are formulating policies to support research and development in an educational infrastructure capable of producing the next generation of the science and technology workforce.[44] Even if such initiatives succeed, the results might be too distant to help solve the immediate workforce issues.

Is this a challenge for intelligent technologies or for the intelligent use of technology? It's primarily the latter, but it's also a challenge for work analysis, at least for the near future.

With regard to the challenge of intelligent use of technology, the methodology of software-supported knowledge elicitation, described earlier, is fairly well understood. There's a missed opportunity here in that knowledge elicitation is typically regarded as a process in which elicitation is the sole activity. However, an organization's apprentices could be participant-observers when the expert's knowledge is being elicited. Also, such methods as "teachback" interviewing[45] and question-asking[46] (in which novices ask experts questions) have some use as an instructional method. If it's true that knowledge elicitation takes experts away from their jobs, we could at least double the return on investment by merging elicitation with mentoring. This idea resembles what Josianne Basque and her colleagues did by having experts collaborate with trainees in creating knowledge models, using a concept-mapping approach, with more than 150 experts and 150 novices at Hydro-Québec.[39]

Regarding the challenge for cognitive work analysis, although the literature on expertise studies is informative on what makes an expert teacher,[47] it doesn't deal with what makes a good mentor in the context of work (as opposed to the context of sports coaching, which has been extensively studied[48]). To help conceptualize a system for mentoring employees along the continuum of expertise, one of us (Robert Hoffman) invoked the middle ages' tradition of craft guilds.[49] A *master* was any practitioner who was "qualified" to teach, meaning he or she embodied the special qualities of a good mentor. So, even a journeyman could be qualified as a master. There's an unresolved need for robust, generalizable methods for identifying individuals having the most experience as a mentor and then conducting cognitive task analysis to reveal the mentors' reasoning strategies, especially as they deal with challenging mentoring situations.

A second step would be to apply the research findings to accelerate the achievement of expertise. Experienced workers often feel motivated to pass along their "tough case" knowledge. However, the bureaucratic habit of expecting that mentoring will succeed can be the culprit when workers are left not knowing how to proceed or even that their tough-case knowledge is critical and highly informative to apprentices. We must refine our understanding of how mentoring activities can occur within the context in which the job tasks themselves must be conducted.

Challenge 4: Costing

None of the challenges we've mentioned can be solved quickly through "accredited training" or "manpower" procedures. We sense a lingering belief that knowledge-retention issues can be solved through normal training, better or newer computers and software, traditional workforce planning, and benefits and retirement packages. Many people possess unique, important, undocumented knowledge, even knowledge that might be captured using simple, routine administrative methods. This leads to the mind set that a little effort spread over many people will manage the risk. Historically this has worked because turnover was slow and the pace of technical change was manageable.

> As long as an organization is at risk because of loss of expertise, any effort to capture and preserve expertise is bound to have some long-term value.

This is no longer the case in many areas of the private sector, such as the utilities. "In order to justify the time and money spent on an embedded-knowledge system, and to assess how well it's working, an organization needs to have a measurement-oriented culture."[42] But what to measure? Some organizations in the electric-utility business are beginning to conduct "knowledge loss risk assessment." This is a matter of intangible-asset valuation, which is difficult and can cloud the issues. We're perplexed to find organizations in a catch-up mode, seeking easy fixes to what are still outstanding problems for an empirical science and methodology of KM. Although we lack good solutions to the tough-nut problem, as long as an organization is at risk because of loss of expertise, any effort to capture and preserve expertise is bound to have some long-term value. Nonetheless, we're continually challenged to justify and calculate the short- versus long-term costs, benefits, and risks of doing (and not doing) knowledge capture.[50]

Of course, each challenge we've mentioned is open for empirical investigation. Such investigation must be a multidisciplinary collaboration of cognitive systems engineering and intelligent systems engineering. We've outlined some difficult scientific and practical problems that seem, at present, to be outside KM's scope. If the needed science is conducted in parallel and in collaboration with organizations that nurture and support a culture of KM practice, we might realize the true promise of knowledge management—if "management" is really even the right word for it. ■

References

1. R.R. Hoffman and L.F. Hanes, "The Boiled Frog Problem," *IEEE Intelligent Systems*, July/Aug. 2003, pp. 68–71.
2. G. Klein, "Using Knowledge Engineering to Preserve Corporate Memory," *The Psychology of Expertise: Cognitive Research and Empirical AI*, R.R. Hoffman, ed., Lawrence Erlbaum Associates, 1992, pp. 170–190.
3. I. Becerra-Fernandez and D. Leidner, eds., *Knowledge Management: An Evolutionary View*, Prentice-Hall, 2008.
4. A. Poulymenakou, T. Cornford, and E.A. Whitley, "Knowledge Acquisition for Organizational Problem Solving: Developing Expert Systems and Beyond," *Expert Systems with Applications*, vol. 5, 1992, pp. 121–130.
5. D. Pringle, "Learning Gurus Adapt to Escape Corporate Axes," *Wall Street J.*, 7 Jan. 2003, p. B1.
6. E. Berkman, "When Bad Things Happen to Good Ideas," *Darwin*, Apr. 2001; www.darwinmag.com/read/040101/badthings.html.
7. R. Sabherwal and I. Becerra-Fernandez, "An Empirical Study of the Effect of Knowledge Management Processes at Individual, Group, and Organizational Levels," *Decision Sciences*, vol. 34, 2003, pp. 225–260.

8. D.W. Haughey, "Leveraging Marine Corps Experience," *Marine Corps Gazette*, Nov. 2000, pp. 45–46.
9. J.A. Ballas, "Human-Centered Computing for Tactical Weather Forecasting: An Example of the 'Moving Target Rule,'" *Expertise Out of Context*, R.R. Hoffman, ed., Lawrence Erlbaum Associates, 2007, pp. 316-326.
10. R.M. Grant, "Toward a Knowledge-Based Theory of the Firm," *Strategic Management J.*, vol. 17, 1996, pp. 109–122.
11. I. Nonaka and H. Takeuchi, *The Knowledge Creating Company*, Oxford Univ. Press, 1995.
12. J.-C. Spender, "Making Knowledge the Basis of a Dynamic Theory of the Firm," *Strategic Management J.*, vol. 17, 1996, pp. 45–62.
13. D.E. O'Leary and R. Studer, "Knowledge Management: An Interdisciplinary Approach," *IEEE Intelligent Systems*, Jan./Feb. 2001, pp. 24–25.
14. M. Gross, L. Hanes, and T. Ayres, "Capturing Undocumented Worker-Job-Knowledge at Electric Utilities: The EPRI Strategic Project," *Proc. IEEE 7th Conf. Human Factors and Power Plants*, IEEE Press, 2002, pp. 6.20–6.24.
15. A. Fisher, "How to Battle the Coming Brain Drain," *Forbes Magazine*, 21 Mar. 2005, pp. 121–131.
16. D. Leonard, "Deep Smarts," *Harvard Business Rev.*, vol. 82, no. 137, Sept. 2004, pp. 88–97.
17. *Workforce Analysis Report*, US Nat'l Aeronautics and Space Administration, 2003.
18. I. Becerra-Fernandez and D.W. Aha, "Case-Based Problem Solving for Knowledge Management Systems," *Proc. 12th Int'l Florida AI Research Soc. Conf.*, AAAI Press, 1999, pp. 219-223.
19. *2006 Long Term Reliability Assessment*, North Am. Electric Reliability Council, 2006.
20. "Loss of Line Workers," *Morning Edition*, Nat'l Public Radio, 22 Mar. 2005.
21. *Interview with NRC Chairman Dale Klein at US WIN 2007*, Women in Nuclear Conf., 6 Sept. 2007, http://video.google.com/videoplay?docid=3549043670358279894.
22. R.R. Hoffman et al., "Eliciting Knowledge from Experts: A Methodological Analysis," *Organizational Behavior and Human Decision Processes*, vol. 62, 1995, pp. 129–158.
23. M. Polanyi, *The Tacit Dimension*, Doubleday, 1966.
24. R.J. Sternberg and J.A. Horvath, eds., *Tacit Knowledge in Professional Practice*, Lawrence Erlbaum Associates, 1999.
25. D.C. Berry and D.E. Broadbent, "On the Relationship between Task Performance and Associated Verbalizable Knowledge," *Quarterly J. Experimental Psychology*, vol. 36A, 1984, pp. 209–231.
26. J. Roberts, "From Know-How to Show-How? Questioning the Role of Information and Communication Technologies in Knowledge Transfer," *Technology Analysis and Strategic Management*, vol. 12, 2000, pp. 429–443.
27. R.R. Hoffman, B. Crandall, and N. Shadbolt, "A Case Study in Cognitive Task Analysis Methodology: The Critical Decision Method for the Elicitation of Expert Knowledge," *Human Factors*, vol. 40, 1998, pp. 254–276.
28. K.R. Hammond et al., "Direct Comparison of the Efficacy of Intuitive and Analytical Cognition in Expert Judgment," *IEEE Trans. Systems, Man, and Cybernetics*, vol. 17, 1987, pp. 753–770.
29. I. Josefson, "The Nurse as Engineer: The Theory of Knowledge in Research in the Care Sector," *Knowledge, Skill, and Artificial Intelligence*, B. Goranzon and I. Josefson, eds., Springer, 1988, pp. 19–30.
30. G.A. Klein, R. Calderwood, and A. Clinton-Cirocco, "Rapid Decision Making on the Fire Ground," *Proc. Human Factors Soc. 30th Ann. Meeting*, Human Factors Soc., 1986, pp. 576–580.
31. J.D. Bransford et al., "New Approaches to Instruction: Because Wisdom Can't Be Told," *Similarity and Analogical Reasoning*, S. Vosniadou and A. Ortony, eds., Cambridge Univ. Press, 1989, pp. 470–497.
32. R. Goffee and G. Jones, "Why Should Anyone Be Led by You?" *Harvard Business Rev.*, Sept. 2000, pp. 62–70.
33. B. Gaines, "Organizational Knowledge Acquisition," *Handbook of Knowledge Management*, vol. 1, C.W. Holsapple, ed., Springer, 2003, pp. 317–347.
34. I. Becerra-Fernandez, A. Gonzalez, and R. Sabherwal, *Knowledge Management: Challenges, Solutions, and Technologies*, Prentice-Hall, 2004.
35. I. Becerra-Fernandez, "Searching for Experts on the Web: A Review of Contemporary Expertise Locator Systems," *ACM Trans. Internet Technology*, vol. 6, 2006, pp. 333–355.
36. R.R. Hoffman, "Protocols for Cognitive Task Analysis," Inst. for Human and Machine Cognition, 2005, http://ihmc.us:16080/research/projects/CTAProtocols.
37. M.T. Hansen, "The Search-Transfer Problem: The Role of Weak Ties in Sharing Knowledge across Organization Subunits," *Administrative Science Quarterly*, vol. 44, 1999, pp. 82–111.
38. E. Stein, "A Look at Expertise from a Social Perspective," *Expertise in Context*, P.J. Feltovich, K.M. Ford, and R.R. Hoffman, eds., MIT Press, 1997, pp. 181–194.
39. J. Basque, B. Pudelko, and M. Léonard, "Collaborative Knowledge Modeling between Experts and Novices: A Strategy to Support Transfer of Expertise in an Organization," *Proc. 2nd Int'l Conf. Concept Mapping*, Univ. of Pamplona, 2004.
40. R.R. Hoffman, "An Empirical Comparison of Methods for Eliciting and Modeling Expert Knowledge," *Proc. 46th Meeting Human Factors and Ergonomics Soc.*, Human Factors and Ergonomics Soc., 2002, pp. 482–486.
41. B. Crandall, G. Klein, and R.R. Hoffman, *Working Minds: A Practitioner's Guide to Cognitive Task Analysis*, MIT Press, 2006.
42. T.H. Davenport and G. Glaser, "Just-in-Time Delivery Comes to Knowledge Management," *Harvard Business Rev.*, vol. 80, 2002, pp. 107–111.
43. R.G. Berger and B.A. Kichak, "Physician Order Entry: Helpful or Harmful?" *J. Am. Medical Informatics Assoc.*, vol. 11, 2004, pp. 100–103.
44. Committee on Science, Engineering, and Public Policy, *Rising above the Gathering Storm: Energizing and Employing America for a Brighter Economic Future*, Nat'l Academies Press, 2006.
45. L. Johnson and N. Johnson, "Knowledge Elicitation involving Teachback Interviewing," *Knowledge Elicitation for Expert Systems: A Practical Handbook*, A.L. Kidd, ed., Plenum Press, 1987, pp. 91–108.
46. R. Mack and J.B. Robinson, "When Novices Elicit Knowledge," *The Psychology of Expertise: Cognitive Research and Empirical AI*, R.R. Hoffman, ed., Lawrence Erlbaum Associates, 1992, pp. 245–268.
47. J. Minstrell, "Expertise in Teaching," *Tacit Knowledge in Professional Practice*, R.J. Sternberg and J.A. Horvath, eds., Lawrence Erlbaum Associates, 1999, pp. 215–230.
48. S.M. Fiore and E. Salas, "Cognition, Competition, and Coordination: Understanding Expertise in Sports and Its Relevance to Learning and Performance in the Military," to be published in *Military Psychology*, 2008.
49. R.R. Hoffman, "How Can Expertise Be Defined? Implications of Research from Cognitive Psychology," *Exploring Expertise*, R. Williams, W. Faulkner, and J. Fleck, eds., Macmillan, 1998, pp. 81–100.
50. W. Zachary et al., "Human Total Cost of Ownership: The Penny Foolish Principle at Work," *IEEE Intelligent Systems*, Mar./Apr. 2007, pp. 22–26.

Robert R. Hoffman is a senior research scientist at the Institute for Human and Machine Cognition. Contact him at rhoffman@ihmc.us.

David Ziebell is manager of Human Performance Technology at the Electric Power Research Institute. Contact him at dziebell@epri.com.

Stephen M. Fiore is a research scientist in the University of Central Florida's Team Performance Laboratory. Contact him at s.fiore@ist.ucf.edu.

Irma Becerra-Fernandez is a professor of management information systems at Florida International University. Contact her at becferi@fiu.edu.

Chapter 30: Metrics, Metrics, Metrics: Negative Hedonicity

R.R. Hoffman, M. Marx, and P. Hancock, "Metrics, Metrics, Metrics: Negative Hedonicity," *IEEE Intelligent Systems*, vol. 23, no. 2, Mar./Apr. 2008, pp. 69–73. doi: 10.1109/MIS.2008.31

Intelligent technologies such as performance support systems and decision aids represent a key aspect of modern sociotechnical systems. When new tools are introduced into the workplace, they represent hypotheses about how cognitive work is expected to change. The tacit hypothesis is that any such change will be for the better, performance will be more efficient, and decisions will be improved—that is, they'll be made faster and on the basis of greater evidence. Experience suggests that technological interventions sometimes have the intended positive effect. However, they often result in negative effects, including unintended cascading failures and worker frustration due to "user-hostile" aspects of interfaces.

Metrics, Metrics, Metrics: Negative Hedonicity

Robert R. Hoffman and Morris Marx, *Institute for Human and Machine Cognition*
Peter Hancock, *University of Central Florida*

Intelligent technologies such as performance support systems and decision aids represent a key aspect of modern sociotechnical systems. When new tools are introduced into the workplace, they represent hypotheses about how cognitive work is expected to change.[1,2] The tacit hypothesis is that any such change will be for the better, performance will be more efficient, and decisions will be improved—that is, they'll be made faster and on the basis of greater evidence. Experience suggests that technological interventions sometimes have the intended positive effect. However, they often result in negative effects, including unintended cascading failures and worker frustration due to "user-hostile" aspects of interfaces.[3]

Concern is rising about the high rate of software procurement failures that are due to the inadequate consideration of human factors. Recent statistics suggest a dismal record, representing the expenditure of billions of dollars for technologies that are unusable, ineffective, and at times even defunct.[4,5] At the same time, funding for developing communication and information technologies has reached record levels (about US$500 billion in the mid-1990s).[6] Recently we've seen entire government-sponsored research programs with titles that state human–system integration as a key goal for new technologies.[7] The notorious frustrations and failures triggered by software interventions in the workplace have led to a significant concern in the software engineering community with evaluation,[8,9] including help for organizations to establish metrics for "key performance indicators."[10,11]

Editors: Robert R. Hoffman, Patrick J. Hayes, and Kenneth M. Ford
Institute for Human and Machine Cognition
rhoffman@ihmc.us

The call for "metrics"

Nearly all announcements of US government-funded research programs for developing large-scale information systems have shown a pervasive concern with "metrics." The following three paraphrased statements from recent program announcements illustrate this point:

- "[The program will] explore methodologies and technologies which achieve substantial improvement and cost reduction in software development, requirements analysis and definition, software management, complexity, and quality metrics, reuse, reengineering, maintenance."
- "Metrics are needed to determine the correct fidelity for attaining training objectives while operating within the boundaries of current technologies, human perception, schedule and cost."
- "Multidisciplinary and cross-domain approaches are highly encouraged especially if useful in the development of metrics for dynamics, complexity and usability."

The sought-for measures have to gauge efficiency, effort, accuracy, and similar reflections of a maximizing process, hearkening to John Henry versus the steam hammer.[12] This is particularly frustrating for the advocates of human-centered computing and work-centered design.[13,14] A valiant effort to think along human-centering lines was a recent report of the US National Institute for Standards and Testing.[15] This highlighted measures such as efficiency but did so with reference to dimensions including effectiveness at hypothesis generation, effectiveness at coping with massive data, and effectiveness of human-machine interaction. Measures also included confidence ratings and assessments of associated mental workload. However, in light of our knowledge of human adaptability, can we provide better methods and procedures to create measures that reflect the meaningful aspects of systems-level cognitive work and activity?

The challenge

We must take the measurement of cognitive work to entirely new levels—addressing, for example, the important trade-offs in cognitive work at the team and systems level. The latter is, after all, where we might realize the final payoff for any investment.

A significant challenge is that studies of human-computer interaction, and the measures that we take, must support the evaluation of hypotheses concerning the nature of cognitive work itself (for example, the effects of synchronous versus asynchronous communication in distance collaboration, effects due to amount of team experience, and so on). At the same time, the study design must support evaluation of the software tools themselves. In other words, new technologies must do double duty: they enable research on cognitive work by supporting cognitive work, including new work methods. We might think of them as part of the materials and procedure comprising the method of an experiment on human-machine interaction. But we must also evaluate the new technologies themselves for effectiveness as components within cognitive-work systems.

We seek a framework for creating a "fast track" for evaluating work methods and the computer technology that's an intrinsic part of our methods.

Table 1 presents the considerable variety of things we might measure.

In a previous essay in this department, we argued that workarounds and kluges were inevitable realities that we can study empirically and cannot tacitly sweep under a carpet as if they had no significance.[16] We can easily conduct ethnographic studies of sociotechnical work systems to find instances of workarounds and kluges on the basis of an ontology.[16] We can then measure such things as time to create and estimate such things as time saved when used. Kluges and similar informal processes and procedures are, we believe, only hard to specify and measure before we bother to take an empirical approach.

There's one other possibility, that of measuring "negative hedonicity" (which we'll define in a moment). This idea stems from a previous essay in this department, which presented the Pleasure Principle of human-centered computing: "Good tools provide a feeling of direct engagement. They simultaneously provide a feeling of flow and challenge."[17] Notions of "hedonomics" and related ideas have emerged in the context of human factors and industrial design.[18,19]

Negative hedonicity

Measures of "raw" performance (efficiency, accuracy, errors) hold work methods hostage to human motivation. Typically, complex cognitive systems (that is, new technologies) do the reverse, holding human motivation hostage to work methods (especially software and interface systems). Thus, it's important to study and understand vital motivational factors. This includes positive affect (for instance, the feeling of "being in the problem" versus "fighting with the technology") and increased intrinsic, goal-oriented motivation.[19] *Negative hedonicity* is the valuation of affect and motivation as negatively impacted by the work experience. This dimension is reflected in frustration, confusion, mental (or data) overload, and automation surprise.

We seek a framework for creating a "fast track" for evaluating work methods and the computer technology that's an intrinsic part of our methods.

Negative hedonic measurement is now possible using a remarkably simple device, the Hancock Switch, which consists of a prominent red button placed next to each workstation operator (see figure 1). The button's normally open circuit connects to a digital signal generator that sends a signal to the main workstation when the switch is closed. Residing on that computer is software that creates a time-stamped flag in the trace of the trial events whenever the workstation operator presses the button. We call these signals *hedonic flags*. Participants are instructed, "At any time during the study, if you feel mentally overloaded, confused, or frustrated for any reason, just press the button."

Theoretically, this causes little or no interference and doesn't change the "ordinary" course of cognitive work. The hedonic flag task leverages the natural human inclination to apply greater force to their tools (the computer keyboard, in this case) at times of frustration (for example, during inadequate feedback from the machine).[20] Although we think of posting a hedonic flag as a form of dual task, it's actually a secondary task. However, it should entail minimal entrainment of additional cognitive resources because the user is already frustrated with the primary task.[21] Posting a flag can occur at the same stage as processing the primary task (the response stage) and can involve the same modality (visual processing) and the same channel (visual focal attention). However, posting occurs only when the primary task has already been frustrated—in other words, when the primary performance has hit a momentary hiatus. Thus, rather than casting this within the dual-task interference paradigm, we see this as affect-induced redirection.

Measures and measurements

The fundamental measure of negative hedonicity would be the number of hedonic flags posted per trial or session per participant (NHF). The NHF trace would have an interesting advantage from the perspective of experimental design—that is, it would immediately enable us to incorporate a method of task reflection. As is sometimes cited in the psychology literature on introspection, Oswald Külpe and his students developed a method they called systematic postexperimental introspection.[22] Today, this would be referred to as a method of retrospection or task reflection and be referred to as the analysis of verbal reports[23] or a form of cognitive task analysis.[24] It's generally understood in cognitive psychology that meaningful and useful data on reasoning come from analyses of verbal reports, sometimes based on

Table 1. A variety of system-level measurables.

Things to increase	Things to reduce	Things to avoid
Usefulness of the technology	The gap between the "actual work" and the "true work"	Working the technology ("make-work")
Usability of the technology	Mental workload	Fighting the technology ("workarounds")
Justified trust in the technology	Time/effort	Misunderstanding the technology ("automation surprises")
Enhanced immersion ("being in the problem") or positive hedonicity	Negative affect/frustration (negative hedonicity)	
Enhanced direct perception, recognition, comprehension	Uncertainty	
Accelerated achievement of proficiency	Unjustified trust in the technology	
Enhanced intrinsic motivation	Unjustified mistrust in the technology	
Effective coping with rare or tough cases		
Rapid recovery from error		

a "think-aloud problem solving" task and sometimes based on task reflection, as in the Critical Decision Method.[25] In a number of communities of practice (sociotechnics, computer-supported collaborative work, work ethnography, ethnomethodology, and others), it's understood that rich, useful data on cognitive work in complex systems come from analyzing the content of communications and well-conducted interviews that scaffold the participant in the recall and analysis of recently encountered tough cases.[25,26]

In the Külpe method, the participant is run through the entire study a second time, this time reviewing the complete trace (using our modern technology, perhaps including video). The marks for hedonic flags would serve as memory cues, allowing for more detailed exploration into the reasons for each posting. Why was a person who performed especially well overall suddenly frustrated? Why was another person repeatedly confused? What was it about the tool that another person didn't understand at some point in a scenario? Such performance-based evaluation would go well beyond the vagaries and vicissitudes of superficial user surveys that shoehorn meanings into designers' categories, or one-off, post hoc questionnaires that leave people prone to bias from task-demand characteristics, or other forms of satisficing that merely serve to show that "some people liked it, more or less, some of the time."

There are additional possibilities. The researcher could

- look at NHFs posted over the length of a single trial or over blocks of trials;
- evaluate individual differences by examining a specific range statistic—for instance, comparing the number of flags posted by two participants, the one who posts the most flags versus the one who posts the fewest flags; or
- evaluate range statistics that are based on the principal performance measure—that is, comparing the number of hedonic flags posted by the best- and the worst-performing participants).

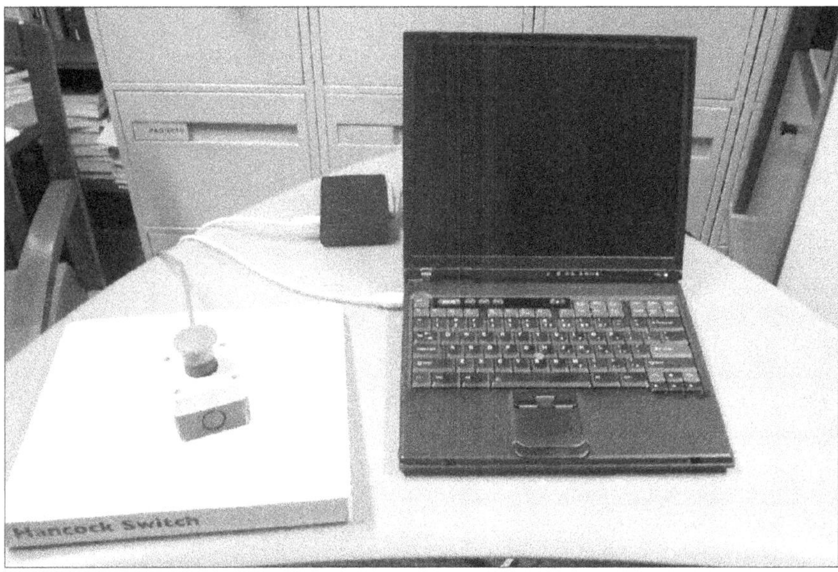

Figure 1. The Hancock Switch linked to a laptop computer.

The researcher could then use independent variables that define the main study design (for instance, easy versus difficult scenarios, or individual versus team work) to guide evaluation of the respective hedonicity measurements. For example, the study could look at the difference between

- the average number of flags posted by participants when working on the scenarios resulting in the best performance, and
- the average number of flags posted by participants when working on the scenarios resulting in the worst performance.

Alternatively, the study could look at the differences of differences, contrasting

- the best- and worst-performing participants on the scenario resulting in the best performance, with
- the best- and worst-performing participants on the scenario resulting in the worst performance.

Such studies might clarify why a tool is low in learnability or usability.

Modeling the NHF data

We postulate that the number of hedonic flags posted in a given time interval will follow a Poisson distribution—that is,

$$p_X(k) = e^{-\lambda} \frac{\lambda^k}{k!}, k = 0, 1, 2, \ldots$$

where λ is the rate of flags over time.

If the participants are somewhat homogeneous in their propensity to post flags, the rate parameter λ alone would enable us to compare work methods. Drawing inferences on the rate parameter of a Poisson distribution is a straightforward process.

If the participants vary in their intrinsic tendency to post hedonic flags, which of course is likely, a Bayesian approach with a distribution assigned to the rate parameter λ would be an appropriate derived measure. For example, placing a gamma distribution on λ results in a negative binomial distribution. In this case too, drawing inferences is straightforward.

Whether or not participants are homogeneous in their propensity to post flags, they'll presumably do so in an experiment's early minutes or trials because the work method will be unfamiliar and confusion more likely. This being the case, and given that the data are discrete, the distribution might take the form of the negative binomial. The most likely approach that is appropriate for data modeling would be inferences based on a cumulative probability function.

Another possibility for analyzing NHF data involves a novel variant on signal detection analysis. Generally, the main measures in traditional signal detection theory (SDT), called d′ and Beta, are intended to separate out response bias and thereby result in a cleaner measure of operator sensitivity. These are always calculated with reference to individuals' performance, making SDT of limited use in the study of sociotechnical systems. One might, however, calculate hit rates from the number of hedonic flags posted by two or more participants referenced to the same trial scenario. For instance, if a particular event resulted in three participants posting hedonic flags, and subsequent retrospections revealed that they had the same reason for that posting (for example, confusion resulting from scenario-induced mental overload), then the number 3 would be added to a sum along with numbers representing all other such consensus postings. We could compare this group hit rate to the number of nonconsensus postings for each individual (to determine false alarms) and to the number of consensus postings that a given individual didn't enter (to determine misses). From these respective calculations, we might derive sensitivity and response bias measures (d′ and Beta) with respect to aspects of the work method or scenario that are linked to operator hedonic response and yet aren't the reflection of any one operator's hedonic responsivity (or bias).

Our ideas for modeling NHF data are speculative, and experimental results will soon permit an evaluation of the utility of what we propose. We've tried in this essay to present, in a concrete and nonspeculative way, some "metrics" that relate directly to customer needs (that is, performance measures). At the same time, we hope these metrics allow meaningful evaluation of the complexity of cognitive work, one might say, sneaking system-level considerations in through the back door. ■

> We must take the measurement of cognitive work to entirely new levels—addressing, for example, the important trade-offs in cognitive work at the team and systems level.

Acknowledgments

Robert Hoffman's contribution was through participation in the Advanced Decision Architectures Collaborative Technology Alliance, sponsored by the US Army Research Laboratory under cooperative agreement DAAD19-01-2-0009.

References

1. S.W.A. Dekker, J.M. Nyce, and R.R. Hoffman, "From Contextual Inquiry to Designable Futures: What Do We Need to Get There?" *IEEE Intelligent Systems*, Mar./Apr. 2003, pp. 74–77.
2. D.D. Woods, "Designs Are Hypotheses about How Artifacts Shape Cognition and Collaboration," *Ergonomics*, vol. 41, 1998, pp. 168–173.
3. E. Hollnagel and D.D. Woods, *Joint Cognitive Systems: Foundations of Cognitive Systems Engineering*, Taylor and Francis, 2006.
4. J. Goguen, "Towards a Social, Ethical Theory of Information," *Social Science Research, Technical Systems, and Cooperative Work*, G. Bowker et al., eds., Lawrence Erlbaum Associates, 1997, pp. 27–56.
5. K. Neville et al., "The Procurement Woes Revisited," *IEEE Intelligent Systems*, Jan./Feb. 2007, pp. 72–75.
6. W.W. Gibbs, "Software's Chronic Crisis," *Scientific Am.*, Sept. 1994, pp. 72–81.
7. R.W. Pew and A. Mavor, eds., *Human-System Integration in System Development: A New Look*, Nat'l Academy Press, 2007.
8. J. Grudin, "Utility and Usability: Research Issues and Development Concepts," *Interacting with Computers*, vol. 4, 1992, pp. 209–217.
9. M.B. Rosson and J.M. Carroll, *Usability Engineering: Scenario-Based Development of Human-Computer Interaction*, Morgan Kaufmann, 2002.
10. M.J. O'Neill, *Measuring Workplace Performance*, 2nd ed., Taylor and Francis, 2007.
11. E. Schaffer, *Institutionalization of Usability*, Addison-Wesley, 2004.
12. E.J. Keats, *John Henry: An American Legend*, Pantheon Books, 1965.
13. R.R. Hoffman, P.J. Hayes, and K.M. Ford, "Human-Centered Computing: Thinking In and Outside the Box," *IEEE Intelligent Systems*, Sept./Oct. 2001, pp. 76–78.
14. R. Scott et al., "Work-Centered Support Systems: A Human-Centered Approach to System Design," *IEEE Intelligent Systems*, Mar./Apr. 2005, pp. 73–81.
15. J. Scholtz, "Metrics for Evaluation of Software Technology to Support Intelligence Analysis," *Proc. Human Factors and Ergonomics Soc. 49th Ann. Meeting*, Factors and Ergonomics Soc., 2005, pp. 918–921.
16. P. Koopman and R.R. Hoffman, "Work-Arounds, Make-Work, and Kludges," *IEEE Intelligent Systems*, Nov./Dec. 2003, pp. 70–75.
17. R.R. Hoffman and P.J. Hayes, "The Pleasure Principle," *IEEE Intelligent Systems*, Jan./Feb. 2004, pp. 86–89.
18. T. Oron-Gilad and P.A. Hancock, "The Role of Hedonomics in the Future of Industry, Service, and Product Design," *Proc. Human Factors and Ergonomics Soc. 49th Ann. Meeting*, Human Factors and Ergonomics Soc., 2005, pp. 1701–1704.
19. P.A. Hancock, A.A. Pepe, and L.L. Murphy, "Hedonomics: The Power of Positive

and Pleasurable Ergonomics," *Ergonomics in Design*, Winter 2005, pp. 8–14.
20. Y. Qi, C. Reynolds, and R.W. Picard, "The Bayes Point Machine for Computer-User Frustration Detection via Pressuremouse," *Proc. 2001 Workshop Perceptive User Interfaces* (PUI 01), vol. 15, ACM, 2001, pp. 1–5.
21. C.D. Wickens, "Multiple Resources and Performance Prediction," *Theoretical Issues in Ergonomics Science*, vol. 3, 2002, pp. 150–177.
22. E.G. Boring, "A History of Introspection," *Psychological Bull.*, vol. 50, 1953, pp. 169–189.
23. K.A. Ericsson and H. Simon, *Protocol Analysis: Verbal Reports as Data*, 2nd ed., MIT Press, 1993.
24. B. Crandall, G. Klein, and R.R. Hoffman, *Working Minds: A Practitioner's Guide To Cognitive Task Analysis*, MIT Press, 2006.
25. R.R. Hoffman, B. Crandall, and N. Shadbolt, "A Case Study in Cognitive Task Analysis Methodology: The Critical Decision Method for the Elicitation of Expert Knowledge," *Human Factors*, vol. 40, 1998, pp. 254–276.
26. R.R. Hoffman and L. Militello, *Perspectives on Cognitive Task Analysis: Historical Origins and Modern Communities of Practice*, CRC Press, 2008.

Robert R. Hoffman is a research scientist at the Institute for Human and Machine Cognition. Contact him at rhoffman@ihmc.us.

Peter Hancock is a professor of psychology at the University of Central Florida and senior research scientist at the Institute for Human and Machine Cognition. Contact him at phancock@pegasus.cc.ucf.edu.

Morris Marx is a senior research scientist at the Institute for Human and Machine Cognition and president emeritus of the University of West Florida. Contact him at mmarx@ihmc.us.

Chapter 31: Accelerated Learning (?)

R.R. Hoffman, P.J. Feltovich, S.M. Fiore, G. Klein, and D. Ziebell, "Accelerated Learning (?)," *IEEE Intelligent Systems*, vol. 24, no. 2, Mar./Apr. 2009, pp. 18–22. doi: 10.1109/MIS.2009.21

We pose accelerated learning as a challenge for intelligent systems technology. Research on intelligent tutoring systems has proved that accelerated learning is possible. The Sherlock tutor for electronics troubleshooting, for example, condensed four years of on-the-job training to approximately 25 hours, compressing the duration of the experience-feedback-learning cycle. But accelerated learning should refer to more than the hastening of basic proficiency. It reaches across the proficiency scale to the question of how to accelerate the achievement of expertise, and whether that is even possible. Paralleling this question are practical issues, including the military's need to conduct training at a rapid pace, and the issues of workforce and loss of expertise. Many organizations such as the US Department of Defense, NASA, and the electric utilities are at risk because of the imminent retirement of domain practitioners who handle the most difficult and mission-critical challenges. To accelerate proficiency, we must facilitate the acquisition of extensive, highly organized knowledge. We must also accelerate the acquisition of expert-level reasoning skills and strategies. But that's just the beginning of the challenge.

Accelerated Learning (?)

Robert R. Hoffman and Paul J. Feltovich, *Institute for Human and Machine Cognition*
Stephen M. Fiore, *University of Central Florida*
Gary Klein, *Klein Associates Division of ARA*
David Ziebell, *Electric Power Research Institute*

We wish to pose accelerated learning as a challenge for intelligent systems technology. Research on intelligent tutoring systems has proved that accelerated learning is possible.[1] The

Sherlock tutor for electronics troubleshooting, for example, condensed four years of on-the-job training to approximately 25 hours, compressing the duration of the experience-feedback-learning cycle:[2]

> Sherlock presented a concentration of useful cases in a brief period of time. The real world mostly provides opportunities to do the routine. Expertise involving the nonroutine is harder to get from everyday work experience because the right situations occur rarely and often are handled by established experts when they do occur, not by students.[3]

But accelerated learning should refer to more than the hastening of basic proficiency. It reaches across the proficiency scale to the question of how to accelerate the achievement of expertise, and whether that is even possible. Paralleling this question are practical issues, including the military's need to conduct training at a rapid pace, and the issues of workforce and loss of expertise. Many organizations such as the US Department of Defense, NASA, and the electric utilities are at risk because of the imminent retirement of domain practitioners who handle the most difficult and mission-critical challenges.[4]

To accelerate proficiency, we must facilitate the acquisition of extensive, highly organized knowledge. We must also accelerate the acquisition of expert-level reasoning skills and strategies.[5] But that's just the beginning of the challenge.

The Challenge

Experts are repositories of vast historical information that enables them to exercise effective technical leadership in ambiguous or complex situations, often by communicating subtle features that other people won't see until those features are pointed out. A classic estimate states that the development of very high-level skills in any complex domain takes at least 10 years.[6] But extraordinary experts who conduct mission-critical activities in industry settings have proven their value and earned extraordinary respect through the course of 25 to 35 years of experience.

It's clear that mere time in grade doesn't enable just anyone to adequately fill such functions; routine practice isn't sufficient for the development of expertise. There needs to be

- a constant stretching of the skill, defined by increasing challenges (tough or rare cases),
- high levels of intrinsic motivation to work hard, on hard problems,
- practice that provides meaningful feedback, and
- practice with an expert mentor's support and encouragement.

Edwin Thorndike, one of the founders of educational psychology, called this "practice with zeal."[7] Appropriate to his milieu, Thorndike focused on classroom learning of simple tasks. More recently in the field of expertise studies, Anders Ericsson has referred to "deliberate practice" to achieve expertise, in such domains as music and chess.[8] But the notion also holds for domains such as weather forecasting, engineering, and military command.[9] At its most general level, the core idea is that mere repetition of what's already known is not enough—what's necessary is practice that systematically engages the learner in increasingly challenging ways and provides a meaningful context for feedback, remediation, and growth.

Let's accept for the moment the finding from studies of experts that 10 years is a lower limit and that a lengthy period of deliberate practice is necessary. In that case, the best that organizations could hope for is to "preburn" a few years during the novice-to-apprentice and apprentice-to-journeyman spans of training. Our vision, in contrast, is that we might accelerate the achievement of proficiency across the journeyman-to-expert span.

Background

We can leverage a few decades of research on "cognition in the wild"—that is, studies of complex problem solving by experts in a variety of domains, including firefighting, nursing, weather forecasting, emergency response, and military command.[10-13] Experts possess rich, detailed, highly organized knowledge. They are distinguished by their ability to

- develop rich mental models of cases or situations to support sensemaking and anticipatory thinking,
- create new procedures on an ad hoc basis,
- cope with novel and tough cases,[14] and
- perform under stress and high levels of mental workload.

Expertise takes a long time to achieve and is bounded in its range.[8] Thus, traditional learning methods that focus on cursory exposure and short-term results might be insufficient to accelerate the achievement of proficiency. It's often assumed that the way to help learners cope with complexity is to simplify the situation and then incrementally introduce increasingly complex elements. However, initial learning that's more difficult and that even demonstrates inferior immediate results can lead to greater flexibility and transfer.[15] Perhaps most importantly, research on high-end learning (for example, in medical education) has shown that when learners are initially exposed to simplifications of complex topics, serious misunderstandings can become entrenched and then interfere with achieving richer, accurate understandings.[16]

> Time in grade doesn't enable just anyone to adequately fill such functions; routine practice isn't sufficient for the development of expertise.

Leverage Points for Acceleration

Background research also provides pointers to ways of achieving acceleration.

Tapping the Right Theories

Two related proposals about high-end learning, based upon findings from expertise research, can inform acceleration: cognitive flexibility and cognitive transformation.

Research on how people deal with difficult problems led to the idea of cognitive flexibility.[17,18] Problems that involve dynamics, interacting processes, nonlinear causation, simultaneous events, and other complexities are particularly difficult for learners. When confronted with gaps and inaccuracies in their knowledge or reasoning regarding these types of complexity, learners invoke what are called knowledge shields—ill-formed counterarguments that let them preserve their simplistic understanding in the face of contradictory evidence.[16] To achieve expertise, a learner must be flexible—that is, willing and able to recognize and overcome the knowledge shields.

Closely related is the idea of cognitive transformation: the hypothesis that to achieve expertise, people must unlearn.[19] That is, they must work through experiences that force them to lose faith in their entrenched, simplistic mental models so that they can move to deeper levels of understanding.

Studying How Mentors Do It

Mentoring has not been studied at the higher levels of expertise and extraordinary expertise. Some researchers have investigated what makes for a good coach in sports[20] and what makes for a good teacher.[21,22] But little is known about how to find good mentors or what makes for a good mentor in the context of the modern sociotechnical workplace. Also, little is known specifically about mentoring from the journeyman level to expert.

In *Sources of Power*, Gary Klein describes the techniques that skilled mentors use and the kinds of skills they need to develop for evaluating mentees and setting the right climate for learning.[23] The good mentor knows how to create appropriate learning content and guide those who are less experienced. The expert mentor can rapidly form a rich mental model of the learner's knowledge and skill. From this, the expert mentor can predict when and why the learner will form a simplistic or inaccurate understanding. The mentor anticipates the kinds of cases that will lead the learner to err and the kinds of practice experiences that will push the learner to greater understanding of complexity.[14,24]

There is an outstanding practical need for methods to rapidly identify good mentors and then apply the right cognitive task analysis methods to reveal their reasoning strategies, especially as they deal with challenging mentoring situations. Many experienced workers are intrinsically motivated to pass along their "tough case" knowledge, but they're often left without organizational support, not knowing how to proceed. They often don't even know that their "tough case" knowledge is critical and highly constructive to apprentices.

Giving Corrective Feedback

Studies of expertise reveal great variability between domains (and specializations within domains) in the extent to which workers receive any feedback, let alone timely, high-quality feedback.[25] In some cases, the inherent nature of the domain (for example, long-term weather forecasting and intelligence analysis for policy projection) makes it impossible for the practitioner to receive timely feedback. This might be one reason why it can take a decade or more for an individual to achieve expertise.

Experts learn more from their mistakes than from what they get right. It's been said that apprentices make the same mistake twice, journeymen make the same mistake once, and experts work until they never make mistakes. Domain specialists are intrinsically motivated and often seek out corrective feedback that allows them to perceive their errors.[26] When everything works the way it's supposed to, practitioners are less likely to receive feedback about what didn't work or what might have been done better. Experts seek out corrective feedback that points out targets for improvement. Cognitive flexibility and cognitive transformation suggest that feedback should help learners transcend the inclination to invoke a knowledge shield (that is, rationalize away a reductive misunderstanding) and help them unlearn notions that incorrectly simplify their understanding of the domain.

Tough-Case Time Compression

People learn what they practice. So, to achieve adaptive expertise, they should practice in many ways, across many kinds of cases (including ones that involve the same basic principles but in different kinds of contexts), using many kinds of conceptual tools, points of view, mental organizational structures, and investigation and practice strategies.[17] The modes and means of training should engage real work practice—the job's challenges, contexts, and duties—to the greatest extent possible.

Training to accelerate proficiency will have to include an appreciation of the importance of dynamic or causal reasoning, anticipatory thinking, problem detection, and other macrocognitive functions.[5] In order for practitioners to better handle complexity, especially unexpected complexity, training must involve helping them acquire a more powerful toolbox and the knowledge of how to build entirely new tools when tough cases arise.

Tough cases, more or less by definition, are rare. This might be another reason why it takes so long to achieve expertise. A library of tough cases could be utilized to accelerate expertise development ... and here we come to the role of intelligent systems.[18,27] We propose that intelligent technologies, including virtual reality and other case-oriented modeling tools, could enable time compression. We could eliminate the time spans between tough cases, and also shrink the chunks of time inside tough cases, when not much is happening.

The initial step would be to generate a case library. This would be a job for cognitive systems engineers. Although laborious and time consuming, this would be a "two-fer." That is, the process of capturing and preserving expert knowledge would merge with the process of generating training materials. Methods of knowledge elicitation and cognitive task analysis would be used to generate cases. For each case, the expert's narrative would weave together the hidden chain of causally related events leading to a particular problem. Each case will have to form around a rich narrative, a timeline, a roster of information requirements, a roster of decision requirements, and other resources spanning the range of media (photos, video, and so on). Each case would be scaled for the level of proficiency, relative to individuals' levels of ability, both for routine practice and for skill stretching. In collaboration with computer scientists, the cases would be formed into instructional materials and exercises, which could range from desktop exercises to full simulated scenario experiences driven by intelligent systems technologies.

We can also use tough, rare cases in unlearning to reveal knowledge shields and help trainees overcome dimensions of difficulty for given cases.[17] Rare cases would be juxtaposed with routine or typical cases in such a way that the learner could experience the

Apprentices make the same mistake twice, journeymen make the same mistake once, and experts work until they never make mistakes.

differences that produce difficulties.

Another application of the case corpus involves the constantly changing sociotechnical workplace.[28] New technologies, and the work methods that they shape, typically must be integrated with legacy work methods and technologies. Conceptually, we can view a set of tough-case scenarios as opportunities for practice at adaptation, not merely to handle familiar and routine cases but also to "stretch" the new technologies and work methods through application in tough cases.

Simulations allow for tremendous flexibility in manipulations of fidelity—differing kinds and amounts of contextual richness. With regard to the application of intelligent systems, the acceleration simulations would be set up such that the simulations would sometimes lead and sometimes mislead the learner in seeking solutions. The idea is that the simulation, like an expert mentor, purposely misguides a learner into a common solution, but the reality is that the error is due to a subtle issue. In addition, an appropriately crafted scenario would manage temporal sequencing. This would juxtapose real-world time with narrative time, so that the learner could experience the event through the expert's perspective (real-world time) and through the more omniscient, third-person perspective of compressed narrative time—that is, presenting events to highlight certain occurrences. These variations would emphasize particular elements of the scenario and promote both perceptual learning and the acquisition of expert strategies.

The modern sociotechnical workplace and the world in which it's embedded present significant challenges that aren't easily solved, in part because they force us to take traditional notions of training and transfer to new levels. The people who work in sociotechnical systems must be trained to be adaptive, so that they can cope with the ever-changing world and an ever-changing workplace. People must be trained to be resilient, so that they can cope with complexity when unexpected events stretch resources and capabilities. And people must be trained faster. Intelligent systems technology, and intelligent use of technology, will certainly play a critical and perhaps necessary role in this.

People must be trained to be resilient, so that they can cope with complexity when unexpected events stretch resources and capabilities.

References

1. K.D. Forbus and P.J. Feltovich, eds., *Smart Machines in Education*, AAAI Press, 2001.
2. A.M. Lesgold, "Sherlock: A Coached Practice Environment for an Electronics Troubleshooting Job," *Computer Assisted Instruction and Intelligent Tutoring Systems: Shared Issues and Complementary Approaches*, J. Larkin and R. Chabay, eds., Lawrence Erlbaum Associates, 1992, pp. 201–238.
3. A.M. Lesgold, "On the Future of Cognitive Task Analysis," *Cognitive Task Analysis*, J.M. Schraagen, S.F. Chipman, and V.L. Shalin, eds., Lawrence Erlbaum Associates, 2001, pp. 451–466.
4. R.R. Hoffman and L.F. Hanes, "The Boiled Frog Problem," *IEEE Intelligent Systems*, July/Aug. 2003, pp. 68–71.
5. G. Klein et al., "Macrocognition," *IEEE Intelligent Systems*, May/June 2003, pp. 81–85.
6. J.R. Hayes, "Three Problems in Teaching General Skills," *Thinking and Learning Skills: Research and Open Questions*, vol. 2, S.F. Chipman, J.W. Segal, and R. Glaser, eds., Lawrence Erlbaum Associates, 1985, pp. 391–406.
7. E.L. Thorndike, *Education Psychology*, Routledge, 1913.
8. K.A. Ericsson et al., *The Cambridge Handbook on Expertise and Expert Performance*, Cambridge Univ. Press, 2006.
9. R.R. Hoffman, ed., *Expertise Out of Context: Proc. 6th Int'l Conf. Naturalistic Decision Making*, Taylor & Francis, 2007.
10. E. Hutchins, *Cognition in the Wild*, MIT Press, 1995.
11. G. Klein and C. Zsambok, eds., *Naturalistic Decision Making*, Lawrence Erlbaum Associates, 1995.
12. J. Lave, *Cognition in Practice: Mind, Mathematics, and Culture in Everyday Life*, Cambridge Univ. Press, 1988.
13. S. Scribner, "Studying Working Intelligence," *Everyday Cognition: Its Development in Social Context*, B. Rogoff and S. Lave, eds., Harvard Univ. Press, 1984, pp. 9–40.
14. R.R. Hoffman, "How Can Expertise Be Defined? Implications of Research from Cognitive Psychology," *Exploring Expertise*, R. Williams, W. Faulkner, and J. Fleck, eds., Macmillan, 1998, pp. 81–100.
15. R.A. Schmidt and R.A. Bjork, "New Conceptualizations of Practice: Common Principles in Three Paradigms Suggest New Concepts for Training," *Psychological Science*, vol. 3, 1992, pp. 207–217.
16. P.J. Feltovich, R.L. Coulson, and R.J. Spiro, "Learners' (Mis)Understanding of Important and Difficult Concepts: A Challenge to Smart Machines in Education," *Smart Machines in Education*, K.D. Forbus and P.J. Feltovich, eds., AAAI/MIT Press, 2001, pp. 349–375.
17. P.J. Feltovich, R.J. Spiro, and R.L. Coulson, "Issues of Expert Flexibility in Contexts Characterized by Complexity and Change," *Expertise in Context*, P.J. Feltovich, K.M. Ford, and R.R. Hoffman, eds., AAAI/MIT Press, 1997, pp. 125–146.
18. R.J. Spiro et al., "Cognitive Flexibility Theory: Advanced Knowledge Acquisition in Ill-Structured Domains," *Proc. 10th Ann. Meeting Cognitive Science Soc.*, Lawrence Erlbaum Associates, 1988, pp. 375–383.
19. G. Klein and H.C. Baxter, "Cognitive Transformation Theory: Contrasting Cognitive and Behavioral Learning," *The PSI Handbook of Virtual Environments for Training and Education: Developments for the Military and Beyond, Vol. I: Learning, Requirements, and Metrics*, Praeger Security Int'l, 2009, pp. 50–65.

20. S.M. Fiore and E. Salas, "Cognition, Competition, and Coordination: Understanding Expertise in Sports and Its Relevance to Learning and Performance in the Military," *Military Psychology*, vol. 20, 2008, pp. S1–S9.
21. J.A. Minstrell and E.H. Van Zee, *Inquiring into Inquiry Learning and Teaching in Science*, Am. Assoc. for the Advancement of Science, 2000.
22. R.W. Proctor and K.-P.L. Vu, *Stimulus-Response Compatibility Principles: Data, Theory, and Application*, CRC Press, 2006.
23. G. Klein, *Sources of Power: How People Make Decisions*, MIT Press, 1998.
24. G. Klein, "Coaching Others to Develop Strong Intuitions," *Intuition at Work*, Doubleday, 2002, pp. 208–226.
25. E. Salas, D.R. Nichols, and J.E. Driskell, "Testing Three Team Training Strategies in Intact Teams: A Meta-Analysis," *Small Group Research*, vol. 38, no. 4, 2007, pp. 471–488.
26. S. Sonnentag, "Excellent Performance: The Role of Communication and Cooperation Processes," *Applied Psychology: An Int'l Rev.*, vol. 49, 2000, pp. 483–497.
27. R.J. Spiro et al., "Cognitive Flexibility Theory: Hypermedia for Complex Learning, Adaptive Knowledge Application, and Experience Acceleration," *Educational Technology*, Sept./Oct. 2003, pp. 5–10.
28. R.R. Hoffman and W.C. Elm, "HCC Implications for the Procurement Process," *IEEE Intelligent Systems*, Jan./Feb. 2006, pp. 74–81.

Robert R. Hoffman is a senior research scientist at the Institute for Human and Machine Cognition. Contact him at rhoffman@ihmc.us.

Paul J. Feltovich is a research scientist at the Institute for Human and Machine Cognition. Contact him at pfeltovich@ihmc.us.

Stephen M. Fiore is director of the Cognitive Science Laboratory at the University of West Florida. Contact him at sfiore@ist.ucf.edu.

Gary Klein is senior scientist at the Klein Associates Division of ARA. Contact him at gary@decisionmaking.com.

David Ziebell is manager of human performance technology at the Electric Power Research Institute. Contact him at dziebell@epri.com.

Chapter 32: Metrics, Metrics, Metrics, Part 2: Universal Metrics?

R.R. Hoffman, P.A. Hancock, and J.M. Bradshaw, "Metrics, Metrics, Metrics, Part 2: Universal Metrics?," *IEEE Intelligent Systems*, vol. 25, no. 6, Nov./Dec. 2010, pp. 93–97. doi: 10.1109/MIS.2010.147

A previous article in this department from 2008 introduced the topic of measures and metrics. The focus of that essay was on measurement of the "negative hedonics" of work—the frustrations, uncertainties, mistrust, and automation surprises caused by poorly designed technology that is not human-centered. This second article focuses on the concept of "metrics" and issues related to it. Following a discussion of relevant issues, we present an immodestly bold proposal for a set of universal metrics.

Metrics, Metrics, Metrics, Part 2: Universal Metrics?

Robert R. Hoffman, *Institute for Human and Machine Cognition*
Peter A. Hancock, *University of Central Florida*
Jeffrey M. Bradshaw, *Institute for Human and Machine Cognition*

A previous article in this department from 2008 introduced the topic of measures and metrics.[1] The focus of that essay was on measurement of the "negative hedonics" of work—the frustrations, uncertainties, mistrust, and automation surprises caused by poorly designed technology that is not human-centered. This second article focuses on the concept of "metrics" and issues related to it. Following a discussion of relevant issues, we present an immodestly bold proposal for a set of universal metrics.

Metrics have been a salient topic of many recent government-funded research programs for developing large-scale information systems. We have counted a multitude of funding program announcements that include statements such as the following abstraction:

> The program seeks metrics quantifying the value and risk added by new information, processes, and modalities ... [The program seeks] the quantitative and qualitative metrics required by the acquisition community to use human systems integration tools and processes in the design process ...

This is an expression of "The Great Hope," to be codified in mathematics in the same manner it has now been reified in the legal language of the procurement process. The doomed expectation is that if something can be measured we therefore will be able to understand it. This is a thinly veneered disguise for the reductionistic obsession to measure the success of everything by its return on investment. The sought-for measures defined in these terms have to gauge efficiency, effort, accuracy, and similar reflections of a maximizing process, hearkening back to the contest between John Henry and the steam hammer. This myopic perspective is particularly frustrating for the advocates of human-centered computing and work-centered design.

Our view is that we must measure cognitive work at the system level—addressing, for example, the important trade-offs and the wider effects of technology-induced changes in the culture of the workplace and the health of the community at large. The quantitative characterization of highly complex interactive effects, or even more problematically, subjective apperceptions of the world, presents one of the greatest challenges to advancing technology in the early 21st century.[2]

Cognitive systems engineers have called for new objective methods for evaluating the performance impact and learnability for software systems,[3–7] including the increasing number of systems requiring human-automation teamwork of a consequential sort.[8,9] In general, there has been a rising concern with the human factors of complex cognitive work, or "metrics and methodologies for evaluating technologies."[10]

So what exactly does it mean to ask for a metric?

Measures versus Metrics

To understand the foundations for a demand for metrics, we illustrate some basic ideas on measurement through the use of the simple example of intelligence testing (see Table 1).

Metrics are thresholds or decision criteria that are used in an evaluation. One has to decide, "This value differentiates." Such decisions arise from policy shaped by goals, value judgments, and other considerations. The policy that leads to the adoption of particular operational definitions (for example, "What do we want to measure?") is external to measurement. Thus, metrics do not arise either immediately or automatically from measures or measurement scales. Assuming that we

Table 1. Some fundamental concepts of measurement.

Steps to get from a theoretical concept to a metric	Meaning	Example
Conceptual measurable	This is a concept from the subject matter of some theory. It is assumed that instances of this concept can be identified and counted.	A theory of cognitive development might assert that there are individual differences in intellectual capacity, referred to as intelligence.
Operational definition	This is a specification of a replicable, dependable procedure for counting instances or making measurements.	This is what an intelligence test does, as in the phrase, "Intelligence is what an intelligence test measures."
Numerical scale	The numerical scale expresses distinctions regarding the conceptual measurable. The distinctions could be categorical or numerical.	"Genius" is a categorical distinction. The IQ is a ratio of mental age and chronological age, which is a numerical distinction.
Measurement scale	The numerical scale values are entered into a calculation that creates a derived measurement scale.	IQ scores expressed as percentile ranks.
Measurement	A specific observation is regarded as an instance of a specific scale value.	A specific measured IQ score and its derived percentile rank is an example of a measurement.
Metric	A decision threshold is expressed as some value (minimum, maximum, or range) on the numerical scale.	If a person's IQ score measured at age 16 is at the 85th percentile or greater, they get to go to college. If a person's IQ score is 145 or greater, they are classified as genius.

have successfully gone from a conceptual measurable to one or more reasonable operational definitions, and assuming further that we have successfully derived specific measurement procedures and linked the measurements to one or more meaningful measurement scales, we cannot then assume some easy step to a metric without having some sort of policy or goal. Without some policy to specify what is desired (or good), how can we determine what a decision threshold should be? In one context, 85 percent correct might represent a useful metric. In another context, it might be misleading or indeed genuinely dangerous. In one context, 35 percent better than before might be a significant gain, whereas in another content, 35 percent might be negligible.

With this understanding as background, we argue that on certain assumptions that apply to the evaluation of computer-supported cognitive work, it might be possible to generate universal metrics that place all performance evaluations essentially on a common playing field.

The Designer's Gamble

In the standard view of hypothesis testing, real-world variability must be restricted either by passive control or more often by active manipulation. Multiple experiments are always required to peg down the determiners of human skill acquisition and performance, especially in macrocognitive work systems. Potentially, any feature of the participants (such as experience, intelligence, motivation, aptitude, and so on), test scenarios (such as interesting, rare, easy, or boring), teams (such as colocated, asynchronous, and dysfunctional), and tools (such as displays and menus) can prove relevant, as can countless other mediating and moderating variables.[7,11]

This means that if an experimental paradigm were conducted properly, the development and procurement process would take even longer than it already does and, in theory, could require a boundless sequence of tests. This would be an untenable situation at a time when the priority is to drastically reduce procurement time.[12–14] Furthermore, by the time the relevant factors have been controlled, key variables isolated, and effect sizes estimated, design requirements changed and reevaluated, and so forth, the cognitive work will almost certainly have evolved or been transformed, sometimes completely.[15]

"It is difficult to sample all the things that must be sampled to make a generalization ... the sheer number [of interacting factors] can lead to unwieldy research plans."[16] We call this the "fundamental disconnect."[17] We need to reduce the time frame required for experimentation so that its length does not preclude effective change in an evermore rapidly changing world. We need to find alternatives to both standard usability testing and standard controlled experimentation so as to expedite evaluation of the performance effects of technological interventions in macrocognitive work systems.[4,7,18]

In light of this conundrum, we think it might be fruitful to question some of the basic methodological assumptions in the standard experimental model. For example, there is the question of controlling for variables in the workplace. Let us ask the following: If all the interacting and uncontrollable factors are in effect when the actual work is being performed, why should we assume that they have to be controlled when work methods are being evaluated? Indeed, we actually need the daunting variability of the world to be represented in the evaluation of new technologies.[7,18] The traditional approach asserts that the only path to scientific truth is to conduct an extended series of controlled factorial experiments resulting in measures of statistical significance. However, in macrocognitive work domains, we need an approach that emphasizes ecological representativeness and utility and leads to measures of practical significance.[19] Thus, we express what we call the Designer's Gamble, which can be stated as follows:

> We, the designers, believe that our new technology is good, and that good work will result from its use. Thus, we can let the daunting variability of the "real world" remain in the summary statistics and measurements, and we can conduct reasonably risky tests of usefulness and usability. We're going to gamble that the new technologies and the work methods they instill are so good that improvements in the cognitive work will be straightforwardly demonstrable despite the daunting variability of the real world.

We think that the Designer's Gamble is no mere fantasy. Just as funding program announcements sometimes appear to ask for the world, research proposals often gladly promise it. Statements of the following general type often appear in grant proposals and preproposal white papers:

> We will develop new modeling strategies leveraging previous research in dynamic networked environments. This architecture will provide near real-time interoperability and robustness and will allow the detection and modeling of information flows and actions and mitigate data overload. This will then be integrated with a suite of algorithms that will automatically reconfigure the running simulation....

Overly confident statements such as these, relying heftily as they do on the word "will," promise more than can ever be guaranteed. Other words, such as "might," would be more appropriate. Phrases such as "we hope will" would be more honest. Organizations, teams, and individuals who seek to create information technology invariably justify their entire approach and design rationale on a tacit Designer's Gamble.

The Designer's Gamble can be an explicit assumption made during the processes of procurement (such as system development and evaluation). As such, it is a leverage point for empirical analysis and, in particular, testing hypotheses about the goodness of software tools. What follows from the Designer's Gamble is a way around the fundamental disconnect, through the explicit use of range statistics in which we look at the extremes of performance.

Range Statistics and Universal Metrics

Comparing the best and worst performers using a new technology, as opposed to their performance when using their legacy methods, informs the evaluator about both the technology's learnability and the quality of the work that results. The best performance of an individual (or team) demonstrates what is possible with the new technology, while results from the worst performing individual (or team) can draw attention to training, work variability, or selection problems. Neither extreme represents an aberration to be glossed over by calculations of averages or standard deviations. This is especially important for a statistical analysis of situations where the participants are beginners with the tools because we know that measurements taken on initial task performance are not normally distributed.[18,20–22] Thus, we can devise a

Table 2. Universal Metrics levels.

Metric level	Definition
Metric level 0 (minimal)	Range statistics are not distinguishable from those in the legacy work.
Metric level 1 (mixed)	The best performer in the new work performs better at achieving the primary task goals than the best performer using the legacy work method, but the worst performer of new work performs worse at achieving the primary task goals than the worst performer at the legacy work method. Metric level 1 is an expected outcome because it is somewhat likely that any intervention will tend to increase performance variability. At this metric level, the performance at the high end improves. Worsened performance at the low end indicates a need for either an improved job selection criterion or improved training.
Metric level 2 (improved)	The worst performer of new work performs better at achieving the primary task goals than the worst performer at the legacy work.
Metric level 3 (good)	The best performer of new work performs better at achieving the primary task goals than the best performer at the legacy work.
Metric level 4 (excellent)	The worst performer of new work performs better at achieving the primary task goals than the worst performer at the legacy work, and the best performer in the new work performs better at achieving the primary task goals than the best performer at the legacy work.
Metric level 5 (superior)	The worst performer of new work performs better at achieving the primary task goals than the best performer at the legacy work.

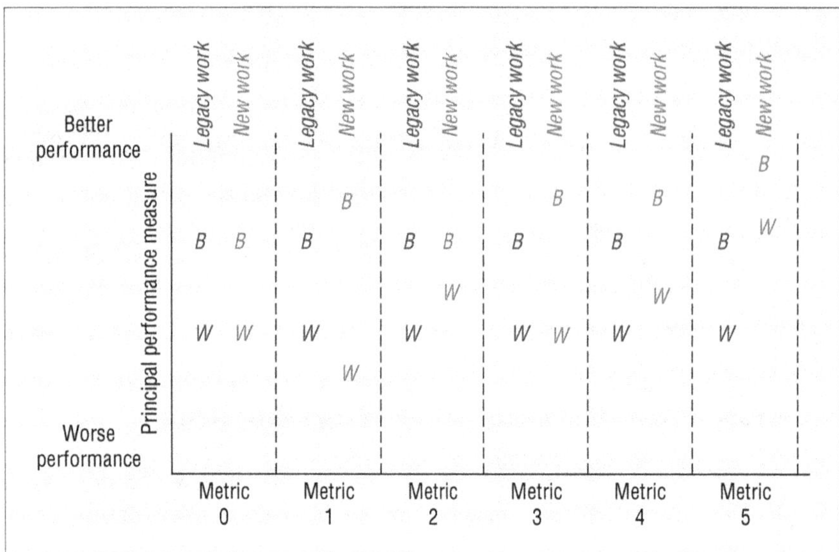

Figure 1. A visual explanation of the meanings of the Universal Metrics levels.

set of universal metric levels for comparing new work methods to legacy work methods, and for evaluating the learnability of work methods. Table 2 presents one such set of metrics.

Figure 1 illustrates these universal metrics levels.

The universal metrics levels presume that the new work involves the same principal task goals as the legacy work, for which data are available to form a baseline used in establishing what counts as "best" and "worst" performance. (For cases in which the work involves completely new kinds of tasks, there might not be an historical baseline and the evaluation will initially have to reference some normative model or theory of the work. An example might be the emerging forms of cyberdefense. This issue of "formative design," however, is a serious and significant topic deserving of its own separate analysis.)

Using these universal metrics levels represents a risk on the part of evaluators. The outcome of an evaluation hinges on the performance of one or two individuals (or teams). Remembering that the performance of all the others will fall between the extremes, in the "real world," operational performance likewise often hinges on the performance of one or two individuals (or teams). If the evaluation is explicitly founded on the Designer's Gamble, and if the desire is to evaluate software in ecologically valid conditions, then the logic of the approach holds firm. It is of course possible, although we hope not likely, that evaluators will try to finesse this method by eliminating poor performers post hoc (for example, on some claim of validity, such as "they were sick"). But such finagling would be transparent and counterproductive.

If, on the other hand, a software tool developer does not wish to adopt the Designer's Gamble up front, then any a priori promises about the performance gains that will result from the to-be-delivered capabilities must be expressed in a far more cautious way than we commonly see today.

Either way, the sponsor wins.

We submit that the concept of universal metrics levels can provide a framework that includes the following:

1. an approach to evaluation that emphasizes ecological representativeness and utility and escapes the constraints imposed by traditional controlled factorial experimentation;
2. a means for measuring practical significance rather than (or in addition to) statistical significance;
3. a common playing field for evaluating performance of software-supported work of all kinds;
4. a common playing field for evaluating the learnability of software-supported work methods and, by implication, the goodness of the software tools; and
5. a means of sensitizing analyses to outliers that might signal training or selection issues.

What we offer here is not a closed-end solution. Rather, it is a first step or a prospectus in a challenging journey to rethink, document, and quantify the character and capacities of large-scale interacting human-machine systems. ■

References

1. R.R. Hoffman, P. Hancock, and M. Marx, "Metrics, Metrics, Metrics: Negative Hedonicity," *IEEE Intelligent Systems*, vol. 23, no. 2, 2008, pp. 69–73.
2. P.A. Hancock, J.L. Weaver, and R. Parasuraman, "Sans Subjectivity, Ergonomics is Engineering," *Ergonomics*, vol. 45, 2002, pp. 991–994.
3. R.R. Hoffman, K.J. Neville, and J. Fowlkes, "Using Cognitive Task Analysis to Explore Issues in the Procurement of Intelligent Decision Support Systems," *Cognition, Technology, and Work*, vol. 11, 2009, pp. 57–70.
4. R. Lipshitz, "Rigor and Relevance in Naturalistic Decision Making Research: How To Study Decision Making Rigorously with Small Samples and Without Controls or Statistical Inference," to be published in *Cognitive Engineering and Decision Making*, 2010.
5. K. Neville et al., "The Procurement Woes Revisited," *IEEE Intelligent Systems*, vol. 23, no. 1, 2008, pp. 72–75.
6. W.M. Newman, "On Simulation, Measurement, and Piecewise Usability Evaluation," *Human-Computer Interaction*, vol. 13, no. 3, 1998, pp. 317–323.

7. E.N. Roth and R.G. Eggleston, "Forging New Evaluation Paradigms: Beyond Statistical Generalization," *Macrocognition Metrics and Scenarios*, E. Patterson and J. Miller, eds., Ashgate, 2010, pp. 204–219.
8. J.M. Bradshaw, P. Feltovich, and M. Johnson, "Human-Agent Interaction," to be published in *Handbook of Human-Machine Interaction*, G. Boy, ed., Ashgate, 2010.
9. G. Klein et al., "Ten Challenges for Making Automation a 'Team Player' in Joint Human-Agent Activity," *IEEE Intelligent Systems*, vol. 24, no. 6, pp. 91–95.
10. J. Scholtz, "Metrics for evaluation of software technology to support intelligence analysis," *Proc. Human Factors and Ergonomics Society 49th Ann. Meeting*, Human Factors and Ergonomics Soc., 2005, p. 918.
11. R.M. Baron and D.A. Kenny, "The Moderator-Mediator Variable Distinction in Social Psychological Research: Conceptual, Strategic and Statistical Considerations," *J. Personality and Social Psychology*, vol. 51, no. 6, 1986, pp. 1173–1182.
12. M. Hewish, "Out of CAOCs Comes Order," *Jane's Int'l Defense Rev.*, May 2003, p. 22.
13. *Weapon Systems Acquisition Reform Act of 2009*, Public Law 111-23, *US Statutes at Large* 123, 2009.
14. R.R. Hoffman and S.V. Deal, "Influencing versus Informing Design, Part 1: A Gap Analysis," *IEEE Intelligent Systems*, vol. 23, no. 5, 2008, pp. 72–75.
15. J.A. Ballas, "Human-Centered Computing for Tactical Weather Forecasting: An Example of the 'Moving Target Rule,'" *Expertise Out of Context: Proc. 6th Int'l Conf. Naturalistic Decision Making*, R.R. Hoffman, ed., Erlbaum, 2007, pp. 317–326.
16. W.A. Firestone, "Alternative Arguments for Generalizing from Data as Applied to Qualitative Research," *Educational Researcher*, vol. 22, 1993, p. 18, 19.
17. L. Chronbach, "Beyond the Two Disciplines of Scientific Psychology," *Am. Psychologist*, vol. 30, no. 2, 1975, pp. 116–127.
18. R.R. Hoffman et al., "Measurement for Evaluating the Learnability and Resilience of Methods of Cognitive Work," *Theoretical Issues in Ergonomic Science*, 2010; http://prod.informaworld.com/smpp/content~content=a920740998~db=all~jumptype=rss.
19. R.R. Hoffman and K.A. Deffenbacher, "An Analysis of the Relations of Basic and Applied Science," *Ecological Psychology*, vol. 5, no. 4, 1993, pp. 315–352.
20. W.F. Book, "The Psychology of Skill with Special Reference to its Acquisition in Typewriting," *Studies in Psychology*, vol. 1, Univ. of Montana Press, 1908.
21. K.M. Newell and P.A. Hancock, "Forgotten Moments: Skewness and Kurtosis Are Influential Factors in Inferences Extrapolated from Response Distributions," *J. Motor Behavior*, vol. 16, no. 3, 1984, pp. 320–335.
22. H.S. Sichel, "The Estimation of Parameters of a Negative Binomial Distribution with Special Reference to Psychological Data," *Psychometrika*, vol. 16, no. 1, 1951, pp. 107–127.

Robert R. Hoffman is a senior research scientist at the Institute for Human and Machine Cognition. Contact him at rhoffman@ihmc.us.

Peter A. Hancock is professor of psychology at the University of Central Florida. Contact him at phancock@pegasus.cc.ucf.edu.

Jeffrey M. Bradshaw is a senior research scientist at the Institute for Human and Machine Cognition. Contact him at jbradshaw@ihmc.us.

Chapter 33: Beyond Simon's Slice: Five Fundamental Trade-Offs that Bound the Performance of Macrocognitive Work Systems

R.R. Hoffman and D.D. Woods, "Beyond Simon's Slice: Five Fundamental Trade-Offs that Bound the Performance of Macrocognitive Work Systems," *IEEE Intelligent Systems*, vol. 26, no. 6, Nov./Dec. 2011, pp. 67–71. doi: 10.1109/MIS.2011.97

Articulating the laws of cognitive work has been a continuing theme in this department. A number of the articles represent an effort to move toward a unified theory of "macrocognitive work systems." These are complex adaptive systems designed to support near-continuous interdependencies among humans and intelligent machines to carry out functions such as sensemaking, replanning, mental projection to the future, and coordination. The effort to identify empirical generalizations and use them to construct a formal theory has led us to the identification of a number of fundamental trade-offs that place boundary conditions on all macrocognitive work systems. This article presents five trade-offs identified to date that define these boundary conditions. It also illustrates how the known empirical generalizations about the performance of human work systems can be systematically organized by the trade-offs.

Beyond Simon's Slice: Five Fundamental Trade-Offs that Bound the Performance of Macrocognitive Work Systems

Robert R. Hoffman, *Institute for Human and Machine Cognition*
David D. Woods, *Ohio State University*

Articulating the laws of cognitive work has been a continuing theme in this department. A number of the articles represent an effort to move toward a unified theory of "macrocognitive work systems."[1] These are complex adaptive systems designed to support near-continuous interdependencies among humans and intelligent machines to carry out functions such as sensemaking, replanning, mental projection to the future, and coordination.

The effort to identify empirical generalizations and use them to construct a formal theory[2] has led us to the identification of a number of fundamental trade-offs that place boundary conditions on all macrocognitive work systems. This article presents five trade-offs identified to date that define these boundary conditions. It also illustrates how the known empirical generalizations about the performance of human work systems can be systematically organized by the trade-offs.

Laws of Cognitive Work

Research in cognitive systems engineering has supported a considerable number of generalizations about macrocognitive work that have held up under empirical scrutiny across work domains.[3] For example, people always develop mental models of the agents, processes, and devices they deal with, including apparently intelligent technology. There is no "cognitive vacuum." The force of this generalization is that the developers bear the responsibility to design the technology such that that people can form accurate mental models of how the device or process works and the capabilities and limitations of that device or process relative to different situational factors.[4] If the design does not do this, one can be certain that people will form a variety of inaccurate explanations.

This inescapability makes the generalization law-like. For illustrative purposes, we present a few additional examples of the established empirical generalizations:

- *Law of Coordinative Entropy.* Coordination costs, continuously. The success of new technology depends on how the design affects the ability to manage the costs of coordinating activity and maintaining or repairing common ground.[5]
- *Law of Systems as Surrogates.* Technology reflects the stances, agendas, and goals of those who design and deploy the technology. Designs, in turn, reflect the models and assumptions of distant parties about the actual difficulties in real operations. For this reason, design intent is usually far removed from the actual conditions in which technology is used, leading to costly gaps between these models of work and the "real work."
- *Mr. Weasley's Law.* Based on their experiences, people develop unjustified trust and unjustified mistrust in their work system and its technology. As Mr. Weasley states in the *Harry Potter* series, "Never trust anything that can think for

itself if you can't see where it keeps its brain." Understanding the intent of others, tracking and adjusting intent as situations change, and maintaining common ground across agents are critical in systems of interdependent agents, roles, and centers of control.[6]

- *The Law of the Kludge.* Work systems always require workarounds, with resultant kludges that attempt to bridge the gap between the original design objectives and current realities or to reconcile conflicting goals among workers. Sets of algorithms, plans, and procedures cannot account for inevitable variability and ongoing changes in the world. Thus, someone has to act responsibly to help plans match situations in order to meet mission goals.
- *The Law of Stretched Systems.* Every system is stretched to operate at its capacity. As soon as there is some improvement or new technology, some stakeholders will identify the opportunities that the change makes possible to achieve some of their goals. The process of exploiting these opportunities will result in a new and greater intensity and tempo of activity as the work system moves toward the edge of its competency envelope.[7]
- *The Law of Fluency.* Well-adapted cognitive work occurs with a facility that belies the difficulty of resolving demands and balancing dilemmas. The adaptation process hides the factors and constraints that are being adapted to or around. Uncovering the constraints that fluent performance solves, and therefore seeing the limits of or threats to fluency, requires a contrast across perspectives.[3]
- *The Reductive Tendency.* Agents at all scales develop and use simplifications, such as relying on decomposition to cope with interdependencies and decoupling to cope with dynamic interactions. Reductive understandings help workers manage what would otherwise be overwhelming complexity.[8]

Looking over the emerging set of empirical laws, now numbering approximately 30, several themes stand out, including interdependence and adaptation. Many of the laws seem to be a consequence of limits on systems that carry out cognitive work—for example, limits on building accurate models of devices (their capabilities and boundaries) and limits on the extent to which plans can match actual situations. Laws often include an interdependency relationship, either across different agents, perspectives, or roles or between system activities and the demands that arise in the environment.[9] Several laws express regularities about adaptation processes, capturing how people are active in a struggle to reach for goals despite the complications that arise regularly.

These observations led us to realize that the empirical generalizations might arise from constraints imposed by a set of more fundamental trade-offs, or "covering laws."

It's Always about Trade-Offs

Discussions in cognitive science make much of a constraint introduced by Herbert Simon, which he called "bounded rationality."[10] Simon argued that there is a limit on the knowledge available to any agent or system and a limit on how that knowledge can be brought to bear in actual situations. Systems scientists have identified another trade-off that limits the performance of complex adaptive systems. Based on studies of biological and physical systems, John Doyle argued that the pursuit of increases in optimality with respect to some criteria guarantees an increase in brittleness with respect to changes or variations that fall outside of those criteria—a trade-off between optimality and fragility.[1] Work on proactive safety management and resilience engineering has identified two trade-offs that bound the performance of organizations that carry out risky activities: a tradeoff between acute and chronic goals, and a tradeoff between efficiency and thoroughness.[11,12] In addition, work on robotics and networks has illustrated limits on perspective taking and coordination across multiple agents.[6,13]

The Five Fundamental Bounds

We realized that the trade-offs organize subsets or "families" of laws as originally proposed by David Woods[7] and discussed in previous articles in this department. The end result is that five fundamental trade-offs seem to define five families of laws. The title of this article comes from our realization that Herbert Simon had found only "one slice" through the trade spaces governing the effectiveness of macrocognitive work systems.

Bounded Ecology

A work system can never match its environment completely; there are always gaps in fitness, and fitness itself is a moving target. There is always a struggle to adapt, which can ease or intensify as events unfold. This problem has been addressed by efforts to develop resilience and avoid brittleness, allowing the work system to either bounce back or gracefully degrade in the face of surprise.[14]

This is an optimality-fragility trade-off—or stated in a way to balance two positives, the *Optimality-Resilience of Adaptive Capacity Trade-Off.* Increasing the scope of the routine increases the opportunities for surprise at the boundaries. Optimizing over some demands leads to brittleness when encountering other demands. As a result, resilience requires a capacity to adapt to surprising events, understanding that the ability to anticipate surprise requires additional resources whose contribution might be missed and might be mistaken for inefficiencies.

Bounded Cognizance

Limited resources and inevitable uncertainties lead to unavoidable gaps in knowledge. There is always "effort after meaning," although the struggle to acquire and deploy knowledge might temporarily ease or intensify. There are always gaps in plans, models, and procedures relative to the situations where they would be implemented to achieve goals. These gaps lead to an impetus to learn and adjust plans to fit the situations at hand. The process of testing the fit between plans and situations leads to a trade-off between being thorough and being efficient—the *Efficiency-Thoroughness of Situated Plans Trade-Off.*[11] Efficient plans mark well-worn paths, but they become cumbersome as the need to incorporate more contingencies and variations grows. Thoroughness expands the scope of the plans, expanding assessments, decisions, and ambiguities, but it constrains the ability to put plans into action and modify plans in progress.

We recast Simon's notion of bounded rationality as bounds on cognition, however, that might be embodied in an agent or agent architecture. We are agnostic with regard to the proposition that computer programs are models of cognition, and we do not adopt a rationalist-normative view of cognition. We therefore sought an alternative phrase to refer to Simon's slice: *bounded cognizance.*

Bounded Perspectives

Every perspective both reveals and hides certain aspects of the scene of interest, and work systems are limited in their ability to shift their perspective cost-effectively. Apprehension gaps can widen because situations differ in how strongly they signal the need to shift perspectives to reveal what has been hidden. Thus, there is always an invitation for reflection—that is, to step out of the current perspective. The work system is compelled to continuously devote resources to the integration of additional perspectives. But this comes at a cost, because the integration of different perspectives always requires an effort to translate or create a shared language to bridge or constructively contrast the perspectives.

Hence, there is a *Revelation-Reflection on Perspectives Trade-off.* Disambiguation for sensemaking arises from the ability to shift and contrast perspectives[13,15] or to rely on multimethod approaches that involve cycles of coactive emergence and convergence among humans and automation.[16] Modeling of complex adaptive systems has benefitted by including the concept of perspective as a basic parameter.[17] The ability to shift and contrast perspectives has proven to be essential to coordinated activity and collaborative work.[18]

Bounded Responsibility

Work systems divide up roles and responsibilities for subsets of goals; there are always gaps in authority and responsibility across the various subgoals. This means that all systems are simultaneously cooperative over shared goals and potentially competitive when goals conflict. Fundamental or chronic goals (such as safety and equity) tend to be sacrificed with increasing pressure to achieve acute goals ("faster-better-cheaper").[12] This, in turn, leads macrocognitive work systems to become blind to risks and sources of brittleness. Acute goals can be assessed through short-run tabulations, but chronic goals such as safety can only be assessed in the long run. They are more difficult to measure, and they function like values.

As a result, we term this bound as reflecting an *Acute-Chronic Goal Responsibility Trade-Off.* Work systems must continuously devote resources to manage responsibility across roles and ensure reciprocity. Without reciprocity across roles, the different agents or centers of control will tend to work at cross purposes in the face of goal conflicts.[18,19]

Bounded Effectiveness

Macrocognitive work systems are restricted in the ways they can act and influence situations. Agents understand that they are not omnipotent. This entails a trade-off between distributing autonomy, initiative, and authority across echelons, versus the more typical approach that concentrates autonomy, initiative, and authority in single centers of control. Distributing activities that define progress toward goals can increase the range of effective action, but increasing the distribution of activities entails difficulty of keeping them coherent and synchronized. Concentrating activities in single roles can produce more immediate and definitive progress toward landmarks, but it also reduces the range of effective action. Coordinating activity across distributed agents, units, or centers expands the scope and scale of factors that can be considered, but distributing macrocognitive work increases the cost of managing coordination as changes occur.[6,18,19] Concentrating the potential for action reduces the ability to consider potentially important interdependencies, whereas distributing the potential for action does just the opposite.

Ultimately, the challenge of the *Concentrated-Distributed Action Trade-Off* is to balance micromanagement with delegation over echelons to insure continuity and avoid fragmentation.

Covering Laws

These five bounds serve as covering laws that organize the first-order empirical generalizations of macrocognitive work. They place those generalizations in a larger theoretical and metatheoretical framework. For example, the Law of Stretched Systems is entailed by bounded ecology—that is, adaptation to become more optimal with respect to some goals and criteria will leave the system poised more precariously than its designers and managers realize. The Reductive Tendency law is entailed by bounded cognizance—that is, adaptation to finite resources inevitably leads to a reliance on simplifications.

Five Bounds and Adaptive Macrocognitive Work Systems

The bounds place inescapable limits on the performance of all macrocognitive work systems. This is seen in the frequency of unintended consequences following technology insertions: change directed only at one part within the system often inadvertently triggers deleterious effects on other aspects of the system that cancel out or outweigh the intended benefits. Technological interventions always produce a mix of desired and undesired effects because the change affects the system's positioning in the five trade spaces. For example, consider brittle but valuable drones that require large numbers of people to make up for the adaptive shortfall, or a system responding to faster, better cheaper pressure keeps eroding its margins and discounting warning signs until a sudden collapse occurs in the form of an accident (such as the Columbia space shuttle mission).[12]

The drones are part of a system that can be designed to be resilient rather than brittle, and organizations can develop cross-checking mechanisms that overcome the tendency to rationalize away warning signs. What are the basic architectural principles that allow systems to improve performance across the interdependencies captured by the five bounds rather than simply trade beneficial effects in one area for deleterious effects in others? Studies and models of complex adaptive systems have begun to identify principles that can be used to manage macrocognitive work systems, ensuring their capacity to maneuver in the trade-off spaces as evidence of risks of different types of adaptive breakdown grow—that is, to be resilient in the face of surprise.[14,20]

Grounding the modeling of human-machine work systems on the five trade-off functions provides a starting point for solving the perennial problem of how to evaluate the performance and adaptive capacity of macrocognitive work systems on principled formal grounds, rather than on the basis of ad hoc tabulations chosen to maximize local tractability and minimize immediate cost. We now see how efforts at measurement and prediction might evolve beyond the traditions of utility and the limits on measuring an individual person's performance.

The trade-offs take the bounds a crucial step closer to things we can actually measure at the system level. Assessing work-system performance requires at least two measurables for each of the five bounds. Numerical scales must address interactions across data types and must be interpretable as measurement scales that address the system's ability to adapt to events.[21] Positions along the bounds represent different solutions to the trade-offs, and as conditions change, the relative costs and benefits of different positions will change. Macrocognitive work systems might improve how they perform with respect to one of the trade-offs, but they cannot escape the inherent risks and the unintended consequences that can propagate across the other trade spaces. This means the set of trade-offs can be used to explain the adaptive history of past insertions of technology into complex fields of practice. Although design intent might attempt to move a work system toward the maximum limit on one of the trade-offs, the intervention can have effects that cascade across all of the trade-offs. Tracing those effects might let us make sense of the multiple and often unintended effects that actually result from technological interventions.

Prospects

The trade-offs can be used to project the potential reverberations or unintended consequences of any proposed injection of technology. We have used the five bounds to chart adaptive histories and reverberation paths for a number of specific cases—for example, the unintended consequences of introducing cockpit automation, networking technology for distributed intensive care in medicine, and nuclear power technologies following the Three Mile Island incident. Such exercises are suggestive of the potential value of the five bounds for modeling macrocognitive work systems. A next step is prospective analysis, tracing paths of reverberation across the linked trade-offs for proposed insertions of new technology, which should allow stakeholders to anticipate unintended consequences in advance of deployment.

One way of understanding the advance that we present here is to say that Herbert Simon only had one slice of the problem when he set out his framework for interpreting computer programs as theories of cognition. Broadening from the context of "one person, one machine" to the context of macrocognitive work systems, we have found additional bounds on performance. The trade-offs provide the theoretical underpinnings that can produce meaningful measures and metrics at the system level.■

Acknowledgments

A preliminary presentation on these ideas was given at the 10th International Conference on Naturalistic Decision Making, sponsored by the University of Central Florida, in June 2011. We are indebted to Stephen M. Fiore and Jeffrey M. Bradshaw for their comments.

References

1. G. Klein et al., "Macrocognition," *IEEE Intelligent Systems*, vol. 18, no. 3, 2003, pp. 81–85.
2. R.R. Hoffman and D.D. Woods, "Steps Toward a Theory of Complex and Cognitive Systems," *IEEE Intelligent Systems*, vol. 20, no. 1, 2005, pp. 76–79.
3. D.D. Woods and E. Hollnagel, *Joint Cognitive Systems: Patterns in Cognitive Systems Engineering*, Taylor and Francis/CRC Press, 2006.
4. D.A. Norman, "Cognitive Engineering," *User-Centered System Design: New Perspectives on Human Computer Interaction*, D.A. Norman and S.W. Draper, eds., Erlbaum, 1986, pp. 31–61.
5. P. Feltovich et al., "Toward an Ontology of Regulation: Support for Coordination in Human and Machine Joint Activity," *Engineering Societies for the Agents World VII*, G. O'Hare et al., eds., Springer-Verlag, 2011, pp. 175–192.
6. G. Klein et al., "Ten Challenges for Making Automation a 'Team Player' in Joint Human-Agent Activity," *IEEE Intelligent Systems*, vol. 19, no. 6, 2004, pp. 91–95.
7. D.D. Woods, "Steering the Reverberations of Technology Change on Fields of Practice: Laws that Govern Cognitive Work," *Proc. 24th Ann. Meeting of the Cognitive Science Soc.*, Cognitive Science Soc., 2002, pp. 1–14.
8. P.J. Feltovich, R.R. Hoffman, and D. Woods, "Keeping it too Simple: How the Reductive Tendency Affects Cognitive Engineering," *IEEE Intelligent Systems*, vol. 19, no. 3, 2004, pp. 90–95.
9. M. Johnson et al., "Beyond Cooperative Robotics: The Central Role of Interdependence in Coactive Design," *IEEE Intelligent Systems*, vol. 26, no. 3, 2011, pp. 81–88.
10. H.A. Simon, *The Sciences of the Artificial*, MIT Press, 1969.
11. E. Hollnagel, *The ETTO Principle: Efficiency-Thoroughness Trade-Off: Why Things that Go Right Sometimes Go Wrong*, Ashgate, 2009.
12. D.D. Woods, "Essential Characteristics of Resilience," *Resilience Engineering: Concepts and Precepts*, E. Hollnagel, D.D. Woods, and N. Leveson, eds., Ashgate, 2006, pp. 19–30.
13. A. Morison et al., "Integrating Diverse Feeds to Extend Human Perception into Distant Scenes," *Advanced Decision Architectures for the Warfighter: Foundation and Technology*, P. McDermott, ed., Alion Science, 2009, pp. 177–200.
14. D.L. Alderson and J.C. Doyle, "Contrasting Views of Complexity and their Implications for Network-centric Infrastructures," *IEEE Systems, Man and Cybernetics, Part A*, vol. 40, 2010, pp. 839–852.
15. D.D. Woods and N.B. Sarter, "Capturing the Dynamics of Attention Control from Individual to Distributed Systems: The Shape of Models to Come," *Theoretical Issues in Ergonomics*, vol. 11, no. 1, 2010, pp. 7–28.
16. J.M. Bradshaw et al., *Sol: An Agent-Based Framework for Cyber Situation Awareness*, Kuenstliche Intelligenz, to be published in May 2012.
17. S.E. Page, *Diversity and Complexity*, Princeton Univ. Press, 2011.
18. P.J. Smith, A.L. Spencer, and C. Billings, "The Design of a Distributed Work System to Support Adaptive Decision Making Across Multiple Organizations," *Informed by Knowledge: Expert Performance in Complex Situations*, K.L. Mosier and U.M. Fischer, eds., Taylor and Francis, 2010, pp. 139–152.
19. E. Ostrom, "Toward a Behavioral Theory Linking Trust, Reciprocity, and Reputation," *Interdisciplinary Lessons from Experimental Research*, E. Ostrom and J. Walker, eds., Russell Sage Foundation, 2003.
20. D.D. Woods and M. Branlat, "Essential Characteristics of Resilience," *Resilience Engineering in Practice*, E. Hollnagel et al., eds., Ashgate, 2011, pp. 127–143.
21. R.R. Hoffman et al., "Measurement for Evaluating the Learnability and Resilience of Methods of Cognitive Work," *Theoretical Issues in Ergonomic Science*, 2011, doi:10.1080/14639220903386757.

Robert R. Hoffman is a senior research scientist at the *Institute for Human and Machine Cognition*. Contact him at rhoffman@ihmc.us.

David D. Woods is a professor at The Ohio State University in the Institute for Ergonomics. Contact him at woods.2@osu.edu.

Part VI:

Procurement Woes: Why Technologies Come to Be NOT Human-Centered

Chapter 34: The Boiled Frog Problem

R.R. Hoffman and L.F. Hanes, "The Boiled Frog Problem," *IEEE Intelligent Systems*, vol. 18, no. 4, Jul./Aug. 2003, pp. 68–71. doi: 10.1109/MIS.2003.1217630

As many of the most knowledgeable personnel in technically complex businesses approach retirement, there is a need to capture their knowledge. The temptation is for management to ignore the problem until it is too late. The article discusses how a company can identify employees who possess valuable undocumented knowledge, evaluate whether the knowledge is worth capturing, elicit, represent, and preserve the valuable knowledge, and share this knowledge with other personnel when needed.

The Boiled Frog Problem

Robert R. Hoffman, *Institute for Human and Machine Cognition*
Lewis F. Hanes, *Electric Power Research Institute*

They say that a frog placed in boiling water will protest vigorously, but one placed in cool water that is slowly brought to a boil will languish happily until it is ready to be a puree. We use this as a metaphor to discuss an outstanding problem in knowledge management—a problem that human-centered computing can perhaps address.

In all complex sociotechnical workplaces, including those in government and industry, knowledge and skill have become widely recognized as increasingly important assets. They are important because expertise is a "must" for proficient performance in these domains. Furthermore, this importance is increasing as we recognize that many of the most knowledgeable personnel are nearing retirement, and there are adverse consequences associated with losing their expertise. An outright panic attack comes when an organization realizes that it does not have a plan for capturing the valuable knowledge about to be lost. Like the frog languishing happily, management will languish happily until it realizes that it is getting into "very hot water" because of a loss of expertise.

Widespread recognition of the boiled frog problem is apparent in the current popularity of the phrases *knowledge preservation* and *knowledge management*, as Gary Klein discussed in his seminal paper, "Using Knowledge Engineering to Preserve Corporate Memory."[1] Many organizations have discovered—either the hard way or too late—that expert wisdom is a corporate asset. For example, NASA encountered problems owing to its loss of engineering expertise from the Apollo era. Similarly, a retiring supervisor at a large soup manufacturing firm possessed a unique skill for controlling the large soup-making machines. On the verge of his retirement, the company realized no one could do what he did, so they brought in a team of knowledge engineers to elicit and preserve his skills.[2]

Editors: Robert R. Hoffman, Patrick J. Hayes, and Kenneth M. Ford
Institute for Human and Machine Cognition, University of West Florida
rhoffman@ai.uwf.edu

Getting into hot water

Another example is the situation in which some electric power utilities have found themselves. For various reasons, including downsizing in the 1990s and early 2000s, loss of expertise has become a critical issue. Several electric utilities have collaborated under the aegis of The Electric Power Research Institute (EPRI) in two projects concerned with capturing valuable undocumented worker and job knowledge.

An early step in the first project was to conduct a survey of a sample of electric utility management. The survey found that 92 percent of 37 respondents representing 21 electric utilities reported that loss of unique valuable expertise would pose a problem within the next five years. However, only 30 percent of the respondents indicated that a planning effort was in place to retain knowledge from experienced workers in a manner that would let new or replacement members access or use it.[3]

The EPRI project goals were to provide guidelines and methods that a utility company might consider for

- Identifying employees who possess valuable undocumented knowledge
- Evaluating whether the knowledge is worth capturing
- Eliciting, representing, and preserving the valuable knowledge
- Sharing this knowledge with other personnel when needed

As part of its Strategic Human Performance Program, the EPRI developed generic guidelines as a major component of the first project.[3,4] The EPRI Nuclear Sector sponsored the second project and developed specific guidance and methods applicable to nuclear power generation stations.

The knowledge management craze

Since Klein's publication first appeared, numerous trade books have been published (see the "Trade Books" sidebar) that discuss expertise (or *core competencies*), knowledge elicitation (or *mapping*), and knowledge representation (or *repositories*). They all include chapters on technologies for knowledge management and example case studies on organizations that have created knowledge management policies and infrastructures. These books manifested the knowledge management craze of the late 1990s, when upwards of 25 percent of Fortune 500 companies had a Corporate Knowledge Office (CKO).[5] These efforts met with some success. For instance, Delta Airlines' Chief Learning Officer developed a knowledge capture program that elicited the job expertise of many retiring employees.[5]

More recently, however, there has been some retrenchment in the corporate sector (fewer than 20 percent of Fortune 500 companies have CKOs). We can't help but wonder if the retrenchment might be occurring for the wrong reasons (such as the phrase "knowledge management" turning people off or companies regarding CKOs as expendable when belt-tightening is needed). In any event, management at some companies continues to recognize that they must preserve expertise so they can reuse it. Norman Kamilkow, editor of *Chief Learning Officer Magazine*, said, "What we saw was that there is a growing role for a chief learning officer type within enterprise-level companies … there is a need to have somebody focused on how to keep the skills of the corporation's work force at a high level."[5]

Trade Books

If We Only Knew What We Know: The Transfer of Internal Knowledge and Best Practice (C. O'Dell and C.J. Grayson, The Free Press, 1998)

Working Knowledge: How Organizations Manage What They Know (T.H. Davenport and L. Prusak, Harvard Business School Press, 1998)

The Knowledge Evolution: Expanding Organizational Intelligence (V. Allee, Butterworth-Heinemann, 1997)

The Knowing Organization: How Organizations Use Information to Construct Meaning, Create Knowledge and Make Decisions (C.W. Choo, Oxford Univ. Press, 1998)

Corporate Memory: Strategies for Knowledge Management (A. Brooking, Int'l Thomson Business Press, 1999)

Continuity Management (H. Beazley, J. Boenisch, and D. Harden, John Wiley, 2002)

Where HCC comes in

HCC involves leveraging and extending the human's ability to perceive, reason, and collaborate, which involves creating information systems that support the human's natural abilities to exercise expertise. This in turn entails one of the principles of HCC, which we refer to as the Fort Knox Principle:

> The knowledge and skills of proficient workers is gold. It must be elicited and preserved, but the gold must not simply be stored and safeguarded. It must be disseminated and utilized within the organization when needed.

"[S]ome CKOs have survived, even thrived, by judiciously distancing themselves from the original craze while still exploiting the concept … the key has been concentrating on practical projects" in such areas as sales, ongoing training on new technologies, and encouragement for innovation.[5] The Fort Knox Principle expresses an important goal for any organization, requiring a change not just in policy but also in the corporate culture. And like our boiled frog, adhering to the Fort Knox Principle involves recognizing that there are two situations in which organizations can find themselves.

The "catch-up" mode

The loss of expertise can continue a degree at a time until an organization recognizes it is nearing or reaching its boiling point. Although many organizations have capabilities to collect and transfer valuable knowledge (through training, procedures, and apprentice and mentoring programs, for example), the approach is often fragmented and unsystematic. When someone recognizes the loss of expertise as a major potential problem, the organization is forced into a "catch-up" situation. It must formalize a knowledge-capture program and devote significant resources to collecting the valuable knowledge before it is lost. This can be especially difficult because the personnel with the most valuable knowledge are usually the busiest, so little time is available for knowledge capture and transfer. In catch-up mode, there is little organizational infrastructure to capture the departing experts' valuable knowledge, except for the ineffective exit interview that human resources conducts.

The "standard operating procedures" mode

Experience has shown little success in burdening the domain practitioner with yet another task—some form of do-it-yourself knowledge elicitation that detracts from the practitioner's main work. An example is the software programs developed several years ago to self-elicit knowledge as part of the process of developing expert systems. Alternatively, the programs might ask the expert to prepare and teach a training module or an entire training course to transfer his or her valuable knowledge. Or they might require that he or she update or create a new procedure documenting the expertise, or mentor one or more workers.

A problem with such methods is that they require significant time and extra effort from the practitioner. As suggested earlier, experts are usually the "go to" person when major problems are encountered, and they have little time for knowledge preservation. Experience suggests that it would be a major problem to burden most domain practitioners with the additional efforts involved in knowledge elicitation.

However, knowledge elicitation and preservation can come as part of the bargain from using cognitive prostheses that make current jobs easier and more effective. An example is Guy Boy's *active design document* technique, in which the documents that describe designs for new technologies include a discussion of the design rationale and justification.[6] Such information is lack-

Table 1. Knowledge preservation: Catch-up mode.

Research needs (two years)	Pilot program (three years)	Organizational policy (five years)
Map knowledge elicitation methods to the domain, according to such features as problem structuredness, situation awareness requirements, and so forth. Systematically map knowledge elicitation methods to the organization (on the basis of size, management philosophy, organizational structure, and so forth). Systematically map knowledge elicitation methods to individual styles of workers in the organization (on the basis of reasoning strategies, metacognitive skills, and so forth).	Offer pilot incentive program for knowledge elicitation of senior and other experts who might not be available when needed. Establish a program whereby experts with extremely valuable undocumented knowledge collaborate with a knowledge engineer. Working together, the two elicit and preserve the worker's wisdom for inclusion in the organization's knowledge base. In extreme cases, such as a senior worker retiring, the individual might be retained or brought back as a consultant not for the purpose of conducting his or her familiar jobs or duty assignments, but from whom expert knowledge can be elicited.	Continually elicit knowledge from all proficient workers, supported by an institutionalized organizational culture and an infrastructure including an incentive program and possibly including someone designated with overall responsibility for the program (trained in the organization and its domain, and in knowledge engineering). Shift over to the standard operating procedures mode.

Table 2. Knowledge preservation: Standard operating procedures mode.

Research needs (two years)	Pilot program (three years)	Organizational policy (five years)
Identify leverage points for the creation of cognitive prostheses to make current jobs easier and more effective. Recreate the jobs in a way that results in knowledge preservation as an added benefit.	Offer pilot program in which the prostheses are utilized and evaluated. Designate someone to have overall responsibility for the program—someone who has supporting resources and derives the organization's knowledge base from the products that the prostheses creates.	Continually enrich the knowledge base (those responsible for the ongoing program should do this).

ing in most design documentation, but it is precisely what practitioners need when analyzing designs retrospectively because it explains the designer's reasoning and the knowledge brought to bear in the design problem. Once the designers realize that filling in the justification information now can save them effort later on, the process of knowledge elicitation becomes a welcome addition to their usual task.

Instituting the Fort Knox Principle

Currently, a "palette" of over two dozen empirically refined knowledge elicitation methods is available.[7,8] Their strengths and weaknesses are fairly clear.[7,8] But even though the notion of knowledge preservation has become current parlance, many organizations lack a supporting infrastructure or organizational culture for knowledge preservation. There is considerable work ongoing in the knowledge management field in setting up and using knowledge portals, knowledge bases, communities of practice, and so forth. Although software programs are available to capture knowledge as it is created (for example, software to capture, evaluate, and store for retrieval certain information in email messages), the knowledge management field has not produced tools to elicit deeply held valuable tacit knowledge.

Tables 1 and 2 present a roadmap for instituting the Fort Knox Principle: Table 1 presents the catch-up mode and Table 2 the standard operating procedures mode.

Perhaps the most challenging entries in Tables 1 and 2 are those for the five-year organizational policy in the catch-up mode (Table 1) and those for the two-year research need for the standard operating procedure mode (Table 2). The two are related—in fact, the former gives way to the latter. Periodic or routine knowledge elicitation must be as painless as possible. The practitioner cannot at any given moment stop what he or she is doing to try and express his or her knowledge or reasoning. But management might ask experts to simply flag cases or experiences that constitute challenges to their expertise so that knowledge officers can subsequently mine them. The practitioner might have to complete a simple form on a periodic basis that asks whether any challenging situations had occurred. A knowledge elicitor can subsequently interview the practitioner. Ideally, the process of knowledge elicitation merges with the practitioner's usual tasks, and this moves us to the two-year research need for the standard operating procedures mode.

As sometimes happens, recognizing one problem gives way to yet another, and in this case recognizing the boiled frog problem gives way to what we call the *tough nut problem*. This is a major challenge for the HCC researcher as well as for the organizational management and culture. There is nearly always some momentum to stick with mandated and legacy systems, which would make knowledge elicitation a gloss. However, finding a best solution to the boiled frog problem involves solving the tough nut problem:

How can we redesign jobs and processes, including workstations, computational aids, and interfaces, in such a way as to get knowledge elicitation as a "freebie" and at the same time make the usual tasks easier?

The example of the active design document technique is a clear case of a solution to the tough nut problem, and we invite readers to suggest others. Of course, part of the tough nut problem is that redesigning jobs and processes can be expensive. Therefore, the gold nuggets (valuable knowledge) associated with the Fort Knox Principle must be assayed to establish whether and how organizations can crack the tough nut problem.

Acknowledgments

Robert Hoffman's contribution to this department was through his participation in the Advanced Decision Architectures Collaborative Technology Alliance, sponsored by the US Army Research Laboratory under cooperative agreement DAAD19-01-2-0009.

Robert R. Hoffman is a research scientist at the University of West Florida's Institute for Human and Machine Cognition and a faculty associate in the Department of Psychology. Contact him at the IHMC, 40 Alcaniz St., Pensacola, FL 32501; rhoffman@ihmc.us.

Lewis F. Hanes works part-time as a project manager at Electric Power Research Institute. Contact him at 2023 Wickford Rd., Columbus, OH 43221; lhanes@columbus.rr.com.

References

1. G. Klein, "Using Knowledge Engineering to Preserve Corporate Memory," *The Psychology of Expertise: Cognitive Research and Empirical AI*, R.R. Hoffman, ed., Erlbaum, 1992, pp. 170–190.
2. K. McGraw and A. Riner, "Task Analysis: Structuring the Knowledge Acquisition Process," *Texas Instruments Technical J.*, vol. 4, 1987, pp. 16–21.
3. M. Gross, L. Hanes, and T. Ayres, "Capturing Undocumented Worker-Job-Knowledge at Electric Utilities: The EPRI Strategic Project," *New Century, New Trends, Proc. 2002 IEEE 7th Conf. Human Factors and Power Plants*, IEEE Press, 2002, pp. 6-20–6-24.
4. L.F. Hanes, and M.M Gross, "Capturing Valuable Undocumented Knowledge: Lessons Learned at Electric Utility Sites," *New Century, New Trends, Proc. 2002 IEEE 7th Conf. Human Factors and Power Plants*, IEEE Press, 2002, pp. 6-25–6-29.
5. D. Pringle, "Learning Gurus Adapt to Escape Corporate Axes," *The Wall Street J.*, 7 Jan. 2003, p. B1.
6. G. Boy, *Cognitive Function Analysis*, Ablex, 1998.
7. R.R. Hoffman et al., "Eliciting Knowledge from Experts: A Methodological Analysis," *Organizational Behavior and Human Decision Processes*, vol. 62, 1995, pp. 129–158.
8. J.M. Schraagen, S.F. Chipman, and V. Shalin, eds., *Cognitive Task Analysis*, Erlbaum, 2000.

Chapter 35: HCC Implications for the Procurement Process

R.R. Hoffman and W.C. Elm, "HCC Implications for the Procurement Process," *IEEE Intelligent Systems*, vol. 21, no. 1, Jan./Feb. 2006, pp. 74–81. doi: 10.1109/MIS.2006.9

Most system designers and human factors engineers have participated in projects that culminated in systems that were highly constrained by short-term cost considerations. In the procurement of information processing and intelligent technology for complex sociotechnical domains, the focus on short-term cost considerations at the expense of human-centering considerations always comes with a hefty price down the road. This price weighs much more heavily on users' shoulders than on those of the technologists or project managers. The authors use as an example the US National Weather Service's Advanced Weather Information Processing System. The authors argue that regarding HCC notions as design challenges or policies for procurement promises to make information technologies more intelligent by making them human-centered.

HCC Implications for the Procurement Process

Robert R. Hoffman, *Florida Institute for Human and Machine Cognition*
William C. Elm, *ManTech International*

Most system designers and human factors engineers have participated in projects that culminated in systems that were highly constrained by short-term cost considerations. In the procurement of information processing and intelligent technology for complex sociotechnical domains, the focus on short-term cost considerations at the expense of human-centering considerations always comes with a hefty price down the road. This price weighs much more heavily on users' shoulders than on those of the technologists or project managers.

We illustrate this with just one of many examples: design of the US National Weather Service's Advanced Weather Information Processing System (AWIPS). Evidence from cognitive task analysis (CTA) had clearly shown that forecasters inspect on the order of seven data types or fields per minute.[1] The traditional meteorological chart wall lets forecasters inspect multiple data types, flip through charts over time, make annotations using colored markers, conduct weather briefings, and so on. When the National Weather Service was revamping the traditional chart wall as a computerized workstation, it was clear from a task analysis that forecasters would need at least four large-screen CRTs, each dedicated to particular data types depending on the day's weather.[1] One might be for computer model outputs, one for showing the satellite image loop, one for showing radar, and one for composing forecasts. However, the initial AWIPS prototype had a single CRT. Subsequent versions had more than one CRT, and the now-operational AWIPS has three. But throughout the reprototyping process, there was a momentum to limit the number of CRT displays because of cost considerations, despite considerable reference to human-factors issues.

A "solution" the designers adopted was to screen-sector the views of various data types. This quick fix didn't go very far for the graphically and symbolically dense displays involved in weather forecasting (that is, sector-minimized displays are illegible). Moreover, sectoring requires a great deal of make-work that burdens forecasters—pointing and clicking to minimize and maximize particular data types' views. And it ignores the fundamental point: that forecasters must be able to see at a glance a number of diverse data types, with the types depending on the forecasting situation at hand.

So, somehow the process of procuring the AWIPS deviated from its purported human-centered intentions. And by the way, following the introduction of the new electronic workstations, some forecasters have reinvented their traditional chart wall by tacking traditional paper charts to their cubicle dividers.

There are many additional stories about how reality hasn't matched information technology's promise.[2–4] Here's a passage from "Out of CAOCs Comes Order," which appeared in *Jane's International Defense Review*, May 2003:[5]

> New technology and revised procedures are greatly enhancing the capabilities of [Air Operations Centers].... "The buzzword for this decade is going to be 'integration.' Why can't we do that today? Why aren't we integrated now?" So said General John Jumper, US Air Force (USAF) Chief of Staff...."[All] the stovepipes in each segment of the chain have to work in separate ways to make it all happen. Certain tribes within each of those stovepipes have taken steps to make sure they can't be interfered with by any other segment. We have formed antibodies to integration. You go into an Air Operations Center (AOC) today, and what will you see? Tribal representatives sitting down in front of tribal workstations, interpreting tribal hieroglyphics to the rest of us who are on watch. And then what happens? They stand up and walk over to another tribal representative, and reveal their hieroglyphics, which are translated by the other tribe into its own hieroglyphics and entered

Editors: Robert R. Hoffman, Patrick J. Hayes, and Kenneth M. Ford
Institute for Human and Machine Cognition, University of West Florida
rhoffman@ai.uwf.edu

into its own workstation. What if machines talked to one another? That would break down the stovepipe ...."

The author has nailed a problem—the AOC systems aren't human-centered. At the risk of being accused of summoning a root cause analysis out of a cauldron, we hasten to add that everyone involved in this AOC project is smart, well-intentioned, and highly motivated: "The USAF leadership is considering how to proceed with further enhancements of its AOCs, with emphasis on achieving true integration of systems rather than mere interoperability."[5]

Clearly the procurement process, at least in the US, leads to the creation of systems that are anything but human-centered. In this essay, we reflect upon the process by which information technologies (including "intelligent" decision aids) are procured, in light of human-centered computing.[6]

Down into the weeds

There is no single procurement process, of course. Looking at any one large organization—say, the US Department of Defense (DoD)—how technologies are procured depends on many guidelines and procedures, including literally thousands of specifications for everything from interface font sizes to stepwise budget-reporting processes. Many technical reference manuals, memoranda, addenda, appendices, and architecture framework standards specify data formats, communication exchange formats, interoperability requirements, software documentation requirements, and more, in a mind-boggling panoply of procedures and acronyms.[7–10]

Standing back from the gory details, the procurement process, or at least some large chunks of it, is typically summarized with reference to either the waterfall or spiral model.[11] (The literature offers a number of waterfall variations, including the rapid-prototyping model and the incremental model.[12]) Figure 1 presents the idealized waterfall model, and figure 2 presents the idealized spiral model.

In the waterfall model in figure 1, the steps are in iterative pairs. For instance, software requirements analysis feeds into preliminary design, but effort at that second step can feed back into software requirements analysis, leading to changes in the requirements. There's also a review process at each step.

In the spiral model in figure 2, the quadrants show four activities that are presumed to be fundamental, and sequential. The spiral model is explicit about system evaluation, but the typical evaluations and verifications for both spiral and waterfall modeling are often based just on a "satisficing" criterion. That is, when users are asked to work with a system prototype for a while and are then queried about their opinions, results show that some people like it, more or less, at least some of the time.

Evidence suggests that we can attribute many of the breakdowns in human-computer interaction (such as automation surprises) to the procurement process. Every technologist has seen it. Even some program managers with whom we've talked bemoan the situation and argue that we must scrap the mandated, legacy procurement process. But they admit that they themselves are handcuffed by it. On the other hand, we've heard strident claims that we must couch the development of information processing systems, including intelligent systems, in terms of the waterfall or spiral model. These models, so it's claimed, express the categories and process that system developers actually follow, that developers must follow, or (for the candid ones among them) that program managers follow because they're forced to. Upstarts who point out nasty empirical facts ("Yeah, but what you say you do is not what you really do!") hear that they must recast their ideas into the waterfall or spiral lingo because that's what system developers use and are comfortable with.

The trap of designer-centered design

Designer-centered design, whether conducted under the guise of either model, goes essentially like this:

1. Specify the requirements.
2. Design the automation to enforce the requirements.
3. Deliver the system as (what is believed to be) a finished product.
4. Force the human user to execute the designer's plan.

The result is just the sort of ubiquitous technology (for example, VCR remote-control devices) that frustrates people at home and at work. Following are the negative and usually unanticipated consequences:

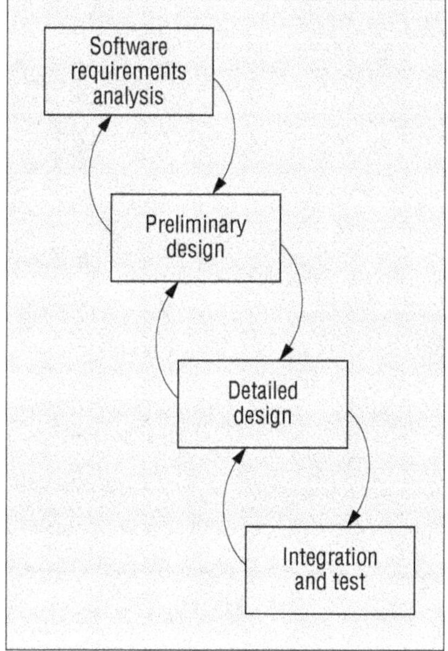

Figure 1. The idealized waterfall model.

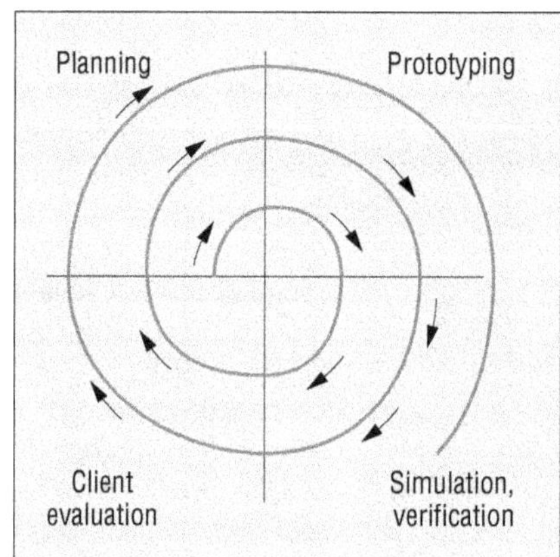

Figure 2. The idealized spiral model.

- *Effort.* The user must adapt to "tasks" defined by the designer and the machine.
- *Bewilderment.* Computers can be difficult to understand or use.
- *Roadblocking.* Computers provide impoverished feedback, limit users' ability to explore and integrate information, and restrict the ability to detect and recover from error.
- *Overload.* Computers don't help people cope with data or mental overload, and in many circumstances actually contribute to it.
- *Error.* Although a new computer system or interface might help you avoid certain kinds of error, they invariably create new forms and patterns of error—error attrib-

utable to the human-machine system, not to the human.

- *Clumsiness*. New technology might make some jobs easier but usually makes some jobs harder. Computers often reduce motivation and create a need for kludges, local solutions, and other means for avoiding make-work.
- *Surprise*. Users are sometimes surprised by the actions that automated agents take (or don't take). Worse, the automated agents don't make their mechanisms (or intent) apparent.

The net result is that people yell at machines, even simple ones such as VCR remote-control devices.

The fundamental problem here is the trap of designer-centered design: The road to user-hostile systems is paved with user-centered intentions, even on the part of smart, well-intentioned people who are aware of this trap.

Acquisition reform?

Reform isn't new to the acquisition process. A streamlining in DoD acquisition occurred in the mid-1990s at the US Secretary of Defense's direction. This new way of doing business included canceling some blocks of specifications without replacing them and leaving more things to contractors' discretion.[10] The effect was to reduce the number of specifications by 62 percent. However, this meant that the burden merely shifted to the documents that laid out non-DoD standards (such as NASA and Human Factors and Ergonomics Society documents). Our point here isn't about the necessary and gory details—font size is a consideration in the human factors of all display design. Rather, our point falls at a higher level, one dealing with human-centering. DoD Instruction 5000.2-R states,[7]

> Program managers shall initiate a comprehensive strategy for [human-system integration] early in the acquisition process to minimize ownership costs and ensure that the system is built to accommodate the human performance characteristics of the user population that will operate, maintain, and support the system. (para. C5.2.3.5.9)

Here we see that human-centering considerations are reduced to maintainability, safety, performance metrics, and training efficiency (with cost-effectiveness always being the cart pulling the horse). All these are surely important. However, in all the procurement documents, we only occasionally see a reference to guaranteeing on the basis of empirical evidence that the eventual technologies will help domain practitioners work on problems rather than forcing them to fight with the technology. Even then, the requirements are stated as "physical/cognitive requirements" or "human performance effectiveness." The acknowledgment that systems should be both usable and useful, that they should motivate and not frustrate, is rarely made explicit. Where the rubber meets the road, information technology needs to support human reasoning, knowing, perceiving, and collaborating. We know that expertise comes from extensive, continuous, deliberate practice, including practice at difficult tasks.[13] But in the standards and procurement documents, we see

The acknowledgment that systems should be both usable and useful, that they should motivate and not frustrate, is rarely made explicit.

no consideration that systems should support the achievement and expression of expertise. Quite to the contrary (and to our shock), there's actually a push, intended or not, to prevent users from achieving or exercising expertise: "Design efforts shall minimize or eliminate system characteristics that require excessive cognitive, physical, or sensory skills"[7] (para. C5.2.3.5.9.1).

Rethinking requirements

There's wide recognition that the development of information technologies hinges upon the interaction of users, systems designers, and systems developers (including systems analysts, computer scientists, and engineers).[14] Designers must understand users' needs and the goals for the system being created.[15] However, the process of designer-user interactions isn't grounded in the empirical methodologies of CTA. Thus, "poor or error-prone communication between the user and analyst remains a major problem"[16] (p. 257).

Miscommunication results in misinterpreted user needs.[17] This leads to design glitches that force users to create work-arounds and cope with user-hostile features such as brittleness and automation surprises when the machine does things the user doesn't understand. Consequently, it's the rare system that doesn't have to go through redesigns, often costly ones.[18] The need to improve this process is a major concern to the entire information systems development industry.[19,20]

A driving factor here is technological backlash—the inevitable negative consequence of "intelligent" technologies that aren't created under human-centering methodologies. The technologies don't work, so it's little surprise that this sometimes creates scandal. The most recent (in a depressingly long series of cases) is the US Federal Bureau of Investigation's discovery that the costly new Trilogy information technology modernization program resulted in software that does not support analysts' cognitive work (referred to as "operational needs").[21] The problems were blamed on a lack of adequate prototyping and testing in the operational context and on the fact that system requirements changed over the course of development.

This critique made us wonder about the assumption that requirements should be fixed, especially in a world that is not. In fact, change in the world seems to vastly outpace our ability to build and adequately test large-scale decision- and performance-support systems. Yet, the default belief seems to be that the world can be frozen and that requirements must be frozen, or nothing will get built. Technological backlash always results in a blame game seeking simple, clear-cut human errors or human limitations, or criticizing a contractor when the root cause is systemic. "Requirements creep" is not a nasty thing to eradicate, but an empirical inevitability to accommodate and understand empirically.

The shortcomings of traditional software engineering and system development, with respect to their ability to support decision making, aren't inherently linked to any particular software engineering approach. The research community has suggested and is vigorously pursuing alternatives to the traditional spiral and waterfall models, including

Extreme Programming,[22] Rapid Application Development,[23] and Joint Application Development.[24] All these procedures

- involve representative end users (but only minimally, mostly in the early stage of system development and basically in the form of focus groups), and
- assume that requirements specification is a clear-cut starting point for the system development process.

In general, software engineering does not regard requirements specification as a process. All the alternative models assume that the requirements are correct, and they seek to build to the requirements in high-quality ways. The system developers might therefore be building the wrong system, even though they might be building it well. The earliest formal approach, the waterfall model, was instantiated in a series of IEEE and military standards that focused on the content of each sequential design artifact in the process. The development effort "flowed downhill" from one approved document to the next. Virtually no attention went to the work activities needed to actually develop those documents' content. This was particularly evident in waterfall's initial requirements definition phase.

Spiral processes addressed some of the limitations of a downhill flow but still assumed that some miraculous insight would provide good system requirements concerning what to build for each spiral. Evaluating the previous spiral improved the odds to some degree, but it was still a long shot. This was true whether the programming language was procedural or object-oriented. An example is James Rumbaugh's Object Modeling Technique,[25] since merged with the Booch method[26] to become the Unified Modeling Language.[27] It's an example of an OO software engineering methodology that still assumes that requirements for effective decision support are divined.

As this recurrent "build the wrong thing well" syndrome became more evident, the community began to offer various techniques in response. Use cases are one example.[28] This approach tries to capture users using the proposed system in an easy-to-understand language—that is, objects. The assumption is that if enough cases are captured, all the needs of the users' interactions with the intended system would be exposed, and these use cases could then be the basis for system requirements definition. Use case notation comes in various forms—for example, what the Object Modeling Technique calls event trace diagrams, now called sequence diagrams in UML. Although this method focuses on users' interactions, it does nothing to help system developers determine what the correct interaction should be. So, in essence, it might be a better way to ensure completeness but not correctness.

Rapid application development and joint application development are becoming fashionable as ways to (supposedly) ensure that developers explicitly incorporate "user needs" into the system development process. The theory is that by holding a user captive within the development team for the first few months of system development,

> Use case notation does nothing to help system developers determine correct system-user interaction. It might be a better way to ensure completeness but not correctness.

you will produce a design that is correct for the user. At best, such a method allows the program manager to say, "We had user involvement, so therefore it is a user-centered system." But this claim doesn't hold water. The difficulty in determining good decision support, even with a domain practitioner in the design team, is evident by the desperate measures that developers employ to achieve those requirement epiphanies. For example, we found the following advice regarding how to get users to "be creative" in describing system requirements:[29]

> The first JAD I facilitated involved a three-day business trip to Florida with the JAD team. At the start of the first session after we returned, I mysteriously found a two-foot rubber alligator on the overhead projector. This "gator" has since become legendary and attends all JAD sessions. I use him as a tool by "speaking through him." Via this character, I get people to speak—or not speak. We consult him on important issues, and involve him in helping the group reach consensus.

And on the cover of this book is the reviewer's statement, "This book is a gold mine of practical advice on the organization and conduct of JAD sessions." Go figure.

Our point is that although software engineering methodologies focus on good construction techniques, they do not yet effectively address what's needed to provide good intelligent technologies or decision support systems. The mistaken belief is that if the initial specifications are correct and complete, the rest of the development process can proceed and will lead to a "final" system.[16]

Both the waterfall and spiral models have advantages and disadvantages (for example, whether they minimize certain kinds of risks, how they trade off effort and cost, or what project scale they're suited for).[12] Both involve feedback and review. Both have worked to the satisfaction of some researchers, at least some of the time. Even when a façade, they still satisfy someone, as indicated by the repeated references to spiral development in DoD documents.[8,9] Both of the models have worked insofar as some of the resulting software products have been put to actual use. However, both models

- represent a trajectory through the wrong kind of design space—the technology-centered, designer's space;
- include some notion of evaluation, but the wrong kind of evaluation—satisficing; and
- have some notion of involving domain practitioners, but the wrong kind of involvement—the designer-users might also be serving as domain experts, or it's too little involvement, or too late.

OK, what if we reach for a better model?

HCC principles as design challenges

By becoming part of the mind-set of how to design and develop systems, HCC might impact the numerous systems that engineers are routinely constructing using desperation measures. That very desperation becomes an opportunity. The challenge to the cognitive systems engineering community is how to adapt the HCC paradigm and methods to produce the outputs needed to integrate the system development processes. The complexities of the modern sociotechnical workplace, and the computational systems that inhabit it, behoove us to reflect on all of HCC's principles and the laws of cognitive work to discover the implications for procurement.

First, HCC mandates using CTA—that is, analyzing work in terms of its macrocognitive functionalities. These include knowledge, reasoning strategies, data integration skills, and decision-making skills. HCC also mandates studying domain practitioners in their actual work context. A string of recent cognitive systems engineering success stories includes using CTA to support the redesign of workstations aboard US Air Force aircraft and US Navy vessels, using CTA to create improved training methods for various important jobs, new interfaces in air traffic control, and new control systems for power plants.[13,30–32]

Glaring by its absence in the spiral and waterfall models is any emphasis on supporting procurement and specification by conducting CTA with domain practitioners (especially experts). The models don't even acknowledge that developers should conduct CTA before, during, and after systems engineers perform requirements specification, planning, and system design. And, we must note, CTA must involve much more than simple interviews or one-off focus groups.[16,33]

The work that people really need to accomplish often differs from their "actual work," since the latter is shaped by legacy technologies and mandated procedures.[32] A palette of CTA techniques from human-factors engineering and cognitive anthropology involves ways of revealing the true work by studying people at work.[13] What are the patterns and cues that decision makers perceive? What are the tough decisions? What knowledge is needed to make good decisions?

A second way in which HCC offers value to procurement will derive from taking HCC principles and the laws of cognitive work as design challenges or policies.

The Zero Tolerance Challenge

If we look closely at procurement standards documents and ferret out a list of what was really important to their authors, we see demands for interoperability and integration, portability, reusability, development efficiency, vendor independence, and manageability. We don't contest the importance of these things, but nowhere do we see a specification like this: *The system must be proven to be usable, useful, and understandable. It must be user friendly and have no user-hostile aspects.* Countless systems (including most VCR remote-control devices) would literally disappear overnight if we applied such a stricture. And we do not lack reports from domain practitioners on what works, what works well, and what needs fixing.[34]

The Sacagawea Challenge

This principle is named after the Indian guide of the Lewis and Clark expedition: *Human-centered computational tools need to support active organization of information, active search for information, active exploration of information, reflection on the meaning of information, and evaluation and choice among action sequence alternatives.*[35] Practitioners must be shown information in a way that's organized in terms of their major goals. Information needed for each particular goal should be shown in a meaningful form and should allow the human to directly comprehend the major decisions associated with each goal.

> **The work that people really need to accomplish often differs from their "actual work," since the latter is shaped by legacy technologies and mandated procedures.**

The Envisioned World Challenge

New technologies are hypotheses about the effects of technologies on work patterns.[36] The introduction of new technology will bring about unanticipated changes in the cognitive and collaborative work of individuals and teams.[37] If new technology does indeed change cognitive work, then the handover of a deliverable can't be the end of procurement; it must be the beginning of a next wave of empirical research, to assure that cognitive work changes for the better.

Hold on, that's not good—procurement would actually take longer than it does now! Worse, if technology changes the work, practitioners in the current world of work won't necessarily carry their expertise over into the envisioned world. The jobs, roles, or tasks that they will conduct in the envisioned system might not be fully formed until after at least some of the technology is in place. Practitioners will have to backpedal to adapt to the new technologies.

The Envisioned World Challenge is this: *Exploration of the envisioned world must be folded into the system development process.* From design notion to design sketch, to initial mock-up, to first prototype, then refined prototype, new technology is embedded in the actual workplace. Designers work with users as users work with and comment on new devices. As the new devices come closer to matching the envisioned world, the users find themselves spending more time conducting their work using the new devices, and over time the legacy systems collect dust. At that point, the new world is essentially ready to become operational.

We've heard a few cases of advanced decision support systems development where, at every iteration (from design sketch to rough mock-up, and so on), users evaluated the prototype in or near their normal work context. They reached a point where the prototype was good enough, even better in some respects than their current systems. At that point, they kept the prototype in the operational facility, and as it was improved, they used it more and more as the primary tool. The old world of practice and the envisioned world coevolved. And the envisioned world included a cohort of individuals who learned within the evolving system context.

The Challenge of Adaptive Design

Two additional empirical facts have strong implications for procurement. The first is expressed by the notion of trickle-off ergonomics: *Prototyping never ceases, it just trickles off.* Complex technologies always undergo iteration and rebuilding after delivery. Software is always upgraded. Individuals, organizations, and teams always create local solutions. They always use Post-Its. The second nasty empirical fact is the Moving Target rule: *The socio-technical workplace is constantly changing, and constant change in environmental constraints may entail constant change in cognitive requirements, even if domain constraints remain constant.*[38] Given the empirical reality of trickle-off and the moving target, why then do procurement processes assume that deliverables must be essentially finished products? Why not admit reality and assume some notion of adaptive design?[36] In adaptive design, deliverables must have built-in (dare we say intelligent?) capabilities to enable them to be easily adapted and evolved so as to better meet the needs of particular organizations, teams, or individuals. The process goes like this:

1. The designers and practitioners identify a constraint space based on domain constraints and support for user control.
2. The designers build the tool so that it shows the constraint boundaries and data for ongoing situations in a way that helps practitioners choose among action sequences.
3. The practitioners "finish" the design on the basis of local information, knowledge, and expertise.

Adaptive design supports workers in tailoring their systems and in adapting to them. Practitioners must be empowered to control and modify their tools. Some factors that practitioners must consider can only be discovered by those practitioners during operation-in-context, which is itself always a moving target. A design should support the continual adaptation of the functionality of the sociotechnical system to local and contextual contingencies.

For example, process control workers sometimes deliberately alter alarm thresholds for various reasons, but usually to either reduce false-alarm rates or to have an alarm serve as an ad hoc notifier. In the Guerlain and Bullemer system,[39] workers could define temporary, context-specific notifications of occurrences or alarm states without altering or overriding the standard alarms. The system supports workers' local adaptation and thus mitigates their need to conduct ad hoc tailoring activities that could otherwise lead to errors, especially in unforeseen circumstances.

The notion of adaptive design brings us back to the problem with requirements.

Stella's Challenge

This principle is named after the character in Tennessee Williams' play, *A Streetcar Named Desire*: *Human-centered systems have a built-in capability to be expanded in the future so as to include functionalities that users desire but that aren't or can't be included in initial versions of the system.* Both the spiral and waterfall models fail to acknowledge that users not only have immediate, definite needs (that should be captured as requirements) but also that they have *desirements*. John MacNamara of the US Air Force Rome Labs suggested this concept (in a personal communication) to refer to desired functionalities that currently can't be included as system requirements but might be at some future time. These are not "bells and whistles" to be scratched off the project's accounting ledgers because managers think users don't really need them or because budget constraints preclude expending time and effort. While appreciating the trade-offs involved here, we're also guided by the common finding from studies of expertise in context that domain practitioners' candid statements about what they really need are often not given due consideration.[13]

> Studies of expertise in context have found that domain practitioners' candid statements about what they really need are often not given due consideration.

To build for desirements, we must create technology from the start so as to anticipate, and not merely allow for, subsequent modification. Modifiability is generally thought of in terms of common operating systems, interoperability, and modularity. A new software bundle might plug and play, making the technology adaptable from an engineering point of view. But there's also a largely neglected human-centering and human-machine system aspect. Because of the complex interactions and contextual dependencies that are always involved in complex cognitive and collaborative work, adding a new capability on the basis of a desirement might alter an existing system capability's work demands. For example, it might lead to goal conflicts.

We submit that regarding HCC notions as design challenges or policies for procurement has promise for making information technologies more intelligent by virtue of making them human-centered. One thing is clear: The legacy procurement process bears some responsibility for resulting in systems that are not human-centered.

We have one final recommendation—perhaps our most far-reaching one. Simply stated, it is to begin now to develop a program to educate a new cohort of individuals in both cognitive systems engineering and information technology project management. The goal will be to groom a generation of project managers who advocate for domain practitioners; who prioritize the creation of demonstrably usable, useful, and understandable technologies; who appreciate CTA's critical role; and who appreciate the significance of empirical generalizations such as the Envisioned World Principle. ■

Acknowledgments

We thank John McNamara of the US Air Force Research Lab for illustrating the concept of a "desirement" and how the notion can have utility in the system design and procurement process.

Robert Hoffman's contribution was made possible in part through his contributions to Chi Systems Inc. on the contract "Embedding Cognitive Systems into Systems Engineering Practice," DoD SBIR topic AF05-071, and through his participation in the Advanced Decision Architectures Collaborative Technology Alliance, sponsored by the US Army Research Laboratory under cooperative agreement DAAD19-01-2-0009.

References

1. R.R. Hoffman, "Human Factors Psychology in the Support of Forecasting: The Design of Advanced Meteorological Workstations," *Weather and Forecasting*, vol. 6, 1991, pp. 98–110.

Robert R. Hoffman is a senior research scientist at the Institute for Human and Machine Cognition. Contact him at IHMC, 40 So. Alcaniz St., Pensacola, FL 32502-6008; rhoffman@ihmc.us.

William C. Elm is the executive director of the Cognitive Systems Engineering Center of ManTech International. He has over 20 years of experience in applying cognitive systems engineering, adapting the science of David Woods, Jens Rasmussen, Erik Hollnagel, and others into a pragmatic systems engineering process. Contact him at Cognitive Systems Eng. Center, ManTech Int'l, 501 Grant St., Ste. 475, Pittsburgh, PA 15219; welm@mindsim.com.

2. G.A. Jamieson, "Bridging the Gap between Cognitive Work Analysis and Ecological Interface Design," *Proc. 47th Ann. Meeting Human Factors and Ergonomics Soc.*, Human Factors and Ergonomics Soc., 2003.

3. D.R. Jones and M.J. Smith, *Implementing New Technology: Proc. Human Factors and Ergonomics Soc. 48th Ann. Meeting*, Human Factors and Ergonomics Soc., 2004, pp. 1601–1604.

4. T.K. Landauer, *The Trouble with Computers*, MIT Press, 1995.

5. M. Hewish, "Out of CAOCs Comes Order," *Jane's Int'l Defense Rev.*, May 2003, p. 22.

6. R.R. Hoffman, P.J. Hayes, and K.M. Ford, "Human-Centered Computing: Thinking in and outside the Box," *IEEE Intelligent Systems*, Sept./Oct. 2001, pp. 76–78.

7. "Mandatory Procedures for Major Defense Acquisition Programs and Major Automated Information Systems Acquisition Programs," Instruction 5000.2-R., US Dept. of Defense, 1996.

8. W. Kaworski, *Handbook of Standards and Guidelines in Ergonomics and Human Factors*, US Dept. of Defense, 2001.

9. *Technology Transition for Affordability: A Guide for S&T Program Managers*, tech. report, Office of the Deputy Undersecretary of Defense (Science and Technology), US Dept. of Defense, 2001.

10. L.M. Adams et al., "Human Factors Engineering and Acquisition Reform," *Ergonomics in Design*, Summer 2003, pp. 10–15.

11. A. Behforooz and F.J. Hudson, *Software Engineering Fundamentals*, Oxford Univ. Press, 1996, chapter 1.

12. S.R. Schach, *Object-Oriented and Classical Software Engineering*, McGraw-Hill, 1996.

13. B. Crandall, G. Klein, and R.R. Hoffman, *Working Minds: A Practitioner's Handbook of Cognitive Task Analysis*, MIT Press, 2006.

14. G.I. Green, "Perceived Importance of Systems Analysts' Job Skills, Roles, and Non-Salary Incentives," *Management Information Systems Quarterly*, vol. 13, 1989, pp. 115–133.

15. K. Holtzblatt and H.R. Beyer, "Requirements Gathering: The Human Factor," *Comm. ACM*, vol. 38, no. 5, 1995, pp. 31–32.

16. L.A. Freeman, "The Effects of Concept Maps on Requirements Elicitation and System Models during Information Systems Development," *Proc. 1st Int'l Conf. Concept Mapping*, Universidad Pública de Navarra, 2004; http://cmc.ihmc.us/papers/CMC2004-126.pdf.

17. Y.-G. Kim and S.T. March, "Comparing Data Modeling Formalisms," *Comm. ACM*, vol. 38, no. 6, 1995, pp. 103–115.

18. P.C. Scott, "Requirements Analysis Assisted by Logic Modeling," *Decision Support Systems*, vol. 4, no. 1, 1988, pp. 17–25.

19. P.J. Guinan, J.G. Cooprider, and S. Faraj, "Enabling Software Development Team Performance during Requirements Definition: A Behavioral versus Technical Approach," *Information Systems Research*, vol. 9, no. 2, 1998, pp. 101–125.

20. D. Teichroew, "A Survey of Languages for Stating Requirements for Computer-Based Information Systems," *Proc. AFIPS 1972 Fall Joint Computer Conf.*, AFIPS Press, 1972, pp. 1203–1224.

21. J.C. McGraddy and H.S. Lin, eds., *A Review of the FBI's Trilogy Information Technology Modernization Program*, tech. report, National Academies Press, 2004.

22. K. Beck, *Extreme Programming Explained*, Addison-Wesley, 1999.

23. M.A. Hirschberg, "Rapid Application Development: A Brief Overview," *Software Tech News*, vol. 2, 2002; www.dacs.dtic.mil/awareness/newsletters/technews2-1/toc.html.

24. M.C. Yatco, *Joint Application Design/Development*, 2004, www.umsl.edu/~sauter/analysis/JAD.html.

25. K.W. Derr, *Applying OMT: A Practical Step-by-Step Guide to Using the Object Modeling Technique*, Prentice Hall, 1995.

26. G. Booch, *Object-Oriented Analysis and Design with Applications*, 2nd ed., Addison-Wesley, 1993.

27. C. Kobryn, "UML 2001: A Standardization Odyssey," *Comm. ACM*, vol. 42, no. 10, 1999, pp. 29–37.

28. I. Jacobson et al., *Object-Oriented Software Engineering: A Use Case Driven Approach*, Addison-Wesley, 1992.

Erratum

J. Frank Yates's biographical information in the printed version of "Decision(?) Making(?)," *IEEE Intelligent Systems*, vol. 20, no. 4, 2005, pp. 76–83, was inaccurate. The following one is correct:

J. Frank Yates, a past president of the Society for Judgment and Decision Making, is a professor of psychology and of business administration and marketing at the University of Michigan. He is also coordinator of the University of Michigan Decision Consortium, associate editor of the *Journal of Behavioral Decision Making*, and author of *Decision Management* (Jossey-Bass, 2003). His research focuses on decision making, with current emphases on decision management, judgment accuracy and processes, indecision, consumer choice, risk perception, and culture/decision-making interactions. Contact him at jfyates@umich.edu.

29. J. Wood and D. Silver, 1995, *Joint Application Development*, 2nd ed., John Wiley & Sons, 1995, p. 225.

30. P.C. Cacciabue and J.-M. Hoc, eds., *Expertise and Technology: Issues in Cognition and Human-Computer Cooperation*, Lawrence Erlbaum & Associates, 1995.

31. M.R. Endsley, B. Bolte, and D.G. Jones, *Designing for Situation Awareness*, Taylor and Francis, 2003.

32. K.J. Vicente, *Cognitive Work Analysis*, Lawrence Erlbaum Associates, 2000.

33. C.T. Bowles et al., "Knowledge Engineering: Applying the Process," *Proc. Human Factors and Ergonomics Soc. 48th Ann. Meeting*, Human Factors and Ergonomics Soc., 2004, pp. 2411–2415.

34. P. Koopman and R.R. Hoffman, "Work-arounds, Make-work, and Kludges," *IEEE Intelligent Systems*, vol. 18, no. 6, 2003, pp. 70–75.

35. M.R. Endsley and R. Hoffman, "The Sacagawea Principle," *IEEE Intelligent Systems*, vol. 17, no. 6, 2002, pp. 80–85.

36. D.D. Woods and S.W.A. Dekker, "Anticipating the Effects of Technology Change: A New Era of Dynamics for Human Factors," *Theoretical Issues in Ergonomics Science*, vol. 1, 2001, pp. 272–282.

37. R.R. Hoffman and D.D. Woods, "Studying Cognitive Systems in Context," *Human Factors*, vol. 42, no. 1, 2000, pp. 1–7.

38. S.W.A. Dekker, J.M. Nyce, and R.R. Hoffman, "From Contextual Inquiry to Designable Futures: What Do We Need to Get There?" *IEEE Intelligent Systems*, vol. 18, no. 2, 2003, pp. 74–77.

39. S. Guerlain and P. Bullemer, "User-Initiated Notification: A Concept for Aiding the Monitoring Activities of Process Control Operators," *Proc. Human Factors and Ergonomics Soc. 40th Ann. Meeting*, Human Factors and Ergonomics Soc., 1996, pp. 283–287.

Chapter 36: Human Total Cost of Ownership: The Penny Foolish Principle at Work

W. Zachary, R.R. Hoffman, K. Neville, and J. Fowlkes, "Human Total Cost of Ownership: The Penny Foolish Principle at Work," *IEEE Intelligent Systems*, Mar./Apr. 2007, vol. 22, no. 2, pp. 88–92. doi: 10.1109/MIS.2007.33

Human-centered computing is about creating technologies that are intelligent in the usual sense of intelligent systems. But we also mean intelligent in the sense that they are usable versus user-hostile; useful because they're designed on the basis of results from cognitive task analysis, so that they actually help people do things that need to be done; and understandable, in that the human can learn what the machine is doing and why. Allocating costs specifically to human-centering and cognitive systems engineering aspects of technology R&D will mitigate human-machine interaction issues and decrease training and maintenance costs, thus benefitting the service or system owner over the technology's life time. If we follow HCC's lead in defining the real costs of software systems, the procurement of technology and intelligent systems can become dollar wise.

Human Total Cost of Ownership: The Penny Foolish Principle at Work

Wayne Zachary, Kelly Neville, and Jennifer Fowlkes, *CHI Systems*
Robert R. Hoffman, *Institute for Human and Machine Cognition*

This essay taps a recurring topic in this department: procurement.[1–4] Human-centered computing is about creating technologies that are intelligent in the usual sense of intelligent systems. But we also mean intelligent in the sense that they are

- usable versus user-hostile;
- useful because they're designed on the basis of results from cognitive task analysis, so that they actually help people do things that need to be done; and
- understandable, in that the human can learn what the machine is doing and why.

Unfortunately, the procurement processes we see often don't achieve these ends. New tools called decision aids or performance aids trigger a need for kluges—that is, they're rarely usable. Machines wind up collecting dust—they're not useful. Menus cause user rage—they're not understandable. All too often we see instances of this Penny Foolish Principle of complex cognitive systems:

> A focus on short-term cost considerations, as a main driving force in procuring new information technology, always comes with a hefty price down the road, a price that always weighs most heavily on users' shoulders.

Countless program managers, system designers, computer scientists, human-factors engineers, and cognitive systems engineers have participated in projects culminating in technologies that were highly constrained by short-term cost factors. In many instances, such short-term considerations came back as hauntings.

Editors: Robert R. Hoffman, Patrick J. Hayes, and Kenneth M. Ford
Institute for Human and Machine Cognition, University of West Florida
rhoffman@ai.uwf.edu

Two examples

We offer two examples, one from weather forecasting and one from finance.

Weather forecasting

In the 1980s, the traditional workstation evolved into the personal computer and entered the weather forecasting domain. Task analyses and workplace observations showed clearly that weather forecasters had to be able to inspect multiple data types at a glance.[5] The meteorological "chart wall" and the dozens of clipboards, each reporting one data type, were evidence of this need. Human-factors studies showed that forecasters would need a workstation with at least four large-screen CRTs, each dedicated to a particular data type (one for charts of observations, one for satellite images and loops, one for radar, and so on).

However, the initial prototype of the Advanced Weather Information Processing System (AWIPS) had a single CRT, just like the "man-machine interaction" prototypes that had been created in the prior decade. Subsequent versions of AWIPS had more than one CRT and today's AWIPS have three, but throughout the reprototyping process, there was a momentum to limit the number of CRT displays because of their cost. With some hand-waving to human-factors considerations, one solution the system designers adopted was screen sectoring. Their clever finesse was to allow for sector-minimizing of displays of data types. However, this quick fix didn't go very far with weather forecasting's graphically and symbolically complex displays (that is, sector-minimized displays can be illegible), and using the sectoring tool required a great deal of make-work (in other words, pointing and clicking). And this solution didn't address the fundamental point—that forecasters must be able to see at a glance a number of diverse data types depending on the forecasting situation at hand.

Mortgage closing

In the home mortgage industry, the job of settlement officers who preside over title transfer at mortgage transactions is called *closing*. This complex process is best conducted by experienced, knowledgeable people. A company we'll call XYZ Inc. procured new job-aiding software and its associated training process using a "minimize immediate costs" model. The job aid turned out to be a confusing array of piecemeal software tools that were created without considering the work's actual cognitive demands. Consequences included the following:

- The extra cognitive work necessitated by the software slowed closing operations. Slower closings meant fewer closings, which meant either less revenue or hiring more closers to accomplish the undone work.
- Inconsistent interfaces and tortured workflow (the user had to adapt to the computer's limitations) increased the frequency and therefore the cost of errors at closing. Each mistake involved potential litigation cost to the closer's employer.
- The software made the closer's job unnecessarily difficult to learn, because the piecemeal aids confounded rather than supported the work's cognitive flow.

People typically learn how to close a mortgage on the job rather than at a school, so XYZ Inc. relied on a craft-style apprenticeship method to train new closers. Expert closers mentored trainees, who observed what their mentors did and gradually began to perform parts of the job. The company believed this method was cost effective because it minimized the costs of instructors and training systems, again a short-term cost minimization goal. But in that approach to training, the new job-aiding software had some negative unanticipated consequences.

First, the experts had to spend most of their time teaching trainees how to use the software rather than instilling knowledge about the hows and whys of the job or the overall closing process. If the software accelerated the achievement of anything, it was skill at working the software, not expertise at mortgage closing.

Second, the apprenticeship training process, tried and true as it might be, took skilled closers away from doing closings to involve them in training, a task for which they might be unprepared or ill suited. Because the bad software unnecessarily lengthened the apprenticeship period, even more of the experienced practitioners' time was lost.

Third, the software increased trainee frustration and contributed to personnel loss (trainees quit, experts retired), so there was a negative repercussive cost, that of training trainees to replace the trainees who quit. XYZ Inc.'s trainees had an attrition rate of about 48 percent during the four- to six-month apprenticeship. Every time a trainee washed out, an apprenticeship started again, further delaying when the company could put an actual closer on the job.

Finally, this created another repercussive cost—opportunity cost, the loss of potential business that couldn't be serviced and instead went to competitors.

So, the software's poor quality resulted in higher human costs, all because of the Penny Foolish strategy of lowest immediate cost.

The human cost of ownership

These examples show that procurement strategies that are driven primarily by the goal of reducing immediate costs are at a considerable risk of failure because they don't recognize the value of the system's human component. (Surprisingly often, procurement ignores even the predicable costs of replacements, upgrades, and maintenance over the artifacts' full lifetimes.) People create weather forecasts; people determine that you really do have title to the property you've mortgaged for 30 years. People pay a price when they must try to work productively using bad technology. This is the Penny Foolish Principle at work, an empirical regularity that is generalizable across all sociotechnical systems and complex cognitive systems, at least all the ones we've seen in recent decades. Table 1 summarizes the human costs of ownership.

The Penny Foolish approach views users as data-entry or data-output devices without considering the role they play or the importance of human motivations and expertise. People have needs, goals, and aspirations, such as acquiring the expertise needed to do their jobs and expanding the range of that expertise. People prefer an information or work environment that's sensitive to what they need (and how they need it) to perform their jobs in a satisfying and gratifying way. Meeting such needs is essential to achieving the ultimate goals of the system or organization. Conversely, not meeting human needs and goals is almost sure to not achieve the overall goals—that is, to not get the desired work performance. If some new piece of technology (that is, the newly envisioned human-machine system) is to succeed, the organization must pay the human costs, whether the procurement process considers them or not.

All the human costs are caused or exacerbated by *designer-centered design* approaches. Indeed, the Penny Foolish approach provides a convenient open door

Table 1. The effects of total human cost of ownership on design and procurement.

Human factor	Design problems	Financial footprint, longer-term impact
Training	Poor designs are harder to learn.	Training takes longer and might increase wash-outs, both of which increase costs.
Frustration	People's engagement with their work is lessened by software that's not usable, not useful, and not understandable.	Work output falls and worker attrition increases, leading to the need for more people (and their attendant costs) just to maintain productivity.
Recruitment	User frustration and training wash-outs mean more recruitment is needed; poor designs might mean that special aptitudes or prior skills must become part of the recruitment agenda.	Recruitment becomes more difficult and takes longer, costing more.
Performance cost	Poor designs increase the frequency of errors of various kinds.	Error mitigation costs accumulate and increase.
Opportunity costs	Longer training and longer recruitment processes result in positions remaining unfilled longer.	Mission goals and customer needs aren't achieved; competitors might benefit.

from this standpoint. Cognitive task analysis (to reveal the cognitive work) can be dismissed as irrelevant (when in fact it should be mandated) or can be conducted as a weak procedure (for example, unstructured interviews with a few "end users"), performed solely at project outset as a one-off activity. Designs can be created out of a designer-centered design playbook for technology that's cheap to build (even if it's known to be hard to learn, use, or maintain). The resulting design flaws become training problems, which become operations problems, which become performance problems, which become human-error problems, which become (re)training problems, and so on. The human-machine system "works," but the technology can't be used well or easily to accomplish the true work. Human costs skyrocket, or human performance, motivation, and growth degrade rather than improve. The low-cost solution suddenly becomes expensive, and then just a quiet failure. Many such bodies are buried in the hills around procurement offices.

So, procurement processes lead to Penny Foolish phenomena largely because the definition of "cost" lets us hide the huge impact of non-human-centric designs. The failure to acknowledge human costs lets us largely ignore these impacts, because those costs are institutionally segregated as if they occur in different universes. And the irony of all this is that when people scrutinize mission-goal achievement, it's often reduced to pitting the human against the machine. Psychologists call this "blaming the victim," and it never works in the long run.

Calculating human costs?

In current practice, *total cost of ownership* (TCO) is taken to be acquisition cost—that is, the cost of systems engineering—which doesn't consider human costs other than the immediate staffing level. The cost of meeting human aspirations is the *human total cost of ownership* of the technology. We could define HTCO in several other ways, and from the conceptual definitions we might generate a number of operational definitions of how to actually calculate things. HTCO would certainly include costs that are ordinarily considered TCO—that is, the cost of acquiring and paying for warm bodies (even it they're perceived only as input or output devices). After that, a number of factors might kick in.

First, we have training costs, including the cost of recruiting, salary during training, and training support (salaries, travel, and so on). Some procurement processes fold in the cost of human error calculated as error frequency times average cost per errors, expressed as a percentage of revenue. (From an HCC viewpoint, most so-called human errors are systemic—that is, they're caused at a system level and are often linked to weak human-centering. The organization singles out an individual just to assign blame.)

A second consideration is the principle of Trickle-Off Ergonomics, another regularity in cognitive work: "Prototyping never ceases, it just sort of trickles off." This principle acknowledges an empirical reality but also jabs at the typical stories about how system development proceeds (that is, waterfall or spiral modeling[1]). Rebuilds disrupt the cognitive work, suggesting that HTCO might include all the costs of rebuilds, right up to the point where steel cabinets end up in a dumpster. It would include repercussive negative costs of rebuilds, such as operational shutdowns, users' lost time (relearning), time for training and employing bug-fixers, help desks, and so on.

The resulting design flaws become training problems, which become operations problems, which become performance problems, which become human-error problems.

In a bizarre world in which things were easily measured, HTCO (see table 1) would include

- the cost of training people to learn to use unusable, unuseful, incomprehensible systems whose sole virtue is that they were cheaper to build;
- the added difficulty of recruiting people to work with those technologies, once the word gets out that the software systems make the job just plain awful;
- all the downstream costs of schedule slippages induced by poor designs; and
- the cost in terms of frustrating workers, decelerating the achievement of expertise, and decreasing workers' intrinsic motivation.

Our intent here, of course, is to emphasize the H in HTCO, which would include all the costs associated with all human users of the system and the negative repercussive costs of weakness in human-centering. But none of these things is easily measured.

Worse, it's immediately obvious to procurement officers that up-front costs will increase if procurement depends on initial cognitive systems engineering activities (for instance, costs during design and development). The cognitive systems engineer will not get terribly far into the procurement decision-making process by pointing out that other phases (operation, maintenance, upgrading, and so on) should have lower long-term human costs if the system is designed from the beginning in a human-centered way. This is true even if the cognitive systems engineer asserts that those additional repercussive costs might dwarf the marginal-cost delta in the design and development phase.

Might there be a way to short-circuit these problems? One relatively easy thing to include in an operational definition of HTCO is the cost of retraining, representing both the cost of training people who quit before starting productive work and the cost of recruiting and training additional people to replace the trainees who quit. Drilling down on this readily calculable aspect of HTCO might let us project the impact of specific cognitive systems engineering and human engineering aspects of procurement.

Let's throw some numbers at this, relying on our example of mortgage closing at XYZ Inc. As we said in the example, the software was so bad that nearly 48 percent of trainees quit within the first three months of training. The turnover rate in the months immediately following training, for those who completed it, was about 7 percent. Because the return-on-investment calculation that the company conducted was blind to these truths, their accounting model seriously underestimated costs and overestimated ROI, and XYZ Inc. went merrily on its way hemorrhaging money. This included trainer salary and travel ($1,300), training materials ($600), new-hire salary and benefits during training ($13,800), salary of on-the-job trainers for a brief period immediately following training

($4,000), opportunity cost (lost revenue during time-to-competency, $36,000), and recruiting costs per hire ($1,000). All this amounted to a total cost per trainee completing training of about $57,000. On top of that, there was a repercussive cost of turnover during training (an average additional cost of $27,000 to fill the empty chair of a trainee who quit before completing the training). The bottom line was a cost of about $110,000 per employee who trained to competency and began creating revenue.

But the story doesn't end there—there was the "human error" component. Company records showed that about 2 percent of sales revenue was lost per year because of closing errors. The average loss of revenue because of error on the part of new closers was about $3,000 per year. Error triggered another $1,500 loss in the administration burden. So, each new revenue-producing employee lost the company about $5,000 per year, blamed on human error but arguably due to the software's poor quality. So, we end up with $115,000 per employee cost to the company because the software wasn't human-centered. (We don't claim that retraining plus error would be zero if the technology had been aptly human-centered. It would be nonzero for a variety of reasons. We do claim it would have been significantly less than $115,000.)

A way forward?

A widely heard aphorism in system-design circles is that "training is somebody else's problem," meaning that the procurement process doesn't consider training or learnability to be part of acquisition cost. As a result, designers know that they can, if they need to, cut costs at the risk of creating technology that's hard to learn or delivered with its true learnability left undetermined.

The HTCO factor we propose involves a deeper analysis of training costs. If included in TCO calculations, it would—we predict—raise some eyebrows. And while they are raised, the eyes might open to the value of basing intelligent systems procurement on substantive cognitive task analyses, thereby creating technology that's human-centered. The costs of training, maintenance, time to competence, "error," and personnel selection and management are real costs and huge contributors to system TCO. So, these cost elements make sense to high-level decision makers.

Much of this discussion is predicated on the context of mortgage closing, but our aim is to create a general acquisition analysis process. This kind of process would bring human-centering considerations in by the back door and would avoid having to justify to program managers such nebulosities as cognitive task analysis or HCC principles.

The case is a little different with usability, which is becoming more widely considered in the procurement process and which will hopefully transcend lip service. Although the sponsors, or buyers, might mandate usability assessment as part of the design process, actual usability typically isn't quantified and made part of the evaluation score that they use to determine who wins a bidding competition or to vet a product. Consequently, developers know they have to talk about but not really pay much attention to usability analysis.

> Our intent here is to emphasize the H in HTCO, which includes all the costs associated with all human users of the system and negative repercussive costs of weakness in human-centering.

The International Council on Systems Engineering (INCOSE) has formed a Human-Systems Integration Working Group that's struggling with the human-centering issues in large-scale software development and the challenges of injecting considerations of cognitive systems engineering into system development. A US Navy program on collaborative knowledge interoperability is struggling with the challenges of how to measure macrocognitive functions at the level of team performance in sociotechnical systems. The US Air Force has sponsored a workshop and a continuing effort at extending our understanding of "systems of systems," a notion that's used to motivate a consideration of human-centering issues.

We might look to a point in time where human-centering considerations have gained entry into major governmental policy documents on system procurement. Any procurement process for intelligent systems that's sensitive to human-centering issues should estimate HTCO in one way or another, using empirical data, historical data, various parameters of component acquisition, and any other pertinent data. HTCO might be specified as a part of the system requirements statements or requests for proposals as evaluation criteria. This would create the "big stick" to enforce the allocation of funds in the intended use—that is, to amplify and extend cognitive work. If procurement can appreciate the footprints of bad design in the all-important bottom-line cost, then eventually designers won't have to be forced to take a human-centered approach or to integrate rich processes of cognitive task analysis into technology R&D. They will take HCC for granted if they're going to eliminate the beast that created those messy footprints in the first place, those unusable, unuseful, incomprehensible system designs. Allocating costs specifically to human-centering and cognitive systems engineering aspects of technology R&D will mitigate human-machine interaction issues and decrease training and maintenance costs, thus benefitting the service or system owner over the technology's lifetime. If we follow HCC's lead in defining the real costs of software systems, the procurement of technology and intelligent systems can become Dollar Wise. ■

Acknowledgments

The authors' contributions were made possible by a Phase II contract, "Joint Systems Engineering Methodology," to CHI Systems under the Small Business Innovative Research Program contract FA8650-06-C-6637, sponsored by the US Air Force Research Laboratory. Robert Hoffman's contribution was also made possible through participation in the Advanced Decision Architectures Collaborative Technology Alliance, sponsored by the US Army Research Laboratory under cooperative agreement DAAD19-01-2-0009. We also thank Amanda Hafich, Jerry Owens, Jack Ennis, Geraldine Burke, and Vassil Iordanov for their contributions to the JSEM effort.

References

1. R.R. Hoffman and W.C. Elm, "HCC Implications for the Procurement Process," *IEEE Intelligent Systems*, Jan./Feb. 2006, pp. 74–81.

2. G. Klein, B. Moon, and R.R. Hoffman, "Making Sense of Sensemaking 1: Alternative Perspectives," *IEEE Intelligent Systems*, July/Aug. 2006, pp. 22–26.

3. P. Koopman and R.R. Hoffman, "Work-arounds, Make-work, and Kludges," *IEEE Intelligent Systems*, Nov./Dec. 2003, pp. 70–75.

4. P. Laplante, R.R. Hoffman, and G. Klein, "Antipatterns in the Creation of Intelligent Systems," *IEEE Intelligent Systems*, Jan./Feb. 2007, pp. 91–95.

5. R.R. Hoffman, "Human Factors Psychology in the Support of Forecasting: The Design of Advanced Meteorological Workstations," *Weather and Forecasting*, vol. 6, 1991, pp. 98–110.

Wayne Zachary is the president of CHI Systems, an OSI Geospatial company. Contact him at wzachary@chisystems.com.

Robert R. Hoffman is a senior research scientist at the Institute for Human and Machine Cognition. Contact him at rhoffman@ihmc.us.

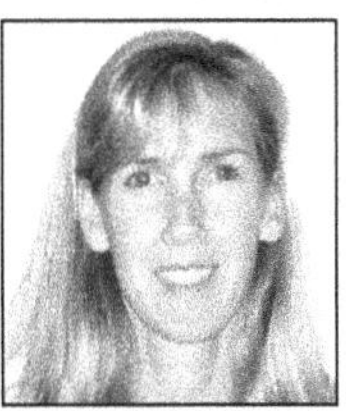

Kelly Neville is a managing cognitive engineer at CHI Systems, an OSI Geospatial company. Contact her at kneville@chisystems.com.

Jennifer Fowlkes is a managing cognitive engineer at CHI Systems, an OSI Geospatial company. Contact her at jfowlkes@chisystems.com.

Chapter 37: The Procurement Woes Revisited

K. Neville, R.R. Hoffman, C. Linde, W.C. Elm, and J. Fowlkes, "The Procurement Woes Revisited," *IEEE Intelligent Systems*, vol. 23, no. 1, Jan./Feb. 2008, pp. 72–75. doi: 10.1109/MIS.2008.15

The set of people who are frustrated every day by badly designed information technology is very large. So is the set of people whose dollars pay for the badly designed technology. A conservative estimate ranges in the billions for the cost of large-scale information systems that end up collecting dust because they're not properly human-centered. Yes, billions and still counting—that's the scary part. Within this large set of frustrated customers (see the sidebar "When Systems Development Neglects Human Considerations") is a subset whose job it is to do something about this situation. That subset includes policymakers, program managers, and systems engineers. It also includes a sub-subset comprising cognitive systems engineers, ethnographers, and many others who, in one vernacular or another, advocate human-centered computing. We must show that intelligent technologies—those designed to interact with humans or play a role in the cognitive work conducted in sociotechnical work systems—are usable, useful, and understandable.

The Procurement Woes Revisited

Kelly Neville, *Embry-Riddle Aeronautical University*
Robert R. Hoffman, *Institute for Human and Machine Cognition*
Charlotte Linde, *NASA Ames Research Center*
William C. Elm, *Resilient Cognitive Solutions*
Jennifer Fowlkes, *CHI Systems*

Our civilization needs to heal the wound between its social and the technical-scientific world views. —Joseph Goguen

The set of people who are frustrated every day by badly designed information technology is very large.[1] So is the set of people whose dollars pay for the badly designed technology. A conservative estimate ranges in the billions for the cost of large-scale information systems that end up collecting dust because they're not properly human-centered. Yes, billions and still counting—that's the scary part.

Within this large set of frustrated customers (see the sidebar "When Systems Development Neglects Human Considerations") is a subset whose job it is to do something about this situation. That subset includes policy-makers, program managers, and systems engineers. It also includes a sub-subset comprising cognitive systems engineers, ethnographers, and many others who, in one vernacular or another, advocate human-centered computing. We must show that intelligent technologies—those designed to interact with humans or play a role in the cognitive work conducted in sociotechnical work systems—are usable, useful, and understandable.

Procurement woes

A review of government documents covering standards and requirements[2] shows that cost is always the horse that's pulling the cart: "The DoD components shall, as part of programs such as Human Systems Integration, minimize system support costs by addressing manpower affordability early in the acquisition process."[3] This emphasis on cost is understandable, and arguably necessary, but the way it's stated means that worker needs can always get jettisoned at the first sign of trouble. As the Penny Foolish Principle states, the true "human costs" always show up further along in development after human-centering considerations have been sacrificed.[4,5]

Other human-centering issues are more subtle. For instance, the DoD requires that software use necessitate minimal effort on the user's part: "Design-induced requirements for operator workload, accuracy, time constraint, mental processing, and communication shall not exceed operator capabilities."[6] Actually, this doesn't make good sense. We know from expertise studies that people achieve high levels of proficiency only after long hours of working hard, on hard problems. Software designed to always minimize difficulty, and not serve as Janus Machines[7] that support tough task training, wouldn't help workers progress along the path to expertise.

In a previous essay in this department,[8] two of us (Hoffman and Elm) discussed John MacNamara's notion of "desirements" as a way to shift terminology away from entrenched tradition and think about requirements differently. We especially challenged the notion that "requirements creep" is a nasty thing to be avoided or somehow done away with. We also suggested that a partial fix would be to train individuals versed in both systems engineering and cognitive systems engineering to be the future managers of large-scale procurements.

Joseph Goguen (1941–2006)

As we've learned, computer scientist Joseph Goguen anticipated these ideas and other HCC notions. He saw the challenge of anticipating and addressing technology's human impacts as tractable as well as ethically, methodologically, and economically necessary. This essay is a homage to him, so that we might highlight one key point: If the procurement woes that we've boldly offered in this HCC department were in fact anticipated a decade or more ago, then the situation now must *really* be bad. We find in Goguen's writings many discussion points and topics for elaboration. Our starting and ending points differ somewhat from his, but we have many interesting commonalities. If this essay stimulates any significant discussion, it will have done its job.

Throughout his distinguished career, Goguen worked to

Editors: Robert R. Hoffman, Patrick J. Hayes, and Kenneth M. Ford
Institute for Human and Machine Cognition
rhoffman@ihmc.us

The *Wall Street Journal* reported that 50 percent of software projects fail to meet CEO expectations and 42 percent of corporate information technology projects are discontinued before completion.[1] A 1995 US Department of Defense study estimated that 46 percent of DoD-funded IT development efforts result in products that are delivered but not successfully used and 29 percent never even produce a product.[2] These statistics translate into workers who lose out because they don't have the technology they need to perform their work effectively, not to mention the billions of dollars squandered. For example, the US Internal Revenue Service spent $4 billion on a decision support system that, in the words of an IRS official, does "not work in the real world,"[3] and the US Federal Bureau of Investigation spent $170 million on a problem-riddled software development effort before abandoning it.[4] Other well-known system development disasters include the London emergency dispatch system released in 1993[5] and the US air traffic control system upgrade.[6] Each of these examples points to the neglect of human considerations during the development of sociotechnical systems.

References

1. P.E. Coyle, "Simulation Based Acquisition for Information Technology," paper presented at the *Academia, Industry, Government Crosstalk Conf.*, 1999; www.dote.osd.mil/presentations/Coyle051899/tsld001.htm
2. T.R. Leishman and D.A. Cook, "Requirements Risks Can Drown Software Projects," *Crosstalk*, vol. 15, 2002, pp. 4–8, www.stsc.hill.af.mil/crosstalk.
3. S. Gardner, *Marketplace*, news archives, Nat'l Public Radio, 31 Jan. 1997; http://marketplace.publicradio.org/shows/1997/01/31_mpp.html.
4. D. Eggen, "FBI Pushed Ahead with Troubled Software," *Washington Post*, 6 June 2005.
5. A. Finkelstein and J. Dowell, "A Comedy of Errors: The London Ambulance Service Case Study," *Proc. 8th Int'l Workshop Software Specification and Design* (IWSSD), IEEE CS Press, 1996, pp. 2–4.
6. D.F. Carr and E. Cone, "Can FAA Salvage Its IT Disaster?" *Baseline*, 8 Apr. 2002, www.baselinemag.com/article2/0,1540,656862,00.asp.

build bridges between rigorous formal systems and the messy, creative ways in which human minds and social groups actually operate. His early work was on fuzzy logic, then on the foundations of computer science, and then on the empirical study of group decision making. Examples include his analysis of the Watergate tapes and an analysis of the black-box recordings of cockpit conversations in aviation accidents. Goguen spanned boundaries. For instance, he considered lessons from jazz in developing a theory of consciousness.[9] His work, taken as a whole, was an attempt to include art, ethics, and group politics within the range of formal description—a mathematics of the complexity of human life.

This is evident in his statement of the procurement problem: "Experience shows that many failures are due to a mismatch between the social and technical aspects of a supposed solution."[10] (p. 97) In works spanning 1994–2000, Goguen argued that we need new thrusts in education and new approaches to system development that integrate the technical and social aspects of work, improve resilience, and enable people to cope with the complexity of the technology itself.[10–13]

A tipping point

Procurement woes bear repeating right now because we might be at a tipping point. The US Navy initiative for "human-system integration" (HSI) has gained voice and office in other branches of the military. With Steven Deal's indefatigable leadership, the Human-System Integration Working Group of the International Council on Systems Engineering has drafted language for a definition of HSI to be included in the *Incose Systems Engineering Handbook*.[14] There is wide agreement that cognitive systems engineering must (somehow) be integrated with systems engineering and not just "injected into" it.[15,16]

Quotables

Goguen's work is chock full of juicy quotables capturing procurement antipatterns. Antipatterns are patterns people follow regularly and with negative repercussions that limit the integration and even the consideration of human and social factors in technology development.[17]

In this essay, we hope to give you a sense of Goguen by sharing some of our favorite quotes. Some of these echo our own thoughts. Others contain insights that widened our eyes to the range of factors contributing to and affected by the current state of human-centering in systems development.

On software engineering

Goguen's arguments about software engineering convey his passion about overcoming designer-centered and reductionist approaches to technology development:

> Experience with real projects shows that there is no such orderly progression from one phase to the next; instead, there is a continual projection forward and backward. ... the nature and limitations of such models [e.g., waterfall and so-called process models] do not seem to have been widely appreciated.[12] (pp. 176–177)

> Indeed, the activities necessary for a successful system development project cannot always be expected to fit in a natural way into any system of pre-given categories.[11] (p. 35)

> Similarly, requirements documents must serve a number of different stakeholders.[11] (p. 37)

Goguen proposed an alternative way to conceive software development on the basis of Humberto Maturana and Francisco Varela's notion of self-organizing or "autopoietic" systems:[18]

> A software development project is not a formal mathematical entity. Perhaps it is usefully seen as an autopoietic process, an evolving organization of informational structures, continually recreating itself by building, modifying, and reusing its structures ... Autopoietic systems are about as far as we know how to get from rigid top-down hierarchical goal-driven control systems; autopoietic systems thrive on error, and reconstruct themselves on the basis of what they learn from their mistakes. Autopoiesis can be considered an implementation technique for postmodernism.[10] (pp. 116–117)

Following this lead, the most recent discussions of alternative approaches to system development rely heavily on notions of evolutionary adaptive development[15] and resilience engineering.[19]

On requirements specification

Goguen recognized that just as controlling a complex sociotechnical system development process is impossible using regimented top-down controls, managing requirements about complex sociotechnical systems within such regimentation is also impossible:[10]

> The very rapid rate of change of requirements, which is so typical of large projects, implies an even more rapid rate of change for specifications. This makes many formal methods very difficult, perhaps even impossible, to apply in practice. (p. 115)

> It is *not* just as easy to find specifications and invariants for the flight control software of a real airplane as it is for a sorting algorithm; in fact, finding specifications and invariants is not an important activity in real industrial work. On the contrary, it turns out that finding requirements (i.e., determining what kind of system to build), structuring the system (modular design), understanding what has already been done (reading documentation and talking to others), and organizing the efforts of a large team, are all much more important for a large system development effort. (p. 101)

We see here that Goguen appreciated the idea that came to be known as the Envisioned World Problem.[20] Seeds for this idea emerged at about the same time in several scientists' writings.[21,22] As Goguen argued, this notion that "designs are hypotheses" calls into question the view that requirements are stable things that can be preformulated:[11]

> This explains why it can be so difficult to determine the requirements for a large system: it only becomes clear what the requirements are when the system is successfully operating in its social and organizational context; requirements evolve as system development proceeds, and a reasonably complete and consistent set of requirements for a large, complex system can only emerge from a retrospective reconstruction … Determining whether some system meets its requirements is the outcome of a complex social process that typically involves negotiation, and may involve legal action. Thus, it is usually entirely misleading to think of requirements as pre-given.[10] (p. 37)

On method

As the quotations show so far, Goguen was concerned with the methods of systems development and whether they provide a sound basis for a design:

> Moreover, the requirements phase of a large system development project … has the greatest economic leverage, … is also the least explored, and has the least satisfactory intellectual foundations.[12] (p. 166)

Goguen sought better and richer ways of measurement and evaluation, advocating the use of observational techniques for understanding the structure of sociotechnical systems and the ways in which people actually work. He acknowledged that using and developing methods that bridge the social and technical aspects of work is a difficult task. He also acknowledged that innovative and multidisciplinary work generally can be difficult and that some attempts are "greeted largely with incomprehension."[10] (p. 109) Particularly, he was concerned about the fact that commonly used techniques lead to a limited understanding of the problem space:

> This means that the needs of the user, both as individual and as organisation, are not addressed systematically; in general, they are only incompletely known to the development team, and there are often some serious misconceptions. [23] (p. 153)

Goguen was convinced that methods used by the social sciences were needed to understand and represent the complexity of cognitive work.

> The problems of requirements elicitation cannot be solved in a purely technological way, because social context is much more crucial.[23] (p. 153)

He argued that ethnographic methods (the observation of people in their natural environments) are genuinely scientific, appropriate for use in developing complex systems, and scalable to software development efforts' needs. He adopted a viewpoint called *ethnomethodology*, which

> tries to reconcile a radical empiricism with the situatedness of social data by looking closely at how competent members of a group actually organize their interactions.[11] (p. 40)

Although ethnomethodology relies on ethnographic methods, it differs from traditional sociology by focusing on the methods (hence, "-methodology") used by individuals and society (hence, "ethno-") to make sense of things and achieve social order. Ethnomethodology has had special impact in the sociology of scientific knowledge. For instance, the dependence of meaning on context has implications for the view that scientific knowledge is "objective."[24] Goguen applied ethnomethodology in his treatment of requirements analysis:

> To sum up, we recommend a "*zooming*" method of requirements elicitation, whereby the more expensive but detailed methods are only employed selectively for problems that have been determined by other techniques to be especially important. From this point of view, the various techniques based on ethnomethodology can be seen as analogous to an electron microscope: they provide an instrument that is very accurate and powerful, but that is also expensive, and requires careful preparation to ensure that the right thing is examined. [23] (p. 162)

Bridging the technological, social, and ethical

Goguen found it astonishing that in the information age,

> there is no adequate theory of information, nor even any adequate definition of information.[10] (p. 112)

He tried to extend traditional information theory to human situations but found it didn't apply:

> Data can only become *information* when people care about it for some reason and are able to interpret it. This means that information technology … is bound up with the social at a very basic level having to do with the nature of information itself.[10] (p. 94)

> Meaning is an ongoing achievement of some social group; it takes *work* to interpret configurations of signs, and this work necessarily occurs in some particular context.[11] (p. 34)

> Information has an intrinsic ethical dimension.[10] (p. 112)

He then tried general systems theory for a complexity-based information theory,

> but again it became clear that no purely formal approach, however abstract and general, could deal with human meaning in any deep sense.[10] (p. 112)

> It follows that a suitable theory of information must be a *social theory of information*, rather than a *statistical theory of information*.[11] (p. 29)

> *An item of information is an interpretation of a configuration of signs for which members of some social group are accountable.* The goal is to get a theory of information adequate for understanding and designing systems that process information.[10] (p. 112)

Goguen considered information to be either "dry" or "humid," a distinction we find both useful and entertaining:

> Formalization is the process of making information drier (i.e., less situated) by using a more explicit and precise metalanguage. (p. 32)

Dry, formalized information is represented by formalized modeling languages. Information can be humid, too—that is, "situated." In the same 1999 article, Goguen cited recipes as an example of humid information. His point was quite serious:

> But we now know that ignoring the situated, social aspect of information can be fatal in designing and building software systems.[10] (p. 97)

> Western civilization is fundamentally entangled with a separation of technology from ethics, based on an untenable instrumental conception of technology (i.e., viewing technologies simply as tools we create rather than as a force shaping our view of the world). (p. 16)

Goguen proposed that developers must learn to take information's qualities into account. Specifically, information is situated, local, emergent, contingent, embodied, vague, and open.

> [Therefore we can] understand why it is not possible to completely formalize requirements: They cannot be fully separated from the social context. More specifically, the qualities explain why so-called life-cycle phases cannot be fully formalized.[11] (p. 35)

An epitaph

The illumination that we see at the end of the tunnel actually comes from behind, not from ahead. It comes from the lanterns of those from whom we've learned, lighting a way forward for us.

References

1. K.J. Vicente, "Crazy Clocks: Counterintuitive Consequences of 'Intelligent' Automation," *IEEE Intelligent Systems*, Nov./Dec. 2001, pp. 73–75.
2. L. Lormann et al., *A Review of Government Requirements and Standards with Regard to Human Factors and Human-Centering of Technology*, to be published; available from Jennifer Fowlkes on request.
3. *Directive No. 1100.4, Guidance for Manpower Management*, US Dept. of Defense, 2005.
4. P. Koopman and R.R. Hoffman, "Work-arounds, Make-work, and Kludges," *IEEE Intelligent Systems*, Nov./Dec. 2003, pp. 70–75.
5. W. Zachary et al., "Human Total Cost of Ownership: The Penny Foolish Principle at Work," *IEEE Intelligent Systems*, Mar./Apr. 2007, pp. 22–26.
6. *DoD Design Criteria Standard: Human Engineering, MIL-STD-1472F*, US Dept. of Defense, 1999.
7. R.R. Hoffman, G. Lintern, and S. Eitelman, "The Janus Principle," *IEEE Intelligent Systems*, Mar./Apr. 2004, pp. 78–80.
8. R.R. Hoffman and W.C. Elm, "HCC Implications for the Procurement Process," *IEEE Intelligent Systems*, Jan./Feb. 2006, pp. 74–81.
9. D. Borgo and J. Goguen, "Rivers of Consciousness: The Nonlinear Dynamics of Free Jazz," L. Fisher, ed., *Jazz Research Proc. Yearbook*, vol. 25, 2005, pp. 46–58; www.iaje.org/iaje.aspx?pid=68.
10. J. Goguen, "Tossing Algebraic Flowers down the Great Divide," *People and Ideas in Theoretical Computer Science*, C.S. Calude, ed., Springer, 1999, pp. 93–129.
11. J. Goguen, "Toward a Social, Ethical Theory of Information," *Social Science, Technical Systems, and Cooperative Work: Beyond the Great Divide*, G. Bowker et al., eds., Lawrence Erlbaum, 1997, pp. 27–56.
12. J. Goguen, "Requirements Engineering as the Reconciliation of Social and Technical Issues," *Requirements Engineering: Social and Technical Issues*, M. Jirotka and J. Goguen, eds., Elsevier, 1994, pp. 165–200.
13. J. Goguen et al., "An Overview of the Tatami Project," *Cafe: An Industrial-Strength Algebraic Formal Method*, K. Futatsugi, A.K. Nakagawa, and T. Tamai, eds., Elsevier, 2000, pp. 61–78.
14. *Incose Systems Engineering Handbook: A Guide for System Life Cycle Processes and Activities*, Int'l Council on Systems Eng. (Incose), 2006.
15. R.W. Pew and R.S. Mavor, "Human-System Integration in the System Development Process: A New Look," *Report of the Committee on Human-System Design Support Changing Technology*, US Nat'l Research Council, 2007.
16. R.G. Eggleston et al., "Tightening the Linkage of CSE and Software Systems Engineering," *Proc. Human Factors and Ergonomics Soc. 48th Ann. Meeting* (HFES), 2004.
17. P. Laplante, R. Hoffman, and G. Klein, "Antipatterns in the Creation of Intelligent Systems," *IEEE Intelligent Systems*, Jan./Feb. 2007, pp. 91–95.
18. H.R. Maturana and F.J. Varela, *Autopoiesis and Cognition: The Realization of the Living*, Kluwer Academic, 1991.
19. E. Hollnagel, D.D. Woods, and N. Leveson, *Resilience Engineering: Concepts and Precepts*, Ashgate, 2007.
20. D.D. Woods and S.W.A. Dekker, "Anticipating the Effects of Technology Change: A New Era of Dynamics for Human Factors," *Theoretical Issues in Ergonomics Science*, vol. 1, no. 3, 2001, pp. 272–282.
21. J.M. Carroll and R.L. Campbell, *Artifacts as Psychological Theories: The Case of Human-Computer Interaction*, research report RC 13454, IBM T.J. Watson Research Center, 1988.
22. T. Winograd and F. Flores, *Understanding Computers and Cognition*, Ablex, 1986.
23. J. Goguen and C. Linde, "Techniques for Requirements Elicitation," *Proc. Requirements Eng. '93*, S. Fickas and A. Finkelstein, eds., IEEE CS Press, 1993, pp. 152–164; reprinted in *Software Requirements Engineering*, 2nd ed., R. Thayer and M. Dorfman, eds., IEEE CS Press, 1997.
24. R.R. Hoffman and L. Militello, *Perspectives on Cognitive Task Analysis*, Taylor and Francis, 2008.

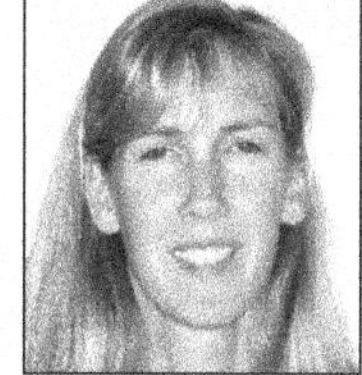

Kelly Neville is a visiting associate professor in human factors at Embry-Riddle Aeronautical University. Contact her at nevillek@erau.edu.

Robert R. Hoffman is a research scientist at the Institute for Human and Machine Cognition. Contact him at rhoffman@ihmc.us.

Charlotte Linde is a senior research scientist in the Computational Sciences Division of the NASA Ames Research Center. Contact her at charlotte.linde@nasa.gov.

William C. Elm is president of Resilient Cognitive Solutions. Contact him at welm@resilientcognitivesolutions.com.

Jennifer Fowlkes is a managing cognitive engineer at CHI Systems. Contact her at jfowlkes@chisystems.com.

Chapter 38: The Practitioner's Cycles, Part 1: Actual World Problems

S.V. Deal and R.R. Hoffman, "The Practitioner's Cycles, Part 1: Actual World Problems," *IEEE Intelligent Systems*, vol. 25, no. 2, Mar./Apr. 2010, pp. 4–9. doi: 10.1109/MIS.2010.54

This is one of three essays on the forces and constraints of procurement versus the goals of human centering, including the creation of intelligent technologies that are usable, useful, and understandable. The procurement process tends to de-emphasize these goals while focusing on strict adherence to rules and regulations. As a result, software system development processes, described in texts and acquisition documents, come to be misaligned with the challenges faced by development teams. This misalignment between "actual world problems" and normative documentation repeatedly results in failed systems. A real-life practitioner's account illustrates this point by describing how a group of individuals, acting on their own initiative and at their own risk, short-circuited the rules and constraints of the procurement process to turn a procurement process failure into a success. In the next essay, we will present a model called the Practitioner's Cycles and discuss how this model applies to the envisioned world problem, which is the challenge of creating intelligent technologies for new work systems.

The Practitioner's Cycles, Part 1: Actual World Problems

Steven V. Deal, *Deal Corp.*
Robert R. Hoffman, *Institute for Human and Machine Cognition*

This is one of two essays on the forces and constraints of procurement versus the goals of human centering, including the creation of intelligent technologies that are usable, useful, and understandable. The procurement process tends to de-emphasize these goals while focusing on strict adherence to rules and regulations. As a result, software system development processes, described in texts and acquisition documents, have come to be misaligned with the challenges faced by development teams. This misalignment between "actual world problems" and normative documentation repeatedly results in failed systems. A real-life practitioner's account illustrates this point by describing how a group of individuals, acting on their own initiative and at their own risk, short-circuited the rules and constraints of the procurement process to turn a procurement process failure into a success.

In the next essay, we will present a model called the *Practitioner's Cycles* and discuss how this model applies to the *envisioned world problem*, which is the challenge of creating intelligent technologies for new work systems.

Actual World Problems

System failures and the concomitant waste of competitive and taxpayer resources seem to be the fare of the day. Woes about issues in major procurements are dramatic due to the magnitude of squandering and the profound setbacks to operational capabilities. Information technology, especially intelligent systems technology, seems to be particularly susceptible to programmatic breakdowns.[1–4]

Several surveys have documented information technology procurement issues.[5] Although some reports criticize the methods that the surveys use,[6] methodological weakness succumbs to the evidentiary tide.

Information technology procurement failure is gauged in various ways. For information technology administrators, operators, and others, deliverables are unsatisfying, related to gaps of usefulness, usability, and understandability. For management, projects fail to achieve their business objectives, and procurements exceed the costs budgeted for their execution.[7] Moreover, projects take far longer than expected to complete.

Several fallacies must be overcome if the chances for project success are to increase. Such fallacies include the belief that "requirements creep" is a bad, unnecessary thing that should be avoided, when it is actually a necessity as well as an empirical fact. There is also a fallacy that one can conduct "concurrent maturation" of enabling technology without anchoring this in cognitive task analysis to understand the actual work of the domain. Project development teams often misunderstand the perspectives of the various stakeholders. Moreover, there is a fallacy that budgeting should be exclusively project centered without embracing human-centering goals. These actual world problems involve a mismatch between the challenges at hand and the available resources and delegated responsibilities.

The Challenge Is Always Today's

Technologies must be relevant to immediate needs. Businesses must address market demand even if, as with innovative new products, they must create that demand themselves. Government sponsors want to solve the problems their people are dealing with today. Technologists have to align themselves with rapid "satisficing" (settling on a solution they think is "good enough") and deliver usable, useful, and understandable products that are achievable in reality.

The Response Is Delayed

Despite these immediate demands, however, it can take years to get a new system into the hands of workers. The 2008 US Government Accountability Office Assessment found that for 39 programs begun since 2001, average system development time was 37 months,[8] a duration that is typical of large software projects. The acquisition process takes years, during which attempts are made to capture all stakeholder requirements, include all the latest technologies, and neutralize risks. New technologies emerge, and sponsors desiring to maintain and obtain additional competitive advantage will contractually insist that these be incorporated into existing product designs, extending the system development process even further. US Army Vice Chief of Staff General Peter Chiarelli stated the problem bluntly: "We have to find better ways to keep up with technology. It doesn't do us any good to have a procurement cycle that takes 10 to 15 years."[9]

The Challenge Is Morphing

Moreover, during the years it takes to bring a product to market or to achieve an initial operating capability, the people who need new systems and upgrades are vulnerable to adaptive circumstances and adversaries. This is a reflection of the *moving-target law* that governs sociotechnical workplaces.[10] Today's needs must be repeatedly redefined to adapt to changing mission requirements and the obsolescence introduced because the process is so lengthy. The operational context changes, and projects must compete for resources. Expertise gets lost due to attrition. New competitors enter the market place; old competitors change their tactics. New alliances emerge. Management incentives reward new and additional tasks, leading to misaligned goals. Job responsibilities and incumbents change.

Complexity Will Kill You

In addition to the above actual world problems, things seem inevitably to become more complex. Congressman Curt Weldon was quoted by the Department of the Air Force as saying: "The [Army Future Command System] software task alone is five times larger than that required for [the] Joint Strike Fighter and ten times larger than the F-22, which after two decades is finally meeting its software requirements."[11] Thus, one of the risk factors affecting the ability to transition research is the difficulty of rapidly validating and verifying the functionality of technologies against realistic problems.

System Development Never Really Ends Anyway

Finally, system development never really ends anyway. The process lives on in rebuilds, procedural modifications, block upgrades, replacements, and altered missions or applications. This has been called the *Law of Trickle-Off Ergonomics*.[2] This never-ending process sort of nullifies the very meaning of the term *deliverable*. One of the most difficult tasks a developer faces is to fully list the assumptions on which system development is based. The complexity of current and emerging systems, and systems of systems, requires breakthrough approaches in system development, including organizational structures, personnel development plans and career tracks, and budgeting mechanisms that span the entire product-line life cycle.

Is Acquisition Reform an Impossibility?

Quite a few US government programs illustrate the consequences of ignoring actual world problems: cost overruns, low usability, software issues, and so on.[1,8] The roster includes cases in which expensive ongoing programs had to be drastically restructured.[12] However, a few government initiatives also present sincere attempts to escape actual world problems.

For instance, recent acquisition programs of the US Department of Defense have sought to apply a method or goal of "rapid acquisition." Indeed, all the DoD branches seek novel methods for rigorous yet rapid testing of technology (for instance, testing for interactions between different software systems). In fact, the DoD has a Rapid Reaction Technology Office charged with addressing this very problem.[13] This push has been motivated by the desire to get new systems (including weapons systems but also robotic systems, software systems, decision aids, and others) to the warfighters as rapidly as possible.[14] This push has also been motivated by recognition of the burdens and roadblocks involved in acquiring complex information technologies.

Alas, reform can end up being a mere piggyback on the status quo. This, of course, is the easy path. And it's illustrated by calls for acquisition reform that effectively just entail additional regulations and reporting requirements, new bureaucracy for cost estimation, more oversight of testing, additional requirements for prototyping (with escape clauses), and more punishments for overruns—and, this, despite there already being a shortage in acquisition personnel. Then, killer complexity comes into play, because the remaining people are unable to keep pace with the regulation sprawl.

New regulations often come in response to a breakdown or other disaster, but they generally try to solve the problem in piecemeal fashion and in ways that don't take into account the actual underlying factors behind the disaster—which are typically systemic but get reduced to a blame game. Also left out of consideration is the issue of how existing regulations will interact with the new piece of regulation—for instance, by creating goal conflicts.

To illustrate this piggybacking approach, we can tap into the 1997 General Accounting Office report on opportunities to reform acquisition.[15] This report recommended two actions: conduct joint mission assessments, and test sufficiently before production. How would these apparently simple and substantive reforms actually be implemented if they were to occur under the umbrella of the current procurement system?

First, "joint" would need to be defined. How many offices or branches would need to participate for an assessment to be considered "joint"? Once the stakeholders were identified, common understandings would have to be achieved. Good luck with that. Next, the steps constituting a mission assessment would need to be delimited and explicated. Then, the criteria for sufficiency would be investigated and detailed (that is, pried from context). Also, the stipulation "before production" would have to be specified: should it be before full production or before low-rate production? Furthermore, the means to measure compliance would have to be identified and carefully specified.

All of this would require timely documentation-processing mechanisms. At the high end, policy would need to be coordinated across all branches. Language accounting for the cultures and specialized procedures of each branch must be agreed upon. Each branch would draft procedures with legalistic precision, which must be reviewed, revised, and finalized. Defense acquisition coursework would be updated. Clauses for agreements and contracts would be revised. Acquisition professionals would need to be made aware of the new guidelines, and contractors would need to become familiar with the new policies.

The end result would be a recreation of the hobbled and intractable process that triggered all the grumbling in the first place: an explosion of documentation, additional regulations, and more oversight.

The root limitation of the piggybacking approach is that legislation, policy, standards, and processes are limited in their capacity to effect change that does not "complexify." Various reforms have been tried and have failed, leading to advice by Harvey Sapolsky,[16] professor of Public Policy and Organization Emeritus at Massachusetts Institute of Technology, to skip acquisition reform, on the basis of the following assertions:

- Everything has been tried. The truth is you can't fix the acquisition system. All the insiders know this.
- Sponsors ask for crazy systems that must do impossible things.
- Existing systems are so good that new systems must be really, really good to justify the government buying new ones.
- Only a few firms have the capability to manage complex, new projects.
- The vendors' claim, "We can build that, cheaper than you think."
- Acquisition rules intentionally slow things down with demands for constant reconsideration, in the hope that support for the project will fade. When we really want something quickly, like new systems urgently needed by warfighters, we have to suspend the rules, set up a fast track, and push aside the bureaucrats.
- The problem with fast tracking as a solution is that everyone must agree that a weapon is needed. Most of the time, there is disagreement.
- Skipping the reform charade might force officials to educate the taxpayers instead of hoodwinking them, because making decisions on which weapons to develop and buy is very difficult: we don't know what wars we'll fight and what weapons we'll have to counter.

This circumstance is not peculiar to government. David Riley, director of Pera International's acquisitions support group, noted in speaking of manufacturing in the United Kingdom: "The current pattern is to spend 80 percent of management time and costs on financing taxation, legal and contractual issues, and 20 percent on the market, technology and people issues. Successful acquisition usually has the reverse equation."[17]

Alternatively, reform can be radical: the unfixable system gets trashed, and the core rules of the game get changed. This requires acknowledging actual world problems, which include satisfying stakeholders by maintaining jobs; sustaining an industrial technology base; and acknowledging that excruciating oversight could waste even more dollars than abuse, capable systems take a long time to create, and the world doesn't wait while you create them.

No wonder insiders believe fixing "the system" is impossible.

What Makes for Success?

On the basis of a survey of software development activities that were arguably successful, Robert Frese and Vicki Sauter presented several *success elements* centering on communication, planning, and management support.[18] Kelly Neville, Jennifer Fowlkes, and Robert Hoffman conducted in-depth interviews with experienced program managers and software engineers about procurement, and they too listed some success elements, including accommodation to changing requirements, management buy-in and support, and communication and coordination among team members.[3]

Some of the success elements revealed in these explorations are fine as general guidance, such as "solicit input to fully understand user needs;" "promote communication among executives, managers, developers, suppliers and users;" and "pay attention to human considerations."[18] But as Neville, Fowlkes, and Hoffman point out, methods and tools for actually accomplishing such communication and facilitation goals are entirely lacking.[3] The result is that program managers and researchers must fend for themselves.

Companies such as Apple have demonstrated the value of addressing one particular element, *user needs*, with products such as the iPod and the iPhone. The importance of understanding user needs is highlighted by cases in which the users of the technology were the ones who were innovative, whether in business[19] or in the military.[20] Technologists and inventors are often surprised at the uses to which people put their innovations. Think back to the original purposes of GPS and the Internet, and compare them with today's applications. People discover techniques and opportunities afforded by product features, which they gradually employ to their (often novel) advantage.

Failure to engage in rich cognitive task analysis to reveal "desirements" can be practically guaranteed to result in software systems that are limited in usability, usefulness, and understandability. Success cases at coping with actual world problems tend to be those in which the technology developers had a deep understanding of the nature of the user's work. The "Practitioner's Tale" sidebar illustrates this point.

The practitioner's tale given in the sidebar is an example of success at coping with actual world problems. Success was achieved by deviating from the rules while appreciating their intent. The technologists complained and said "No!" The program manager felt ill at ease, since he was put at considerable risk. But he and his team "got away with it." By implication, perhaps the only way to achieve human centering in the face of actual world problems is by deviating from the rules, because of the strictures of the mandated or traditional concepts and processes of procurement.

The next essay in this department will continue this extrapolation all the way to a model we call the *Practitioner's Cycles*, which represents one path for escaping actual world problems but also for coping with the envisioned world problem.

References

1. D. Graham-Rowe, "Fifty Years of DARPA: Hits, Misses and Ones to Watch," *NewScientist*, 15 May 2008; www.newscientist.com/article/dn13907-fifty-years-of-darpa-hits-misses-and-ones-to-watch.html.
2. R.R. Hoffman and W.C. Elm, "HCC Implications for the Procurement Process," *IEEE Intelligent Systems*, vol. 21, no. 1, 2006, pp. 74–81.
3. R.R. Hoffman, K.N. Neville, and J. Fowlkes, "Using Cognitive Task Analysis to Explore Issues in the Procurement of Intelligent Decision Support Systems," *Cognition, Technology & Work*, vol. 11, no. 1, 2009, pp. 57–70.
4. K. Neville et al., "The Procurement Woes Revisited," *IEEE Intelligent Systems*, vol. 23, no. 1, 2008, pp. 72–75.
5. "Failure Causes: Statistics," IT Cortex; www.it-cortex.com/Stat_Failure_Cause.htm.
6. "Herding Cats: Ideas, Comments and Resources about Project Management from Field Experience and Materials from www.niwotridge.com," 2007; http://herdingcats.typepad.com/my_weblog/2007/12/2007-books.html.
7. W. Zachary et al., "Human Total Cost of Ownership: The Penny Foolish Principle at Work," *IEEE Intelligent Systems*, vol. 22, no. 2, 2007, pp. 88–92.
8. *Defense Acquisitions: Assessments of Selected Weapons Programs*, Report to Congressional Committees, GAO-08-467SP, Government Accountability Office, 2008; www.gao.gov/new.items/d08467sp.pdf.
9. S.I. Erwin, "Army's Vice Chief: 'We Have to Speed up How We Procure Things,'" *National Defense*, Oct. 2009, pp. 22–23; www.nationaldefensemagazine.org/archive/2009/October/Pages/Army%E2%80%99sViceChief%.
10. R.R. Hoffman and D.D. Woods, "Studying Cognitive Systems in Context," *Human Factors*, vol. 42, no. 1, 2000, pp. 1–7.
11. *Software and Systems Text Track*, solicitation no. Reference-Number-BAA-06-13-IFKA-PART-2, Air Force Materiel Command, Dept. of the Air Force, AFRL: Rome Research Site, 2009; https://www.fbo.gov/index?s=opportunity&mode=form&id=355fbd80a0d621c61d5fe6f93cb13cca&tab=core&_cview=1.
12. "Crusader," *GlobalSecurity.org*; www.globalsecurity.org/military/systems/ground/crusader.htm.

The Practitioner's Tale

The following story was told to us by a government program manager with decades of experience at leading software development teams. This manager had first-hand experience (and frustration) with the *actual world problems* we discuss in this essay. In our retelling of the tale, we have scrubbed certain identifying information to protect the guilty. With the exception of this and some minor editorial changes and paraphrasing, we retell this real-life account in the practitioner's own words.

The job at an aviation radar facility was to ensure safety by coordinating aviation operations. Though the analog scopes worked well, they were hard wired. It was difficult to integrate the data. The operators wanted more flexibility. So a contractor was tasked to create a totally new radar facility—the building, the system, the scopes, the operations floor, the works—with one large screen, one large computer to integrate the data.

So, at the Preliminary Design Review, they set the ground rules. Developers had to follow the government specifications. They had to use a waterfall development model. It was a nightmare. Everything had to be modular, so the people who built the new building never talked to the people who would use it—the people who were still using the old scopes at the old building. The old building, with the current operators, stood less than 100 yards away, but no one ever went over to find out how the operators performed their jobs.

The new facility was built and the users came in. They took one look at the new radar picture and knew it was wrong. For instance, the code was generating bogus tracks due to weather. The operator could not credibly keep the real tracks clear. The procurement people had followed the rules: do the specifications and build to the requirements by government specifications. The result was trash.

So they brought in my team to fix the code. We looked at the code and predicted its failure modes, which the operators subsequently confirmed but hadn't spoken up about. Our team said the new building was OK, the big screen was OK, but everything else had to go, especially a lot of the software. But the parts of the code that had to be trashed could not be isolated. Though it had been modularized, it relied on a shared memory. Overwrites and shares meant that the functions could not be split out—like trying to remove an octopus from a barrel of them without disturbing any of the others. The developers had violated the intent of the rules because they followed the rules blindly.

The program manager asked what they would have to do to replace it all. Our team had anticipated this. We had to work with the actual operators to find the intent of the coded rules. Our coders needed to understand the needs of the radar operators. We sent some junior engineers to the site, telling them, "Go there, get training, and come back when you have reached the point where the director would say he would let you do the actual job."

That took about three weeks. With their input, our team reached agreement on what the system really needed to do, using the operator's jargon. The engineers came back two weeks later with a summary document that made sense. Then they went back to the operators again and got a list of their "desirements" that could be incorporated in the rebuild. We played a set of older mission data into the new tracker. Our team was able to craft the look and feel that the operators wanted. We checked the buttonology with the operators and had the first build in three months.

The program manager said we could not write code prior to the Preliminary Design Review. That would be a violation of the government-specified waterfall. The intent of that is to not write code before the problem is specified. But our development team already knew more about the problem than the procurement and contracting people. The project directors set these ground rules; we were going to do it their way. But when we got to the Critical Design Review (when you decide on the hardware), our team was told we had to decide on the machines and the operating system. We said "No! The technology is improving too fast." We wanted to test the alternative hardware later on. In a few months there would be better computers available and a compiler extension that would simplify the code and make compilation easier in the long run.

The program director was aghast. But our team continued in another refinement of the build. One desirement was for a training capability, the reuse of tough cases. We did some of that, at no extra cost. We tested a rebuild, delivered it, and it went operational. Some operators came over from the old analog facility. One said he could not do his job with the new screen. But we were prepared. Our system had tools to develop screens, because we had anticipated the need. We had built in the flexibility. So this operator came in the next day and we had made the screen he wanted. He was shocked, and loved it. "How did you do that so fast?" That's what our screen development tools allowed.

A radar facility at another location had also started all over to recreate a new system. But they were not learning from the users. They fell back on the rules and the comfortable process. Some operators that had worked with our team moved to this other location and called in our team to observe and help. (Our team had made the software so that it could be exported to other facilities.)

Then there was some new leadership on the government side. People started moving to our new spiral model, which by then our team had been using for some years. Users cannot specify requirements, as these are understood by software people. Users can specify their needs and their desirements. Now, people were starting to do this, but we saw a tendency for them to warp this new approach back into their traditional procedures. You need to go by the intent of the rules, not the rules themselves.

13. *Experimentation and Rapid Prototyping in Support of Counterterrorism*, Committee on Experimentation and Rapid Prototyping in Support of Counterterrorism, National Research Council, 2009.
14. K. Osborn, "Bolton: U.S. Army Should Keep Pursuing Rapid Acquisitions," *Defense News*, 14 Jan. 2008; www.mail-archive.com/osint@yahoogroups.com/msg52830.html.
15. *Defense Programs: Opportunities to Reform Key Business Practices*, GAO/NSIAD-97-99R, Nat'l Security and Int'l Affairs Division, General Accounting Office, 1997; http://archive.gao.gov/paprpdf1/158389.pdf.
16. H. Sapolsky, "Let's Skip Acquisition Reform This Time," *Defense News*, 8 Feb. 2009; www.defensenews.com/story.php?i=3938405.
17. "UK: Acquisitions—Fewer Buyers but Failure Rate Steady," *Management Today*, 1 Mar. 1993; www.managementtoday.co.uk/search/article/409368/uk-acquisitions-fewer-buyers-failure-rate-steady.
18. R. Frese and V. Sauter, "Project Success and Failure: What Is Success, What Is Failure, and How Can You Improve Your Odds for Success?" white paper, College of Business Administration, University of Missouri–St. Louis, 2003; www.umsl.edu/~sauterv/analysis/6840_f03_papers/frese.
19. Knowledge@Wharton, "Gadgets at Work: The Blurring Boundary between Consumer and Corporate Technologies," *Technology First*, Jan. 2009; www.technologyfirst.org/magazine-articles/45-january-2009/325-g.
20. J.R. Lindsay, "War upon the Map: The Politics of Military User Innovation," doctoral dissertation, Dept. of Political Science, Massachusetts Inst. of Technology, 2006; www.mit.edu/~lindsayj/Projects/WarUponTheMap%20v30.pdf.

Steven V. Deal is vice president and systems engineer at Deal Corp. Contact him at s.deal@sbcglobal.net.

Robert R. Hoffman is a senior research scientist at the Institute for Human and Machine Cognition. Contact him at rhoffman@ihmc.us.

Chapter 39: The Practitioner's Cycles, Part 2: Solving Envisioned World Problems

R.R. Hoffman, S.V. Deal, S. Potter, and E.M. Roth, "The Practitioner's Cycles, Part 2: Solving Envisioned World Problems," *IEEE Intelligent Systems*, vol. 25, no. 3, May/June 2010, pp. 6–11. doi: 10.1109/MIS.2010.89

Previous Human-Centered Computing department articles have reflected on the mismatch that can occur between the promise of intelligent technology and the results of technological interventions. Part 1 on the Practitioner's Cycles illustrated ways in which actual world problems—the forces and constraints of procurement—are at odds with the goals of human centering. This article culminated in a practitioner's tale, in which individuals acted on their own initiative and at their own risk, short-circuiting the rules and constraints that limit success at procurement. This paper presents a model based on the tale and focuses on how the model applies to envisioned world problems—the creation of intelligent technologies for new work systems.

The Practitioner's Cycles, Part 2: Solving Envisioned World Problems

Robert R. Hoffman, *IHMC*
Steven V. Deal, *Deal Corporation*
Scott Potter, *Charles River Analytics*
Emilie M. Roth, *Roth Cognitive Engineering*

Previous Human-Centered Computing department articles have reflected on the mismatch that can occur between the promise of intelligent technology and the results of technological interventions.[1,2] Part 1 of this article on the Practitioner's Cycles illustrated ways in which actual world problems—the forces and constraints of procurement—are at odds with the goals of human centering.[3] That article culminated in a practitioner's tale, in which individuals acted on their own initiative and at their own risk, short-circuiting the rules and constraints that limit success at procurement.

This Part 2 presents a model based on the tale and focuses on how the model applies to envisioned world problems—the creation of intelligent technologies for new work systems.

Envisioned World Problems

New technologies are hypotheses about the effects of interventions on macrocognitive work patterns.[4] New technology, especially intelligent technology, always triggers unanticipated changes in cognitive and collaborative work.[5] This being the case, the handover of a deliverable cannot be the end of procurement; it must be the beginning of a next wave of empirical research, to ensure that cognitive work changes for the better. In addition, the expertise of the current work's practitioners will not necessarily carry over into the envisioned world, raising a significant expertise gap and an associated training challenge.

Does this mean that procurement will actually take longer than it does now? We think not. One reason is that acquisition is actually much longer than plans and charts say it is.[3] Our substantive argument is that a different sort of process could shorten acquisition, if we define it as the time between identifying a need and fielding a response.

The Current Procurement Process

Currently, the procurement process organizes and funds its trajectory as a series of discrete activities where a system is conceived, designed, built, tested, fielded, refurbished, upgraded, redesigned, retired, and replaced (and repeat). This is the approach advocated by practitioners of the Spiral and Waterfall models.[6,7]

Researchers have discussed numerous variations of these models in the literature, including the Rapid Prototyping[7] and Incremental Commitment[8] models. The Spiral model repeats the basic activities of planning, prototyping, testing, and client evaluation. In the Waterfall approach, steps are taken in interactive pairs. For instance, software requirements analysis feeds into a preliminary design, but efforts at that second step might feed back into software requirements analysis, leading to changes in the requirements. In addition, each step includes a review process to assess progress and evaluate risk. In following the Waterfall process, engineers decompose a system into subsystems that are treated in progressively greater detail, using diagrams, spreadsheets, and statements that enable manufacturers and software developers to cut metal or write code.

Neither traditional Spirals nor Waterfalls explicitly embrace the role of cognitive work analysis and the requirement that it be conducted before, during, and after replanning as well as throughout the system development effort. Developers should begin system design and development with cognitive task analysis to understand the current work and then continue investigating the envisioned world as new technologies and work methods are created and tested.[9,10]

Successfully Applying Cognitive Work Analysis

A project aimed at developing new intelligent systems for weather forecasting and monitoring in a military airlift command and control organization provides a case study that clearly shows the value of cognitive analyses.[11,12] Scott Potter, Emilie Roth, and their colleagues conducted cognitive work analyses that revealed the knowledge and strategies that forecasters employed to generate weather forecasts and monitor weather conditions. These analyses included field studies where cognitive systems engineers shadowed forecasters as they developed forecasts and interacted with personnel responsible for mission planning and execution. They also conducted structured interviews with weather forecasters and other stakeholders in the organization to elicit first-person perspectives with respect to the challenges they faced and the opportunities they saw to enhance operational effectiveness.

The work identified leverage points where performance improvements in weather forecasting and monitoring could have substantial operational impact (such as fewer mission delays and cancellations). They also discovered areas where integrated visualizations and automated alerts would enable forecasters to more finely tailor their forecasts and more quickly detect mission-relevant weather changes.

In a series of prototype and test activities, weather forecasters were encouraged to work with the software and provide feedback on prototypes of increasing maturity. With each design and test cycle, the prototypes became successively more comprehensive and accurately tuned to forecaster requirements. At the same time, the test conditions became successively more representative of actual situations that forecasters confront. The prototype eventually reached a level of maturity where it became operationally useful. The forecasters then requested that the developers leave the prototype in place to be used in actual operation.

As it happened, the pace of operations in the forecasting center dramatically increased over the development period. Hence, developers identified some requirements that had been previously missed as well as new, emerging requirements. These stimulated additional design and evaluation cycles. A parallel activity was initiated to implement the prototype concepts in a new module within the legacy system. Ultimately, this allowed for a graceful transition from the legacy work to a more sustainable capability within a system of record.

Practitioner's tales such as this have contributed to ideas about how to innovate procurement. One of these innovations, the *Incremental Commitment model*,[8] is a new approach to spiral development. This model recognizes the role of participatory analysis and usability analysis. Furthermore, in the Spiral model's operating, architecting, and development steps, products are released to operators and user experiences are used to inform architecture evolution and continued development.

The Practitioner's Cycles

The practitioner's tale in Part 1 told how a project leader took the initiative, deviated from mandated processes and rules (while appreciating their intent) and met with success. We hasten to point out that this approach is not a singular anomaly. A related approach, called *user innovation*,[13] is exemplified in the project that resulted in the FalconView standard for the US government's digital mapping. The FalconView moving map software application was created by the US Air National Guard F-16 community based on its need for automated planning tools.[14] It was not created by vendors.

Figures 1 through 5 show the five cycles that can be found in the practitioner's tale. (A single diagram that integrates all five cycles is available from the first author upon request.)

The prototype (see Figure 5) was not merely "good enough;" it was better in some respects than their legacy system. Across the cycles, the old world of practice faded away as the envisioned world emerged. Over time, it was the legacy system that began to collect dust. At that point, the new prototype was declared ready for operational testing. Furthermore, the envisioned world included a cohort of individuals who had learned within the evolving system context and could subsequently train and mentor another cohort.

What's Different?

Spiral models, as generally understood, present a sequence of activities that repeats a traverse through supplier activities. In contrast, each of the practitioner's cycles presents a trajectory through workplace activities. The work of designers is aligned with the work of the users for whom they are designing; that is, the work of both is macrocognitive. In all forms of complex macrocognitive work, activities are continuous and highly interacting, not just concurrent.[15–18]

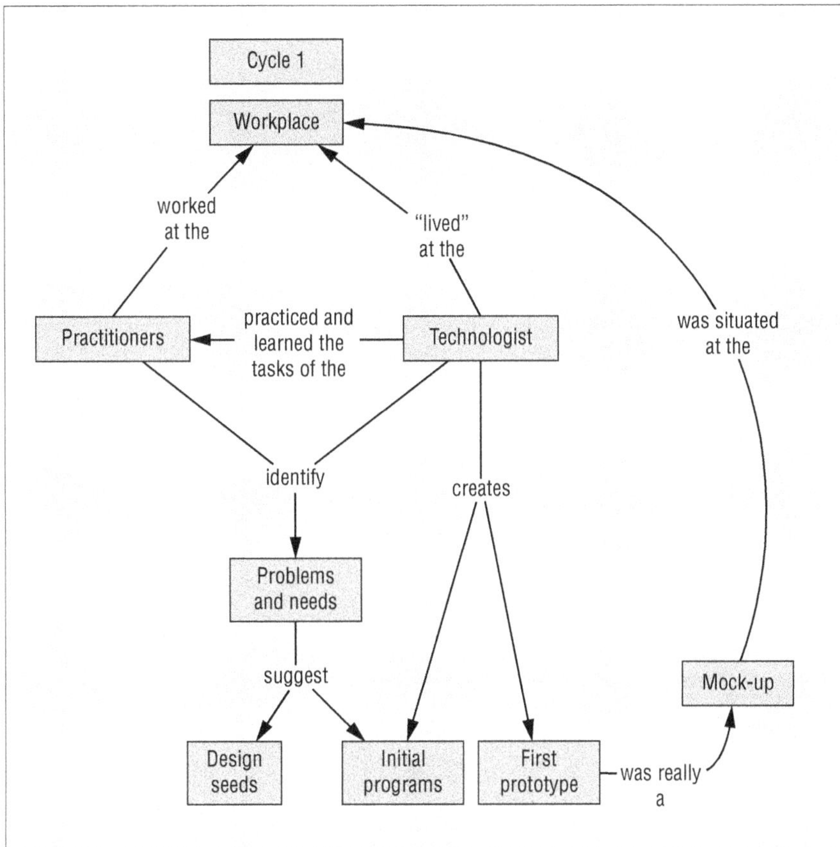

Figure 1. Cycle one of the Practitioner's Cycles.

Core processes of sense-making, coordinating, mental projection, and the like are parallel; they are not delimited by schedules or tools. Designers hardly stop thinking about design when someone checks off a milestone on some chart. Planners hardly stop replanning once they have closed a spreadsheet.

Advantages

Throughout system development, there must be continual evaluations of usefulness, usability, and understandability. The intent of the Practitioner's Cycles approach is to fold as much of this as possible into the development process. Worker discovery and expression of useful functions is necessary for achieving useful, usable, and understandable capabilities.

The Practitioner's Cycles approach might support the evolution of mission needs better than any alternative model by rapidly putting new capabilities into worker's hands. The evolutionary improvement path rewards resilient, extensible architectures, and it accommodates evolution of the cognitive work. The process could be highly responsive to changing markets and competitors. Testing in the workplace would assure a validated result and might eliminate adjunct cost surprises during manufacturing and logistics. Investment and capabilities can be strongly linked—you pay for what you need, and you get what you pay for.

Because the exploration of the envisioned world is situated in the operational environment, worker satisfaction becomes the focus, and the performance benchmark of operational metrics is ever-present. Risks that have been introduced by isolating developers from the workforce are retired. The value of the evolving capability should be apparent to managers, maintainers, and other stakeholders. The maintainers, who have customarily been relied on to service the legacy system, also shape the envisioned world through their impacts to the new system design.

The Practitioner's Cycles has implications for the management of project funding. Sponsors could set up an annual budget and fund development through a series of task orders targeted at adding capabilities. Together, stakeholders and the design team would identify the next pressing need, describe it in a proposal, and rapidly receive funding. Progress toward the task order goal would be easy to evaluate because the prototypes could be implemented gradually, and the sponsor, seeing the improvements, could both perceive and measure return on investment by operational performance gains and user satisfaction.

Limitations

As with any system development model, the Practitioner's Cycles model is no panacea. As always, momentum from designer-centered design approaches can always reemerge and be difficult to overcome. Programmatic emphasis on management and technical control processes, or on the technology itself, can undermine the goals of human centering—that is, getting useful, usable, understandable systems, and beyond-the-horizon-desired capabilities quickly to the worker.

The Practitioner's Cycles approach is not like crossing a finish line. The Waterfall and Spiral models look at the problem, then focus on delivering technology to stakeholders and close out the project. The Practitioner's Cycles emphasizes human centering and recognizes that relevance and effectiveness depend on a continuous evolutionary approach.

And this brings us to our final argument.

How Did We Get into This Mess?

Development models supporting procurement were devised to coordinate and evaluate the efforts of large teams. Risk management—of spending too much money, taking too long, or generating an unnecessary or unacceptable system—is at the core of most development models. For both Spiral and Waterfall modeling, a verification methodology is specified at the time that requirements and specifications are crafted. Software is subjected to reviews that are progressively more integrated, going from configured item to operational system. The engineering advantage of this is that the hardware and software developers have a means of determining when they've adequately completed the predefined task. But why are reviews necessitated? The risk that the product will not satisfy operator needs is created by segregating the development team from the system operators.

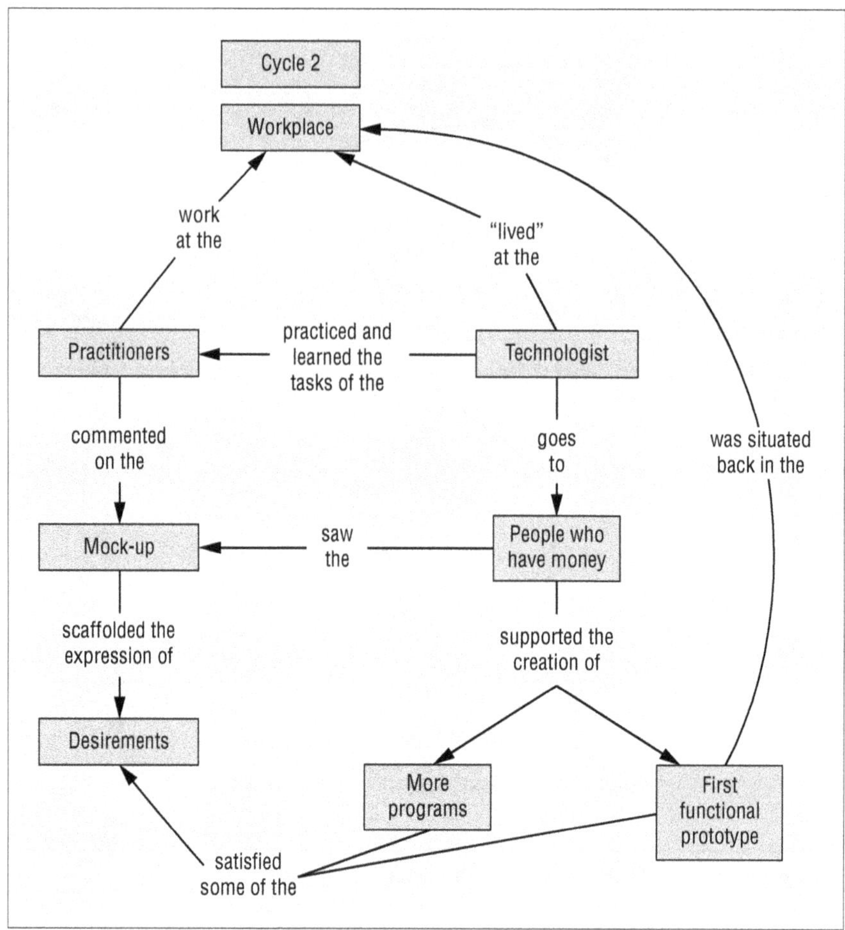

Figure 2. Cycle two of the Practitioner's Cycles.

Of course, there must be a means for manufacturers and reviewers to assess that the job has been done correctly and executed to greatest advantage. However, the precise statement of requirements, combined with a strictly followed Spiral or Waterfall process, lets software engineers abrogate responsibility, or not see it as part of their job description. If the software ends up being glitchy or otherwise defective, the developer can simply say, "Hey, we built to the requirements."

The Practitioner's Cycles approach highlights the view that excellence is achieved by tailoring the system to environmental and worker demands, artistically balancing goal conflicts and competing demands, and paying as you go. So while some might regard this approach as radical, we hold that is a return to the model that was in place prior to industrialization and mass production—the artisan's approach to work.

An Artisan's Approach

A master craftsman begins as an apprentice, becomes a journeyman, and after creating a masterpiece, earns the title of master.[19] Journeymen setting out on their own would've had the resources and essential tools to set up a shop. As they gained experience, they would devise and create their own specialty tools designed to speed up production, ease the workload, or improve safety. The tools would change as the articles their clients brought in changed with the times, or as the craftsmen conceived improvements. At guild meetings, they might have been made aware of new technologies or tools that would further improve their return and would craft those.

Nothing the craftsmen used as a tool would be regarded as a finished article. It might be retired in favor of a better concept or replaced because of wear, but the craftsmen's work continued. They employed a build-and-test method and discarded the items that didn't meet their needs. It was likely that some of the tools developed were incomplete before being used on the job. This cycle of conception, implementation, test, and improvement was organic to successful craftsmen. It was an approach that led to success and assured a steady stream of customers.

In the industrial era, the craftsman's shop gave way to the machine shop, and connections between tool inventor and worker started to break down. In the 200 years since, the connection has been broken further, the distance between developer and user

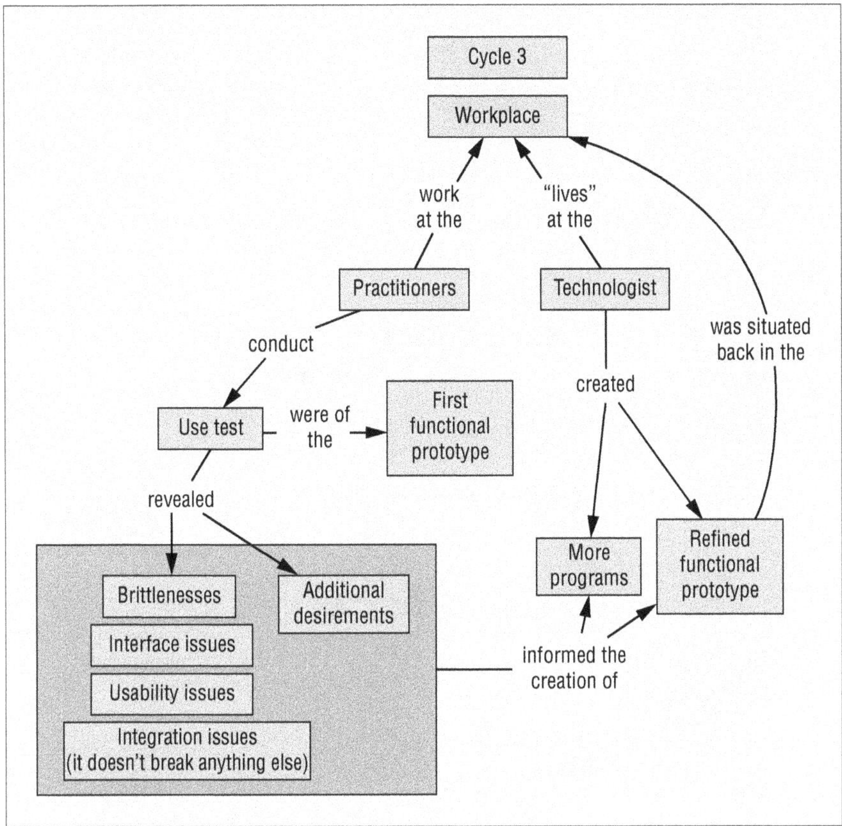

Figure 3. Cycle three of the Practitioner's Cycles.

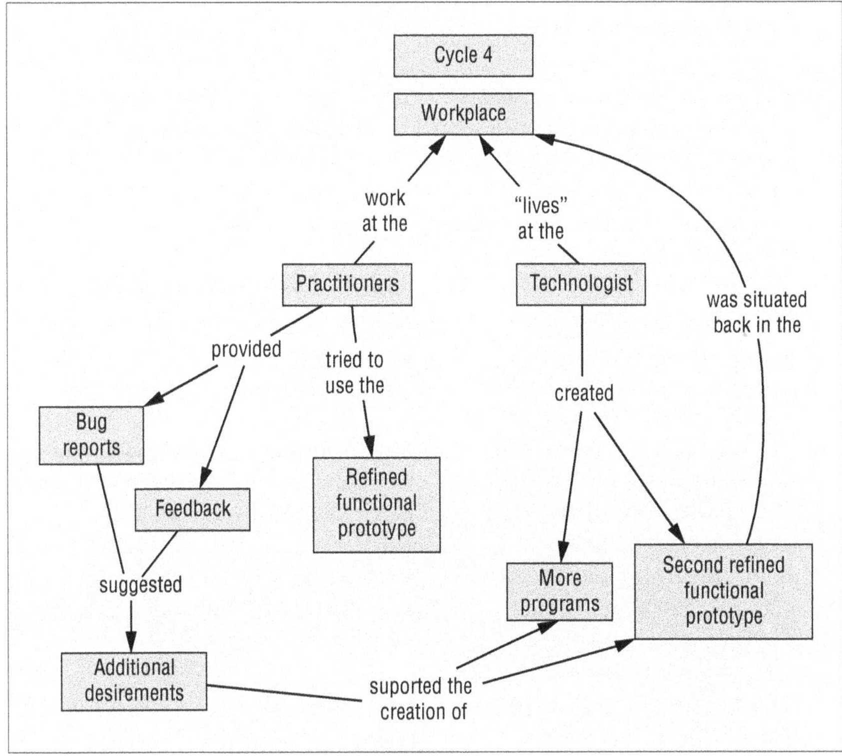

Figure 4. Cycle four of the Practitioner's Cycles.

has grown. Today's acquisition system takes the artistry out of creation by relying on procedures that foster the abrogation of responsibilities and that create goal conflicts. The artistry gets stifled due to burdens of statute, truckloads of documentation, and organization forms that poorly integrate specialist expertise and user perspectives. It seems that the actual goal of acquisition is to take degrees of freedom out of the development process and restrict the ability of technologists to respond with experience to the unique situation that each project presents, while still expecting excellence to result. By removing the artistry, the procurement process limits the capacity of technologists to be flexible to the context of changing circumstances and emerging opportunities.

The moral of the practitioner's tale is that hardware and software engineering might be thought of as a scientific and mathematical approach to artisanship. The advantage we see in the Practitioner's Cycles model is that it suggests one way of bringing artisanship back into the procurement process—and getting human-centered intelligent systems to users more expeditiously.

Current procurement methods were based on a logic of appropriateness and were developed in parallel with bureaucracies that were meant to allow nonartisans to perform at a minimally acceptable level of functionality through standardization of procedures and functions. Is it likely that industry and government will ever be willing to take on the risk of escaping the bureaucratic mindset and begin the cultivation of artisans? ■

References

1. R.R. Hoffman and S.V. Deal, "Influencing versus Informing Design, Part 1: A Gap Analysis," *IEEE Intelligent Systems*, vol. 23, no. 5, 2008, pp. 72–75.

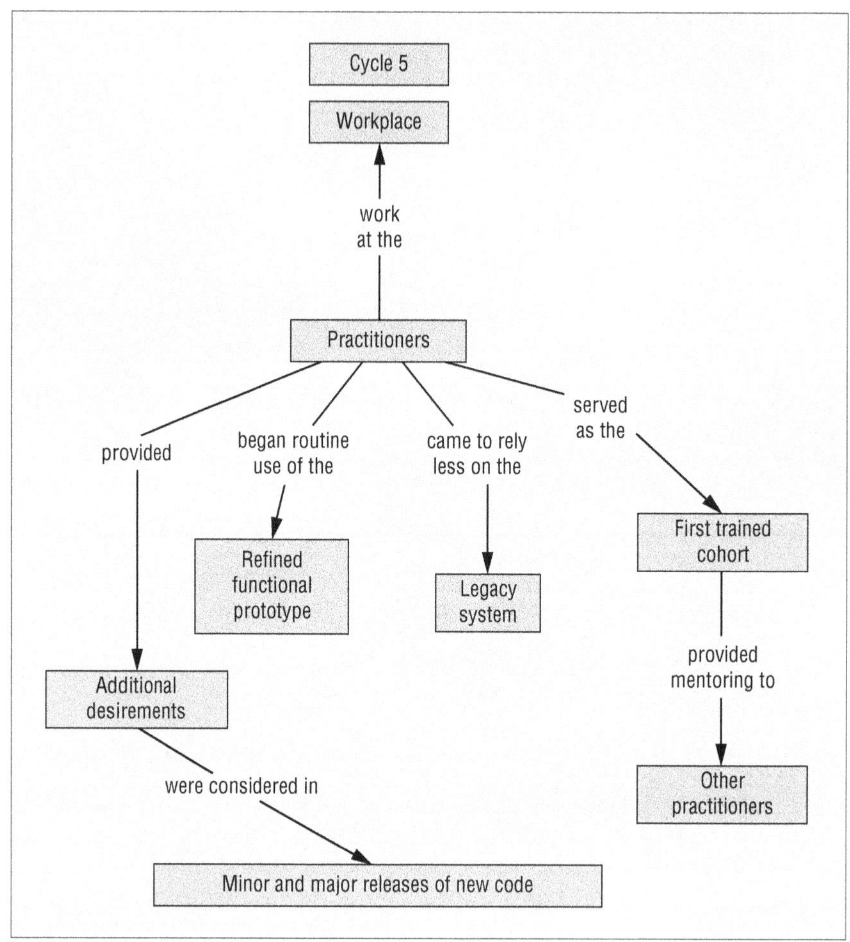

Figure 5. Cycle five of the Practitioner's Cycles.

2. K. Neville et al., "The Procurement Woes Revisited," *IEEE Intelligent Systems*, vol. 23, no. 1, 2008, pp. 72–75.
3. S. Deal and R.R. Hoffman, "The Practitioner's Cycles, Part 1: The Actual World Problem," *IEEE Intelligent Systems*, vol. 25, no. 2, 2010, pp. 4–9.
4. D.D. Woods and S.W.A. Dekker, "Anticipating the Effects of Technology Change: A New Era of Dynamics for Human Factors," *Theoretical Issues in Ergonomics Science*, vol. 1, no. 3, 2001, pp. 272–282.
5. R.R. Hoffman and D.D. Woods, "Studying Cognitive Systems in Context," *Human Factors*, vol. 42, no. 1, 2000, pp. 1–7.
6. A. Behforooz and F.J. Hudson, *Software Engineering Fundamentals*, Oxford Univ. Press, 1996, chapt. 1.
7. S.R. Schach, *Object-Oriented and Classical Software Engineering*, McGraw-Hill, 1996.
8. R.W. Pew and A.S. Mavor, *Human-System Integration in the System Development Process: A New Look*, Nat'l Academy Press, 2007.
9. R.G. Eggleston, E.M. Roth, and R. Scott, "A Framework for Work-Centered Product Evaluation," *Proc. Human Factors and Ergonomics Soc. 47th Ann. Meeting*, Human Factors and Ergonomics Soc., 2003, pp. 503–507.
10. S.S. Potter et al., "Bootstrapping multiple converging cognitive task analysis techniques for system design," *Cognitive Task Analysis*, J.M. Schraagen and S.F. Chipman, eds., 2000, Erlbaum, pp. 317–340.
11. R. Scott et al., "Work-Centered Support Systems: A Human-Centered Approach to Intelligent System Design," *IEEE Intelligent Systems*, vol. 20, no. 2, 2005, pp. 73–81.
12. E. Roth et al., "Evolvable Work-Centered Support Systems for Command and Control: Creating Systems Users Can Adapt to Meet Changing Demands," *Ergonomics*, vol. 49, 2006, pp. 688–705.
13. E. Von Hippel, *The Sources of Innovation*, Oxford Univ. Press, 1988.
14. J.R. Lindsay, "War Upon the Map: The Politics of Military User Innovation," doctoral dissertation, Dept. of Political Science, Massachusetts Inst. of Technology, 2006.
15. S.W.A. Dekker, J.M. Nyce, and R.R. Hoffman, "From Contextual Inquiry to Designable Futures: What Do We Need to Get There?" *IEEE Intelligent Systems*, vol. 18, no. 2, 2003, pp. 74–77.
16. R.R. Hoffman and W.C. Elm, "HCC Implications for the Procurement Process," *IEEE Intelligent Systems*, vol. 21, no. 1, 2006, pp. 74–81.
17. R.R. Hoffman, A. Roesler, and B.M. Moon, "What Is Design in the Context of Human-Centered Computing?" *IEEE Intelligent Systems*, vol. 19, no. 4, 2004, pp. 89–95.
18. G. Klein et al., "Macrocognition," *IEEE Intelligent Systems*, vol. 18, no. 3, 2003, pp. 81–85.
19. G. Renard, *Guilds in the Middle Ages*, A.M. Kelley, 1968.

Robert R. Hoffman is a senior research scientist at the Institute for Human and Machine Cognition. Contact him at rhoffman@ihmc.us.

Steven V. Deal is vice president and systems engineer at Deal Corporation. Contact him at s.deal@sbcglobal.net.

Scott Potter is research scientist at Charles River Analytics. Contact him at spotter@cra.com.

Emilie Roth is principal scientist of Roth Cognitive Engineering. Contact him at emroth@mindspring.com.

Chapter 40: The Practitioner's Cycles, Part 3: Implementation Opportunities

S.V. Deal and R.R. Hoffman, "The Practitioner's Cycles, Part 3: Implementation Opportunities," *IEEE Intelligent Systems*, vol. 25, no. 5, Sep./Oct. 2010, pp. 77–81. doi: 10.1109/MIS.2010.129

The Practitioner's Cycles Part 1 illustrated ways in which actual world problems—the forces and constraints of procurement—are at odds with the goals of a human-centered approach. In Part 2, we presented an application of the Practitioner's Cycles model to envisioned world problems—the creation of intelligent technologies for new work systems. (See the "Synopsis of the Practitioner's Cycles" sidebar for a quick review.) This essay (Part 3) describes formative implementations of the Practitioner's Cycles. We propose the Practitioner's Cycles concept as a solution to the simultaneous problems of maturing new technologies and rapidly transitioning those technologies into new products.

The Practitioner's Cycles, Part 3: Implementation Opportunities

Steven V. Deal, *Deal Corporation*
Robert R. Hoffman, *IHMC*

The Practitioner's Cycles Part 1 illustrated ways in which actual world problems—the forces and constraints of procurement—are at odds with the goals of a human-centered approach.[1] In Part 2, we presented an application of the Practitioner's Cycles model to envisioned world problems—the creation of intelligent technologies for new work systems.[2] (See the "Synopsis of the Practitioner's Cycles" sidebar for a quick review.) This essay (Part 3) describes formative implementations of the Practitioner's Cycles. We propose the Practitioner's Cycles concept as a solution to the simultaneous problems of maturing new technologies and rapidly transitioning those technologies into new products.

The Importance of First-Mover Advantage—Rapid Fielding

Being first to market is often all the advantage an organization needs to dominate competitors.[3] Because some organizations are unable to capitalize on the favorable strategic position, however, this is not a guarantee of long-term market supremacy. However, first-mover advantage provides the high ground from which resources can be manipulated to weaken, bracket, and eliminate competitors. Commercial firms have developed techniques such as rapid application development, design patterns, and set-based concurrent engineering;[4] integrated modular design;[5] and plug-n-play architectures largely with the view of achieving speed to market.

In military systems, the problem addressed by first-mover advantage is expressed in terms of difficulties in the rapid fielding of new capabilities. Stephen Welby, the director of systems engineering in the Office of the Director of Defense Research and Engineering, expresses the problem in this way: "Development takes too long, change takes too long, replacement takes too long. The environment is highly uncertain and complex."[6] Uncertainty and complexity collapse the required response time from tens of years to months or weeks.[7]

For both commercial and military systems, the importance of retaining process rigor while increasing speed of deployment is critical. Loss of rigor can result in disaffected customers, squandered investments, and lawsuits in the commercial world. In the military domain, it can result in

Synopsis of the Practitioner's Cycles

The development team is colocated with practitioners (the "users") and the maintainers. Together, they define needs and the initial concept. Practitioners have seeded development discussions with their ideas, as one seeds clouds to generate rain. Technologists develop an initial prototype—a mockup—that is situated and validated in the workplace. The mockup generates discussion, which bootstraps the next prototype. Additional funding supports a more mature prototype, which is again validated by practitioners. Subsequent cycles introduce user testing, revealing shortcomings and missing requirements, and more mature prototypes result. The prototype gradually insinuates itself into the practitioners' workflow. Those at the workplace become the first trained cohort as the prototype evolves to become a verified, valid, successful new product.

Table 1. Department of Defense technology readiness levels (TRLs).

TRL	Definition
1	Basic principles observed
2	Concept formulation
3	Proof of concept
4	Breadboard (experimental assembly for feasibility testing) in laboratory
5	Breadboard in representative environment
6	[Subsystem] Prototype in representative environment
7	System prototype in operational environment
8	System qualified
9	Mission proven

unusable implementations that are poorly coordinated with other capabilities and enterprise requirements and that waste taxpayer dollars.

Technology Transition Challenges

New technologies must move through a trajectory from basic research to a mature application. The final steps from applied research to a mature application are customarily the most difficult to achieve. Table 1 presents the US Defense Department's technology readiness level schema, one of several ways to view the technology transition trajectory.

Technology readiness levels (TRLs) 1 through 3 are considered basic research. At TRL 3, feasibility has been demonstrated. The path from TRL 3 to TRL 7 is often referred to as the "valley of death."[8] Organizations with demanding operational needs are reluctant to include conceptual technologies when developing essential capabilities. Doing so has too often resulted in costly delays and compromises in the desired capability. This tendency to avoid new technologies is most notable in space systems where a paradigm exists that precludes incorporating technologies that have not been previously qualified for space.

The valley-of-death phenomenon results in frustrated practitioners who are unable to employ new technologies in a timely fashion and in stymied researchers whose inventions have no path to application.

Models for Implementation

Implementation of the Practitioner's Cycles concept strongly depends on the context of the business environment. We offer two concrete examples to show that the Practitioner's Cycles need not be viewed as revolutionary.

A Model for Commercial Implementation

Durable goods and information technology goods firms have developed cost-saving techniques for rapidly developing and producing products. In the durable goods arena, the Toyota Production System and the Toyota Product Development System have, until recently, been exemplars of efficiently delivering products to market. The production system creates a "community of scientists" that continuously applies the scientific method.[9] Administrators ask questions that spur the team to solve manufacturing problems. The product development system also creates a community of engineering scientists whose materials are knowledge and information. Product development cycles are measured in weeks and months, which is similar to the US Defense Department's stated needs.

IT manufacturers have also developed techniques for rapidly bringing products to market. Rapid development techniques (such as agile, Extreme Programming, and joint application development) are intended to accelerate software development, reduce cost risk, and maintain process rigor. They depend on prototypes of increasing fidelity, effective team communication, collaboration, and requirements management by user prioritization. The rapid and joint application development methods explicitly include customers in feature identification and test definition. Extreme programming requires developers to work in pairs; this method has sometimes been implemented with client employees comprising half the pair. Most rapid processes feature short development cycles that conclude with product delivery to customers, who then must implement the product in their organization.

It is not difficult to conceive implementations of the Toyota and rapid techniques that would move processes closer to the domain practitioner. If automobile drivers were to be included in the incremental build-up of a prototype model—defining, advising on construction, and evaluating the emergent system to the point where the new model supplants the one in current use—the result would be the Practitioner's Cycles.

This could be done by implementing the Practitioner's Cycles at a dealership. Assuming important logistics issues could be worked out, there might be considerable competitive advantages. For example, executing portions of the process publicly could be a marketing advantage, demonstrating the emphasis the company places on aligning products with customer desires. Additionally, the speed with which the process lets the development team sift through the trade space and select features and technologies that drivers value would decrease the likelihood that a competitor could appropriate the design. The competitor would have to move even more rapidly to produce a knock-off and preemptively get it to market.

In the IT domain, rapid techniques could be implemented at the client's facility. Instead of handing off a CD at the end of a cycle, the new system would be developed in parallel with operational systems and employed by domain practitioners at the earliest opportunity. Then, as with the automobile example, the Practitioner's Cycles concept would have been implemented. The characteristic transparency and employee involvement would also generate secondary benefits to the client firm. Employees would gain insight into the firm's integrated processes. The firm would cohere as a team. Middle managers and employees would take ownership of the changes catalyzed by the new system. There would be shared pride in the accomplished product.

A Model for Military Implementation

It is a considerable understatement to say that the US Defense Acquisition process mandates rigorous supervision. The process operates under the constant tension between the need for oversight to mitigate risk and the goal of reducing development time.

System reform oscillates between doing research in-house versus outsourcing. The former can lead to poor quality (because there are no external controls on quality and no real competition), and the latter can lead to contractor excesses (because the few internal researchers do not have the skills to adequately evaluate and control contractor results). The best of the internal researchers end up leaving (in normal economic times) because they want to do something more than contract monitoring.

Another oscillatory aspect of system reform has to do with this tension between the need to reinvigorate—a buzzword for adding documentation and review requirements—and the need to streamline.[10] The latter has become so compelling in the face of a rapidly adaptive adversary, that a "rapid acquisition authority" has been established to "ensure that the needed equipment is acquired and deployed as quickly as possible."[11] The need for comprehensive oversight is necessitated by the functional separation of acquisition personnel—those purchasing the product from practitioners who will use the product.

The following is a notional example of a Practitioner's Cycles response to a deficiency in military capability that resulted in combat casualties. Immediately after an urgent operational need has been validated—a process that can take days or weeks—a solution team is resourced with an initial response team that consists of a small management and technologist staff resourced to implement the cycles process at a point as close to the operational site as possible. The greater the separation between the military fighter and the technical team, the greater the risk that the solution will fail to meet all operational demands and be delayed. The initial response team executes the first cycle by generating a mockup of the solution.

The mockup serves to identify the additional resourcing required to generate the functional prototypes in subsequent cycles. It helps management plan subsequent cycles, estimate and request funding, and begin addressing the process requirements of the Joint Capabilities Identification and Development System. The management team's primary responsibility is to ensure clear lines of communication remain open between technologists and practitioners; the larger the practitioner-technologist team, the greater this effort will be for project manager.

By the third cycle, a prototype suitable for practitioner testing and system-of-systems evaluations exists. By the fourth cycle, a prototype suitable for the field exists. A manufacturing contractor is onsite to define requirements for scaling up from prototype production. This accelerated achievement has been made possible because of the intimate involvement of military personnel in prototype definition and the operational urgency of getting the capability into the field. By the fifth cycle, military personnel who contributed to capability development are already familiar with its use, and units are being supplied to the field. Minor capability refinements can be initiated as required. Associated legacy capabilities are retired because they are no longer acceptable when compared against the new product's functionality.

Each of the cycles could be independently funded, which reduces risk. Practitioners, managers, and service decision makers decide jointly when the product is sufficiently mature to allow development to slow its pace or to cease. This enables the efficient allocation of resources to problems with the greatest priority.

This example describes the process for an urgent need, but we believe the Practitioner's Cycles can also be effectively implemented for all major defense acquisition programs. For example, a warship's overall design could be developed in conjunction with practitioners executing similar missions. Hull design mockups and prototypes would be developed in collaboration with practitioners who would be responsible for maneuvering it and who would eventually maintain it. Practitioners would staff the development team because their expertise, either in operations or sustainment, is required to define and evaluate the emerging prototypes. If this approach were adopted, a task force from the Office of the Secretary of Defense could revisit documentation and oversight requirements to establish the minimum necessary to ensure delivery of operationally suitable, safe, and effective capabilities.

Simultaneously Solving Rapid Fielding and Technology Transfer Challenges

We have so far described the cycles in terms of first-mover benefits. The method also offers a pathway for rapidly maturing new technology. If we were to define the proximal-to-practitioner development location as a laboratory situated in a highly representative environment, then it is not too difficult to see that implementing the Practitioner's Cycles surmounts the valley-of-death obstacle. The initial mockup builds on the basic research proof of concept (TRL 3 in Table 1). TRL conditions four through seven are satisfied by the second, third, and fourth cycles in which prototypes are developed in a location that is simultaneously a laboratory (recall Toyota's "community of scientists"), a representative environment (the practitioner's workplace), and the operational environment.

System qualification is thus integrally accomplished as part of the development cycle as practitioners continue to work with and improve the prototype until it supplants the unacceptable legacy equipment or becomes a new capability in the practitioner's toolkit. A method of directly incorporating practitioner requirements and desires and holistically incorporating change from technical, planning, and funding perspectives virtually ensures the resultant product's ability to address mission needs. The new system has been globally optimized to the greatest extent possible. If this is not the case, the cycles development team is on hand to address remaining shortfalls.

Focused Demonstrations

Our description of the Practitioner's Cycles does not explicitly address the oversight that the Defense Department would characterize as process rigor. A focused demonstration could help to identify a minimum set of oversight processes and artifacts required to meet these organizational needs. Each of the two candidate demonstrations we describe here has potential for high business return and practitioner value. Both require disciplined multiorganizational coordination for success.

Candidate Demonstration One

Corporate business systems for accounting, travel planning, expense reporting, and collaboration are moving to a Web 2.0 paradigm. Unlike commercial social-networking products that evolve in response to consumer feedback, corporate workers are often at the mercy of software design teams who perform a one-time requirements collection and then develop in isolation from "end users." These systems regularly frustrate employees because the practitioners' desires have not been considered in development and their work needs remain unsupported. The result can be, and often is, hours of squandered productivity.

Imagine, instead, a development team that works at the same tasks the employees perform and then iteratively and collaboratively develops usable, understandable prototypes that incrementally replace systems that waste hours of time with ones that require only minutes.

Candidate Demonstration Two

The sensors of military intelligence systems produce data streams that overwhelm analysts' cognitive abilities. We assert that this is because sensor and information technology through TRL 4 have been developed without input from practitioners. Although this is appropriate for basic and applied research, the chasm between technical requirements and practitioner desires results in a transition valley of death.

Implementing the Practitioner's Cycles in the intelligence analysts' environment could increase the value of new technologies in application by inculcating the practitioner's perspectives in laboratory technologists and the design team.

Codicil

In this series of three essays, we have described how the Practitioner's Cycles might—and we believe can—solve real-world and envisioned world problems. Applying the cycles to their implementation will strengthen the method so that it demonstrably serves speed to market, technology transition, and process rigor. Looking across the 40 articles that have appeared in this department, it would seem that the core stance of human-centered computing has forced a consideration of procurement issues. Articles have presented a great many of the "procurement woes" that have been expressed by researchers, and articles have proposed a number of solutions and ideas for a way forward. We do not expect the Practitioner's Tale to be the final story in this saga.■

References

1. S. Deal and R.R. Hoffman, "The Practitioner's Cycles, Part 1: The Actual World Problem," *IEEE Intelligent Systems*, vol. 25, no. 2, 2010, pp. 4–9.

2. R.R. Hoffman et al., "The Practitioner's Cycles, Part 2: Solving Envisioned World Problems," *IEEE Intelligent Systems*, vol. 25, no. 3, 2010, pp. 6–11.
3. T. Hatton, *Small Business Management, Entrepreneurship and Beyond*, Houghton Mifflin, 2003.
4. D.K. Sobek, II, A.C. Ward, and J.K. Liker, "Toyota's Principles of Set-Based Concurrent Engineering," *Sloan Management Rev.*, vol. 40, no. 2, 1999, pp. 67–83.
5. "Integrated Modular Avionics (IMA) Development Guidance and Certification Considerations," RTCA DO-297, RTCA Inc., 2005.
6. S. Welby, "DoD Systems Engineering Update," presentation at the Nat'l Defense Industrial Assoc. Systems Eng. Division Meeting, June 2010; www.ndia.org/Divisions/Divisions/SystemsEngineering/Pages.
7. D. Honey, "Address from the Research Office of the Director, Defense Research and Engineering, United States Air Force," presentation at the Wright Dialogue with Industry, Dayton Area Defense Contract Assoc., June 2010.
8. A. Vu, "Small Business Innovation Research/Small Business Technology Transfer Program," presentation at the Wright Dialogue with Industry, Dayton Area Defense Contract Assoc., June 2010.
9. J. Cleveland, "Toyota's Other System—This One for Product Development," *Automotive Design and Production*, Feb. 2006, pp. 18–22.
10. US Dept. of Defense, "Acquisition Documentation Streamlining Task Force," memorandum from principal deputy under secretary, Acquisition Technology and Logistics, 2010.
11. Acquisition Community Connection, "What Exactly Is 'Rapid Acquisition Authority'?" Defense Acquisition Univ., 2010; https://acc.dau.mil/CommunityBrowser.aspx?id=22114.

Robert R. Hoffman is a senior research scientist at the Institute for Human and Machine Cognition. Contact him at rhoffman@ihmc.us.

Steven V. Deal is vice president and systems engineer at Deal Corporation. Contact him at s.deal@sbcglobal.net.

Appendix A: Article Details

Part I: Human-Centered Computing Foundations and Principles

Chapter 1: Human-Centered Computing: Thinking In and Out of the Box

R.R. Hoffman, P.J. Hayes, and K.M. Ford, "Human-Centered Computing: Thinking In and Out of the Box," *IEEE Intelligent Systems*, vol. 16, no. 5, Sep./Oct. 2001, pp. 76–78. doi: 10.1109/5254.956085

The motion picture *AI* lets the AI profession squirm in the glory of misrepresentation. It's not fun, especially when one's field suffers from waves of innovation/hype/backlash. The problem is that the film *AI* reinforces the dream of the android just when many who work toward "truly" intelligent technologies are cutting loose from the dream's more surrealistic aspects. People are asking new questions: Is the Turing test really the right kind of standard? If not, what is better? Must we define intelligence in reference to humans? Must intelligent technology be boxes chock-full of this thing we call intelligence, or should it operate as a "cognitive orthosis" to amplify or extend human perceptual, cognitive, and collaborative capabilities? Must intelligence always be in some individual thing—either a headbone or a box—or is intelligence a system property that is definable only in terms of the triple of humans-machines-contexts?

Chapter 2: The State of Cognitive Systems Engineering

R.R. Hoffman, G. Klein, and K.R. Laughery, "The State of Cognitive Systems Engineering," *IEEE Intelligent Systems*, vol. 17, no. 1, Jan./Feb. 2002, pp. 73–75. doi: 10.1109/5254.988462

The widespread introduction of the personal computer, beginning about 1970, helped spawn the field of inquiry called cognitive engineering, which concerns itself with such things as interface design and user friendliness. Since then, this field has taught us many important things, including two major lessons. First, the road to user-hostile systems is paved with designers' user-centered intentions. Even smart, clever, well-intentioned people can build fragile, hostile devices that force the human to adapt and build local kludges and workarounds. Worse still, even if you are aware of this trap, you will still fall into it. Second, technology developers must strive to build truly human-centered systems. Machines should adapt to people, not the other way around. Machines should empower people. The process of designing machines should leverage what we know about human cognitive, perceptual, and collaborative skills.

Chapter 3: The Sacagawea Principle

M. Endsley and R.R. Hoffman, "The Sacagawea Principle," *IEEE Intelligent Systems*, vol. 17, no. 6, Nov./Dec. 2002, pp. 80–85. doi: 10.1109/MIS.2002.1134367

Many software tools and systems restrict the availability of information and make information integration and exploration difficult. Poorly designed tools are often brittle, because they prescribe task sequences. But in complex sociotechnical contexts, workers do not perform tasks; they engage in knowledge-driven, context-sensitive choices from among alternative activities in order to achieve goals. So, good tools must be flexible—they must provide the information that workers need to generate appropriate action sequences by which they can achieve the same goal in different situations. Adapted from the writings of Donald Norman is a principle we call the Sacagawea Principle: Human-centered computational tools need to support active organization of information, active search for information, active exploration of information, reflection on the meaning of information, and evaluation and choice among alternative activities. Context-conditional variation includes variation due to the worker—each worker has his or her own needs, entailing different requirements and constraints. This implies that individuals should be able to choose different trajectories to achieve the desired outcome in different ways. A good tool gives users discretion to generate various action sequences and express their preferences. As with many HCC principles, we have named this one after a person to give it a concrete and meaningful label. Sacagawea served as a guide, without whose help the Lewis and Clark expedition might not have achieved the successes it did. The name is also somewhat ironic, because Sacagawea was, for part of her life, a captured slave. The theme of machines and robots as slaves is arguably the oldest in the robotics literature, and it is still often used as a metaphor to describe the tools people use to accomplish their work. In this essay, we explore an approach for fulfilling the Sacagawea Principle in system design—an approach based on empirical study of the way in which people process their environments in complex worlds.

Chapter 4: The Triples Rule

R.R. Hoffman, P. Hayes, K.M. Ford, and P. Hancock, "The Triples Rule," *IEEE Intelligent Systems*, vol. 17, no. 3, May/June 2002, pp. 62–65. doi: 10.1109/MIS.2002.1005633

A fundamental stance taken in human-centered computing is that information processing devices must be thought of in systems terms. At first blush, this seems self-evident. However, the notion has a long history, and not just in systems engineering. In this new age of symbiosis, machines are made for specific humans for use in specific contexts. The unit of analysis for cognitive engineering and computer science is a triple: person, machine, and context. The triples rule asserts that system development must take this triple as the unit of analysis, which has strong implications, including a mandate that the engineering of complex systems should include detailed cognitive work analysis. It also has implications for the meaning of intelligence, including artificial intelligence.

Chapter 5: The Janus Principle

RR. Hoffman, G. Lintern, and S. Eitelman, "The Janus Principle," *IEEE Intelligent Systems*, vol. 19, no. 2, Mar./Apr. 2004, pp. 78–80. doi: 10.1109/MIS.2004.1274915

We find here an allegory to the apprentice-expert continuum in the acquisition of knowledge, and so we name a principle of human-centered computing after Janus. This principle deals with the distinction between performance and training, and its implications for intelligent technologies. The notion of a Janus Machine is the following: if a software tool works well as an intelligent training aid (for apprentices), it should also work as an actual operational support tool (for experts). We illustrate such machines.

Chapter 6: The Pleasure Principle

R.R. Hoffman and P.J. Hayes, "The Pleasure Principle," *IEEE Intelligent Systems*, vol. 19, no. 1, Jan./Feb. 2004, pp. 86–89. doi: 10.1109/MIS.2004.1265891

The list of "concepts that psychology really can't do without" includes such notions as neuronal connectionism, degrees of consciousness, mental representation of information, and dissociation. Of the pantheon of contributors to the history of psychology, Aristotle outranks all others in terms of the number of critical concepts he introduced, including the notion of the association of ideas, the law of frequency and the affiliated concept of memory strength, the notion of stage theories of development, the idea of distinguishing types of mental processes or faculties, the idea of scales of nature and comparisons between humans and animals, and last but not least, the pleasure principle. Unfortunately, computers don't always provide an unmixed increase in pleasure. Recent evidence suggests, contrary to what we might hope or suppose, that the computerization of the modern workplace has actually led to productivity declines. The negative impacts are likely due, at least in part, to the user unfriendliness of computers.

Chapter 7: Toward a Theory of Complex and Cognitive Systems

R.R. Hoffman and D.D. Woods, "Toward a Theory of Complex and Cognitive Systems," *IEEE Intelligent Systems*, vol. 20, no. 1, Jan./Feb. 2005, pp. 76–79. doi: 10.1109/MIS.2005.18

We present nine propositions that we've referred to as principles of human-centered computing. We discussed the reductive tendency, which is a necessary consequence of learning. We pointed out that this tendency also applies to those who are creating new information technologies, especially complex and cognitive systems. Indeed, the people who try to create new complex and cognitive systems are themselves prone to generate reductive understandings, in which complexities are simplified.

Chapter 8: Complex Sociotechnical Joint Cognitive Work Systems?

R.R. Hoffman, D.O. Norman, and J. Vagners, "Complex Sociotechnical Joint Cognitive Work Systems?," *IEEE Intelligent Systems*, vol. 24, no. 3, May/June 2009, pp. 82–89. doi: 10.1109/MIS.2009.39

This essay continues a tradition in this department: deconstructing the meanings of various buzz phrases. It calls out a cluster of phrases that use the word system. Notions of emergence and complexity are meaningfully related with regard to systems in general, and related in turn to notions of resilience, agility, and robustness. This is arguably true for engineered work systems and for biological systems. But a path to sorting all this out remains hidden by brambles. We are hostages to our language and especially to our fondness for Cartesian dualisms. We need to say that something is both a "structure" and a "dynamic." So far, the word "system" may be our best option even though the search for a definition continues. The editors of this department invite definitions of the word "system" and its modifiers.

Part II: Human-Machine Systems: From Interaction to Interdependence

Chapter 9: Work-Arounds, Make-Work, and Kludges

P. Koopman and R.R. Hoffman, "Work-Arounds, Make-Work, and Kludges," *IEEE Intelligent Systems*, vol. 18, no. 6, Nov./Dec. 2003, pp. 70–75. doi: 10.1109/MIS.2003.1249172

Paradigms are often defined partly in terms of what they are not, or in terms of what they are reacting against. The paradigm of human-centered computing is no exception. We discuss a user-hostile system. We decided that the terms kludge and work-around, and also the related concept of make-work, have yet to be clearly defined for the intelligent systems community. Human-centered systems are different from user-hostile systems as well as from systems based on a designer-centered approach. We try to clarify the senses of these three terms and suggest ways we might study work-around, make-work, and kludges as an integral part of human-computer systems—rather than as embarrassing necessities that are best swept under the computing research rug.

Chapter 10: Ten Challenges for Making Automation a "Team Player" in Joint Human-Agent Activity

G. Klein, D.D. Woods, J.M. Bradshaw, R.R. Hoffman, and P.J. Feltovich, "Ten Challenges for Making Automation a 'Team Player' in Joint Human-Agent Activity," *IEEE Intelligent Systems*, vol. 19, no. 6, Nov./Dec. 2004, pp. 91–95. doi: 10.1109/MIS.2004.74

We propose 10 challenges for making automation components into effective "team players" when they interact with people in significant ways. Our analysis is based on some of the principles of human-centered computing that we have developed individually and jointly over the years, and is adapted from a more comprehensive examination of common ground and coordination.

Chapter 11: Antipatterns in the Creation of Intelligent Systems

P. Laplante, R.R. Hoffman, and G. Klein, "Antipatterns in the Creation of Intelligent Systems," *IEEE Intelligent Systems*, vol. 22, no. 1, Jan./Feb. 2007, pp. 91–95. doi: 10.1109/MIS.2007.3

A design pattern is a named problem-solution pair that enables large-scale reuse of software architectures or their components. Ideally, patterns explicitly capture expert knowledge, design trade-offs, and design rationale and make these lessons learned widely available for off-the-shelf use. They can also enhance developers' vocabulary—for example, by easing the transition to object-oriented programming. Conventionally, patterns consist of four elements: a name, the problem to be solved, the solution to the problem (often termed the refactored solution), and the consequences of the solution. Numerous sets of patterns (collectively known as pattern languages) exist for software design, analysis, management, and so on. Shortly after the notion of design patterns emerged, practitioners began discussing problem-solution pairs in which the solution did more harm than good. These have come to be known as antipatterns, and they are well known in the design and management communities.

Chapter 12: The Dynamics of Trust in Cyberdomains

R.R. Hoffman, J.D. Lee, D.D. Woods, N. Shadbolt, J. Miller, and J.M. Bradshaw, "The Dynamics of Trust in Cyberdomains," *IEEE Intelligent Systems*, vol. 24, no. 6, Nov./Dec. 2009, pp. 5–11. doi: 10.1109/MIS.2009.124

This essay examines some human-centering issues for the Networld, placed primarily for convenience into five categories: antitrust in technology, a concensus on what "trust" is, interpersonal trust versus trust in automation, trusting as a dynamic process, and resilience engineering for the active management of trust. We describe our approach for designing the active management of trust in cyberdomains and generating multiple measures for different forms of trust relationships.

Chapter 13: Beyond Cooperative Robotics: The Central Role of Interdependence in Coactive Design

M. Johnson, J.M Bradshaw, P.J. Feltovich, R.R. Hoffman, C. Jonker, B. van Riemsdijk, and M. Sierhuis, "Beyond Cooperative Robotics: The Central Role of Interdependence in Coactive Design," *IEEE Intelligent Systems*, vol. 26, no. 3, May/June 2011, pp. 81–88. doi: 10.1109/MIS.2011.47

This article argues that the concept of levels of autonomy is incomplete and insufficient as a model for designing complex human-machine teams, largely because it does not sufficiently account for the interdependence among their members. Building on a theory of joint activity, we introduce the notion of coactive design, an approach to human-machine interaction that takes interdependence as the central organizing principle among people and agents working together as a team.

Part III:
Design of Human-Machine Systems: From Requirements to Desirements

Chapter 14: A Rose by Any Other Name... Would Probably Be Given an Acronym

R.R. Hoffman, P.J. Feltovich, K.M. Ford, D.D. Woods, G. Klein, and A. Feltovich, "A Rose by Any Other Name... Would Probably Be Given an Acronym," *IEEE Intelligent Systems*, vol. 17, no. 4, July/Aug. 2002, pp. 72–80. doi: 10.1109/MIS.2002.1024755

In this article, we concern ourselves with characterizations of the "new" approaches to the design of complex sociotechnical systems, and we use a biological classification scheme to organize the discussion. Until fairly recently, the design of complex sociotechnical systems was primarily known as "cognitive engineering" or "cognitive systems engineering" (CSE), a term introduced to denote an emerging branch of applied cognitive psychology. A number of new terms have since emerged, all of which might be considered members of the genus "human-centered computing" (HCC). A number of varieties have entered the fray, resulting in an "acronym soup" of terms that have been offered to designate "the" new approach to cognitive engineering. Using the rose metaphor, and taking some liberties with Latin, this article is organized around a set of "genuses" into which the individual "varieties" seem to fall.

Chapter 15: From Contextual Inquiry to Designable Futures: What Do We Need to Get There?

S.W.A. Dekker, J.M. Nyce, and R.R. Hoffman, "From Contextual Inquiry to Designable Futures: What Do We Need to Get There?," *IEEE Intelligent Systems*, vol. 18, no. 2, Mar./Apr. 2003, pp. 74–77. doi: 10.1109/MIS.2003.1193660

Human-centered systems result when software engineers or developers give attention to the orientations, expectations, and understandings of the people who will be part of the sociotechnical system. Human factors researchers often take certain agendas, terms, and theories for granted or rely on them out of habit. This paper takes a special look at contextual enquiry as a putatively (and indeed potentially) superior way of giving end users a serious say in the procurement process of complex cognitive systems.

Chapter 16: The Borg Hypothesis

R.R. Hoffman, J.M. Bradshaw, P.J. Hayes, and K.M. Ford, "The Borg Hypothesis," *IEEE Intelligent Systems*, vol. 18, no. 5, Sep./Oct. 2003, pp. 73–75. doi: 10.1109/MIS.2003.1234774

What if intelligent computing were centered inside humans? Portending an even braver and newer world, it's now possible to insert wires into a person's nerves to control appliances. We can even send such signals over the Internet, where they are decoded by computer and then fed into another person's nervous system. Human bodies are getting more and more plugged in. It's not easy to set aside questions of ethics and choice. It is not even possible. However, in this essay we simply overlook them in order to work toward our hypothesis. To do that, we must take you on a trip into space. Our argument is that if humanity decides to continue human exploration of space, we will sooner or later—probably sooner—be forced to center some intelligent computing inside humans.

Chapter 17: What Is Design in the Context of Human-Centered Computing?

R.R. Hoffman, A. Roesler, and B.M. Moon, "What Is Design in the Context of Human-Centered Computing?," *IEEE Intelligent Systems*, vol. 19, no. 4, July/Aug. 2004, pp. 89–95. doi: 10.1109/MIS.2004.36

We deal with design in human-centered computing. Problem solving often involves recognizing and fiddling with tacit assumptions. Such realization can often come from seeing things from new perspectives. Appreciating the human-centered perspective may offer some hope for enriching design's scientific foundations and for crafting new and better approaches to it. Certainly this suggests a constraint on or a goal for design, but how do we go from such statements to actual designs that accomplish the stated goals? We approach this class of question by considering the origins of and historical influences on the notion of design, then by considering the assumptions underlying our modern conception of design in light of the principles of human-centered computing.

Chapter 18: Keeping It Too Simple: How the Reductive Tendency Affects Cognitive Engineering

P.J. Feltovich, R.R. Hoffman, D. Woods, and A. Roesler, "Keeping It Too Simple: How the Reductive Tendency Affects Cognitive Engineering," *IEEE Intelligent Systems*, vol. 19, no. 3, May/June 2004, pp. 90–94. doi: 10.1109/MIS.2004.14

Certain features of tasks make them especially difficult for humans. These constitute leverage points for applying intelligent technologies, but there's a flip side. Designing complex cognitive systems is itself a tough task. Cognitive engineers face the same challenges in designing systems that users confront in working the tasks that the systems are intended to aid. We discuss these issues. We assume that the cognitive engineers will invoke one or more knowledge shields when they are confronted with evidence that their understanding and planning involves a reductive understanding. The knowledge shield phenomenon suggests that it will take effort to change the reductive mindset that people might bring to the design of a CCS.

Chapter 19: Influencing versus Informing Design, Part 1: A Gap Analysis

R.R. Hoffman and S.V. Deal, "Influencing versus Informing Design, Part 1: A Gap Analysis," *IEEE Intelligent Systems*, vol. 23, no. 5, Sep./Oct. 2008, pp. 78–81. doi: 10.1109/MIS.2008.83

The collaboration of cognitive systems engineers with systems engineers is motivated by the goal of creating human-centered systems. However, there can be a gap in this collaboration. In presentations at professional meetings about cognitive systems engineering projects, we often hear that one or another method of cognitive task analysis was employed in order to inform design. But what software developers need is designs. This is the first of two essays about the gap between the products of cognitive task analysis and the needs of the software engineers. We discuss a success story of cognitive systems engineering for a large-scale system, a project that coped with the practical constraints of time pressure and the challenge of designing for an envisioned world when system elements could not be fully specified in advance. This project relied on a particular product from cognitive task analysis, the abstraction-decomposition matrix, that speaks in a language that corresponds with the needs and goals of the software designers.

Chapter 20: Influencing versus Informing Design, Part 2: Macrocognitive Modeling

R.R. Hoffman, "Influencing versus Informing Design, Part 2: Macrocognitive Modeling," *IEEE Intelligent Systems*, vol. 23, no. 6, Nov./Dec. 2008, pp.86–89. doi: 10.1109/MIS.2008.105

Cognitive-systems engineers study the cognitive work conducted in sociotechnical contexts and, from that understanding, provide guidance to software engineers. The previous essay in this department discussed how there can be a gap—the guidance from cognitive-systems engineers can inform design, but what software engineers actually need are designs. The gap has been successfully crossed in one direction, in projects in which cognitive-systems engineers expressed the requirements in a way that captured key functionalities and their rationale, thereby speaking to the software engineer's needs. This essay works in the other direction: providing systems engineers with an easy-to-use method—the macrocognitive modeling procedure—that might enable them to ramp up their understanding of the cognitive work. The procedure involves creating and then validating models of domain practitioners' reasoning. The method is easy to use and can enable software engineers to ramp up their understanding of end users' cognitive work.

Chapter 21: Once More, Into the Soup

P.J. Stappers, R.R. Hoffman, "Once More, Into the Soup," *IEEE Intelligent Systems*, vol. 24, no. 5, Sept./Oct. 2009, pp. 9–13. doi: 10.1109/MIS.2009.100

In one of the earlier essays in this department, we discussed a number of acronyms all having to do with system design, and all having the form "x-centered design." The purpose of that essay was to demonstrate a broad framework within which to understand human-centered computing (HCC), and also to show the various convergences and divergences of the communities of practice that have introduced their own x-centered-design designations. Among them are learner-centered design, client-centered design, designer-centered design, decision-centered design, and work-oriented design.

Part IV: Expertise and Cognitive Skill

Chapter 22: The Limitations of Limitations

J.M. Flach and R.R. Hoffman, "The Limitations of Limitations," *IEEE Intelligent Systems*, vol. 18, no. 1, Jan./Feb. 2003, pp. 94–97. doi: 10.1109/MIS.2003.1179200

The authors consider human-centered computing and argue that human factors and applied cognitive psychologists have not just been selective in regarding certain human characteristics as limitations, but have also selected the wrong things and for the wrong reasons. Throughout the literatures of cognitive science, computer science, and human factors, one finds all sorts of references to the idea that humans have limitations in memory, attention, and reasoning. Humans have many characteristics, any of which can be regarded as a limitation *if one chooses to*. The heart of the problem is a preference for easily quantifiable answers to the wrong questions and avoidance of the right questions because they are messy. There are many people within the human factors community who cling to the belief that their primary function is to catalog human limitations. We hypothesize that this resistance is partly due to a misconception about the needs of designers.

Chapter 23: Macrocognition

G. Klein, K.G. Ross, B.M. Moon, D.E. Klein, R.R. Hoffman, and E. Hollnagel, "Macrocognition," *IEEE Intelligent Systems*, vol. 18, no. 3, May/June 2003, pp. 81–85. doi: 10.1109/MIS.2003.1200735

If we engineer complex cognitive systems on the basis of mistaken or inappropriate views of cognition, we can wind up designing systems that degrade performance rather than improve it. The results stemming from the application of any cognitive systems engineering methodology will be incomplete unless they include a description of the cognition that is needed to accomplish the work. Traditionally, cognitive researchers have conducted laboratory experiments on micro-level topics such as puzzle solving, serial versus parallel attention, and other standard laboratory paradigms for psychological research. In contrast, the methodology for macrocognition focuses on contexts such as the "field setting," the "natural laboratory." In such contexts the adaptation of cognition to complexity involves functions such as sensemaking and problem detection. Macrocognitive modeling also differs from modeling in the microcognitive distinction (e.g., stages, steps, flowcharts) in that the core processes are regarded as continuous, parallel, and highly interacting. This view has many implications for the goals of intelligent systems and for processes for creating human-centered work systems.

Chapter 24: Decision(?)Making(?)

R.R. Hoffman and J.F. Yates, "Decision(?)Making(?)," *IEEE Intelligent Systems*, vol. 20, no. 4, July/Aug. 2005, pp. 76–83. doi: 10.1109/MIS.2005.67

Computers, including intelligent systems, assist human decision making in many ways. One aspect of decision making is the "final point" notion, that decision making leads up to a commitment to action. This aspect is what makes it too easy for us to think of decisions as things that are made. We argue otherwise, that all acts of deciding can be decomposed into a set of underlying issues and conditional dependencies. The decomposition we present has implications for the design of human-centered decision support systems.

Chapter 25: Making Sense of Sensemaking 1: Alternative Perspectives

G. Klein, B. Moon, and R.R. Hoffman, "Making Sense of Sensemaking 1: Alternative Perspectives," *IEEE Intelligent Systems*, vol. 21, no. 4, July/Aug. 2006, pp. 70–73. doi: 10.1109/MIS.2006.75

Sensemaking has become an umbrella term for efforts at building intelligent systems. This essay examines sensemaking from various perspectives to see if we can separate the things that are doable from the things that seem more like pie-in-the-sky.

Chapter 26: Making Sense of Sensemaking 2: A Macrocognitive Model

G. Klein, B. Moon, and R.R. Hoffman, "Making Sense of Sensemaking 2: A Macrocognitive Model," *IEEE Intelligent Systems*, vol. 21, no. 5, Sep./Oct. 2006, pp. 88–92. doi: 10.1109/MIS.2006.100

In this paper, we have laid out a theory of sensemaking that might be useful for intelligent systems applications. It's a general, empirically grounded account of sensemaking that goes significantly beyond the myths and puts forward some nonobvious, testable hypotheses about the process. When people try to make sense of events, they begin with some perspective, viewpoint, or framework—however minimal. For now, let's use a metaphor and call this a frame. We can express frames in various meaningful forms, including stories, maps, organizational diagrams, or scripts, and can use them in subsequent and parallel processes. Even though frames define what count as data, they themselves actually shape the data. Furthermore, frames change as we acquire data. In other words, this is a two-way street: frames shape and define the relevant data, and data mandate that frames change in nontrivial ways. We examine five areas of empirical findings: causal reasoning, commitment to hypotheses, feedback and learning, sense-making as a skill, and confirmation bias. In each area the Data/Frame model, and the research it's based on, move us beyond commonsense views.

Chapter 27: Perceptual (Re)learning: A Leverage Point for Human-Centered Computing

R.R. Hoffman and S.M. Fiore, "Perceptual (Re)learning: A Leverage Point for Human-Centered Computing," *IEEE Intelligent Systems*, vol. 22, no. 3, May/June 2007, pp. 79–83. doi: 10.1109/MIS.2007.59

At least since Adrianus Dingeman de Groot conducted his pioneering work on the reasoning of chess masters, perceptual skill has been regarded as key to the advantage of experts. Here we explore the conjunction of two facts: 1. experts can perceive things that are invisible to the novice; 2. it takes a decade or more for someone to become an expert in most significant domains; 3. this conjunction represents a leverage point for intelligent systems—not from the Turing Test perspective of building machines that emulate humans but from the human-centered computing (HCC) perspective of amplifying and extending human capabilities.

Chapter 28: Franchise Experts

R.R. Hoffman, D. Ziebell, P.J. Feltovich, B.M. Moon, and S.M. Fiore, "Franchise Experts," *IEEE Intelligent Systems*, vol. 26, no. 5, Sep./Oct. 2011, pp. 72–77. doi: 10.1109/MIS.2011.85

This article harks back to the origins of this periodical as *IEEE Expert Systems*. Even while expert systems as a field or paradigm was morphing into intelligent systems, it was recognized that cognitive task analysis was critical in the design of new technologies. Furthermore, as a part of cognitive task analysis, it is crucial to conduct some form of proficiency scale to help identify the experts whose knowledge and skill might be revealed and specified in the creation of reasoning and knowledge-based systems. In this article, we will advance the claim that identifying and studying franchise experts can contribute to the design of intelligent systems. Of further interest is the possibility that the knowledge elicited from such experts might be invaluable for the practice of accelerated learning. We refer to "franchise" experts because they are not only expert in their chosen technical domain but also expert with regard to the organizations to which they belong. As a concept map organizer within a "knowledge model," some of the nodes are appended with icons that link to other concept maps that drill down into details, technical documentation, schematics, URLs, and so forth. This concept map shows that the franchise expert's knowledge refers to organizational structures and topics.

Part V: Methodology and Metrics: Making What's Important Measurable

Chapter 29: Knowledge Management Revisited

R.R. Hoffman, D. Ziebell, S.M. Fiore, and I. Becerra-Fernandez, "Knowledge Management Revisited," *IEEE Intelligent Systems*, vol. 23, no. 3, May/June 2008, pp. 84–88. doi: 10.1109/MIS.2008.51

A number of social, economic, technological, and scientific trends have led to the emergence of communities of practice centered on the notion of the knowledge-based organization. However, the scientific foundation (knowledge elicitation methodology) and the commercial growth of knowledge management (KM) have largely developed in parallel. So, the creation of human-centered systems faces lingering challenges. In the KM process, company management establishes a program whereby experts who possess valuable knowledge collaborate with a knowledge engineer. Working together, they elicit the expert's wisdom for inclusion in the organization's knowledge base.

Chapter 30: Metrics, Metrics, Metrics: Negative Hedonicity

R.R. Hoffman, M. Marx, and P. Hancock, "Metrics, Metrics, Metrics: Negative Hedonicity," *IEEE Intelligent Systems*, vol. 23, no. 2, Mar./Apr. 2008, pp. 69–73. doi: 10.1109/MIS.2008.31

Intelligent technologies such as performance support systems and decision aids represent a key aspect of modern sociotechnical systems. When new tools are introduced into the workplace, they represent hypotheses about how cognitive work is expected to change. The tacit hypothesis is that any such change will be for the better, performance will be more efficient, and decisions will be improved—that is, they'll be made faster and on the basis of greater evidence. Experience suggests that technological interventions sometimes have the intended positive effect. However, they often result in negative effects, including unintended cascading failures and worker frustration due to "user-hostile" aspects of interfaces.

Chapter 31: Accelerated Learning (?)

R.R. Hoffman, P.J. Feltovich, S.M. Fiore, G. Klein, and D. Ziebell, "Accelerated Learning (?)," *IEEE Intelligent Systems*, vol. 24, no. 2, Mar./Apr. 2009, pp. 18–22. doi: 10.1109/MIS.2009.21

We pose accelerated learning as a challenge for intelligent systems technology. Research on intelligent tutoring systems has proved that accelerated learning is possible. The Sherlock tutor for electronics troubleshooting, for example, condensed four years of on-the-job training to approximately 25 hours, compressing the duration of the experience-feedback-learning cycle. But accelerated learning should refer to more than the hastening of basic proficiency. It reaches across the proficiency scale to the question of how to accelerate the achievement of expertise, and whether that is even possible. Paralleling this question are practical issues, including the military's need to conduct training at a rapid pace, and the issues of workforce and loss of expertise. Many organizations such as the US Department of Defense, NASA, and the electric utilities are at risk because of the imminent retirement of domain practitioners who handle the most difficult and mission-critical challenges. To accelerate proficiency, we must facilitate the acquisition of extensive, highly organized knowledge. We must also accelerate the acquisition of expert-level reasoning skills and strategies. But that's just the beginning of the challenge.

Chapter 32: Metrics, Metrics, Metrics, Part 2: Universal Metrics?

R.R. Hoffman, P.A. Hancock, and J.M. Bradshaw, "Metrics, Metrics, Metrics, Part 2: Universal Metrics?," *IEEE Intelligent Systems*, vol. 25, no. 6, Nov./Dec. 2010, pp. 93–97. doi: 10.1109/MIS.2010.147

A previous article in this department from 2008 introduced the topic of measures and metrics. The focus of that essay was on measurement of the "negative hedonics" of work—the frustrations, uncertainties, mistrust, and automation surprises caused by poorly designed technology that is not human-centered. This second article focuses on the concept of "metrics" and issues related to it. Following a discussion of relevant issues, we present an immodestly bold proposal for a set of universal metrics.

Chapter 33: Beyond Simon's Slice: Five Fundamental Trade-Offs that Bound the Performance of Macrocognitive Work Systems

R.R. Hoffman and D.D. Woods, "Beyond Simon's Slice: Five Fundamental Trade-Offs that Bound the Performance of Macrocognitive Work Systems," *IEEE Intelligent Systems*, vol. 26, no. 6, Nov./Dec. 2011, pp. 67–71. doi: 10.1109/MIS.2011.97

Articulating the laws of cognitive work has been a continuing theme in this department. A number of the articles represent an effort to move toward a unified theory of "macrocognitive work systems." These are complex adaptive systems designed to support near-continuous interdependencies among humans and intelligent machines to carry out functions such as sensemaking, replanning, mental projection to the future, and coordination. The effort to identify empirical generalizations and use them to construct a formal theory has led us to the identification of a number of fundamental trade-offs that place boundary conditions on all macrocognitive work systems. This article presents five trade-offs identified to date that define these boundary conditions. It also illustrates how the known empirical generalizations about the performance of human work systems can be systematically organized by the trade-offs.

Part VI: Procurement Woes: Why Technologies Come to Be NOT Human-Centered

Chapter 34: The Boiled Frog Problem

R.R. Hoffman and L.F. Hanes, "The Boiled Frog Problem," *IEEE Intelligent Systems*, vol. 18, no. 4, Jul./Aug. 2003, pp. 68–71. doi: 10.1109/MIS.2003.1217630

As many of the most knowledgeable personnel in technically complex businesses approach retirement, there is a need to capture their knowledge. The temptation is for management to ignore the problem until it is too late. The article discusses how a company can identify employees who possess valuable undocumented knowledge, evaluate whether the knowledge is worth capturing, elicit, represent, and preserve the valuable knowledge, and share this knowledge with other personnel when needed.

Chapter 35: HCC Implications for the Procurement Process

R.R. Hoffman and W.C. Elm, "HCC Implications for the Procurement Process," *IEEE Intelligent Systems*, vol. 21, no. 1, Jan./Feb. 2006, pp. 74–81. doi: 10.1109/MIS.2006.9

Most system designers and human factors engineers have participated in projects that culminated in systems that were highly constrained by short-term cost considerations. In the procurement of information processing and intelligent technology for complex sociotechnical domains, the focus on short-term cost considerations at the expense of human-centering considerations always comes with a hefty price down the road. This price weighs much more heavily on users' shoulders than on those of the technologists or project managers. The authors use as an example the US National Weather Service's Advanced Weather Information Processing System. The authors argue that regarding HCC notions as design challenges or policies for procurement promises to make information technologies more intelligent by making them human-centered.

Chapter 36: Human Total Cost of Ownership: The Penny Foolish Principle at Work

W. Zachary, R.R. Hoffman, K. Neville, and J. Fowlkes, "Human Total Cost of Ownership: The Penny Foolish Principle at Work," *IEEE Intelligent Systems*, Mar./Apr. 2007, vol. 22, no. 2, pp. 88–92. doi: 10.1109/MIS.2007.33

Human-centered computing is about creating technologies that are intelligent in the usual sense of intelligent systems. But we also mean intelligent in the sense that they are usable versus user-hostile; useful because they're designed on the basis of results from cognitive task analysis, so that they actually help people do things that need to be done; and understandable, in that the human can learn what the machine is doing and why. Allocating costs specifically to human-centering and cognitive systems engineering aspects of technology R&D will mitigate human-machine interaction issues and decrease training and maintenance costs, thus benefitting the service or system owner over the technology's life time. If we follow HCC's lead in defining the real costs of software systems, the procurement of technology and intelligent systems can become dollar wise.

Chapter 37: The Procurement Woes Revisited

K. Neville, R.R. Hoffman, C. Linde, W.C. Elm, and J. Fowlkes, "The Procurement Woes Revisited," *IEEE Intelligent Systems*, vol. 23, no. 1, Jan./Feb. 2008, pp. 72–75. doi: 10.1109/MIS.2008.15

The set of people who are frustrated every day by badly designed information technology is very large. So is the set of people whose dollars pay for the badly designed technology. A conservative estimate ranges in the billions for the cost of large-scale information systems that end up collecting dust because they're not properly human-centered. Yes, billions and still counting—that's the scary part. Within this large set of frustrated customers (see the sidebar "When Systems Development Neglects Human Considerations") is a subset whose job it is to do something about this situation. That subset includes policymakers, program managers, and systems engineers. It also includes a sub-subset comprising cognitive systems engineers, ethnographers, and many others who, in one vernacular or another, advocate human-centered computing. We must show that intelligent technologies—those designed to interact with humans or play a role in the cognitive work conducted in sociotechnical work systems—are usable, useful, and understandable.

Chapter 38: The Practitioner's Cycles, Part 1: Actual World Problems

S.V. Deal and R.R. Hoffman, "The Practitioner's Cycles, Part 1: Actual World Problems," *IEEE Intelligent Systems*, vol. 25, no. 2, Mar./Apr. 2010, pp. 4–9. doi: 10.1109/MIS.2010.54

This is one of three essays on the forces and constraints of procurement versus the goals of human centering, including the creation of intelligent technologies that are usable, useful, and understandable. The procurement process tends to de-emphasize these goals while focusing on strict adherence to rules and regulations. As a result, software system development processes, described in texts and acquisition documents, come to be misaligned with the challenges faced by development teams. This misalignment between "actual world problems" and normative documentation repeatedly results in failed systems. A real-life practitioner's account illustrates this point by describing how a group of individuals, acting on their own initiative and at their own risk, short-circuited the rules and constraints of the procurement process to turn a procurement process failure into a success. In the next essay, we will present a model called the Practitioner's Cycles and discuss how this model applies to the envisioned world problem, which is the challenge of creating intelligent technologies for new work systems.

Chapter 39: The Practitioner's Cycles, Part 2: Solving Envisioned World Problems

R.R. Hoffman, S.V. Deal, S. Potter, and E.M. Roth, "The Practitioner's Cycles, Part 2: Solving Envisioned World Problems," *IEEE Intelligent Systems*, vol. 25, no. 3, May/June 2010, pp. 6–11. doi: 10.1109/MIS.2010.89

Previous Human-Centered Computing department articles have reflected on the mismatch that can occur between the promise of intelligent technology and the results of technological interventions. Part 1 on the Practitioner's Cycles illustrated ways in which actual world problems—the forces and constraints of procurement—are at odds with the goals of human centering. This article culminated in a practitioner's tale, in which individuals acted on their own initiative and at their own risk, short-circuiting the rules and constraints that limit success at procurement. This paper presents a model based on the tale and focuses on how the model applies to envisioned world problems—the creation of intelligent technologies for new work systems.

Chapter 40: The Practitioner's Cycles, Part 3: Implementation Opportunities

S.V. Deal and R.R. Hoffman, "The Practitioner's Cycles, Part 3: Implementation Opportunities," *IEEE Intelligent Systems*, vol. 25, no. 5, Sep./Oct. 2010, pp. 77–81. doi: 10.1109/MIS.2010.129

The Practitioner's Cycles Part 1 illustrated ways in which actual world problems—the forces and constraints of procurement—are at odds with the goals of a human-centered approach. In Part 2, we presented an application of the Practitioner's Cycles model to envisioned world problems—the creation of intelligent technologies for new work systems. (See the "Synopsis of the Practitioner's Cycles" sidebar for a quick review.) This essay (Part 3) describes formative implementations of the Practitioner's Cycles. We propose the Practitioner's Cycles concept as a solution to the simultaneous problems of maturing new technologies and rapidly transitioning those technologies into new products.

Author Index

C

D

E

F

G

H

I

J

K

N

O

P

Q

R

S

T

V

Subject Index

D

E

F

G

H

I

J

K

L

M

N

U

W

Z

www.ingramcontent.com/pod-product-compliance
Lightning Source LLC
Chambersburg PA
CBHW080149060326
40689CB00018B/3903

* 9 7 8 0 7 6 9 5 4 7 1 5 2 *